A Piece of Cake

BOOKS BY SUSAN G. PURDY

A Piece of Cake

Susan G. Purdy

Illustrated by Susan Martin

COLLIER BOOKS
MACMILLAN PUBLISHING COMPANY • NEW YORK
Maxwell Macmillan Canada • *Toronto*
Maxwell Macmillan International
New York • Oxford • Singapore • Sydney

For My Father,
Harold A. Gold,
with love

Collier Books
Macmillan Publishing Company
866 Third Avenue
New York, NY 10022

Maxwell Macmillan Canada, Inc.
1200 Eglinton Avenue East
Suite 200
Don Mills, Ontario M3C 3N1

Macmillan Publishing Company is part of the Maxwell
Communication Group of Companies.

Library of Congress Cataloging-in-Publication Data
Purdy, Susan Gold, 1939–
    A piece of cake / Susan G. Purdy; illustrated by Susan Martin.
    p.   cm.
    Originally published: New York: Atheneum, 1989.
    Includes index.
    ISBN 0-02-036085-1
    1. Cake.   I. Title.
TX771.P87   1993   93-16077   CIP
641.8'653—dc20

Macmillan books are available at special discounts for bulk purchases
for sales promotions, premiums, fund-raising, or educational use.
For details, contact:

Special Sales Director, Macmillan Publishing Company,
866 Third Avenue, New York, NY 10022.

First Collier Books Edition 1993

10   9   8   7   6   5   4   3   2   1

Printed in the United States of America

Contents

BUTTER AND/OR SHORTENING CAKES 71

CONTENTS

CONTENTS

Meringue Cakes and Dacquoise 244

ABOUT MERINGUE; ALL-PURPOSE MERINGUE, COLD AND SWISS METH-
ODS; ITALIAN MERINGUE; MERINGUE OR DACQUOISE CAKE LAYERS
AND VARIATION: CHOCOLATE DACQUOISE; TOFFEE CREAM DACQUOISE
AND VARIATION: RASPBERRY CREAM; CHOCOLATE MOUSSE DAC-
QUOISE AND VARIATION: CHOCOLATE RUFFLE; HUNGARIAN COFFEE
MERINGUE CAKE

Tortes 261

ABOUT TORTES; HAZELNUT TORTE; WALNUT TORTE; ALMOND TORTE;
ITALIAN ALMOND-CHOCOLATE TORTE; PASSOVER NUT TORTE; POP-
PYSEED TORTE; SACHERTORTE; MOCHA TORTE; DOBOSTORTE; CARROT
TORTE

ELEGANT AND SPECIAL CAKES 285

INTRODUCTION; HAZELNUT WHITE-CHOCOLATE MARQUISE; BLACK
FOREST CHERRY CAKE; SAVARIN; LIME MOUSSE CAKE; BERRIES IN WINE
GÂTEAU; CASSIS GÂTEAU; CHESTNUT MOUSSE CAKE; GÉNOISE AND
SPONGE CAKE VARIATIONS: CHOCOLATE MARQUISE, STRAWBERRY
MOUSSE CAKE (AND RASPBERRY VARIATION), LYNN'S DEVON LEMON
CREAM CAKE, GRAND MARNIER GÉNOISE, GÂTEAU MOKA, ORANGE-
CHOCOLATE DREAM CAKE; FEATHER-TOPPED TRUFFLE CAKE; CHOCO-
LATE MOUSSE CAKE; CHOCOLATE CHESTNUT FUDGE CAKE; SEVEN- OR
EIGHT-LAYER CHOCOLATE CAKE; ANNA TERESA CALLEN'S TIRAMISÚ;
TRIFLE; JO'S BLITZ TORTE; BAKED ALASKA; ICE-CREAM FILLED ANGEL
CAKE; ZUCCOTTO; PUMPKIN-PECAN ICE-CREAM BOMBE; PANFORTE
DI SIENA

CHARLOTTES 327

ABOUT CHARLOTTES; CHOCOLATE MINT CHARLOTTE; RED AND WHITE
CHARLOTTE AND VARIATION: CHARLOTTE RUSSE; VANILLA BAVARIAN
CREAM; STRAWBERRY CHARLOTTE ROYALE AND VARIATIONS: FRESH
BERRY, PASSION FRUIT OR MANGO, TANGERINE, CRANBERRY-ORANGE;
APPLE CHARLOTTE; APRICOT CHARLOTTE

CONTENTS

CONTENTS

MOCHA; CLASSIC FRENCH EGG-YOLK BUTTERCREAM AND VARIATIONS: DELUXE FRENCH CHOCOLATE, COFFEE, ORANGE, LEMON OR LIME, ORANGE-CHOCOLATE, CLASSIC FRENCH BUTTERCREAM WITH ME-RINGUE; FRENCH BUTTERCREAM MÉNAGÈRE (HOMESTYLE) AND VARI-ATIONS: LEMON, ORANGE, CHESTNUT, CHOCOLATE VELVET, HAZELNUT-CHOCOLATE; CREAM-CHEESE ICING AND VARIATIONS: OR-ANGE, CHOCOLATE; QUICK COCONUT ICING; SOUR-CREAM NUT ICING; PEANUT BUTTER ICING; PENUCHE ICING; BROWN-SUGAR CARAMEL ICING AND VARIATION: SUGAR 'N' SPICE; BROILED CARAMEL-NUT ICING; MOCHA FROSTING; ORANGE WINE ICING; SEVEN-MINUTE ICING AND VARIATIONS: SEAFOAM, MAPLE, COCONUT, ORANGE, LEMON, PEPPERMINT; BOILED ICING AND VARIATIONS: ROCKY MOUNTAIN, BEIGE MOUNTAIN, LANE, LADY BALTIMORE, LORD BALTIMORE FILLING AND ICING, LEMON, ORANGE, COCOA, COCONUT; SWISS MERINGUE BUTTERCREAM; ITALIAN MERINGUE BUTTERCREAM AND VARIATION: DELUXE; TANGERINE GLAZE FOR CHEESECAKE; STRAWBERRY GLAZE; ABOUT ICING GLAZE; BASIC ICING GLAZE; ORANGE ICING GLAZE AND VARIATION: LEMON; GANACHE ICING GLAZE OR CHOCOLATE FILLING AND VARIATION: FRANNI'S GANACHE GLAZE; FABULOUS CHOCOLATE GLAZE; CHOCOLATE WATER GLAZE; COCOA ICING GLAZE; APRICOT GLAZE; FIRM APRICOT GLAZE; CLASSIC POURED FONDANT; QUICK MOCK FONDANT

Sauces and Syrups 416

CRÈME FRAÎCHE; VANILLA CUSTARD SAUCE (CRÈME ANGLAISE); HARD SAUCE; WARM BERRY SAUCE; HOT LEMON SAUCE; BUTTERSCOTCH SAUCE; RICH CHOCOLATE SAUCE; STRAWBERRIES ROMANOFF AND STRAWBERRIES À LA RITZ; CAKE SOAKING SYRUP AND VARIATIONS: ORANGE OR GRAND MARNIER, ALMOND, RUM, COFFEE; STOCK SYRUP

DECORATING CAKES 423

. . . .

TO PREPARE CAKES FOR FILLING AND DECORATING; ABOUT CAKE FROSTING AND DECORATIONS; HOW TO FROST A CAKE; PASTRY BAGS AND TIPS; CAKE DECORATING IDEAS AND TECHNIQUES; FEATHERED CHOCOLATE GLAZE; SHAPED CAKES

CONTENTS

xi

· ACKNOWLEDGMENTS ·

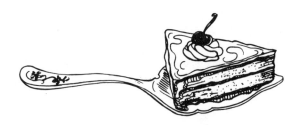

A CEREMONIAL PIECE OF CAKE is offered with love to the memory of Bruce Whitney Bacon (1940–1984). Friend, artist, connoisseur of food and wine, he wanted the world to know that "he was right, but he was zany."

AND THANKS TO . . . nearly everyone involved in my life, from family to friends, neighbors, teachers, and professional colleagues. A project as big and diverse as this one necessarily involves a great number of people. To all who visited our home and shared cakes, recipes, and reminiscences, to all the new friends we made traveling in search of cakes and recipes, to anyone inadvertently omitted from the following list, I say a grateful thank-you. It is only by tasting, talking, and testing many times over that recipes and techniques become refined enough for publication.

For their encouragement, support, and helpful critiques of hundreds of cakes as well as for their enthusiasm and culinary judgment during extensive research and traveling, I thank my husband, Geoffrey, and our daughter, Cassandra. For family recipes, I thank my parents, Frances and Harold Gold; my sister, Nancy G. Lieberman; my aunts, Phoebe Vernon and Beatrice Joslin. For suggesting literary quotations, I thank Lucille Purdy, Alexandra and Sesyle Hine; for help in tracing the British background of the phrase "it's a piece of cake," I thank Robin and Thérèse Davies. For endless hours in the kitchen working out the details of each recipe with patience, good humor, and skill, I am grateful to my baking assistant, Barbara Went Cover. For advice on writing technique and style I thank my editor at Gannett Newspapers, Meryl Harris. For research, especially during travel to Vienna, I thank Marylois Purdy Vega, Jesse Birnbaum, and Mrs. Traudel Lessing. For lending us their home in Venice as well as for sharing travel advice and culinary wisdom throughout our cake-eating European holidays, we thank Molly and Walter Bareiss.

For technical consultation on the introductory chapters, I am indebted to Chef Albert Kumin of the Country Epicure's International Pastry Arts Center, Bedford Hills, New York. I will always appreciate his good humor and wisdom. I thank, too, Jeanne Harper for facilitating my visits to the school. For recipe ideas as well as for organizing a remarkable visit with his family in France, I thank Chef Jacques Pépin, and his mother, Jeannette Pépin. For expertise on the use of the food processor in cake baking, I am indebted to Carl G. Sontheimer, Suzanne Jones, and Mayburn Koss of Cuisinarts, Inc. For editorial skill, understanding, and enthusiastic support, I thank my editor, Pam Hoenig, my art director, Wendy Bass, my production editor, Patricia McEldon, and Manohla Dargis. For moral support and encouragment throughout the development of this project I thank Olivia Blumer, Marilyn Abraham, and my literary agent, Susan Lescher.

For sharing recipes, research, techniques, and ideas as well as for tasting and testing, I thank Charley, Marleni, and Katia Kanas; Chef Lynn Pageau; Chef Michael La Croix; Fran and Wally Sheper of Franni's Café-Pâtisserie, Montreal; Chef Vicky Zeff; Pâtissier Robert Dause of Azay-le-Rideau, France; Pastry Chef Fredrich Pflieger of the Hotel Sacher, Vienna; Sandra Calder Davidson; Jill, John, and Elizabeth Guthrie; Corinne and Marc Debavelaere; Jo Trogdon Sweatt; Nina Bacon; Gene Fogarty; Marie Swanson; Norma Went; Nancy German; Pat and Terry Glaves; Michele Peasley; Shirley Johansen; Grace and Jack Johnson; Elizabeth MacDonald; Sofia Stirling; Joan Moore; Martha Schindhelm; Roberta Dehman Hershon; Francine Scherer; Mr. Schooner Sherman; Mrs. Diane Skor; Carolyn Klemm; Leslie Sutten; Annie Evans; Gerry Martin Hearn; George and Leslie Hearn; Hugh Bareiss; Gunnar Anderson; Janet and Strother Purdy; the students and faculty of the Washington Montessori School as well as my students in baking classes at the Silo Cooking School in New Milford, Connecticut, and at the Complete Kitchen in Darien, Connecticut.

The beautiful drawings that enhance these pages are the work of Susan Martin, whose intelligent understanding of the text, sensitivity and skill as an artist, and enthusiastic support as a friend made working together a joy.

Introduction

The idea for this book evolved over a period of years from the classes I have taught in pastry making. It has become more and more apparent to me that while many people are interested in learning one or two particularly showy cakes for a grand finale dessert, they rarely consider adding cake baking to their general cooking repertoire. Coffee cakes, which can take less time to prepare at home than a salad, are automatically bought boxed in the supermarket. For birthday cakes, people head for a bakery or reach for a cake mix rather than consider the healthier and more delicious alternative of baking from scratch.

Even many restaurant chefs who are expert entrée cooks are intimidated by serious baking. Usually, they rely on a pastry chef or buy cakes from an outside pastry shop. A chef may toss together a berry cobbler and serve its biscuity crust slathered with whipped cream, but he or she will more often than not "bring in" a 9-layer Dobostorte iced with Swiss mocha buttercream and topped by wedges of crisp amber caramel. Maybe a restaurant chef has too many other things on his mind, but for the home cook, cakes are completely within the realm of possibility, even pleasurable probability.

Anyone can bake cakes. There is no magic to it, although there seems to be when you watch a simple mixture of eggs, butter, flour, and sugar mount into thick waves of luxuriously silken batter, then bake into delicate flavorful crumbs that literally melt in the mouth.

While there is no magic, there is chemistry, and there is technique. Both can be explained, taught, and learned. Simply read the introductory theory and follow the recipes in this book. Unlike baking pies, which can require getting your hands into the dough, rolling it, and otherwise relying on some manual dexterity, cake batters can if you wish be prepared entirely with an electric mixer. If you stop short of making icing decorations, you can be a complete klutz and still turn out a respectable cake. My premise is that everyone can, and should, bake cakes. We should all treat our souls, our palates, and our families to the delectable tastes, textures, and aromas of home-baked cakes.

As a matter of fact, so-called environmental scents, or room potpourri, were a popular gift item this Christmas season. They are part of an extraordinary phenomenon: the marketing of what I call baking perfume—herbs and spices one simmers in water on the stovetop to impart "the scent of home-baking," as the copy reads. Available in "flavors" such as Gingerbread Cake or Apple Crumble, these products are a sad simulation, not even a whiff, of the real thing. Why do they exist? Because everyone loves a home to smell as if there were a cake in the oven, but no one wants to put it there. We are too busy, or too intimidated by the "science" of baking. Science plays a part, to be sure, but baking is also an art, a craft, and fun.

This book is not intended to be the ultimate, complete cake collection. Rather, it is a group of personal favorites, student-tested recipes, and selected classics. For a period of over three years, I have refined the recipes, testing them many times myself, then passing them on to other home bakers for independent scrutiny. Recipes had to be consistently reliable to be considered for inclusion. And of course, they had to taste good, very, very good. I have shared the cakes with family, friends, and neighbors and listened to all comments.

Some recipes were dropped because the cakes did not pass our taste tests at dessert parties where friends gathered to help me "work" on the book. "This is not for fun," I would caution them, "this is serious cake eating. Pay attention." They did, and those who did not gain too much weight even returned for additional sessions. My own weight-prevention secret, to answer a question I am often asked, is to eat a slice of a cake, rather than the whole thing, to see if it is worthy. I quickly learned another trick, the art of giving away cakes rather than leaving them around as temptation. It is hard to cut a slice from a pie and have something presentable to give away, but my great breakthrough with round cakes was simply to cut them into squares. By slicing off four sides, I had plenty to taste and a perfectly good-looking "whole" cake to share with a friend.

The recipes in this book range from the quick and easy-to-make to the complex and time-consuming; pound cakes are a breeze to whip up compared to a Dobostorte, but there are recipes for both, should the spirit move you. I hope it does, for you will be amply rewarded by the praise you receive and the pleasure you share with family and friends. Another significant reward is the improvement in nutrition you will bring to those raised on preservative- and chemical-laden cake mixes and commercial bakery cakes.

Recognizing the pressures of time facing today's baker, I have included tips and hints for advance preparation, storage, and freezing of ingredients and complete cakes.

I don't dispute the fact that some cake recipes are difficult, but many are not. Start with the coffee cakes; they are casual, easy to mix, trouble free to bake, and require no frosting other than an occasional sifting of sugar on top. Many elegant cakes are also easy to prepare and often can be made ahead and frozen.

I have tried in this book to use the style of my classes, including background for each recipe, the types of equipment used, the ingredients and their function, and the meaning of specific baking terms and techniques. If you are a beginner, I advise you to read the introductory material for each category of cakes as well as the opening chapters on ingredients so you will understand the reason for each procedure. It will help you, for example, to read through "What Happens When a Cake Bakes" in order to comprehend the reaction between ingredients and oven heat. After this, the importance of folding egg whites gently into a batter will make more sense to you. If you are already a confident baker, you may pick up a few ideas from reading the problem-solving hints and tips that follow each introductory chapter; see Cheesecakes, for example. A skilled baker seeking new ideas will know what material to skim in the text, and will work from the Index, going straight to specific information.

While some techniques require no special skills, others demand more precision and care. If the recipe instructions at times appear lengthy, please do not be put off; length is directly related to the degree of detail required for a specific procedure. Instead of leaving you alone at a critical moment in a certain technique, I prefer to have you feel you are at a cooking class, with a teacher by your side.

The cakes are divided into categories, depending upon the type of, or lack of, fat used in the recipe: shortening and/or butter cakes versus non-shortening cakes. In addition, there are sections on Elegant and Special Cakes; Finger Cakes, Petits Fours, and Cupcakes;

Fillings, Icings, and Cake Decorating. If you are looking for a particular type of cake, chocolate for example, use the Index to see a listing of all the chocolate cakes, regardless of category. If you have trouble finding an ingredient or piece of equipment, see the index or list of mail-order Suppliers.

To gather background material and recipes, I have drawn on a wide range of sources and experiences. In preparation for this book, my husband, daughter, and I set ourselves the somewhat less than arduous task of tasting cakes and collecting recipes in several famous pastry-making regions of Europe. To this end we visited Paris, Lyons, northern Italy, Venice, Vienna, Munich, and their surrounding regions.

We lingered for hours in Viennese coffeehouses, tasting yet another torte and having yet another dollop of *Schlag* long after the late-afternoon regulars had gone. We breakfasted in our hotel rooms on cake slices gleaned the evening before from Konditorei and restaurants; we snacked midmorning on astonishing cakes plucked from the lavish jewel-box windows of every bakery we passed. We sat by the canals in Venice sampling cream-filled, rum-soaked, marzipan-topped sponge cakes, and and we shared the crumbs of our all-cake picnic lunch with sparrows in the gardens of Munich's Nymphenburg Palace. We spent scrumptious hours in the back kitchen of a small bakery in Azay-le-Rideau in France's Loire valley, tasting new cake concoctions and learning techniques from a marvelous young *pâtissier*. We filled notebook after notebook with sketches and detailed descriptions of ingredients, layers, and fillings. In preparation for a magazine article, we visited with an extraordinary chef, Jeannette Pépin, mother of Jacques Pépin, at her home near Lyons, France. Cooking and marketing with her, then working side by side with this delightful and generous woman at her niece's restaurant in the village of Port high in the Jura Mountains, we discovered new dimensions to the baker's art.

When this project began, I had for over two years been a food columnist for Gannett Newspapers' Sunday magazine, *Suburbia Today,* published in a dozen newspapers in the New York area. During that period, my column, my readers' questions, and particularly my skillful editor, Meryl Harris, provided material and queries in the baking field that added depth to my research.

To refine my skills, I studied cake baking with Chef Albert Jorant at École de Cuisine La Varenne, in Paris, and with Chef Albert Kumin, at the Country Epicure's International Pastry Arts Center in Bedford Hills, New York. In addition, Chef Kumin graciously and generously shared his time and talent by reading several manuscript chapters and answering many technical questions for this book (though I accept all errors as my own).

I am often asked where I get my recipes. I reply that I have been collecting them for as long as I can remember. Whenever possible in this book, I have tried to give credit for the recipe, to acknowledge its source. Sometimes it is impossible to determine the exact origin of a cake. Many recipes were shared with me by members of my family, friends, students, colleagues, and teachers. Some cakes are variations on traditional themes, others are international classics. Often, even classics appear in a variety of forms from a variety of sources. A prime example is the famed chocolate cake known around the world as the Sachertorte. Nearly every bakery and restaurant has served it at one time, and nearly all claim to be using the original recipe of Frau Sacher. Nevertheless, every Sachertorte (see Index) is different. In cases like this, I have experimented with many variations until I developed one that seemed the very best to me.

I have never knowingly used another baker's recipe without credit. If this has happened, it was inadvertent. In any case, the procedure will be mine for, as a teacher, I strive to create my own style of practical and precise instructions. They are presented in the hope that you will try a few of the recipes and discover that "it's a piece of cake" to bake.

· IT'S A PIECE OF CAKE ·

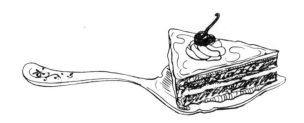

*I*t's a piece of cake . . . as the old saying goes. Just how old? Where does it come from? Eric Partridge's *A Dictionary of Slang and Unconventional English* (Macmillan, 8th edition, 1985) tells us it refers to "something easy to handle . . . ," while the same Partridge, in his *A Dictionary of Catch Phrases* (Routledge & Keegan and Paul, 1977) notes, "It is, was, will be something very easy to do, a 'snip'; occasionally, it's a wonderful opportunity . . . also something as easy to dispose of as a piece of cake."

Partridge notes that the first recorded use of the phrase "it's a piece of cake," meaning something easy to do, appeared in Britain about 1938. As a catch phrase, it became a popular Royal Air Force expression during World War II, referring to the (hopeful) ease of a mission. In C. H. Ward-Jackson's *It's A Piece of Cake, or, R.A.F. Slang Made Easy* (Sylvan Press), reference is made to a cartoon published during the 1948 Berlin Airlift in which the phrase appears. In the cartoon, one RAF pilot is saying to another

"It's a piece of Gatow, old boy." Gatow was the name of a Berlin airfield vital to the British supply operation, and its use was a play on the French word, *gâteau,* meaning cake.

Looking farther back, the *Oxford English Dictionary* notes the slang definition of "cake" as a "foolish, silly, or stupid person." Someone simple, in a word, was "a cake, or cakey." And in the extreme, the fool was called "half-baked."

My guess is that it took but a short leap of language for cake to refer just as easily to a simple thing or simple activity as to a simple person. Hence, I hope you will bake from this book, it's a piece of cake!

The word "cake" itself derives not as one might guess from Latin *coquere,* to cook, but rather from the Old Norse *kaka,* Middle English *Kake,* Middle High German *Kuoche,* and German *Kuche.* The venerable *Oxford English Dictionary* defines cake as "a baked mass of bread or substance of similar kind, distinguished from a loaf or other ordinary bread, either by its form or by its composition . . . In England, cakes have long been treated as fancy bread, and sweetened or flavoured; hence the current sense:

A composition having a basis of bread but containing additional ingredients as butter, sugar, spices, currants, raisins, etc. . . . "

It is true that except for egg sponge leavening, first used in the late 1600s, and the development of chemical leaveners in the mid-1800s, early cakes were simply sweetened breads with various additions. As a sweet treat, cake was well known and so well loved that from the earliest times it entered our language as a synonym for pleasure.

Dost thou think, because thou art virtuous, there shall be no more cakes and ale?

Shakespeare, *Twelfth Night,* II, iii (Sir Toby)

And in a political sense, cake signified life's rewards:

If I stay in [office], I must now have my share of the Cake.

Earl of Holderness, 1750, *Original Letters, II*

And everyone is familiar with the proverb "You can't have your cake and eat it too."

We often hear that things are so popular they sell "like hot cakes," probably a reference to pancakes rather than raised cakes, and when something is the best of its kind, we say it "takes the cake," wins the prize. The origin of this expression dates back to ancient Greece, where a cake made of wheat and honey was awarded to the night guard who kept watch with the greatest vigilance. Early Irish lore records the winning dancer in a competition receiving a cake:

A churn-dish stuck into the earth supported on its flat end a cake, which was to become the prize of the best dancer . . . a young man . . . who taking the cake, placed it gallantly in the lap of a pretty girl to whom . . . he was about to be married.

Bartlett and Coyne, *Scenery and Antiquities of Ireland,* vol II, quoted in *Brewer's Dictionary of Phrase and Fable,* ed. Ivor H. Evans, Harper & Row, 1981

A variation on the expression "take the cake" is the phrase "cake walk." In World War I, "cake-walk" was military slang for a raid or attack that turned out to be easy. A more common reference for the "cake walk" is a Southern Black event wherein couples walked, or promenaded, around a cake and were judged on their grace, elegance, and fancy steps. The winning couple received the cake. In the early twentieth century, this "walk" developed into a popular strutting-style dance step known as the cakewalk.

The name of Marie-Antoine (Antonin) Carême (1783–1833), master chef and baker, comes to the forefront of any history of cake baking. Because of his incredible skill and style, he elevated the baker's art to its greatest heights, though the man himself began at the most humble level; in fact, his life parallels in microcosm the history of cakes in general. For this reason, Carême is an appropriate introduction to a historical survey.

Carême was one of twenty-five children born to a very poor Parisian family. Unable to support the entire brood, his father sent him out at the age of nine to seek his fortune. Whether by luck or destiny, the frightened young boy found his way to a cookshop *(gargotier)* where the owner took him in and gave him his first opportunity to work in a kitchen. By the age of fifteen, Carême had begun his apprenticeship with Bailly, a famed pastry chef who worked for the house of Talleyrand.

Also at this time, Carême began to study foreign cuisines and architectural design as it applied to the culinary arts. It was not long before Carême became a chef himself, working directly for Talleyrand. As his experience grew and his fame spread, Carême's clientele soon included Louis XVIII, the Prince Regent of England (later King George IV), Czar Alexander I, the Court of Vienna, the British Embassy in Paris, and the Rothschild family. Carême became known as "the king of cooks and the cook of kings." Though he was a famed *chef de cuisine,* creative culinary inventor, and author of many books on cooking, Carême's fame came in large part from the application of his architectural designs to the art of pastry making. He devoted such enormous energy to designing *pièces montées,* elaborately ornate architectural structures made of cake, that his fans called him the "Palladio of pastry," in honor of the famous

Italian architect. Before his death at the age of 49, Carême wrote ". . . the fine arts are five in number, to wit: painting, sculpture, poetry, music, architecture—whose main branch is confectionery" (*L'Art Culinaire au XlXe Siècle,* Antonin Carême, Mairie du IIIe Arrondissement, 1984, Orangerie de Bagatelle).

Looking back through history, Carême's dazzling cake creations stand in stark contrast to man's first attempts at cake baking.

The first cakes were really breads, primitive forms of dough made from hand-gathered grains pounded flat with rocks, softened with water, and baked on stones over a fire. These crude pastries were an important part of life's sustenance at least as early as the Stone Age. Over time, herbs, seeds, oils, nuts, honey, even dried fruits were added to the rough, flat dough to add flavor. The evolution of dough from that stage to the fancy dessert cakes we enjoy today parallels the history of civilization—and of machines for harvesting grain, milling grain into flour, and baking doughs. As this brief survey will show, each advance in equipment produced an advance in the baker's product. But through it all the thread was never broken, for whatever the stage of man's development, pastry in some form was always a significant part of life.

Plain and sweetened breads and cakes have been important in man's ceremonial life since prehistoric times. There is evidence suggesting that even the earliest people dedicated some form of grain product to their gods in seasonal rituals. In these pagan sacrifices, men offered life's most important foods, among them bread/cake, to their god(s) along with prayers for help, hope, or thanksgiving for the harvest.

There is a direct connection between these first offerings and our current practice of using cakes to celebrate life's significant events—births, christenings, weddings, and seasonal holidays.

As an example, consider the Christmas Yule log cake (Bûche de Noël). The shape of this cake derives directly from the Yule logs and bonfires that early Norse tribes burned to dispel the darkness of the season and frighten away the demons of winter who they believed were stealing the sun. It was traditional for a piece of the burned Yule log to be saved for starting the next year's fire; the ash or twig of this log was considered a symbol of good luck and strength. These customs, and the burning of Yule logs, are still holiday rituals in many European countries. As a substitute for the real log, the log-shaped cake, or *Bûche de Noël,* became a tradition during the Christmas and New Year holidays.

To understand progress in the baker's art, one must look at the ingredients and tools available at each period of history.

We know that the early people of Mesopotamia cultivated grains, which they crushed with flat stones. The ancient Egyptians also cultivated grains. Their bread, called *ta,* was a flat loaf made from a barley sourdough. For ceremonial offerings, it was seasoned with sesame seeds or honey. To produce their flour, the Egyptians used a saddle-stone mill, a grooved flat rock that held the grain while a stone rolling pin was pushed over it by hand. The Greeks improved on this with a stone mill worked by a lever. This improvement produced a more refined, nearly white flour with a light texture. Because of this advance, the Greeks became the first to make light-textured pastries and sweet cakes, including plain honey cake (the Greeks added honey to their cakes so they would retain moisture and keep longer), fried cake soaked in honey syrup (an ancestor of baklava), and even cheesecake. The Romans learned these arts from the Greeks, and carried them several steps farther.

The Romans invented the rotary mill in the first century B.C., and were then able to produce refined flour in large quantities for the first time. Bread was commercially produced on a large scale in public bakeries. Cakes, also commonly made, were baked by a sweetmeat maker, who was not to be confused with the bread baker. These specialized pastry chefs devised elaborate sweets for the splendid, if often outrageous, banquets for which the Romans became known.

As the Roman Empire spread to the West, Roman food and customs spread as well. Medieval French, Italian, and English cuisines thus derived directly from the Roman. However, baking in Europe also owes much to the Far and Middle East, primarily because this was the area where sugar cane was first grown and used as a food sweetener.

Since prehistoric times, honey and fruit were used throughout the world to sweeten foods. But in Asia, India, and the islands of the South Pacific, sugar cane was indigenous and was long used as a sweetener. Some authorities believe the first manufactured cane sugar came from India, but we know that it was grown in the Middle East as early as the fourth century. In addition to sugar, Arab bakers also had many spices and flavorings that were products of their trade with the Far East.

In seventh-century Persia, for example, cakes were made with sugar cane, cinnamon, nutmeg, cloves, almonds, walnuts, and rosewater. At this time, and for centuries to come, the Arabs were way ahead of the West in the knowledge of the baking arts. In fact, even in the Middle Ages, the Arabs knew how to leaven their cakes with wood ash, which produced carbon dioxide when mixed with an acid such as sour milk; this advance was unknown in the West until the 1800s.

The use of sugar in baking, along with other customs, spread to the West through the forces of war, power, and progress in methods of transportation. The Crusades and the development of trade routes in the Middle Ages helped the cause.

As Venice had the most vital trading ports for contact with the East, the Venetians and other regional chefs of the Italian city-states were the first to adopt Arab ingredients and translate Arab treatises on cooking and baking. This contact was an essential factor in the development of the craft of Italian pastry making as the first and most advanced in the West.

Sugar as well as pastries from the Arab world were introduced to the rest of Europe by Italian chefs, who then influenced the French. The French, in turn, spread their culinary arts to England when William the Conqueror took his Norman cooks with him across the English Channel in 1066.

The culinary arts reached dizzying heights in the Middle Ages as feudal lords strove to produce ever-more elaborate banquets. In addition to the proverbial "four and twenty blackbirds," live rabbits, frogs, other small animals, and occasionally dwarves were encased in pastry crusts by inventive chefs. This "subtletie," as the fun was called in the fifteenth century, was the origin of the modern custom of hiding show girls inside fancy cakes, to leap out at the guest of honor during a birthday or stag party.

It was during this period that the horticulture and culinary uses of sugar cane spread from East to West. Sugar cane was grown on the island of Sicily from the twelfth century onward. Fifteenth-century Portuguese explorers discovered the cane and took it from Sicily to Madeira and Spain, and from there to Brazil. But except in these tropical areas where it grew and was accessible, sugar was often unknown, or at best a rare luxury. It was prohibitively expensive for all but royal or noble households, and in some places was sold only by chemists for medicinal purposes. In Western Europe, this remained the case until the mid-1800s, when it was discovered that sugar could also be produced from the sugar beet, which could be cultivated in northern climates. The widespread production of sugar from the beet, aided by a decree from Napoleon to increase acreage devoted to the sugar beet, brought its price down to a level the common householder could afford and made it economical, for the first time in history, to use sugar for home cake baking.

Leavening was another essential factor in cake baking. Until the seventeenth century, cakes were leavened primarily with yeast. In fact, most cakes were really sweetened and flavored yeast breads.

The yeast used for cake leavening came from many sources: airborne yeast was used to make a starter from a soft dough, and yeast was scooped from the scum of fermenting wine, beer, and cider. Chemical leavenings did not develop until the early 1800s and were not commercially sold until the mid-nineteenth century. In the 1850s the first commercially prepared bakers' yeast became available, developed in Germany and imported to the United States. Dried yeast was not sold commercially until after World War II.

The use of egg foams for leavening cakes first became widely known in the West at about the beginning of the seventeenth century. With this advance, egg-lightened cakes grew in popularity, and by the nineteenth century sponge cakes were standard fare. So too were cakes made with generous quantities of eggs. Granted, the eggs of that time were smaller than ours, but it was not uncommon to see a cake recipe calling for 3 dozen eggs, or an extra-large wedding cake made with ninety.

The first colonists arriving in America, at the beginning of the seventeenth century, brought their recipes with them, but they could not bring the ingredients, and among the hardships they faced was a scarcity of fine wheat flour. However, they incorporated indigenous ingredients such as the rye and corn used by the Indians. Thus, "rye 'n' injun" became a staple New England bread/cake, made from rye flour, corn, molasses, and yeast.

On the frontier, "hardtack" was the most common cake, made of whatever type of flour was at hand mixed with water, an occasional wild bird's egg, and baked in a frying pan on an open fire. This same bread was also known to sailors as sea bread or ship's biscuit because it remained edible for so long. Another staple of the frontier was a flat cornmeal cake which originated with the Shawnee Indians of the Algonquin Tribe. They shared their recipe with Colonial trappers, who called the cakes "Shawnee-cakes," later corrupted to "journey cakes," then "johnny cakes." Indians taught the settlers to sweeten their food with syrup made from maple trees and cornstalks. They also taught them to pound corn, peas, and beans into flour to make ashcakes, dough

On the subject of yeast breads, it is interesting to note that it was really a yeast-risen brioche that was referred to in the famous quotation:

"Let them eat cake," attributed to Marie Antoinette at the time of the French Revolution.*

Her callous remark, of course, referred to the peasants who could not get ordinary bread. In point of fact, what she really said, was "Qi'ils mangent de la brioche," "Let them eat brioche," which was a refined type of bread rather than a fancy cake.

While on the subject of Marie Antoinette, one should remember that she was the eleventh daughter of Empress Maria Theresa, ruler of eighteenth-century Austria, where no excess was too lavish in the invention or consumption of cakes. The princess grew up in Vienna's Hofburg Palace, famous to this day for its "Zuckerbackerstiege," or Sugar-bakers' staircase, named for the passageway where a constant stream of cakes and pastries was delivered. If, in fact, Marie Antoinette actually did mean "cake" when she made her fatuous remark, it is no wonder, since she grew up thinking everyone had cake whenever they wished.

*Although attributed to Marie Antoinette, the line was actually written several years before she is supposed to have said it by Jean Jacques Rousseau, Sixth Book of Les Confessions, *1781–1788 (written about 1768 or 69). See Bartlett's* Familiar Quotations, *p. 436-b, 14th Edition, Little Brown, 1968.*

wrapped in leaves and cooked in the ashes, and hoecakes, dough cooked on the blade of a hoe held over an open fire. By the nineteenth century, hoecakes and ashcakes had become specialties of the American South. Corncakes were another. At first called cornpones, from the Algonquin *oppone,* (also spelled *appone*) or corn cake, these cornmeal cakes were dropped from a spoon onto a tin set over the fire. They were also called corn dodgers, because they were so hard you had to dodge or risk injury if one was thrown at you.

Sugar cane and molasses were brought to the American colonies by traders after 1650, giving bakers new products to work with. As the ports were in the South, Southerners developed many cakes utilizing molasses and brown sugar. In the nineteenth century refined white sugar also became available, in the South as well as across the country at a price. It was sold in pressed cones that were broken into chunks with iron pincers. The chunks were then pounded fine and sifted for use.

Flavorings for cakes had remained the same for centuries—primarily nuts, spices, seeds, citrus in the tropics, and orange-flower water or rosewater—until 1791, when Thomas Jefferson brought vanilla back from a visit to France and introduced it to the American kitchen.

For the American baker, the nineteenth century brought the greatest technological changes. New inventions in every field including farming aided the cultivation of grains and the production of flour, the essential ingredient of cakes.

Before this time, farmers had been dependent upon horses and oxen for power; the new industrial development brought machines powered by steam, then by gasoline. Among the new inventions were the steel plow, patented in 1837, the reaper, the steam thresher and sheaf binder for harvesting grain, and windmills for irrigating the prairies. In 1902 the first gasoline tractors were introduced to the market. The building of the railroads made possible the settlement of the West, and the perfecting of the steel plow made possible the cultivation of the fertile prairies and the planting of wheat as a staple crop.

In the mid nineteenth century, Minneapolis became the capital of America's flour industry. Here a middlings purifier was invented, to remove the bran from spring wheat, making a finer flour. In 1856, a miller in Indiana developed a method of grinding soft winter wheat to produce the first fine cake flour. During this period, grain elevators were developed to store wheat, and in 1862 Abraham Lincoln signed a bill opening the transcontinental railroad, which made it possible to ship wheat cheaply. By the end of the Civil War wheat flour had become a reliable, accessible, and inexpensive ingredient for the home baker.

Before the nineteenth century, American home cooking was done on an open hearth. Breads and pastries were baked in brick beehive ovens above and behind an open fire, or on an open hearth in special iron pots with lids that held ashes for overhead heat. In the Southwest, baking was done in dome-shaped ovens made of adobe.

The first American cookstove was cast in Pennsylvania in 1765, but it was not until the 1840s that wood or coal stoves popularly began to replace fireplaces for cooking.

These freestanding metal cookstoves were more modern to be sure, and easier to use than fireplaces in many ways. But neither offered much help in the way of oven heat control. Judging the heat when baking a cake was one of the baker's most difficult tasks. In the seventeenth century, bakers had been cautioned not to put cake in a beehive oven so hot it scorched your hand. Early nineteenth-century cookbooks are full of homey advice for judging oven temperatures. Some recommend baking a cake once the oven was hot enough to brown a sheet of white writing paper or white cake flour tossed on the oven floor in 10 seconds, or when the fire chamber was glowing a particular cherry red color.

Knowing how long to bake a cake was an equally mystifying problem. Recipes might specify leaving a cake in the oven for as long as one could recite a specified number of Ave Maria's or the Pater Noster.

Gas stoves were introduced to American cooks in the 1850s, but were not widely accepted for many years because bakers feared they would blow up. These ranges were easier to use than coal or wood, but the early models still lacked heat-regulating thermostats. Recipes from the turn of the century, and into the 1920s in fact, require the cake baker to test the oven temperature before putting in the cake. One test: If you could leave your hand in the oven for 20 to 35 seconds, it was a "quick" oven; from 35 to 45 seconds, it was a "moderate" oven; from 45 to 60 seconds, it was "slow."

Electric stoves were first shown at the World's Fair of 1893 but were not accepted widely in homes for at least twenty years.

Progress in the field of baking owes a great deal to Fannie Farmer, a determined redhaired cooking expert who graduated from the Boston Cooking School, eventually became its director, and went on to write *The Boston Cooking-School Cook Book* and found her own cooking school. Aspiring cookbook authors might note that her manuscript was at first rejected by her publisher, Little, Brown and Co. of Boston. Finally, they agreed to print an edition of 3,000 if Fanny paid for the printing herself. She did, and in 1896 the book was published.

Fannie Farmer is sometimes called the mother of the level measurement. Up to that time, tea cups, coffee spoons, "butter the size of an egg," or "butter the size of a walnut" were common measuring units. Many cookbook writers before her had tried to specify level or at least standard measurements, but Farmer wrote the most specific instructions and preached the virtues of level measurements and standardized methods for reliable baking. She also recommended the virtues of oven thermometers and oven thermostats and wrote recipes specifying baking times and temperatures, a real innovation.

Cakes were baked in cast-iron pans until the 1870s, when light coated steel pans were introduced. Also in 1870, the first egg beater was patented. Before this, egg foams and stiffly beaten egg whites were laboriously whipped up by the combined forces of strong arms and forks, or arms and a branch, or a bundle of twigs. One famous Shaker recipe for Mother Ann's birthday cake recommends beating the egg whites with peach twigs to impart the delicate flavor of peaches to the batter. (I tested this recipe for inclusion in this collection, but found the cake too bland and uninteresting; the failure was probably mine, as I confess I did not use the peach twigs.)

Refrigeration through the nineteenth century was still dependent upon ice—ice boxes and ice chests—for the first electric refrigerators were not on the market until 1916. By the 1940s they were common, however, and the first household freezers began to be popular around the middle of that decade.

One glance at the array of baking appliances, gadgets, and ingredients in today's kitchen should impress us with just how far we have come.

· BAKING EQUIPMENT ·

*I*n this age of ubiquitous food processors and electric gadgets, it is important to remember that not too long ago arm power was the home bakers' primary tool. Cake batters were beaten with wooden spoons in wooden or earthenware bowls and egg whites were whipped with a fork or a bundle of twigs. The wooden spoon blended ingredients perfectly well (and still does); the fork- or twig-whipped whites foamed well, given enough time and effort. There's the key: time and effort are the things technology has saved us from. Machines can do our work and free us for other tasks, and by and large, as far as baking goes, quality has not suffered too much in the bargain. However, if you ever really want to "feel" the transformation of raw ingredients into a cake batter, you can do so only by beating it by hand. I suggest that my

baking students mix butter cake by hand at least once just to get the feel of it. Professional bakers use industrial-strength electric mixers for beating, but they still use their hands, and arms, for folding mixtures together; they insist this is the only way to maintain control. For the home baker, it is usually more practical to use a spoon or rubber spatula for folding, and to beat batters with an electric mixer to save time.

While hands are still a basic tool, there are certain pieces of equipment that are essential to today's baker. These are described in this chapter. Be aware that baking is a creative art, and part of that creativity may involve improvisation with equipment. Feel free to substitute what you find in your cupboard before you run out to buy something new. Put a saucepan into a frying pan to make a double boiler. Use a wine bottle for a rolling pin. Consult the Pan Volume and Serving Chart (see index) to substitute baking pan sizes based on cake batter quantities given in the recipes.

Note: I assume that since you are reading this book, your kitchen has the basic cooking essentials: liquid and dry measuring cups, measuring spoons, mixing bowls, whisks, a rubber spatula, a wire rack for cooling pans, potholders, and a hand-held or stand-type electric mixer. Each cake recipe carries a list of "special equipment" needed. This refers only to items *beyond* the above-mentioned basics, such as extra bowls or pots, a double boiler, grater, decorating tubes and tips, sifter, wax paper, etc.

CAKE PANS

■

The first thing to note when selecting cake pans is the size. Every manufacturer measures by a different system: some across the top, others across the bottom, some to the outer edge of the lip, others inside. In this book, all pans are measured across the top inner edge and volume is measured in cups of water needed to fill the pan to the brim. The Pan Volume and Serving Chart (see Index) compares different pan sizes and volumes. Many cakes can be baked in a variety of shapes and sizes, and for these cakes, the recipes note the number of cups of batter the recipes yield. Select alternate pan sizes from the chart by comparing volumes. Note that pans should be filled about ⅔ full so there is room left for

the batter to rise; for this reason, the chart notes maximum batter amounts for each size, as well as the number of cups of water needed to fill the pan to the brim.

You can calculate the comparative pan sizes by square inches: An 8 × 8 square has 64 square inches, while an 11 × 7 pan has 77. Deeper pans hold more batter even if dimensions are otherwise the same. Remember that a round 9-inch diameter pan equals ¾ the area of a 9-inch square pan because the corners add more area.

To modify the size of a large pan, line it with foil, fold foil into a lip at cut-off point, and fill excess area with dry beans.

The wrong size pan may result in baking failure. Batter must be at least 1 inch deep in the pan, preferably deeper, for the cake to rise properly. Batter that is too thin bakes into a cake that is too flat. On the other hand, if the pan is too small and the batter too near the top, it may overflow while the cake is rising, causing the cake to sink after baking and the overflow to burn onto your oven floor.

Buy layer-cake pans in pairs or threes. For cake baking basics, you will eventually need two 8- × 1½-inch rounds, two 9- × 1½-inch rounds, one 8-inch square 2 inches deep, one jelly-roll pan 15 × 10 inches and 1 inch deep, one 9-inch tube pan (6-cup capacity), one 10-inch tube or bundt pan (12-cup capacity), one 8- or 9-inch diameter springform pan with a flat bottom, and one loaf pan 9 × 5 × 3 inches. If you like to split one cake into several thin layers, as for a torte, buy one or two layer pans 2 or 3 inches deep.

As a general rule, I prefer to bake cakes in aluminum or heavy, tin-plated steel. Look for well-sealed seams and good construction. You do not need Teflon or nonstick cake pans if you grease your pans properly. Black steel or iron is fine for some types of baking, but not for cakes. The blackness causes a dark, heavy crust that is undesirable in delicate cakes.

Springform pans are two-piece pans that have either a flat or tubed center panel surrounded by a hoop fastened with a spring latch; these are used for delicate tortes and cheesecakes that might be damaged by inverting from a solid-bottom pan. Note: Cheesecakes can be baked in solid-bottom pans set in a water bath, but cake removal can be a delicate process. Therefore in this book, we always use springforms for cheesecakes. It is essential to check the strength of the spring latch before using your pan. Fix it if it is weak, or replace the pan; or wire the hoop into a fixed position for baking and untwist the wire to unlatch. I have had weak springs unlatch, spilling my half-baked cake into the oven, and I promise you it is not a wonderful baking experience.

Removable-bottom layer-cake pans make unmolding easy. These are simply round pans containing a central flat disk that is a removable bottom. The cake is inverted onto a wire rack, the side piece lifted off, then the bottom disk removed. Avoid this type of pan for very liquid batters, as they may leak from beneath the bottom while in the oven.

Professional bakers like to use metal hoops or flan rings of varying depths set on parchment-lined baking sheets.

Tube pans vary amazingly in manufacture, size, and shape. Plain tubes, ring molds, bundt pans, and kugelhopf molds are all variations on the same theme, and can be used interchangeably as long as the size is correct; check volume in cups of water needed to fill to capacity. The tube shape is designed to conduct heat to the center of the batter, allowing the dough to rise and bake evenly. For this reason, the tube is excellent for heavy or dense batters like pound cakes and their relatives. The kugelhopf and other yeast doughs are baked in a tube because it gives the rising yeast dough more surface to cling to, thus helping the rise. Angel-food cakes are also baked in tube pans because the added surface area gives the fragile batter structure something to cling to as it rises. The best angel-food pans have removable bottoms as well as small feet sticking up on the rim so the baked cake may be inverted and suspended as it cools. If your pan has no feet, invert your baked angel cake onto a funnel or tall bottle until thoroughly cool (see page 70). As a general rule when selecting tube pans, the heavier the metal, the more evenly the cake will bake.

Square, oblong, or rectangular pans 1½ to 2½ inches deep are used for sheet cakes. They come in a wide variety of dimensions; in the home, one can use a lasagna pan or turkey roasting pan. Again, refer to the chart (see page 57) for volumes and dimensions.

Jelly-roll pans have many uses. Select a sturdy, nonwarping pan with a firm lip all around, a good 1 inch deep. A nonstick surface is not essential, though it works well. I use the jelly-roll pan for roulades, for fairly thin sheet cakes from which to make *petits fours,* and I have also been known to invert the pan and use it as a cookie sheet. In addition, I like to use the jelly-roll pan beneath the springform when baking cheesecakes, for ease in handling and to catch any leaks or drips of batter.

CHARLOTTE MOLDS

∎

A charlotte is a molded dessert in which bread, cake, or biscuits line a container holding a filling of fruit and/or a sweetened cream. Because the charlotte must be unmolded for serving, the shape of the mold itself is important: it must be wide-mouthed, with sides that are either straight or tapered outward. The classic charlotte mold, imported from France, is a slightly tapered cylindrical form made of tinned steel. It has two heart-shaped handles, an optional lid, and is available in graduated sizes from 6 ounces to 2 quarts. The recipes in this book use the 1½-quart (6-cup capacity) and 2-quart (8-cup capacity) sizes. Beware of charlotte molds made of aluminum, because the metal can interact with certain cream fillings and/or acidic fruits, causing them to darken unappetizingly. If you are using an aluminum mold, line it with a piece of Saran or plastic wrap before adding the unbaked filling. Instead of the French metal mold, you can substitute a fluted metal brioche mold, a porcelain soufflé mold, or any other flared or straight-sided container of comparable capacity. For nonbaked charlottes, you can use a round plastic freezer container. For some charlottes, round-bottomed Pyrex bowls or mixing bowls may be used as well.

STEAMED PUDDING MOLDS

∎

Pudding molds come in a great variety of sizes, shapes, and materials. They can be as simple as a pottery "basin," as the English call a pudding bowl, which is lined with cloth, filled with batter, then covered with cloth and foil before being tied and set into a steamer. Or they can be as elaborate as a 2-piece tinned steel Turk's-head or melon mold. In addition to steaming puddings, the mold can be used for making all types of gelatin desserts or Bavarian creams. A good quality metal mold is not expensive, and if you plan to steam more than one pudding a year, it is worth investing in one. Select one with a lid that fastens securely to the body so that no water will seep into the batter during the steaming process. Metal molds are very decorative, and most come with a hanging loop so that they can be displayed on the wall. Molds are available in 1-, 1½-, 2-, and 2½-quart sizes.

DOUBLE BOILERS

∎

Commercial double boilers have a bowl or basin with a lip that sits inside a saucepan; usually there is a pot lid as well. Hot or boiling water goes in the lower pot, the item to be melted or cooked sits in the raised container. The purpose is to provide gentle, indirect heat for cooking.

ELECTRIC MIXERS

∎

All cakes can be mixed by hand with a spoon and a bowl. Some, like Swedish Butter Cake, (see Index), are even best made that way.

However, I have written the recipes in this book assuming the availability of an electric mixer because it gives good results and saves time.

There is a wide variety of electric mixers available today. I like to use a heavy-duty KitchenAid with its wire whisk or flat paddle-type beater for all general-purpose cake baking. I use a KitchenAid Model K45SS, with the head that tips back to raise the beater; I find this model practical because the design makes it easy to add ingredients or scrape down the sides of the bowl. Models with fixed heads are larger but make these tasks awkward at best.

For whipping cream, I prefer using a hand-held beater and a small, deep stainless-steel bowl that has been well chilled. (I finish whipping cream, however, with a hand whisk, so I can control the degree of stiffness.) The hand-held beater is excellent for beating yolks or sauces in a double boiler, as for zabaglione, but a whisk or egg beater will work well, too.

FOOD PROCESSORS

■

While most bakers think of preparing cake batters in electric mixers, the ubiquitous food processor can be a great help and time-saver when baking cakes. It is not suitable for for every type of cake or icing of course, but for some it can save from a quarter to half of the preparation time.

How to Adapt Traditional Cake Recipes to the Food Processor

To take advantage of this popular kitchen tool and apply it to the techniques of cake baking, you must first analyze your cake recipe to see what techniques it requires. Then consider the functions the processor performs well and try to put them together. It will take some experimentation, but you will quickly find many recipes that are best done in the processor. My favorites are Carrot Cake and Cream-Cheese Icing (see Index).

As a general rule, the processor works well for creamed butter cakes or nut or fruit cakes with oil as the fat. Often the sequence of steps and the order of adding ingredients must be changed when using the processor. As an example, first pulse flour, baking powder and/or baking soda, and salt to blend and aerate them (instead of sifting as in a conventional recipe), then remove them from the bowl. The flour mixture should be added to the ingredients *last*.

Without washing the bowl, go on to process other dry ingredients, grind bread crumbs or chop nuts (for another technique with nuts, see Chops Nuts, page 19), shred carrots, apples, etc. Remove them from the bowl and set aside. Without washing the bowl, add shortening or oil, eggs, and sugar. Process for about 15 seconds to blend, then scrape down the workbowl. Add other liquids and flavorings and pulse to combine. Return to the bowl the prepared crumbs or fruit, nuts, etc. Finally, add the flour, salt, baking powder and/or soda and pulse only 4 or 5 times, just to blend. Do not overwork the batter. That is the one danger with this machine, for overprocessing the flour develops its gluten and can produce a tough cake.

For creamed cakes, where butter and sugar are conventionally beaten together, pulse the flour, salt, baking powder mixture to aerate, then remove from the workbowl; this step is optional. Then process the butter (which can be cold from the refrigerator) until smooth, add the sugar, and process until the mixture forms a ring around the metal blade, about 30 seconds. Scrape down the workbowl often. Then add eggs, liquid, and flavorings, pulsing to blend. Last, add the flour mixture and pulse 3 or 4 times just to blend.

For a sponge cake or torte that calls for whipped egg whites, the whites can be whipped first, in the workbowl fitted with a whisk attachment. Remove the whites and reserve them until they are added back at the end of the recipe by pulsing 2 or 3 times to incorporate them with the rest of the batter. Be careful about overprocessing whipped whites or they will deflate. If you do not have the whisk attachment, use a regular beater or electric mixer and hold the whipped whites aside until ready to add them to the ingredients in the processor.

I do not recommend the processor for angel-food cakes because the recipe requires so many egg whites that the volume is more than most processor bowls can handle.

Cake mixes can be made in the processor. Most processor workbowls will hold a standard 18.5-ounce packaged mix. Use the metal blade. Add the cake mix to the workbowl, then turn on the machine and add the eggs and liquid through the feed tube. Process for a few seconds, scrape down the workbowl, then process for 1 full minute (unlike most batters where dry ingredients are quickly pulsed).

You can use the processor fitted with the metal blade for whipping chilled heavy cream; just watch carefully and stop processing when the cream is nearly stiff. Note that this method makes the cream more dense than when whisked, and thus, while it has slightly less volume, it holds its shape well when piped through a pastry bag.

Things the processor does very well:
- Chops nuts—When they are to be ground very fine in order to replace flour as in a torte, they can be combined with some of the flour or sugar in the recipe and ground to powder with the metal blade.
- Chops dried fruit pieces—Add a little sugar or flour to keep the pieces dry.
- Melts chocolate easily—Simply break up block chocolate and powder it by processing with the metal blade. With machine running, pour hot liquid (melted butter, very hot water, coffee) through the feed tube onto the chocolate. Process until the chocolate is completely melted and smooth.
- Chops citrus zest—Remove the zest with a vegetable peeler and cut it into 2-inch lengths. Add to the workbowl fitted with the metal blade and process with some of the flour or sugar from the recipe. Leave in bowl and continue recipe.
- Eliminates need for sifting by aerating flour and blending it evenly with baking powder or baking soda and salt
- Makes icing glazes (sifted confectioners' sugar plus liquid) or creamed butter or cream-cheese icing in seconds.

MIXING BOWLS

∎

I prefer to use heavy pottery or stainless-steel bowls, with wide, flat bottoms. Avoid metal bowls with rounded bottoms, as they can tip over if you leave a spatula or whisk inside. It is good to have a variety of sizes, and a small, deep metal bowl is handy for whipping small amounts of cream. I also like my heavy Pyrex glass bowl that is microwave safe, has a handle and pouring spout, and is marked with graduations up to 2 quarts. It is great for whipping cream, for blending batters by hand, or for whipping eggs. Avoid plastic bowls for general use because they cannot be perfectly cleaned. The plastic surface retains grease, damaging beaten egg whites for instance, and occasionally plastic bowls retain odors that may be passed on to your cakes.

SIFTERS/STRAINERS

■

Flour settles in packing and shipping, and even brands labeled "presifted" are not, for our purposes. For most cake baking, it is important to sift flour before measuring by the scoop and sweep method (see page 50) and again with the other dry ingredients. This second sifting blends the dry ingredients together, distributing them evenly throughout the batter. For most cakes, I find this method sifts sufficiently; I rarely use a triple-tier sifter, though I own one; I do use it occasionally for a génoise, an especially fine sponge cake. My regular sifter is actually a sieve, or strainer, with a very fine mesh.

DRY AND LIQUID MEASURING CUPS

■

Dry measuring cups are designed so you can fill them to the brim and level the top by passing a straight edge over it. These cups are available in graduated sizes, with a separate cup for each unit from ⅛ or ¼ cup up to 2 cups; usually they nest together for storage. By contrast, liquid measuring cups are usually Pyrex (select this type) or plastic, with a handle and pouring spout. They are commonly available in 1-, 2-, and 4-cup sizes. To use a liquid measure, you simply fill the cup to the desired mark and read it at eye level. Another feature of liquid measuring cups is the space left just above the topmost measuring mark. If you fill the cup with liquid to the highest mark, there will still be a space above this mark so that the liquid will not spill while being moved. If you were to fill this cup with dry ingredients and level it off, you would have much too much. If you filled it to a measurement below the brim, you would have no way to level it off; the cup will not work properly for dry ingredients. Be sure to use each type of cup for its designated purpose. Read How To Measure Ingredients (see page 49).

SCALES

■

Scales are used for accurate measuring of flour, sugar, fat, and some other ingredients in cake baking. Read About Using Scales (page 50). There are two types of scales—balance and spring. Both are accurate, but professionals use the balance system in bakeshops. The spring-type can be checked for accuracy by weighing a known quantity: a pound (454 grams) of butter, for example. After practice, you will find it much more practical to measure 100 grams of flour on a scale than to measure 1 cup; your cups may be of differing sizes, you may compact the flour by tapping the cup, in any number of ways the volume may vary, but the scale weight will not. Butter and other solid fats, of course, are easy to measure on a scale, as opposed to packing them into a measuring cup and hoping no air holes lodge in the bottom.

PASTRY BRUSHES

■

A pastry brush is essential for applying egg washes and jelly glazes to tarts. It is also excellent for spreading soaking syrups on cake layers and fruit glazes atop finished cakes. For the most delicate tasks, I prefer an imported European goose-feather brush with a handle of braided quills. This is lovely to look at, lasts a very long time, and is inexpensive. After use, you simply wash it in warm soapy water, rinse, and air dry. Find it in gourmet cookware shops or catalogues. Ordinary pastry brushes from 1 inch to 2½ inches wide are better for spreading jam glazes on sponge layers.

SPATULAS

■

There are two types of spatulas referred to in this book. Rubber spatulas are tools used for mixing, folding, and scraping out the inside of a bowl or mixer beater. They come in all sizes, but the most common for home kitchen use has a plastic or wood handle about 6 inches long, topped by a flexible tongue. The most common household size has a tongue roughly 2 × 3½ inches. One edge of the flexible top is curved, to ride neatly against the side of a curved bowl. Life would not be the same without this device.

A metal spatula is equally essential in baking. It resembles a blunt-edged, round-ended knife with a metal blade, and is useful for all spreading tasks—fillings and icings, for example. The basic icing spatula that I use is about 10 inches long overall, with a 1- × 6-inch blade that will flex but is not flimsy. For smoothing icing on the tops and sides of large layer cakes, for icing broad sheet cakes, and for lifting individual layers or whole cakes, I love my large 17-inch metal spatula. It is built like a fine knife, with a good wooden handle and a strong 12-blade 1¾ inches wide. Also for lifting, I use an offset, or step-down spatula with a broad long blade. For fancy decorative work with icing, I use an artist's palette knife, kept just for this purpose.

DOUGH SCRAPER

■

My favorite tool for working with yeast doughs is the dough scraper, called a *coupe-pâte* in French. It is simply a rectangular metal scraper with a wooden handle on one edge. Similar tools are made of flexible plastic. Use this ingenious device for cutting, kneading, lifting, and scraping dough, as well as for cleaning off countertops. You can substitute a wide putty knife or pancake turner, but the long handle gets in the way.

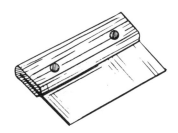

CARDBOARD CAKE DISKS

■

For baking cakes, you will quickly find it hard to live without these disks of corrugated cardboard sold in dimensions that correspond to cake pan sizes—6, 8, 9, 12, 14 inches. Some manufacturers refer to them as "cardboard cake circles." They come covered with glazed white or plain brown paper or gold or silver foil and with plain or fluted edges. They are available in restaurant supply houses, party and paper goods shops, and more and more frequently in bakeware shops. If you have trouble finding them, ask at a local pizzeria; these are the same boards put under baked pizzas. If you cannot find these boards, simply cut your own out of any corrugated box and cover them with foil. They are indispensable for handling cakes, especially when spreading on icing or pressing crumbs or chopped nuts onto the iced cake sides.

COOLING RACKS

■

Wire cooling racks are essential in cake baking. As soon as the cake comes from the oven, the pan is set on the rack, which has short feet lifting it off the counter. The air circulating beneath the pan prevents condensation on the cake bottom and helps it cool evenly. Most cakes have a fairly fragile structure that needs to cool in the baking pan, on a wire rack, for at least 10 minutes before unmolding. After unmolding, cakes should continue cooling on a wire rack so air circulation will remove the moisture or steam given off by the hot cake. If contained inside the cake, this steam would make it soggy.

CAKE TESTERS

■

One sticks a cake tester into a baking cake to see if the batter is completely baked. If the tester comes out clean, the baking is complete; if there is raw batter clinging to the tester, the cake must cook longer. Cake testers can be simple or elaborate. In the old days, the most common tester was a clean broom straw. My favorite is a thin bamboo skewer, also called a cocktail or saté skewer (available in gourmet or Oriental shops). A toothpick may be used, but for some cakes it is not long enough to penetrate to the center of the batter. Metal cake testers are sold in hardware or baking shops. These are simply metal needles with a handle, but I prefer wood to the metal, for metal gets hot fast and may cause batter to cling to it even when the cake is completely baked.

CAKE STANDS

■

A revolving cake stand is a lazy Susan made for the baker. The fact that the stand is raised above table height makes it easy to see decorations at eye level. One hand can rotate it while the other applies the decoration, making efficient and regular patterns more easily than on a flat and stationary surface. Select a stand of heavy-duty aluminum, with a platform about 12 inches in diameter that turns very easily. For tips on using the stand for decorating, see Index.

THERMOMETERS

∎

Specialized thermometers are important for accuracy in different stages of pastry and confectionery work. For making candy, sugar syrups, and pastry creams, I use a "candy-jelly-deep-fry" thermometer with a mercury-filled glass tube fastened to a stainless-steel casing. It is widely available, made by Taylor. Buy one of these, or the best quality you can find. Do not settle for inferior thermometers, there is no point in having them. Take care of your thermometers; never put a cold one directly into boiling syrup, but rather warm it in hot water first. Thermal shock can crack the glass tubes if you are not careful. Always read your thermometer at eye level; when it is fastened to your saucepan, bend down in order to see the reading correctly at eye level.

For instant read-out temperatures for sauces or other foods, I like to use a stainless-steel stemmed thermometer with a large dial. This device is not meant to be left in a food throughout the time it is cooking. Instead, it is placed in food periodically for a few seconds, reacts immediately, and is then removed. These are made by Tel-Tru and by Taylor among others and are called Instant Bi-Therm thermometers. Note that instant-type thermometers often have a shorter temperature range than regular thermometers.

OVENS AND OVEN THERMOMETERS

∎

Even heat is vital in a baking oven, whether gas or electric. My own ovens are gas, and they have distinct and rather obstinate personalities. Fortunately, we are old friends, and I know how to cajole them into behaving. No matter how carefully I have their thermostats recalibrated, they go right out of whack. I have learned to rely on auxiliary thermometers that I place inside the ovens. I use two thermometers, front and back, and I replace them every few months to be sure I have reliable instruments. One should never rely on the built-in oven thermometer alone. Instead, buy a small, mercury-type thermometer, mounted on a metal stand, and put it in your oven. These gadgets are available at modest cost in hardware stores. Once it is in place, adjust your outer oven thermostat so the internal oven temperature is correct at all times. And remember not to blame a cookbook until you are sure the fault for a failed cake does not lie within your own oven.

Always preheat your oven 15 to 20 minutes before starting to bake. If a batter is set into a cool oven, the ingredients will react entirely differently from when set into the correct temperature; results will be disastrous. Glance at your auxiliary oven thermometer inside the baking chamber to check that the heat is correct before putting in the cake.

Some bakers prefer electric baking ovens, saying the heat is more even than gas, which surges on and off as it regulates the temperature. However, I get consistently good results and cannot complain. Learn to know your oven, but never trust it. Constantly monitor its hot spots. Sometimes a back corner may suddenly bake more quickly than the front and your cake will overbrown in one spot only, or sink on one side. If you have this problem, rotate cakes from one shelf to another, or front to back, *after* half of the baking time is past, but only do this if you must. Never have cake pans on the shelf touching each other or the oven walls. Allow at least an inch or more between pans and the oven wall for good heat circulation. If you are baking several layers at one time, stagger them on two shelves so one is not directly above the other and heat can circulate freely.

Positioning Oven Shelves

Recipes in this book specify the position of the oven shelf upon which the cake is to be baked. This may sound silly, but placement makes a difference. The point is to locate the direction of the heat source in the oven, and figure out where the hottest and coolest areas will be. For example, the floor of my large gas oven contains a border of holes that release heat from the gas jets below up into the oven chamber. As the heat comes from these holes, the oven sides deflect it right up to the top of the chamber. Therefore, the topmost shelf will be hotter than the middle, and the floor will be the hottest of all. Single-layer cakes can be baked in the lower third of the oven because there the heat is moderately hot. Single layers can bake fairly quickly, drying all the way through before either the top or bottom crust overbakes. Thicker cakes, with more than 2 inches of batter, or cakes with delicate structure, should be baked in the center of the oven where the heat is more moderate. For these cakes it is important to heat the batter evenly throughout, without forming an overcooked crust before the center dries out.

Convection Ovens

Convection ovens contain an interior fan that blows the heat around. This constant circulation causes the ovens to cook about 25 percent faster than regular ovens. For baked goods, this produces a nicely browned crust and fine interior crumb. Follow your manufacturer's directions, but as a guide, most convection ovens are about 20 degrees warmer than regular ovens. When converting ordinary recipes designed for regular ovens to use in a convection oven, most books recommend lowering baking temperatures about 25 to 50 degrees and reducing baking time about 25 percent. Baking will certainly be completed sooner than the ordinary recommended times, so don't forget to modify temperature and time and check the oven to observe the baking if you are not used to convection timing.

Microwave Ovens

I was the last kid on my block to give in, but I finally own a microwave oven. For baking, I use it primarily to melt or soften butter and to melt chocolate. I love the microwave for defrosting everything, however, and always use it when coffeecakes, muffins, or scones are frozen. Remember to remove any foil or freezer wrapping, then envelop the frozen baked goods in a piece of paper toweling and bake at medium power for 40 to 60 seconds. Test to see if the product is defrosted and is warm; if necessary repeat in 5 to 10-second bursts. Do not overbake or the texture will be unalterably turned to concrete.

My baking students continue to ask about baking cakes in the microwave, and I continue to think it is not a wonderful idea. The subject, however, can no longer be ignored, as new products and recipes constantly appear. Our experiments are disappointing at best, unreliable and irregular, and not even close to baking in a conventional oven, which doesn't take too much longer and gives superior results. For our tests, my baking assistant Barbara Cover used a simple chocolate cake recipe baked in microwave-safe cake pans, comparing it to other recipes and to specially formulated Microwave mixes.

In our opinion, the commercial microwave mixes do not work any better than ordinary scratch recipes, and they taste like mixes. *Consumer Reports* (June, 1987) summed it up this way: "Microwave ovens do many things well, but baking isn't one of them."

That said, we have developed a few guidelines to help you if you want to experiment. Following ordinary microwave manufacturer's baking instructions, the "scratch" cake came out lumpy, rubbery, and tough. This was improved, and the texture softened, when Barbara beat the batter smooth (longer mixing time than most manufacturers advise), greased the pan, then lined the bottom with wax paper, added no more than 2 cups of batter to the 7-inch pan (more did not cook through evenly), and pressed another piece of wax paper directly on top of the batter. The paper prevents a skin or crust from forming and encourages even baking. Many manufacturers advise raising the cake off the oven floor by setting the pan on an overturned plate, and this is essential.

The actual baking times and temperatures turn out to vary depending on what type of cake is baked; yellow cakes baked in slightly less time than chocolate. The best times and temperatures for the chocolate cake: 7 minutes on defrost, rotate the cake ½ turn, 2 minutes on high power, rotate the cake ½ turn, 2 minutes on high power. Invert the cake immediately onto a rack to cool. In our opinion, this is too bothersome a process to make only 1 small 7-inch layer; with very little more time and effort, you can make several full-size layers in an ordinary oven. The baking time for this microwave cake was a total of 11 minutes in the oven, while a conventional chocolate cake baked in a conventional oven requires 30 minutes. Maybe it is longer, but you don't have to stand at the ready to turn the pans, and the results are guaranteed.

BAKING PARCHMENT

∎

This specially formulated paper is made for lining baking pans to prevent baked goods from sticking. Some parchments are treated with silicone, some with paraffin, but whatever the material, it works. The paper is easily marked with a pencil, unlike wax paper, and can be cut to fit into any shape pan. If using it as a pan liner, you need to grease only the sides of the pan. Wax paper is a satisfactory substitute but not as durable, and it should be greased. Parchment paper is also ideal for making paper decorating cones; it is slightly stronger and less fragile than wax paper for this purpose.

Precut parchment rounds may be purchased to fit various cake pan sizes; large sheets of parchment are sold in bulk, as well as in small, home-size dispenser rolls. They are available in some gourmet shops and in baker's and restaurant supply houses.

· UNDERSTANDING INGREDIENTS ·

While it is true that anyone who can read can, more or less, follow a cake recipe, you know from experience that the same recipe can produce different results with different cooks. This is the reason baking competitions often are based upon one distributed recipe, with entrants' results compared. Some cooks, of course, have a natural "feel" for baking, but more than anything else, success in the kitchen depends upon understanding the properties of each ingredient, why they are used, and how they are best blended together.

Although the proportions of ingredients in bread or even pie doughs can be rather flexible, cake batters must be precise. Good cakes are the product of good recipes—carefully balanced chemical compositions that blend protein foams with flour, fat, liquid, leavening, and flavoring. Each ingredient has a specific function and causes a specific reaction

with its partners. Professional bakers characterize cake batter ingredients in functional groups. This particular system was devised by William J. Sultan in his book *Practical Baking* (Avi Publishing Company, Inc., 1981), though I have modified it somewhat. You will find it a handy quick reference guide.

· BINDERS AND TOUGHENERS (provide structure, bind the ingredients): flour, milk solids, egg whites

· TENDERIZERS (soften cake by cutting development of gluten in wheat flour, prevent toughness): sugar, fat, egg yolks, chocolate, and a variety of other acidic foods including sour cream, yogurt, honey, molasses

· MOISTENERS (moisten cake, lengthen storage time): milk, water, eggs, sugar syrups, honey, some other liquids

· DRIERS (absorb and retain moisture, give cake body): flour, milk solids, starches

· FLAVORERS (enhance or provide flavor): chocolate, butter, eggs, extracts and other specific flavoring agents including citrus zests, coffee, nuts, for example

FLOUR

■

Wheat flour contains gluten, the stretchy elastic cell walls that develop when two of wheat's unique proteins are mixed with liquid and worked together. Gluten is actually made up of two of the several proteins present: gliadin (located in the endosperm, or core of the wheat kernel) and glutenin (located in the outer layer of the kernel). Gliadin provides elasticity and glutenin provides strength; both are needed to give flour the characteristics required for baking. The proportions of these two elements in flour are affected by the method of milling as well as by the type of wheat (hard or soft) and where it was grown. Some flours are more elastic, others more delicate and tender, and each has a specific purpose.

For a tender, flaky, or short piecrust, low gluten flour is most desirable. On the other hand, the rich development of a large quantity of gluten is essential for kneaded yeast doughs, which require a strong elastic structure to support the gases given off by the expanding yeast. For a cake, you need very little gluten, but some is required to support the carbon dioxide given off as a leavening agent by the baking powder and/or baking soda. The ability of flour to absorb and retain moisture from the batter stage through the final baking de-pends upon the amount and quality of the protein in the flour; it is critical to a good cake to select the best flour.

Bread flour is milled from hard wheat and has a high gluten content, 12 to 15 percent. All-purpose flour is milled from a blend of hard and soft wheats and contains roughly 10 to 13 percent gluten; pastry flour is milled from soft wheats only and has a lower gluten content, 8 to 12 percent. Cake flour, also milled from soft wheat, has somewhat less gluten, about 6½ to 10 percent, and is specifically designed to produce a tender grain in cakes. Self-rising cake flour is another item altogether and should not be substituted for regular cake or pastry flour; it contains added calcium acid phosphate or monocalcium phosphate, bicarbonate of soda, and salt. I prefer not to use self-rising cake flour for two reasons. First, I like to control the amount of salt and leavening in my recipes. Second, and most important, baking powder loses its strength after about three months; if the flour has been stored too long (and the consumer never knows for sure), your cakes may not rise properly.

Many commercially available brands of all-purpose flour are actually prepared blends of all-purpose flour (80 percent) and cake flour (20 percent). These are excellent for many cakes, and are specified in many recipes in this book. When the texture of the cake is particularly light and delicate, the finest and lightest flour, cake flour, is called for instead.

You can make your own cake flour from all-purpose flour by substituting 2 tablespoons cornstarch for 2 tablespoons flour in every cup. To substitute cake flour for all-purpose flour, use 1 cup plus 2 tablespoons cake flour for every cup of all-purpose flour.

If you are not sure of the protein content of your flour, read the flour package label, or write to the flour company if the label is not helpful. Under "Nutritional information," many brand labels note that per 1 cup flour there are a specific number of grams of protein. For example, Pillsbury's Best All Purpose Enriched contains 11 grams per 1 cup (4 ounces) flour; Gold Medal All Purpose and Hecker's Unbleached All Purpose are the same. King Arthur Unbleached All-Purpose has 12 grams protein per 4 ounces flour, and Swans Down *Cake* Flour contains 8 grams protein per 4 ounces flour. Remember that flour varies depending upon where the grain was grown and milled and how it was processed.

Though it varies depending upon the type of wheat, most flour that is newly milled contains quite a high moisture content and is yellowish in color because of the zanthophyll and other natural carotenoid pigments in the wheat. If left in storage at controlled temperatures, it will age after a period of many weeks, and oxygen will bleach it white while it oxidizes the proteins. The aging process strengthens the stretching and bonding characteristics of gluten, thus developing better baking qualities than are found in freshly milled flour. This process can be speeded up and made more efficient with chemicals. Thus flour is bleached with chlorine dioxide or a similar gas; this ages the flour and removes the yellowish color naturally present in the wheat while also removing many vitamins. These are returned artificially in a later process.

Unbleached flour is said to be more nutritious because some of the wheat bran is retained during the milling and refining process. In fact, however, most commercially milled American flours, both bleached and unbleached, are actually bleached and highly refined. Some are chemically bleached with either potassium bromate or iodate, others are bleached by aging in the air. Unbleached flours are usually a little heavier than bleached flours, and and thus less desirable for use in very delicate cakes.

Instant-blending flour is processed to be granular so that it will mix with water without lumping. It is fine for making gravy, but not suitable for baking cakes. Do not use it as a substitute for all-purpose or cake flour.

Flour should be stored in a cool, dry place, raised off the floor, and well ventilated. It will absorb odors if stored next to a strongly scented product or kept in a damp location. Flour stored for any length of time in a warm location or in warm weather can develop insects even when chemically bleached. The best solution is to store all flour in the freezer or refrigerator. At 0°F, flour keeps for about a year.

Sifting Flour

Sifting flour has two purposes: it removes lumps and foreign objects and aerates the flour. Good aeration ensures proper moistening of the flour during mixing of the batter. Flour is also sifted with other dry ingredients (baking powder, salt, sugar) to blend these ingredients evenly. Ignore flour labels that say "presifted"; store handling and shipment have effectively settled and compacted that flour if it ever was aerated. Cake flour is finer than all-purpose flour and tends to lump or settle even more; it must always be sifted.

Before sifting flour, read How To Measure Dry Ingredients, About Sifters/Strainers, and Dry and Liquid Measuring Cups (see Index).

It is important in cake baking to remember that too much flour makes a heavy and/or tough cake. You should use the precise amount of flour called for. Note that 1 cup of cake flour weighs more (4½ ounces; 120 grams) before sifting than after (3½ ounces; 100 grams). In recipes where sifting is not critical to the texture of the cake, unsifted flour is specified.

LIQUIDS

∎

The liquid category in cake batters includes eggs, honey, molasses, oil, melted butter, and coffee, as well as water, milk, cream, sour cream or yogurt, and fruit juices. Liquids are added to a batter to dissolve the salt and sugar, and to create steam that pushes apart the cells of the batter, giving the cake a good rise and fine texture.

In addition, liquids moisten the leavening agent, whether baking soda, baking powder, or both, to begin production of carbon dioxide gas, which will cause the cake to rise. Liquid should be used carefully: too much will activate the gluten in the flour, causing extra elasticity and toughness, qualities undesirable in a cake. Acid liquids such as citrus juices, vinegar, and sour milk products cut the development of gluten and help produce short or flaky baked goods and tender cakes. Honey, molasses, sour cream and yogurt also add acidity to a cake batter and change its Ph balance. See Leavening Agents (Index). Milk products add moisture, color, and richness to cakes and help prolong their freshness. Some bakers like to add a little milk as part of the liquid in any cake, just to improve these qualities. Liquid quantities must be adjusted when baking at high altitudes.

Milk

Homogenized milk is used in this book whenever plain milk is called for in a recipe. Homogenized milk is treated so the fat and milk are blended and will not separate. Skim milk is regular milk minus the cream content. Low-fat milk is skim milk that still contains a small portion of its cream. When a recipe requires buttermilk, it is so specified. Buttermilk is the liquid by-product created when milk or cream is churned into butter. Cultured buttermilk is pasteurized skim milk treated with a lactic-acid bacteria culture. Cultured buttermilk powder is a dried mix that is reconstituted by blending with water.

Cream

There are many types of cream on the market and all have specific uses in baking. The butterfat content of the cream is what determines the way it can be used, although package labeling information is often lacking. Heavy Cream, also called Heavy Whipping Cream (not the same as Whipping Cream), has between 36 and 40 percent butterfat. This is sufficient to whip and hold its form. Use a chilled bowl and chilled beater for maximum volume. If you use an electric mixer to whip the cream, stop before it reaches medium-soft peaks; finish the whipping with a hand whisk to control stiffness perfectly. Note that cream doubles in volume when whipped (1 cup heavy cream makes about 2 cups whipped cream).

Whipping Cream has only 30 percent butterfat; it will whip, but not very well; it will never hold its foam for very long, and will droop maddeningly if you use it for decoration on pastry.

Light Cream has a butterfat content of between 18 and 20 percent, while half-and-half has 10½ to 12 percent; both are used primarily for beverages; neither will whip.

EGGS

∎

Eggs are one of the most important ingredients in cakes. They aid in leavening, contribute to the structure, texture, color, and flavor, and add richness and nutritive value.

Eggs add an important liquid to the cake batter and help bind it together. The proteins in eggs work with the proteins in flour to support the structure of the risen cake. When eggs are beaten, they incorporate air, which expands in the heat of the oven to leaven the cake.

Yolks contain all of the fat of the egg and more protein than the white. Eggs add tenderness to a cake because of the high fat content of the yolk. Yolks also contain natural lecithin, an emulsifying agent, which helps yolks whip to a stabilized foam that will stand longer than egg-white foam before breaking down.

The food value of eggs is substantial. They add fat, protein, vitamins, and minerals to any product. There is no difference to the baker between brown and white eggs, but eggs do vary in freshness, size, and whipping qualities. For whipping to greatest volume, eggs should be at least 2 days old. The size of your eggs is vital to the success of your cakes. The recipes in this book are based upon large eggs, weighing 2 ounces in the shell. Sixteen of these large eggs equal 1 quart; 4 to 4½ eggs equal 1 cup. By United States law, one dozen large eggs must weigh 24 ounces; however, the individual eggs within that dozen may have varying weights. For this reason, keep an eye on your eggs; if they look small, weigh them to be sure. Or use whatever weight of egg you prefer, but calculate the quantity to be sure it is equivalent to the number of 2-ounce, "large" eggs given in the recipe. If you need to add a little more egg to increase the weight, simply beat an egg and pour in the needed additional amount. The white of 1 large egg equals about 2 tablespoons, or 1 ounce; the yolk equals 1 tablespoon, or about ½ ounce.

Eggs separate most easily when cold, but whites beat to their fullest volume when at room temperature. Eggs should be at room temperature for use in cake batters. If your eggs are cold from the refrigerator, simply set them, whole in the shell, in a bowl of very warm water for 10 to 15 minutes. If eggs must be separated, do this as soon as they come from the refrigerator, then let them sit a while; or set the bowls of whites and/or yolks inside other bowls of warm water to warm them quickly.

Separated egg whites can be stored, refrigerated, in a partially covered bowl or jar for up to 1 month. Be sure your egg whites come from pure, fresh eggs with unbroken shells. Always open an egg carton in the market to see that no shells are cracked. Bacteria causing a common food poisoning, salmonellosis, are sometimes present in unsanitary egg whites and cannot be destroyed by quick cooking. For the same reason, be sure to refrigerate meringue-topped cakes or pies and cheesecakes because they contain eggs.

Eggs can be frozen for storage. Whites and yolks can be frozen separately or lightly beaten whole eggs can be mixed with a few grains of salt or sugar and frozen in ice-cube trays (1 cube equals 1 egg). Theoretically, frozen egg whites should be thawed overnight in the refrigerator before bringing them to room temperature for whipping. However, I often forget to thaw my frozen whites long enough in advance, and have to set them in a bowl of warm (not hot) water to thaw. These thawed whites will make a fine angel-food cake, so you can collect whites in the freezer as you go along, and bake a cake once enough whites are stockpiled. Never refreeze thawed eggs.

How to Separate Eggs

There are several techniques for separating eggs. Whichever you select, be sure to scrape out and use the white that tends to cling inside the shell; about 15 percent of the white can be lost in the separation process if this is not done.

The first method is to break the egg into halves, then hold the half-shell containing the yolk upright in one hand while you pour the egg white from the other half-shell into a cup. Then tip the yolk out into the empty half-shell while the white that surrounds it falls into the cup below. Place the yolk in another cup. The next method is fun and infallible if you don't mind getting your hands dirty. Crack the egg by tapping it sharply against the side of the bowl. Holding the egg over a bowl, pull the halves of the shell apart, simultaneously turning one half-shell upright so it will contain the entire egg. Holding this full half-shell upright with one hand, discard the empty half-shell. Then turn your empty hand

palm up, and dump the whole egg into it. Spread your fingers slightly to let the white slip through them into a bowl below. The yolk will remain in your palm and can be turned into another container. Instead, you can use a gadget known as an egg separator. This is a disk with a ring-shaped slot cut out just inside the edge. When the egg is broken onto the disk, the yolk is retained in the center and the white slides through the slot into a cup below.

FATS

■

Fat is the generic term for butter, margarine, lard, oil, or vegetable shortening. The richness and tenderness of a baked product depends upon the type of fat used and the manner in which it is blended with the other ingredients in the batter. Fats also provide for aeration to help the leavening of a batter, contribute flavor, impart desirable grain and texture, act as emulsifiers for holding liquids in the batter, and, in the case of yeast doughs, lubricate the gluten in the flour.

As a general rule, the colder and harder the fat, the less it is absorbed by the starch in the flour. The more separate the fat remains, the more it layers with the flour. This creates desirable flakiness in pie crust but is wrong for cake batters. Here the fat must be at room temperature, roughly 70°F, to be soft and pliable enough to stretch around air bubbles as they are creamed or whipped into the batter. If the fat is too cold, the cell walls will be brittle, will break and let out the air, causing the cake to lose volume or fall completely. If the fat is warm enough to melt, it will not mold itself around air cells at all; however, good cakes can be made with melted butter or oil if their particular characteristics are taken into account in the blending method. As fats are not soluble in liquid, they must be well blended so that their particles are evenly distributed throughout the batter. Only in this way will they produce a tender cake.

Butter has the best flavor of all the fats used in baking. You may have to taste several brands before you find one that has good taste and texture, without too much moisture. Unsalted butter is the preferred type for cake baking. It tends to be fresher than salted butter, perhaps because it is often sold frozen. Check freshness dating on the packages. I prefer unsalted butter not only for its freshness and its taste, but also because I like to be the one to control the amount of salt in my recipe. Salted butter has between .5 and 6 percent salt added to enhance flavor and extend shelf life. Butter is made from pasteurized sweet cream, with a butterfat content of 80 to 86 percent. It has a melting point slightly lower than body temperature; for this reason butter melts in the mouth. Liquid content of butter varies, and in cake-baking you should select butter with the least liquid. Compare liquid content of various butters by melting an equal amount of each type, then chilling them and observing the quantity of liquid that settles out.

Margarine was invented by a French chemist during the late nineteenth century when Napoleon III needed a long-lasting and inexpensive fat for his army. It was patented in England in 1869 and in America in 1873. A wide variety of oils and solid fats is used in making margarine. Blends of both are heated;

water, milk emulsifying agents, and flavorings are added; and the mixture is cooled. Excess liquid is extracted; preservatives, coloring, and vitamins are added; and the product is packaged to resemble the "real thing." It does, in some ways: both have roughly the same water and salt content and margarine is 85 to 100 percent fat. However, margarine has a higher melting point (110°F) than butter, and because it is created from oils, it remains softer and more oily. Since margarine is not an animal fat, it contains less (or in some cases nonexistent amounts of) cholesterol. To satisfy Kosher dietary laws, one can select a brand of margarine made without either milk solids or animal fats. The taste of margarine is not as good as butter and in most cakes this makes a difference. Do not use soft tub-type margarine for cake baking; it is too soft. Use only solid margarine. In the cake recipes in this book, use butter or margarine where each is indicated. Margarine can be substituted for butter where dietary considerations are a factor or where spices, chocolate, or other strong flavors will mask the flavor of the fat, as in certain coffee or spice cakes.

Solid shortenings are created by forcing pressurized hydrogen gas through oils made from vegetable or animal fats. These artificially created hydrogenated fats contain 100 percent fat and are good for creaming and whipping; they are soft and flexible and will envelop a multitude of air bubbles, thus aiding the leavening of cakes. Crisco is one widely used brand of hydrogenated shortening, available both flavorless and butter-flavored. I use flavorless. Solid shortening can be used in place of margarine in cakes with strong flavors such as spice or chocolate. This type of fat gives cakes a soft crumb and fine grain but, unlike butter, adds no flavor.

Emulsified shortening is a commercially used product in which mono- and di-glycerides are added to ordinary shortening to give it greater absorptive and moisture-retaining qualities. Bakeries use this type of shortening for cakes that contain a large amount of sugar (high-ratio cakes). Emulsified shortening gives these cakes a finer grain and more volume than would regular shortening.

Vegetable oils are used as the fat in chiffon cakes. When oil is called for in a recipe, select one with a neutral flavor such as safflower, sunflower, peanut, or corn. Safflower oil is the most polyunsaturated of all vegetable oils, and my own preference for cakes. Oil or melted fat added to cake batter coats the starch particles and reduces the strength of the protein, weakening the gluten's elasticity and contributing to the tenderness of a cake. Store oils for short periods at room temperature. Refrigerated oil remains fresh longer but clouds when cold; it clarifies on reaching room temperature. Note that vegetable oils contain no cholesterol. Certain brands of vegetable oil contain silicates which inhibit foaming, a quality essential to most cake batters. Check the label and select only silicate-free oil for cakes.

Lard is rendered pork fat (100 percent animal fat containing cholesterol), plus a small percentage of water. It produces a marvelously flaky piecrust, but because of its distinct flavor it is rarely used in making cakes.

Cocoa butter is a by-product of processing cocoa beans to make chocolate (see page 46). This fat is primarily used in icings and confections. It is added to chocolates or chocolate products to increase the tenderness and gloss, and to help carry or hold the chocolate flavor.

SUGARS

.

Sugar

Sugar is used in cakes to provide sweetness, to aid the creaming and whipping of air into the batter, and to contribute to grain and texture. It also helps cakes to stay fresh longer, aids in yeast fermentation, and provides good color, especially to cake crusts.

It is sugar's ability to attract and absorb moisture that helps to keep a cake fresh. Sugar also slows down the development of gluten in wheat flour, causing the cell walls to stretch slowly so that the cake can rise to the maximum before the structure is set by the oven heat. Sugar also raises the point at which the proteins in the batter will coagulate and set. High-ratio cakes are those having more than 1 cup of sugar per cup of flour; these cakes have an especially fine texture because of the slowness with which their cell walls have stretched.

Granulated sugar needs to be sifted only if it has been in storage for a long time and looks lumpy. Confectioners' sugar should always be sifted before use.

There are many forms of sugar; the one most commonly used in baking is sucrose, a natural sugar found in plants. It is obtained from sugar beets and sugar cane, processed and refined to 99.9 percent purity. Sucrose is a complex sugar, or disaccharide, composed of 1 fructose and 1 glucose molecule joined to form a simple carbohydrate; it can be rapidly absorbed by the body to provide quick energy.

There are many types of sucrose available to the baker: white, dark or light brown sugar, and molasses. Each type comes from a different stage of the refining process. When crushed sugar cane or sugar beet juice is turned into sugar, it is first dissolved in water; the resulting syrup is boiled in steam evaporators. After evaporation, the sugar remaining is crystallized in heated vacuum pans, and molasses, the liquid by-product, is separated out by a series of spinnings in a centrifuge. At this stage, the raw sugar contains many impurities. Once it is steam-washed, it is sold as turbinado sugar. For further purity and clarification, refining continues as turbinado is heated and liquefied, centrifuged, clarified, and filtered.

Granulated brown sugar is crystallized from liquid sugar drawn from the filtering process before all the molasses, caramelized sugar juices, and minerals are removed. To remove remaining traces of color, minerals, and mineral salts, the liquid sugar is then percolated and filtered through a deep bed of bone char. Some refineries also use chemicals to bleach the sugar. Finally, the colorless liquid sugar is boiled in steam-heated vacuum pans and recrystallized, forming granulated white sugar.

□ WHITE SUGAR

White sugar is available in a variety of crystal sizes, from regular granulated to superfine or bar sugar, and 4, 6, and 10X confectioners' sugar. The size of the crystals is directly related to the amount of air that can be incorporated into a cake batter by creaming or whipping the sugar with fat. The sharp edges of these crystals are essential to bite into the fat and open up pores that grow to become air cells. Sugar thus contributes to a cake's structure and volume. Obviously, powdered confectioners' sugar cannot incorporate as much air as granulated sugar. The size of the crystals is also a factor in how quickly the sugar will dissolve in the batter; the tiny crystals of superfine sugar dissolve much faster than the larger crystals of regular granulated sugar. Superfine is thus best for drinks or meringues. Superfine sugar can be made by grinding granulated sugar in the food processor; the resulting crystal size will be uneven, although appearing fine to the naked eye, but this does not affect its use. Superfine is also called ultrafine or bar sugar and is the finest granulated sugar produced; it is commonly sold in supermarkets only in 1-pound boxes. Extrafine sugar is slightly finer than granulated and is used primarily by professional bakers. Baker's Special sugar is slightly finer than extrafine and is used by commercial bakeries. British "castor sugar" is similar to Baker's Special; superfine sugar can be substituted. The British term "icing sugar" refers to confectioners' sugar.

□ CONFECTIONERS' SUGAR

This is granulated sugar that has been ground to a specified degree of fineness. For home baking use, powdery 10x is generally used and widely available. The baker should be aware that approximately 3 percent cornstarch is added to each box of confectioners' sugar to prevent lumping and crystallization. Cornstarch gives this sugar a raw taste that is best masked by cooking or adding flavorings to hide the taste of the cornstarch. Because it dissolves almost instantly, confectioners' sugar is primarily used for meringues, icings, and confections; in France, it is sometimes substituted for granulated sugar in preparing sweet tart pastry. Confectioners' sugar is occasionally added to cake batters to produce a denser and more silken texture than that created with granulated sugar.

□ BROWN SUGAR

Turbinado and dark and light brown sugars are less refined than white sugar. The darker the sugar, the more molasses and moisture (both by-products of refining) it contains. Turbinado sugar has a coarser grain than granulated white sugar. It is usually sold in natural-food stores, though it is available in some supermarkets. Its moisture content varies with its molasses content, and as this is unpredictable, it is not very reliable for use in cake baking.

Brown sugars are added to cakes, streusel toppings, and icings to give color, flavor, and moisture. Brown sugars tend to make products heavy and are usually to be avoided in very light cakes. In general, the darker brown the sugar, the more intense the flavor; light brown sugar has a light, honeylike taste while dark brown sugar tastes more of molasses. Both dark and light brown sugar have the same sweetening power as an equal weight of white sugar. However, white sugar is more dense; therefore, to achieve an equivalent degree of sweetness, the brown sugar must be firmly packed before measuring by volume.

To avoid lumping, store brown sugar in a covered glass jar or strong plastic bag in a cool, dry location. If, in spite of your best efforts, your brown sugar hardens, put it in a plastic bag with a slice of apple for a few days. Or sprinkle a few drops of water on it and seal it into a closed plastic bag for a few days. Do not try to crush hardened brown sugar with the metal blade of your food processor; you may break the blade.

To make 1 cup of your own brown sugar, combine 1 cup granulated sugar with 4 tablespoons unsulfured molasses.

□ SUGAR SYRUPS

When solutions of sugar are boiled, they form syrup. Syrups are used for poaching fruit, blending with buttercreams or meringues, or are caramelized to form threads or candies.

When sugar is added to cold water, it dissolves and blends—up to the point where the water is saturated and can hold no more sugar; this is a saturated solution. Beyond this point, excess sugar remains in crystals and is visible in the water. Cold water can hold double its weight in sugar. When heated, it can absorb more sugar, almost twice as much as when cold. The greater the heat, the more sugar the water can absorb. Maximum saturation is achieved at boiling point. A supersaturated solution contains more sugar than will dissolve in water at room temperature.

When a sugar-water syrup boils, the water evaporates, leaving a sugar concentration of varying density; the less water, the more sugar and the harder the sugar will set when cold. The degree of evaporation can be measured with a candy thermometer, or determined by testing the consistency of the syrup when dropped into a glass of ice water, or the density of the sugar in the syrup can be measured with a saccharometer or Baumé sugar weight scale.

Sugar in solution has a natural tendency to recrystallize whenever there is not enough moisture to maintain the solution. Controlling the crystallization of the sugar is the essential factor in controlling the texture of fudge, fondant, icing, or candy. Crystals form when the syrup is worked, but the temperature of the syrup will determine the size of the crystal. A very hot syrup forms large crystals, a cool syrup, small crystals. Premature crystallization can ruin the final product. There are several tips that will guard against this.

First, always use an absolutely clean pot, completely free of any fat or food residues. A copper pot is ideal for cooking sugar, but any heavy-bottomed nonreactive metal or ceramic pot with a smooth surface will work.

Second, combine your sugar with water, as per the recipe, and add a pinch of cream of tartar or lemon juice. This acid is added to the sugar, or sucrose, to change it during heating into its components, glucose and fructose. This chemical reaction, called inversion, will prevent recrystallization of the sugar. Corn syrup, called an invert sugar, is an acid, and will also prevent recrystallization in sugar syrup.

Let the mixture stand for a while to form a cold saturated solution; extra sugar will sink to the bottom and remain visible. When the syrup cooks, be sure all the sugar is dissolved before boiling starts. Use a wooden spoon, never a metal one, which would pull heat from the syrup and leave cool spots. It is best not to stir the cooking syrup at all; the stirring motion pushes the sugar molecules into one another and may start crystallization. Instead of stirring, swirl the pan gently to distribute the heat and speed dissolving of the sugar. To avoid crystals on the pan sides, wash down the pan sides with a pastry brush dipped into cold water; do this several times during the boiling process.

Use a candy thermometer to determine the correct temperature of the sugar syrup. Also, at the same time, I like to perform the old-fashioned ice-water test.

First test the accuracy of your candy thermometer by rinsing it in warm water (to prevent shock), then setting it in boiling water to be sure it registers 212°F (100°C). Set the thermometer on the edge of your syrup pan, with the tip resting in the syrup. Alongside the stove, set out a Pyrex measuring cup containing ice cubes and water. Professional bakers and confectioners test the stages of sugar by plunging their fingers into ice water, then immediately into the syrup; they feel the consistency of the sugar most accurately with their fingertips. My students are, naturally, intimidated by this technique, as I was the first time I saw Albert Jorant, pastry instructor at École de Cuisine La Varenne in Paris, literally drag a screaming student to the stove and hold her hand while guiding her in this process. It worked and the girl was both unburned and converted. It takes courage the first time, however.

Note that it takes quite a while for sugar to begin to reach the thread stage, but once there it passes quickly from one stage to the next. As the desired temperature approaches, begin to test the syrup in ice water, and watch the thermometer. Do not leave the room. After 250° or 260°F, changes happen by the second, and the syrup can overcook before you realize it.

Stages of Boiled Syrup

215° to 219°F (102° to 104°C) Thin Thread Stage: Syrup drips from the spoon edge in a thin thread. If you touch the syrup with your fingers, join your fingers, then pull them apart, a thin thread forms between them. This is used for cake soaking syrups.

230° to 234°F (110° to 112°C) Thread Stage, also called Blow or Soufflé Stage: Similar to thin thread stage, bubbles in the boiling syrup look like snowflakes, and the thread is slightly thicker and firmer. This is used primarily for candy and syrups.

235° to 240°F (113° to 115°C) Soft Ball Stage: When a drop of syrup is put into ice water, you can pick it up between your fingers, but it feels very soft and nearly loses its shape when worked. This is usually used for fondants, fudge, and some buttercreams.

244° to 248°F (117° to 120°C) Firm Ball Stage: When a drop of syrup is put into ice water, you can pick it up between your fingers and it will hold a firm shape although it is still a little flexible. This is used for caramels, toffees, nougats, etc.

250° to 266°F (121° to 130°C) Hard Ball Stage: When a drop of syrup is put into ice water, you can pick it up between your fingers and it forms a hard ball. This is used for many candies.

270° to 290°F (132° to 143°C) Soft Crack Stage: A drop of syrup put into ice water forms a string that cracks when broken although it is still slightly pliable. This is used for candies. The color is pale yellow.

295° to 310°F (145° to 154°C) Hard Crack Stage: A drop of syrup put into ice water forms a string that is completely brittle and cracks when broken; it is not at all pliable. This is used for nut brittles and coated or glacéed fruit. The color is light amber.

320° to 355°F (165° to 179°C) Caramel: The color darkens from gold to medium-amber, 340°F (171°C) to brown, then quickly blackens and burns. Use for caramel coating of pans at amber stage. Beware of overcooking.

Molasses

Molasses is the liquid separated from sugar crystals during the first stages of refining. The color and strength of the molasses depends on the stage at which it comes in the separation process. When liquid molasses is separated from sugar crystals, it is put through a series of spinnings in a centrifuge. "First" molasses is drawn off in the first centrifuging and is the finest quality. "Second" molasses, from the second round, contains more impurities, and the third, known as "blackstrap" molasses (from the Dutch word *stroop,* or syrup), is the blackest, and strongest in flavor. Most molasses used in cooking is of the first type, often blended with cane syrup to standardize quality.

Some processors treat their sugar cane with sulfur dioxide to clarify and lighten the color of its juice; this produces a sulfur taste in the molasses that many find distasteful. "Unsulfured" molasses has not been so treated; it has the best flavor for cooking and is the type of molasses recommended in this book.

Honey

While not a sugar, honey is a sweetener used in baking. Beside sweetness, it adds moistness, softness, and chewiness to a cake or baked product. Honey has the same sweetening power as sugar, but it cannot replace sugar entirely because it does not work the same way during creaming or whipping of the batter. Honey caramelizes quickly at a low temperature, and causes baked products to appear dark in color. Its degree of natural acidity varies, and baking soda is used with it as a neutralizer. Note: To substitute honey for granulated sugar, use about ⅞ the quantity called for and decrease the liquid in the recipe by 3 tablespoons. One cup granulated sugar equals ⅞ cup honey.

The flavor of honey varies depending upon the area in which it is produced and the type of flowers visited by the nectar-gathering bees. For cake baking, use clear liquefied honey rather than honey in solid or comb form. If your honey solidifies or turns granular, set the opened jar on a rack in a pot of gently simmering water until the honey melts and clarifies.

Maple Syrup

Pure maple syrup comes from the sap of the sugar maple tree boiled down until evaporated and thickened. It takes about 30 gallons of maple sap to produce 1 gallon of syrup. Grade A or Fancy Grade syrup is light amber in color, delicate in flavor, and very expensive. Grade B, usually kept for family use by the syrup producer, is my favorite. It is darker brown in color, richer in maple flavor, and less expensive, though hard to find. Store opened maple syrup in the refrigerator. If you see mold forming, put the syrup in a saucepan, heat just to boiling, and skim off the mold. Bring to a boil quickly, then cool, pour into a clean container, and refrigerate for further use.

Try to avoid imitation maple syrups. They are basically corn syrups with artificial maple flavoring, butter flavors, and caramel color added.

LEAVENING AGENTS

∎

Leavening agents are added to cake batters to make cakes rise and to produce a light and porous texture. Air, steam, and carbon dioxide gas are the principal leaveners.

Air bubbles beaten into fat or eggs constitute one type of leavening agent for cake batters. In the heat of the oven, the air in these bubbles expands, causing the cake to rise. The steam produced by heating the liquids in the batter is another rising agent. The steam expands the air cells and lifts the batter. Read What Happens When a Cake is Baked (page 66).

Baking Powder

Baking powder is a chemical leavening agent composed of acid-reacting materials (tartaric acid or its salts, acid salts of phosphoric acid, compounds of aluminum) and alkali bicarbonate of soda. When baking powder is mixed with the liquid in the batter it forms a solution, causing a reaction between the acid and the alkali, which then begin to release carbon dioxide gas. When the batter is placed in the heat of the oven, the reaction is completed, releasing no less than 12 percent carbon dioxide; double-acting commercial baking powder releases about 14 percent carbon dioxide.

There are three main types of baking powders. The first is single, or fast-acting, baking powder in which baking soda is combined with tartaric acid or with a combination of cream of tartar and tartaric acid. This is known as tartrate baking powder, and it releases gas quickly when mixed with liquid; a batter containing this powder must be baked promptly. The second type is slow-acting baking powder, also called phosphate baking powder. This type combines baking soda with calcium acid phosphate or sodium acid phosphate. It releases very little gas until placed in the heat of the oven, so batters can be held a long time before being baked. This slow-acting baking powder is often used in commercial bakeries. The third type is double-acting baking powder, also called SAS baking powder. It is the only one recommended in this book, and it is the type most commonly used in home kitchens today. This product is composed of cream of tartar, tartaric acid, sodium aluminum sulfate or sodium acid pyrophosphate, and the mono-calcium phosphates. Double-acting powder produces two separate reactions. When it is first mixed with the batter at room temperature, it releases a small amount of gas, which begins to form many tiny air cells. When the batter is exposed to oven heat, the second reaction occurs. At this point, the baking powder releases its full power, expanding the gas cells as the batter sets, giving a full rise to the cake.

Starch filler is included as a stabilizer in baking powder, to keep the acid salts from reacting with the bicarbonate of soda and to act as a buffer in case any moisture is absorbed in the mixture. On the average, baking powder contains from 23 to 30 percent cornstarch.

In an emergency, if you run out of baking powder, you can make your own (but do not try to store this): for every 1 cup of flour in your recipe, combine 2 teaspoons cream of tartar, 1 teaspoon baking soda, and a few grains of salt (optional).

The amount of baking powder must be adjusted when baking at high altitudes where the air pressure is lower and gas expansion in the batter is increased; read about High Altitude Baking (see Index).

Note that if too much baking powder is used in a cake, the taste may be very bitter, and the cake may rise rapidly, then collapse.

Baking powder absorbs moisture from the air and can deteriorate quickly. It has a shelf life of about 3 months. For home baking, you should buy it in small cans and replace it if it is old. To test its effectiveness, combine 1 teaspoon baking powder with ½ cup hot water; if it bubbles up vigorously, the baking powder is still usable; if no reaction occurs, toss out the can and buy more. If in doubt, throw it out. Store baking powder and baking soda in a cool, dry place away from dampness.

Baking Soda

Baking soda is another common leavening agent. Originally known as saleratus, it is now called baking or bicarbonate of soda. This alkaline product is used in cake batters when there is an acid agent present (buttermilk, sour milk, yogurt, molasses, honey, chocolate, cocoa, etc.) in order to neutralize some of the acidity as well as to provide leavening powder. The alkaline soda needs the acid in order to react, releasing carbon dioxide gas. This action is similar to that of fast-acting baking powder, for the reaction takes place as soon as the batter is mixed. Batters risen entirely with soda must be baked as soon as possible, before the rising effect is dissipated.

Bicarbonate of soda has other properties as well. Because it is an alkali, it has the ability to darken the color of chocolate or cocoa in a cake. It also causes the reddening of cocoa, giving Devil's Food Cake its name.

If you use too much baking soda without a balancing acid in the batter, you will darken or yellow a white cake and produce off-odors and a soapy flavor.

Years ago, baking soda was coarsely ground, and for that reason was mixed with boiling water before being added to batter. Many cookbooks still refer to this method. Today, however, soda is ground very fine and may be sifted into the other dry ingredients for even distribution throughout the batter.

Yeast

There are over 160 different species of the single-celled fungus known as yeast. The particular species used in baking and brewing is *Saccharomyces cerevisiae* (brewer's sugar fungus). When combined with water, sugar, and/or flour, certain proteins, and the correct degree of warmth, this yeast has the ability to divide and grow, converting most of the sugar and starch into alcohol and carbon dioxide. When making beer, wine, or spirits, the alcohol is kept and the carbon dioxide is discarded; when baking, the carbon dioxide gas is utilized to raise the batter or dough and the alcohol evaporates in the heat of the oven.

There are two main types of yeast available to the home baker: fresh compressed and active dry granulated, which is the most readily available and which I have used exclusively in this book. As a general rule, you can substitute one cake of fresh compressed yeast (1 packed tablespoon; 3/5 ounce; 22 grams) for one envelope of dry active granulated yeast (2 1/4 teaspoons; 1/4 ounce; 7 grams). The temperature of the liquid used for dissolving each type of yeast is different and critical to the success of

the yeast growth; however, both types will die if exposed to temperatures above 120°F. If kept at excessively cold temperatures, the yeast will hibernate, or be unable to multiply. Many recipes advise keeping rising dough away from drafts because cool air slows the multiplication of yeast cells. Once yeast growth has begun, the cells will multiply best in a temperature of between 70°F to 85°F (average home kitchen temperature).

Active dry granular yeast, which contains only about 8 per cent moisture, is sold in envelopes weighing 1/4 ounce (7 grams, about 1 tablespoon) and also in jars containing larger amounts. Look for freshness dates on the packages and be sure your yeast is not outdated; if too old, it will probably be dead. Store unopened envelopes or jars in a cool, dark place, ideally at temperatures of 32°F to 34°F, or in the refrigerator. Open envelopes must be stored in the refrigerator.

To use, sprinkle the yeast granules into water that is 105°F to 115°F (just hotter than lukewarm to the touch), and allow the mixture to sit about 5 minutes. To hasten the growth of the yeast, a little sugar can be added. After a few minutes, a healthy, active batch of yeast will "proof," or bubble up and look frothy; after 5 or 6 minutes it will expand in volume. If the mixture is still dormant, it is too old and should be discarded. Rapid-rising yeast requires a special procedure for success in cake baking. I prefer to use the original regular-type dry yeast. Beware of proofing rapid-rise yeast; it may exhaust its rising power during the proof period.

Note that while some sugar (or flour that the yeast enzymes can convert to sugar) is essential for yeast growth, a high proportion of sugar in a batter or dough slows yeast multiplication. For this reason, rich sweet coffee-cake dough often requires a longer rising time than plain bread.

SALT

∎

Common salt, or sodium chloride, is the type used in baking. It contributes many factors: it enhances flavors and improves taste, aids digestibility, and strengthens the gluten in yeast products. Keeping in mind today's concerns about salt in relation to high blood pressure and general health, I have tried to cut the salt included in the cake recipes to a minimum. Always bake with unsalted butter so that you can control the amount of salt added to the cake; different brands of butter vary in salt content.

GELATIN

∎

Gelatin is a natural product derived from collagen, the protein found in bones and connective tissue. It is sold most often in the United States in dry granulated form. For making fillings, Bavarian creams, and puddings, use unsweetened flavorless gelatin sold in bulk or packaged in small envelopes. Bulk packages are usually freshness–dated; it is worth checking. Each individual envelope contains 1 scant tablespoon of granulated gelatin (¼ ounce; 7 grams), enough to set 2 cups of liquid. To dissolve gelatin, sprinkle it on top of a small amount of cold water and let it sit for 3 to 5

minutes to swell and soften. Then set the mixture over moderate heat and stir until the granules dissolve completely. Do not boil, or the gelatin will lose some of its setting strength. Beware of using too much gelatin, it makes products rubbery.

FLAVORINGS

∎

Spices, extracts, citrus rind (zest), liqueurs, coffee, and chocolate all add flavoring to baked products, fillings, and icings. They vary widely in their properties and purity, so pay careful attention to recipe requirements.

Spices
Once a spice is ground, the aroma is volatile and fades when exposed to the air or to heat for a period of time. If you buy ground spices, they must be kept in well-sealed jars in a cool, dry cupboard. Whole seeds and spices have a longer shelf life, but should also be stored in sealed containers away from heat, air, and moisture. It is always preferable to use freshly ground spices if you possibly can; they impart a stronger and more aromatic flavor to baked goods than do the pallid powders lingering in the back of the spice rack.

Extracts
Extracts are the concentrated natural essential oils of the flavoring agent, usually dissolved in alcohol. Some flavors are made from the oils found in the rind of citrus fruits (lemons and oranges, for example); others are made from fruit pulp.

Extract bottles are labeled "pure" or "imitation." The distinction is important. Most liquid flavors are volatile and thus dissipate in the heat of baking. To have a good flavor in the finished cake, you must start with the purest and strongest flavoring. Pure extracts cost more, and are worth it. Imitation flavors are produced synthetically, and often impart a chemical taste to cakes; at best, they are weaker and less aromatic than pure extracts. Some flavors are unavailable in pure extracts—coconut or pistachio, for example. You can use the fresh nuts for flavoring instead, or use the extract in moderation. Some natural flavors do need a little enhancement from extracts. I find that pure maple syrup (even grade B, which has a stronger flavor than the lighter-colored Fancy, or grade A) may not flavor a cake enough; the flavor benefits from a very tiny bit of artificial maple extract.

The purest vanilla extract is that which you make yourself. To do this, buy 4 pliable aromatic vanilla pods (in a gourmet or baking supply shop) and slit each pod lengthwise. Soak the pods in 2 cups of vodka in a covered glass jar for at least 2 weeks. After this time, you can remove the pods or leave them in, as you wish. Use this flavored vodka, strained, for your extract. Homemade vanilla extract makes an excellent holiday gift for a baker.

Liquid extracts should be stored in dark-colored, tightly closed bottles in a cool, dark cupboard. Extracts are volatile in the presence of heat and light.

Zests
Zest is simply the bright-colored part of the peel of a citrus fruit. The zest contains all the essential oils, or flavors, of the peel. Just below the zest is a bitter-tasting white pith, which should not be used. When the recipes in this book call for grated lemon, orange, or tangerine zest, for example, I mean that only the brightest-colored part of the peel should be used. When you have a bunch of lemons, oranges, or limes to squeeze for juice, grate them first, or cut off the zest in long thin strips, and freeze it for later use in baking; then extract the juice.

Grating citrus zest with a box or panel grater is hard, because of the struggle required to free the fruit. Food writer and cook Richard Sax once showed me his method, which works for most purposes and avoids the worst of the problem. He uses a gadget called a citrus peeler, a tool with a wooden handle and a flat metal head containing 5 tiny, sharp-edged round holes. This tool is scraped across the skin of the fruit, shredding it into long very thin slivers. I love to use these slivers just as they are for decorations on a buttercream-covered orange or lemon cake. Richard puts the slivers on a wooden board and minces them with a sharp knife, creating a texture nearly as fine as grating, with less waste.

Nuts
The preparation technique for nuts is determined by their use. Toasting nuts brings out their flavor and darkens their color somewhat. For cake batters with a good strong nut flavor, it is best to toast nuts before grinding or chopping them. However, for cookies, meringue cake layers (dacquoise) or streusel toppings, where the chopped nuts will be exposed more directly to the heat source, they will effectively be toasted during baking so it is not necessary to do so in advance. Do toast nuts to be used as a garnish on cake sides or top.

□ TO DRY OR TOAST AND
SKIN NUTS

Some nuts, walnuts in particular, have a high oil content and tend to make a paste when ground; to avoid this and improve ease of grinding, dry the nuts in the oven before grinding them. Spread the nuts on a shallow pan and set them in a preheated 300°F oven for 5 to 6 minutes, 8 minutes for hazelnuts. To toast nuts instead of simply drying them, increase oven heat to about 325°F. Heat the nuts for 5 to 7 minutes or longer, until they are aromatic and show a light golden color. Toss or stir several times for even heating. Or toast the nuts until golden in a heavy-bottomed frying pan set over low to moderate heat; watch the nuts and stir them constantly.

Beneath their shells, some nuts have skins that must be removed.

To remove the brown skin from hazelnuts, toast the nuts as described. As soon as the nuts come from the oven, wrap them in a coarse-textured towel for several minutes to steam. Then rub the skins off with the towel; discard the skins and pick out the nuts to use. A few bits of skin will still cling to the nuts; ignore this.

To remove the skins of almonds or pistachios, they should be blanched. This is easily accomplished by boiling the shelled nuts (skins still on) in water for 2 or 3 minutes. Drain and cool them under cold running water. Pinch off the skins with your fingers.

□ TO GRIND NUTS

Some nut cakes, especially European tortes and Swedish pastries, use finely ground nuts, especially almonds, hazelnuts, and walnuts. The end product must be fine and very dry, almost like a shaved powder rather than oily chopped beads. It is easiest to accomplish this with a hand-held food or nut mill in which a presser bar pushes on the nuts, forcing them onto a rotating cutting disk. This gadget is available from specialty cookware supply houses (see list of Suppliers, page 482).

A meat grinder can be used to grind nuts, but sometimes it tends to press the oils out, and this may not be desirable. A blender can also be used, but remember to add only ½ cup of nuts at a time and pulse for about 4 seconds. Stop the blender and stir the nuts before repeating the chopping action. The food processor does an excellent job of fine-chopping nuts, but may create a paste if the nuts are oily; the best way to fine-chop nuts in the processor is to add a tablespoon or two of granulated sugar (take this sugar from the measured amount used in the recipe) before turning on the machine. The sugar keeps the nuts spinning and prevents packing, thus enabling the blades to a finer texture.

Poppyseeds

Many Austrian and Hungarian recipes require ground poppyseeds, which are richly flavorful, highly aromatic, and moist. Certain specialty markets sell ground poppyseeds (see list of Suppliers, page 482) but grinding is a task easily accomplished at home with an imported poppyseed or spice grinder. The seeds can also be ground in a regular meat grinder (fitted with the finest blade) or an electric herb mincer, which I prefer. The mincer I use, made by Varco, came from a cookware shop. It consists of a small cup containing a set of sharp thin blades. Seeds or spices (or garlic, shallots, or herbs) are placed in the cup, which is pushed down onto a base, engaging a motor on contact. Simple to use and effective, it grinds poppyseeds to perfection. A regular electric blender will also work if you grind only ½ cup of seeds at a time and stir them down once or twice. Grind them in the blender on high speed for at least 1 full minute. Note that the regular food processor will not grind poppyseeds, as they are too small to be cut by the blade.

Dried Fruits

Dried fruits are used in many types of baked products: coffee and tea cakes, for example, as well as fruitcakes. It is important to use fruits that are not too hard and dried out, for baking will not soften them. Before adding dried fruits to a batter, taste them for flavor and texture. If they are too hard, place them in a strainer over (not in) boiling water, cover, and steam them for a few minutes until you can bite into them without breaking your teeth.

Dates and prunes are available pitted as well as with pits. The pitted products are easier to work with and can easily be chopped. Avoid packaged prechopped dates as they rarely have good texture; their skins are usually encrusted with undesirable crystalized sugar.

Raisins are grapes dried either by the sun or by artificial heat. In this book, I use both dark seedless raisins and golden raisins, which are regular raisins that have been treated with sulfur dioxide to prevent darkening. The flavor of golden raisins is lighter and sweeter than that of dark raisins.

Dried currants used in baking are actually small raisins made from dried Zante grapes. This product is sold in the supermarket next to dried raisins, and the box is labeled "Zante Currants." Store currants and raisins in covered glass jars in the refrigerator. Note: Dried Zante currants are not related to fresh, bush-grown currants, which are white, black, or red berries.

Dried figs come primarily from California, Greece, or Turkey. Select figs that are flexible when pressed rather than hard and dried out. Store dried figs in a covered jar in a dry cupboard.

Coconut

The coconut is the fruit of the palm *Cocos nucifera,* one of the oldest food plants known. Its name has been documented in Sanskrit, but our word coconut, according to the *Oxford English Dictionary,* probably derives from the Portuguese and Spanish *coca,* meaning "grinning face or grimace." Portuguese explorers thought the eye pattern on the coconut looked like the grinning face of a monkey.

Botanically, the coconut is not a nut at all, but a "drupe" fruit. The coconut consists of a thick fibrous husk and a hard inner shell that contains the white meat and coconut liquid, correctly termed coconut water, not milk. Coconut oil is a highly saturated fat, but this is not really a problem for cake eaters because the amount of coconut consumed is relatively small.

When buying a fresh coconut, generally available as the hard, brown fiber-covered shell freed from the thick outer husk, be sure it is heavy for its size. You should hear the liquid inside when you shake the coconut, and there should be no sign of mold around the eyes or cracks in the shell, which might allow bacteria to grow inside.

The coconut can be stored at room temperature. When opened, the meat should be white; if it looks gray and smells fermented, it is spoiled and should be discarded.

□ TO PREPARE A COCONUT

Set the coconut on a towel so it does not roll and pierce the eyes with a screwdriver and a hammer. Drain the coconut water into a bowl and store it in the refrigerator for baking or to drink. Strain the liquid if it contains fibers. Set the drained coconut on a roasting pan and bake at 350°F for about 30 minutes. The heat should cause the shell to crack. If it needs to be cracked more, wrap it in a towel and give it a few blows with a hammer. Use the screwdriver to pry the shell away from the meat. Use a vegetable peeler to remove the brown skin from the white meat.

Break up the prepared coconut meat into small pieces and grate it in several small batches in the blender or food processor, or by hand on a box grater. Slice chips from the edges of the coconut sections and toast these with salt in a 300°F oven for about 25 minutes, tossing occasionally, to make a delicious snack.

To make true "coconut milk," cover the grated coconut meat with about 1¼ cups boiling water, let sit for about 10 minutes, then strain the liquid into a clean container. Or pour the boiling water through the feed tube of the food processor containing the grated coconut and process for 20 to 30 seconds; let stand for 10 minutes, then strain. This strained liquid is the milk. Repeat the process if you need more liquid, or add water or milk to the first batch of liquid.

To make "coconut cream," pour no more than 2 cups boiling water over 1 grated coconut, let it sit until cold, then drain through cheesecloth, squeezing the coconut dry. Let this liquid sit until a waxy cream rises and forms on top. Remove this and refrigerate to use in baking.

Chocolate

As an unabashed chocoholic, I consider chocolate an essential element, right up there with fire, air, and water. I have devoted considerable time and thought to the subject, and I find its story, from cacao tree to candy bar, both complex and fascinating.

The chocolate tree is *Theobroma cacao,* a tropical evergreen native to South and Central America, also cultivated in Africa and Southeast Asia. The Aztecs were the first to appreciate the fruit of this tree, making a cocoa beverage so venerated that it was reserved exclusively for the Emperor Montezuma and his ministers. It is said that Montezuma drank as many as 50 golden cups a day of this frothy cold drink, prepared from roasted and ground cacao beans flavored with peppers and spices. Among chocolate's many virtues, the Aztecs considered it an aphrodisiac, a fact modern science has explained by isolating phenylethylamine, a natural ingredient of chocolate that produces a euphoric sensation some say is akin to the feeling of falling in love. Our words chocolate and cocoa derive from the Nahuatl *xochuatl* or *chochuatl,* meaning "bitter juice."

The tree produces large pods, which are cut from the trunk, and opened. The inner beans and pulp are scooped out, air-dried, fermented, and cured to remove the bitter taste, impart aroma, enrich the flavor, and darken the color. As beans from different geographical areas have particular qualities, most manufacturers blend them to combine the best taste, texture, and aroma, much as coffee beans are blended.

At the factory, the beans are roasted to develop their "chocolaty" taste and flavor. Their hulls are removed, and the inner nibs, containing 50 to 54 percent cocoa butter, a natural fat, are crushed and ground, or rolled between steel disks. The heat produced in this process liquefies the cocoa butter, most of which is removed. The dark brown paste remaining is called chocolate liquor. A churning procedure called conching further refines the product and enhances its quality.

Chocolate liquor can be molded and solidified. This is then sold as unsweetened or bitter chocolate. When varying amounts of sugar and cocoa butter are combined with the chocolate liquor, the results are bittersweet, semisweet, and sweet chocolate, depending on the proportions. Bittersweet is the least sweet of these. When dry milk solids are added to sweetened chocolate, it becomes milk chocolate. Depending on your taste preference and the requirements of your recipe, the different types of chocolate can be used interchangeably in cakes and icings.

□ COCOA

To make cocoa, chocolate liquor is pressed to remove more than half of its remaining cocoa butter. The dry cake of residue is then pulverized and sifted, making fine unsweetened cocoa powder. Note: Instant cocoa mixes for drinks have dry milk solids and sugars added and should not be substituted for baking cocoa.

Natural processed cocoa, like chocolate, is acidic and has the fruity flavor of the cocoa bean. To neutralize some of the acid, and to darken and redden the color, some cocoas are Dutch-processed, or factory-treated with alkali. The name comes from the fact that a Dutchman, Coenraad van Houten, discovered the process. Examples of brands using this method are Droste, Van Houten, Fedora, and most other imports. The most widely available American brands of unsweetened cocoa powder, Hershey's and Baker's, are "natural," not Dutch-process, and thus have higher acidity. Both types are used in recipes calling for baking soda, which interacts with their natural acidity to balance the Ph, darken and redden the color, and at the same time create a leavening agent by releasing carbon dioxide when the acid and alkaki mix. However, Dutch-process cocoa requires less baking soda to neutralize its acid than does natural processed cocoa. For this reason, you should take care when substituting Dutch-process cocoa for natural cocoa. It is best to use the specific type called for in the recipe. To adjust the recipe yourself, be aware that for Dutch-process cocoa you decrease the amount of baking soda slightly and add a little baking powder; excess baking soda may result in a soapy flavor in the cake.

Note: To substitute cocoa powder for solid unsweetened chocolate, use 3 level tablespoons natural (not Dutch-process) cocoa plus 1 tablespoon solid vegetable shortening or unsalted butter for each 1 ounce unsweetened chocolate. However, the flavor and texture will be slightly different because solid chocolate contains cocoa butter, which is lacking in cocoa.

□ WHITE CHOCOLATE

White chocolate is not a true chocolate because it contains no chocolate liquor. In its simplest form, it is a blend of whole milk and sugar, cooked, condensed, and solidified; sometimes, in the best types, cocoa butter is added to enhance the chocolate flavor. Whey powder, lecithin, vanillin, nuts, and even egg whites may be added. Though labeling leaves a lot to be desired, often the most expensive imported brands do have cocoa butter added (Tobler and Lindt, for example).

Take care when melting white chocolate, as it tends to solidify easily. Too much heat transforms the protein in the milk additives and lumps the chocolate; at over 110° to 115°F the chocolate will start to recrystallize and become grainy. Always melt white chocolate slowly over warm (125°F) water, stir it often to prevent crusting, and use it as soon as it is melted. White chocolate can be used just like regular dark chocolate to make chocolate leaves, curls, and decorations.

☐ IMITATION CHOCOLATE
Artificial chocolates, sold in supermarkets alongside the Real Thing, are not at all the same and should be avoided in baking. These products do not contain the chocolate liquor and cocoa butter that distinguish real chocolate. They are made of vegetable fats (other than cocoa butter) such as palm kernel, coconut, or cottonseed oil. Some brands contain paraffin as a hardener.

☐ COATING CHOCOLATE OR COUVERTURE
These chocolates are processed specially for coating purposes or confectionery work; if they contain cocoa butter, they have to be tempered, or kept at specific temperatures, to maintain their texture and gloss. Couverture chocolates, usually sold in specialty or gourmet shops or baker's supply houses, are good for making chocolate curls and decorations; they are softer and less brittle than regular chocolates. However, for the purposes of this book, they are not usually required.

☐ TO TEMPER CHOCOLATE
When chocolate that contains cocoa butter is melted, then resolidified, it tends to dull in color and lose its "snap," or clean-breaking quality; professionals say the chocolate has lost its "temper." To restore the original quality of the chocolate, restabilizing the crystals of cocoa butter within it, the chocolate should be tempered as follows: Chop the chocolate into matchstick-size pieces. Melt about two thirds of the chocolate in the top pan of a double boiler over hot (120°F) water until the chocolate registers 110°F on a candy thermometer. Remove the pot of chocolate from the heat, place on the counter, and stir in remaining chopped chocolate until the mixture registers 75°F on the thermometer. Set the top pan again over hot water in the lower pan and stir until the chocolate is completely melted and registers 91°F on the thermometer (85°F for milk chocolate). If some of the solid chocolate remains unmelted when the mass reaches its correct temperature, remove the solid pieces. At this point, the chocolate is ready to use—to spread on a cake, to coat candies or whole fruits, to pour onto baking parchment to solidify into a sheet that can be sliced into wedges or cut into other shapes for cake decorations. To speed setting, chocolate can be chilled. Note that tempered chocolate can be stored in the refrigerator for several days. It can also be retempered if the result is not acceptable to you—if the chocolate is not glossy or crisp after the first tempering.

☐ TO MELT WHITE AND DARK CHOCOLATE
Chocolate is an emulsion; unless handled carefully, the fat will separate out. For this reason, it must be melted very slowly, preferably in

the top pan of a double boiler set over hot (125°F) water. Ideally, you melt only about half of the chocolate in the double boiler, then remove it from heat and stir until remaining chocolate is melted. Dark chocolate should never be heated above 120°F because it will turn grainy. White chocolate will become grainy if heated above 115°F; ideally you should hold melting white chocolate to 100° to 110°F. To speed up the melting process, chop the solid chocolate into matchstick-size pieces before heating.

Beware of getting liquid into pure white or dark chocolate as it melts. A drop of water added by mistake, or present in a damp pan, can cause the chocolate to seize and harden. This is not always salvageable, but you can try smoothing it out by stirring in 1 teaspoon solid white shortening for each ounce of chocolate.

To avoid the moisture problem, you can melt dark chocolate in the microwave oven. For each ounce, heat at medium-low (7) for 2 to 3 minutes. The chocolate will not lose its shape when melted, so remove it from the microwave oven and stir until it is all evenly melted; this is especially important if melting several ounces at once. It usually melts unevenly and needs stirring plus a few more seconds in the microwave. In baking, never use chocolate that is unevenly melted; check by stirring until uniformly smooth.

□ TO STORE CHOCOLATE

Store chocolate in a cool, dry place at about 60°F. At warmer temperatures, a grayish bloom develops on the surface of the chocolate; this is the cocoa butter rising to the surface. It does not affect the flavor but may be unsightly. The color returns to normal if the chocolate is melted. Some commercial candy bars are treated to have higher melting points and prevent bloom in warm stores or warm weather; this means the chocolate will no longer melt in your mouth, as the original quality has been altered.

Chocolate stored at excessively cold temperatures may sweat when brought to room temperature. It is not a good idea to store chocolate in the refrigerator or freezer.

□ CHOCOLATE TYPES AND SUPPLIERS

For chocolate suppliers, see the list of mail-order houses in the back of the book.

For the recipes in this book, I have used only pure semisweet, bittersweet, or unsweetened chocolate available in local stores or from mail-order specialty shops. As a general rule, you can substitute chocolate morsels for block chocolate, chopped, and vice versa. As a guide, ⅛ cup regular-size chocolate morsels = 1 ounce = 2 tablespoons. Hershey's, Nestle's, Maillard Eagle, Ghirardelli, Baker's, and Baker's German Sweet are some of the most widely known brands I use. Imports I like especially include Lindt Extra-Bittersweet and Lindt Excellence, Tobler Tradition and Tobler Bittersweet, Callebaut Semi-Sweet or Bittersweet, and Poulain Bittersweet for Baking. For white chocolate I use Tobler Narcisse and Van Leer White Chocolate (purchased through a baking supply house). Some gourmet shops sell white chocolate blocks in small quantities as well as white chocolate morsels.

· HOW TO MEASURE INGREDIENTS ·

*I*n the United States, we use volume measurements for both dry and liquid ingredients. Elsewhere in the world, people tend to measure dry ingredients by weight on a scale. This is a much more accurate system, and once you are used to it, it is easy to work with. A quick look at 1 cup of cake flour will explain: 1 cup of sifted cake flour spooned into a 1-cup measure and leveled off will weigh 3½ ounces or 100 grams. If I tap this cup sharply, the contents will compact so that I can then spoon in as much as 2 tablespoons more flour, for a weight of about 4 ounces, or 113 grams. As we all handle measuring tools differently, we can unwittingly use more of an ingredient than we mean to. Excess flour, for example, can toughen baked goods, so one wants to use the minimum required. Thus, it is more reliable to weigh out 100 grams of flour than to measure 1 cup by volume.

Since accuracy with flour, sugar, and fat measurements are especially critical in cake baking, I have included the weights for these ingredients in both ounces and grams alongside their volume measurements. Ideally, you will weigh these items (directions for using a scale follow) and measure the other ingredients by volume. If scales daunt you, of course use the conventional method; simply measure with care.

HOW TO MEASURE LIQUIDS

■

Use a liquid measuring cup (see page 20). Set the cup flat on the counter, fill it to the desired amount, and bend down to read the mark at eye level. Note: Eggs are considered liquids, and are measured in a liquid measuring cup.

How to Measure Dry Ingredients

∎

☐ SCOOP AND SWEEP METHOD

When the recipe does not specify sifting, use this method. Simply dip your dry measuring cup (see page 20) into a canister of flour or sugar and scoop up a heaping amount. Then take the back of a knife or other straight edge and sweep off the excess, leveling the top.

☐ SCOOP AND SWEEP METHOD WHEN YOU ARE IN A HURRY

One level cup of unsifted flour contains about 2 tablespoons more flour than 1 cup that is sifted; therefore, if you are in a hurry and feel you must cheat, not bothering to sift when the recipe tells you to, be aware that while you are skipping the aeration value of the sifter, you can compensate for the volume difference by scooping and sweeping a *scant* cup of flour, about 2 tablespoons less than a full cup. Do your cheating on coffee cakes and their like rather than sponge cakes or génoise, or you will have disappointing results.

☐ TO SIFT AND MEASURE BY VOLUME

When the recipe specifies sifting, use this method. Scoop flour or confectioners' sugar or cocoa from the canister and put it into a strainer (which I prefer) or sifter set over a piece of wax paper or a bowl. Sift. Spoon the item into the appropriate size of dry measuring cup, heaping the top slightly. Take the back of a knife or other straight edge and sweep off the excess, leveling the top. Lift the edges of the piece of wax paper and pour the excess back into the canister.

Note: Unless granulated sugar looks lumpy and has been in storage too long, it is not necessary to sift it before measuring.

☐ TO SIFT AND MEASURE BY WEIGHT

First read About Using Scales, following. Line the scale container with plastic wrap. Scoop flour or other dry ingredient from the canister into a strainer and sift it onto the scale container until the correct weight is reached. Or sift onto a piece of plastic wrap or wax paper, then spoon it onto the scale.

☐ UNSIFTED MEASURING BY WEIGHT

First read About Using Scales, following. If no sifting is required, simply weigh the item directly on the scale platform. When weighing berries or other juicy items, first line the scale container with plastic wrap.

About Using Scales

∎

For information about types of scales, see page 20. Select a type that is made for cooking, not a dieter's scale, which will only hold very small quantities. It should have a container or platform large enough to hold at least 2 cups of flour or sugar; ideally, it should measure at least 16 ounces or 500 grams. Line the container or platform with a piece of plastic wrap before measuring. The wrap helps prevent washups and also can be used to transfer the measured item to the mixing bowl.

If your scale does not have a deep container, set a plastic freezer-type container on the platform to hold the ingredients; be sure to reset the dial to zero to compensate for the weight of the container before adding the ingredients to be weighed. Reset the dial when the auxiliary container is no longer in use.

In addition to using the scale for all dry ingredients, it is also useful for measuring solid fats and eggs. The size and weight of eggs varies (see page 30) and while the recipes in this book call for large, 2-ounce eggs, you may use other sizes, if the combined weight is correct.

To Measure Fats

■

Oil is liquid fat; it is measured in a liquid measuring cup, as for other liquids. There are several methods for measuring solid fats, but the easiest is with a scale, as described.

The second choice is to use butter or margarine sold in quarter-pound sticks. Each stick is marked on the wrapper indicating tablespoon and cup divisions. One stick = 8 tablespoons = ½ cup; ⅓ cup = 5⅓ tablespoons; ¼ cup = 4 tablespoons.

To measure solid shortening without a scale, it is best to pack it into a dry measuring cup, taking care to eliminate any air pockets that may be trapped in the bottom of the cup. Level off the cup, and use. The water displacement method for measuring solid fats is not a good choice for baking cakes, because water clings to the fat and may upset the balance or chemistry of the other ingredients in the batter. However, for the record, to measure ¼ cup of shortening, you would fill a 1-cup liquid measure ¾ full of water, then add shortening until the water reaches the 1-cup mark. Pour off the water and use the measured shortening.

· A NOTE ABOUT RECIPE ·
MEASUREMENTS

Standard volume measurements (cups and spoons) are given for all the ingredients used in the recipes in this book; in addition, weight measurements in ounces and grams are given for certain ingredients (flour, sugar, fat, and some other items) so that they may be weighed on a scale for greater accuracy. If you are using a scale, you will notice that our ounce and gram weights have been rounded off. Do not worry about discrepancies here because the amounts will all be in correct proportion to one another. See the table below for examples of our measurements.

Ounces:	Grams (exact)	Grams (rounded off)	Ounces:	Grams (exact)	Grams (rounded off)
¼	7.0	7	7	198.45	200
½	14.17	15	8	226.80	230
1	28.35	30	9	255.15	255
1¾	49.61	50	10	283.50	280
2	56.70	60	10½	297.67	300
2¾	74.85	75	11	311.85	310
3	85.05	85	12	340.20	340
3½	99.22	100	13	368.55	370
4	113.40	110	14	396.90	400
5	141.70	140	15	424.25	425
6	170.10	170	16 (1 pound)	453.60	454

Examples of Weight Equivalents

■

	Unsifted ounces grams	Sifted ounces grams
ALL-PURPOSE FLOUR		
1 cup	5 oz; 140 g	4¼ oz; 120 g
(Note: 1 cup sifted flour = 1 cup unsifted flour minus 2 tablespoons.)		
CAKE FLOUR		
1 cup	4½ oz; 120 g	3½ oz; 100 g
GRANULATED SUGAR		
1 cup	7 oz; 200 g	—
CONFECTIONERS' SUGAR		
1 cup	4½ oz; 130 g	3½ oz; 100 g
DARK BROWN SUGAR, firmly packed		
1 cup	9 oz; 255 g	—

	Tbsp.	oz/lb	stick(s)	cup(s)	Grams (exact)	Grams (rounded off)
BUTTER						
	1	½ oz	⅛	—	(14)	15
	2	1 oz	¼	—	(28)	30
	4	2 oz	½	¼	(57)	60
	8	4 oz; ¼ lb	1	½	(113)	110
	16	8 oz; ½ lb	2	1	(227)	230
	32	16 oz; 1 lb	4	2	(453.6)	454

Equivalents and Substitutions

■

Note that all measurements used in this book are level.
All eggs used in the recipes are U.S. Grade A large.

Equivalents

BREAD CRUMBS
    1 cup fresh bread crumbs   = 2 ounces; 60 grams
    1 cup dry or toasted bread crumbs   = scant 4 ounces; 110 grams

BUTTER
    1 pound butter   = 2 cups; 454 grams
    ¼ pound butter   = ½ cup; 1 stick; 113 grams; 8 tablespoons

CHOCOLATE
    1 ounce solid semisweet chocolate   = 1 premeasured square = 25 grams
    1 ounce regular-size chocolate morsels   = ⅛ cup = 2 tablespoons
    ½ cup regular chocolate morsels   = 3 ounces; 85 grams
    1 cup regular chocolate morsels   = 6 ounces; 170 grams
    1 cup mini-chip chocolate morsels   = 5½ ounces; 155 grams

COCONUT
    1 average size coconut, 4-inch diameter   = 3½ cups grated coconut, loose; 2 cups, hard packed
    4 ounces coconut, dried and flaked or shredded   = 1 scant cup

CREAM
    1 cup heavy cream (36 to 40 percent butterfat)   = 2 cups whipped cream

EGGS
    1 U.S. Grade A large egg   = 2 ounces = 3 tablespoons
    1 large egg yolk   = 1 generous tablespoon
    1 large egg white   = 2 tablespoons = ⅛ cup
    2 large eggs   = scant ½ cup = 3 medium eggs
    4 to 5 large eggs   = 1 cup

EGGS (continued)

6 to 7 large yolks	= ½ cup
4 large whites	= ½ cup
3 large whites, beaten stiff	= 3 cups meringue, enough to top a 9-inch cake

FLOUR

1 pound all-purpose flour	= 4 cups
5 pounds all-purpose flour	= 20 cups
1 pound cake flour or pastry flour	= 4½ cups plus 2 tablespoons

FRUITS

1 8-ounce box dried apricots	= 2 cups, packed
1 pound seedless raisins	= 3½ cups; 454 grams
1 whole lemon	= 2 to 3 tablespoons juice plus 2 to 3 teaspoons grated zest
1 whole orange	= 6 to 8 tablespoons juice plus 2 to 3 tablespoons grated zest
1 quart fresh berries	= 4 cups

GELATIN

1 envelope unflavored gelatin	= 1 scant tablespoon (¼ oz; 7 g); to hard-set 2 cups liquid

NUTS

1 pound whole almonds, shelled	= 3¼ cups; 454 grams
1 cup blanched almonds, shelled	= 5 ounces; 140 grams
1 pound walnuts, shelled	= 4 cups; 454 grams
1 cup walnuts, shelled	= 4 ounces; 110 grams
1 pound whole pecans, shelled	= 4½ cups; 454 grams
1 cup shelled pecan halves	= 3½ ounces; 100 grams
1 cup shelled peanuts	= 5 ounces; 140 grams
1 pound whole hazelnuts, shelled	= 3¼ cups; 454 grams
1 cup shelled whole hazelnuts	= 5 ounces; 140 grams

SUGAR

1 pound granulated sugar	= 2¼ cups
5 pounds granulated sugar	= 11¼ cups
1 pound brown sugar	= 2¼ cups, packed
1 pound confectioners' sugar	= 4 to 4¼ cups, unsifted

1 ounce solid chocolate	= 3 tablespoons cocoa plus 1 tablespoon solid vegetable shortening or vegetable oil
1 cup sour milk	= 1 cup sweet milk plus 1 tablespoon vinegar, let sit for 2 to 3 minutes
1 cup whole sweet milk	= 3 to 4 tablespoons dry milk solids plus 1 cup water
1 cup buttermilk	= 1 cup plain yogurt, stirred
1 cup crème fraîche	= 1 cup heavy cream plus ½ cup sour cream (see recipe, page 416)
1 cup all-purpose flour	= ⅞ cup rice flour
2 tablespoons flour for thickening 1 cup liquid in medium-thick sauce	= 1 tablespoon cornstarch, potato starch, or arrowroot, or 3 tablespoons quick-cooking tapioca
1 cup granulated sugar	= 1 cup molasses plus ½ teaspoon baking soda and omit baking powder in recipe. Also decrease recipe liquid by ¼ cup for each cup of molasses.
1 cup granulated sugar	= ⅞ cup honey and decrease recipe liquid by 3 tablespoons.
1 cup brown sugar	= 1 cup granulated white sugar plus 2 tablespoons unsulfured molasses
1 cup cinnamon sugar	= 1 cup granulated sugar plus 1 to 2 tablespoons ground cinnamon, to taste
1 teaspoon baking powder	= ¼ teaspoon baking soda sifted together with ½ teaspoon cream of tartar. Or, for each 1 cup flour in the recipe, use 1 teaspoon baking soda plus 2 teaspoons cream of tartar and a few grains of salt sifted together.

· PAN VOLUME AND SERVING CHART ·

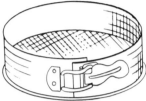
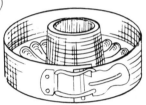

*U*se this chart as a guide when substituting other pans for those called for in the recipes. The pan sizes given are those most frequently used in this book. The number of cups of batter is indicated in the notes preceding each recipe. Except where so-noted in recipes, pan sizes may be changed without affecting baking results. Pans are measured across the top, from rim to rim. To find the full capacity of a pan, fill it to the brim with measured cups of water;

slight variations from the chart are caused by differences in the shape of the pan; pans with slightly sloping or fluted sides have a different volume from pans with straight sides. Batter is usually added to a depth of no more than half to two thirds of the pan because room must be left to allow the cake to rise.

The number of servings indicated is for a 2- or 3-layer cake; yield depends upon the richness and the size of the pieces.

Pan shape and size	Maximum cups fluid to full pan capacity	Maximum cups batter for pan (allowing for rise)	Approximate number of servings
ROUND LAYERS			
6×2 inches	4	2 to 2½	6
8×1½ or 8×2	4½ to 5	2	8 to 10
9×1½ or 9×2	6 to 6½	3 to 3½	8 to 10
10×2	10	4½ to 6	14
12×2	14	7½ to 9	22
14×2	19½	10 to 12	36 to 40

Pan shape and size	Maximum cups fluid to full pan capacity	Maximum cups batter for pan (allowing for rise)	Approximate number of servings
SQUARE LAYERS			
8×2	8	3½ to 5	9 to 12
9×1½	8 to 9	4½ to 5	9 to 12
9×2	10	5½	9 to 12
10×2	12⅓	6	20
12×2	16	10 to 12	36
14×2	24	12 to 14	42
OBLONG (SHEET CAKES)			
8×12 (7½× 11¾×1¾)	8	4 to 5	12
9×13 (8¾× 13½×1¾)	16	8 to 9	20 to 24
11×17 (11⅜× 17¼×2¼)	25	14 to 15	24 to 30
10½×15½×1 (jelly-roll pan)	10	4 to 5 for butter cake or 8 for génoise	35
HEART			
9×1½	5	3 to 3½	16
TUBE, RING, BUNDT, KUGELHOPF			
9×2¾ plain tube	6 to 7	4 to 4½	8 to 10
9×2 springform tube	9 to 10	6 to 7	10 to 12
9¼×3¼ fluted tube or bundt	9 to 10	5 to 6	10 to 12
9½×3¾ or 10-inch plain tube or springform	12	6 to 7	12 to 14
9×4 kugelhopf	10	5 to 6	10 to 12
9¾×4¼ kugelhopf	12	6 to 7	12 to 14
10×3½ bundt	12	6 to 7	14

Pan shape and size	Maximum cups fluid to full pan capacity	Maximum cups batter for pan (allowing for rise)	Approximate number of servings
LOAVES			
6×3½×2 (baby)	2	1¼ to 1½	6 to 8
7½×3½×2 or 8½×4½×2¾ (average)	5 to 6	3	7 to 8
9×5×3 (large)	8 to 9	4 to 5	9 to 10
CHARLOTTE MOLDS			
5½-inch base, 3½-inch height	6	—	8
6-inch base, 4-inch height	8	—	10
SOUFFLÉ MOLDS			
6½-inch base, 3¼-inch height	6	4 to 5	8
7-inch diameter, 3¾-inch height	8	6 to 7	10
COFFEE CANS			
4-inch diameter, 5½-inch height (1-pound size)	4	2 to 3	7 to 8
CUPCAKES			
1¾×¾ (baby)	4 teaspoons	3 teaspoons	1
2×1	3 tablespoons	2 tablespoons	1
2½-inch diameter	4 tablespoons	2½ tablespoons	1
2¾-inch diameter	½ cup	¼ cup	1
3×1¼	½ cup	5 tablespoons	1

*T*o prevent cake batters from sticking to pans during baking, most pans are specially coated or lined. From the time of the ancient Egyptians to the early nineteenth century, beeswax was commonly used for this purpose, as was oil of various types. Beeswax was preferred, because oil could turn rancid and impart off-flavors to cakes. Butter, of course, was often used, and in the 1880s vegetable shortening was introduced, providing another alternative.

Pans should be prepared before you mix your batter, so that, once made, the cake can be placed directly into the oven. If a whipped batter must stand around while you prepare the pans, volume may be lost as the batter deflates.

Pans for shortening or butter cakes are greased with shortening and flour; pans for chocolate butter cakes are greased with short-ening, then dusted with cocoa powder instead of flour; the cocoa powder works well and gives a browner, less gray appearance to the surface of the baked chocolate layers. I like to use solid white vegetable shortening for greasing pans as it contains no water that may cause the batter to stick. Margarine and butter do contain water. Solid shortening also has the ability to withstand high temperatures without burning, and it films on the pan with ease, holding the coating powder (flour or cocoa) perfectly. I prefer to spread this shortening on the pans with my fingers to achieve a more even coating than I can with a piece of wax paper or paper towel, though these will work, as will a medium-stiff pastry brush (preferred by professional bakers). Note: Cocoa clings more easily if it has been sifted first.

To apply flour or cocoa, sprinkle a tablespoon, or more if the pan is large, over the greased surface, then rotate and tap the pan to let the powder coat all the bottom; turn the pan on edge and rotate it to coat the sides with powder. If adding powder to a greased tube pan, the only way to coat the greased tube properly is to sprinkle the powder on it with with a small sifter or with your fingers. Turn the pan upside down over wax paper or over the sink and tap it sharply to remove excess powder.

When I am making many cakes at one time, I follow a professional baker's tip and mix up a blend of solid shortening and flour (4 parts shortening to 1 part all-purpose flour). I store this in a covered jar in a cool cupboard or in the refrigerator and apply it to my cake pans with a medium-stiff pastry brush, not a feather brush. Pam is an odorless nonstick vegetable spray useful when working with fondant or nut brittle; Baker's Joy combines flour and oil in a spray made for coating baking pans. It is excellent for cake and muffin pan preparation.

Pans are not greased at all for angel-food cakes or some chiffon cakes. This is so the egg-white batter can cling to the sides of the pan as it rises; it would slide and fall if the pan were greased. Sponge cakes usually have a paper liner on the bottom, for easy removal of the cake, but sometimes the sides are left un-greased, again so that the fragile egg-white batter can cling as it rises.

Pans with decorative shapes like bundt, kugelhopf, and Turk's-head molds must be generously buttered and floured to prevent the batter from sticking in their patterned depressions. Spray coating such as Baker's Joy is especially helpful for these decorative pans.

Paper liners are often added on pan bottoms and sometimes also the sides, to prevent cakes from sticking. To hold the liners in place, you can dab a little shortening on the pan sides before adding the paper.

To cut liners to fit your pans, see the diagrams that follow. For round and ring liners, there are a several techniques. Chef Albert Jorant, of École de Cuisine La Varenne in Paris, has a quick and neat method. He holds the parchment paper sheet on top of the inverted cake pan with one hand, while the other hand wields a sharp long-bladed knife. With the knife at roughly a 45-degree angle, he makes long clean downward strokes against the bottom edge of the pan, trimming the paper to an exact fit as he slowly rotates the pan (diagram a). A simpler way is to set the pan down on the paper and draw around it with a pencil; then cut out the paper disk (diagram b). If you will be baking many lay-

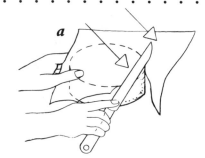

ers, cut out several disks at one time. My shortcut method is to set the pan and paper on protective stiff cardboard, then "draw" around the pan bottom with an Exacto knife, cutting the shape in one step. Don't do this directly on a tabletop or you will mar the surface.

Pans for baking fruitcakes are often completely lined. The easiest way to line a rectangular loaf pan on the bottom and sides is to cut 2 long paper strips, a narrow strip to fit over the bottom and short ends and a wide strip to cover the sides and again cover the bottom. Overlap these strips in the greased pan (diagram a). Another method is to place the pan in the center of a piece of parchment or wax paper. Draw around the pan bottom (b), then tip the pan on its side and mark the side depth. Then tip the pan on its end and mark the end depth. Repeat for the other side and end. You now have two rectangles. Cut wedges out of each corner as shown (diagram c), and fit the liner into the pan (diagram d).

To line a tube pan, there are several choices,

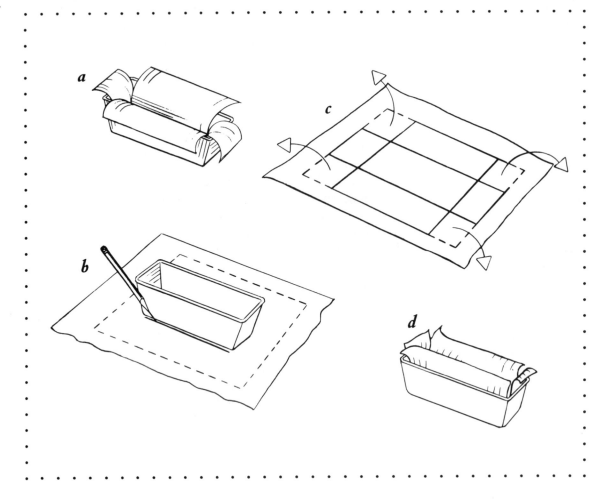

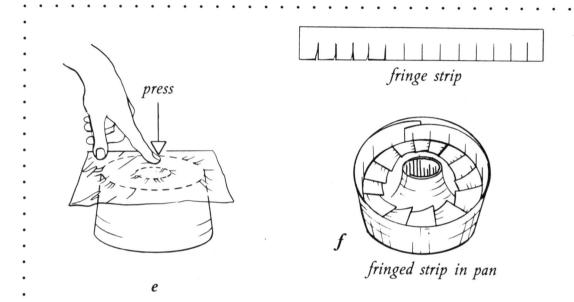

press

fringe strip

f

fringed strip in pan

e

all easy. First, you can set the pan on a piece of parchment or wax paper and draw around the pan bottom. If possible, stick the pencil inside the tube and draw around its base; if you can't reach, hold the pan upside down and press the paper onto its base with your fingers to mark the outer and inner edges of the bottom surface (diagram e). Cut out this paper ring. Then measure the height of the pan side and the tube side and cut 2 paper strips, each slightly longer than the circumference of the pan or tube. Spread a little shortening on the inside surface of the pan. Fit both the side papers in place overlapping them at the ends. Note: If your pan has very sloping sides cut a 1-inch-wide fringe in the side and tube strips. First position these strips with fringe facing the bottom, and overlap the fringe flaps as much as necessary to make the paper fit the slope (diagram f). Finally, add the bottom paper ring. If you must grease and flour the

paper liners, it is easiest to do so before putting them into the pan; stick them to the pan with a little grease. Dust with flour and tap very gently to remove excess without loosening papers.

To line jelly-roll pans, cut paper to fit, then anchor it to the pan with a few dabs of shortening. For ease in removing the cake, you can also cut the paper about 4 inches longer than the length of the pan and let 2 inches overhang at each short end. Grab these ends to lift the cake out of the pan. Peel off the paper after the baked cake is inverted.

Baking parchment does not have to be greased; wax paper should be greased and floured.

Cupcakes are baked in muffin tins. To prepare them for baking, line them with store-bought paper or foil muffin tin liners, coat them with solid shortening, or spray with store-bought nonstick baking coating.

· BEFORE YOU BEGIN TO BAKE... ·

Before you begin to bake there are a few basic procedures and techniques that are important to review. Most are mentioned elsewhere in this book, but they bear repetition. First, read the recipe all the way through to the end before starting. This helps you organize your ingredients and your equipment. It also helps you plan your time, noting whether a recipe is quick and easy or time-consuming and intricate.

Second, set out all the ingredients on the counter. By doing this, you can see whether you have omitted anything as you mix the batter. Bring all ingredients to room temperature (70°F) before beginning. An icy cold milk added to a warm batter can harden the blended shortening and cause the delicate cell walls of beaten air to become brittle and col-

lapse; thus the cake loses volume.

Sift the dry ingredients; chop, grate, and in general prepare all ingredients that need advance attention before beginning to mix the batter. Preheat the oven at least 15 minutes before using it; never set a cake into a cold oven. Put an auxiliary oven thermometer inside the baking chamber and check it before setting the cake inside to bake. Be sure the heat is correct.

If you are going to need whipped cream, place an extra bowl and beater(s) into the freezer or refrigerator before beginning the cake; they will be chilled and ready when you need them. Prepare (grease and flour) your baking pans before mixing your batter. Set out cooling racks while the cake is in the oven, so they are ready when needed.

BASIC CAKE TYPES AND
TECHNIQUES

.

We divide the cakes in this book into two basic categories: shortening or butter cakes and non-shortening (sponge or foam cakes). This determination is based upon the leavening, or rising method used; understanding the techniques involved in each will help you control the results. For specific mixing instructions and technical details about both Shortening Cakes and Non-Shortening Cakes, see Index.

The following material is discussed in greater detail in the specific sections noted above. Here, our purpose is simply to define terms for the beginning baker.

Shortening, or butter cakes, are the largest category of American cakes. These use either baking soda or baking powder for the primary leavening, with air as a secondary source. Of course, they contain a large amount of shortening (butter, margarine, oil, etc.) in proportion to the number of eggs used.

Cakes in this family include layer cakes, loaf and tea cakes, coffee cakes, pound cakes, fruitcakes, etc. There are specific methods for combining ingredients when making a butter cake (see page 73).

☐ CREAMING is the basic technique common to cakes in this category. For butter cakes, one usually creams the butter or shortening and sugar together first. To do this by hand, use a wooden spoon and smooth the ingredients back and forth against the sides of the bowl, blending them together. Eventually, the mixture will lighten in color, as air bubbles begin to mix into the fat, and soften,

smoothing out into a creamy, slightly fluffy paste. Some recipes ask you to "cream butter and sugar until light and fluffy"; however, they never really get fluffy, so do not feel you are missing something. Just look for a smooth, even blend. The mixture will be granular, because the sugar does not dissolve at this stage. If you are using an electric mixer, beat on medium-low speed so that many small bubbles will be created, with the fat opening up as the sugar crystals beat against it. Beating is slow at first to protect the fragile air cells; increase the speed gradually. Even though chemical leavening is added, the air cell structure must be protected as the batter is mixed.

☐ BLENDING is stirring or mixing ingredients until uniformly combined.

☐ BEATING is mixing rapidly to blend the ingredients. You can use a wooden spoon in a round-bottomed bowl, or an electric mixer, or an egg beater. Generally, in beating the purpose is not necessarily to increase the volume of air, as in whipping.

☐ FOLDING is a specific mixing method used for several jobs: adding whipped egg whites to a batter, adding whipped cream to a batter, or combining melted chocolate with whipped egg whites, for example. To fold, you must understand the first principal: be slow and gentle and protect every air bubble; do not deflate the volume of the whipped mixture while blending in the second ingredient. Use a large bowl and a rubber spatula. Begin by adding a small amount of the whipped ingredient to the heavier mass. Hold the bowl with one hand and the spatula with the other. Cut the spatula down through the center of the mixture, turn it, and draw it up along the side of the bowl. Give the bowl a quarter turn.

Again cut down through the center of the mixture, right down to the bottom, then up and over the top, turning the spatula upside down as it comes over the top. Repeat. Never stir, never push the spatula from side to side. Simply turn it over and over in a light up-down motion, cutting through the mass to blend it gently.

☐ KNEADING is a technique reserved for yeast doughs. In this book, it is used for yeast-risen coffee cakes. Kneading means working the mass of dough in a specific pattern in order to develop the gluten in the flour and enable it to stretch and contain the carbon dioxide gas given off by the yeast as the bread rises.

To knead, set the dough out on a lightly floured work surface. Flour your hands. Fold the mass of dough in half toward you, then push it away while leaning on it with the heels of your hands. Give the dough a quarter turn and repeat the folding and pushing. Soon the flour will work itself into the dough, as the mass turns inside out. Add a little more flour as necessary. Continue to fold and push the dough for 5 to 10 minutes, until it looks smooth and has a stretched, satiny skin that no longer feels sticky to the touch.

Non-shortening cakes are leavened primarily with air whipped into the eggs, hence the name "foam cakes." This family includes sponge cakes, angel cakes, roulades, meringues, and flourless tortes. While many foam cakes contain no shortening, some sponge cakes and tortes do.

☐ WHIPPING is the primary technique for this type of cake. Whether whipping whole or separated eggs, or even cream, the important thing is to use a balloon whisk or beater. If whipping by hand, use a whisk in a large, deep bowl. Use generous arm motions, lifting the mass and carrying it up and down, incorporating as much air as possible into the mixture. Do not stir or mix from side to side, or you will deflate the air bubbles. With an electric mixer, use the whip-type beaters; begin on low speed to create a lot of tiny air cells; gradually increase the speed to whip as much air into the mass as possible. Beware, with cream, however, for overwhipping makes butter. Use a chilled bowl and beater to whip cream quickly. Whipping egg whites requires an immaculately clean bowl and beaters.

WHAT HAPPENS WHEN A CAKE IS BAKED

▪

In the heat of the oven chemical reactions take place that transform the thick liquid batter into a cake with a light-textured crumb. It looks like magic, and partly it is, but the basics are understandable.

Oven heat causes flour and other starches to absorb moisture from the batter and begin to swell. Proteins in the flour, starch, eggs, and milk coagulate and set; starch gelatinizes. Heat causes the liquids in the batter to boil and make steam, which expands. The air bubbles beaten into the fats and coated with sugar and eggs also expand from the heat, as does air in egg foams or stiffly beaten egg whites. This expansion pushes up the batter, causing the cake to rise. Also, the moisture and heat cause chemical leaveners such as baking soda and baking powder to release carbon dioxide gas, which expands and rises, further pushing up the batter.

Finally, the risen batter sets into a firm shape while the sugars continue to cook and darken the color of the cake's surface.

Metal pans absorb heat quickly and retain it; therefore, the batter touching the pan walls will heat and set before the inner areas; hot spots in the oven can overbake or even burn some sections of the cake before others are heated through. Occasionally, cake pans must be turned during the baking process to ensure even heating. If it is hard to control your oven temperature, you may want to put a cookie sheet beneath the cake pan to deflect the heat, or wrap a heat insulating pad (sold in specialty stores for this purpose) around the sides of your cake pan. You can make your own pads by cutting pan-width strips of old Turkish toweling. Soak them in water, wring them out, and pin or paper clip them to the outside of the batter-filled pans before putting them into the oven to bake. I have tried this but do not do it on a regular basis; however, I have a friend who never bakes without insulating her pans. Suit yourself and your oven.

Most cakes are baked at a temperature between 325° and 375°F (165° to 190°C). The most common temperature is 350°F (175°C). These temperatures are sufficiently high to cause steam and gas in the batter to expand and rise quickly and the batter texture to set, holding the rise. The cake bakes through evenly without drying out.

At a cooler temperature, the heating of the batter takes place too slowly, the rise is incomplete, and the cake dries out too much because it takes so long to bake through. In a very hot oven, the batter agitates excessively, the gases rise too quickly, and the cake may rise unevenly. Also the top and bottom of the cake will overbake before the inside has had time to cook through.

A Note About the Recipes in this Book

■

1. All measurements are level.

2. All eggs are U.S. Grade A large (2 ounces).

3. Butter is unsalted unless otherwise stated.

4. Grated zest of orange or lemon refers to the bright-colored part of the peel; the white pith under the zest can have a bitter flavor and is best not used except for candied citrus peel.

5. Most of the recipes in this book are written with the assumption that you will be using an electric mixer, either hand-held or stand-type. However, all recipes for cakes, icings, and fillings can also be prepared by hand, with a bowl and a wooden spoon or wire whisk.

6. For reliable results, use the type of flour specified in the recipe (cake flour or all-purpose). Sift the flour where specified. When unsifted flour is called for, measure it by the "scoop and sweep" method (page 50). When the recipe reads "1 cup sifted flour," it is sifted before measuring.

7. Granulated sugar is only sifted if obviously lumpy, as after long storage. Confectioners' and superfine sugars are always sifted unless otherwise specified.

8. It is important to have cake-baking ingredients at "room temperature." However, room temperatures vary widely. In the recipes this phrase means approximately 70°F.

9. In most recipes nuts are chopped or ground *before* measuring. Hence, ½ cup shelled and chopped walnuts, (2 oz; 60 g) means ½ cup (2 oz; 60 g) of *chopped* nuts.

· HOW TO TEST A CAKE'S DONENESS ·

*T*o be sure that your cake is thoroughly baked through the center as well as on the top and bottom where the heat has been more direct, you should perform some simple tests. First, set your oven timer for the minimum time given. If you are inclined to be a voyeur, restrain yourself from opening the oven door until at least three quarters of this time is past. And then, only sneak a peek. A cold draft could cause the cake to fall. At the minimum specified time, open the oven, slide out the shelf, and observe the cake.

If the cake is done, the color of the top should be golden brown, the edges should (usually) just begin to pull away from the pan sides, and the mass should appear to be firm, rather than ripply or jiggly beneath the top, as if filled with liquid. Touch the top surface lightly with your finger; under light pressure, the cake should feel a little springy. (Don't poke it hard enough to make a dent!) To be sure the center is cooked through, stick a cake tester into the center or side, as specified in the recipe. The tester should come out clean and dry if the cake is done, wet and covered with batter if it needs to bake longer. If longer cooking is required, bake until the next specified time and retest.

Note that some cakes, cheesecake in particular, have special qualities and tests for doneness; refer to About Cheesecake (page 184).

· HOW TO COOL CAKES ·

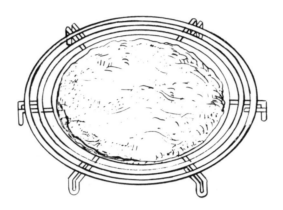

To Cool Butter Cakes

■

As a general rule, baked cakes are left in their pans, set on a wire rack, for 5 to 10 minutes after coming from the oven. At this point, you can take a paring knife, or a long thin-bladed knife if the cake is deep, and run it between the side of the cake and the pan, to loosen the cake and to free any sticking crumbs. Top the cake with a wire rack or flat platter, and invert. Lift off the cake pan. If it sticks, tap it gently and try again. If you have used paper to line the pan bottom, peel it off the cake now, while the cake is warm. At this point, the cake is bottom up on the wire rack. It can

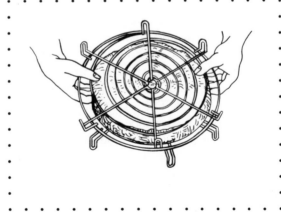

be left this way to cool completely, or you may prefer to invert it once more, so it cools top up (see diagram). The wire rack is used for cooling because it permits air to circulate beneath the cake, preventing condensation of moisture on the hot surface.

If you are planning to frost the cake with a thin icing in which the cake's own surface may show, you may prefer not to cool the cake on a wire rack because it sometimes leaves indentations in the cake. Instead, you can sprinkle granulated sugar onto baking parchment, wax paper, or foil set on the counter and invert your cake layer directly onto that. The sugar will prevent the cake from sticking to the paper, while it also absorbs any moisture from condensation. The cake will remain perfectly flat as it cools.

To Cool Sponge, Angel, and Chiffon Cakes

■

Angel, chiffon, and most sponge cakes are leavened primarily with air. Lacking chemical leaveners or fats to support their delicate structures, they would shrink or collapse if left right side up to cool. To prevent this, they should be inverted immediately after coming from the oven and hung upside down until completely cooled. The easiest way to do this is to bake the cake in a tube pan that has "feet" on the rim that will raise the inverted cake above the countertop. If your pan has no feet, invert the pan over a funnel or tall bottle for several hours, until the cake is thoroughly cold. Then slide a sharp long-bladed knife between the cake and the pan side to free any sticking crumbs. Work the knife gently between the cake and the tube as well. Top the cake with a platter and invert it. Lift off the

pan sides, then the removable pan bottom. See Index for specific instructions on Angel Cakes and Chiffon Cakes.

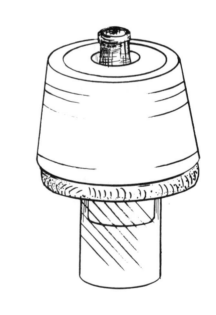

Butter &/or Shortening Cakes

About Butter and/or Shortening Cakes

∎

Cakes made with butter or shortening are the most popular and widely known American cakes. They are our classics, the cakes familiar since our childhood birthday parties, beloved for their moist sweet crumb and high-stacking layers filled and frosted with buttercreams.

For some new ideas, consider the birthday cake suggestions that follow. See the Index for recipe pages. For a child's birthday, try making a Shaped Cake, Molded Cake, or Checkerboard Cake. For a classroom birthday party, it may be useful to make deco-

Birthday cakes have a long history. The Roman emperors celebrated their birthdays with offerings of cakes to the gods as well as to the common people. In the Middle Ages, people celebrated with a cake on the feast day of their name saint instead of their birthday.

It is believed that the first birthday cake candles were used in Germany during the Middle Ages as symbols of earlier religious votive candles. The candle in the center of the cake was called the Lebenslicht, *or "light of life"; today we call this the "one to grow on," or the "good luck candle."*

There are many customs related to the candles on the cake. The most universal is for the celebrant to make a wish before blowing out the candles. The number of puffs it takes equals the number of months or years before the wish comes true. Some families also add little cups of brandy to the cake top and drink a toast for good luck after blowing out the candles. In my family, each guest puts a finger ring on the central candle—there may be quite a number stacked up on that post. The idea is that when the candles are blown out, the rings, and their donors, reinforce the good luck going to the birthday person. After the candle ceremony, the rings are returned, and there are always some who say the tradition is just a trick to get your ring on the bottom so that you can have a lick of icing.

rated cupcakes, one for each guest, with the birthday child having the cupcake with the candle on top.

My daughter's favorite birthday cake is Anna's Swedish Butter Cake, which has many flavor variations. Ice-cream cakes are much loved by adults as well as children and can be prepared well in advance, a help to the partygiver; a favorite in this category is Angel-Food Ice Cream Cake. Sheet cakes are helpful for big crowds as are tiered cakes (see the Wedding Cake) decorated with a birthday theme.

For an especially elegant adult birthday cake, consider a mousse-filled Dacquoise or Meringue Cake, any one of the Génoise Cake Ideas, or Chestnut Mousse Cake, or Cassis Gâteau. In the extravagantly lush category, try the 3-layer Lane Cake, the Dobostorte, or the Black Forest Cherry Cake. My own birthday choice this year is a Chocolate Sponge Roll, filled with Deluxe White Chocolate Mousse, while my husband's favorite birthday cake is a pie, proving that on this special day, one's whim should be indulged.

Some butter cakes are so moist they defy icing and require only the faintest sifting of confectioners' sugar for presentation. Compared to sponge cakes, butter cakes have a fairly firm texture and hold their shape well; they can be baked into any shape in any type pan from a bundt to a bunny mold. Cakes in this category include basic 2-, 3-, and 4-egg cakes; the nineteenth century 1-2-3-4 Cake; a vast array of layer and sheet cakes including traditional white, yellow, and chocolate as well as many less common varieties; bundt and tube cakes; coffee cakes and kuchens; tea cakes and loaf cakes; pound cakes, fruitcakes, and upside-down cakes.

Butter or shortening cakes are distinguished from other types of cake by the fact that they contain a large amount of fat in relation to the number of eggs used. Success with these cakes depends upon understanding how to incorporate ingredients correctly to achieve a perfectly creamy batter with good aeration. Butter cakes are leavened by whipping air into the batter plus the additional use of baking powder or baking soda; only true pound cakes use no baking powder.

Because fat is the essential ingredient here, it is critical to select the best one for your purposes. Read about Fats (see Index). Butter is 80 to 86 percent butterfat; it contains varying amounts of liquid and salt, plus some solids. For cake baking, select unsalted butter so that you can control the salt content of the cake. Also important, select butter with the highest possible butterfat content and the least amount of liquid. Solid vegetable shortening is 100 percent fat and contains no liquid, so it will cream more easily than butter and hold more air bubbles; however, it has less flavor. For the best creaming properties plus the best flavor, you can combine both fats, using butter and solid shortening or margarine, up to half of each, in your cake recipe.

There are three traditional methods of mixing butter or shortening cakes: creaming, combination, or blending. In all methods it is essential for all ingredients to be at room temperature, approximately 70°F, in order to blend properly.

□ CREAMING METHOD: Butter, margarine, or shortening is creamed together with the sugar until light and smooth. During this process, sugar crystals cut into the fat, opening holes that are enlarged and multiplied as beating continues, creating small air bubbles surrounded by fat and sugar. The fat must be warm and pliable enough to wrap around the air bubbles; if the fat is too cold, the bubble walls will be brittle and will burst; if too warm, the fat may melt. In both cases air, and therefore volume, are lost.

Beating is begun on medium-low speed to prevent excessive friction damaging the fragile air bubbles as they are formed. As more ingredients are added and the cell walls strengthen, the speed can be increased. Work up to medium speed, but avoid the highest speed, as it may break down the air cells. Anything that breaks down the number and build-up of air cells results in loss of volume and a less-leavened, somewhat heavier cake.

The curdling of batter, which sometimes results when eggs are added to creamed butter and sugar, also causes loss of air and volume. However, this is not exactly fatal, so don't panic if it occurs. In fact, curdling is unavoidable in some batters, and is so noted in those recipes. To prevent it, eggs are always added slowly to the creamed butter-sugar mixture. Ideally, whole eggs are lightly beaten first, then very slowly dripped into the creamed mixture while the beater runs on low speed. Or unbeaten whole eggs, or just yolks, can be added one at a time, with beating after each addition. This is done because the yolk contains all the fat of the egg; during beating this fat clings to the surface of the air cells, allowing them to expand and hold the cake's liquids. The category of liquids includes egg whites as well as milk or juice. When eggs are added too fast, or liquid is added all at once, the batter curdles because more liquid has been added than the batter emulsion can absorb at once. When eggs are beaten in a little at a time, as in a mayonnaise, the fat in the yolk

is slowly incorporated into the emulsion and it does not break down or curdle. If you do see the batter begin to curdle, hold back the eggs and beat the mixture faster to smooth it out before adding more eggs.

After incorporating the eggs, the sifted dry ingredients are usually added alternately with the room temperature liquid. You begin and end with the flour mixture, the better to bind the batter together. Adding these ingredients alternately helps prevent curdling and keeps the batter light and creamy.

While the creaming can be accomplished with an electric mixer, many bakers swear by the old-fashioned method of hand beating. They willingly forego the speed and ease of electricity in order to have complete control over the texture of the batter. I appreciate the theory and vote for electricity.

□ COMBINATION METHOD: This is used when the creamed ingredients are to be combined with others that are whipped. For example, when whipped egg whites are added to a butter-sugar-egg-yolk batter. In this case, the whites are whipped in a separate bowl, then a small amount of the whites is stirred into the heavier and stiffer creamed batter to lighten it. Finally, remaining whites are gently folded into the batter. Combination method cakes sometimes utilize baking powder to supplement the leavening action of the air whipped into the egg whites.

□ BLENDING OR ONE-BOWL METHOD: This is the quickest and easiest method: All the ingredients are simply combined in one bowl and beaten together. The temperature of the ingredients and the speed of the mixer are critical to this method, so follow the recipe guidelines carefully. The one-bowl method works best when the fat used is oil or solid vegetable shortening or butter that has been warmed (not melted) to the *pommade* stage. Do not use cold butter; it will not blend properly with this technique. Eggs must be warm, at room temperature, for proper blending of the batter.

Baking powder or baking soda provides the principal leavening for the one-bowl technique because, unlike the situation in the creaming method, the fat here cannot be whipped up enough to hold sufficient air bubbles for leavening. Instead, the fat melts into the batter, marrying with all ingredients. This causes one-bowl cakes to be very moist, with a dense and close-grained texture. They are easy to make, but are never as light-textured as cakes made by the creaming method.

☐ CHANGING METHODS: Many creamed or blended butter cake recipes that contain whole eggs can be changed, if you wish, to the combination method, whereby you separate the eggs and fold the stiffly whipped whites into the batter. This provides additional leavening and lightens the texture of the cake.

Shortening Cakes

A well-prepared butter cake is moist and fine-grained with an even texture. Sometimes it is dense (pound cake), other times light (layer cake) but it always has tiny, evenly distributed air holes and a delicate crumb.

The basic rule for these cakes is to select the correct mixing method to suit the fat used (creamed method for butter, combination or blending method for softer fats). Always grease and flour cake pans. Bake cakes in the preheated oven as soon as the batter is set into the pans. Layer or sheet cakes are baked in the lower third of the oven; taller cakes with thicker quantities of batter (pound cakes, fruit cakes, and tube cakes) need less direct heat and a slower, more even temperature. They are baked in the center of the oven.

Troubleshooting

· If the cake does not rise enough: The fat was too cold or too warm, and did not incorporate a sufficient amount of air into the batter. Butter and shortening must be at approximately 70°F to be flexible enough to surround and trap air bubbles in the batter.

· If the cake sinks or rises unevenly: The eggs and liquid were too cold. If straight from the refrigerator, they can cause the creamed butter surrounding the air cells to chill, solidify and crack, letting out the air. Similarly, hot liquids will melt the fat around the air bubbles and destroy the aeration. Either of these problems causes curdled batter, breaks the emulsion, and results in a loss of volume and lightness in the baked cake. Baking powder added to the batter helps prevent disasters but will not stop them entirely if all air is lost. Beating technique also affects rising of the cake. Note that, especially in the early stages of mixing, creaming the butter and sugar at too high a speed on the electric mixer can break down air cells from excess friction.

· If the cake collapses or sinks in the center: It contains too much baking powder or was overbeaten and became overaerated.

Layer &

Sheet Cakes

Basic 1-2-3-4 Cake

.

A nineteenth-century classic that forms the basis for many of today's recipes, this is a light, moist, flavorful vanilla layer cake. It is easy to remember (1 cup butter, 2 cups sugar, 3 cups flour, 4 eggs), simple to prepare, and foolproof, so it was one of the first cakes taught to beginning bakers. According to James Beard's *American Cookery* (Little Brown & Co., 1972), the cake was originally made in a loaf and contained no liquid. Its popularity was due to the ease of remembering the measurements and the fact that, in the days before standardized measuring utensils were common, one could use the same cup for measuring all ingredients and ensure repeatable success.

There are many references to this formula in old cookbooks. One, *The Pocumtuc Housewife,* a New England Cookbook dating from 1805, has a version called Aunt Emily's Cake, which shows how every housewife made it her own; Aunt Emily added "a little lemon extract, nutmeg, a dash of brandy, one cup of raisins, and a cup of citron sliced fine" to the basic recipe. You can add your own touches to personalize the cake. Our suggestions, which follow, include Basic Yellow, Coconut, Lemon, Almond, Spice, and Rocky Mountain Cake. Top the basic cake with your favorite icing (see Index).

Note: For the lightest texture, follow the

recipe as written, separating the eggs and beating the whites stiff. For an even simpler method with just a slightly more compact texture, you can beat in whole eggs in place of the yolks, omitting the stiffly beaten whites.

□ ADVANCE PREPARATION: The cake can be made in advance, wrapped airtight, and frozen. Thaw before frosting.

□ SPECIAL EQUIPMENT: two 8- or 9-inch round cake pans or one sheet pan 13 × 9 × 1¾ inches, wax paper, extra bowl and beater for beating egg whites

□ BAKING TIME: 30 to 35 minutes at 350°F (175°C) for layers, slightly longer for sheet

□ QUANTITY: 5¾ cups batter with stiffly beaten whites added; 5 cups batter with whole eggs beaten in; one 2-layer 8- or 9-inch cake (serves 8) or one sheet cake 9 × 13 inches (serves 12)

□ PAN PREPARATION: Spread solid shortening all over the bottom and sides of the pans, then dust evenly with flour; tap out excess flour.

3 cups sifted all-purpose flour (12¾ ounces; 360 g)
1 tablespoon baking powder
½ teaspoon salt
1 cup unsalted butter (2 sticks; 230 g), at room temperature
2 cups granulated sugar (14 ounces; 400 g)
4 large eggs, separated (see note in introduction)
1 cup milk
1 teaspoon vanilla extract

1. Prepare pans as described. Position shelf in lower third of oven. Preheat oven to 350°F (175°C).

2. Sift together flour, baking powder, and salt. Set aside.

3. In the large bowl of an electric mixer, beat the butter until soft and smooth. Add the sugar and beat until light and smooth. Add egg yolks, one at a time, beating after each addition. Stop the mixer and scrape down the sides of the bowl and the beaters several times.

4. With the mixer on low speed, alternately add the flour mixture and milk, beginning and ending with flour. Stir in the vanilla. At this point, add any personal flavoring touches (grated lemon zest, coconut, etc.).

5. In another bowl, with a clean beater, beat the whites until stiff but not dry. Stir about ½ cup of whites into the batter to lighten it, then fold in remaining whites in several additions.

6. Divide the batter evenly between the pans. Smooth the batter level, then spread it slightly from the center toward the edges of the pan so it will rise evenly. Bake in the preheated oven for 30 to 35 minutes, or just until a cake tester inserted in the center of each layer comes out clean and the cake tops are lightly springy to the touch.

Cool the cakes in their pans on a wire rack for 10 minutes. Top with a wire rack and invert; lift off pans. Completely cool layers on the rack before frosting. Or you can leave a sheet cake in its pan to cool, and frost and serve it from the pan.

· *Variations:* ·

BASIC YELLOW CAKE:

Prepare Basic 1-2-3-4 Cake but use 5 eggs; do not separate them. Add whole eggs in step 3. Increase milk to 1¼ cups.

COCONUT CAKE:

Prepare Basic 1-2-3-4 Cake but in step 3, stir in 1 cup shredded sweetened coconut and ¾ teaspoon coconut extract. Frost cake with Coconut Icing (see page 394).

ORANGE CAKE:

Prepare Basic 1-2-3-4 Cake but replace milk with orange juice. In step 3, stir in grated zest of 1 orange. Bake the cake in a 10-inch tube pan, greased and floured. Ice cake with Orange Wine Icing (page 398).

LEMON CAKE:

Prepare Basic 1-2-3-4 Cake but in step 3 stir in 1 teaspoon lemon extract and 2 teaspoons grated lemon zest. Ice cake with Lemon Buttercream (page 389).

ALMOND CAKE:

Prepare Basic 1-2-3-4 Cake but in step 3 add 1 teaspoon almond extract along with the vanilla. Ice with your favorite icing, but press sliced almonds into the icing around the sides.

SPICE CAKE:

Prepare Basic 1-2-3-4 Cake, but add and sift with dry ingredients 1½ teaspoons ground cinnamon; ½ teaspoon each of ground nutmeg, allspice, ginger, and cloves; 1 tablespoon unsweetened sifted cocoa.

ROCKY MOUNTAIN CAKE:

Prepare Basic 1-2-3-4 Cake but fill and frost with Rocky Mountain Icing (page 400).

Two-Egg White Cake

■

This was the first cake I ever made more or less by myself, and I can still recall the pleasure and pride I felt at age seven, when I served the slightly uneven, probably overbaked layers to my parents. Flushed with success, I made it repeatedly, in endless variations including orange and nut, which were my favorites. Perhaps it is true that we all get what we deserve in the end, for my youthfully egotistical boast that "I could bake any basic two-egg cake" became one of those family legends that comes back to haunt. Probably my writing of this book is an attempt to exorcise the story.

Regardless, the cake, also called a One-Bowl Cake, is still easy enough for a child to make and very good to eat. Frost with the icing of your choice (see Index). Variations follow for Light 2-Egg Cake, Berry Cake, Easy Nut Cake, and Marble Cake.

□ ADVANCE PREPARATION: The cake can be made in advance, wrapped airtight, and frozen. Thaw before frosting.

□ SPECIAL EQUIPMENT: two 7- or 8-inch layer pans or one 9-inch (6-cup capacity) tube pan, wax paper

□ BAKING TIME: 20 to 25 minutes at 350°F (175°C)

□ QUANTITY: About 3¼ cups batter; one 2-layer small 7- or 8-inch cake (serves 8) or one 9-inch ring (serves 8)

□ PAN PREPARATION: Spread solid shortening all over bottom and sides of pan(s), then dust evenly with flour; tap out excess flour.

*1¾ cups sifted cake flour (6 ounces;
     170 g)*
2 teaspoons baking powder
½ teaspoon salt
*⅓ cup unsalted butter (5⅓
     tablespoons; 80 g)*
1 cup granulated sugar (7 ounces; 200 g)
2 large eggs, lightly beaten
½ cup milk
2 teaspoons vanilla extract

1. Prepare pan(s) as described. Position shelf in lower third of oven. Preheat oven to 350°F (175°C).

2. Sift onto wax paper the flour, baking powder, and salt. Set aside.

3. In the large bowl of an electric mixer, cream together butter and sugar until well blended. Stop mixer and scrape down sides of bowl and beater several times. Add beaten eggs, a little at a time, mixing well after each addition.

4. Stirring by hand or with mixer on low speed, alternately add flour mixture and milk to batter, beginning and ending with flour. Stir in vanilla.

5. Turn batter into prepared pan(s). Smooth batter level, then spread it slightly from the center toward the edges of the pan so it will rise evenly. Bake for 25 to 30 minutes, or until a cake tester inserted in the center comes out clean and the cake top is golden brown and springy to the touch.

Cool the cake in its pan(s) on a wire rack for 10 minutes. Top each layer with a rack and invert; lift off pan. Cool cake completely on the rack. Frost when cold.

·Variations:·

LIGHT 2-EGG CAKE:

Prepare Two-Egg White Cake, but separate the eggs and beat the whites until stiff but not dry. Beat the yolks into the creamed butter and sugar. After combining dry ingredients, milk, and vanilla, fold in the beaten whites. Bake as directed.

BERRY CAKE:

Prepare Two-Egg White Cake, with the following changes: Prepare a sheet pan 11¾ × 7½ × 1¾ inches (8½-cup volume). Pick over, wash, and hull a generous ½ cup fresh berries (raspberries, huckleberries, or blueberries, for example). Toss berries lightly with ¼ cup of the measured flour. Prepare batter as directed, and fold the berries in at the end. Top the baked cake with a sifted-on layer of confectioners' sugar or sweetened whipped cream; garnish with whole berries.

EASY NUT CAKE:

Prepare Two-Egg White Cake, with the following changes: Add ¾ cup chopped walnuts or almonds to the regular cake batter, folding in the nuts at the end. If using almonds, add ½ teaspoon almond extract to the batter along with the vanilla. Frost the cake with your favorite icing (see Index) and garnish with halved or chopped nuts.

MARBLE CAKE:

Prepare Two-Egg White Cake, with the following changes: In the top pan of a double boiler set over hot, not boiling, water, melt 1½ ounces semisweet chocolate. Remove from heat, stir until smooth, and set aside to cool. After preparing the batter as directed, pour half of the batter into a second bowl. Stir the chocolate into one half, blending well. Put the batter into the prepared pan by alternating spoons of vanilla and chocolate batter. With a table knife, gently draw swirls through the batter to marbleize it slightly (don't touch pan bottom or sides with knife). Bake as directed. Frost with any rich chocolate icing (see Index).

Orange Velvet Cake

■

My inspiration for this cake came from the 1941 edition of Fannie Merritt Farmer's *Boston Cooking School Cook Book.* You will find this a reliable and easy-to-make recipe; the Lemon Velvet Variation is equally delicious.

□ ADVANCE PREPARATION: The cake can be baked ahead, wrapped airtight, and frozen. The filled and frosted cake can also be frozen, but for no longer than a month without losing flavor.

□ SPECIAL EQUIPMENT: two 8- or 9-inch layer pans 1½ inches deep or one 9-inch tube pan (6½-cup capacity) or one sheet pan 11¾ × 7½ × 1¾ inches; extra bowl and beater for egg whites, grater, small saucepan, pastry brush

□ BAKING TIME: 30 to 40 minutes at 350°F (175°C) for layers, slightly longer for tube or sheet pan.

□ QUANTITY: about 4½ cups batter, one 2-layer 8- or 9-inch cake, one 9-inch tube, or one sheet cake 11¾ × 7½ inches (serves 10 to 12)

□ PAN PREPARATION: Spread solid shortening on bottom and sides of pan(s), then dust evenly with flour; tap out excess flour.

1½ cups sifted cake flour (5¼ ounces; 150 g)
½ cup sifted cornstarch (2¼ ounces; 65 g)
2 teaspoons baking powder
½ teaspoon salt
½ cup unsalted butter (1 stick; 110 g), at room temperature
1½ cups granulated sugar (10½ ounces; 300 g)
4 large eggs, separated
½ teaspoon orange extract
Grated zest of 1 large orange
½ cup freshly squeezed orange juice

GLAZE:

½ cup freshly squeezed orange juice
2 tablespoons granulated sugar
Grated zest of 1 orange
1 tablespoon butter

ICING:

Orange Wine Icing (page 398) or Orange Buttercream (page 389)

1. Prepare pan(s) as described. Position rack in lower third of oven. Preheat oven to 350°F (175°C).
2. Sift together dry ingredients. Set aside.

3. In the large bowl of an electric mixer, cream together the butter and sugar until light and smooth. Add the egg yolks, one at a time, beating after each addition. Beat in the orange extract and grated zest. Alternately add to batter the flour mixture and orange juice, beginning and ending with flour. Beat slowly to blend after each addition. Scrape down the sides of the bowl often.

4. In a clean bowl with a clean beater, beat the egg whites until stiff but not dry. Stir about 1 cup of whites into the batter to lighten it, then gently fold in remaining whites.

5. Turn batter into the prepared pan(s). Level the batter, then spread it slightly from the center toward the edges of the pan so it will rise evenly. Bake for 30 to 35 minutes, or until a cake tester inserted in the center comes out clean, and the top is golden and lightly springy to the touch.

6. While the cake bakes, prepare the orange glaze. Combine the ingredients in a small saucepan, bring to a boil, and stir to dissolve the sugar. Set the glaze aside, but warm it just before using.

When the cake is baked, set the pans to cool on a wire rack. With a bamboo skewer or 2-tine roasting fork, prick holes over the cake. With a pastry brush, paint the warm glaze all over the hot cake, wait a few minutes, and apply remaining glaze; if you have made 2 layers, divide glaze between them.

Cool the cake completely, top with another rack, invert, and lift off pan. Serve cake as is, or fill and frost with Orange Wine Icing made with orange juice instead of wine, or Orange Buttercream. Or, if the cake was baked in a sheet pan, leave it in the pan to cool, then frost and serve from the pan.

LEMON VELVET CAKE

Prepare Orange Velvet Cake, but substitute lemon juice, grated zest of 2 lemons, and lemon extract for the orange flavoring. Use lemon juice and zest in the glaze as well. Ice with Lemon Glaze (page 407), or Orange Wine Icing made with lemon juice.

Gold Layer Cake

■

This marvelous gold layer cake was shared with me by my good friend Mary Alice McCulloch. Mary is originally from Kentucky, and this cake, now a family heirloom, was the specialty of her grandmother, Lela Ducker. It is traditionally baked in two layers and filled and frosted with Sour-Cream Nut Icing, though any buttercream would do as well.

☐ ADVANCE PREPARATION: The cake is best the day after it is baked; wrap it airtight and store it at room temperature for a day or two. Or wrap and freeze.

The icing takes about 1½ hours to cook and cool before using, so make this in advance.

☐ SPECIAL EQUIPMENT: two 8-inch layer pans 1½ inches deep, sifter, wax paper

☐ BAKING TIME: 25 to 30 minutes at 350°F (175°C)

☐ QUANTITY: about 4 cups batter, one 2-layer 8-inch cake (serves 8)

BUTTER &/OR SHORTENING CAKES

81

□ PAN PREPARATION: Spread solid shortening on bottom and sides of pans, then dust evenly with flour; tap out excess flour.

1½ cups sifted all-purpose flour (6¼ ounces; 180 g)
¼ teaspoon salt
1 teaspoon cream of tartar
½ teaspoon baking soda
¾ cup unsalted butter or margarine (1½ sticks; 170 g)
1 cup granulated sugar (7 ounces; 200 g)
8 large egg yolks, lightly beaten
½ cup milk
1 teaspoon vanilla extract

ICING:

1 recipe Sour-Cream Nut Icing (page 395), made in advance and cooled

1. Prepare pans as described. Position rack in lower third of oven. Preheat oven to 350°F (175°C).
2. Sift together the flour, salt, cream of tartar, and baking soda onto wax paper. Set them aside.
3. In the large bowl of an electric mixer, cream together the butter and sugar until well blended. Add the beaten yolks slowly, beating constantly as they are added.
Alternately add the flour mixture and the milk, beating after each addition, beginning and ending with flour. Stir in the vanilla. The batter will be thick and dark yellow in color.
4. Divide batter evenly between the pans. Spread the tops evenly. Set the pans in the preheated oven to bake for 25 to 30 minutes, or until the top of each is golden brown, a cake tester inserted in the cake comes out clean, and the cake starts to pull away from the pan sides. Cool the cakes on a wire rack for about fifteen minutes, then top with another rack, invert, and lift off pans. Cool the cake completely before filling and frosting.

Lord Baltimore Cake

■

Lady Baltimore Cake is made with 8 egg whites, and Lord Baltimore was given his due with a cake made from the yolks. Culinary history is still unsure whether this famous pair of cakes was actually named for the third Lord Baltimore, sent from England in 1661 to govern the land that was to become Maryland. It is possible that, because of his despotic and unpopular rule, the cake was named instead for the city given his name. In any event, both these cakes are now classics of the Southern baking repertoire.

This is an excellent all-purpose basic yellow cake, light in texture, with an open grain resembling that of a sponge cake. Tradition is divided about its presentation, so you can select the method you prefer. Bake the cake in 3 layers, fill it with Lord Baltimore Filling (Boiled Icing with macaroon crumbs and pecans) and frost it with Plain Boiled Icing (page 400). Or bake it in a tube pan and top it with brown sugar-flavored Seafoam Icing (page 399).

□ ADVANCE PREPARATION: The cake can be made in advance, wrapped airtight, and frozen. Thaw before filling and frosting.

□ SPECIAL EQUIPMENT: three 8- or two 9-inch layer pans; or one 9-inch tube pan (6½-cup capacity), sifter, extra mixing bowl, wax paper, grater, 8- or 9-inch cardboard cake disk (optional)

□ BAKING TIME: 20 to 25 minutes at 350°F (175°C) for layers, slightly longer for tube pan

□ QUANTITY: 4½ cups batter, one 3-layer 8-inch cake or 2-layer 9-inch cake or one 9-inch tube cake (serves 10 to 12)

□ PAN PREPARATION: Spread solid shortening all over the bottom and sides of the pan(s), then dust evenly with flour; tap out excess flour.

2½ cups sifted cake flour (8¾ ounces; 250 g)
1 tablespoon baking powder
½ teaspoon salt
¾ cup unsalted butter (1½ sticks; 170 g), at room temperature
1¼ cups granulated sugar (8¾ ounces; 250 g)
8 egg large yolks
¾ cup milk
½ teaspoon lemon extract
1 teaspoon grated lemon zest

FILLING AND ICING:

Double recipe Boiled Icing, Lord Baltimore Variation (page 401)

1. Prepare pan(s) as described. Position shelf in lower third of oven. Preheat oven to 350°F (175°C).

2. Sift together flour, baking powder, and salt onto a sheet of wax paper. Set aside.

3. In the large bowl of an electric mixer, beat the butter until soft. Add the sugar and cream with the butter until completely blended. In another bowl, beat the egg yolks until thick and lemon-colored. Slowly beat the yolks into the butter-sugar mixture. Beat to combine well.

4. By hand with a spoon or with electric mixer on lowest speed, alternately add flour mixture and milk to batter, beginning and ending with flour. Stir in lemon extract and lemon zest.

5. Divide batter between the prepared pans. Smooth it level, then spread it slightly from the center toward the edges of the pan so it will rise evenly. Bake in the preheated oven for 20 to 25 minutes, or until the top is lightly springy to the touch and a cake tester inserted in the center comes out clean. Cool the cake in its pan(s) on a wire rack for 10 minutes. Top with another rack and invert; lift off pans. Cool completely on the rack.

6. Fill and frost cake: Set a dab of icing in the center of a cardboard cake disk or a serving platter to hold the cake steady. Cut several wax paper strips and fit them between cake and plate to protect the plate edges from icing (see page 425). Spread icing on the bottom layer, top with another cake layer, add more icing. Top with final cake layer, align the layers neatly, then ice the sides. Finally, ice the cake top.

Lane Cake

■

This famous Southern cake originated in Alabama. The recipe is generous, making a 3-layer white cake with a fine grain and velvet texture. It is also known as White Cake, Silver Cake, or Snow Cake because the batter uses only egg whites and is pure white. This is a fine recipe for wedding cakes or petits fours. Traditionally, Lane Cake is filled with Lane Cake Filling, a rich custardy fruit and nut mixture, and iced with Boiled Icing. This basic recipe is the foundation for several famous variations that follow, including Lady Baltimore Cake, White Mountain Cake (also called Colorado Cake), and Cornstarch Cake. The recipe is also used for Checkerboard Cake (page 85).

Note: To make a 2-layer Lane Cake, simply halve the recipe and use 3 or 4 egg whites.

□ ADVANCE PREPARATION: The cake can be made in advance, wrapped airtight, and frozen. Thaw before frosting.

□ SPECIAL EQUIPMENT: three 8-inch round pans, wax paper, 8-inch cardboard cake disk (optional)

□ BAKING TIME: 20 to 25 minutes at 375°F (190°C)

□ QUANTITY: about 6 cups batter, one 3-layer 8-inch cake (serves 10 to 12)

□ PAN PREPARATION: Spread solid shortening on bottom and sides of pan, then dust evenly with flour; tap out excess flour.

3¼ cups sifted cake flour (11½ ounces; 330 g)
3½ teaspoons baking powder
¼ teaspoon salt
8 egg whites (reserve yolks for filling)
2 cups granulated sugar (14 ounces; 400 g)
1 cup unsalted butter (2 sticks; 230 g), at room temperature
2 teaspoons vanilla extract
1 cup milk

FILLING:

Lane Cake Filling (page 383)

ICING:

Boiled Icing (page 400)

1. Prepare pans as described. Position shelf in lower third of oven. Preheat oven to 375°F (190°C).

2. Sift together the flour, baking powder, and salt onto a sheet of wax paper. Set them aside.

3. In a large mixing bowl, whip egg whites until foamy, then add 2 tablespoons of the measured sugar and whip until nearly stiff but not dry. Remove bowl from mixer and set aside. Scrape whites from beaters into bowl. Without washing beaters, return them to the mixer.

4. In another large bowl, use the mixer to beat butter until soft. Add remaining sugar, and cream with the butter until completely blended to a smooth granular paste. Beat in vanilla.

5. With mixer on low speed, or mixing by hand, alternately add flour mixture and milk

to butter-sugar mixture, beginning and ending with flour.

With rubber spatula, give whipped whites several gentle folds to be sure they are amalgamated. Gradually fold whites into the batter, using a light touch.

6. Divide batter evenly among the prepared pans. Smooth batter level, then spread it slightly from the center toward the edges of the pan so it will rise evenly. Arrange pans on one shelf in a triangular pattern and bake for 20 to 25 minutes, or until a cake tester inserted in the center of each layer comes out clean and the cake is lightly springy to the touch. Cool the layers in their pans on a wire rack for 10 minutes. Top with a wire rack and invert; lift off pans. Completely cool cake on the rack.

7. Frost the cake: Dab a little icing in the center of a cardboard cake disk, then add the first cake layer. Alternate icing and cake layers, then frost the cake sides and top. If not using the cardboard cake disk, protect the serving plate with strips of wax paper. Remove paper after frosting is complete.

·Variations:·

LADY BALTIMORE CAKE:

Prepare Lane Cake. Fill with Rocky Mountain Filling (page 400), a regular boiled icing with chopped pecans, figs, and raisins added, and frost with regular Boiled Icing (page 400). Garnish cake top with halved pecans and arrange fresh roses around the base of the platter for a gracious Southern presentation.

WHITE MOUNTAIN CAKE:

Also called Colorado Cake, this recipe is sometimes baked in 3 graduated pans which, when stacked resemble a mountain. Prepare Lane Cake in 3 regular layers or 3 graduated tiers. Fill and ice with double recipe of Boiled Icing.

CORNSTARCH CAKE:

Prepare Lane Cake but reduce flour to 2¼ cups and add 1 cup sifted cornstarch. Cornstarch produces a finer texture.

. . . .

Checkerboard Cake

■

The checkerboard cake is a neat trick: 3 layers of alternating chocolate and vanilla rings that make a checkerboard pattern when stacked and sliced. Special gadgets for dividing the rings of batter are sold in cookware shops (see Suppliers' List, page 482) but they are not necessary; you can get the effect almost as neatly simply by carefully spooning or piping the batter into rings in plain round pans. Use a fairly thin layer of icing between the layers so the checkerboard pattern is not interrupted.

☐ ADVANCE PREPARATION: Make Lane Cake (preceding recipe).

☐ EQUIPMENT: three 8- or 9-inch round pans or checkerboard cake pan set (see Suppliers, page 482); wax paper, scissors, 8- or 9-inch cardboard cake disk (optional)

☐ BAKING TIME: 20 to 25 minutes at 375°F (190°C)

☐ QUANTITY: About 6 cups batter, one 8- or 9-inch 3-layer cake (serves 8 to 10)

☐ PAN PREPARATION: see Lane Cake.

FILLING AND ICING:

Any Chocolate or Vanilla Buttercream (see Index).

CAKE:

Lane Cake, plus 3½ tablespoons unsweetened cocoa, preferably Dutch-process, and ¼ teaspoon baking soda.

Prepare the cake as directed with the following changes:

1. After completing the batter in step 5, remove half of the batter to another bowl. Sift the cocoa and baking soda into the second bowl of batter and fold them together lightly to blend, making an even chocolate color.

2. Arrange the batter in the greased and floured pans as follows: In one pan, spoon a 1½-inch-wide ring of chocolate batter around the outside edge, nearly half the depth of the pan. Alongside this ring, spoon a 1½-inch-wide ring of white batter of the same depth. Fill the center with a circle of chocolate batter of the same depth (diagram a). Make a second pan in exactly the same pattern (chocolate, white, chocolate). In the third pan, spoon white batter in the outside ring, chocolate next, and white in the center (diagram b). Bake the layers as directed for 20 to 25 minutes, cool them for 10 minutes, then invert them onto wire racks to cool completely.

3. Prepare the icing of your choice. Dab a little icing on a cardboard cake disk and set down one of the cake layers with the outer chocolate ring. On top of this spread a fairly thin layer of icing. Add the cake layer with the white outer ring, and top it with a fairly thin layer of icing and the second layer with the chocolate outer ring (diagram c). Finally, ice the cake sides and top with as much icing as you wish. When the cake is sliced, you will see the checkerboard pattern (diagram d).

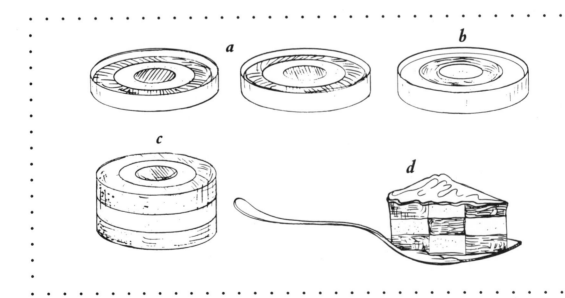

Fresh Coconut Cake

∎

They drawe a mylke of the coco-nut
which the Christian men of those
regions put in the tortes or cakes which
they make of the grayne of Maizium . . .
by reason of the sayde mylke of Cocus,
the tortes are more excellent to be eaten
without offence to the stomake.

> The Decades of the Newe Worlde
> or West India,
> Richard Eden, 1555

As one sixteenth-century explorer of the tropics noted, the milk of the fresh coconut does indeed make an excellent cake. One of the best I have ever tasted is made from this recipe, which I have adapted from one shared with me by my friend Joan Moore, a photographer now living in Cape May, New Jersey. Joan is originally from Kentucky, and this cake is a family recipe she fondly recalls being made for her childhood birthdays.

Those who analyze the recipe will note that it is a variation on the classic 1-2-3-4 Cake. Utilizing both the liquid and the grated meat of a fresh coconut, this cake is very moist, with a fine grain and a distinct coconut flavor. The recipe makes 2 layers, which are split to make a big 4-layer cake filled and iced with coconut-flavored Seven-Minute Icing, the perfect selection for a birthday party!

☐ ADVANCE PREPARATION: The cake can be made in advance, wrapped airtight, and frozen.

☐ SPECIAL EQUIPMENT: two 9-inch layer pans 1½ inches deep, serrated knife, 9-inch cardboard cake disk (optional), wax paper. For coconut: screwdriver, hammer, bowl, roasting pan, vegetable peeler, blender or food processor

☐ BAKING TIME: 35 minutes at 350°F (175°C)

☐ QUANTITY: 7½ cups batter, one 4-layer 9-inch cake (serves 10 to 12)

☐ PAN PREPARATION: Spread solid shortening on bottom and sides of pan, then dust evenly with flour; tap out excess flour.

1 fresh coconut (read about Coconut,
page 44), to yield 1 cup fresh coconut
liquid and 2 cups firmly packed
grated fresh coconut meat (1 cup for
cake batter and 1 cup for icing)
3 cups sifted cake flour (10½ ounces;
300 g)
3 teaspoons baking powder
½ teaspoon salt
4 large egg whites
1 cup unsalted butter (2 sticks; 230 g),
at room temperature
2 cups granulated sugar (14 ounces;
400 g)
1 teaspoon vanilla extract

ICING:

Double Recipe Seven-Minute Icing, Coconut Flavor (page 398), to which you add 1 cup freshly grated coconut

1. Prepare the coconut as described, piercing the eyes with the screwdriver, and reserving the strained coconut liquid for the cake. If you do not have a full cup of liquid, make up the difference with milk or cream. Bake the whole coconut at 350°F for about 30 minutes, then crack the shell with a hammer, break off the shell, and use a vegetable peeler to remove the brown skin. Break up the meat and grate it in small batches in the blender or food processor. Save 1 cup well-packed grated meat for the cake, another cup for the icing.

2. Prepare pans as described. Position rack in lower third of the oven. Preheat oven to 350°F (175°C).

3. Sift together the flour, baking powder, and salt onto a sheet of wax paper. Set them aside.

4. In the medium-size bowl of the electric mixer, whip the egg whites until stiff but not dry. Remove bowl from the mixer and scrape the beaters into the bowl. Without washing the beaters, return them to the mixer.

5. In a large bowl, cream together the butter and sugar until completely blended into a smooth granular paste. Add a little of the flour mixture and a little of the coconut liquid and beat on slow speed just to blend; this may be done by hand, as well. Continue alternately adding a little of the flour mixture and liquid, blending after each addition and ending with the flour. Stir in the vanilla and about 1 cup of the whipped egg whites, just to lighten the batter.

With a rubber spatula, fold the whipped whites over onto themselves once or twice to be sure they are amalgamated. With a light touch, fold the egg whites into the batter in several additions. Spread 1 cup grated coconut onto a piece of wax paper and crumble it to break up any clumps. Gradually sprinkle this coconut onto the batter and fold it in.

6. Turn batter into the prepared pans and bake in the preheated oven for about 35 minutes, or until the cake tops look golden brown, start to pull away from the edges, and a cake tester inserted in the center comes out clean. Allow the layers to cool on a wire rack for about 10 minutes, then run a knife around the edge of each layer to release it from the pan. Top each layer with a wire rack and invert; lift off the pan. Allow layers to cool completely on the rack.

7. When completely cold, cut each layer into halves horizontally, using a long-bladed serrated knife (see page 424).

While the cake is cooling, prepare the icing. To assemble the cake, put a dab of icing in the center of the cardboard cake disk or serving platter to hold the cake, then top with 1 cake layer, cut surface up. Spread icing on this layer, then top with another layer, and repeat. After adding the top cake layer, check to see that all 4 layers are lined up. Ice the sides, then the top. If you wish, sprinkle any leftover grated coconut on top. Note: If frosting the cake on a serving platter, protect the platter by covering it with strips of wax paper; remove the paper after icing the cake.

Anna's Swedish Butter Cake

•

Anna Olson's Swedish Butter Cake has been a tradition in my family since Anna shared her recipe with my mother over 35 years ago. Not only is it easy to make, but it is rich without being too sweet, has a fine tender crumb, and seems to taste better the longer it stands. In short, it is the perfect cake for every day, and every occasion. To serve with tea or coffee in the afternoon, we bake it in a tube pan and dust it lightly with confectioners' sugar, all the topping it really needs. For birthdays, we bake 2 heart-shaped layers and fill and frost them with buttercream. For weddings, this cake is ideal; it can be stacked in many tiers. Over the years, we have devised all sorts of variations, from chocolate to marzipan to orange (see recipes following), but we always come back to Anna's original—plain butter cake; it is the best. My daughter proved this for us all when, at the age of eleven, she won two blue ribbons with this recipe for Best Cake at the Bridgewater Connecticut Firemen's Country Fair and Best Butter Cake at the Goshen Connecticut 4-H Fair.

Note: As a young girl in Sweden, Anna learned to hand-mix this cake with a wooden spoon, and she steadfastly held to her preference for this method, which produces a rather dense texture. I usually use the electric mixer, which lightens the cake somewhat but does not, in my opinion, detract in any way from its success.

□ ADVANCE PREPARATION: The cake can be baked in advance, wrapped airtight, and stored at room temperature for a week. It can also be frozen. One day after it is baked, the cake's flavors mellow to perfection and it is more easily sliced than when fresh from the oven.

□ SPECIAL EQUIPMENT: One 9-inch tube pan (6½-cup capacity) or two 9-inch layer pans, or one 8-inch-square pan 2 inches deep; large mixing bowl and wooden spoon, or electric mixer (preferably fitted with paddle attachment)

□ BAKING TIME: 55 to 60 minutes at 350°F (175°C) for tube pan; 30 to 35 minutes for layers.

□ QUANTITY: about 4½ cups batter, one 9-inch tube cake or one 2-layer 9-inch cake (serves 8)

□ PAN PREPARATION: Spread solid shortening on bottom and sides of pan(s), dust evenly with flour; tap out excess flour.

2 cups (8½ ounces; 240 g) plus 2 tablespoons sifted all-purpose flour
1 teaspoon baking powder
¼ teaspoon salt
1 cup lightly salted butter (not margarine) (2 sticks, 230 g), at room temperature
1½ cups granulated sugar (10½ ounces; 300 g)
2 large eggs
¾ cup milk
1 teaspoon almond extract (vanilla extract can be substituted)
Confectioners' sugar (optional)

1. Prepare pans as described. Position rack in center of oven. Preheat oven to 350°F (175°C).

2. Sift together flour, baking powder, and salt onto a piece of wax paper. Set aside.

3. With a wooden spoon in a mixing bowl or with an electric mixer, cream together the butter and sugar until smooth and well blended. Add the eggs, one at a time, beating after each addition.

Alternately add the dry ingredients and milk, beating after each addition, beginning and ending with flour. Scrape down the sides of the bowl and the beaters. Stir in the almond or vanilla extract.

Note: If you are doubling the recipe—as for a wedding cake, for example—remove the bowl from the mixer after beating in the eggs and stir in the dry ingredients and milk by hand. After all ingredients are blended well, you can return the bowl to the mixer for a few seconds.

4. Spoon batter into the prepared pan(s), level the top, then spread the batter slightly toward the pan edges. Bake in the preheated oven for 55 to 60 minutes for a tube cake or 30 to 35 minutes for layers, or until the top is golden and a cake tester inserted in the center comes out clean.

Cool the cake in its pan(s) on a wire rack for about 10 minutes, then run a knife blade around the edge of the cake. Top with another rack or plate, invert, and lift off the pan(s). Cool the cake completely before sifting on confectioners' sugar or adding a frosting of your choice.

·Variations:·

ANNA'S ORANGE BUTTERCAKE

Prepare Anna's Swedish Butter Cake, but add the grated zest of 1½ oranges and replace the milk with ¾ cup freshly squeezed orange juice. Use 1 teaspoon orange extract instead of almond or vanilla. Ice with Orange Buttercream or Orange Glaze or Orange Wine Icing (see Index).

MARZIPAN BUTTERCAKE:

Prepare Anna's Swedish Butter Cake, but add to the batter along with the eggs 4 ounces of canned almond pastry filling (Solo Brand, for example, sold in supermarkets). Top the cake with a sheet of rolled Marzipan (see page 426) tinted a faint yellow color with a little food coloring; or put a sheet of rolled marzipan between the 2 layers before frosting with almond-flavored buttercream.

ANNA'S CHOCOLATE
BUTTERCAKE:

Prepare Anna's Swedish Butter Cake, but replace ⅓ cup flour with ⅓ cup sifted unsweetened cocoa, preferably Dutch-process, and add ¼ teaspoon baking soda.

Swedish Sandcake

■

This traditional Swedish *Sandkaka* is one of my old standbys—a reliable cake that is quick and easy-to-prepare, and sure to be loved by everyone. It is not too sweet, has a most delicate tender crumb that literally melts in the mouth, and needs no icing. It is perfect when served with a light dusting of confectioners' sugar, and sublime when accompanied by fresh raspberries or strawberries. Be sure to have one of these on hand, in the freezer, in case company drops by.

Note: The tenderness of this cake is the result of the potato flour, also called potato starch, in the batter. This is sold in most supermarkets and gourmet shops.

The classic flavoring for *Sandkaka* is brandy, but you can vary this to suit your taste. Try any fruit- or nut-flavored liqueur, or omit the spirits and substitute vanilla, almond, or another pure extract.

☐ ADVANCE PREPARATION: The cake can be prepared ahead, wrapped airtight, and frozen. Wrapped well, or in a cake box, it will also keep at room temperature for at least a week.

☐ SPECIAL EQUIPMENT: 9-inch tube pan (6½-cup capacity) or two 7″ layers

☐ BAKING TIME: 45 minutes at 300°F (150°C) for tube, 25 to 30 for layers

☐ QUANTITY: 3¾ cups batter, one 9-inch tube cake (serves 8 to 10)

☐ PAN PREPARATION: Generously spread solid shortening on inside of pan, then dust evenly with flour; tap out excess flour.

¾ cup sifted cake flour (2½ ounces; 70 g)
2 teaspoons baking powder
Pinch of salt
1 cup unsalted butter (2 sticks; 230 g), melted and cooled
1 cup granulated sugar (7 ounces; 200 g)
¾ cup sifted potato flour (4½ ounces; 130 g)
3 large eggs

2 tablespoons brandy (for a stronger brandy flavor, use 3 tablespoons), or 1 teaspoon vanilla or other extract

TOPPING:

1 tablespoon confectioners' sugar, sifted on the cake

1. Prepare pan as described. Position rack in center of oven. Preheat oven to 300°F (150°C).

2. Sift together the flour, baking powder, and salt into a small bowl. Set aside.

In the large bowl of an electric mixer, combine the melted and cooled butter, the sugar, and potato flour. Beat slowly until well blended and creamy. Slowly add flour mixture, beating well for 2 full minutes to blend. Add 1 egg and beat batter until it looks creamy and smooth. Scrape down bowl and beaters. Add remaining eggs, one at a time, beating after each addition. Finally, beat in brandy or other flavoring.

3. Pour batter into the prepared pan and bake in the center of the preheated oven for about 45 minutes, or until the top is golden brown and well risen (it will crack in the center), and the sides begin to pull away from the pan. A cake tester inserted in the center should come out clean.

Let the cake cool in its pan on a wire rack for 10 minutes. Slide a knife between the cake sides and the pan to loosen crumbs if necessary, then top the cake with a rack or plate and invert. Lift off pan. Leave cake upside down on a wire rack until completely cold.

To serve, sift on about 1 tablespoon of confectioners' sugar.

Shaker Maple Sugar Cake

•

This lightly spiced, maple-scented applesauce cake is my adaptation of a Shaker recipe from the North Union community. Years ago, maple sugar was widely available; today you have to look for it in Vermont general stores, mail-order catalogues, and gourmet shops. It is worth the hunt, for it lends a delicious flavor to baked goods. Note: Granulated maple sugar tends to dry out and lump, so before using it, you should check to be sure it is granular. If necessary, pulse the sugar in a food processor or put it in a plastic bag and pound it with a rolling pin. Sift out any remaining hard lumps.

☐ ADVANCE PREPARATION: This cake may be made ahead, wrapped airtight, and frozen.

☐ SPECIAL EQUIPMENT: two 8-inch layer pans 1½ inches deep or one sheet pan 11¾ × 7½ × 1¾ inches, nut chopper or food processor, sifter

☐ BAKING TIME: 30 to 40 minutes at 350°F (175°C)

☐ QUANTITY: 4 cups batter, one 2-layer 8-inch cake (serves 8), or one sheet cake 11¾ × 7½ inches (serves 12)

☐ PAN PREPARATION: Spread solid shortening on bottom and sides of pans, then dust evenly with flour; tap out excess flour.

2½ cups sifted all-purpose flour (10½ ounces; 300 g)
1 teaspoon baking powder
1 teaspoon baking soda
½ teaspoon salt
½ teaspoon ground cinnamon
½ teaspoon ground nutmeg
½ cup currants (2¼ ounces; 65 g) or seedless raisins
1 cup shelled walnuts (4 ounces; 110 g) or hickory nuts, chopped
¼ cup unsalted butter or margarine (4 tablespoons; 57 g)
1 cup granulated maple sugar (5¼ ounces; 150 g), sifted
½ cup granulated white sugar (3½ ounces; 100 g)
2 large eggs
1½ cups unsweetened applesauce

ICING:

Maple Icing (page 399)

1. Prepare pans as described. Position rack in center of oven. Preheat oven to 350°F (175°C).

2. Sift together flour, baking powder, baking soda, salt, cinnamon, and nutmeg. Set aside. In a small bowl, combine currants and walnuts. Stir about 2 tablespoons of the flour mixture into the currant-nut mixture, tossing to coat pieces well.

3. In the large bowl of an electric mixer, cream together the butter and both sugars until very well blended. Scrape down the sides of the bowl. Add the eggs, one at a time, beating after each addition.

4. Alternately add to the batter the flour mixture and the applesauce, beating very slowly after each addition. Stir down the sides of the bowl often. Gently fold in the currants and nuts.

5. Divide batter evenly between the prepared pans, smoothing the top evenly, then spreading it slightly from the center toward the pan edges. Bake in the preheated oven for 30 to 40 minutes, or until a cake tester inserted in the center comes out clean and the cake top is lightly springy to the touch. Cool on a wire rack for about 10 minutes. Top each layer with a second rack, invert, and lift off pan. Cool completely on racks. Fill and frost with Maple Icing.

Peanut Cake

∎

This recipe—known locally as Goober Cake—was shared with me by a friend from Georgia, the leading state in peanut production. The peanut is native to South and Central America, and was eventually introduced into West Africa. During the seventeenth and eighteenth centuries, peanuts were exported from the West Coast of Africa to the American South. Africans who came to the area called the nuts *nguba,* Bantu for ground-nut, and goober became the Americanized corruption of this word. The peanut is not a true nut, but a member of the pea family, hence goober peas.

Children love the strong peanut flavor of this light-textured, fine-grained cake. It is a perfect choice for a Fall Harvest or Halloween Party. Top the cake with Peanut Butter Icing and chopped peanuts.

☐ ADVANCE PREPARATION: The cake can be made in advance, wrapped airtight, and frozen. Thaw before frosting.

☐ SPECIAL EQUIPMENT: one sheet pan 9 × 13 × 2 inches, wax paper

☐ BAKING TIME: 40 to 45 minutes at 350°F (175°C)

☐ QUANTITY: 7 cups batter, one sheet cake 9 × 13 inches (serves 12)

☐ PAN PREPARATION: Spread solid shortening over bottom and sides of pan, then dust evenly with flour; tap out excess flour.

2 cups unsifted all-purpose flour (10 ounces; 280 g)
2 teaspoons baking powder
½ teaspoon salt
Pinch of ground cinnamon
1 cup smooth peanut butter (9 ounces; 255 g), at room temperature
⅔ cup lightly salted butter or margarine (10⅔ tablespoons; 160 g), at room temperature
2 cups firmly packed dark brown sugar (18 ounces; 510 g)
6 large eggs
2 teaspoons vanilla extract
¾ cup milk

ICING:

Peanut Butter Icing (page 395) plus ½ cup dry-roasted peanuts (2½ ounces; 70 g), chopped

1. Prepare pan as described. Position shelf in lower third of oven. Preheat oven to 350°F (175°C).

2. Sift together flour, baking powder, salt,

and cinnamon onto a sheet of wax paper. Set aside.

3. In the large bowl of an electric mixer, cream together the peanut butter and butter. Slowly add the sugar, beating until creamy. Add the eggs, one at a time, beating after each addition. Beat in the vanilla.

4. With the mixer on lowest speed, alternately add flour mixture and milk to batter, beating after each addition, beginning and ending with flour.

5. Turn the batter into the prepared pan. Smooth the surface and spread it slightly from the center toward the edges of the pan so the cake will rise evenly. Bake in the lower third of the oven for 40 to 45 minutes, or until a cake tester inserted in the center comes out clean and the top is springy to the touch. Cool the cake completely in its pan on a wire rack. When cold, top with icing and sprinkle with chopped peanuts. Cut into 3-inch squares and serve from the pan.

Chocolate Buttermilk Cake

∎

This is a marvelous old-fashioned chocolate fudge cake. In fact, of all the chocolate layer cakes in this book, this is my favorite, the one I invariably turn to for "Chocolate Cake Occasions," a special category in our family. The cake is moist, with a fine grain and excellent flavor. The tiny touch of nutmeg lends a barely detectable hint of spice, which enhances the chocolate. You can go even further (as I

do) to create Double-Chocolate Cake by adding mini-chocolate chips to the batter.

Since it is loved equally by adults and children, this recipe is a perfect choice for family gatherings and birthday parties. It can be made equally well in cupcake tins, in a sheet pan, or in 2 layers. For a gala, you can split the 2 layers into 4, filling them with whipped cream, fresh raspberries, and shavings of semisweet chocolate. You can also use this cake as the basis for Black Forest Cherry Cake (see page 289).

☐ ADVANCE PREPARATION: The cake can be made in advance, wrapped airtight, and frozen. Thaw before icing. Store iced cake in an airtight container.

☐ SPECIAL EQUIPMENT: two 9-inch layer pans 1½ inches deep or one sheet pan 9 × 13 × 1½ inches, double boiler

☐ BAKING TIME: 40 to 50 minutes at 325°F (165°C) for sheet cake, 35 to 45 minutes for 2 layers

☐ QUANTITY: About 7 cups batter, one 2-layer 9-inch cake (serves 8); one sheet cake 9 × 13 inches (serves 12)

☐ PAN PREPARATION: Spread solid shortening on bottom and sides of pan(s), then dust evenly with unsweetened cocoa or flour; tap out excess cocoa or flour.

2 cups sifted all-purpose flour (8½ ounces; 240 g)
¼ teaspoon salt
¼ teaspoon freshly grated nutmeg
1½ teaspoons baking soda
4 ounces unsweetened chocolate (110 g; ½ cup)
1 cup unsalted butter (2 sticks; 230 g), at room temperature (margarine can be substituted, or use half of each)

1¾ cups granulated sugar (12¼ ounces; 350 g)
4 large eggs
1⅓ cups buttermilk
1 teaspoon vanilla extract

ICING:

Seven Minute Icing, Caramel Icing, or Chocolate Buttercream Icing (see Index). Or fill and frost with flavored whipped cream (page 368). Note: if slicing cake into 4 layers, adjust icing quantities accordingly.

1. Prepare pan(s) as described. Position shelf in lower third of oven. Preheat oven to 325°F (165°C).

2. Sift together the flour, salt, nutmeg, and baking soda. Set aside.

3. Melt the chocolate in the top pan of a double boiler set over hot, not boiling, water. Remove chocolate from heat, stir to make sure it is completely melted and smooth, then set aside to cool until comfortable to touch.

4. In the large bowl of an electric mixer, cream together the butter and sugar until light and fluffy. Stop the mixer and scrape down the bowl and beaters several times. Add the eggs, one at a time, beating well after each addition.

5. With the mixer on low, add the flour mixture and buttermilk alternately to batter, beginning and ending with flour. Stir in the vanilla and cooled chocolate, blending until the color is even.

5. Turn the mixture into the prepared pan(s). Smooth it level, then spread it slightly from the center toward the edges of the pan so it will rise evenly. Bake in the lower third of the oven for 40 to 50 minutes for the sheet cake, 35 to 45 minutes for layers, or until the top is lightly springy to the touch and a cake tester inserted in the center comes out clean. Leave the cake in its pan(s) on a wire rack for 10 minutes. Top with a second rack and invert; lift off pan(s). Cool the cake completely on the rack. To split layers, use a serrated knife (see page 424). Fill and frost the layers. Or leave the sheet cake in its pan to cool, and frost and serve it from the pan, making 3-inch squares.

·*Variation:*·

DOUBLE-CHOCOLATE CAKE:

Prepare Chocolate Buttermilk Cake, but add 1 cup semisweet mini-chips (5½ ounces; 160 g), tossed together with 1 tablespoon of the flour mixture from step 2. Stir chips into batter after adding the melted chocolate.

. . . .

Chocolate Mayonnaise Cake

■

The first version of this exceptionally quick and easy-to-prepare recipe, also known as Salad Dressing Cake, was created in 1937 by Mrs. Paul Price, the wife of a sales distributor for Hellmann's Mayonnaise. Her rich, moist chocolate cake was an overnight success and a great promotional device for her husband's company. If the recipe sounds odd to you, remember that mayonnaise is made of oil and eggs, and both contribute richness and moisture to any cake.

Mrs. Price's original recipe, supplied to me by the Hellmann's Company (Best Foods) in honor of their seventy-fifth anniversary, is nearly identical to my recipe except that hers uses 6 tablespoons grated unsweetened chocolate instead of the cocoa, and adds a little salt and 1 cup each of chopped dates and walnuts.

My recipe comes from a friend and neighbor, Norma Went, who contributed it to *Roxbury Cookery* published by the Women's Auxiliary of the Roxbury, Connecticut, Volunteer Fire Department in 1974. With this pedigree, it is no wonder the cake is a staple at country fairs and bake sales across the country.

The Chocolate Mayonnaise Cake can be split into 2 layers for filling and frosting, or the recipe may be baked into cupcakes.

☐ ADVANCE PREPARATION: This cake can be made in advance, wrapped airtight, and frozen. Thaw before frosting.
☐ SPECIAL EQUIPMENT: one 9-inch-square pan or one sheet pan 11¾ × 7½ × 1½ inches, wax paper
☐ BAKING TIME: 35 to 40 minutes at 350°F (175°C)
☐ QUANTITY: about 3½ cups batter, one single layer 9-inch cake (serves 9 to 12); sheet cake serves 12

☐ PAN PREPARATION: Spread solid shortening over bottom and sides of pan, then dust evenly with unsweetened cocoa or flour; tap out excess cocoa or flour.

2 cups sifted all-purpose flour (8½ ounces; 240 g)
1½ teaspoons baking soda
¼ teaspoon salt
4 tablespoons sifted unsweetened cocoa (¾ ounce; 20 g), preferably not Dutch-process
1 cup good-quality commercial mayonnaise
1 cup granulated sugar (7 ounces; 200 g)
1 cup cold water
1 teaspoon vanilla extract

1. Prepare pan as described. Position shelf in lower third of oven. Preheat oven to 350°F (175°C).
2. Sift together the flour, baking soda, salt, and cocoa onto a piece of wax paper. Set aside.

In the large bowl of an electric mixer, beat together the mayonnaise and sugar. With the mixer on lowest speed, alternately add the flour mixture and water to the mayonnaise-sugar batter, beating after each addition and beginning and ending with flour. Stir in the vanilla and beat for 2 minutes longer.

3. Turn the batter into the prepared pan. Smooth it level, then spread it slightly from the center toward the edges of the pan so it will rise evenly. Bake in the lower third of the oven for 35 to 40 minutes, or until a cake tester inserted in the center comes out clean and the cake is lightly springy to the touch.

Leave the cake in its pan on a wire rack for 10 minutes, then top with another rack and invert; lift off pan. Cool completely on the rack before frosting. Or cool, frost, and serve the cake from its baking pan.

Devil's Food Cake

∎

I have been sorely tempted by Devil's Food Cake ever since I can remember, and for nearly that long I have wondered about its name. A study of the chemistry of chocolate solved the mystery. The very rich taste of the cake is not, as I suspected, the reason for the devilish reference; it is the reddish-brown color of the cake itself. The characteristically reddish color is caused by the baking soda used to neutralize the natural acidity of chocolate and at the same time leaven the cake. Baking soda has the effect of reddening and darkening certain types of cocoa.

It is important that a Devil's Food recipe specify the type of cocoa to be used, i.e., natural or Dutch-process (factory-treated with alkali; read about Chocolate, page 45). A soapy taste in the cake can be the result of an incorrect balance between the acidity of the chocolate and the quantity of baking soda.

This recipe follows the traditional method, using "natural" un-Dutched cocoa with baking soda. The result is a full-bodied, moist chocolate cake with excellent flavor.

Note: There are two different methods you can use for preparing this cake: the traditional method, as written, or the "dump and blend" quick method, which follows as a variation. They are completely opposite in technique, and produce slightly different results, but both work and taste good.

□ ADVANCE PREPARATION: The cake can be made in advance, wrapped airtight, and frozen. Thaw before icing. Or ice with buttercream, chill, then wrap and freeze. Thaw, wrapped, in the refrigerator.

□ SPECIAL EQUIPMENT: two 8-inch round pans 1½ inches deep, or one sheet pan 11¾ × 7½ × 1¾ inches

□ BAKING TIME: 30 to 35 minutes at 350°F (175°C)

□ QUANTITY: 5 cups batter, one 2-layer 8-inch cake (serves 8)

□ PAN PREPARATION: Spread solid shortening on bottom and sides of pan(s), dust evenly with unsweetened cocoa powder or flour; tap out excess powder.

2¼ cups sifted all-purpose flour (9½ ounces; 270 g)
1¼ teaspoons baking soda
¼ teaspoon salt
½ cup sifted Hershey's unsweetened cocoa, not Dutch-process
½ cup margarine or butter (1 stick; 110 g)
1½ cups granulated sugar (10½ ounces; 300 g)
2 large eggs
1 teaspoon vanilla extract
1½ cups buttermilk

ICING:

Chocolate Buttercream of your choice (see Index).

1. Prepare pan(s) as described. Position rack in lower third of oven. Preheat oven to 350°F (175°C).

2. Have ingredients at room temperature. Sift together all dry ingredients and set them aside.

3. In the large bowl of an electric mixer, cream together the margarine and sugar until light and fluffy. Add eggs, one at a time, beating after each addition. Beat in vanilla. Alternately add flour mixture and buttermilk, beginning and ending with flour and beating slowly to blend after each addition.

4. Divide batter between the prepared pans. Level the top, then spread the batter slightly from the center toward the edges of the pan so it will rise evenly. Bake in the preheated oven for about 35 minutes, until a cake tester inserted in the center comes out clean and the cake feels lightly springy to the touch. Cool on a wire rack for 10 minutes. Run the tip of a knife around the edge of each layer to release it from the pan. Top with another rack and invert. Lift off pan. Cool completely before frosting.

·*Variation:*·

"Dump and Blend" Quick Method: This gives a softer, more compact texture to the cake, with very tiny crumbs that melt in the mouth. The rise is the same as with the traditional method. Dump and Mix is literally that. Have all ingredients at room temperature. In the large bowl of an electric mixer, beat margarine until soft, beat in sugar, dump in eggs and vanilla, sift on all dry ingredients, and pour in milk. Now, carefully beat on very low speed for 60 full seconds (KitchenAid mixer #2 speed). Scrape down inside of bowl. Beat on high speed for 3 full minutes (KitchenAid, #8), until batter is very light and fluffy. Scrape down inside of bowl. Bake as directed.

Mocha Fudge Cake

■

This is a moist, fine-grained, intensely chocolate cake. If you are looking for a reliable fudge cake for your repertoire, this is an excellent choice. The recipe was shared with me by my friend and neighbor Linda Adams, who is well known in our town for her superb baking. For parties, Linda splits each of the 2 cake layers and fills them with sweetened whipped cream before topping the entire 4-layer extravaganza with Mocha Icing. Garnished with Chocolate Leaves (see page 449), the cake is guaranteed to be a show-stopper.

Note: The preparation of this recipe is quite unusual. Boiling water is added at the last minute to a fluffy creamed batter, and this will seem like a mistake. It is not. As you beat in the water, the batter reconstitutes, and the cake will bake perfectly. Try it.

☐ ADVANCE PREPARATION: The cake can be made in advance, wrapped airtight, and frozen. Thaw before icing.

☐ SPECIAL EQUIPMENT: two 9-inch layer pans 1½ inches deep; note that batter is watery; use solid-bottom pans rather than those with removable bottoms; double boiler

☐ BAKING TIME: 35 minutes at 350°F (175°C) for layers

☐ QUANTITY: about 5 cups batter, one 2-layer 9-inch cake (serves 8); or split into a 4-layer cake to serve 10 to 12

☐ PAN PREPARATION: Spread solid shortening over bottom and sides of pan, dust evenly with unsweetened cocoa; tap out excess cocoa. Note: If cocoa is lumpy, sift before using.

2¼ cups sifted cake flour (8 ounces; 230 g)
2 teaspoons baking soda
½ teaspoon salt
3 ounces unsweetened chocolate (85 g), chopped
½ cup lightly salted butter (1 stick; 110 g), at room temperature
2¼ cups firmly packed light brown sugar (15¾ ounces; 450 g)
3 large eggs
1½ teaspoons vanilla extract
1 cup sour cream or coffee-flavored yogurt
1 teaspoon instant coffee dissolved in 1 cup boiling water

FILLING:

2 cups heavy cream
½ cup sifted confectioners' sugar (2¼ ounces; 65 g)
½ teaspoon vanilla extract

ICING:

1 recipe Mocha Frosting (page 397); double the recipe if icing is to be used for filling as well as frosting 2 layers, or if frosting top and sides of 4-layer cake. Note: If using whipped cream to fill cake, make icing for top and sides soft enough to spread without pressing on layers, or cream will be forced out.

1. Prepare pans as described. Position rack in lower third of oven. Preheat oven to 350°F (175°C).

2. Sift flour, baking soda, and salt together onto a sheet of wax paper. Set aside. Melt the chocolate in the top pan of a double boiler set over hot, not boiling, water. Set chocolate aside to cool.

3. In the large bowl of an electric mixer, cream butter until very smooth and fluffy. Beat in brown sugar, then add eggs, one at a time, beating after each addition. Beat the mixture on medium-high speed for 4 to 5 minutes, until very fluffy and light.

4. With mixer on low speed, beat in vanilla and cooled chocolate. Add flour mixture to batter alternately with sour cream or coffee yogurt, beginning and ending with flour. Beat on low speed until smooth. Finally, blend in boiling water with coffee dissolved in it. Note: Water should be at boiling temperature when added to batter. Beat just until batter is blended and smooth.

5. Divide batter between pans. Level the batter, then spread it slightly from the center toward the edges of the pan so it will rise evenly. Bake in the preheated oven for 35 minutes, or until the top is lightly springy to the touch and a cake tester inserted in the center comes out clean.

6. Cool layers in pans on a wire rack for 10 minutes, then run a knife around sides of each layer to release it from the pan. Top each layer with a second rack and invert; lift off pan. If pan sticks, tap bottom gently. Cool cakes completely on the wire rack. Wrap airtight and freeze at this point, or fill and frost cakes. To split layers horizontally, use a serrated

knife (see instructions, page 424).

Note: If whipped cream is used for filling, the cake should be stored in the refrigerator.

Eggless Chocolate Cake

■

This quick and easy-to-make egg-free chocolate cake is good for those on special diets. However, the flavor is intense and the cake delicious for any one, any time. Fill and frost with your favorite eggless icing (see Recipes for Special Needs, page 474). Note that the cake, though moist, tends to be fragile and slightly crumbly when freshly baked.

☐ ADVANCE PREPARATION: The cake can be made in advance, wrapped airtight, and frozen. Thaw before icing.

☐ SPECIAL EQUIPMENT: two 8-inch cake pans 1½ inches deep

☐ BAKING TIME: 20 minutes at 375°F (190°C)

☐ QUANTITY: 4 cups batter, one 2-layer 8-inch cake (serves 8)

☐ PAN PREPARATION: Spread solid shortening over bottom and sides of pan, then dust evenly with unsweetened cocoa; tap out excess cocoa.

1⅔ cups sifted all-purpose flour (7 ounces; 200 g)
1 cup granulated sugar (7 ounces; 200 g)
¾ cup unsweetened cocoa, not Dutch-process (2 ounces; 60 g), sifted
1 teaspoon baking soda
1 teaspoon salt
1 cup buttermilk (or sour milk made by adding 1 tablespoon white vinegar to whole milk and letting stand for 5 minutes)
½ cup unsalted butter or margarine (1 stick; 110 g), melted and cooled
2 teaspoons vanilla extract

1. Prepare pans as described. Position shelf in lower third of oven. Preheat oven to 375°F (190°C).

2. Place a sifter over the large bowl of the electric mixer. Add to it all the dry ingredients, and sift them into the bowl.

Mixing by hand or with an electric mixer on lowest speed, stir in the buttermilk, melted butter, and vanilla. Blend well. The batter will look like a thick brownie batter.

3. Divide batter between prepared pans. Smooth it level, then spread it slightly from the center toward the edges of the pan so it will rise evenly. Bake in the preheated oven for about 20 minutes, or until a cake tester inserted in the center comes out clean and the top of the cake is lightly springy to the touch.

Cool layers in their pans on a wire rack for 10 minutes. Top each layer with a second rack and invert; lift off pans. Cool cake on the rack. Frost when completely cool.

Marvelous Mud Cake

■

Dense, dark, moist, and addictive, this easy-to-prepare chocolate tube cake is my variation of Maida Heatter's 96-Proof Chocolate Cake (used with permission, from *Maida Heatter's Book of Great Chocolate Desserts,* Alfred A. Knopf, 1980). I have added sour cream and another egg to give a more moist crumb. The original recipe uses bourbon for flavoring; rum, Amaretto, or Cognac are equally successful. This is a great dinner party cake because it is reliable to make and freeze in advance, yet it looks special and tastes heavenly with a dollop of whipped cream and a few fresh raspberries.

□ ADVANCE PREPARATION: When wrapped in plastic wrap and stored in an airtight container, this cake keeps very well at room temperature for up to a week. It may also be frozen.

□ SPECIAL EQUIPMENT: 9-inch (10-cup capacity) bundt, kugelhopf, or tube pan, double boiler, 2-cup glass measuring cup, sifter, flat paddle for electric mixer if available

□ BAKING TIME: 65 to 70 minutes at 325°F (165°C)

□ QUANTITY: about 7 cups batter, one 9-inch tube cake (serves 18 to 20)

□ PAN PREPARATION: Generously spread solid shortening inside pan, taking care to cover all indentations. Dust inside of pan with unsweetened cocoa or flour or fine dry unflavored bread crumbs; tap out excess.

5 ounces unsweetened chocolate (140 g)
2 cups sifted all-purpose flour (8½ ounces; 240 g)
1 teaspoon baking soda
¼ teaspoon salt
¼ cup powdered instant coffee or instant espresso
2 tablespoons boiling water
1 cup plus 2 tablespoons cold water
½ cup bourbon, or rum, Amaretto, or Cognac
1 cup unsalted butter (2 sticks; 227 g), at room temperature
1 teaspoon vanilla extract
2 cups granulated sugar (14 ounces; 400 g)
3 large eggs plus 1 large extra yolk
4 tablespoons sour cream or buttermilk

OPTIONAL ICING:

Chocolate Water Glaze (page 410) or sifted unsweetened cocoa or confectioners' sugar

1. Prepare pan as directed. Position rack in center of oven. Preheat oven to 325°F (165°C).

2. Melt the chocolate in the top pan of a double boiler set over hot, not boiling, water. Remove chocolate before it is completely melted and stir until smooth. Set aside off heat.

3. Sift together flour, baking soda, and salt and set aside. In a 2-cup glass measure, dissolve the instant coffee in the boiling water. Stir in the cold water and bourbon or other flavoring and set mixture aside.

4. In the large bowl of an electric mixer fitted with a paddle-type beater (if available), cream the butter with vanilla and sugar until well blended and smooth. Beat in eggs, one at a time, beating after each addition; beat in the extra yolk and sour cream. Scrape down the bowl and beater. Add melted and slightly cooled chocolate and beat until the batter is smooth.

5. Remove bowl from the mixer stand. By hand, using a spoon or rubber spatula, alternately stir in small amounts of the flour mixture and the coffee-bourbon liquid. Beat until batter is smooth; it will be quite thin. Don't worry if the batter looks slightly curdled.

6. Pour the batter into the prepared pan. Bake in the center of the preheated oven for 65 to 70 minutes, or until the cake top is springy to the touch and slightly crackled looking, and a cake tester inserted in the center comes out clean. Do not overbake, or the cake will dry out.

7. Cool the cake on a wire rack for 15 minutes, then top with another rack or plate and invert. Lift off pan. Cool cake completely.

To serve, top with Chocolate Water Glaze or a light sifting of cocoa or confectioners' sugar. Or leave the cake unadorned. Serve with bourbon-flavored, slightly sweetened whipped cream (page 368) or vanilla ice cream. Or slide a cardboard cake disk underneath the baked and cooled cake, wrap airtight, and freeze.

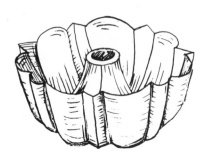

Crazy Mixed-up Chocolate Cake

∎

This is the cake that beat the cake mix in our time tests, clocked at 4 minutes 35 seconds from measuring ingredients to popping the cake into the oven! Probably the oddest, quickest, and easiest cake in this book, it is known by many names: Three-Holes-In-One, Mix-in-Pan, and Crazy Cake, for example. All the names refer to the fact that the ingredients are simply dumped in the pan, stirred, and baked. The result is a surprisingly delicious, moist, unsweet, eggless chocolate cake. Usually Crazy Cake is served without icing, but you can sift unsweetened cocoa on top, or confectioners' sugar, or add buttercream icing, or whipped cream and raspberries if you wish a more elegant presentation.

☐ ADVANCE PREPARATION: Cake can be baked ahead, wrapped airtight, and frozen.

☐ SPECIAL EQUIPMENT: one sheet pan 13 × 9 × 1½ inches, mixing spoon, sifter

☐ BAKING TIME: 30 to 35 minutes at 350°F (175°C)

☐ QUANTITY: 5 cups batter, one sheet cake 13 × 9 inches (serves 20)

☐ PAN PREPARATION: Note: Although the pan is not greased the cake pieces are easily removed when the cake is cut and served from the pan.

3 cups unsifted all-purpose flour (15 ounces; 425 g)
½ cup unsweetened cocoa, Hershey's or Baker's, preferably

1 teaspoon salt
2 cups granulated sugar (14 ounces; 400 g)
2 teaspoons baking soda
2 tablespoons white or cider vinegar
2 teaspoons vanilla extract
⅔ cup vegetable oil
2 cups lukewarm water

TOPPING (OPTIONAL):

Confectioners' sugar or unsweetened cocoa

1. Position rack in center of oven. Preheat oven to 350°F (175°C).

2. Set the sifter in the baking pan. Into the sifter put the flour, cocoa, salt, sugar, and baking soda. Sift everything into the ungreased baking pan. (If you are really rushed, forget the sifter, just combine the ingredients and stir them together.)

Make 3 depressions in the dry mixture. Into one put the vinegar, in another the vanilla, and in the third, the oil. Pour the water over all, then stir gently with a spoon. Be sure to cover the entire pan bottom and go into the corners so no pockets of dry ingredients remain unmixed. Stir until batter looks creamy and smooth. Wipe off the edges of the pan.

3. Place the pan in the preheated oven and bake for 30 to 35 minutes, until a cake tester inserted in the center comes out clean and the cake feels lightly springy to the touch. Cool completely in the pan set on a wire rack. Cut into squares and serve from the pan. If you wish, you can ice the top or dust it lightly with a sifting of confectioners' sugar or cocoa.

Carrot Cake

■

This is a classic carrot cake, easy-to-prepare, nutritious, and everyone's favorite. It is very moist, not too sweet, and keeps well (if hidden). Serve it plain or topped with the traditional Cream-Cheese Icing. This recipe lends itself to several intriguing variations: Parsnip Cake, Zucchini Cake, and Chocolate-Zucchini Cake, following.

Note: This recipe may be prepared two ways, by the traditional mixing method or in the food processor. Instructions for both methods follow.

☐ ADVANCE PREPARATION: The cake can be baked ahead, wrapped airtight, and frozen. It can also be iced before freezing.

☐ SPECIAL EQUIPMENT: 9-inch tube pan (6½-cup capacity) or 9-inch round or square layer pan, grater, nut chopper or food processor

☐ BAKING TIME: 40 to 45 minutes at 350°F (175°C)

☐ QUANTITY: 4 cups batter, one 9-inch tube cake (serves 8 to 10)

☐ PAN PREPARATION: Spread solid shortening on bottom and sides of pan, then dust evenly with flour; tap out excess flour.

1 cup sifted all-purpose flour (4¼
  ounces; 120 g)
1 teaspoon baking soda
½ teaspoon salt
2 large eggs
1 cup granulated sugar (7 ounces; 200 g)
¾ cup vegetable oil
1 tablespoon vanilla extract
1 teaspoon ground cinnamon
½ teaspoon ground nutmeg
4 to 5 raw carrots, peeled and grated to
  make 1½ cups (6 ounces; 170 g)
¾ cup canned crushed pineapple,
  drained well (optional)
1½ tablespoons toasted wheat germ
  (optional)
½ cup walnuts (2 ounces; 60 g),
  chopped

ICING:

Cream-Cheese Icing (page 393)

1. Prepare pan as described. Position rack in center of oven. Preheat oven to 350°F (175°C).

Note: For the traditional mixing method, follow steps 2, 3, and 4. To make the cake in the food processor, follow steps 5 and 6.

2. Sift together flour, baking soda, and salt. Set aside.

3. In the large bowl of an electric mixer, beat together the eggs and sugar. Add oil, vanilla, and spices and beat slowly to combine. Add flour mixture, stirring until blended. Finally, add grated carrots, pineapple (if using it), wheat germ, and chopped nuts. Stir well.

4. Spoon batter into prepared pan. Level top of batter. Set pan in center of preheated 350°F (175°C) oven to bake for 40 to 45 minutes, or until a cake tester inserted in the center comes out clean. Cool cake in its pan on a wire rack for about 15 minutes. Slide a knife blade between cake and side of pan to loosen it, then invert cake onto a platter or another wire rack and cool completely before frosting.

FOOD PROCESSOR METHOD:

5. Shred the carrots, using a medium shredding disc. Remove shredding disc and replace it with the metal blade. Leave carrots in workbowl and pulse 2 or 3 times, to cut the shreds. Turn carrots out on wax paper. Do not wash workbowl.

6. Combine in the workbowl the eggs, sugar, oil, vanilla, and spices. Process for about 3 seconds. Add walnut pieces (not previously chopped) and dry ingredients. Pulse until combined, about 6 times. Stop machine and scrape down workbowl one or twice. Stir in carrots, pineapple (if you use it), and wheat germ. Turn batter into pan and bake as directed in step 4.

·Variations:·

PARSNIP CAKE:

The Parsnip
The parsnip, children I repeat,
Is simply an anemic beet.
Some people call the parsnip edible;
Myself, I find this claim incredible.

Ogden Nash, from *Verses From 1929 On,*
  © 1941 by Ogden Nash. Used
  by permission of Little, Brown and
  Company.

Even if you agree with Nash's wit, this cake will restore the parsnip to culinary favor. It really tastes good, with a flavor and texture similar to carrot cake. I have adapted this recipe from one shared with me by my friend and real estate colleague Carolyn Klemm.

Prepare Carrot Cake, with the following changes: Instead of using carrots, substitute 8 ounces (230 g) parsnips, peeled and coarsely grated (2 cups). Omit pineapple. Bake for 35 to 40 minutes, or until a cake tester inserted in the center comes out clean.

ZUCCHINI CAKE:

This is rather like the Carrot Cake, but has a more moist texture resembling a steamed pudding. This moisture is from the zucchini, and will vary, depending upon the moisture content of the vegetable. Drier zucchini makes a drier cake, but either way it is very tasty.

Prepare Carrot Cake, with the following changes: Instead of using carrots, substitute 12 ounces (340 g) zucchini, washed, grated, and well drained; press firmly on grated zucchini in a strainer (2 cups). Omit pineapple. Bake for 45 to 50 minutes, or until a cake tester inserted in the center comes out clean. Note: Extramoist cakes take slightly longer to bake.

CHOCOLATE ZUCCHINI CAKE:

This is one of my favorite cakes—unusual, seductively moist and chocolaty, with a smooth, almost puddinglike texture. Note that the moisture results from the moisture content of the zucchini, which varies somewhat. The baking time for this cake is almost 20 minutes longer than for the preceding vegetable cakes.

Prepare Carrot Cake, with the following changes: Add to the sifted flour mixture $\frac{1}{3}$ cup sifted unsweetened Baker's cocoa ($\frac{4}{5}$ ounce; 25 g). Instead of using carrots, substitute 12 ounces (340 g) zucchini, washed, grated, and well drained; press firmly on grated zucchini in a strainer (2 cups). Along with the walnuts, add $\frac{1}{4}$ cup semisweet chocolate mini-bits ($1\frac{1}{3}$ ounces; 40 g). Bake cake for 50 minutes, test with a cake tester, then bake for 10 to 20 minutes longer, or just until the cake tester inserted in the center comes out clean but wet. The cake will be springy to the touch and will pull away from pan edges. Cool on a wire rack for 10 minutes, then invert and remove from pan. Complete cooling on wire rack. Serve at room temperature or warm, with Crème Anglaise Sauce or Zabaglione Sauce (see Index).

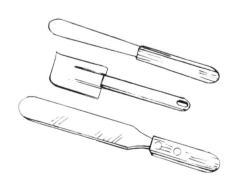

ABOUT WEDDING CAKES

∎

I sing of brooks, of blossoms, birds, and bowers:
Of April, May, of June, and July flowers.
I sing of maypoles, hock-carts, wassails, wakes,
Of bridegrooms, brides, and of their bridal
  cakes.

Robert Herrick, *Hesperides,* 1648

The ceremonial wedding cake has its roots in ancient cultures. Since earliest times, men have believed in the magical and religious powers of offerings made to spirits and/or gods. When a couple came together to form a family unit, grains were among the first offerings given—to the gods as well as directly to the couple. The grain symbolized their hope for fertility and for an abundance of food. This was the beginning of the tradition, and although variations occur from one country and one people to the next, the basic symbolism remains the same to this day. For example, the first Anglo-Saxons in the British Isles used grains of wheat in their wedding ceremony. Guests threw wheat at the bride; to underscore the symbolism, the bride also carried wheat stalks in her hand. Guests then gathered the tossed wheat grains and ate them to add their strength to the magic.

It was not long before the wheat grains were ground into flour and baked into flat cakes, and then the cake itself was crumbled and thrown over the bride's head. In some areas corn flour was used, as corn is also a symbol of fertility. This throwing of grain, or grain products, is the origin of throwing rice, though in some parts of Britain cake crumbs are still favored.

The custom of placing small figurines representing the bride and groom atop a wedding cake recalls another ancient practice: modeling small totems to attract the blessings of the spirits. Today, as in ancient times, we hope good spirits will reflect on the symbolic figures and that, through them, the real bridal couple will absorb good fortune.

Historians believe our wedding cake may be related to the cake used in ancient Roman weddings. After the wedding ceremony, the newly married couple traveled to their own home. The groom carried the bride over the threshold (to avoid offending any household spirits) and the couple attended a special ceremony in the presence of a priest and witnesses. During this *confarreatio,* consecrating the moment when the bride was delivered from the control of her father to that of her husband, the couple ate pieces of a ceremonial barley cake dedicated to Jupiter.

In the seventeenth and eighteenth centuries in England, it was the custom to pass small pieces of linen-wrapped wedding cake through the bride's wedding ring a certain magical number of times: 3, 7, or 9, to ensure good luck. These "magical" cakes were then given to the bridesmaids, who slept on them in the hope of dreaming of a future spouse. Similarly, small pieces of wedding cake were boxed and shared with the wedding guests. This custom is still popular today, and promises good luck in love and dreams of a future spouse to those who sleep with the cake beneath their pillow.

During the Tudor period in England, spices and dried fruits were added to the plain wheat flour wedding cake, but it was not until the Restoration period in the 1660s, when King Charles II returned to England from France with his entourage of French chefs, that icing was added to decorate the plain fruited wedding cake. Since the custom of crumbling pieces of the cake over the bride continued in most places well into the nineteenth century, it became practical to stack several cakes together under one coat of icing. In this way, one or two cakes could be crumbled for throwing at the bride, while the others were reserved for serving later.

Before the introduction of baking powder and baking soda as leaveners in the nineteenth century, wedding cakes—like most other cakes—were leavened with eggs or yeast and flavored with dried fruits and nuts. The English continue to use dried fruits in their wedding cakes, and to coat their fruitcake with a layer of marzipan and royal icing. By contrast, once baking powder came along, American bakers turned to lighter wedding cakes, often called bride's cakes, while continuing to make the fruitcakes for the groom's cake. Today, groom's cake is often served at a bachelors' party the night before the wedding.

□ DECORATING WEDDING CAKES
WITH FRESH FLOWERS AND HERBS

Herbs and plants with special significance have long been a part of the marriage ceremony as well as part of the decoration of the wedding cake. One of the most common examples is rosemary, symbol of wisdom, remembrance, love, fidelity, and luck in marriage. In Eastern Europe, notably Hungary and Romania, brides still wear sprigs of rosemary on their gowns or in their bouquets just as English brides did in the seventeenth century. The orange blossom, popular since the early 1800s, is still seen in many weddings today. The aromatic blossoms symbolize virginity, purity,

and fertility; it is not unusual to see orange blossoms in the bridal bouquet as well as on an orange-flavored wedding cake (see our recipe, page 89). Other plants of "significance" still in use today include the rose (love), rue (understanding), ivy (marriage, friendship), violets (faithfulness), sweet marjoram (joy), and thyme (courage). Many of the herbs have lovely flowers, which can add color as well as meaning to bridal bouquets and cakes. Other plants that make fine cake decorations include stephanotis blossoms, wild strawberries and their leaves, baby's breath, mint leaves, jasmine, acacia, lilac, honeysuckle, pear and apple blossoms, pinks and mini-carnations, citrus blossoms (including orange, grapefruit, lemon), and scented geraniums.

Fresh flowers provide a lovely and easy way to decorate a wedding cake, but you should be sure the flowers are edible; some, notably lilies of the valley, for example, might seem like good choices but are actually poisonous. You do not want to have flowers with unsavory oils that can penetrate the icing or cake. Some suggested flowers are noted herein, but if you have any doubts consult your state agricultural extension service or a local botanist.

There are several tricks to adding fresh flowers to a cake. First, the flowers and leaves must look fresh when the cake is served. Therefore, the flowers and leaves should be held separately, in water, until the very last moment, when they are trimmed of their stems and placed on the cake. Fresh mint leaves may be scattered near sugar icing roses. Real rosebuds and full-size roses can be set atop the cake at the last moment; the tigher the buds the longer they will look fresh. Remove thorns from rose stems. Scatter additional blossoms or petals on the tray holding the cake. My favorite technique is to hollow a small depression in the top cake layer; into this hole I set a small baby-food jar filled with waterlogged florist's foam holding an arrangement of roses or mixed flowers. You can also set the flower stems directly into the cake or into water-filled rubber-stoppered plastic tubes sold by florists to hold individual long-stemmed roses. Fresh flowers or individual petals may also be brushed with egg whites, then sprinkled with granulated sugar. These air-dry in about one hour and make sparkling decorations on a cake.

□ FROSTING FLOWERS

In place of real flowers, you can make marzipan roses and leaves or White Chocolate Plastic Roses (page 454) left white or tinted a pale color. Marzipan or Royal Icing or Buttercream can be used to form roses or other flowers that are made ahead, refrigerated, and set in place on the iced cake after the basic ornamentation has been added.

□ DECORATING TIPS

In addition to using fresh and frosting flowers, you can decorate the cake with narrow white satin bows placed on the cake to complement swags and bows of white icing.

There are a few basic rules about decorating wedding cakes that are good to keep in mind: first, unless you are a professional decorator, less is more; don't overdo the decorations. Simplicity is elegant. Second, the color scheme of the cake should follow the color scheme of the wedding itself—yellows and greens, for example, or shades of rose. However, in icing, the colors should be very pale tints, not bold tones.

Be conservative in icing the layers. The weight of multiple layers will tend to compress the cake even if posts and boards are used in the construction; keep icing layers thin so they do not press out. Remember that the decorations add plenty of richness to the cake sides. Thick icing between the layers encourages the layers to slide as well, and this can be fatal in a multitiered cake.

□ TYPES OF ICING FOR
WEDDING CAKES

Consider the weather and conditions when selecting the cake icing. My favorite icing for taste and texture is Classic French Egg Yolk Buttercream, which can be made well in advance. However, egg yolks are highly perishable, and if the cake must stand in the sun on a hot summer afternoon, you will be safer from a health standpoint, to use Italian Meringue Buttercream with an egg-white base, which will stand up longer.

Use American-style buttercream with some solid shortening added to form roses; the shortening gives the icing more body and will enable it to hold shape longer. For delicate tracery, use Royal Icing (page 387).

□ WEDDING CAKE SIZES
AND SERVINGS

For good proportions, ease in serving, and space for decorations, the layers should be 3 to 4 inches apart in size: 18, 15, 12, 9, and 6 inches; or 14, 10, and 6 inches, for example.

In figuring quantities of cake, consider the type of function and how the cake will be served. Will it be for an afternoon Champagne reception—when no meal will be served, and therefore cake pieces may be fairly large—or will it be served after a banquet, when only tiny slices will be required? Will you need a second cake that can be cut up and boxed as good luck tokens for the guests to take home? Will the top layer of the cake be reserved for the bride and groom to save until their first anniversary or the christening of their first child? In this case, you may want to add an extra layer or two to have enough servings for the wedding party.

As a general rule, a cake containing three 3-inch-thick layers, each layer made up of two 1½-inch-thick layers, 14, 10, and 6 inches in diameter, should serve 85 if the cake top is used. Figure about 48 slices (1 × 2 inches) from the 14-inch layer, 27 slices from the 10-inch layer, and 12 slices from the 6-inch layer.

□ THE MOVABLE WEDDING FEAST
If transporting the cake, be sure to use an air-conditioned vehicle in hot weather. If possible, transport each layer separately in an insulated box (see How To Transport Cakes, page 471). Construct the cake and complete final decorations at the party site. Plan to take with you extra icing and a pastry bag, tips, and extra ornaments or flowers just in case the cake needs touch-up work at the last moment. Transport fresh flowers in bouquets with their stems wrapped in wet newspaper, then watered down and stuck into large cans partly filled with water; place the cans in cardboard cartons packed with crumpled newspaper for stability.

Wedding Cake

•

The ideal wedding cake should be flavorful and delicate of crumb, yet firm enough to support the weight of several tiers. In addition, it should be able to be made in advance, and not lose quality on standing a day or two. All these characteristics and more are present in our recipe for Anna's Swedish Butter Cake (page 89). It is moist and flavorful and improves the longer it stands. Its texture is similar to, but lighter than, a pound cake, and best of all, it is very easy to make and extremely reliable.

Because orange blossoms are a popular wedding flower, we have flavored our cake with oranges. You might instead choose almond flavoring for the cake, almond buttercream or custard or marzipan for the filling, and a coat of rolled marzipan over the layers before icing with buttercream. If you prefer to follow the English tradition of making a fruitcake, you can adapt this same recipe simply by adding chopped brandy-soaked currants and golden raisins. For other flavor ideas, see the cake recipe. To make a separate cake for the groom, prepare the Groom's Cake (Bourbon-Pecan Cake, page 131), and trim it with sprigs of fresh rosemary.

It is fun, and completely within the realm of possibility to make at home a multitiered wedding cake for 50 to 100 people; our recipe serves about 85. To serve a larger crowd, make additional batches of the same recipe baked in sheet pans. Coat with buttercream but do not decorate; cut and serve from the kitchen, displaying only the 3-tiered decorated cake. It is a project that takes advance planning, to be sure. Make certain you have all the equipment: special pans, decorating bags and tips, cardboard cake disks, dowels or plastic straws for supporting the various layers. Plan your time: It will take a good afternoon to bake all the layers, and another several hours to frost and assemble the cake. The final elaborate decorations can take anywhere from a morning to all day, depending on your skill and energy; or you can decorate with fresh flowers added at the last minute—equally effective and much easier than a lot of fussy sugar icing. I like to freeze the 3 double-layers separately before assembling them into one cake. Before icing the cake, I return it to the freezer to set the layers firmly in place. It helps to locate freezer space large enough: our cake is 14 inches in diameter, sitting on a cardboard disk 16 inches in diameter, and the 3 layers stacked up and decorated reach a height of 15 to 16 inches. If you don't have freezer space, the refrigerator will do as well, but you probably will have to remove a shelf to accommodate the cake's height. If you have to transport the cake, locate a large cardboard box and have it ready; if transporting the cake in separate layers (the preferred method), have a box ready for each layer. In hot weather, have ice packs taped inside each box, or use styrofoam insulation panels (read How To Transport Cakes, see page 471).

□ ADVANCE PREPARATION: The cake layers may be made in advance, wrapped airtight, and stored at room temperature for 3 or 4 days, or they may be frozen several weeks ahead. Once iced, the layers can be frozen, as can the assembled cake. Bring the cake to room temperature by thawing it in the refrigerator overnight. Buttercream icing can be made 2 weeks in advance and refrigerated. Note: Classic French Egg Yolk Buttercream made in advance must be brought to room temperature, then whipped to soften it before spreading on the cake. Beware of whipping the buttercream while still too cold, for it may tend to separate, or break (curdle). To remedy this, whip the buttercream over a pan of slightly warm water.

□ SPECIAL EQUIPMENT: Graduated wedding cake pans are sold in kitchen supply shops. For a cake to serve 85, you will need at least one 14- × 2-inch, one 10- × 2-inch, and one 6- × 2-inch round layer pan; 2 cake layers are baked in each pan; for convenience, it helps to have two 10-inch and two 6-inch pans so both these sizes can be baked at the same time. To trim the domed tops of the baked layers, you will need a serrated knife with a blade 12 to 14 inches long. To support the tiers when stacked, you will need matching-size round cardboard cake disks (6, 10, and 14 inches) covered with foil plus 12 strong dowels such as plastic drinking straws, and scissors.

As a sturdier alternative to plastic straws, you can use chopsticks or ¼-inch wooden dowels (sold in hardware stores) cut with a small coping saw or strong shears. You will need about 48 inches of doweling plus one ¼-inch dowel that is about 20 inches long, the total height of your cake, depending upon the number of layers, to pierce the entire assembled cake, holding the layers in place. Beneath the largest layer (14 inches), you will need a 16-inch foil-covered cardboard cake disk or a flat tray. Note: It is important to use a bottom disk at least 2 inches larger than the base of the cake; this protects the cake sides during lifting and moving.

To cool the largest baked cake layers you will need 1 or 2 large wire racks about 16½ × 24½ inches (or substitute clean oven shelves) and several smaller racks (10 and 14 inches in diameter). For icing, you will need large (12 × 1¾ inches) and small (6 inches × 1 inch) icing spatulas, a 16- to 18-inch nylon pastry bag fitted with a variety of tips (2-inch-long tips for the large bags) depending upon the type of decoration to be added (large and small star tips for shells and borders, small round open tips for writing or strings, etc.). See page 435 for decorative ideas.

For ease in applying the icing, it helps to have a rotating cake stand or a lazy Susan. To cut the cake, you will need 2 or 3 knives: a ceremonial knife that is attractive, traditionally tied with a white satin bow, and a second, utilitarian knife for actually cutting the cake. For this purpose I usually use 2 knives: a long thin serrated blade for making vertical cuts around the layers, and a sturdy 6-inch carving knife with a straight blade for cutting the slices.

□ BAKING TIME: at 350°F (175°C), 14-inch layers need 40 to 45 minutes; 10-inch layers need 35 to 40 minutes; 6-inch layers need 25 minutes.

□ QUANTITY: one 3-tier cake (made up of double layers 14, 10, and 6 inches) to serve about 85. Note: If the top layer is to be saved, the cake will only serve about 75: 48 slices from the 14-inch layer and 27 slices from the 10-inch layer. If you want to have extra, add an 18-inch layer on the bottom or make a sheet cake.

□ PAN PREPARATION: Spread solid shortening on the bottom and sides of the pans; line the pans with wax paper or baking parchment cut to fit; it is okay to piece the paper if it is not large enough. Grease the paper, then dust the pans with flour; tap out excess flour.

GROOM'S CAKE:

Bourbon-Pecan Cake (page 131). Ice with Orange Icing Glaze (page 407) and garnish with sprigs of fresh rosemary

BRIDE'S CAKE
(WEDDING CAKE):

Anna's Swedish Butter Cake (page 89), Orange Flavor variation. Note the following modifications:
· For the wedding cake layers, line the pans with paper and grease and flour the paper even though this is not done in the original recipe.
· With the pan sizes specified, you will use a ¾-inch-thick layer of batter in each pan, giving a baked layer of 1½ inches. Make 2 layers of each size. When assembled, each pair of layers equals 3 inches.
· Follow baking times given here rather than those in the original recipe.

□ BAKING PROCEDURE:
Make 1 original recipe (4½ cups batter) to divide between two 6-inch pans.

Double the original recipe (9 cups batter) to divide between two 10-inch pans. Note: If you only have one 10-inch pan, make one recipe and bake it, then repeat.

Double the original recipe (9 cups batter)

for one 14-inch layer. Repeat, doubling the recipe again for the second 14-inch layer.

WEDDING CAKE FILLING:

Double recipe (3 cups) Light Orange Buttercream (page 382)

WEDDING CAKE ICING:

(You need 8 cups, total) Classic French Egg Yolk Buttercream (page 390), orange-flavor variation, *but use the following ingredients,* equal to 4 times the basic recipe:

2 cups granulated sugar, 1/2 teaspoon cream of tartar, 1 cup water, 12 large egg yolks, and 4 cups (2 pounds) unsalted butter, softened. Flavor with 3 teaspoons pure orange extract and 6 tablespoons orange liqueur, or to taste.

□ WEDDING CAKE ICING NOTES
· Omit the grated orange zest so the icing is smooth. It will have an ivory color.

· You will have enough icing (8 cups) to frost the sides and top of 3 layers (6 cups) plus extra to use for piping shell borders between the layers. For making other border decorations you need to make an additional double recipe (4 cups) of this buttercream. For roses or more elaborate details, see Decorative Icing (procedure following).

· Read Advance Preparation notes, regarding making this buttercream in advance.

· For a summer wedding, substitute heat-resistant Italian Meringue Buttercream (page 403). Prepare a triple recipe (about 11 cups) flavored with 3 teaspoons orange extract and

orange liqueur to taste; omit grated orange zest.

DECORATIVE ICING:

To make icing roses, prepare the basic All-Purpose Frosting (page 387), using half solid shortening, half soft butter. Tint the roses to match the ivory buttercream, or use a drop or two of food coloring to give them another light shade.

To make delicate lines or string work or writing, make Royal Icing (page 387). You can use this white, or tint it with a drop or two of undiluted frozen orange-juice concentrate to match the ivory tone of the original buttercream. Start with 1 recipe and make more as needed. Note that white chocolate matches the ivory color of this icing. If you want to decorate with white chocolate curls or roses, see page 455.

□ WEDDING CAKE ASSEMBLY
1. Bake and cool all cake layers. Prepare the filling and icing and have them at spreading consistency. If they have been made in advance, bring them to room temperature and stir or whip smooth. Be sure you have the required foil-covered cardboard cake disks, dowels or plastic straws, and scissors or shears to cut the dowels. See the construction diagram c, page 114.

2. With the long-bladed serrated knife, cut off the domed top of each cake layer, making sure all cake layers are absolutely flat. Brush crumbs from each layer.

3. Begin by assembling the 2 largest layers. Set out the 14-inch cardboard cake disk. Put a dab of buttercream icing in the center to anchor the cake, then set down the first layer. Top this with 1 1/3 to 1 1/2 cups of Light Or-

ange Buttercream Filling spread in an even layer. Do not make the filling too thick, or the layers will tend to slip. Top this with the second 14-inch layer. Line up the sides carefully.

4. At this point, supporting dowels are added in the center of the cake to hold the weight of the next layer. Some bakers do this after the cake is frosted, but I find that too messy; this system works well.

To position the straws or dowels that will support the weight of the next layer, take a 10-inch cake disk (or whatever size your next layer will be) and set it on top of your base cake. With the tip of a knife, mark the edges of the cardboard disk (diagram a), then lift off the disk. Poke 6 evenly spaced plastic straws (straight stemmed, not flexed) or wooden dowels just inside these marks. For more than 3 layers, use 8 dowels. One at a time, poke a straw or dowel down into the cake, and mark it with your finger or with a felt pen where it meets the cake top. Pull it out and cut it off at the mark (diagram b); use scissors for the straw or a coping saw or shears for the dowel.

Reposition the post and repeat. All posts should be level with the cake top. None should stick up, or the next layer will be raised; if the posts are sticking up and are uneven, the next layer will be tilted. Repeat, positioning posts in every layer that will support another above it.

5. After adding the supporting posts, frost the bottom layer. Spread about 1½ cups of Classic Egg Yolk Buttercream around the cake sides, and a scant 1⅓ cups on the top. Leave icing fairly thin in the center of the top where the second layer will be positioned. Spread the icing smooth all around. Place the iced cake in the refrigerator or freezer.

6. Set out the 10-inch foil-covered cardboard cake disk and spread a dab of buttercream in the center to anchor the cake. Top it with one 10-inch cake layer. Spread on this about 1 cup of filling, then top with the second 10-inch cake.

Follow the instructions in step 4 to position supporting posts (straws or dowels) to carry the weight of the next layer. After the posts are in place, frost the cake: spread the sides

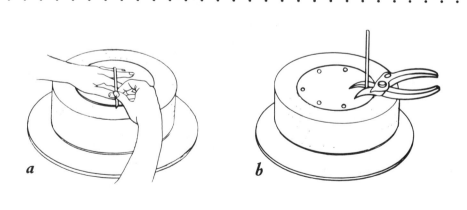

a   *b*

with about 1¼ cups Classic Egg Yolk Buttercream, putting about 1 cup on the top. Check that the icing on the sides and top is as smooth as possible. Place the iced cake in the refrigerator or freezer.

7. Set out the 6-inch foil-covered cardboard cake disk and spread a dab of buttercream in the center to anchor the cake. Top it with one 6-inch cake layer. Spread on this about ⅓ cup of filling, then top with the second 6-inch cake. This is the top layer and requires no supporting posts. Frost the sides with about ¾ cup Classic Egg Yolk Buttercream, putting slightly less on top. Smooth the icing and refrigerate the cake.

8. When all layers are chilled so their buttercream feels firm, you can assemble the cake (diagram c).

Put a dab of buttercream in the center of the 16-inch cake disk; this is the bottom "carrying" tray. Center the 14-inch double layer cake on this larger disk.

Put a dab of buttercream in the center of the 14-inch layer, to anchor the cake disk, then set down the 10-inch layer, taking care to center it. Put a dab of buttercream in the center of the 10-inch layer and position on it the 6-inch layer. Look at the cake carefully from all angles to be sure the layers are evenly lined up.

With a knife or pencil sharpener, sharpen a point on the end of the longest wooden dowel. Stand it on the table next to the cake, mark the cake's height on the dowel, then cut it to this height. Poke the dowel through the exact center of all the layers; this will keep the layers from sliding sideways.

In extremely hot weather, you can refriger-

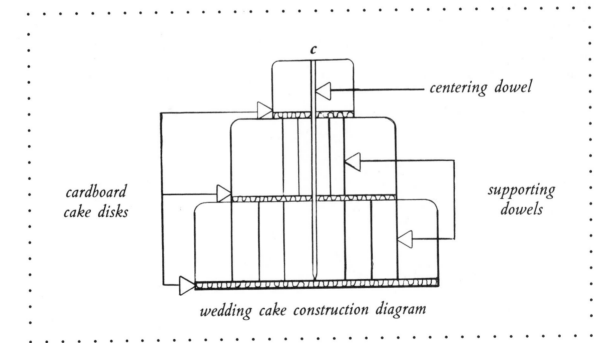

c

— *centering dowel*

cardboard cake disks

supporting dowels

wedding cake construction diagram

ate the cake now, just until the layers are firmly fastened to each other.

9. To decorate the cake, the first job is to apply delicate borders of shells around the base of each layer (diagram d), to conceal the cardboard disks. Then add any side borders or roses, vines, swags, or string loops if you wish (diagram e). Roses can be piped onto foil and refrigerated until ready to set on the cake (diagram f). To add a raised mound of roses on the top layer, frost a small scrap of cake trimmings into a raised dome and set this atop the center of the cake; apply the roses to this dome. Note: Even if fresh flowers will be used for decorations, you still need to pipe borders between the layers to conceal the disks and around the top cake edges to give the cake a finished appearance. Once decorated, the cake can be refrigerated until ready to transport or set on display.

10. To cut and serve the cake, set out the ceremonial knife for the bride and groom as well as the 2 utilitarian knives and a broad, long spatula for lifting the layers.

The bride and groom make the first cuts in the lower level, cutting just up to the side of the second tier. To remove the first slice, make a perpendicular cut at the side of the second tier, releasing the slice (diagram g). This slice is shared by the bride and groom. After this ceremony, the cake is cut by professionals in the following manner:

First, use the long serrated knife to cut completely around the base of the middle tier down through the bottom tier. Then cut 1-inch wedge-shaped slices around the outer edge of the lower tier (diagram h). Serve these slices. Lift off the top tier (i); set it aside to cut and serve or to save for first anniversary. Cut a ring around the base mark left by the top tier (j), then cut wedge-shaped slices from the middle tier (k). Pull the centering dowel out of the cake and discard it. Pull out the four straws or dowels in the middle layer. Cut the middle core cake into serving wedges (diagram l). Lift off the middle cardboard disk, and remove the final straws or dowels. Cut the lowest tier into serving slices; this tier may still be large enough to make another circular cut and remove wedge-shaped slices before cutting up the central core. If serving the top tier, use the broad spatula to remove the mound of roses on top, then cut the cake into wedges.

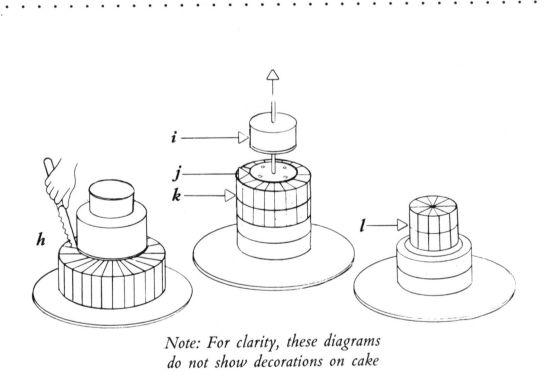

Note: For clarity, these diagrams do not show decorations on cake

Pound Cakes

ABOUT POUND CAKE

■

American pound cake came from England; it is named for the fact that it traditionally contained 1 pound each of flour, butter, eggs, and sugar. In France, pound cake is known as *quatre quarts,* or four quarters, referring to the quantities of principal ingredients used: to arrive at the proportions for a classic *quatre quarts,* one weighs 3 or 4 eggs, then uses an equal weight of flour, butter, and sugar. Originally, no baking powder was used in either the classic French or English pound cake; the eggs provided both the leavening and the liquid. Sometimes the eggs were separated and the whites stiffly whipped to supplement the leavening. This is still done, though today baking powder is also added.

In spite (or because) of its density, pound cake became the cornerstone (no pun intended) for generations of bakers. Why? Because it was easy to make, reliable, delicious, and would keep practically forever. It still is, and does. Though its fine grain and weight are part of its charm, it is fairly dry. Modern tastes favor more moisture and a lighter texture. There are many updated recipes for pound cake that vary the proportions of ingredients so they are no longer "1 pound each"; Best Pound Cake (page 121) is my choice in this category.

In the nineteenth century, bakers flavored pound cake with nuts or seeds such as caraway, cardamom, or anise; today pound cakes are glamorized with everything from chocolate bits to chopped ginger.

The recipes following are a sampler of styles, including the old-fashioned classic, a lightened up-to-date version, Best Pound

Cake (with nine variations), and a faintly tangy Sour-Cream Pound Cake, which is my own personal favorite.

Hints and Tips for Pound Cakes

· Bake pound cakes in loaf, tube, or bundt pans, preferably of shiny metal rather than dark steel. Dark pans cause the outside of the cake to brown too fast, before the inside is baked through.

· For a closer-grained, more dense cake, mix the batter by hand. For a lighter texture, incorporate air by using an electric mixer to cream the butter and sugar until fluffy. If the batter is not mixed enough, the texture will be coarse. If overwhipped, however, too much air can be incorporated, causing the cake to fall, or to overflow the pan when it bakes.

· To avoid curdling the batter, add the liquid slowly, and beat after each egg, or yolk, is added.

· After baking, allow pound cake to cool in its pan on a rack for at least 20 minutes, and be sure it is away from drafts. Then tip the cake out of the pan, set it upright on a rack, and cool completely. If unmolded too soon or in a cool place, the freshly baked cake can sink or break apart.

Troubleshooting Pound Cakes

· Batter overflows in pan: Too much batter in the pan, or batter overwhipped.

· Top crust sticky or white spots visible: White spots are undissolved sugar in the batter. The cake may be underbaked, or too much sugar was used, or the sugar was not completely dissolved in the batter. To remedy, add about half of the sugar with the egg yolks and the other half with the whipped whites.

· Top of cake splits: This is normal, caused by pressure from the steam that escapes during baking.

· Cake sinks in center: Batter overwhipped, so it rose too quickly, then fell in the oven. Or cake underbaked; or cake unmolded from pan too soon; or excess liquid or sugar in batter.

· Dense, heavy texture: Underbeating; or insufficient leavening; or old baking powder used; or insufficient oven heat.

Classic Pound Cake

■

This is a true pound cake in which the butter, sugar, eggs, and flour each weigh 1 pound. In its classic form, this recipe does not include baking powder; it appears here as an option I generally use. The eggs are separated, and the whites are whipped to lighten the texture somewhat. The flavor is very bland unless you add sufficient brandy, rum, juice, or extract. In the nineteenth century, Seed Cake was a popular variation including a tablespoon of spices or caraway seeds. For this recipe as well as the Spice, Marble, Citrus, Nut, and Chocolate Chip Pound Cake variations, see Index.

Note: This is a large recipe, making 2 loaves. To make a single loaf, prepare half the classic recipe but use only 2 cups flour and ¾ teaspoon salt.

□ ADVANCE PREPARATION: The cake can be prepared in advance, wrapped airtight, and kept at room temperature for a week, or refrigerated for several weeks. Or the cake can be frozen.

☐ SPECIAL EQUIPMENT: two loaf pans 9 × 5 × 3 inches, electric mixer fitted with paddle if available, large extra bowl and beater for egg whites

☐ BAKING TIME: 1 hour and 15 minutes at 325°F (165°C)

☐ QUANTITY: 8 cups batter, 2 loaves (serves 16 to 18)

☐ PAN PREPARATION: Spread solid shortening on bottom and sides of pans, dust evenly with flour; tap out excess flour.

4½ cups sifted cake flour (15¼ ounces; 450 g)
1 teaspoon baking powder (optional)
1 teaspoon salt
2 cups lightly salted butter (4 sticks; 454 g)
2¼ cups granulated sugar (15¾ ounces; 450 g)
8 large eggs, separated, at room temperature
2 teaspoons vanilla extract
2 tablespoons flavoring: brandy or dark rum or fruit juice, or a combination

1. Prepare pans as directed. Position rack in center of oven. Preheat oven to 325°F (165°C).
2. Sift together the flour, baking powder if using it, and ½ teaspoon of the salt onto a sheet of wax paper. Set aside.
3. In a mixing bowl with a sturdy spoon, or in the electric mixer fitted with a paddle if

possible (so as not to whip excess air into the batter), beat the butter until soft and fluffy, then gradually add 1½ cups of the sugar, beating until the mixture is very light and creamy. Add the egg yolks, one at a time, beating after each addition. The batter should be a pale yellow color, and very creamy. Scrape down the inside of the bowl and the beaters. Beat in the vanilla and other flavoring; some nineteenth-century cookbooks blend both rum and lemon juice, or brandy and orange juice. Be creative, but keep the total amount to 2 tablespoons.

4. By hand or with the mixer on lowest speed, gradually add the flour mixture to the batter in 5 or 6 additions. The batter will be quite stiff.

5. In a clean bowl with a clean beater, whip the egg whites with remaining ½ teaspoon salt until fluffy. Gradually beat in remaining ¾ cup sugar, whipping until the whites are stiff but not dry.

Stir about 1 cup of the whites into the batter to soften it. A little at a time, fold in remaining whites. At first this is hard going, but the batter smooths out quickly.

6. Divide batter between the prepared pans and bake in the preheated oven for about 1 hour and 15 minutes, or until the cake tops are golden brown, the centers are well risen, and a cake tester comes out clean. Cool both cakes in their pans on a wire rack for about 20 minutes. Then slide a knife around the cake sides to loosen it. Tip each cake out of its pan, set it upright on the rack, and cool completely. Do not frost the cakes. Note that the cakes mellow in flavor and also cut more easily the day after they are baked.

Sour-Cream Pound Cake

■

This cake is lighter than the classic pound cake, velvety in texture, buttery and moist, moderately sweet, with a slightly tangy flavor. The top crust is slightly crunchy, with an eggy taste. With all these virtues, you can see why it remains a favorite cake in our family, one we never tire of. When I began to research pound cakes for this chapter, three different friends sent me this recipe from three different parts of the country, proving its popularity.

Note: Double the recipe to bake this cake in a 10-inch tube or bundt pan.

☐ ADVANCE PREPARATION: The cake can be baked in advance, wrapped airtight, and kept at room temperature for about a week, or refrigerated for 2 to 3 weeks. Or it can be frozen.

☐ SPECIAL EQUIPMENT: one loaf pan 8½ × 4½ × 2¾ inches, or one 9 × 5 × 3 inches, electric mixer fitted with paddle attachment if possible, extra bowl and beater for whipping egg whites

☐ BAKING TIME: 1 hour and 15 minutes at 325°F (165°C)

☐ QUANTITY: 4½ cups batter, 1 loaf (serves 8)

☐ PAN PREPARATION: Spread solid shortening on bottom and sides of pan; dust evenly with flour; tap out excess flour.

1½ cups sifted all-purpose flour (6¼ ounces; 180 g)
⅓ teaspoon baking powder
⅛ teaspoon baking soda
½ cup lightly salted butter (1 stick; 110 g), at room temperature
1½ cups granulated sugar (10½ ounces; 300 g)
3 large eggs, separated, at room temperature
½ cup sour cream
1 teaspoon vanilla extract

1. Prepare pans as described. Position rack in center of oven. Preheat oven to 325°F (165°C).

2. Sift together the flour, baking powder, and baking soda and set aside.

3. In a mixing bowl with a sturdy spoon or an electric mixer, cream together the butter and ¾ cup of the sugar until very well blended and light. Add egg yolks, one at a time, beating after each addition.

4. Alternately add flour mixture and sour cream, beating slowly after each addition and beginning and ending with flour. Stir in the vanilla. The batter will be quite stiff.

5. In a clean bowl with a clean beater, whip the egg whites until fluffy. Gradually add remaining ¾ cup sugar while beating until the whites are stiff but not dry. Stir about 1 cup of whipped whites into the batter to soften it, then gradually fold in remaining whites.

6. Turn the batter into the prepared pan and bake in the preheated oven for 1 hour and 15 minutes, or until the cake is golden brown, well risen, and a cake tester inserted in the center comes out clean.

Cool the cake in its pan on a wire rack for 20 minutes. Then slide a knife around the cake sides to loosen it. Tip the cake out of the pan, set it upright on the rack, and cool completely. Do not ice the cake.

Best Pound Cake

•

This is a contemporary pound cake, a little sweeter and lighter than the classic version. The recipe makes a marvelously flavorful, moist loaf; in our taste tests it won all the votes for flavor, texture, appearance, and general delectability. Following the recipe, you will find nine variations: Mother's Whiskey Cake, Seed Cake, New England Spice Pound, Citrus Pound, Nut Pound, Praline Pound, Chocolate Chip Pound, Marble Pound, and Rose Geranium Pound Cake.

☐ ADVANCE PREPARATION: The cake can be baked in advance, wrapped airtight, and stored at room temperature for a week or refrigerated for several weeks. Or the cake can be frozen.

☐ SPECIAL EQUIPMENT: one loaf pan 9 × 5 × 3 inches or one 9-inch (6½-cup capacity) tube pan, mixing bowl and wooden spoon, or electric mixer fitted with paddle attachment if available

☐ BAKING TIME: 1 hour and 15 minutes at 325°F (165°C)

☐ QUANTITY: 4½ cups batter, one loaf 9 × 5 inches or one 9-inch tube (serves 8 to 10)

☐ PAN PREPARATION: Spread solid shortening on bottom and sides of pan, dust evenly with flour; tap out excess flour.

2 cups unsifted cake flour (9 ounces; 260 g)
1 teaspoon baking powder
½ teaspoon salt
1 cup unsalted butter (2 sticks; 230 g), at room temperature
1⅔ cups granulated sugar (11½ ounces; 330 g)
5 large eggs
1½ teaspoons vanilla extract

1. Prepare pans as described. Position rack in center of oven. Preheat oven to 325°F (165°C).

2. Sift together flour, baking powder, and salt. Set aside.

3. In a mixing bowl with a sturdy spoon, or in the electric mixer, preferably fitted with the paddle (to avoid whipping excess air into the batter), beat the butter until soft and fluffy. Gradually add the sugar and beat until very light and creamy. Add the eggs, one at a time, beating well after each addition. Beat in the vanilla.

4. By hand or with the mixer on lowest speed, gradually stir in the flour mixture. Blend well.

5. Turn batter into the prepared pan and bake in the preheated oven for 1 hour and 15 to 20 minutes, or until cake is well risen and golden on top, and a tester inserted in the center comes out clean. Cool the cake in its pan on a wire rack for 20 minutes. Then slide a knife around the sides to loosen it. Tip the cake out of the pan, set it upright on the rack, and cool completely.

·Variations:·

MOTHER'S WHISKEY CAKE:

Prepare Best Pound Cake, but bake it in a 9-inch (6½-cup capacity) tube pan. While the cake bakes, prepare a syrup by combining in a small pan ½ cup lightly salted butter and ½ cup granulated sugar. Set over low heat and stir until the butter melts. Remove from heat and stir in ½ cup whiskey (for example, Canadian Club). As soon as the cake is baked, set the pan on a wire rack. Use a thin skewer or cake tester to prick holes all over the cake. Pour warm syrup over the hot cake and allow it to cool completely in the pan. When cold, top with a plate, invert, and lift off pan. Sift on confectioners' sugar. Note: This syrup can also be poured over a larger pound cake baked in a bundt pan; it is sufficient for a 10-inch cake.

SEED CAKE:

Prepare Best Pound Cake and add 2 teaspoons caraway seeds, ⅓ cup finely chopped citron, and 1 teaspoon grated lemon rind to the finished batter.

NEW ENGLAND SPICE POUND CAKE:

Prepare Best Pound Cake, but add 1 teaspoon ground cinnamon and 1 teaspoon ground nutmeg to the finished batter.

CITRUS POUND CAKE:

Prepare Best Pound Cake, but add the grated zest of both 1 lemon and 1 orange to the finished batter.

NUT POUND CAKE:

Prepare Best Pound Cake, but add 1 cup finely chopped walnuts (4 ounces; 110 g) plus ½ teaspoon ground cinnamon and ½ teaspoon ground mace to the finished batter.

PRALINE POUND CAKE:

Prepare Best Pound Cake, but add ½ cup chopped toasted almonds or hazelnuts and ½ cup almond or hazelnut Praline Powder (page 444) to the finished batter.

CHOCOLATE CHIP POUND CAKE:

Prepare Best Pound Cake, but toss ⅔ cup semisweet miniature chocolate chips with 2 or 3 tablespoons of the sifted flour mixture and set them aside. Fold the chips into the batter at the end. You may need to increase baking time 10 to 15 minutes, baking just until a cake tester comes out clean.

MARBLE POUND CAKE:

Prepare Best Pound Cake, but place half of the batter in a second bowl. Melt 2½ ounces semisweet chocolate in the top pan of a double boiler. Stir the chocolate into half of the batter. Spoon vanilla and chocolate batters alternately into the prepared baking pan. Draw a knife blade through the batter to create a marbleized effect; do not stir.

ROSE GERANIUM POUND CAKE:

Scented geraniums are available in an astonishing number of varieties including orange, lemon, apple, mint, and rose. The leaves of these plants are highly aromatic, and their oils impart a delicate flavor to foods. In the nineteenth century, when over 300 varieties were cultivated, this romantic cake was very popular.

Prepare Best Pound Cake, but line the greased and floured pan with rose geranium leaves *(Pelargonium graveolens)* before adding the batter. Bake the cake as directed, remove it from the pan with the leaves in place, and dust on a light sifting of confectioners' sugar before serving.

Fruitcakes

ABOUT FRUITCAKE

■

Fruitcakes are great "occasion" cakes, traditionally baked for special events and holidays. Certainly they can be baked well in advance and "aged," but that is not their only virtue. The fact that they are show-off cakes has something to do with their appeal, rather like a culinary potlatch, demonstrating wealth by using lavish quantities of rich ingredients. Most fruitcakes are virtual cornucopias of brandy-soaked fruits and nuts minimally bound by cake crumbs. In Great Britain, fruitcake is the traditional Christmas cake, usually enrobed in a sheet of marzipan coated with royal icing textured like snow and topped by a miniature Father Christmas or holly sprig. With more elaborate and less seasonal trimming, fruitcake is also the traditional English wedding cake.

Unfortunately, many of us shy away from fruitcakes because of overexposure to sickeningly sweet supermarket glacéed fruits. A homemade fruitcake made with the best-quality ingredients bears no resemblance to the store-bought variety; if you make the cake yourself, you can use only those ingredients you prefer. Try, for example, dried peaches, mangoes, papaya, apples, pineapple, apricots, figs, pears, dates, and prunes in place of candied citron and cherries.

One of the most famous American fruitcakes was the Great Cake baked by Martha Washington for the president's family holidays. The handwritten recipe, penned by her granddaughter and signed "This was wrote by Martha Custis for her Grandmama" reads:

Take 40 eggs and divide the whites from the yolks & beat them to a froth [ed. a bunch of twigs was used for this purpose] then work 4 pounds of butter to a cream & put the whites of eggs to it a Spoon

Fruitcakes have been popular since the ancient Romans, who made many dishes blending dried fruits, nuts, and sweet wine. One such cake, known as satura, *combined barley mash, raisins, pine nuts, pomegranate seeds, and mead, a honey wine. The Latin word "satura" meaning a "full dish," or "one containing many different types of fruit" according to the* Oxford English Dictionary, *is the root of the word satire, referring to the fact that a variety of points of view or different ingredients, both sweet and sour, are addressed in the literary satire.*

full at a time till it is well work'd then put 4 pounds of sugar finely powderd to it in the same manner then put in the Youlks of eggs & 5 pounds of flower & 5 pounds of fruit. 2 hours will bake it add to it half an ounce of mace & nutmeg half a pint of wine and some frensh brandy.

Collection of Mount Vernon Ladies
Association, Mount Vernon

Today the whole process is much easier. You will find that this is one cake you don't have to be afraid of; the mixing is casual—a tossing together of your favorite blend of fruits, nuts, and brandy, which is left to macerate for a day or two, then a simple stirring up of a pound cake batter to bind the fruit.

Hints and Tips for Fruitcakes

• Buy the best-quality dried fruits you can find, usually available at food coops and health-food stores or gourmet shops; supermarket "dried candied fruits" or "glacéed fruits" are oversweet and often of poor quality. To improve these supermarket fruits, set them in a strainer and pour boiling water over them to remove some of the sugar, then soak them in brandy before using. Don't worry about dicing all fruits to the same size; when you slice the cake, you will cut the fruit anyway; a variety of sizes makes an attractive mosaic when the cake is cut. Instead of spirits, you can make nonalcoholic fruitcake, using fruit juice, honey, molasses, maple syrup, or flavorful tea.

• Use an assortment of pans; for gifts, make small or baby loaves. Use regular loaf pans of any size, or pressed aluminum "disposable" pans. For large cakes you can use any angel-food tube pans, or springform pans with or without a tube. Fluted kugelhopf or bundt pans can be used, but are more difficult to line with paper; I use aluminum foil to line these pans, pressing the foil into the greased flutes of the pan.

• Use shiny metal pans, avoiding black nonstick or black steel pans whose dark surface will cause the outside of fruitcakes to bake too quickly. Be sure to grease the pan lightly, then always carefully line the bottom *and* sides with wax paper, baking parchment, or brown paper cut from paper bags. Grease the paper after it is cut, fit, and neatly positioned in the pans (see page 62). Paper prevents too-quick baking of the exterior of the cake and prevents the fruit pieces from sticking to the pan. Make individual fruitcakes in muffin pans, but line the pans with fluted paper or foil liners and reduce baking time accordingly; the danger with tiny cakes is that they overbake and dry out.

• Bake fruitcake in a slow oven, 300°F to 325°F. Small cakes take between 45 and 60 minutes, while large ones can take 2½ hours or longer. To tell when a cake is done, look for a nicely browned, slightly risen top and sides that begin to pull away from the pan. Insert a cake tester in the center; it should come out moist from fruit but with no visible trace of raw batter.

• Note that freshly baked fruitcakes, especially the large ones are rather fragile while still warm. It is best to let the cakes sit in their pans for about 20 minutes, then top them with a cardboard cake disk or flat plate or wire rack, invert, and lift off the pan. Peel off the paper while the cake is still slightly warm. Invert the cake and cool completely in an upright position. Some recipes direct you to wrap the warm cakes immediately in brandy-soaked cloth, others to wait until the cakes are cold. In any case, handle warm cakes as little as possible to prevent breakage. I prefer to let the cake sit under a tea towel for several hours until cold before storing.

• For brandy-soaking wrappers, select the best-quality cheesecloth you can find and use 3 layers; cheap cleesecloth pulls apart and covers the cakes with unsightly threads. Or use clean sheets or tea towels or muslin. Cut a piece large enough to envelop the cake, soak the cloth in the spirits, then wrap it around the cake. Cover the cake with plastic wrap, then place it inside a large heavy-duty plastic bag, well fastened, or in a plastic or metal container with a lid. Don't cover the alcohol-wrapped cake with foil unless first placed in a plastic bag, for the spirits sometimes dissolve the metallic wrap. If storing them in the basement, put the plastic-bag-wrapped cakes in a tin box or the mice will quickly arrive to feast. Occasionally check the cloth and replenish the spirits when needed to keep the cloth moist. The easiest way to add spirits is to paint them onto the cloth-wrapped cake instead of removing the wrapping. Store the cakes in a cool, dry place, but not in the refrigerator. Age them as long as you wish—for 1 week or 1 year or anything in between. A good cake full of good ingredients will taste fine even when freshly baked. Fruitcakes can also be frozen. Before serving, garnish with Apricot Jam Glaze or Icing Glaze, decorated with halved cherries or nuts and angelica.

English Fruitcake

•

This is a dark, moist fruitcake with a moderate amount of delectable cake binding the fruit and nuts. Bake it in cupcakes or loaves or tubes of any size or shape. To change the flavoring, see the Ginger, Victorian Orange, and Chocolate Fruitcake variations following the basic recipe. Read About Fruitcake (page 123).

☐ ADVANCE PREPARATION: Prepare the cake, wrap with brandy-soaked cloth, and store for up to a year. Or freeze the cake after aging.

□ SPECIAL EQUIPMENT: One tube pan 10 × 4 inches, or two loaf pans 8½ × 4½ × 2¾ inches *plus* 2 baby loaf pans 6 × 3½ × 2 inches, or 2½-inch-diameter muffin cups; wax paper or baking parchment or fluted paper muffin liners, scissors, extra-large mixing bowl, wooden spoon, plastic wrap, muslin or cotton or cheesecloth, heavy-duty plastic bags, metal or plastic tins for storing cakes; electric mixer fitted with paddle attachment if available

□ BAKING TIME: about 2 hours at 325°F for 10-inch tube cake; 1 hour and 25 minutes for large loaves; 1 hour and 20 minutes for baby loaves; 40 to 45 minutes for muffins

□ QUANTITY: 11 to 12 cups batter, one 10-inch tube cake, or 2 regular plus 2 baby loaves, or 36 to 40 muffin-size individual fruitcakes

□ PAN PREPARATION: Lightly grease the pan(s), cut aluminum foil or paper liners to fit bottom and sides of pan(s), press paper in place, then grease the paper. Do not grease inside of paper muffin liners.

1 cup seedless raisins (6 ounces; 170 g)
1 cup golden raisins (5 ounces; 140 g)
1 cup currants (4 ounces; 120 g)
1 cup mixed candied fruits, chopped (7 ounces; 200 g)
1 cup firmly packed pitted and chopped dried dates (7 ounces; 200 g)
1 cup whole candied cherries (8 ounces; 225 g)
1½ cups broken walnuts (6 ounces; 170 g)
¾ cup dark rum or brandy, or bourbon or port or cider

1 cup lightly salted butter or half margarine (2 sticks; 230 g), at room temperature
2⅓ cups firmly packed light brown sugar (16¼ ounces; 465 g)
4 large eggs
½ cup honey
Grated zest of 1 lemon
1 cup unsifted whole-wheat pastry flour (4½ ounces; 120 g; available in health food stores)
1⅔ cups unsifted all-purpose flour (8 ounces; 225 g)
1½ teaspoons baking powder
¼ teaspoon salt
1 teaspoon ground cinnamon
½ teaspoon ground nutmeg

GLAZE:

Apricot Glaze (page 411) or Icing Glaze (page 406)

GARNISH:

Halved candied cherries, halved blanched almonds and/or walnuts or pecans, angelica

AGING:

Brandy or rum or port

1. A day or two before baking the cakes, combine all the fruits and nuts in a large bowl, toss with the rum or brandy, and top with a piece of wax paper. Set aside for 24 hours.

2. On the baking day, prepare pans as described. Position racks to divide the oven in thirds if baking several pans at once; otherwise, place rack in center of oven. Preheat oven to 325°F (165°C).

3. To make the cake batter, use a spoon and a mixing bowl or an electric mixer. Cream together the butter and sugar until well blended. Add eggs, one at a time, beating after each addition. Stir in the honey and grated lemon zest. Set a strainer over the bowl and add the flour, baking powder, salt, and spices. Sift these dry ingredients into the batter, stir to blend well. Stir in the macerated fruits and nuts, and blend well.

4. Spoon the batter into the prepared pans, filling them about ⅔ full. Mound the batter somewhat in the center. Bake for the time specified, or until cake is well browned and starting to pull away from the pan sides. A cake tester inserted in the center should show no visible sign of raw batter though it may be sticky from the fruit. Be sure not to overbake muffins or they will dry out. If any cake starts to overbrown on top, cover it with a piece of aluminum foil for protection.

Set the baked cakes on a wire rack for about 20 minutes. Top with cake cardboards cut to fit, or with a plate, invert, remove pans, and peel off paper or foil liners. Invert cakes again and cool completely right side up.

5. At this point, the cakes can be glazed with Apricot or Icing Glaze and garnished with candied cherries or nut halves, and angelica cut into small shapes and arranged as flowers on the cake tops. Wrap the cakes and give as gifts, or slice and serve, or freeze to serve later.

Or the cakes can be wrapped in brandy-soaked cloth and stored for aging. To do this: Cut cloth or cheesecloth, 3 layers, large enough to envelop the cake(s), soak the cloth in brandy, and wrap the cake(s) completely. Do not use fruit juices for this, as only alcohol will preserve the cake. Wrap the moist cloth in a generous piece of plastic wrap, then put the entire package inside a heavy-duty plastic bag and twist the end to seal well. Set this inside a plastic or tin box, covered, and store in a cool dry place. Periodically, check the cake and brush more spirits on the cloth if it is dry. Store for up to a year. Before serving, garnish the cake with a glaze and fruit and nut topping if you wish.

· *Variations:* ·

GINGER FRUITCAKE:

Prepare English Fruitcake but add 1 teaspoon ground ginger to the spices and ¼ to ½ cup finely chopped candied ginger to the fruits.

VICTORIAN ORANGE FRUITCAKE:

Prepare English Fruitcake with the following changes: Omit the candied mixed fruits and candied cherries; substitute ½ cup almond paste, at room temperature, crumbled up, and 1 cup coarsely chopped blanched almonds (5 ounces; 140 g) or halved pecans. Omit the lemon zest and add the grated zest of 2 whole oranges and 1 teaspoon orange extract to the beaten butter-sugar-egg batter. If you wish, substitute Candied Orange Peel (page 448) for the candied cherries. Use Madeira wine instead of rum in the cake and also as a soaking liquid during the aging, or use a combination of orange liqueur and orange juice.

CHOCOLATE FRUITCAKE:

Prepare English Fruitcake with the following changes: Substitute ½ cup sifted unsweetened cocoa, preferably Dutch-process (1⅓ ounces; 40 g) for ½ cup all-purpose flour. Add ¼ teaspoon baking soda along with the salt. Omit the lemon zest. Substitute 2 cups semi-sweet chocolate morsels or chopped bitter-sweet chocolate for 1 cup mixed candied fruits and 1 cup candied cherries.

. . . .

Apricot-Nut Fruitcake

■

This is the fruitcake for those who hate candied fruits. A moderately sweet cake containing chopped apricots, 3 types of nuts, 2 types of raisins, and grated fresh apples, it is wonderful to give as a gift or to serve for the holidays. Read About Fruitcakes (page 123).

□ ADVANCE PREPARATION: The dried fruits and the nuts are combined with the rum and soaked for 24 hours before making the batter. Plan ahead. Prepare the cake, glaze, and garnish, and wrap airtight. Store the cake in the refrigerator for about 2 weeks for the flavors to mellow, then serve or freeze. Of course, it is also fine to eat right after baking. Do not wrap this cake with alcohol-soaked cloths for storage.

□ SPECIAL EQUIPMENT: one tube pan 10 × 4 inches or one 9¼-inch tube pan (9-cup capacity) plus 2 baby loaf pans, each 6 × 3½ × 2 inches, or the equivalent in capacity; nut

chopper or food processor, extra-large mixing bowl, electric mixer, wax paper or baking parchment, scissors

□ BAKING TIME: 1½ to 1¾ hours at 325°F (165°C) for a 9- or 10-inch tube cake, about 1 hour and 15 minutes for baby loaves

□ QUANTITY: about 12 cups batter, one 10-inch tube cake or one 9-inch tube plus 2 baby loaves

□ PAN PREPARATION: Lightly grease pan(s), cut paper liners to cover both bottom and sides (see page 62), press paper in place, then grease paper.

2 cups broken walnuts (8 ounces; 230 g)

1 cup hazelnuts or filberts (5 ounces; 140 g), toasted, skinned (see page 43), halved or coarsely chopped

1 cup Brazil nuts (6 ounces; 170 g), coarsely chopped, or halved pecans

1 cup seedless raisins (6 ounces; 170 g)

1½ cups firmly packed golden raisins (7 ounces; 210 g)

2 cups firmly packed dried apricot halves (12 ounces; 340 g), cut into quarters

¾ cup dark rum or Calvados, plus ½ cup unsweetened apple cider, or use all spirits

1½ cups unsifted whole-wheat pastry flour (6¾ ounces; 185 g; available in health food stores)

2 cups unsifted all-purpose flour (10 ounces; 280 g)

1½ teaspoons baking powder

¼ teaspoon baking soda

½ teaspoon salt

1 teaspoon each of ground cinnamon and nutmeg

1½ cups lightly salted butter (3 sticks; 340 g), at room temperature, or use ½ cup margarine plus 1 cup butter

1½ cups firmly packed light brown sugar (10½ ounces; 300 g)

5 large eggs

2 teaspoons vanilla extract

1 cup unpeeled grated apple, cooking type such as Granny Smith (6 ounces; 170 g)

1 cup applesauce

GLAZE:

Apricot Glaze (page 411) or Icing Glaze (page 406)

GARNISH:

Halved walnuts, almonds, or pecans, cut-up dried apricots

1. A day or two before baking the cake, combine all the dried fruits and nuts in a large bowl and toss well with the rum or Calvados and cider. Cover with plastic wrap and set aside in a cool place for at least 24 hours. Toss the mixture occasionally.

2. On the baking day, prepare pans as described. Position rack in center of oven for 1 large cake, or divide oven in thirds for several cakes. Preheat oven to 325°F (165°C).

3. Sift both flours, the baking powder, baking soda, salt, and spices together onto wax paper. Set aside.

To make the cake batter, use a spoon and a mixing bowl or the electric mixer to cream together the butter and sugar until well blended. Add eggs, one at a time, beating after each addition. Stir in vanilla.

Add the flour mixture in 3 or 4 additions, beating very slowly to blend after each addition. The batter will be quite stiff. Stir in the grated apple and applesauce. Stir the macerated fruit-nut-rum mixture, then add it to the batter along with all the liquid. Stir the batter with a sturdy wooden spoon until well blended; really the best way to blend is with your bare hands.

4. Spoon the batter into the prepared pan(s), filling them about ⅔ full. Bake in the preheated oven as directed until the cake top(s) are golden brown (cracking is normal as the steam escapes) and a cake tester inserted in the center shows no visible raw batter.

Cool each cake on a wire rack for 20 minutes. Run a knife blade around the cake sides to loosen, then top with a cardboard cake disk or plate and invert; remove the pan and peel off the paper. Invert again and cool the cake completely, right side up. Once cold, the cakes may be served or stored.

If you wish, wrap the cold cakes in plastic wrap, then in foil, and refrigerate them for a week or two. Before serving, brush the cake top with Apricot Glaze or Icing Glaze and set a few halved nuts and cut pieces of apricot into the soft glaze. Allow about 30 minutes for the glaze to set.

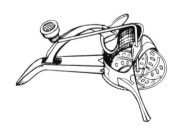

Williamsburg Orange
Wine Cake

•

Culled from the historic papers, journals, and household books of Virginia's first settlers, versions of this recipe came to light during the development of the Colonial Williamsburg restoration. In 1938 the first recipe for the cake appeared in print in *The Williamsburg Art of Cookery Or, Accomplish'd Gentlewoman's Companion,* compiled by the project's archivist Mrs. Helen Bullock. Today, the cake is served at many of the restoration's dining rooms, and its fame has spread across the country. There are still many variations, but all have a strong orange flavor, with a texture flecked with nuts and currants. Traditionally, the cake is baked in a tube pan and iced with Orange Wine Icing, though it can also be formed in layers. Orange Madeira Cake is a variation on this recipe, using Madeira wine instead of sherry. Both are moist, moderately sweet cakes served in small pieces.

□ ADVANCE PREPARATION: Cake keeps well, wrapped airtight, at room temperature for at least a week. Cake can be baked ahead, wrapped airtight, and frozen.

□ SPECIAL EQUIPMENT: One 9-inch tube pan (8½- to 9-cup capacity) or two 9-inch layer pans, nut chopper or food processor

□ BAKING TIME: 55 to 60 minutes at 350°F (175°C) for tube pan; 30 to 35 minutes for layer cake pans

□ QUANTITY: 6 cups batter, one 9-inch tube cake (serves 10) or one 2-layer 9-inch cake (serves 8 to 10)

□ PAN PREPARATION: Spread solid shortening on bottom and sides of pan, then dust evenly with flour; tap out excess flour.

3½ cups sifted cake flour (12¼ ounces; 350 g)
2 teaspoons baking soda
½ teaspoon salt
1 cup shelled pecans, chopped (4 ounces; 110 g)
½ cup currants (2¼ ounces; 65 g)
½ cup unsalted butter (1 stick; 110 g), at room temperature
½ cup margarine (4 ounces; 110 g), at room temperature
1½ cups granulated sugar (10½ ounces; 300 g)
4 large eggs
1¼ cups buttermilk
¼ cup dry sherry
2 teaspoons orange extract
Grated zest of 1½ large oranges, about 5 tablespoons

ICING:

Orange Wine Icing (page 398)

GARNISH:

Halved pecans or thin threads of orange zest

1. Prepare pan as described. Position rack in center of oven. Preheat oven to 350°F (175°C).
2. Sift together the flour, baking soda, and salt. Set aside. Combine nuts and currants in a bowl and toss with ¼ cup of the flour mixture. Set aside.
3. In the large bowl of an electric mixer,

cream together butter, margarine, and sugar until very light and fluffy. Add the eggs, one at a time, beating after each addition. The batter will look curdled; don't worry.

4. With the mixer on lowest speed, alternately add flour mixture and buttermilk to the batter, beginning and ending with flour. Beat to blend after each addition. Scrape down sides of bowl often. Beat in sherry and orange extract. Stir in grated orange zest and nut-currant mixture.

5. Spoon batter into prepared pan and smooth the top. Place in the oven to bake as directed, or until a cake tester inserted in the center comes out clean, and the top is golden and lightly springy to the touch. Cool the cake on a wire rack for 10 minutes, then top with another rack and invert. Lift off pan. Cool completely. Fill and frost a layer cake with Orange Wine Icing. For a tube cake, make the icing slightly softer than for a layer cake. Spread icing on the cake top and allow it to run down the sides. Garnish the cake top with halved pecans or fine threads of orange zest.

·*Variation:*·

ORANGE MADEIRA CAKE:

Prepare Williamsburg Orange Wine Cake with the following changes: In the batter, replace dry sherry with Madeira wine. For icing, make Orange Wine Icing, but replace dry sherry with Madeira wine. For topping: make a syrup of ¾ cup water, ½ cup granulated sugar (3½ ounces; 100 g), and ¼ cup Madeira. Boil for 3 or 4 minutes. Peel 2 or 3 oranges and cut out the sections, taking care to remove the membrane from each piece. Poach the peeled sections in the syrup for 4 to 5 minutes. Remove the orange sections with

a slotted spoon and drain on paper towels. Discard syrup. Ice the cake and top it with an arrangement of orange sections, or garnish with Candied Orange Peel (page 448).

Bourbon-Pecan Cake

■

This cake is a Southern classic, recommended especially for bourbon lovers. The liquor flavor is strong, and the cake is moist and rich with fruit and nuts. Serve it at holiday time, with a bourbon-sugar glaze decorated with candied cherries and halved pecans.

☐ ADVANCE PREPARATION: The cake may be baked well ahead, wrapped in a tea towel soaked with bourbon, and set in a plastic bag, then covered with heavy-duty foil or placed in a tin and stored in a cool place for several weeks. Or it can be baked ahead and frozen. Allow cake to age at room temperature for at least 2 days to mellow flavors before serving.

☐ SPECIAL EQUIPMENT: one 9-inch tube pan (6½-cup capacity) or springform tube pan, nut chopper or food processor, wax paper or baking parchment, scissors

☐ BAKING TIME: 40 to 45 minutes at 325°F (165°C)

☐ QUANTITY: 4 cups batter, one 9-inch tube cake (serves 10)

☐ PAN PREPARATION: Spread a little solid shortening on bottom and sides of tube pan, then line with wax paper or baking parchment. Spread solid shortening on paper.

*1½ cups sifted all-purpose flour (6¼
    ounces; 180 g)*
1 teaspoon baking powder
⅛ teaspoon salt
½ teaspoon ground cinnamon
2 teaspoons ground nutmeg
½ cup bourbon
*1½ cups shelled pecans, toasted (page
    43) and chopped fine (6 ounces; 180 g)*
½ cup currants (2¼ ounces; 65 g)
*½ cup lightly salted butter (1 stick;
    110 g)*
*1 cup (7 ounces; 200 g) plus 2
    tablespoons granulated sugar*
*3 large eggs, separated, at room
    temperature*

ICING:

Bourbon-flavored Icing Glaze (page 406)

1. Prepare pan as described. Position rack in center of oven. Preheat oven to 325°F (165°C).

2. Sift together flour, baking powder, salt, and cinnamon. Set aside. In a small bowl, combine nutmeg and bourbon and set aside to soak. In another bowl, combine the chopped pecans and the currants and toss with ½ cup of the flour mixture, coating fruit and nuts well.

3. In the large bowl of electric mixer, cream butter and 1 cup of the sugar until light and smooth. Add the egg yolks, one at a time, beating after each addition. Little by little, stir in the flour mixture, beating slowly to blend after each addition.

4. Add the bourbon-nutmeg mixture, and beat well to blend. Stir in floured nuts and currants, taking care to distribute them evenly throughout the batter. Batter will be quite stiff.

5. In a separate bowl with a clean beater, beat the egg whites until foamy. Add remaining 2 tablespoons sugar and beat until stiff peaks form. Stir about 1 cup of the beaten whites into the fruit batter to lighten it. Fold in remaining whites.

6. Spoon batter into prepared pan. Bake in the preheated oven for 40 to 45 minutes, or until a cake tester inserted in the center comes out clean and the top of the cake is lightly springy to the touch. Cool cake on a wire rack for 10 minutes. Top with another rack, invert, and lift off pan. Peel off paper. Cool completely. Wrap in a bourbon-soaked tea towel and set in a plastic container or other airtight wrapping to age, if you wish. Or prepare bourbon-flavored Icing Glaze and drizzle it on the cake top. While the glaze is still soft, set halved cherries and pecans into top for decoration.

Scripture Cake

■

Full of fruits and references from biblical times, this is a marvelous moist fruitcake. Checking chapter and verse while nibbling the cake will nourish your spirit as well as your body. There are many versions of this classic, and the citations vary depending on the source. This recipe was sent to me by a dedicated fan of my cookbooks, Mr. Schooner Sherman of Oak Park, Michigan, who notes that the original, with Old Testament citations, came to him from Rabbi Haim Halevy Donin of Oak Park.

□ ADVANCE PREPARATION: This cake can be made well ahead and frozen. It can also be wrapped airtight in heavy-duty foil and kept at room temperature for at least a week.

□ SPECIAL EQUIPMENT: one 10-inch bundt pan or springform tube, nut chopper or food processor; wax paper

□ BAKING TIME: 1½ to 2 hours at 300°F (150°C)

□ QUANTITY: About 6 cups batter, 10-inch tube cake (serves 12 to 14)

□ PAN PREPARATION: Spread bottom and sides of pan with solid shortening, then dust evenly with flour; tap out excess flour.

1½ cups sifted all-purpose flour (6¼ ounces; 180 g) [Leviticus 24:5]

2 teaspoons baking powder [Amos 4:5]

⅛ teaspoon salt [II Kings 2:20]

1 tablespoon ground cinnamon [Song of Solomon 4:14]

½ teaspoon ground cloves [II Chronicles 9:9]

½ cup unsalted butter (1 stick; 110 g), at room temperature [Genesis 18:8]

2 cups granulated sugar (14 ounces; 400 g) [Jeremiah 6:20]

2 tablespoons honey [I Samuel 14:25]

6 eggs, separated [Isaiah 10:14]

½ cup milk [Judges 4:19]

1 cup seedless raisins (5¾ ounces; 160 g) [I Samuel 30:12]

10 dried figs, chopped fine [Song of Solomon 2:13]

2 cups shelled almonds, chopped fine (10 ounces; 280 g) [Genesis 43:11]

1. Prepare pan as directed. Position rack in center of oven. Preheat oven to 300°F (150°C).

2. Sift together the flour, baking powder, salt, and spices on wax paper. Set aside.

3. In the large bowl of an electric mixer, cream together butter, sugar, and honey until light and smooth. Add egg yolks, one at a time, beating after each addition. With mixer on lowest speed, alternately add flour mixture and milk to batter, beginning and ending with flour. Beat after each addition just to blend.

4. Stir in raisins, chopped figs, and chopped almonds. The batter will be quite stiff.

5. In a separate bowl with a clean beater, beat the egg whites until they form stiff peaks. Stir about 1 cup of the whites into the batter to lighten it. Fold remaining whites into batter, 1 cup at a time. Spoon batter into prepared pan.

6. Place cake in the preheated oven and bake for about 1½ hours, or longer if necessary, until a cake tester inserted in the center comes out clean and the cake is well risen and golden brown. Cool on a wire rack for 10 minutes. Slide a knife blade between cake and sides of pan to loosen it, then top cake with another rack and invert. Lift off pan. Cool cake completely. Top with a serving platter and invert, so cake is right side up to serve.

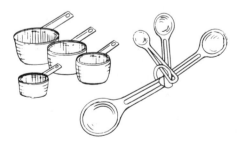

Old English Plum Pudding

•

Hallo! A great deal of steam! The pudding was out of the copper. A smell like a washing-day! That was the cloth. A smell like an eating-house and a pastrycook's next door to each other with a laundress's next door to that! That was the pudding! In half a minute Mrs. Cratchit entered—flushed but smiling proudly—with the pudding, like a speckled cannon-ball, so hard and firm, blazing in half of half a-quartern of ignited brandy, and bedight with Christmas holly stuck into the top.

Charles Dickens, *A Christmas Carol*, 1843

Often called simply Christmas Pudding, this steamed fruit-suet cake is the traditional grand finale to the English Christmas banquet. It is brought to the table as the dining room lights are lowered; the cake is decorated with a sprig of holly, set ablaze with warm brandy, and served with Brandy Hard Sauce. There is an old custom, still observed in some parts of England, whereby a silver charm or sixpence coin is wrapped in foil and tucked into the batter before the pudding is steamed. Whoever finds the charm or coin will have good luck in the coming year. Another custom has to do with the preparation of the batter itself. It is essential that every member of the family take a turn stirring the batter, always in a clockwise direction, while making a secret wish.

☐ ADVANCE PREPARATION: The fruits used in the pudding require at least an hour to macerate in the beer or brandy before the batter is prepared. After steaming, the pudding is wrapped in a brandy-soaked cloth and can be stored in a cool place for up to a month. The pudding may also be wrapped airtight and frozen. Always heat the pudding through just before serving.

☐ SPECIAL EQUIPMENT: Large, medium-size, and small mixing bowls, grater, wax paper, nut chopper, two 1-quart metal steaming molds with tight-fitting lids, or two heatproof bowls of equivalent size; steaming kettle (either 1 large kettle to hold 2 molds or 2 large pots with lids); rack set in bottom of pot to lift mold, aluminum foil, cotton string, scissors, knife with narrow blade, soup ladle or small syrup-server, serving platter

☐ FRUIT MACERATING TIME: 1 hour to 1 week

☐ STEAMING TIME: about 3 hours

☐ QUANTITY: two 1-quart puddings (serves 12)

☐ PAN PREPARATION: Generously butter the inside of the molds or heatproof bowls. Also butter sheets of foil for mold covers, and set out lengths of cotton string to tie foil onto the molds if they do not have their own lids. Set the molds in the steaming kettle to be sure they fit with the kettle covered. Fill the steaming kettle about half full of water, place the rack in the bottom, and set it aside.

PUDDING:

½ cup dried pitted dates (3½ ounces; 100 g), chopped
¾ cup seedless raisins (4½ ounces; 120 g)

½ cup golden raisins (2½ ounces; 70 g)

¼ cup currants (1⅛ ounces; 32 g)

¼ cup candied orange peel, chopped (1¾ ounces; 50 g) or citron

1 medium-large cooking apple such as Granny Smith, peeled, cored, and chopped to make 1 cup (4½ ounces; 120 g)

Grated zest and juice of 1 lemon

1½ cups beer or brandy or dark rum or cider or cranberry juice or buttermilk

4 large eggs

1¼ cups firmly packed dark brown sugar (11¾ ounces; 320 g)

2 tablespoons unsulfured molasses

½ cup shelled walnuts, coarsely chopped (2 ounces; 60 g)

1 cup firmly packed suet (4 ounces; 130 g), chopped by the butcher or ground in the food processor or meat grinder, membranes removed

½ cup fine dry unflavored bread crumbs (2 ounces; 60 g)

1 cup unsifted all-purpose flour (5 ounces; 140 g)

1 teaspoon salt

1½ teaspoons baking powder

¾ teaspoon baking soda

1 teaspoon ground cinnamon

½ teaspoon each of ground nutmeg, allspice, and mace

¼ teaspoon ground cloves

HARD SAUCE:

1 recipe Hard Sauce (page 417)

BRANDY:

¼ cup brandy, to pour over pudding and ignite

1. In a medium-size mixing bowl, combine all the dried and candied fruits. Add chopped apple, grated lemon zest and juice. Add beer or brandy, or other liquid, stir well, and set aside for 1 hour or longer while other ingredients are readied. Prepare molds as directed and set aside.

2. In a small bowl, beat together the eggs, brown sugar, and molasses. Set aside.

In the largest bowl, combine nuts, ground suet, and bread crumbs. Set a strainer over the bowl and add to it the flour, salt, baking powder, baking soda, and spices. Sift in all the dry ingredients. Stir to blend, then stir in the egg and brown-sugar mixture and the soaking mixture of fruits and brandy. Now stir in a clockwise direction, while making a wish, until very well blended.

3. Check to be sure the molds are well greased. If using bowls, cut 2 lengths of string to tie the foil around the tops during steaming. Fill the steaming kettles half full of water, set a rack in the bottom, cover the steamers, and set them on low heat until ready to use.

Spoon the batter into the greased molds, filling ¾ full. The batter will rise about 1 inch during baking, so leave room. To make the foil lid covers, cut the foil to fit inside a metal mold and butter one side of the foil. Top the mold with foil, buttered side down, attach the mold lid, securing it well. For a bowl, cut a piece of foil large enough to take a 1-inch pleat and still wrap generously around the bowl top. Pleat the foil in the center, butter it generously, and set it, buttered side down, over the filled mold. Crimp the foil to the bowl and tie with string to fasten. Fold the foil edge up over the string to secure (diagram a).

4. Set the filled and covered molds on a rack in a steamer. Add boiling water until it reaches about ½ to ⅔ of the way up the side of the mold (diagram b). Cover the steamers, bring the water to a boil, then lower the heat and boil slowly for about 3 hours. Check and add more boiling water if necessary to keep water level constant.

After 3 hours, check to see if pudding is baked. With potholders, remove a mold from the steamer. Remove the lid and/or foil. The pudding should look and feel spongy; a cake tester inserted in the center should come out clean. Rewrap and steam the pudding longer if necessary.

When done, remove molds from the steamers and set aside to cool, uncovered, for 10 to 15 minutes. When the pudding shrinks away from the sides of the mold, run a knife around the edge to loosen, then top with a plate and invert. Lift off the mold. The pudding may be prepared up to this point in advance.

5. Cool the steamed pudding completely, wrap in plastic wrap, and refrigerate; or wrap it airtight and freeze. Or wrap it in a brandy-soaked cloth, then place in a heavy-duty plastic bag and refrigerate for several weeks.

6. The pudding can be served while still warm from steaming; if stored, it should be returned to a bowl set in a steaming kettle and warmed through; this can take 45 to 60 minutes. Or wrap the pudding in foil and set it to bake on a pan in a 325°F oven for about 45 minutes. Transfer the hot pudding to a serving platter.

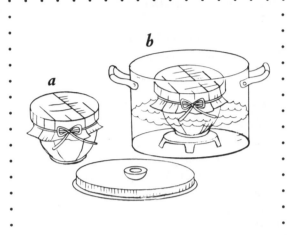

7. In a small syrup server or soup ladle, warm about ¼ cup brandy. Top the pudding with a sprig of holly. Just as the pudding is served, touch a match to the warm brandy and pour it over the top of the pudding (diagram c). As soon as the flames have died down, serve the pudding with a dollop of Hard Sauce.

Upside-Down

Cakes

Old-Fashioned Pineapple Upside-Down Cake

■

This old-fashioned country favorite is easy to prepare and tastes as good as it looks. Originally it was baked in an iron skillet, or "spider," and to my mind this is still the best method, though enameled cast-iron skillets are fine, and any pan that can go from stove top to oven can be used. The method is simple: Butter and brown sugar are melted together in a skillet on top of the stove, fruits and nuts are arranged in this sugar glaze, cake batter is poured on top, and the cake is placed in the oven to bake. When done, the cake is inverted onto a serving platter so that the glazed fruit is on top.

This process is a great one for kindling the interest of young bakers. I always remembered the fun I had as a child, making careful arrangements of fruit, covering them up with batter, then watching with eager anticipation (and a little breath-holding) for them to reappear when the cake was oh-so-carefully flipped upside down.

For the cake, you can use almost any plain sponge or 2-egg butter recipe. Mine is the latter, scented with a little cinnamon and honey. I find this combination goes well with the topping, which, though sweet, is balanced with tart fruit flavors (pineapple, apricot, cranberry).

Note: Old-Fashioned Pineapple Upside-Down Cake is actually a master recipe which lends itself to the many variations that follow: Ginger-Pear, Apple-Cranberry, Cranberry-Raisin, Apricot-Prune, and Peach-Pecan. Make up other fruit combinations to create your own favorites. Serve upside-down cake by itself or topped with lightly sweetened whipped cream.

□ ADVANCE PREPARATION: While this cake may be baked ahead and kept for a day or two if well covered, it is best by far when baked fresh and served warm.

□ SPECIAL EQUIPMENT: one 10-inch ovenproof heavy-bottomed skillet, such as cast iron or enameled iron, with ovenproof handle, or 10-inch round or square baking pan; 12-inch or larger flat serving platter, paper towels for draining fruit

□ COOKING TIME: butter-sugar glaze: 3 to 4 minutes; cake: 40 to 45 minutes in 325°F (165°C) oven

□ QUANTITY: 2½ cups cake batter, one 10-inch cake (serves 8 to 10)

□ PAN PREPARATION: butter-sugar glaze (see recipe)

PINEAPPLE TOPPING:

7 canned pineapple rings, drained, with
¼ cup juice reserved
7 Maraschino cherries, drained, or whole fresh or frozen cranberries
5 tablespoons lightly salted butter (2½ ounces; 70 g)
1 cup firmly packed dark brown sugar (9 ounces; 255 g)
12 to 15 halved pecans or walnuts (optional)

CAKE:

1½ cups sifted all-purpose flour (6¼ ounces; 180 g)
1 teaspoon baking powder
¼ teaspoon baking soda
⅛ teaspoon salt

½ teaspoon each of ground cinnamon and nutmeg
⅓ cup unsalted butter (5⅓ tablespoons; 80 g)
½ cup granulated sugar (3½ ounces; 100 g)
¼ cup honey (see Note)
2 large eggs
½ teaspoon vanilla extract
⅓ cup milk

Note: You can substitute ¼ cup granulated sugar for the honey; to do so, omit the baking soda and add 2 tablespoons additional milk to the batter.

SAUCE (OPTIONAL):

1 cup heavy cream, whipped with 2 tablespoons superfine sugar and 1 teaspoon vanilla extract

1. Preheat oven to 325°F (165°C).
2. Prepare topping: Drain pineapple rings, reserving ¼ cup juice and setting the fruit along with the cherries on paper towels to dry. Melt 5 tablespoons butter in a 10-inch ovenproof skillet set over moderate-low heat. Stir in the brown sugar, breaking it up with the back of a wooden spoon. Stir continually for 3 or 4 minutes, or until the mixture is creamy and begins to bubble. The sugar does not have to dissolve completely. Remove pan from heat. Stir in reserved ¼ cup pineapple juice. Take care here as the juice may splatter. Stir until smooth. Arrange 1 pineapple ring in the center of the pan with other rings around it. Set a cherry or cranberry in the center of each ring. Place nut halves, rounded side down,

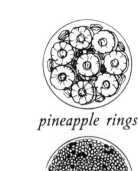
pineapple rings

ginger-pear

apple-cranberry-nut

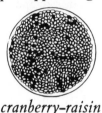
cranberry-raisin

apricot-prune

peach-pecan

between pineapple rings. Set pan aside.

3. Prepare cake batter: Sift together flour, baking powder, baking soda, salt, and spices. Set aside. In the large bowl of an electric mixer, beat together butter and sugar until creamy. Add the honey and beat until smooth. Add the eggs, one at a time, beating after each addition. Add the vanilla. Alternately add flour mixture and milk to the batter, beating slowly after each addition.

Note: This step can easily be done in a food processor, creaming butter, sugar, and honey first, then adding eggs and vanilla and pulsing briefly to blend. Add dry ingredients and milk and pulse only until smooth. Scrape down inside of workbowl several times.

4. Spoon batter over fruit in skillet. Bake in center of the preheated oven for 40 to 45 minutes, or until a cake tester inserted in the center comes out clean and the cake top is lightly springy to the touch.

5. Cool the cake on a wire rack for 3 or 4 minutes, until the glaze stops bubbling. Top the skillet with a large flat serving platter and, holding them together with potholders (the pan will be hot!), invert. Lift off skillet. Reposition on the cake any pieces of fruit that may have stuck to the pan. Serve cake while still warm so the sugar glaze will be soft and slightly runny. If you wish, prepare whipped cream with sugar and vanilla to serve alongside the cake.

·*Variations:*·

GINGER-PEAR
UPSIDE DOWN CAKE:

This is my family's favorite. The flavors are unusual and sophisticated, with maple syrup in both the topping glaze and the cake, and the bright tang of ginger to cut the sweetness.

Prepare Old-Fashioned Pineapple Upside-Down Cake with the following changes:

Replace pineapple topping with:

5 tablespoons lightly salted butter (2½ ounces; 70 g)
⅓ cup firmly packed light brown sugar (2¼ ounces; 70 g)
⅓ cup granulated sugar (2¼ ounces; 70 g)
¼ cup pure maple syrup
3 ripe pears, each about 6 to 7 ounces (200 g), peeled, cored, each one cut in 8 lengthwise slices and sprinkled with a little lemon juice to prevent discoloration; or use canned pears, sliced and well drained
3 tablespoons finely minced crystallized candied ginger

CAKE:

Prepare master recipe with the following changes:

Increase baking powder to 1½ teaspoons, increase salt to ¼ teaspoon, add 2 teaspoons ground ginger, substitute maple syrup for honey.

SAUCE:

Add to master recipe for whipped cream:

½ teaspoon ground ginger and 2 tablespoons finely minced crystallized candied ginger

Prepare topping as in master recipe, melting butter in a skillet and stirring in both sugars until smooth and bubbling. Stir in maple syrup. Add pear slices and cook in glaze for about 3 minutes, turning gently with 2 forks; cook for 1 minute after turning. Remove pan from heat. Arrange pears like flower petals with thin ends toward the center. If using canned pear halves, place them cut side up. Cut 1 piece to fit in the center. Sprinkle on the minced ginger.

Prepare cake as in master recipe.

APPLE-CRANBERRY-NUT UPSIDE-DOWN CAKE:

Use a good tart cooking apple for this cake; cranberries contribute brightness as well as flavor to balance the sugar glaze. Note: When cooked in a cast-iron skillet, the apples tend to darken in color somewhat after baking. To improve appearances, use a nonreactive skillet or sprinkle on a little nutmeg or brush warmed red currant jelly over the baked cake.

Prepare Old-Fashioned Pineapple Upside-Down Cake, with the following changes:

TOPPING:

Replace pineapple topping with:

5 tablespoons lightly salted butter (2½ ounces; 70 g)
1 cup firmly packed light brown sugar (7 ounces; 200 g)
½ teaspoon ground nutmeg
3 large tart cooking apples such as Granny Smith, each about 7 ounces (200 g), peeled, cored, and cut into ½-inch-thick rings
12 pecan or walnut halves
12 fresh or frozen whole cranberries, or substitute Maraschino cherries

Prepare topping as in master recipe, melting butter in the skillet, adding light brown sugar, and stirring over moderately low heat for 3 to 4 minutes, until creamy and bubbling. Add nutmeg and remove from heat. Arrange apple rings in the sugar glaze, placing 1 ring in the center and the others around it. Cut extra apples into pieces to fit between the rings. Add a cranberry or cherry in the center of each ring, and position remaining cranberries and nuts, rounded sides down, among the apples.

CAKE:

Prepare as in master recipe.

SAUCE:

Prepare as in master recipe. ·

CRANBERRY-RAISIN UPSIDE-DOWN CAKE:

This cake makes the most colorful presentation, with the sugar-glazed cranberries glowing like rubies. Be sure to use the light brown sugar because dark brown sugar dims the visual effect slightly. To retain the brightest berry color, use a nonreactive pan of stainless steel, enamel, or ovenproof glass; cast iron darkens the color of the sauce.

Prepare Old-Fashioned Pineapple Upside-Down Cake with the following changes:

TOPPING:

Replace pineapple topping with:

5 tablespoons lightly salted butter (2½ ounces; 70 g)

1 cup firmly packed light brown sugar (7 ounces; 200 g)
2 cups cranberries (8 ounces; 240 g), fresh or frozen, picked over and stems removed
½ cup seedless raisins (3 ounces; 85 g)
Grated zest of 1 orange

Prepare topping as in master recipe, melting butter in skillet, adding light brown sugar, and stirring over moderately low heat for 3 to 4 minutes, until creamy and bubbling. Toss cranberries and raisins together, then add them to the butter-sugar in the pan in an even layer and sprinkle them with orange zest. Set pan aside to cool while you prepare cake.

CAKE:

Prepare as in master recipe, and add grated zest of 1 orange to the finished batter. If you wish, you can replace the milk with orange juice.

SAUCE:

Use Vanilla Custard Sauce, Crème Anglaise (page 416), or serve with slightly sweetened heavy cream, unwhipped.

APRICOT-PRUNE UPSIDE-DOWN CAKE:

The color contrast between concentric rings of sugar-glazed bright orange apricots and blue-black prunes makes a particularly attractive presentation. Prepare Old-Fashioned Pineapple Upside-Down Cake, with the following changes:

Replace pineapple topping with:

*16 prunes, with or without pits (with
pits in, use about 5 ounces, 140 g)*
*46 dried apricot halves, about 1 cup
packed (9 ounces; 250 g)*
*5 tablespoons lightly salted butter (2½
ounces; 70 g)*
*1 cup firmly packed light brown sugar
(7 ounces; 200 g)*
½ teaspoon grated lemon zest

1. Combine prunes and apricots in a 2-quart
saucepan and cover them with water. Simmer
over moderate heat for about 20 minutes, until
fork tender. Drain the fruit. When cool
enough to touch, pit prunes if necessary. Set
fruit out on paper towels to dry.

2. Prepare topping as in master recipe, melting butter in skillet and stirring in sugar for
about 3 minutes, until creamy and bubbling.
Remove from heat and stir in lemon zest.
Arrange apricots, cut side up and overlapping
slightly, in a ring around outside edge of skillet. Arrange a ring of prunes, end to end, just
inside apricots. Make another ring of apricots,
then fill the center with remaining prunes.

CAKE:

*Prepare as in master recipe but omit cinna-
mon, nutmeg, and baking soda and in place
of honey use granulated sugar along with 2
tablespoons extra milk.*

SAUCE:

Prepare as in master recipe.

PEACH-PECAN UPSIDE-DOWN CAKE:

A marvelous cake, especially when made with
fresh ripe peaches.

Prepare Old-Fashioned Pineapple Upside-
Down Cake with the following changes:

TOPPING:

Replace pineapple topping with:

*5 tablespoons lightly salted butter (2½
ounces; 70 g)*
*1 cup firmly packed light brown sugar
(7 ounces; 200 g)*
½ teaspoon ground nutmeg
*3 medium-size ripe peaches, each about
4 ounces (120 g), peeled, halved, and
pitted. Cut each half into 5
wedge-shaped slices; or use about 30
canned peach slices, well drained*
½ cup pecan halves (2 ounces; 60 g)

Prepare topping as in master recipe, melting
butter in skillet, stirring in light brown sugar
for about 3 minutes, until creamy and bubbling. Add nutmeg and remove from heat.
Hold out 6 peach slices, then arrange the rest
side by side in a ring around the pan. In the
center, arrange 4 of the reserved slices end-to-
end; put the last 2 slices facing each other in
the middle. Arrange nuts, curved side down,
among peach slices.

CAKE:

Prepare as in master recipe.

SAUCE:

Prepare as in master recipe.

Coffee Cakes,

Tea Cakes, Kuchen &

Pudding Cakes

Basic Yeast-Risen Coffee Cake

This is a basic recipe for a moderately sweet yeast-risen coffee cake; the dough is breadlike in texture. It can be used with any type of filling and molded into any shape. You can vary the flavor by adding, for example, orange juice and grated orange zest, or almond extract; vary the sweetness of the dough by adding more or less sugar. Recipes for fillings follow. For a richer dough, see the variation for Honey-Yogurt Yeast Coffee Cake, following the basic recipe.

□ ADVANCE PREPARATION: Dough must rise twice, for a total of about 2 to 2½ hours, so plan your time accordingly. Dough can be prepared ahead and kept refrigerated for a couple of days (see step 5). Baked cakes can be wrapped airtight and frozen. Thaw and serve warm for best flavor.

□ SPECIAL EQUIPMENT: large heavy mixing bowl, baking sheet, wire wisk, wooden spoon, pastry brush, aluminum foil

□ BAKING TIME: about 30 minutes at 350°F (170°C)

□ QUANTITY: 2 loaves or cakes

□ PAN PREPARATION: Spread butter, margarine, or oil on pan.

½ cup warm water (105° to 110°F)

1 teaspoon granulated sugar

2 packages active dry yeast (each ¼ ounce; 7 g)

⅔ cup granulated sugar (4½ ounces; 130 g)

1 teaspoon salt

1 cup lukewarm milk, or orange juice for orange-flavored cake

2 large eggs, at room temperature, lightly beaten

2 teaspoons grated orange or lemon zest (optional)

1 teaspoon ground cardamom

½ cup unsalted butter (1 stick; 110 g), melted and cooled to room temperature

4 to 6 cups all-purpose flour (20 to 30 ounces; 560 to 840 g), or more as needed

FILLING:

See recipe ideas that follow; note that fillings are for half of the dough.

EGG GLAZE:

1 egg beaten with 1 tablespoon water

ICING GLAZE (OPTIONAL):

Any icing glaze (see Index)

1. In a large heavy mixing bowl, combine warm (105 to 115°F) water (use thermometer to be accurate) and 1 teaspoon sugar. Sprinkle on the yeast and let sit for about 5 minutes until the mixture looks bubbly.

2. Use a wire whisk to blend in sugar, salt, warm milk or orange juice, beaten eggs, grated zest if using it, cardamom, and melted and cooled butter.

3. With a wooden spoon, stir in 1 cup of flour at a time, mixing until the dough forms a soft ball. Note that the total amount of flour used will vary with dampness of weather, type of liquid used in recipe, etc. Add a little more flour if necessary, to make dough ball pull away from bowl sides.

4. Turn dough out onto a floured work surface and knead for about 5 minutes, adding flour, 1 tablespoon at a time, to prevent dough from sticking. When dough feels smooth and appears to be satiny, place it in a large, oiled mixing bowl. Turn dough ball once to oil all its surfaces. Top dough with a piece of oiled wax paper or plastic wrap and set aside in a draft-free location to rise for 1½ hours, until doubled in bulk. The dough has risen enough when you poke 2 fingers into the top and the depressions remain. Punch down the dough ball to deflate it and remove excess gas bubbles.

5. Turn the dough out onto a floured work surface and divide it into halves.

Note: To hold the dough for later use, refrigerate all the dough in a bowl, covered with a plate. Check under the plate several times and punch down dough each time it rises; dough will keep overnight. Bring dough to room temperature before continuing recipe.

Select fillings. To shape and fill cakes try the following techniques. To bake cakes, follow steps 6 and 7.

6. Place shaped cake on a buttered baking sheet and top with oiled wax paper or plastic wrap. Set aside in a draft-free location to rise until not quite doubled in bulk; better to un-

derrise dough now than to overdo it; it will rise more as it bakes. Preheat oven to 350°F (170°C).

7. When the dough has risen, brush the top with the egg glaze. Place the cake in the preheated oven and bake for about 30 minutes, or until the cake is golden brown on top and sounds hollow when tapped with your knuckle. If top browns too quickly, protect it with a piece of foil while continuing to bake. Use a spatula to help slide the cake off the flat baking sheet. Cool on a wire rack. If you wish, the cake can be topped with Icing Glaze. For holiday cakes, set blanched almonds or pecans and halved candied cherries into the glaze before it sets.

ROLLED HORSESHOE

Use half of the dough to make 1 horseshoe. After the first rising, punch down the dough, then press it out into a flat rectangle about 11 × 15 inches and ¼ inch thick. Brush the dough with melted and cooled butter (omit butter if filling with jam) to within ½ inch of edges. Spread filling mixture over butter, or spread jam filling directly on dough (a). Beginning at one long side, roll up dough like a jelly roll. Seal edges and ends with brushed-on egg glaze, pinching dough together (b). Carefully slide dough onto a buttered baking sheet, placing the seam side down. Curve the roll into a horseshoe shape. With a sharp knife or razor blade, make several slashes about ⅛ inch deep in the top of the dough (c).

SPIRAL TWIST

Use half of the dough to make 1 twist. Prepare Rolled Horsheshoe, but leave cake in a straight line. Slide the cake onto a buttered baking sheet, seam side down. The roll will now be about 14 inches long. Along one side of the roll, make 6 cuts 2-inches apart reaching

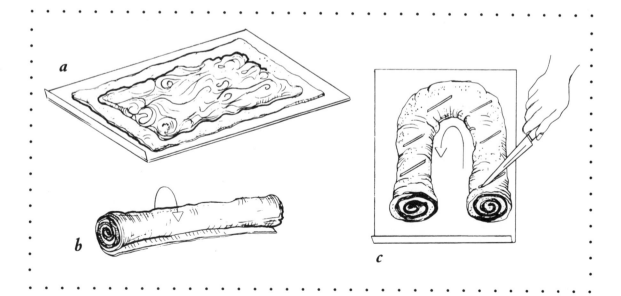

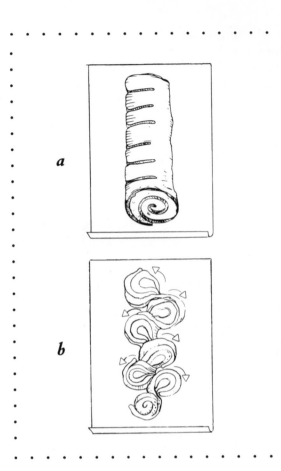

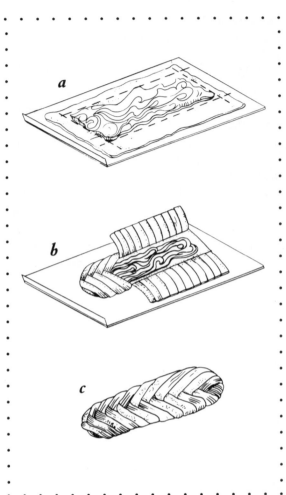

¾ of the way across the roll (a). Lift the first segment, turn it cut side up, and set it flat, with the filled spiral facing up. Lift the next segment, turn it cut side up, and pull it toward the right side of the roll; set it flat. Lift the third segment cut side up and position it to the left side, as shown (b). Repeat.

TOP BRAID

Use half of the dough to make 1 braid. After the dough has had the first rising, press it out into a rectangle about 11 × 15 inches and ¼ inch thick on a buttered baking sheet. Mark-

ing the dough very lightly with the back of a knife, divide it lengthwise into thirds and mark 1-inch borders on each short end. Brush melted butter over the central area, then sprinkle on the filling; omit the butter if using jam (a). With a sharp knife, cut slanted parallel strips about 1 inch wide on each side of the filling (b). To make the top braid, fold the strips alternately across the filling. Overlap the strips so the end of each one hides the start of the next (c).

HONEY-YOGURT YEAST COFFEE CAKE:

This is also an all-purpose yeast-risen dough. It is a little richer and more flavorful than the Basic Yeast-Risen Coffee Cake.

½ cup warm water (105° to 110°F)
1 teaspoon granulated sugar
2 packages active dry yeast (each ¼ ounce; 7 g)
⅓ cup honey
1 teaspoon salt
1 cup plain yogurt or sour cream
2 eggs, at room temperature, lightly beaten
1 teaspoon grated lemon or orange zest
1 teaspoon ground cinnamon
½ cup unsalted butter (1 stick; 110 g), melted and cooled to room temperature
4 to 6 cups all-purpose flour (20 to 30 ounces; 560 to 840 g), as needed

EGG GLAZE:

1 egg beaten with 1 tablespoon water

Follow procedure for Basic Yeast-Risen Coffee Cake, but in step 2, whisk into yeast mixture the honey, salt, yogurt or sour cream, beaten eggs, grated zest, cinnamon and melted and cooled butter.

Fillings for Yeast-Risen Coffee Cakes

■

Each recipe is enough to fill 1 cake, made from half of the total yeast dough recipe.

APPLE-NUT FILLING

☐ QUANTITY: about 2¼ cups, for 1 coffee cake

1½ cups coarsely chopped peeled apples (6 ounces; 170 g)
3 tablespoons golden raisins, optional
½ cup currants (2¼ ounces; 65 g)
½ cup granulated sugar (3½ ounces; 100 g) or firmly packed light brown sugar
1 teaspoon ground cinnamon
½ cup shelled and chopped walnuts or pecans, (2 ounces; 60 g)
3 tablespoons unsalted butter, melted and cooled

In a large bowl, combine apples, raisins, currants, sugar, cinnamon, and nuts. Toss them well. Shape the dough according to directions, then brush the dough with melted butter. Sprinkle on filling. Complete the shaping and baking as directed.

STREUSEL FILLING

☐ QUANTITY: about 1¼ cups, enough to fill 1 coffee cake

⅓ cup firmly packed dark brown sugar
  (3 ounces; 85 g)
3½ tablespoons butter (lightly salted
  has best flavor for this purpose), at
  room temperature, cut up
5 tablespoons all-purpose flour,
  unsifted
½ cup shelled and finely chopped
  walnuts (2 ounces; 60 g)
Generous ⅛ teaspoon each of ground
  cinnamon and nutmeg
3 tablespoons unsalted butter, melted
  and cooled

In a mixing bowl, combine brown sugar, cut-up butter, flour, nuts, and spices. With your fingertips, pinch ingredients together to make crumbs. If the butter is too warm, the mixture will clump rather than crumble and should be chilled for a while.

Shape the dough, brush melted butter over it, sprinkle on the filling, and complete shaping and baking as directed.

POPPYSEED-STREUSEL FILLING

☐ QUANTITY: 1 ⅓ cups, for 1 coffee cake

Make Streusel Filling and add ⅓ cup poppyseeds (1½ ounces; 45 g).

JAM FILLING

☐ QUANTITY: 1 cup, for 1 coffee cake

1 cup thick preserves or jam such as
  apricot, raspberry, blackberry,
  lingonberry

BUBBLE RING COFFEE CAKE:

In this variation on yeast-risen coffee cake, the dough is filled with raisins and nuts, coated with cinnamon sugar, and formed into small balls that rise together in a tube pan.

☐ SPECIAL EQUIPMENT: one tube pan 10 × 4 inches, small saucepan, 2 small bowls

☐ BAKING TIME: 45 to 50 minutes at 350°F (175°C)

☐ PAN PREPARATION: Generously butter the tube pan.

CAKE:

½ recipe for either Basic Yeast-Risen Coffee Cake or Honey-Yogurt Yeast Coffee Cake

TOPPING:

¼ cup lightly salted butter (2 ounces;
  57 g), melted
1 cup granulated sugar (7 ounces;
  200 g)
2 teaspoons ground cinnamon

FILLING:

⅓ cup seedless raisins (2 ounces, 57 g)
  or currants
⅓ cup shelled walnuts, chopped (1¼
  ounces; 40 g)

1. Prepare dough, following steps 1 through 5; allow the dough to rise once and punch it down.

2. Set the melted butter on the counter near the dough and the buttered tube pan. In one small bowl combine sugar and cinnamon. In the second bowl combine raisins and nuts.

3. Pinch off pieces of dough about 1 inch in diameter and roll them into balls between your palms. Dip each ball into butter, shake off excess, then roll the ball in the cinnamon sugar. Set the ball in the bottom of the buttered tube pan. Repeat, covering the pan bottom with 1 layer of balls (diagram a).

Sprinkle on all the raisin-nut filling. Top this with another layer or two, depending on size of your pan, of buttered and sugared dough balls. Sprinkle on any remaining cinnamon-sugar.

4. Set the pan in a draft-free location and let the dough rise until not quite doubled in bulk. Bake in the preheated oven as directed, or until the cake top is golden brown and the topping feels crisp (diagram b). When the cake is tapped, it should sound hollow. Tip the cake out of the pan and cool it on a plate or a wire rack. To serve it, pick off the bubbles of dough. For best flavor, serve warm.

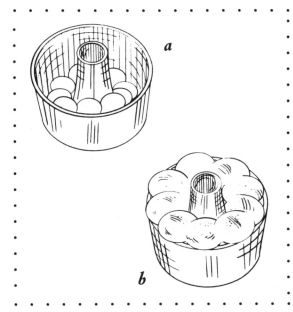

Kugelhopf

∎

Kugelhopf is a delicious Eastern European coffee ring with as many variations in the spelling of its name as there are regional differences in the recipe. You may see it listed as *gugelhapf, kugelhuf, gugelhopf* or *kugelhoff*. In Alsace, it is a sweet yeast bread containing dried fruits; in Poland it is a plain yeast cake; in Germany it is a sandy-textured pound cake lightened with egg whites. In Austria, it can be either a sweet yeast cake studded with kirsch-soaked raisins or a rich raisin pound-cake with plain vanilla or marbled batter, occasionally—in Vienna's most elegant coffeehouses—napped with vanilla or bitter chocolate icing glaze.

The one thing all of these have in common is their shape, for kugelhopf is traditionally baked in a fluted ring or Turk's-head mold that is buttered and lined with sliced almonds before the batter is put in to rise. Once baked, the kugelhopf is garnished with a light dusting of confectioners' sugar.

The following recipe was given to me by a Viennese baker. It is a moderately sweet yeast dough that, curiously, is also lightened with stiffly beaten egg whites. Unlike most yeast recipes, this one has just one very short (25-minute) rising period, and produces a fine-grained, tender-crumbed product halfway between a bread and a cake. It is perfect for late afternoon tea or coffee, or for breakfast, toasted and covered with melting sweet butter.

I am aware of only one variation on the traditional shape of the kugelhopf: in France on the first day of April, bakeries set their kugelhopf dough to rise in molds with the shape of fish. This curious "fish cake" owes its origin to the April first holiday known as April Fool's Day. Before the sixteenth century, many countries celebrated their New Year at the end of March, near the time of the spring equinox. It was not until late in the sixteenth century when Pope Gregory XIII devised a new calendar, that the date of the new year was permanently changed to January 1 in western countries. France was the first country to adopt this new Gregorian calendar.

News traveled slowly in those days, and many people, either because they did not know of the changed date or because they were loathe to accept it, continued to celebrate the new year in the spring. Those who insisted on maintaining the old date were called poissons d'Avril, *literally, April Fish, though the expression entered the English language as April Fool(s). French children receive chocolate fish on this day, and play jokes on one another as we do in the United States, while bakers display fish-shaped kugelhopf.*

□ ADVANCE PREPARATION: Raisins are soaked in kirsch or rum for about 30 minutes before adding them to the batter. Prepare this in advance. The cake rises for about 25 minutes before baking, so plan your time accordingly. The cake can be baked ahead, wrapped airtight, and frozen.

□ SPECIAL EQUIPMENT: one 8-cup kugelhopf mold 9 inches in diameter, strainer that fits into a saucepan with lid, separate bowl and beater for egg whites, small soup bowl

□ RISING TIME: 25 minutes

□ BAKING TIME: 40 minutes at 400°F (204°C)

□ QUANTITY: one 9-inch Kugelhopf tube cake (serves 10 to 12)

□ PAN PREPARATION: Generously spread solid shortening on inner surface of pan, taking special care in the depths of each flute. Sprinkle about ⅓ cup sliced blanched almonds in greased pan and shake to coat sides and bottom. Tap out excess. Place 1 whole blanched almond into each flute in the bottom of the pan; these will form a decorative nut ring on top of the baked cake.

15 whole blanched almonds
⅓ cup sliced blanched almonds
    (1 ounce; 30 g)
⅓ cup seedless raisins (2 ounces; 60 g)
⅓ cup golden raisins (1⅓ ounces;
    40 g)
3 tablespoons kirsch or rum
½ cup warm milk (110°F)
½ cup (3½ ounces; 100 g) plus 2
    tablespoons granulated sugar
2 packages active dry yeast (each ¼
    ounce; 7 g)
4 large eggs, separated, plus 1 extra
    egg white
½ cup lightly salted butter (1 stick;
    110 g), plus 2 tablespoons, melted
    and cooled
Grated zest of 1 lemon
½ cup milk
¼ teaspoon salt
4⅓ cups sifted all-purpose flour (18½
    ounces; 525 g)

ICING:

1 or 2 tablespoons confectioners' sugar
(optional)

1. Prepare the Kugelhopf pan as directed. Measure a couple of inches of water into the bottom of a saucepan. Set the strainer over the pan and add both types of raisins. Cover the strainer with the pan lid and set over high heat. Bring the water to a boil and steam the raisins for about 5 minutes. Remove from heat. The raisins should be soft and plump. Place them in a small bowl with the kirsch or rum, stir well, and macerate for about 30 minutes.

2. In another small bowl, combine the warm (110°F) milk with 1 tablespoon of the measured sugar. Sprinkle on the yeast and let stand for about 5 minutes, until the mixture bubbles.

3. In a very large mixing bowl, combine egg yolks, remaining sugar, melted and cooled butter, grated lemon zest, ½ cup milk, the salt, and the raisins with their liqueur. Stir well to combine. Stir in the yeast mixture.

4. Stir about 2 cups of flour into the mixture, stirring hard to combine. At this point, set the dough aside for a few minutes, and use the electric mixer to beat the 5 egg whites until stiff but not dry.

Stir 1 more cup flour into the dough. When well blended, gently stir in about 1 cup of the stiff whites. It looks impossible at first, but the whites will blend after a few stirs, and will soften the dough. Little by little, fold in remaining whites; have patience and a light hand, because quick stirs will flatten the whites. Finally, sprinkle on remaining 1⅓ cups flour, a little at a time, folding it into the dough.

5. Turn the dough into the prepared pan, smooth the top, and cover the pan with a piece of oiled wax paper. Set in a warm, draft-free location for about 25 minutes.

6. Preheat oven to 400°F (204°C). Place the kugelhopf on the center rack and bake for about 40 minutes, or until the top is a rich golden brown and a cake tester inserted in the center comes out clean. Cool the pan on a wire rack for about 5 minutes, then invert the cake onto the rack, lift off the pan, and cool the cake completely. Sift on a tablespoon or two of confectioners' sugar before serving.

Fresh Berry Coffee Cake

■

This quick and easy-to-prepare coffee cake is filled with plump fresh berries and topped with cinnamon-scented crumbs. This is a great cake to make in the late summer berry season, using whichever berries are ripe. My favorites are blueberries and raspberries, but you can use strawberries, blackberries, or even fresh ripe peaches, sliced thin and mixed in with the berries. For a great breakfast or brunch treat, serve this cake warm from the oven, topped with Warm Berry Sauce (page 418).

□ ADVANCE PREPARATION: The cake can be made ahead, though the flavor is best when served warm from the oven. Freezing changes the texture of the fruit and lessens its quality.

□ SPECIAL EQUIPMENT: one 8- or 9-inch-square baking pan 2 inches deep, colander, paper towels

□ BAKING TIME: 30 to 35 minutes at 350°F (175°C)

□ QUANTITY: 2½ cups batter, one 8- or 9-inch-square cake (serves 8 or 9)

□ PAN PREPARATION: Spread solid shortening on bottom and sides of pan.

1½ cups sifted all-purpose flour (6¼ ounces; 180 g)
1 teaspoon baking powder
¼ teaspoon salt
½ cup unsalted butter or margarine (1 stick; 110 g), at room temperature
1 cup granulated sugar (7 ounces; 200 g)
2 large eggs

1 teaspoon vanilla extract
3 tablespoons sour cream
⅓ cup milk
1½ cups fresh blueberries (7½ ounces; 210 g), or other berries, washed, picked over, and dried on paper towels. Note: Frozen whole berries, unthawed, ice crystals removed, may be substituted, or you can combine peeled and sliced peaches with the berries

CRUMB TOPPING:

3 tablespoons butter (1½ ounces; 45 g), at room temperature
⅓ cup granulated sugar (2¼ ounces; 65 g)
¼ cup unsifted all-purpose flour (1¼ ounces; 35 g)
½ teaspoon ground cinnamon

1. Prepare pan as described. Position rack in the center of oven. Preheat oven to 350°F (175°C).

2. Sift together flour, baking powder, and salt. Set aside.

3. In the large bowl of an electric mixer, cream together butter and sugar until smooth. Add eggs, one at a time, beating after each addition. Add vanilla and sour cream and mix well. Alternately add flour mixture and milk to batter, beginning and ending with flour.

4. Spread half of the batter into the prepared pan and smooth the top. Spread berries on top of batter. Cover berries with remaining batter and spread the top as even as possible with a rubber scraper; some berries will show through and the top will look a little rough. Never mind.

5. Prepare the crumb topping. In a medium-size bowl, combine all topping ingredients and pinch them together with your fingertips to blend, making crumbs. Spread the crumbs evenly over top of cake. Place pan in the oven and bake for 30 to 35 minutes, or until a cake tester inserted in the center comes out clean and the cake top is a golden brown. Cool cake on a wire rack for a few minutes, then cut into squares and serve warm or at room temperature from the pan.

Date Nut Coffee Cake

·

The texture of this recipe is more like a cake than a common quick-bread style date-nut loaf. This is moist and dark, topped with melted brown-sugar icing, and perfect for dunking into a morning's cup of coffee.

☐ ADVANCE PREPARATION: Cake can be prepared ahead and frozen. Thaw and serve warm for best flavor.

☐ SPECIAL EQUIPMENT: one sheet pan 9 × 13 inches, 3 mixing bowls, 2-cup measure, table knife or icing spatula

☐ BAKING TIME: 45 minutes at 350°F (175°C)

☐ QUANTITY: about 8½ cups batter, 1 sheet cake 9 × 13 inches (serves 12)

☐ PAN PREPARATION: Spread solid shortening on bottom and sides of pan, dust pan with flour; tap out excess flour.

1½ cups pitted dates (10½ ounces; 300 g), chopped
1 cup hot water
3 cups sifted all-purpose flour (12¾ ounces; 360 g)
1 cup shelled walnuts, chopped (4 ounces; 110 g)
2 teaspoons baking powder
2 teaspoons baking soda
¼ teaspoon salt
½ cup lightly salted butter (1 stick; 110 g), softened
1 cup granulated sugar (7 ounces; 200 g)
2 large eggs
1 cup hot strong coffee
¾ cup milk
1 teaspoon vanilla extract

ICING:

⅔ cup firmly packed dark brown sugar (6 ounces; 170 g)
¼ cup lightly salted butter (2 ounces; 60 g)

1. Prepare pan as described. Position rack in lower third of oven. Preheat oven to 350°F (175°C).

2. In a mixing bowl, combine dates and hot water. Stir and set aside to soak.

3. In a small mixing bowl, combine ¼ cup of the sifted flour with the chopped walnuts. Set aside. Sift together remaining flour, the baking powder, baking soda, and salt. Set aside.

4. In the large bowl of an electric mixer, cream together butter and sugar until well blended. Add eggs, one at a time, beating after each addition. In a 2-cup measure, combine

coffee, milk, and vanilla. Add flour mixture alternately with coffee mixture to batter, beating slowly after each addition, beginning and ending with flour. Finally, stir in dates and soaking liquid and walnut-flour mixture, and blend well.

5. Pour batter into prepared pan and bake in the preheated oven for 45 minutes, or until a cake tester inserted in the center comes out clean. While cake bakes, prepare icing by mixing together the brown sugar and butter. As soon as the cake comes from the oven, spread the icing over the cake with a knife or spatula. The icing will melt onto the cake. When the cake is cold, cut into squares and serve from the pan.

- -

Yogurt Crumb Cake

∎

This delightfully moist orange-scented cake is made with fruit-flavored yogurt and has crunchy cinnamon-walnut crumbs for both filling and topping.

□ ADVANCE PREPARATION: This cake can be baked ahead and frozen. Thaw and serve warm.

□ SPECIAL EQUIPMENT: nut chopper or food processor, grater, one sheet pan 11¾ × 7½ × 1¾ inches or 9-inch-square pan 2 inches deep, small bowl

□ BAKING TIME: 35 to 40 minutes at 350°F (175°C)

□ QUANTITY: 2½ cups batter, one sheet cake 11¾ × 7½ inches (serves 12), or one 9-inch-square cake (serves 9)

□ PAN PREPARATION: Spread solid shortening on bottom and sides of pan.

1½ cups sifted all-purpose flour (6¼ ounces; 180 g)
1½ teaspoons baking powder
¼ teaspoon baking soda
Pinch of salt
6 tablespoons lightly salted butter or margarine (3 ounces; 90 g), at room temperature
¾ cup granulated sugar (5¼ ounces; 150 g)
1 large egg
1 teaspoon vanilla extract
1 teaspoon orange extract
Grated zest of 1 orange, about 1 tablespoon
¾ cup orange-flavored yogurt, or lemon- or apricot-flavored yogurt, or substitute plain yogurt or sour cream

CRUMB TOPPING:

3 tablespoons dark brown sugar
1 teaspoon ground cinnamon
¾ cup shelled walnuts, chopped (3 ounces; 85 g)

1. Prepare pan as directed. Position rack in center of oven. Preheat oven to 350°F (175°C).
2. Sift together flour, baking powder, baking soda, and salt. Set aside. In a small bowl, combine all ingredients for Crumb Topping. Set aside.

3. In the large bowl of an electric mixer, cream together the butter and sugar until well blended. Beat in the egg, vanilla and orange extracts, and grated orange zest.

4. Alternately add flour mixture and yogurt to the batter, beating slowly after each addition. When well blended, spoon half of the batter into the prepared pan. Sprinkle half of the crumb topping mixture over the batter, then top with remaining batter. Sprinkle on remaining crumb topping.

5. Bake in center of preheated oven for 45 to 50 minutes, or until a cake tester inserted in the center comes out clean and top is golden brown. Cool on a wire rack. Cut into 2½- or 3-inch squares and serve warm or at room temperature directly from the pan.

Patsy Stroble's Oat Scones

■

Leeze me on thee [Commend me to],
  John Barleycorn,
    Thou king o'grain!
On thee aft Scotland chows her cood [chews
    her cud]
In souple scones, the wale [pick]
    o'food.

  "*Scotch Drink,*" Robert Burns, 1787

Scones are small tea cakes, classics of the British Isles and particularly of Scotland, which, as Robert Burns notes, claims them as one of her national dishes.

There are innumerable regional variations on the scone and devotees partial to each. They can be made with butter or cream, white or whole-wheat flour, potatoes or potato flour, oats, wheat germ, sweet milk, buttermilk, or sour cream. They can contain chopped nuts, cheese, raisins, or currants, like the version from Northern England known as Singing Hinnies, whose name refers to the sound made as the batter sizzles on the stovetop griddle.

I suppose that a case could be made against including scones in a cake book, but I have two compelling reasons for doing so. The first is that scones are often baked in a round cake form before they are cut into serving wedges; they are traditionally related to shortcakes, crumpets, and muffins—all loosely connected to the coffee cake family. The second reason is that I want to know where to find this recipe at all times, for these are the best scones I have ever had, and they are an essential part of my life.

This is the first public appearance of the recipe, which has, until she agreed to share it with me for the book, been the closely guarded secret of Patsy Stroble, the charming baker/owner of the Stroble Baking Company in Kent, Connecticut. Patsy and her scones are a treasure in Litchfield County, and customers drive from states around to find them. Born in Indiana, Patsy opened her small attractive shop here in 1983, and with the help of her two daughters, Karen and Laura, she literally built the business from scratch, making her own kitchen cabinets and shelves with just as much love as she puts into the scones. She raises chickens, sells their eggs, and is proud to advertise that she bakes exclusively with butter, avoids all preservatives, and has never had a baking mix in the shop. Her fans are true believers. At the height of the summer season, when the small New England village of Kent caters to many weekending New Yorkers, Patsy sells up to 20 dozen oat scones a day, to say nothing of the myriad cakes, pastries, and armloads of freshly baked French bread that disappear at an alarming rate.

☐ ADVANCE PREPARATION: Scones may be baked in advance, wrapped airtight, and frozen. Thaw and warm in the oven before serving, or thaw in the microwave.

☐ SPECIAL EQUIPMENT: mixing bowl and wooden spoon, medium-size bowl and whisk, small saucepan, 9-inch cake pan, sharp knife with blade at least 10 inches long, flat baking sheet, baking parchment (optional), rubber spatula, flat spatula or pancake turner.

☐ BAKING TIME: 15 to 17 minutes at 400°F (205°C)

☐ QUANTITY: 12 scones

☐ PAN PREPARATION: Spread solid shortening on the flat baking sheet or cover it with ungreased baking parchment

2/3 cup lightly salted butter (10 2/3 tablespoons; 160 g), melted and cooled; do not use unsalted butter

1/3 cup milk

1 large egg

1 1/2 cups unsifted all-purpose flour (7 1/2 ounces; 210 g)

1 1/4 cups "old-fashioned" rolled oats, not instant oats (3 1/2 ounces; 100 g)

1/4 cup granulated sugar (1 3/4 ounces; 50 g)

1 tablespoon baking powder

1 teaspoon cream of tartar

1/2 teaspoon salt

1/2 cup currants (2 ounces; 60 g)

1. Prepare pan as described. Position rack in lower third of oven. Preheat oven to 400°F (205°C).

2. In a medium-size bowl, whisk together the melted butter, milk, and egg. In a large mixing bowl, combine without sifting all remaining ingredients. Stir or toss to blend the dry ingredients and coat the currants with flour.

3. Add the liquid ingredients to the dry and stir with a rubber spatula or wooden spoon just to blend them together. The batter will be quite stiff and will quickly form into a ball. Do not overwork the batter; the less handling it has the lighter the scones will be.

4. Place the 9-inch pan upside down on the counter and lightly dust the pan bottom, now facing up, with flour. Put the scone batter on the floured surface and pat it into a flat cake about 3/4 inch thick. It should reach out to the rim of the pan.

With a sharp long-bladed knife, cut the cake into 12 even wedges. To do this, simply divide the cake into quarters and cut each quarter into thirds. With a metal spatula or pancake turner, transfer the scone wedges to the prepared baking sheet, setting them about 1 inch apart, in alternating directions, so they fit on one pan.

Bake the scones in the preheated oven for 15 to 17 minutes, or until the tops are slightly browned and the bottoms are a rich golden brown. Cool the scones on a wire rack. Serve them warm or at room temperature, accompanied by hot tea or coffee.

Date-Nut Chocolate Bundt Cake

■

This rich moist coffee cake is chock-full of dates, walnuts, and bits of chocolate—perfect for a picnic, an elegant brunch, or afternoon tea.

□ ADVANCE PREPARATION: The cake can be prepared ahead, wrapped airtight, and frozen. Bring to room temperature before serving.

□ SPECIAL EQUIPMENT: small mixing bowl, chopping board and knife, 9-inch bundt or tube pan

□ BAKING TIME: 45 to 55 minutes at 350°F (175°C)

□ QUANTITY: 4 cups batter, one 9-inch bundt cake (serves 10 to 12)

□ PAN PREPARATION: Spread solid shortening on bottom and sides of pan, dust evenly with flour; tap out excess flour.

7 ounces pitted dates, cut into ½-inch chunks (1 cup; 200 g)
1 teaspoon baking soda
1 cup very hot water
½ cup margarine or butter (1 stick; 110 g), at room temperature
1 cup granulated sugar (7 ounces; 200 g)
2 large eggs
1 teaspoon vanilla extract
1⅓ cups sifted all-purpose flour (5¾ ounces; 165 g)
½ teaspoon ground cinnamon
2 tablespoons unsweetened cocoa, any type

½ cup shelled and coarsely chopped walnuts, (2 ounces; 60 g)
6 ounces semisweet chocolate morsels (1 cup; 170 g)
Confectioners' sugar for icing (optional)

1. Prepare pan as directed. Position rack in center of oven. Preheat oven to 350°F (175°C).

2. In a small mixing bowl, combine cut-up dates with baking soda and hot water. Stir and set aside.

3. In the large bowl of an electric mixer, cream together margarine or butter and sugar until completely blended. Add the eggs, one at a time, beating after each addition. Scrape down inside of bowl. Stir in vanilla extract. Add unsifted flour, cinnamon, and cocoa and combine with mixer on lowest speed. Again scrape down inside of bowl.

4. Stir the date mixture, then add it to the batter and beat very slowly just to combine. Don't overbeat.

Sprinkle half the nuts and chocolate morsels into the bottom of the prepared baking pan. Stir remaining chocolate and nuts into the batter. Spoon the batter into the pan, leveling it on the top. Place pan in oven and bake for 45 minutes, or until a cake tester inserted in the center comes out clean and the cake feels lightly springy to the touch. Cool cake in the pan on a wire rack for about 5 minutes, then top with another rack and invert. Lift off pan and cool cake completely. Leave cake bottom up, so nuts and chocolate bits are visible on the surface. Dust very lightly with confectioners' sugar just before serving.

Buttermilk Spice Cake

•

To make excellent spice cakes, take halfe a pecke of very fine Wheat-flower, take almost one pound of sweet butter, and some good milke and creame mixt together, set it on the fire, and put in your butter, and a good deale of sugar, and let it melt together; then straine Saffron into your milke a good quantity; then take seven or eight spooneful of good Ale barme, and eight egges with two yelkes and mix them together, then put your milke to it when it is somewhat cold, and into your flower put salt, Aniseeds bruised, Cloves and Mace, and a good deale of Cinamon: then worke all together good and stiffe, that you need not worke in any flower after; then put in a little rose water cold, then rub it well in the thing you knead it in, and worke it thoroughly; if it be not sweet enough, scrape in a little more sugar, and pull it all in peeces, and hurle in a good quantity of Currants, and so worke all together againe, and bake your Cake as you see cause in a gentle warme oven.

from *Countrey Contentments: or The English Housewife* by G.M.; London, 1623

Spice cakes are among our oldest cakes, though early versions such as the one above used "ale barme," a form of yeast, to raise the dough, giving a more breadlike texture than the tender cake that follows.

This spicy down-home recipe is delicious topped by either cream-cheese or caramel icing. It is made with a blend of black and golden raisins, but these may be omitted if you prefer, or you can add chopped walnuts to the recipe. Bake the cake in a square and serve it casually from the pan, or make layers, filled and frosted for a fancier presentation. In the summer I decorate the iced spice cake with edible nasturtium flowers.

☐ ADVANCE PREPARATION: Cake can be baked in advance, wrapped airtight, and frozen.

☐ SPECIAL EQUIPMENT: one 8- or 9-inch-square pan 2 inches deep or two 8-inch round layer pans

☐ BAKING TIME: 40 to 45 minutes at 350°F (175°C) for 9-inch square, or 35 minutes for 2 layers

☐ QUANTITY: 5 cups batter, one 8- or 9-inch-square, or one 2-layer 8-inch cake (serves 8 or 9)

☐ PAN PREPARATION: Spread solid shortening on bottom and sides of pans, dust pans with flour; tap out excess flour.

2½ cups sifted all-purpose flour (10½ ounces; 300 g)
1 teaspoon baking soda
½ teaspoon salt
1 tablespoon ground cinnamon
1 teaspoon ground allspice
1 teaspoon ground nutmeg
½ teaspoon ground cloves
¼ teaspoon ground ginger
¾ cup margarine or lightly salted butter (1½ sticks; 170 g), at room temperature
1 cup granulated sugar (7 ounces; 200 g)
1 large egg
½ cup unsulfured molasses
1 cup buttermilk
1 cup seedless raisins, half black and half golden (5¾ ounces; 160 g)

½ *cup chopped walnuts (optional; 2*
ounces; 60 g)

ICING:

Cream-Cheese Icing (page 393) or Brown-
Sugar Caramel Icing (page 396)

1. Prepare pans as described. Position rack in lower third of oven. Preheat oven to 350°F (175°C).

2. Sift together flour, baking soda, salt, and spices. Set aside.

3. In the large bowl of an electric mixer, cream together margarine or butter and sugar until well blended. Beat in the egg and molasses. Alternately add flour mixture and buttermilk, beating after each addition, beginning and ending with flour. Stir in raisins and/or walnuts if using them.

4. Spread batter in prepared pan(s), and bake as directed, or until a cake tester inserted in the center comes out clean and the top is lightly springy to the touch. Cool cake on a wire rack in the baking pan(s) for 5 minutes. To serve, cut into squares and serve from pan, or invert cake layers and cool completely on a wire rack before filling and frosting.

. . . .

Coriander-Ginger Spice Cake

■

I have adapted this Colonial recipe from the 1796 cookbook, *Fanny Pierson Crane—Her Receipts,* published by The Montclair, New Jersey, Historical Society. In the early 1800s,

Fanny and her husband, Israel, owner of the town's general store, were the most prominent citizens of Cranetown (now Montclair). The home where they lived from 1796 to 1826 has been restored, is now open to the public on Sundays, and the Crane House Kitchen is used to demonstrate open-hearth cooking techniques. Originally, Fanny's Coriander-Ginger Cake was baked in a covered cast-iron Dutch oven, hung from a crane in the fireplace. I am grateful to our friend, Chef Gene Fogarty, for bringing this recipe to my attention.

You will find an unusual combination of spices in this moist, fine-grained cake. Flavorful, aromatic, and not too sweet, it is full of fresh gingerroot, coriander, cloves, and cinnamon, a heady brew even without the scent of wood smoke from the fireplace. Serve the cake topped with a light sifting of confectioners' sugar or a glaze of blended sugar, cream, and maple syrup.

Note: All spices lose their flavor with age and exposure to heat and light. Ground coriander is especially sensitive, so smell your spices to be sure they have a strong perfume before using them for baking.

□ ADVANCE PREPARATION: The cake can be baked ahead, wrapped airtight, and frozen. Thaw and serve warm for best flavor.

□ SPECIAL EQUIPMENT: one sheet pan 11¾ × 7½ × 1¾ inches, grater, nut chopper or food processor

□ BAKING TIME: 35 minutes at 350°F (175°C)

□ QUANTITY: 5 cups batter, one sheet cake 11¾ × 7½ inches (serves 12)

□ PAN PREPARATION: Spread solid shortening on bottom and sides of pan.

2½ cups sifted all-purpose flour (10½ ounces; 300 g)
½ teaspoon baking powder
1 teaspoon baking soda
½ teaspoon salt
1 teaspoon ground cloves
1 teaspoon ground cinnamon
4 teaspoons ground coriander (yes, amount is correct)
½ cup unsalted butter or margarine (1 stick; 110 g)
½ cup granulated sugar (3½ ounces; 100 g)
½ cup unsulfured molasses
2 large eggs
1 tablespoon peeled and grated fresh gingerroot
1 cup hot water
½ cup buttermilk
½ cup currants (1¾ ounces; 50 g), or golden raisins
½ cup chopped walnuts (2 ounces; 60 g)

TOPPING:

Confectioners' sugar or glaze

GLAZE:

⅓ cup confectioners' sugar blended with enough cream and maple syrup to bring it to pouring consistency

1. Prepare pan as described. Position rack in center of oven. Preheat oven to 350°F (175°C).
2. Sift together flour, baking powder, baking soda, and salt. Add cloves, cinnamon, and coriander. Set mixture aside.

3. In the large bowl of an electric mixer, cream together butter and sugar until well blended. Add molasses. Beat to blend, then scrape down inside of bowl. Add eggs, one at a time, beating after each addition. Batter will appear to be curdled; this is normal. Blend in freshly grated gingerroot. Alternately add flour-spice mixture, hot water, and buttermilk, beating very slowly to blend after each addition. When thoroughly mixed, stir in currants or raisins and the nuts. The batter will be fairly thin.

4. Turn mixture into prepared pan and bake in the preheated oven for 30 to 35 minutes, or until a cake tester inserted in the center comes out clean and the cake feels lightly springy to the touch. Cool on a wire rack, cut into 2½-inch squares, and serve from pan. If you wish, top with sifted confectioners' sugar or a thin glaze made by beating together confectioners' sugar with cream and a little maple syrup.

Gingerbread

▪

They fette hym first the sweete wyn,
And mede eek in a mazelyn,
And roial spicerye
Of gyngebreed that was ful fyn,
And lycorys, and eek comyn,
With sugre that is so trye.

The Tale of Sire Thopas, The Canterbury Tales, Geoffrey Chaucer

The spice we call ginger *(Zingiber officinale)* is a native of tropical Asia cultivated for its pungent flavor and aroma. The spice has a long culinary history; it was a favorite of the ancient Greeks and Romans, who used it in various types of gingerbread, but its popularity dimmed in Europe after the fall of the Roman Empire. According to John F. Mariani in his *Dictionary of American Food and Drink* (Ticknor & Fields, 1983), ginger was reintroduced to the West by Marco Polo, who brought it back from the Orient. Gingerbread was common in sixteenth-century England, and was especially enjoyed by Queen Elizabeth I. Ginger was unknown in America until introduced by the English colonists, but it quickly became an important and popular spice. Its enthusiastic reception was recorded by Amelia Simmons in her book *American Cookery,* published in Hartford, Connecticut, in 1796. One of the first truly American cookbooks, it contained the first published recipe for American soft-style gingerbread, which departed from the more traditional crisp, cookielike European gingerbreads.

Molasses is another essential ingredient of gingerbread, as well as being "an essential ingredient of American independence," in the words of John Adams, referring to the Molasses Act passed by the English in 1733. This punitive act imposed prohibitive duties on molasses (as well as on sugar and rum) imported into North America from non-English islands. Colonists virtually ignored the act, and smuggling became commonplace, for these ingredients were basic to the Colonial economy and its cuisine.

An 1830 gingerbread recipe from a hand-written "receipt" book in Atlanta, Georgia (courtesy of Florence Phillips, in *Tullie's Receipts;* Kitchen Guild of the Tullie Smith House Restoration, Atlanta Historical Society, Inc., Atlanta, Georgia, 1976) shows the use of both these ingredients as well as illustrating nineteenth-century free-form recipe style:

GINGER BREAD
1 PT Molafses, ½ lb Butter, To a cup full Sugar, 1 cup Milk, 1 Wine Glafs Brandy, 4 Eggs, a little Pearl-Ash [as leavening], Nutmeg, Mace, Cloves, & Ginger. Flour sufficient To make it as Thick as Pound Cake.

The popularity and versatility of gingerbread is evident in the many variations that can be built on the basic recipe. We include four: Orange Gingerbread, Applesauce Gingerbread, Vermont Maple-Syrup Gingerbread, and Parkin, an English oatmeal gingerbread. Whatever recipe you follow, serve the gingerbread warm, with a generous dollop of lightly sweetened whipped cream.

□ ADVANCE PREPARATION: Gingerbread may be prepared ahead, wrapped airtight, and frozen. Thaw and serve warm.

□ SPECIAL EQUIPMENT: one 8- or 9-inch-square baking pan 2 inches deep, or sheet pan 11¾ × 7½ × 1¾ inches; 2-cup Pyrex measuring cup

□ BAKING TIME: 35 minutes at 350°F (175°C)

□ QUANTITY: 4 cups batter; one 8- or 9-inch square (serves 9) or sheet cake 11¾ × 7½ inches (serves 12 to 15)

□ PAN PREPARATION: Spread bottom and sides of pan with solid shortening.

*2½ cups sifted all-purpose flour (10½
ounces; 300 g)*
½ teaspoon baking powder
1 teaspoon baking soda
½ teaspoon salt
2 teaspoons ground ginger
1 teaspoon ground cinnamon
*½ cup lightly salted butter or
margarine (1 stick; 110 g), at room
temperature*
*½ cup plus 2 tablespoons granulated
sugar (4¼ ounces; 125 g)*
1 large egg
½ cup sour cream
½ cup unsulfured molasses
1 cup very hot water

1. Prepare pan as described. Position rack in center of oven. Preheat oven to 350°F (170°C).

2. Sift together flour, baking powder, baking soda, salt, and spices. Set aside.

3. In the large bowl of an electric mixer, cream together butter and sugar until completely blended to a granular paste. Scrape down inside of bowl. Beat in egg and sour cream.

4. In a 2-cup Pyrex measure, combine molasses and very hot water, stirring until molasses is nearly dissolved. With the mixer on low speed, add about one quarter of the flour mixture to the batter. Alternately add remaining flour and the molasses-water, beating slowly to blend after each addition.

5. Spoon batter into prepared pan, smooth top evenly, then spread batter slightly toward pan edges. Bake in the preheated oven for about 35 minutes, or until a cake tester inserted in the center comes out clean and the top of the cake is lightly springy to the touch. Cool on a wire rack. Cut into squares and serve directly from pan, accompanied by sweetened whipped cream or vanilla ice cream.

·Variations:·

ORANGE GINGERBREAD:

Prepare basic Gingerbread, but add 1 tablespoon grated orange zest and ⅓ cup chopped walnuts (1¼ ounces; 35 g), stirring them into the batter at the end. Note: Hot orange juice may be substituted for the water if you wish.

APPLESAUCE GINGERBREAD:

This is a slightly larger cake than the basic gingerbread, making 5½ cups batter but it can safely be baked in a sheet pan 11¾ × 7½ × 1¾ inches or 13 × 9 × 1¾ inches. Note that because of the moisture and weight of the applesauce, this cake does not rise quite as high as the basic recipe. For added nutritional value, use half white and half whole-wheat flour.

Prepare basic Gingerbread with the following changes:

Add ¼ cup toasted wheat germ to sifted flour-spice mixture. Add ⅔ cup applesauce alternately with flour and molasses. Stir in at end ⅓ cup chopped walnuts (1¼ ounces; 35 g).

PARKIN (ENGLISH OATMEAL GINGERBREAD):

This is an English version of gingerbread, made with oatmeal and treacle (English molasses). It is a full-bodied, dark, moist cake with a wonderful texture; some people prefer it to basic gingerbread because the flavor is a little stronger. If you can hide it from little fingers, it keeps wonderfully.

☐ ADVANCE PREPARATION, Equipment, Pan Preparation, Baking Time, and Quantity are the same as for basic Gingerbread. Follow recipe and procedure below.

½ cup unsalted butter or margarine (1 stick; 110 g)
⅔ cup unsulfured molasses or treacle
¼ cup light brown sugar (1¾ ounces; 50 g), packed
1 cup plus 3 tablespoons sifted all-purpose flour (4¾ ounces; 135 g)
½ teaspoon baking powder
½ teaspoon baking soda
½ teaspoon salt
1 teaspoon ground ginger
1 teaspoon ground cinnamon
¼ teaspoon ground cloves

¾ cup old-fashioned rolled oats (2¼ ounces; 60 g)
1 large egg
⅔ cup milk

1. Prepare pan as directed. Preheat oven to 350°F (175°C). Position rack in center of oven.

2. In a medium-size saucepan, combine butter, molasses, and brown sugar. Set over moderate heat, stirring occasionally, until butter is melted. Cool to lukewarm.

3. Sift together flour, baking powder, baking soda, and salt. Add spices and oats and toss to blend. Set aside.

4. In a 2-cup Pyrex measure, beat together the egg and milk.

5. In the large bowl of an electric mixer, or by hand, alternately add cooled butter-molasses, egg-milk, and dry ingredients, beating very slowly after each addition until the batter is blended; it will be quite thin. Pour batter

In England, Parkin is traditionally served at Guy Fawkes Day celebrations on November 5. This holiday commemorates a seventeenth-century religious conflict: Roman Catholic priests were banished from Protestant England in 1604. In retaliation, several Catholic Englishmen organized a plot to blow up the Houses of Parliament in the name of religious freedom. The Gunpowder Plot of 1604 was discovered a year later, and the conspirators executed. Guy Fawkes is most remembered because he was the one chosen to ignite the hidden barrels of gunpowder. Today, Guy Fawkes Day is mainly a children's holiday, with costumes, parades, fireworks, straw dummies of Guy Fawkes, and, of course, Parkin to eat.

into the greased pan and bake in the preheated oven for 30 to 35 minutes, or until a cake tester inserted in the center comes out clean and the top of the cake is lightly springy to the touch. Cool on a wire rack. Cut into squares and serve from pan. For a special treat, serve warm, with a little heavy cream poured over the top.

VERMONT MAPLE-SYRUP GINGERBREAD:

This is a mildly flavored, moist gingerbread. The strength of the maple flavor depends upon the quality and grade of the syrup used. To be sure of a definite maple flavor in the cake, add a little maple extract to the batter along with the syrup. To make Maple-Nut Gingerbread, add ½ cup chopped butternuts, walnuts, black walnuts, or hickory nuts to the final batter.

□ ADVANCE PREPARATION, Equipment, Pan Preparation, Baking Time, and Quantity are the same as for basic Gingerbread. Follow recipe and procedure that follows.

2⅓ cups sifted all-purpose flour (10 ounces; 280 g)
½ teaspoon baking powder
1 teaspoon baking soda
¼ teaspoon salt
1½ teaspoons ground ginger
½ teaspoon ground cinnamon
1 large egg
1 cup pure maple syrup
1 cup sour cream
4 tablespoons lightly salted butter or margarine (½ stick; 60 g), melted and cooled
1 teaspoon maple extract (optional)

1. Prepare pan as directed. Preheat oven to 350°F (170°C). Position rack in center of oven.

2. Sift together flour, baking powder, baking soda, and salt. Add ginger and cinnamon. Set aside.

3. In the large bowl of an electric mixer, or in a mixing bowl beating by hand, beat together egg, maple syrup, sour cream, melted butter, and maple extract. A little at a time, stir flour mixture into batter, blending well after each addition.

4. Turn batter into prepared pan and bake in the preheated oven for 30 to 35 minutes, or until a cake tester inserted in the center comes out clean and the top of the cake is lightly springy to the touch. Cool on a wire rack. Cut into squares and serve from the pan.

Honey Cake

■

This recipe has been handed down through several generations of my family. Moist and flavorful, it is traditionally served as a part of the Jewish New Year, Rosh Hashanah, because honey symbolizes the sweetness wished for the New Year. For a variation made with neither honey nor sugar, see Susan Richman's Sugarfree, Honeyfree Orange Cake (page 165).

□ ADVANCE PREPARATION: The cake may be baked in advance and frozen.

□ SPECIAL EQUIPMENT: two loaf pans 9 × 5 × 3 inches, saucepan, sifter, serving platter

□ BAKING TIME: 55 to 65 minutes at 325°F (165°C)

□ QUANTITY: two loaves, each 9 × 5 × 3 inches (serves 16)

□ PAN PREPARATION: Spread bottom and sides of pans with margarine.

1½ cups honey
1 cup strong coffee, or 1½ teaspoons
*   instant coffee dissolved in 1 cup*
*   boiling water*
3½ cups unsifted all-purpose flour
*   (17½ ounces; 495 g)*
2 teaspoons baking powder
1 teaspoon baking soda
Pinch of salt
4 large eggs
2 tablespoons vegetable oil
1 cup granulated sugar (7 ounces;
*   200 g)*
1 teaspoon ground cinnamon
½ teaspoon ground nutmeg
¼ teaspoon ground cloves
⅛ teaspoon ground ginger

1. Prepare pans as described. Position rack in center of oven. Preheat oven to 325°F (165°C).

2. Measure the honey into a saucepan and set over moderate heat just until it comes to a boil. Immediately remove pan from the heat and set aside to cool. Do not let honey continue to boil. Once the honey has cooled slightly, stir in the coffee and set the mixture aside.

3. Sift together flour, baking powder, baking soda, and salt. Set aside.

4. In a large mixing bowl, combine eggs, oil, sugar, and spices and beat well. Alternately add small amounts of the flour mixture and the honey-coffee liquid, beating to blend after each addition and beginning and ending with flour.

5. Divide better evenly between the prepared pans and set to bake in the preheated oven for 55 to 65 minutes, or until a cake tester inserted in the center comes out clean. Cool cakes in their pans on a wire rack until completely cold. To remove cakes, slide a knife blade around the edge of each loaf to release it from the pan, then invert onto a serving plate.

·*Variation:*·

SUSAN RICHMAN'S SUGARFREE, HONEYFREE ORANGE CAKE:

Omit honey and sugar in recipe above. Substitute 2⅓ cups mixed fruit concentrate (a natural sweetening syrup made from pineapples, peaches, and pears, sold in health food stores). Instead of 1 cup of coffee, substitute ¾ cup orange juice and add 1 teaspoon orange extract and grated zest of ½ orange to finished batter.

Cranberry Orange Loaf

■

This easy-to-make cranberry orange loaf is a traditional Thanksgiving and Christmas treat. Because the cake freezes so well, I like to bake it in advance, making many small loaves in new baking pans with the recipe attached to give as holiday gifts. For an unusual variation, try the Apricot Loaf, following.

□ ADVANCE PREPARATION: The cake

can be baked in advance, wrapped airtight, and frozen.

□ SPECIAL EQUIPMENT: sifter, 2 mixing bowls, pastry blender or 2 table knives or forks, nut chopper or food processor, grater, wax paper, 1 loaf pan 9 × 5 × 3 inches or 3 baby loaf pans 5¾ × 3¼ × 2 inches

□ BAKING TIME: 1 hour at 350°F (175°C) for regular large loaf, 35 to 40 minutes for baby loaves

□ QUANTITY: 1 regular loaf or 3 baby loaves (serves 8)

□ PAN PREPARATION: Generously coat bottom and sides of pan(s) with margarine or solid shortening

2 cups unsifted all-purpose flour (10 ounces; 280 g)
1½ teaspoons baking powder
½ teaspoon baking soda
1 teaspoon salt
1 cup granulated sugar (7 ounces; 200 g)
3 tablespoons wheat germ, toasted or plain
¼ cup margarine or unsalted butter (2 ounces; 57 g), at room temperature, cut up
Grated zest of 1 orange
¾ cup orange juice
1 large egg
2 cups whole fresh cranberries, rinsed and picked over; or use frozen whole cranberries, unthawed
½ cup shelled walnuts (2 ounces; 60 g)

1. Prepare pan(s) as described. Position rack in center of oven. Preheat oven to 350°F (175°C).

2. Sift together flour, baking powder, baking soda, and salt into a mixing bowl. Add sugar and wheat germ. Add the cut-up margarine or butter and work it into the dry ingredients as for a piecrust, blending the ingredients with a pastry blender or 2 cross-cutting knives until the dough forms crumbs.

3. In another bowl, combine grated orange zest, orange juice, and egg. Beat well. Set bowl aside.

With nut chopper or food processor, coarsely chop nuts and then cranberries.

4. Add orange-egg mixture to flour-butter crumbs and mix to combine. Stir in chopped nuts and cranberries. Mix well.

5. Spoon batter into prepared pans, smooth the top, then spread batter toward pan sides to aid in rising. Bake in the preheated oven as directed or until the cake is golden and a cake tester inserted in the center comes out clean. Cool cake in pans on a wire rack for about 5 minutes, then tip cakes out of pans and cool completely on the rack. Note that the loaves will cut most neatly the day after they are baked.

·*Variation:*·

APRICOT LOAF:

Prepare Cranberry Orange Loaf with the following changes: Instead of cranberries and orange juice substitute apricots and apricot juice prepared as follows:

Measure 2 cups packed dried apricots (340 g), then chop or slice them into small pieces. Add just enough water to cover the fruit in a saucepan. Cover the pan and bring water to a boil. Lower the heat and simmer for only about 2 minutes.

Save the fruit. Strain and reserve the liquid; you need ¾ cup. Pour a little more water over the apricots in the strainer if you need more liquid. Use the chopped apricots instead of the cranberries, and the liquid instead of the orange juice.

··

Ukranian Poppyseed Loaf

■

This old-world specialty is moist, full of flavor, and very easy to prepare. It is my idea of the perfect comfort food, just the thing to serve with a strong cup of hot tea to restore one's energy.

Because this cake keeps so well, it is good to bake in small pans for holiday gifts. Generally, the cake is topped with only a light dusting of confectioners' sugar. but for holiday giving, if you wish to add a bit of color, use the Icing Glaze (page 406) and stick on a halved candied cherry or two.

Note: To buy poppyseeds in bulk, see list of Suppliers, page 482.

☐ ADVANCE PREPARATION: The poppyseeds must soak in milk for at least 1 hour after being ground and before making the batter; plan your time accordingly. The cake can be made in advance, wrapped airtight, and kept at room temperature for at least a week. It can also be frozen.

☐ SPECIAL EQUIPMENT: 2 loaf pans 8½ × 3½ × 2¾ inches or three 1-pound coffee cans, tops removed, 5½ inches tall × 4 inches in diameter, or 4 baby loaf pans 6 × 3½ ×

2 inches; small saucepan, extra bowl and beater for whipping egg whites

☐ BAKING TIME: 45 to 50 minutes at 350°F (175°C) for either small cylinders or baby loaves; for larger pans, increase time slightly (see doneness tests, page 68).

☐ QUANTITY: 5½ cups batter, 2 loaves or 3 small cylinders or 4 baby loaves

☐ PAN PREPARATION: Spread solid shortening on bottom and sides of pans, then dust evenly with flour; tap out excess flour.

1 cup ground poppyseeds (see grinding techniques, page 43) (5 ounces; 140 g)
1 cup milk
1 cup unsalted butter (2 sticks; 230 g), at room temperature
1½ cups granulated sugar (10½ ounces; 300 g)
3 large eggs, separated
2 teaspoons vanilla extract
2 cups sifted all-purpose flour (8½ ounces; 240 g)
½ teaspoon salt
2½ teaspoons baking powder

TOPPING:

2 tablespoons confectioners' sugar (optional)

1. In a small saucepan, combine ground poppyseeds with milk and bring just to a boil over moderate-high heat. Stir once or twice. Remove from heat and allow to stand for 1 hour. Don't cheat on time because the seeds need time to absorb the milk in order to have the correct flavor and texture.

2. Prepare pan(s) as described. Position shelf in center of oven. Preheat oven to 350°F (175°C).

3. In the large bowl of an electric mixer, cream together butter and sugar until well blended. Stop mixer and scrape down inside of bowl and beater several times. Add egg yolks, one at a time, beating after each addition. With mixer on low speed, slowly beat in poppyseeds and milk, and the vanilla. Scrape down inside of bowl and beater.

4. Combine flour, salt, and baking powder. Stir this mixture into batter in several additions.

5. In a separate bowl with a clean beater, beat egg whites until stiff but not dry. Fold whites into the batter in several additions.

6. Turn batter into pan(s): divide evenly between 2 loaf pans, or put 2 cups batter into each coffee can, or 1½ cups batter into each baby loaf. Bake all sizes for 45 to 50 minutes, or until a cake tester inserted in the center comes out clean and the cake top is lightly springy to the touch. Leave cake in its pan(s) on a wire rack for 10 minutes. Top with a wire rack and invert; lift off pan(s). Cool cake completely on the rack. Sift on sugar when cake is cold.

· ·

Lemon Tea Cake

∎

This is a light, tart cake that is spread with lemon-sugar glaze when fresh from the oven. The hot glaze penetrates the cake thoroughly and keeps it moist and flavorful.

Lemon Tea Cake is one of my favorites for holiday giving, because it can be made in advance and freezes very well. I have included 2 versions of the recipe: Lemon Tea Cake I, and Lemon Tea Cake II, which is a larger batch. If you have a long Christmas list, or are cooking for a bake sale, use the larger recipe, which was developed by my friend and neighbor Marie Swanson. Marie is well known in town for her generosity in sharing this cake and recipe.

LEMON TEA CAKE I

A Note about Lemons: Though lemons vary greatly in size and juiciness, an average lemon yields 2 to 3 teaspoons grated zest and 2 to 3 tablespoons juice. The first Lemon Tea Cake recipe plus its glaze and icing will require 7 teaspoons of grated zest plus 8 tablespoons of juice (a total of 4 lemons, depending upon their size and juiciness). To speed preparation you can grate the zest of 4 lemons, squeeze their juice, and set both aside before beginning to bake.

□ ADVANCE PREPARATION: Once the cakes are glazed, iced, and completely cooled, they can be individually wrapped airtight in heavy-duty plastic bags and frozen.

□ SPECIAL EQUIPMENT: 3 baby loaf pans 6 × 3½ × 2 inches, or 1 loaf pan 9 × 5 × 3 inches, grater, wax paper, lemon squeezer, nut chopper or food processor, small bowl, pastry brush, small nonreactive saucepan

□ BAKING TIME: 40 to 45 minutes at 350°F (175°C) for baby loaves, 50 to 60 minutes for large loaf

□ QUANTITY: about 4½ cups batter, 3

baby loaves or 1 standard loaf (serves 8)

□ P A N   P R E P A R A T I O N : Spread solid shortening on bottom and sides of pans.

1 cup shelled walnuts (4 ounces; 110 g)
1 cup granulated sugar (7 ounces; 200 g)
1½ cups sifted all-purpose flour (6¼ ounces; 180 g)
1 teaspoon baking powder
½ teaspoon salt
6 tablespoons unsalted butter or margarine (3¼ ounces; 90 g), at room temperature
2 large eggs
4 teaspoons grated lemon zest plus 2 tablespoons fresh juice (about 2 lemons)
6 tablespoons milk

HOT LEMON GLAZE:

⅓ cup granulated sugar (2¼ ounces; 65 g)
2 to 3 teaspoons grated lemon zest (save for garnishing iced cakes) and 6 tablespoons fresh juice (save 1 tablespoon juice for Icing) (2 lemons)

LEMON ICING:

½ cup confectioners' sugar (1¾ ounces; 50 g)
1 tablespoon lemon juice (saved from Lemon Glaze)

1. Prepare pans as described. Position rack in center of oven. Preheat oven to 350°F (175°C).

2. To chop walnuts in the food processor, combine them with 2 or 3 tablespoons of the measured sugar. Or chop them with a nut chopper, or in the blender, ¼ cup at a time. Set nuts aside.

3. Sift together flour, baking powder, and salt. Set aside.

In the large bowl of an electric mixer, cream together butter and remaining sugar until well blended. Add eggs, one at a time, beating after each addition. Beat in lemon zest and juice. With mixer on lowest speed, or by hand, alternately add flour mixture and milk, beginning and ending with flour. Beat well, then stir in nuts.

4. Spoon batter into prepared pans. Smooth the tops, and bake them in the preheated oven as directed, or until tops are golden brown and a cake tester inserted in the cake center comes out clean.

While cakes bake, prepare the glaze: Stir together glaze ingredients in a small nonreactive saucepan. Set it over moderate heat and stir until the sugar dissolves. Set pan aside. Rewarm glaze just before using it.

5. As soon as cakes come from the oven, set the pans on a wire rack. Brush the cake tops with the hot lemon glaze. Wait several seconds for the glaze to penetrate, then repeat, using up all the glaze.

6. Stir together the Lemon Icing ingredients until smooth. Before cakes are completely cold, drizzle a little icing on each cake, then garnish with a sprinkling of reserved grated lemon zest or a few very thin strips of lemon zest.

When the cakes are completely cold, wrap each one in plastic wrap, then place in a heavy-duty plastic bag, label, and freeze.

·*Variation:*·

LEMON TEA CAKE II

Note: This carefully proportioned enlargement of the first recipe is more or less three times as big, making 10 cups of batter for 8 or 9 baby loaves or 3 regular loaves.

A Note about Lemons: This recipe, plus its glaze and icing, requires between 6 and 7 lemons, depending on size and juiciness, to make a total of 10 teaspoons grated zest and 16½ tablespoons lemon juice, 1 generous cup. To speed preparation, grate the lemons and squeeze the juice before starting to prepare the batter.

☐ ADVANCE PREPARATION: See Lemon Tea Cake I.

☐ EQUIPMENT: 9 baby loaf pans 6 × 3½ × 2 inches, or 3 average-size loaf pans 8½ × 4½ × 2¾ inches; grater, wax paper, lemon squeezer, nut chopper or food processor, small bowl, pastry brush

☐ BAKING TIME: See Lemon Tea Cake I.

☐ QUANTITY: about 10 cups batter, 8 or 9 baby loaves (serves 48) or 3 regular loaves (serves 24 to 30)

☐ PAN PREPARATION: Spread solid shortening on bottom and sides of pans.

1½ cups shelled walnuts (6 ounces; 170 g)
3 cups granulated sugar (21 ounces; 600 g)
4½ cups sifted all-purpose flour (19 ounces; 540 g)
3 teaspoons baking powder
¾ teaspoon salt
1 cup margarine (2 sticks; 230 g)
½ cup unsalted butter (1 stick; 110 g)
6 large eggs
6 teaspoons grated lemon zest
9 tablespoons freshly squeezed lemon juice
1½ cups milk

HOT LEMON GLAZE:

½ cup granulated sugar (3½ ounces; 100 g)
4 teaspoons grated lemon zest (save for garnishing iced cakes)
7½ to 8 tablespoons lemon juice (save 1 to 1½ tablespoons for Icing)

LEMON ICING:

½ cup sifted confectioners' sugar (1¾ ounces; 50 g)
1 to 1½ tablespoons lemon juice (saved from Lemon Glaze)

☐ PROCEDURE:
Follow procedure for Lemon Tea Cake I, but combine margarine with butter and sugar in step 3. Note that this recipe makes a large quantity of batter and may overfill your large mixing bowl; it is preferable to mix in flour and milk by hand rather than with an electric mixer, thereby avoiding splashes. Once well blended, you can beat the batter with the mixer. In step 4, divide batter evenly among the prepared pans. Use about 1¼ cups batter for each of the baby pans. For ease in handling the baby pans, set them on a jelly-roll pan before placing them in the oven. Stagger the placement of the pans so heat can circulate in the oven. Bake, glaze, and ice the cakes as directed.

Clara Joslin's Banana Nut Cake

■

The recipe for this moist and flavorful banana-nut cake was handed down to me from my maternal grandmother, Clara Joslin, who set great store by bananas as a cure-all. She also believed in the restorative powers of honey, prunes, grains, and fiber in the diet. For years I was more impressed by her fine operatic singing voice than by her cooking, but lately popular medicine has caught up with her nutritional theories and my youthful skepticism has turned to admiration.

The recipe is followed by 2 variations: Banana Streusel and Banana Chocolate-Chip.

□ ADVANCE PREPARATION: The cake can be made ahead, wrapped airtight, and frozen.

□ SPECIAL EQUIPMENT: one 9-inch-square pan 2 inches deep, or sheet pan 11¾ × 7½ × 1¾ inches, or 16 cupcake pans 2¾ inches in diameter; nut chopper or food processor

□ BAKING TIME: 30 to 35 minutes at 350°F (175°C) for 9-inch-square or sheet cake 11¾ × 7½ × 1¾ inches; 20 to 25 minutes for cupcakes

□ QUANTITY: 4 cups batter, 9-inch square (serves 9), larger sheet (serves 12 to 20), 16 cupcakes

□ PAN PREPARATION: Spread solid shortening on bottom and sides of pan.

2 cups sifted all-purpose flour (8½ ounces; 240 g)
1 teaspoon baking powder
½ teaspoon baking soda
⅛ teaspoon salt
½ cup margarine (1 stick; 110 g)
1 cup granulated sugar (7 ounces; 200 g)
2 large eggs
3 large ripe bananas, thoroughly mashed, about 1 cup (9 ounces; 260 g)
½ cup chopped walnuts (2 ounces; 60 g)
¼ cup toasted wheat germ (optional; 1 ounce; 30 g)

1. Prepare pan as directed. Position rack in center of oven. Preheat oven to 350°F (170°C).

2. Sift together flour, baking powder, baking soda, and salt. Set aside.

3. In the large bowl of an electric mixer, cream together margarine and sugar until light and fluffy. Add eggs, one at a time, beating after each addition. Alternately add the dry ingredients and the mashed bananas to the batter, beating slowly after each addition. Stir in nuts, and wheat germ if used. Spoon batter into prepared pan, smooth top evenly, then spread batter slightly toward pan edges.

4. Bake in center of preheated oven as directed, or until a cake tester inserted in the center comes out clean and cake is lightly springy to the touch.

·Variations:·

BANANA STREUSEL CAKE:

Prepare Banana Nut Cake. Prepare 1 recipe Streusel Nut Topping (page 385). Before baking, sprinkle the top of a 9-inch-square cake with about 1½ cups of streusel crumbs. For a sheet cake 11¾ × 7½ inches, use 1¾ cups streusel. Extra streusel crumbs may be frozen in an airtight container for later use.

BANANA CHOCOLATE-CHIP CAKE:

Prepare Banana Nut Cake. Add ½ cup miniature semisweet chocolate morsels to batter along with nuts.

Oatmeal Cake

∎

This easy-to-make cake is moist, flavorful, and highly nutritious. The recipe was shared with me by my friend, caterer Lynn Pageau, owner of Fancy Fare in North Hatley, Quebec. The cake has a marvelous texture, keeps well, and is ideal for picnics or brown bag lunches. To increase the nutritional value further, add ⅓ cup toasted wheat germ or oat bran; for variety, add ½ cup dried currants.

☐ ADVANCE PREPARATION: Cake can be baked ahead and frozen.

☐ SPECIAL EQUIPMENT: 1 sheet pan 13 × 9 × 1½ inches, nut chopper or food processor (Note: You can also use this recipe for cupcakes; for a slightly thicker cake, bake it in a sheet pan 12 × 8 × 1½ inches.)

☐ BAKING TIME: 40 to 45 minutes at 350°F (175°C) for sheet cakes, 20 minutes for cupcakes

☐ QUANTITY: 5 cups batter, 1 sheet cake 9 × 13 inches (serves 20 to 24), or 24 cupcakes, 2½ inches in diameter

☐ PAN PREPARATION: Spread solid shortening over bottom and sides of pan, dust evenly with flour; tap out excess flour.

1 cup old-fashioned rolled oats (3 ounces; 85 g)
1¼ cups boiling water
1⅓ cups sifted all-purpose flour (5¾ ounces; 165 g)
1 teaspoon ground cinnamon
1 teaspoon baking soda
½ teaspoon salt
⅓ cup toasted wheat germ or oat bran
½ cup lightly salted butter (1 stick; 110 g)
1 cup firmly packed dark brown sugar (9 ounces; 255 g)
1 cup granulated sugar (7 ounces; 200 g)
2 large eggs
1 teaspoon vanilla extract
1 cup chopped walnuts (4 ounces; 110 g)
½ cup dried currants (1¾ ounces; 50 g) or chocolate mini-chips

TOPPING:

Broiled Caramel-Nut Icing (page 397)

1. Prepare pan as described. Position rack in center of oven. Preheat oven to 350°F (175°C).

2. In a medium-size mixing bowl, pour boiling water over the oatmeal. Stir mixture and let it stand for about 20 minutes to soften and cool.

3. In a large bowl, sift together flour, cinnamon, baking soda, and salt. Stir in wheat germ if using it. Set bowl aside.

4. In the large bowl of an electric mixer, cream together butter, brown sugar, and granulated sugar until light and fluffy. Add eggs, one at a time, beating after each addition. Stir in vanilla and cooled oatmeal. Fold in flour, then stir in walnuts and currants if using them.

5. Turn batter into prepared pan, smooth top, and set to bake in center of preheated oven for about 40 minutes, or until cake pulls away from pan edge and a cake tester inserted in the center comes out clean. Set cake to cool on a wire rack. While cake is baking, prepare the topping. Apply topping while cake is still warm.

Applesauce Cake

∎

This is a rich, moist applesauce cake that I like to fill with a variety of chopped fruits and nuts. For Christmas, I often double the recipe and make several small loaves for gifts.

☐ ADVANCE PREPARATION: The cake can be baked in advance, wrapped airtight, and kept in a cool place for about a week. Or it can be frozen.

☐ SPECIAL EQUIPMENT: one 9-inch tube pan (6½-cup capacity), nut chopper or food processor

☐ BAKING TIME: 50 to 60 minutes at 350°F (175°C)

☐ QUANTITY: 4 cups batter, one 9-inch tube cake (serves 10)

☐ PAN PREPARATION: Spread solid shortening on bottom and sides of pan, dust pan evenly with flour; tap out excess flour.

1 cup sifted all-purpose flour (4¼ ounces; 120 g)
½ cup unsifted whole-wheat pastry flour (2¼ ounces; 65 g) Note: if you do not have this, use all white flour.
¼ cup wheat germ (1 ounce; 30 g)
½ teaspoon salt
1 teaspoon baking soda
1 teaspoon ground cinnamon
½ teaspoon each of ground cardamom and nutmeg
¼ teaspoon ground cloves
1 cup currants (4½ ounces; 130 g) or raisins
1 cup finely chopped walnuts (4 ounces; 110 g)
1 cup firmly packed light brown sugar (7 ounces; 200 g)
½ cup unsalted butter (1 stick; 110 g), at room temperature
2 tablespoons honey
1 large egg
¼ cup apple cider or apple juice
1 cup thick applesauce

ICING (OPTIONAL):

Icing Glaze (page 406), flavored with vanilla or bourbon

1. Prepare pan as described. Position rack in center of oven. Preheat oven to 350°F (175°C).
2. In a bowl, combine both flours and wheat germ. Sift on salt, baking soda, and spices. In another bowl, combine currants and chopped nuts. Add ¼ cup of flour mixture and toss to coat fruit and nuts well. Set both bowls aside.
3. In the large bowl of an electric mixer,

cream sugar, butter, and honey until light and smooth. Add egg and cider and beat well. Little by little, stir the flour mixture into the batter, beating slowly after each addition. Stir in currant and nut mixture and applesauce.

4. Spoon batter into prepared pan and bake in the preheated oven for 50 to 60 minutes, or until a cake tester inserted in the center comes out clean though wet, and the top feels springy to the touch. Cool on a wire rack for 10 minutes. Top with another rack and invert. Remove baking pan. Cool completely. Serve the cake plain, or top with Icing Glaze.

- -

Marleni's Apple Cake

■

This is our family's all-time favorite apple cake. We were introduced to it years ago by my Parisian goddaughter, Marleni Kanas, who used to make it when she was a little girl visiting her American grandmother, Helen Everitt, in Long Island. Perhaps it is love by association, for we spent many warm summer afternoons nibbling on this cake in Helen's flower-filled garden. The cake is easy enough for a child to make. While it is not too sweet, it is extremely moist, full of fruit, nuts, and spices. This cake was adapted from a recipe in a slim paper volume called *The Way to the Heart Cookbook* (Viet Nam Tree Memorial Committee of Huntington Township, New York, 1976).

□ ADVANCE PREPARATION: Cake can be baked ahead and frozen, though flavor is best when freshly baked.

□ SPECIAL EQUIPMENT: one 9- or 10-inch plain angel-food tube or springform tube pan, nut chopper or food processor

□ BAKING TIME: 90 minutes at 350°F (175°C)

□ QUANTITY: 8 cups batter, one 9- or 10-inch tube cake (serves 10 to 12)

□ PAN PREPARATION: Spread solid shortening on bottom and sides of pan, dust evenly with flour; tap out excess flour.

3 cups sifted all-purpose flour (12³⁄₄ ounces; 360 g)
½ teaspoon baking powder
½ teaspoon baking soda
¼ teaspoon salt
½ teaspoon each of ground nutmeg and cinnamon
3 tablespoons wheat germ (optional)
1½ cups light vegetable oil
2 cups granulated sugar (14 ounces; 400 g)
2 teaspoons vanilla extract
3 tablespoons milk
3 large eggs
3 large cooking apples, about 6½ ounces each (550 g altogether), peeled, cored, and cut into ½-inch dice to make about 3 cups
1 cup seedless raisins (5³⁄₄ ounces; 170 g)
1 cup coarsely chopped walnuts (4 ounces; 110 g)

TOPPING (OPTIONAL):
3 tablespoons confectioners' sugar

1. Prepare pan as described. Position rack in center of oven. Preheat oven to 175°F (350°C).

2. Sift together flour, baking powder, baking soda, salt, and spices. Add wheat germ if using it. Set mixture aside.

3. In the large bowl of an electric mixer, combine oil, sugar, vanilla, and milk. Beat well. Add eggs and beat again. Little by little, stir in flour mixture, beating slowly to blend. Stir in apples, raisins, and nuts. Batter will be very stiff.

4. Spoon batter into prepared pan and smooth the top. Bake in the preheated oven as directed, or until a cake tester inserted in the center comes out clean and the cake feels lightly springy to the touch. Cool on a wire rack for 15 minutes. Slide a knife blade between cake and sides of pan to loosen it, then top cake with a plate and invert. Lift off pan. Top cake with a plate and invert again, so cake is right side up. Cool completely. Sift a little confectioners' sugar on top just before serving.

· ·

Quick Chopped Apple Cake

■

I developed this recipe one fall when inundated with apples from a nearby orchard. There is really more fruit here than cake, and the result is very moist and flavorful. For a brunch treat, serve this warm, with a little heavy cream or Vanilla Pastry Cream (see Index) poured on top.

□ ADVANCE PREPARATION: This cake can be prepared ahead, wrapped airtight, and frozen.

□ SPECIAL EQUIPMENT: one 9-inch-square pan, 2 inches deep, or sheet pan 11¾ × 7½ × 1¾ inches; nut chopper or food processor

□ BAKING TIME: 50 to 55 minutes at 350°F (175°C)

□ QUANTITY: 4 cups batter, one 9-inch cake (serves 9)

□ PAN PREPARATION: Spread solid shortening on bottom and sides of pan.

3 tablespoons unsalted butter or margarine, at room temperature
⅓ cup firmly packed dark brown sugar (3 ounces; 85 g)
⅔ cup granulated sugar (4½ ounces; 130 g)
1 large egg
3 tablespoons toasted wheat germ
1 teaspoon vanilla extract
3 tablespoons sour cream
¾ cup (3¾ ounces; 105 g) plus 7 tablespoons unsifted all-purpose flour
¼ teaspoon salt
1 teaspoon baking powder
¾ teaspoon ground cinnamon
½ teaspoon ground nutmeg
2½ large cooking apples such as Granny Smith, each about 7 ounces (550 g altogether), peeled, cored, and chopped into ¼-inch pieces to make 3 cups
¼ cup dried currants (scant 1 ounce; 25 g), or raisins or diced dried apricots
⅓ cup chopped walnuts or pecans (1¼ ounces; 40 g)

1. Prepare pan as described. Position rack in center of oven. Preheat oven to 350°F (175°C).

2. In the large bowl of an electric mixer, cream together butter and both sugars until completely blended. Add egg and beat well. Scrape down inside of bowl. Add wheat germ, vanilla, and sour cream and beat well.

3. In a small bowl, combine ¾ cup of the flour, the salt, baking powder, cinnamon, and nutmeg. With the mixer on very low speed, or beating by hand, add the flour mixture, a little at a time, to the butter-egg batter.

4. In a large bowl, toss the chopped apples with the currants and nuts. Stir in remaining 7 tablespoons flour, coating the apples. By hand, stir fruit-nut mixture into the batter.

5. Spoon batter into prepared pan. Bake in the preheated oven for 50 to 55 minutes, or until a cake tester inserted in the center comes out clean and the top of the cake is lightly golden. Cool cake on a wire rack. Cut into 3-inch squares and serve warm from the pan.

. . . .

Lauren's Peach Crumb Cake

∎

This quick and easy-to-make recipe comes from my friend Lauren Lieberman, who bakes with the same great enthusiasm she shows when selling country homes. Lauren makes this versatile cake with whatever fruit is in season. She recommends rhubarb, sliced apples, or blueberries.

□ ADVANCE PREPARATION: The dough can be prepared ahead and held, covered, in the refrigerator for a day or two.

□ SPECIAL EQUIPMENT: one 9-inch springform pan and flat serving platter, or 9- or 10-inch deep-dish pie plate

□ BAKING TIME: 35 minutes at 425°F (220°C), or less, depending on type of fruit

□ QUANTITY: one 9-inch cake (serves 8)

□ PAN PREPARATION: none

1½ cups sifted all-purpose flour (6¼ ounces; 180 g)
½ cup granulated sugar (3½ ounces; 100 g)
Pinch of salt
½ cup unsalted butter (1 stick; 110 g), at room temperature, cut up
½ teaspoon ground cinnamon
8 to 10 fresh ripe peaches, peeled (see Note), sliced to make 4 cups, or use 4 cups other fruit
    Note: To peel peaches effortlessly, drop them into a pot of boiling water for 3 or 4 minutes. Remove with a slotted spoon to a bowl of cold water. Drain when cool, then slip off peach skins.
½ cup granulated sugar (3½ ounces; 100 g) or firmly packed light brown sugar; adjust sugar to sweetness of fruit.
2 tablespoons quick-cooking tapioca
1 tablespoon lemon juice
3 tablespoons fruit juice, orange or apple, or water, used as needed

1. Position rack in lower third of oven. Preheat oven to 425°F (220°C).

2. Combine flour, ½ cup sugar, and the salt

in a mixing bowl. Cut in pieces of butter and combine until the mixture resembles dry rice. You can accomplish this by pinching the ingredients together with your fingertips, or cutting them together with 2 cross-cutting knives, or using a wire-loop pastry blender. Or you can pulse the ingredients in the workbowl of a food processor just until you begin to see clumps form; do not form a dough ball. You will have about 2½ cups of dough crumbs.

3. Measure ¾ cup of these crumbs and place them in a small bowl. Stir in the cinnamon; set this aside for the cake topping. Press remaining dough onto the bottom and ¾ inch up the sides of the baking pan.

4. In a large bowl, combine the sliced fruit, ½ cup sugar (more or less, depending on sweetness of fruit), the tapioca, and lemon juice. If your fruit has no juice of its own (dry peaches or apples, for example), add 3 tablespoons fruit juice or water. If fruit is juicy, you can omit this extra liquid. Stir mixture well, taking care to moisten the tapioca with fruit juice. Let mixture stand for a few minutes to soften the tapioca, then arrange fruit on the dough in the pan. Sprinkle on an even layer of the reserved dough crumbs.

5. Bake in the preheated oven for about 35 minutes, or until a knife tip easily pierces the fruit slices and the cake top is golden brown. Note that hard apples may require longer baking time than peaches or berries. Cool cake on a wire rack; release sides of springform pan and slide cake onto a flat serving platter. If cake was baked in a pie plate, serve it from the pan, omitting the serving platter. Cut the cake into wedges and serve warm with lightly sweetened whipped cream or Crème Anglaise (page 416).

·*Variation:*·

APPLE CRUMB CAKE:

Prepare Peach Crumb Cake, but substitute 4 cups peeled, cored, and sliced apples. Use either cooking apples such as Granny Smith or softer varieties such as McIntosh or Delicious. This is a good recipe for apples that are too soft to hold their shape in pies. Add ½ teaspoon ground nutmeg to the crumb topping.

Jeannette Pépin's Pear Cake

■

Lyons, one of France's primary culinary regions, boasts an extra dimension in its tradition of *haute cuisine*—the *mères de Lyon*: women chefs who, since the late eighteenth century, have specialized in superb regional cuisine. Jeannette Pépin is clearly a member of this distinguished group, having presided over two restaurants near Lyons, Le Bressan and Le Pélican. Jeannette now claims to be retired, though she continues to cook and to travel at an exhausting pace. Her son Jacques, who has also carved a significant niche in the culinary world, readily credits his mother with influencing his career. In fact, he would have been hard pressed to avoid it with so many members of his immediate family involved with food. His father was in charge of the restaurant wine cellers, and several aunts, uncles, and cousins owned or worked in restaurants.

I had the good fortune to get to know some

of Jacques' extended culinary family during a recent trip to France. In preparation for an article I was writing, my husband, daughter, and I spent several days shopping and cooking with Jeannette Pépin at her home near Lyons. We also spent an unforgettable day working with her at Le Relais Bressans, a family restaurant tucked into the mountain village of Port, near Nantua in the Jura. Founded by Jeannette's sister and her husband, this gem of Bressan cooking is now run by Jeannette's nieces, Colette and Christiane. Because Colette was ill, we all pitched in to prepare a banquet of *pâté en croûte,* and *poulet aux morilles* (chicken with morels) to serve sixty-five members of the local Lions' Club. Dessert that evening was a relatively modest fresh *salade de fruits* with *fromage blanc* from the local dairy. While at home with Jeannette, we sampled more elaborate dessert fare. Among her Lyonnais specialties, *clafoutis aux poires,* her pear cake, was our favorite.

The following quick and easy-to-make cake is my adaptation of the recipe she presented to us with a casual nod to conventional measurements and a flourish of her special Gallic charm and humor.

☐ ADVANCE PREPARATION: This quickly prepared cake is best made just before serving warm from the oven, or at least no more than 3 or 4 hours in advance.

☐ SPECIAL EQUIPMENT: one 10-inch quiche pan, pie plate, or solid-bottom tart pan; paring knife, vegetable peeler, food processor or mixing bowl, and large spoon or fork

☐ BAKING TIME: 15 minutes at 425°F (217°C), then 30 minutes at 350°F (175°C)

☐ QUANTITY: one 10-inch cake (serves 8)

☐ PAN PREPARATION: Spread unsalted butter on bottom and sides of baking pan. Set pan aside.

4 large ripe Bartlett pears (about 2 pounds, 900 g)
¼ cup (1¾ ounces; 50 g) plus 3 tablespoons granulated sugar, or slightly more if pears are not ripe
½ cup all-purpose flour (2½ ounces; 70 g)
¼ teaspoon salt
½ teaspoon baking powder
3 large eggs
1 cup milk

1. Prepare pan as described. Position rack in center of oven. Preheat oven to 425°F (217°C).

2. To prepare the pears, peel them, then slice each lengthwise into halves. Remove the core with tip of a paring knife. Set each half flat side down on a cutting board and cut crosswise into ⅛-inch slices. Slip the knife blade beneath the entire pear half and lift it up, transferring it to the buttered pan; set the pear half down with the narrow stem end pointing to the center. Repeat, arranging the sliced halves like the petals of a flower in the pan. Now press gently on each pear half, fanning the slices toward the pan center. Sprinkle 2 tablespoons of the sugar over the pears; use more sugar if the pears are underripe.

3. In a mixing bowl, or in the workbowl of a food processor fitted with the metal blade, blend the flour, salt, baking powder, ¼ cup of sugar, the eggs and milk. When smooth, scrape down the inside of the bowl, blend for another second, then pour the batter on top of the pears. Sprinkle on remaining 1 tablespoon of sugar.

4. Set the cake in the preheated oven and

bake as directed, or until the top has puffed, is golden brown, and a cake tester inserted in the center comes out clean. Cool pan on a wire rack for about 10 minutes before serving warm, or serve at room temperature. The cake will sink somewhat as it cools.

Ginnie Hagan's Blueberry Cake

∎

Ginnie Sweatt Hagan is, to my mind, the berry-picking queen of Vermont's Northeast Kingdom. It is a rare summer morning she is not off before dawn on a long-distance trek in pursuit of the perfect wild berry. Perhaps it is the magic of the mountains, or perhaps, as I suspect, Ginnie has a touch of the leprechaun about her, but uncannily she always comes home with a full berry bucket. Ginnie never tells the location of her favorite berry patches, and they stretch from her home in Albany, Vermont, across at least two states and into Quebec, but it doesn't matter because she generously shares her bounty. She picks just for the fun of it and gives most of the berries away to her friends, among whom I gratefully count myself.

Ginnie also organizes church suppers, ice cream socials, village fairs . . . and me. My family is still talking about the day Ginnie dressed me in a bonnet and pinafore, sat me on a hay wagon holding a little black lamb, and entered me in the August Old Home Day town parade as "Mary Had a Little Lamb, His Fleece Was Black as Coal." My reward for this folly (and fun—it was worth every min-

ute) was a morning in her kitchen pouring over berry recipes . . . blueberry chutney, berry muffins, berry ice creams, and this fabulous blueberry cake. It is dark in color, but not as spicy as a gingerbread, and the molasses and cinnamon never overpower the blueberries. I bake this cake often, and find it is just as good made with cranberries. The cake can also be made with frozen berries, unthawed, though fresh wild berries are the best.

□ ADVANCE PREPARATION: The cake can be made ahead and frozen. Thaw and warm before serving.

□ SPECIAL EQUIPMENT: one 9-inch-square baking pan 2 inches deep, 2-cup Pyrex measure

□ BAKING TIME: 40 to 45 minutes at 350°F (175°C)

□ QUANTITY: 3¾ cups batter, one 9-inch square cake (serves 9)

□ PAN PREPARATION: Spread solid shortening on bottom and sides of pan.

2 cups sifted all-purpose flour (8½
  ounces; 240 g)
1 teaspoon baking soda
½ teaspoon salt
1 teaspoon ground cinnamon
¼ cup margarine (½ stick; 60 g), at
  room temperature
1 cup granulated sugar (7 ounces; 200 g)
1 large egg
½ cup unsulfured molasses
1 cup boiling water
1 to 1½ cups fresh blueberries (about
  7½ ounces; 210 g), picked over,
  stemmed, rinsed, and thoroughly
  drained on paper towels; or
  substitute unthawed frozen berries

1 cup heavy cream

1. Prepare pan as described. Position rack in center of oven. Preheat oven to 350°F (175°C).

2. Sift together flour, baking soda, salt, and cinnamon. Set aside.

3. In the large bowl of an electric mixer, cream together margarine and sugar until well blended. Add the egg and beat well. In a 2-cup Pyrex measure, stir together the molasses and boiling water until the molasses is dissolved.

4. Alternately add to the batter the flour mixture and the molasses-water, beginning and ending with flour. Beat very slowly after each addition until well blended. Finally, stir in the blueberries. The batter will be quite thin.

5. Spoon batter into the prepared pan, spread the top evenly, and bake in the preheated oven for 40 to 45 minutes, 50 minutes if using frozen berries, or until a cake tester inserted in the center comes out clean and the top is lightly springy to the touch. Cool the cake on a wire rack, cut it into 3-inch squares, and serve it warm with a little heavy cream poured over each slice.

·Variation:·

CRANBERRY-BLUEBERRY CAKE:

Prepare Ginnie Hagan's Blueberry Cake, but add ½ cup whole fresh or unthawed frozen cranberries to the recipe. Don't decrease quantity of blueberries. Or substitute cranberries (whole or chopped) for all the blueberries.

Lemon-Blueberry Pudding Cake

■

Pudding cake is an old-fashioned favorite now staging a comeback. Unfortunately, however, it has returned primarily in the form of cake mix. It is too bad, because this is just as quick to prepare from scratch; in fact my time tests show that once the ingredients are measured and the eggs separated, preparation time is barely 5 minutes.

This is a recipe novice bakers and children love; a few basic ingredients are simply whisked together, and the only skill needed is turning on the electric mixer to whip egg whites. In the heat of the oven, an ordinary looking batter is magically transformed into a rich creamy pudding studded with fruit and topped by a layer of delicate sponge cake. Serve pudding cake warm for brunch; it is pure heaven.

Note: To achieve the correct texture, it is essential that this cake be baked in a water bath. For flavor variations, the lemon zest may be omitted and other fruit juices substituted for lemon juice. Raspberries may be substituted for blueberries.

□ ADVANCE PREPARATION: The cake can be baked ahead and served cold, but it is exceptionally good warm from the oven, and is best made fairly soon before serving.

□ SPECIAL EQUIPMENT: one 8-inch-square baking pan 2 inches deep or 1½-quart ovenproof casserole, roasting pan large enough to hold the cake pan or casserole with at least an inch or two of space all around, for a water bath; grater, whisk or food processor fitted with steel blade, bowl and beater for whipping egg whites

☐ BAKING TIME: 25 to 35 minutes at 350°F (175°C)

☐ QUANTITY: 4-cups batter, one 8-inch cake (serves 4 or 5)

☐ PAN PREPARATION: Generously coat pan with butter or margarine, not solid shortening. Set out roasting pan and pitcher of water for the water bath.

1 cup granulated sugar (7 ounces;
  200 g)
⅛ teaspoon salt
3 tablespoons unsifted all-purpose flour
Generous pinch of ground cinnamon
2 tablespoons unsalted butter, melted
  and cooled
Grated zest of 1 lemon
¼ cup freshly squeezed lemon juice
3 large eggs, separated, at room
  temperature
1 cup milk
1 cup fresh blueberries or raspberries.
  Note: frozen whole berries can be
  used, but be sure they are drained
  and dry.

1. Prepare pan as directed. Position rack in center of oven. Preheat oven to 350°F (175°C).

2. In a large mixing bowl or the workbowl of a food processor, combine ¾ cup plus 2 tablespoons sugar with the salt, flour, and cinnamon. Stir or pulse for 2 or 3 seconds to mix. Add the melted butter, grated lemon zest and juice, and the egg yolks. Whisk by hand or pulse for a few seconds to blend, then blend in the milk. Do not overbeat.

3. In a clean bowl, beat the egg whites with an electric mixer until foamy. Add remaining 2 tablespoons sugar and beat until the whites are nearly stiff but not dry. Fold the whites into the lemon batter in several additions. Gently fold in the berries.

4. Turn batter into the prepared pan and set cake pan in the larger roasting pan. Carefully pour water into the side of the larger pan until it reaches ⅓ to ½ way up the sides of the baking pan. Gently place the cake in its water bath in the preheated oven and bake for 25 minutes, or until the top is golden brown. Remove cake from the water bath, cool for a few minutes, and serve warm, directly from the pan.

Chocolate Pudding Cake

■

"Quick, easy, and great" read my batter-stained notes for this recipe. You simply toss ingredients together, stir, and top with boiling water. Never mind the fact that it looks weird before baking. It emerges from the oven like a crisp-topped brownie rippled with dark chocolate pudding. Note that the batter is egg-less and uses cholesterol-free vegetable oil—a health bonus, if you need an excuse. Throw in some nuts or chopped white chocolate if you want to get creative, and serve the pudding cake warm, spooned from its baking pan and topped with heavy cream.

☐ ADVANCE PREPARATION: Cake can be baked ahead and rewarmed, but it is never quite as wonderful as when fresh. It will, however, keep fresh, covered, at room temperature for a day or two. In very hot weather, store in the refrigerator.

□ SPECIAL EQUIPMENT: 8-inch-square baking pan 2 inches deep

□ BAKING TIME: 35 minutes at 350°F (175°C)

□ QUANTITY: one 8-inch dessert (serves 4 to 6, or 1 chocoholic)

□ PAN PREPARATION: Spread butter or margarine on bottom and sides of pan.

1 cup unsifted all-purpose flour (5 ounces; 140 g)
1⅓ cups granulated sugar (9¼ ounces; 265 g)
6 tablespoons unsweetened cocoa, preferably Dutch-process
2 teaspoons baking powder
¼ teaspoon ground cinnamon
½ teaspoon instant espresso coffee powder
Generous ¼ teaspoon salt
½ cup milk
¼ cup light vegetable oil, such as corn or safflower oil
1 teaspoon vanilla extract
1 cup boiling water

1. Prepare pan as described. Position rack in center of oven. Preheat oven to 350°F (175°C).

2. In a mixing bowl, combine flour, ⅔ cup of the granulated sugar, 4 tablespoons of the cocoa, the baking powder, cinnamon, coffee powder, and salt. Stir well to blend. With a wooden spoon, stir in milk, oil, and vanilla extract. The batter will feel quite stiff.

3. Spoon batter into the prepared pan and smooth the top more or less even. In a small bowl, stir together remaining 2 tablespoons cocoa and ⅔ cup granulated sugar. Spread this mixture evenly over the batter in the pan. On top of this, pour the boiling water. Do not stir.

4. Carefully set the pan in the preheated oven and bake as directed, or until the top looks crisp and crackled and a cake tester inserted into a cakey area comes out clean. Cool for a few minutes. Serve directly from the pan, topped by unsweetened heavy cream or vanilla ice cream.

Cheesecakes

ABOUT CHEESECAKE

∎

Who can resist the appeal of a rich, creamy, satin-smooth cheesecake? Never mind the calories . . . we include a low-calorie version for the die(t)-hards. Take a smaller slice if you must, but take it. Life is too short. Since this is one luxury that is well within reach, and it is easy to make and freezes well, it is worth preparing for a special occasion.

The following recipes are all winners; in fact, one actually garnered first prize in a cheesecake contest. Read the following tips and notes on ingredients so that you will understand the reasons for each technique.

Equipment

If your mixer has a flat paddle attachment, use it in place of a regular whipping beater, because it will incorporate less air; cheesecakes should be creamed, not whipped. In fact, if you happen to overbeat the batter with a whipping beater, the excess air may cause the cake to crack during baking, though there can be other reasons, explained below. If you do use regular whisk-style beaters, use them on low to low-medium speed, never high; this way, they will not whip excess air into the batter.

When setting the cake into the oven to bake, it is best to place it on a sturdy jelly-roll pan with a lip. This is especially important when using springform pans, because they can leak if not tightly fastened. Once, I experienced the disaster of having a spring come unsprung just as I removed a gorgeous Tangerine Cheesecake from my oven. Naturally, the sides fell away, and the cake landed half in the oven, half on the floor. A baking sheet could at least have saved the cake from the garbage pail.

Batter

For a cheesecake to taste smooth and creamy, the batter must be smooth and creamy at every stage. To accomplish this, all ingredients must be at room temperature (approximately 70°F) when you begin. Beat the cream cheese until smooth and soft before adding any other ingredients to your mixing bowl. Stop the mixer several times to scrape down the inside of the bowl and beater, taking care that there are no lumps in the batter and no ingredients stuck to the bowl bottom.

Cracks

Sometimes cracks appear in the top of a cheesecake while it is baking or cooling. There are as many reasons for this as there are cures or preventive measures. Most cracks occur because the cake has released its moisture or steam too quickly, causing fissures in the delicate warm structure. This can happen when the cake is exposed to extreme changes in temperature, such as baking in too hot an oven, baking for too long a time, or being placed in a cool spot or a draft immediately after baking. Deep cavernous cracks mean the egg-white structure has partially collapsed and the cake's texture may resemble a pudding; it will be edible, but not what you expected, so top it with fruit and don't serve it to company. Shallow cracks often occur despite our best efforts, and generally can be ignored. If they show up during baking, remember that the cake will sink down as it cools and these cracks will get somewhat smaller. Also, you can cover the top with sour cream or a fruit glaze.

To help prevent cracks, professional bakeries often add steam to their ovens; some recipes call for solid-bottom (nonspringform) pans to be baked in a water bath. This procedure adds both moisture and temperature control to give slow, even heat. However, in this book I have chosen the less cumbersome procedure of using the springform pan and baking in a low oven. Be sure to put an auxiliary oven thermometer inside your oven to moniter the heat; oven thermostats are notoriously irregular. (Oven thermometers are inexpensive and sold in hardware stores.) If you can avoid it, never open the oven door during the first half of the baking time for a cheesecake, to keep temperatures steady. Most of my recipes advise leaving the cake in the oven after baking, with the heat off, for an additional hour or so to allow the cake to cool off very slowly, away from drafts. You should follow recipe cooling procedures carefully; they make a difference. One unusual technique, described in the Tangerine Cheesecake recipe, calls for topping the cooling cake with a cardboard disk. The cardboard absorbs the moisture as the cake cools and keeps away drafts. Odd, but it works well. And remember, nothing is infallible.

Crusts

Cheesecakes are so rich that I prefer a light crust. My favorite technique is simply to butter the sides and bottom of the springform pan, then dust the butter with toasted and ground nuts, or cookie crumbs. This produces a light coating that enhances the cake without intruding, and the work involved is minimal. Be sure to select nuts or crumbs with a flavor that is compatible with that of the cake. The recipe for New York Cheesecake does have a pastry crust.

Baking

To tell if your cheesecake is done, observe the top surface carefully. For most cheesecakes, the edges of the baked cake puff up slightly and may turn just faintly golden. You do not want a deeply browned crust. The top surface should look dull, not shiny, and when the side of the pan is lightly tapped, the center should move slightly from side to side but not jiggle as if it were liquid. It is normal for the center to be softer than the edges when the cake is baked. The entire cake will rise during baking, then settle and solidify as it cools. If any cracks appear, they usually get smaller as the cake cools and sinks down.

Transferring Cakes

If you want to freeze a cheesecake but need to reuse the springform pan, you can transfer the cake to another surface. To do this, chill your cake in the refrigerator in the springform pan for at least 4 hours, or overnight, so you are sure the cake is very firm. Then cover a sturdy corrugated cardboard disk of the cake's diameter, or larger, with foil. Set out your largest longest spatula, preferably one with a blade about 1¾ inches by 12 inches. After removing the sides of the springform, very cautiously slide the spatula beneath the bottom of the cake; ease the cake off the baking pan and onto the cardboard. It helps to have a partner to hold the cardboard for you, but it works anyway if your spatula is big enough. Do not attempt this with a thin-bladed knife or a stubby pancake turner, and never try to transfer a warm cake! After transferring the cake, wrap it airtight with plastic wrap and heavy-duty foil before labeling and freezing.

Cutting Cheesecake

Cheesecake tends to stick to the serving knife, making neat slices difficult to achieve. It helps to heat the knife blade under hot running water between cuts, but this is not too convenient during a dinner party. One solution is simply to have at hand an extra knife with which to scrape the cutting knife clean after each slice. My favorite method also makes for good conversation: use dental floss or heavy button thread for cutting. Cut a length about 20 inches long, or the diameter of the cake plus enough to wrap around both hands. Then simply pull the thread taut between your hands, poise it above the cake, and press down right to the cake bottom. Release the thread in one hand and pull it out with the other hand. Repeat, making slices of desired width across the cake like the spokes of a wheel.

Ingredients

□ CREAM CHEESE

Cheese is what this cake is all about; while a variety of cheeses may be used, cream cheese is one of the most common. It is the basic element for most of the recipes here.

Cream cheese contains 35 to 40 percent butterfat. Generally speaking, the higher the butterfat content, the creamier and richer will be the cheesecake. Brands of cream cheese vary in quality and flavor. Cut-rate or generic cream cheese is often less creamy, rich, and delicate of flavor than one would wish, and usually the butterfat content is the minimum permissible. Avoid at all costs using either "imitation cream cheese" or whipped cream cheese for these recipes.

One of the most widely available national brands, and the one I prefer, is Kraft's Philadelphia Brand Cream Cheese, sold in 3- and 8-ounce foil-wrapped blocks that are freshness-dated. Be sure to check dates.

Cream cheese must be brought to room temperature before combining with the other ingredients in your batter. If you are in a hurry and have just removed the cream cheese from the refrigerator, open the packages and put the cheese in the microwave on high speed for 2 or 3 seconds only. Test it; it should be soft to touch but not even near melting. Heat for another second if necessary.

□ HOMEMADE YOGURT CHEESE

This low-calorie substitute for cream cheese is a Middle-Eastern specialty called *labna*. It is simply plain yogurt hung in a cheesecloth bag until all the water is drained out, leaving a creamy, mild, low-fat cheese. It resembles the French cheese, Boursin, and makes a great cracker spread when mixed with herbs. Try it in the recipe for Low-Calorie Yogurt Cheesecake (page 204).

□ RICOTTA CHEESE

Ricotta is a fresh, unripened cheese with a bland, slightly nutty flavor. It is moist, with a soft fine curd that gives a slightly granular texture. While ricotta in Italy is often made from the whey of sheep's milk, American ricotta is usually made from cow's-milk whey. It contains between 4 and 10 percent butterfat and has half the calories of cream cheese per ounce (about 50 as compared with 100). For cheesecakes, whole-milk ricotta is preferable to that made with skim milk.

□ COTTAGE CHEESE

Cottage cheese is a mild-flavored, soft-curd, unripened cheese made from either whole or skim milk. Its flavor is usually slightly sweeter or tangier than ricotta. Depending upon whether or not it has been creamed (by having whole milk or cream added to the curds), the butterfat content can vary between 4 and 15 percent; indeed, some dairies claim it to be as low as ½ to 2 percent. For cheesecake, I prefer to use creamed cottage cheese with a butterfat content of at least 3 or 4 percent.

□ SOUR CREAM

Sour cream, with a butterfat content of about 20 percent, contributes both smoothness and richness to cheesecake. Be sure to check the freshness date on the carton, and bring the cream to room temperature before adding it to the batter.

□ FLOUR

A little flour is sometimes added to cheesecake as a thickening agent. Beware, for too much can cause toughness. You can use either all-purpose or cake flour, sifted before measuring. Cornstarch and potato starch can also be used for thickening cheesecakes.

□ EGGS

Eggs are added to cheesecakes for several reasons. They provide body and texture because they solidify when exposed to heat, but in addition they have the ability to hold the high percentage of moisture present in the cheeses.

The lecithin found in egg yolks also helps congeal the butterfat from the cheese and cream. As a general rule, the greater the amount of butterfat in a recipe, the greater the number of eggs used.

Stiffly beaten egg whites encapsulate a great deal of air between the bubbles of a fine protein web. When gently folded into a cheese batter, they add a light texture to the finished cake. Remember that eggs separate most easily when cold but whites beat to fullest volume when at room temperature. Cold whites can be warmed by setting the bowl of whites into a second bowl of warm water for a few minutes.

Frances's Light Cheesecake

■

When I was growing up, my mother made this delicious cheesecake for special family occasions. It has a satin-smooth texture and the addition of stiffly beaten egg whites makes it lighter than a classic cheesecake. Occasionally, we like to top the cake with a glaze of strawberries, or other berries in season, because the tang of fruit balances the cake's richness. You can use this recipe to create the Light Marble Cheesecake variation that follows.

Though it is not as dense as the classic cheesecake, this version also freezes well. And it travels. I proved this recently when I carried one, frozen, foil-wrapped, and packed in a cardboard cakebox, from our Connecticut home to an uncle in Florida. I am delighted to report that the cake survived both a tumble onto the floor of the plane and a toss by an overzealous baggage handler. It arrived intact and still frozen; at room temperature, no one would have guessed it was imported.

□ ADVANCE PREPARATION: Allow 2 to 3 hours for the baked cake to cool, then 4 hours minimum to become firm in the refrigerator before serving. In fact, this cake benefits from mellowing and firming overnight in the refrigerator. It can be made a day or two before serving, or wrapped airtight and frozen for a week or two without flavor loss. Refrigerate leftovers.

Strawberry Glaze can be prepared a day in advance and refrigerated, or the cake can be topped with glaze and refrigerated.

□ SPECIAL EQUIPMENT: one 9½-inch springform pan, sturdy baking sheet or jelly-roll pan, blender or food processor for chopping nuts, electric mixer with paddle attachment if available, extra bowl and beater for whipping egg whites

□ BAKING TIME: 1 hour and 20 minutes at 300°F (150°C), then cool in oven with heat off but door closed for 60 minutes. Prop oven door open leaving cake inside, and cool completely for at least 60 minutes longer.

□ QUANTITY: one 9½-inch cake (serves 10 to 12)

□ PAN PREPARATION: Generously spread softened butter on bottom and sides of springform pan.

CRUMB CRUST:

½ cup hazelnuts (2½ ounces; 70 g), toasted (page 43), or almonds
1 tablespoon granulated sugar (optional)

CAKE:

3 tablespoons all-purpose flour
¼ teaspoon salt
1½ cups (10½ ounces; 300 g) plus 3 tablespoons granulated sugar
18 ounces cream cheese (1 lb. 2 ounces; 515 g), at room temperature
6 large eggs, separated, at room temperature
2 cups sour cream
1 teaspoon vanilla extract

TOPPING (OPTIONAL):

Strawberry Glaze (page 405)

1. Read About Cheesecake (page 184). Position rack in center of oven. Preheat oven to 300°F (150°C). Prepare pan as directed. After toasting nuts, mix them with 1 tablespoon sugar and grind them in the food processor. Sprinkle ground nuts evenly over sides and bottom of prepared pan. Pat any excess nuts onto the bottom. Set pan aside; in hot weather, store pan in refrigerator.

2. If your mixer has a flat paddle, attach it in place of the regular beaters. Sift together flour, salt, and 1½ cups of sugar into a small bowl. In the large bowl of an electric mixer, beat cream cheese until smooth and soft. Add flour mixture and beat well. Stop mixer and scrape down beater and inside of bowl several times.

3. Lightly whisk egg yolks together in a medium-size bowl, then add them to the cheese batter and beat until very smooth and creamy. Stop mixer and scrape down inside of bowl once or twice. Add sour cream and vanilla and beat smooth.

4. In a separate mixing bowl with a clean regular whipping beater, beat egg whites until foamy. Add remaining 3 tablespoons sugar and beat until stiff but not dry. Gradually fold the whites into the cheese batter. Turn batter into the prepared pan and set on a sturdy baking sheet or jelly-roll pan for ease in handling.

5. Place cake in center of preheated oven and bake for 1 hour and 20 minutes, or until the cake edges are slightly puffed up and the top has a dull finish but is dry to the touch. When side of pan is tapped, the cake center should move slightly, but not jiggle in waves as if liquid. Turn off heat, leave cake inside, and set timer for 60 minutes. After this time, prop open oven door and leave cake inside until completely cool to the touch, at least 1 hour longer. Finally, place cake on a wire rack until cold if not already so, then cover with plastic wrap to protect flavor and refrigerate for a minimum of 4 hours, or overnight, to become firm before serving.

Strawberry Glaze can be added to cold cake before chilling in the refrigerator, or it can be added just before serving. Remove cake from refrigerator at least 30 minutes before serving. Or, after firming in the refrigerator for 4 hours, wrap unglazed cake airtight and freeze.

·Variation:·

LIGHT MARBLE CHEESECAKE:

Prepare Frances's Light Cheesecake through the first half of step 4, when stiff whites are folded into the batter. Measure 2 cups of finished batter into a small bowl and lightly fold in 3 tablespoons sifted unsweetened cocoa.

Then pour about half of the original vanilla batter into the prepared pan. Alternate half-cups full of chocolate and vanilla until the batter is used up. Pull and swirl the blade of a table knife or spatula through the batter to make a marbleized pattern. Be careful not to touch pan bottom or sides with the knife or spatula while swirling or crumb crust will be dislodged and batter may stick to pan. Bake as directed. Omit fruit topping.

Leslie's Black and White Cheesecake

•

Leslie Sutton, of Darien, Connecticut, won first prize with this recipe in a cheesecake contest sponsored by the Complete Kitchen cookware shop in her hometown. With over 40 entries, the competition was stiff, but once you have tried her delectable recipe you will understand why the hands-down winner was this two-tone cake with one intensely chocolate layer topping a creamy vanilla base. For a gala presentation, Leslie suggests decorating the cake top with a cluster of small Chocolate Leaves (see Index). To turn this basic cake into Marble Cheesecake, Chocolate Cheesecake, Mocha Cheesecake, or Brownie Mosaic Cheesecake, see the variations following.

☐ ADVANCE PREPARATION: Allow 2 to 3 hours for baked cake to cool, then 4 hours minimum in the refrigerator for the cake to become firm before serving. In fact, this cake benefits from mellowing and firming overnight in the refrigerator; it can be made a day or two before serving, or wrapped airtight and frozen for several weeks without flavor loss.

☐ SPECIAL EQUIPMENT: one 9½-inch springform pan, sturdy baking sheet or jelly-roll pan, double boiler

☐ BAKING TIME: 40 minutes at 350°F (175°C), then 10 minutes at 450°F (230°C)

☐ QUANTITY: one 9½-inch cake (serves 12 to 14)

☐ PAN PREPARATION: Spread softened butter on bottom and sides of springform pan.

CRUMB CRUST:

1¾ cups chocolate wafer crumbs
    (8½-ounce package of wafers; 240 g)
7 tablespoons unsalted butter (3½
    ounces; 100 g), melted
    Note: ¾ cup toasted, ground
    hazelnuts (3 ounces; 85 g), almonds,
    or walnuts can be liberally sprinkled
    over buttered pan sides and bottom
    instead of butter-wafer mixture. Or
    ground nuts can be combined with
    wafer crumbs and butter if you
    prefer.

CAKE:

7 ounces semisweet chocolate (200 g),
    Poulain Bittersweet or other
    fine-quality chocolate, chopped or in
    morsels
Three 8-ounce packages cream cheese
    (690 g), at room temperature
1 cup granulated sugar (7 ounces;
    200 g)

⅛ teaspoon salt
3 large eggs
1 cup sour cream
1 teaspoon vanilla extract

TOPPING:

2 cups sour cream
¼ cup granulated sugar (1¾ ounces;

1. Read About Cheesecake (page 184). Position rack in center of oven. Preheat oven to 350°F (175°C). Prepare pan as directed. Combine chocolate wafer crumbs and melted butter; press crumbs evenly onto bottom and sides of pan. Set pan aside. If weather is hot, store pan in refrigerator.

2. Place chocolate in the top pan of a double boiler over, not in, very hot water and heat until melted. Stir until smooth. Or melt in the microwave following manufacturer's directions (power 7 for 4½ to 5 minutes is average), but be very sure all the chocolate is melted and can be stirred absolutely smooth. Remove from heat and set aside to cool.

3. If your mixer has a flat paddle, attach it in place of the regular beaters. In the large bowl of an electric mixer, beat the cream cheese until smooth and soft. Add sugar and salt and beat until mixture is very creamy and smooth. Stop the mixer and scrape down the beater and the inside of the bowl several times. Add eggs, one at a time, and beat after each addition. Add 1 cup sour cream and the vanilla and beat until well combined.

4. Pour half of this batter into the prepared springform pan. Test temperature of melted chocolate; if it is comfortable to the touch, stir well, then pour chocolate into batter remain-

ing in the mixing bowl. Beat just to blend well, then pour chocolate batter on top of vanilla layer in the pan.

5. Smooth cake top flat. Set filled cake pan on a sturdy baking sheet or jelly-roll pan for ease in handling. Set cake in center of pre-heated oven to bake for 40 minutes, or until the top has a dull finish but is dry to the touch; the surface should move slightly when you tap the side of the pan, but it should not jiggle in waves as if it were liquid. Remove cake from oven and set on a heatproof surface in a draft-free location. Increase oven heat to 450°F (230°C).

6. While oven is heating, combine 2 cups sour cream and sugar for topping. When oven heat is reached (allow at least 10 minutes), spread topping over cake and return it to the oven. Bake for 10 minutes. Remove cake from oven, set on a wire rack away from drafts, and bring to room temperature. When cold, cover with plastic wrap to protect flavors and refrigerate for at least 4 hours to allow cake to become firm before cutting. For best flavor, remove from refrigerator 30 minutes before serving. Release sides of spring-form but leave cake on pan bottom. Or, after firming in refrigerator for at least 4 hours, wrap cake airtight and freeze. Refrigerate leftovers.

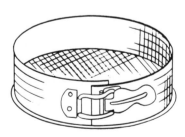

·*Variations:*·

MARBLE CHEESECAKE:

Prepare Leslie's Black and White Cheesecake with the following changes: in step 4, pour half of the vanilla batter into a medium-size bowl or 4-cup liquid measure. Blend melted chocolate into batter remaining in the original mixing bowl. To create the marbleized effect, pour vanilla batter into the prepared pan until bottom is covered. Then pour about 1 cup of the chocolate batter into the pan, then 1 cup of vanilla. Continue alternating colors until all batter is used. Pull and swirl the blade of a table knife or spatula through the batter to make a marbleized pattern. Be careful not to touch pan bottom or sides with knife or spatula while swirling or crumb crust will be dislodged and batter may stick to pan. Omit sour cream topping.

Bake as directed for 50 to 55 minutes. Check for doneness as in master recipe. Turn off oven heat, prop door open, and leave cake in oven until completely cool.

CHOCOLATE CHEESECAKE:

I prefer to bake this variation in an 8½-inch springform pan. Add ½ teaspoon ground cinnamon to the crumb crust. The crust will take slightly fewer crumbs than with the larger pan. As usual, the cake rises as it bakes, but it sinks quite a bit as it cools.

Prepare Leslie's Cheesecake through step 3. In step 4, make the following changes: Stir 1 cup of cheese batter into the melted and cooled chocolate. Stir until the color is uniform. Then turn all the chocolate mixture back into the rest of the cheese batter and beat just to blend. Pour into the prepared pan and bake as for Marble Cheesecake. Use sour cream topping, or omit it, as you prefer.

MOCHA CHEESECAKE:

Prepare Chocolate Cheesecake. Dissolve 1½ teaspoons instant espresso or regular instant coffee powder in 1 teaspoon boiling water. Stir until smooth and cool. Add to batter along with vanilla. Bake as for Marbleized Cheesecake. Use sour-cream topping, or omit it, as you prefer.

BROWNIE MOSAIC CHEESECAKE:

Franni's Pâtisserie-Café on Monkland Avenue is one of Montreal's favorite lunch, tea, and after-theater dining spots. This small, elegant restaurant offers a short, select entrée menu but a sumptuous and lavish array of desserts including over 22 types of freshly baked cheesecakes. I spent one glorious summer day on their outdoor terrace tasting each and every cake, and learning about the fresh ingredients and loving care that my friends Fran and Wally Sheper, the talented young owners, put into their product.

Brownie Mosaic Cheesecake is one of Fran's original inventions, combining two of her favorite sweets in a way that may at first sound like overkill, but is surprisingly successful and delicious. In fact, it is one of their most requested desserts. The brownies are deliberately underbaked and very moist; they are excellent served as is or topped with ice cream. When cubed and added to the cheesecake batter, they meld with the cream filling, absorbing some of its moisture while providing a contrast in flavor and texture. When the slices are cut, the brownies provide the mosaic pattern. This cake is topped with an unbaked dark chocolate glaze, made quickly and easily in the food processor. Note: The brownies may also be added to Mocha Cheesecake or to Café Au Lait Cheesecake.

□ PROCEDURE:
Line the 9½-inch springform pan with the chocolate wafer crumb crust as directed in step 1 of Leslie's Cheesecake. Bake the brownies, using the recipe that follows. Make Leslie's Cheesecake batter with the following changes:

Omit all melted chocolate, making a plain vanilla cheese batter. Gently fold the cubed brownies (about 2 cups) into the cheese batter; avoid making crumbs by stirring. Pour the mixture into the prepared pan. Bake in the preheated 350°F (175°C) oven for 50 minutes. Omit the sour-cream topping and the 10-minute bake at higher heat. Remove from the oven and cool on a wire rack set away from drafts. Note that the brownies may cause the cake top to appear uneven and lumpy; this is fine. When the cake is thoroughly cooled (see step 6), top it with ½ recipe (½ cup) of Franni's Ganache Glaze, (page 409). Smooth the glaze over the top of the cake while the glaze is warm. This cake freezes well.

FRANNI'S BROWNIES:

□ SPECIAL EQUIPMENT: one 8-inch-square pan 1½ inches deep, or a pan 9 × 6 × 1½ inches; 2-quart saucepan, wooden spoon

□ BAKING TIME: 22 to 25 minutes at 350°F (175°C)

□ PAN PREPARATION: Spread solid shortening on bottom and sides of pan, line bottom with wax paper or baking parchment, grease paper.

2 ounces bittersweet or semisweet chocolate, chopped (about ⅓ cup; 60 g)
½ cup unsalted butter (1 stick; 110 g), cut up
⅞ cup granulated sugar (6 ounces; 170 g)
2 large eggs, lightly beaten
¼ teaspoon almond or vanilla extract
½ teaspoon baking powder
½ teaspoon salt
½ cup unsifted all-purpose flour (2½ ounces; 70 g)

In a 2-quart saucepan set over low heat, melt together the chocolate and butter. Stir to blend, then stir in sugar. Remove pan from heat. Add the eggs, stirring constantly until well blended. Add remaining ingredients, stirring until smooth. Pour batter into the prepared pan and bake in the center of the preheated oven for 22 to 25 minutes, until a cake tester comes out just slightly moist rather than completely clean. The top will look shiny, with a slightly crackled surface. Do not overbake; the brownies should be moist rather than dry. Cool in the pan on a wire rack for a few minutes, then invert and peel off paper. Cool brownies, then cut them into ¾- to 1-inch squares for use in the cheesecake. You will have approximately 2 cups of loosely measured cubes. Add brownies to cheesecake batter as directed above, or serve by themselves as a dessert.

Café Au Lait Cheesecake

■

If you like coffee, you will love this mellow, richly coffee-flavored, silken cheesecake. I developed the recipe to take advantage of a new brand of coffee liqueur I was testing and found, somewhat to my surprise, that this cake quickly became a favorite of family and friends.

□ ADVANCE PREPARATION: Allow 2 to 3 hours for baked cake to cool, than 4 hours minimum, refrigerated, to become firm before serving. In fact, the cake benefits from mellowing a day or two in the refrigerator. Wrapped airtight, it may be frozen for several weeks. Thaw, wrapped, in refrigerator overnight. Bring to room temperature before serving.

□ SPECIAL EQUIPMENT: one 8½-inch springform pan, sturdy baking sheet or jelly-roll pan, flat paddle beater for electric mixer if available
Note: You can also use a 9½-inch springform pan, but the cake will be a little less thick than with the smaller pan.

□ BAKING TIME: 45 minutes at 325°F (165°C); Cool in the oven with heat off and door closed for 30 minutes, then prop oven door open and cool cake to room temperature, about 60 minutes.

□ QUANTITY: one 8½-inch cake (serves 12)

□ PAN PREPARATION: Generously butter sides and bottom of springform pan.

CRUMB CRUST:

*¾ cup hazelnuts (3¾ ounces; 105 g),
  toasted and skinned (page 43)*
2 tablespoons granulated sugar

CAKE:

*Two 8-ounce packages cream cheese
  (460 g), at room temperature*
*1 cup granulated sugar (7 ounces;
  200 g)*
3 large eggs
2 tablespoons best-quality coffee liqueur
*2 teaspoons instant espresso powder
  dissolved in 1 teaspoon boiling
  water, stirred smooth*
*7 tablespoons sifted cake flour (3¾
  ounces; 105 g)*
*1 tablespoon sifted unsweetened cocoa
  powder*
¼ teaspoon baking powder
⅛ teaspoon salt
1 cup sour cream
*1 teaspoon undissolved instant espresso
  powder*

1. Read About Cheesecake (page 184). Place rack in center of oven. Prepare pan as directed. Preheat oven to 325°F (165°C).

In a food processor or blender, combine nuts with 2 tablespoons sugar and grind fine. Sprinkle nut mixture on bottom and sides of prepared pan. Pat any excess nuts evenly over the bottom. Set pan aside; if weather is hot, store pan in refrigerator.

2. If your mixer has a flat paddle, attach it in place of the regular beaters. In the large bowl of an electric mixer, beat the cream cheese until smooth and soft. Add 1 cup sugar and beat until very creamy and smooth. Stop mixer and scrape down beater and inside of bowl several times. Beat in eggs, one at a time, along with coffee liqueur and dissolved coffee powder.

3. Sift together flour, cocoa, baking powder, and salt onto a sheet of wax paper. In 3 additions, add dry ingredients to cheese batter, beating to blend each time. Add sour cream and beat to combine thoroughly, but do not whip air into batter. Stir in the undissolved espresso powder. Pour batter into prepared pan. Set pan on a sturdy baking sheet for ease in handling.

4. Place cake, on baking sheet, in center of the preheated oven and bake for 45 minutes. Then turn off oven heat but leave door shut and set timer for 30 minutes. Finally, prop oven door open and allow cake to cool to room temperature, about 1 hour. Remove cake from oven, set on counter until really comfortable to touch, then cover with plastic wrap and chill in the refrigerator for at least 6 hours, or overnight. Note: You can cover the cake with a cardboard disk instead of plastic wrap before chilling it if you are worried that it may crack further.

5. Remove cake from refrigerator 30 minutes before serving. Remove sides of springform pan but leave cake on pan bottom to serve. Serve plain or, if you wish, place a paper doily atop the cake, then sift on a light coating of unsweetened cocoa and carefully remove doily. Or garnish by placing a ring of candied coffee beans around the edge of the cake.

Tangerine Cheesecake

■

This rich cheesecake sparkles with the unique tang of tangerine flavoring. Topped with tangerine-scented sour cream and garnished with tangerine zest, it is a party showstopper. You can use this as a master recipe to create lemon or lime cheesecake, as well as Nut Cheesecake or Roberta's Lemon Sambuca Cheesecake. The basic formula is my variation of a recipe shared with me by my friend Shirley Johansen.

☐ ADVANCE PREPARATION: Allow 2 to 3 hours for the baked cake to cool, then 5 to 6 hours minimum, refrigerated, to become firm before serving. This cake benefits from mellowing and firming overnight in the refrigerator and is best made a day or two in advance. It can be wrapped airtight and frozen for several weeks without flavor loss. Thaw in refrigerator while still wrapped. Bring to room temperature before serving.

☐ SPECIAL EQUIPMENT: one 10-inch springform pan, sturdy baking sheet or jelly-roll pan, flat paddle-type beater instead of regular whipping beater for mixer, if available, 10 to 12-inch corrugated cardboard disk (use a standard cardboard cake disk or a pizza disk, or cut your own from heavy cardboard), grater

☐ BAKING TIME: 45 to 50 minutes at 350°F (175°C) for plain cake; 10 minutes longer after topping is added

☐ QUANTITY: one 10-inch cake (serves 12).

☐ PAN PREPARATION: Spread softened butter on bottom and sides of 10-inch springform pan

CRUMB CRUST:

2 cups graham cracker or cinnamon crisp cracker crumbs (9 ounces; 255 g). Note: 1 cup lightly toasted and ground pecans or almonds may be substituted for half of the crumbs.

   If you substitute a different type of crumbs, you may need up to ½ cup extra, as they compact differently.
7 tablespoons lightly salted butter (3½ ounces; 105 g), melted
3 tablespoons granulated sugar

CAKE:

Four 8-ounce packages cream cheese (920 g), at room temperature
1¼ cups granulated sugar (8¾ ounces; 250 g)
4 tablespoons frozen tangerine-juice concentrate, thawed but undiluted
2 tablespoons tangerine or orange liqueur (Mandarine or Grand Marnier, for example)
1 teaspoon orange extract
1 tablespoon grated tangerine zest (if not available, substitute orange zest; do not use dried grated peel)
4 tablespoons all-purpose flour
⅛ teaspoon salt
4 large eggs plus 1 extra egg yolk

2 cups sour cream (16½ ounces; 470 g)
¼ cup granulated sugar (1¾ ounces; 50 g)
1 tablespoon frozen tangerine-juice concentrate, thawed, or substitute orange liqueur

GARNISH:

2 teaspoons grated tangerine or orange zest

1. Read About Cheesecake (page 184). Arrange rack in center of oven. Preheat oven to 350°F (175°C). Prepare pan as directed. To prepare crust, combine crumbs, melted butter, and 3 tablespoons sugar, and toss well to blend. Press crumbs evenly onto bottom and sides of prepared pan. Set pan aside. If weather is hot, store pan in refrigerator.

2. If your mixer has a flat paddle, attach it in place of the regular beaters. In the large bowl of an electric mixer, beat the cream cheese until smooth and soft. Add 1¼ cups sugar and beat until creamy. Add remaining cake ingredients except eggs and beat until smooth. Add eggs and extra yolk, one at a time, beating for just a second after each addition. Beat to be sure batter is well blended, but don't incorporate too much air.

3. Pour batter into prepared pan and set on a sturdy baking sheet or jelly-roll pan. Place in center of preheated oven and bake for 45 to 50 minutes, or until the edges of the cake are slightly puffed up and turning light golden brown. The center surface will be firm to the touch though softer than the edges. Don't be troubled if you have slight cracks around the edges; the topping will cover them.

4. Remove cake from oven and set on a heatproof surface away from drafts while you prepare topping. In a medium-size bowl, beat together topping ingredients, stirring until smooth. Spread evenly over top of cake. With cake still on its sturdy pan, return it to the oven and bake for an additional 10 minutes.

5. Remove cake from oven, let it set for 3 minutes, then cover with a cardboard disk. Note that the cake will be recessed about ½ inch below the pan top, so the disk will not rest atop the cake, but rather balance on the edge of the pan. Cool pan covered with the cardboard on a wire rack for about 60 minutes, then put the cake, still covered with cardboard, directly into the refrigerator and leave it there overnight. At this point, the cake can be served, or wrapped airtight and frozen. Take cake out of refrigerator 30 minutes before serving. Remove sides of springform pan but leave cake on pan bottom.

· *Variations:* ·

NUT CHEESECAKE:

Prepare Tangerine Cheesecake, with the following changes: Use at least 1 cup ground toasted nuts in the crumb crust. Any nut cookie can be used in place of graham or cinnamon crackers, if you wish. I use Italian Amaretti cookies.

In the filling, omit tangerine juice, liqueur, orange extract, and grated tangerine or orange zest. Substitute 6 tablespoons heavy cream, ½ teaspoon almond extract, 1 teaspoon vanilla extract, and 1 cup toasted and finely ground nuts; use hazelnuts with skins removed (see page 43), or pecans, walnuts, or blanched almonds. Add all substitutions to batter after mixing in the eggs. Beat just to blend mixture well. Bake as directed.

In the topping, omit the tangerine juice. Garnish cake with toasted and ground or thin-sliced nuts.

ROBERTA'S LEMON
SAMBUCA CHEESECAKE:

This recipe comes from Roberta Dehman Hershon, good friend, cook, and food writer, who's firm, Culinary Creations, Inc., specializes in corporate catering in the Boston area. This cake is often requested by Roberta's clients.

Prepare Tangerine Cheesecake, with the following changes: Use 1¼ cups graham-cracker crumbs in place of nuts in the crumb crust. In the filling, omit tangerine juice, orange liqueur, orange extract, and tangerine zest. Substitute ¼ cup lemon juice, ⅓ cup Sambuca Romana Liqueur and 2 teaspoons grated lemon zest. In the sour-cream topping, omit the tangerine juice and substitute 1 teaspoon vanilla extract.

While the sour-cream topping is baking, prepare this lemon glaze: In a small saucepan combine and cook together until thick:

⅓ *cup lemon juice*
¾ *cup water*
1 egg yolk
½ *cup granulated sugar (3½ ounces;*
   100 g)
2½ tablespoons cornstarch

When glaze is thick enough to coat a spoon, remove from heat and cool for a few minutes. After cake has cooled for about 5 minutes, spoon lemon glaze on top of sour cream. Do not top with a cardboard disk. Instead, cool completely in a draft-free location, then refrigerate. Garnish the cake with grated lemon zest or finely minced Candied Lemon or Orange Peel (page 448).

New York Cheesecake

∎

The biggest and the best, this is the state of the art classic, also known as Lindy's Cheesecake because it is supposed to be the cake served at that famous New York restaurant. Unlike the other cheesecakes in this section, this one has a pastry crust on the bottom and sides.

☐ ADVANCE PREPARATION: This cake is best made a day ahead. The pastry can be prepared in advance and chilled for 30 minutes before using, or frozen way ahead. Allow 2 to 3 hours for the baked cake to cool, then 5 to 6 hours minimum, refrigerated, to become firm before serving. The chilled cake can also be wrapped airtight, put in a box, and frozen for several weeks without flavor loss. Thaw in the refrigerator while still wrapped. Bring to room temperature before serving.

☐ SPECIAL EQUIPMENT: one 9½-inch springform pan, wax paper, rolling pin, electric mixer fitted with flat paddle beater if available, grater, flat serving platter

☐ BAKING TIME: 8 to 10 minutes at 400°F (204°C) to bake bottom pastry crust. For cake: 12 to 15 minutes at 500°F (260°C), then 1 hour at 200°F (93°C)

□ QUANTITY: one 9½-inch cake (serves 12 to 14)

□ PAN PREPARATION: Remove sides from bottom disk of springform pan. Generously spread softened butter on both the bottom and sides.

PASTRY CRUST:

1 cup sifted all-purpose flour (4¼ ounces; 120 g)
¼ cup granulated sugar (1¾ ounces; 50 g)
Pinch of salt
1 teaspoon grated lemon or orange zest
½ cup unsalted butter (4 ounces; 110 g), at room temperature, cut up
1 large egg yolk
½ teaspoon vanilla extract

CAKE (TO MAKE 8 CUPS BATTER):

Five 8-ounce packages cream cheese (1150 g), at room temperature
1¾ cups granulated sugar (12¼ ounces; 350 g)
¼ teaspoon salt
½ teaspoon each of grated zest of orange and lemon
½ teaspoon vanilla extract
5 large eggs plus 2 extra egg yolks
¼ cup heavy cream

TOPPING (OPTIONAL):

Strawberry Glaze for Cheesecake (page 405)

1. Read About Cheesecake (page 184). Position rack in center of oven. Prepare pan as directed. Preheat oven to 400°F (204°C).

2. Prepare the pastry: In a food processor fitted with the steel blade, or in a large bowl, combine the flour, sugar, salt, and lemon zest. Pulse or stir, then add the cut-up butter and pulse or pinch together until large crumbs form. Add the egg yolk and vanilla and pulse or pinch until the dough just begins to clump together. If using the processor, do not process long enough to form a dough ball; stop the machine as soon as the dough begins to clump. Turn the dough out onto a piece of wax paper and pat it into a ball; the warmth of your hands will soften the butter and allow the dough to be molded even if it looks powdery at first. At this stage, you can wrap the dough in wax paper and refrigerate for 30 minutes or longer. Or, if dough is not too warm and soft, use it immediately.

Take a little more than one third of the dough and pat it into a thin layer over the buttered, detached bottom of the springform pan. Cover the dough with a piece of wax paper, roll over it with a rolling pin, then trim the edges. Remove wax paper and prick dough with a fork to prevent puffing in the oven. Wrap and reserve remaining dough; refrigerate in hot weather.

Set dough-covered disk in the oven and bake for 8 minutes, or until the dough is a light golden brown color. Set the disk on a wire rack and cool completely while preparing the cake batter.

3. If your mixer has a flat paddle, attach it in place of the regular beaters. In the largest bowl of the mixer, beat the cream cheese until smooth and soft. Add sugar and beat until creamy. Add remaining ingredients except

eggs and cream and beat until smooth. Add eggs and extra yolks, one at a time, beating after each addition. Scrape down the bowl and beater(s). Finally, stir in the cream.

4. Raise oven heat to 500°F (260°C). To line the pan sides with pastry, set the spring-form ring on its edge. With your fingers, gently but firmly press remaining dough (brought to room temperature if chilled) onto the buttered inner surface in an even layer. Avoid getting dough into the track that holds the pan bottom. The dough will stick easily to the pan sides and should be about ³⁄₁₆ inch thick.

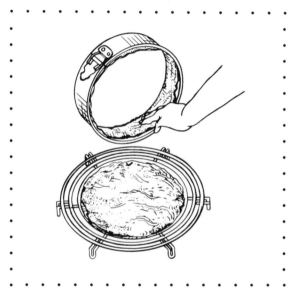

Fasten the dough-covered pan sides to the bottom disk containing the prebaked pastry and secure the spring. Set the dough-lined pan on a sturdy baking sheet or jelly-roll pan.

5. Pour the batter into the prepared pan. Place cake in the center of the preheated oven and bake for 12 to 15 minutes to cook the pastry sides. Then reduce heat to 200°F (93°C)

and continue baking for 1 hour. Turn off the heat and open the oven door completely. Cool the cake in the oven for 30 minutes.

Remove cake from the oven and set in a draft-free location for several hours to cool completely. If you are baking the cake in advance, top it with plastic wrap and refrigerate it, in its pan, overnight.

Or, instead, you can run a knife around the cake edge, release the spring, and lift off the pan sides. Leave the cake sitting on the pan bottom. Spoon on the berry glaze if using it. Refrigerate cake until the glaze is set and the cake thoroughly chilled, 3 to 4 hours minimum. For best flavor, remove cake from the refrigerator 30 minutes before serving to come to room temperature. Leave cake on the pan bottom but set it on a serving platter for presentation.

John the Blacksmith's Cheesecake

■

John the Blacksmith is a character as colorful as his name. Born in Ohio, he's lived most of the last thirty years in Connecticut and upstate New York, making a modest living by the work of his hands. His forge is the focus of his life, and he usually lives right alongside it, accompanied by a fierce dog named Ahab and a family of playful goats. John is the stuff poetry is made of—a great burly figure, strong as an oak, with a thick shock of curly gray hair, intense black eyes full of warmth and humor, and a voluble manner. He loves to talk, about life and work, and especially about what is right and wrong in this world. We have known John for over 25 years, and his life has often been very hard. But one of the things that has always been right is his creative spirit. From horseshoes to abstract sculpture, from ornate iron tracery to homemade cheesecake, John can make anything. As exciting as it is to see this Vulcan at his forge, he is just as fascinating in the kitchen. When my husband and I first met John, his hobby was baking bread to give away to his friends. Enormous double or triple loaves full of raisins were his specialty. Today, John specializes in cheesecakes, experimenting with his own proportions and ingredients, changing traditional methods, creating his own design as usual. The following recipe is his, though I accept responsibility for adapting it slightly for the kitchens of mortals.

John's cheesecake is made primarily with egg yolks. Because yolks contain the fat of the egg, their presence in quantity increases the richness of the cake. Egg whites, which add lightness, are virtually absent (only one is used), though you may use whole eggs if you prefer a lighter version. This cake is dense and intense, with a smooth buttery texture and a yellow color. The flavor reminds me of a heavy egg custard. Note that the cake is self-crusting, so no crumbs or crust are required; the batter is simply turned into a buttered pan. It's easy to make and so rich that it will serve 10 to 12, though only 8 inches in diameter. I like to serve it with Strawberry Glaze because the tang of the fruit cuts the cake's intensity, although John serves the cake plain, "without distractions."

□ ADVANCE PREPARATION: Allow 1 hour for the cake to cool in the oven after baking, then another hour at room temperature before refrigerating for 3 or 4 hours, or overnight, to firm the texture and mellow the flavors before serving. Note, however, that because this is a dense cake, it can also be served at room temperature after the initial cooling period of about 2 hours minimum at room temperature.

□ SPECIAL EQUIPMENT: one 8½-inch springform pan, sturdy baking sheet or jelly-roll pan, flat paddle-type beater for electric mixer if available, aluminum foil

□ BAKING TIME: 50 minutes at 325°F (165°C); plus 1 hour in oven with heat turned off

□ QUANTITY: one 8-inch cake, 1½ inches thick (serves 10 to 12).

□ PAN PREPARATION: Butter sides and bottom of 8½-inch springform pan.

Three 8-ounce packages cream cheese (690 g), at room temperature
1 cup granulated sugar (7 ounces; 200 g)
5 large egg yolks plus 1 whole large egg
1 tablespoon vanilla extract
2 tablespoons all-purpose flour
¼ cup heavy cream
2 teaspoons lemon juice

1. Read About Cheesecake (page 184). Prepare pan as directed. Position rack in center of the oven. Preheat oven to 325°F (165°C). If your electric mixer has a flat paddle, attach it in place of the regular beaters. In the large

bowl of the mixer, beat the cream cheese until smooth and soft. Add sugar and beat until creamy. Add yolks, whole egg, and vanilla and beat smooth. Sprinkle on the flour and slowly blend it into the batter, then beat in cream and lemon juice.

2. Turn batter into the prepared pan, and set pan on a sturdy baking sheet or jelly-roll pan. Place cake in center of the preheated oven and bake for 50 minutes, or until the edges of the cake are slightly puffed up and the center is firm to the touch though softer and flatter than the edges. The cake should not have started to color. When you tap the side of the pan the center of the cake should move slightly but not jiggle as though liquid. Turn off oven heat, but leave cake in the oven. Prop oven door open slightly for 5 minutes to reduce heat, then close the door and leave cake in oven for 55 more minutes.

3. Remove cake from the oven and set the pan on a wire rack. Fold a piece of aluminum foil into a 2-sided tent and place it atop the cake to shield it from drafts as it continues to cool. The foil tent is John's technique—a clever solution devised from metal, his trademark—to help prevent cracks in the cake top. This cake does sink down as it cools, and small cracks occasionally appear. They are not serious, but can be covered with a strawberry topping (page 405) spooned over the cake once it is completely cool.

When cake is cool, cover it with plastic wrap or foil, arranged so it does not touch the cake's surface, and refrigerate for 4 hours, or overnight, to firm texture and mellow flavors before serving at room temperature.

Italian Ricotta Cheesecake

■

An Italian specialty, *torta di ricotta,* is made in a variety of ways depending upon where you are in the country. This delicately flavored cake is neither too sweet nor too fattening and has a grain particular to ricotta, unlike the silken smoothness of a cream cheese-based American-style cheesecake. Though there are several variations offered, the master recipe is lightened by stiffly beaten egg whites and the flavor is enhanced by a hint of lemon, rum-soaked golden raisins, and chopped apricots; other additions might be pine nuts, chopped candied fruit, or chopped chocolate.

Ricotta (page 186) still forms the basis for Italian cheesecakes. It has a rather bland, nutty taste, milder than cottage cheese, which it somewhat resembles in appearance. Note that sieved cottage cheese may be substituted, but will change the flavor of the cake.

You can use Italian Ricotta Cheesecake as a master recipe with which to create the variations that follow: Plain Ricotta, Holiday Ricotta, and Passover Cheesecake.

□ ADVANCE PREPARATION: Soak raisins in rum overnight before making cake, or see step 2.

This cake can be served 2 or 3 hours after it has completely cooled from baking, still at room temperature, when the texture will be at its lightest. However, you can also bake it in advance and refrigerate it overnight to allow the flavors to blend and mellow. In this case, the texture will be slightly denser than when freshly baked. In my experience, this cake freezes less well than a regular cream cheese-based cheesecake. The texture changes quickly and freezing is not recommended.

☐ SPECIAL EQUIPMENT: one 9½-inch springform pan, sturdy baking sheet or jelly-roll pan, grater

☐ BAKING TIME: 45 to 50 minutes at 325°F (165°C); plus 60 minutes in oven with heat turned off

☐ QUANTITY: one 9-inch cake (serves 10 to 12)

☐ PAN PREPARATION: Generously butter bottom and sides of springform pan.

CRUMB CRUST:

1 cup shelled walnuts (5 ounces; 140 g), or macadamia nuts
1 tablespoon dark brown sugar
2 tablespoons granulated sugar
¼ teaspoon ground cinnamon

CAKE:

⅓ cup golden seedless raisins (1⅓ ounces; 50 g)
⅓ cup dark rum or orange juice or water
⅓ cup firmly packed dried apricot halves (2 ounces; 50 g)

Like so many of our sweets and pastries, cheesecake is an invention of the ancient Romans. They baked both an unsweetened version called libum *made of flour, cheese, and egg, and a sweetened one called* savillum. *It had a batter made of flour, cheese, honey, and egg, and after baking was topped with honey and sprinkled with poppyseeds. The cheese the Romans used for these cakes was an ancestor of ricotta, made from the milk of sheep. For another example, consider this sweet wine cake made with cheese given to the famous first century gourmet and cookbook writer, Marcus Gavius Apicius by Cato (234–149 B.C.,) in his writing,* De Agricultura:

Sweet wine-cakes are made as follows: Moisten 1 peck of wheat flour with must (new wine). Add aniseed, cumin, 2 lb. of fat, 1 lb. of cheese, and some grated bark of a laurel twig; shape and place each cake on a bay leaf; then bake.

Apicius, The Roman Cookery Book, *translated by Barbara Flower and E. Rosenbaum (London: George G. Harrap, 1958)*

*3 ounces cream cheese (85 g), at room
temperature*
*1³/₄ cups whole-milk ricotta (1 lb;
454 g), or creamed cottage cheese,
pressed through sieve*
¹/₄ cup plain yogurt
*³/₄ cup granulated sugar (5¹/₄ ounces;
150 g)*
3 large eggs, separated
1 teaspoon grated lemon zest
2 teaspoons lemon juice
4 tablespoons all-purpose flour
Pinch of salt
3 tablespoons pine nuts (optional)

1. Position rack in center of oven. Preheat oven to 325°F (165°C). Prepare pan as directed. In a blender or food processor, combine nuts, sugars, and cinnamon and process until finely ground. Press crumbs evenly onto bottom and sides of prepared pan. Pat excess crumbs onto pan bottom. Set pan aside; in hot weather, store pan in refrigerator.

2. Plump raisins either by covering them with rum to stand overnight, or more quickly, by combining them in a small saucepan and warming the rum over low heat for about 5 minutes, covered. Remove from heat and let stand, covered, for at least 30 minutes. Drain before using raisins. Note: This rum may be used in place of lemon juice in the batter if you wish. Cut apricots into ¹/₄-inch dice and set them aside.

3. If your mixer has a flat paddle, attach it in place of the regular beaters. In the large bowl of an electric mixer, beat the cream cheese until smooth and soft, then beat in the ricotta and yogurt. Stop mixer and scrape down beater and inside of bowl several times. When the mixture is smooth, beat in sugar,

then egg yolks, lemon zest, and lemon juice. Scrape down bowl again. Finally, with mixer on low speed, gradually add flour and salt. Last, stir in the drained raisins and chopped apricots.

4. In a clean bowl with a regular whisk beater, beat egg whites until stiff but not dry. Gently fold whites into the cheese-fruit batter. Turn batter into prepared pan, and set pan on a sturdy baking sheet or jelly-roll pan.

5. Place in the center of the preheated oven and bake for 45 to 50 minutes, or until the cake edges are slightly puffed up and just beginning to look golden. The center surface will be firm to the touch though softer than the edges. When you tap the side of the pan, the center of the cake should move slightly but not jiggle as though liquid. When baked, turn off oven heat but leave cake in oven, with door closed, for an additional 60 minutes. Then set cake on a wire rack in a draft-free location until completely cool. After another 2 hours at room temperature, the cake will be set enough to serve, though it can also be wrapped in plastic and refrigerated.

· *Variations:* ·

PLAIN RICOTTA
CHEESECAKE:

Prepare basic cake, but omit raisins and apricots.

HOLIDAY RICOTTA
CHEESECAKE:

Prepare Italian Ricotta Cheesecake, but replace lemon zest and juice with 1 teaspoon almond extract and replace raisins and apricots with 1 cup candied mixed fruits, chopped (7 ounces; 200 g) or ½ cup chopped semisweet chocolate (3 ounces; 30 g).

PASSOVER CHEESECAKE:

Prepare Italian Ricotta Cheesecake with the following changes: Use an 8- or 8½-inch springform pan.

To prepare the crust, spread softened margarine on the bottom and sides of the pan. Dust the pan with a mixture of ¼ cup matzoh meal (1½ ounces; 40 g), 3 tablespoons granulated sugar, and ½ teaspoon ground cinnamon. Tilt the pan to get an even coating. Pat excess crumbs onto pan bottom.

For the filling, combine the golden raisins with ⅓ cup orange juice in a small pan, cover, and warm over low heat for about 5 minutes. Remove pan from heat and let stand for at least 30 minutes. Use apricots as per recipe. Instead of ricotta cheese, substitute 2 cups 4 percent milkfat cottage cheese (1 lb; 454 g), pressed through a sieve. Use sour cream instead of yogurt, and instead of the flour, substitute 2 tablespoons potato starch. Omit pine nuts. If you wish to cover the cake with sour-cream topping, combine 2 cups sour cream with 4 tablespoons granulated sugar, spread the mixture over baked but not cooled cake, and return it to the oven, at 350°F (175°C) for 10 minutes. Remove cake from oven and set to cool in a draft-free place, topped by a folded tent of aluminum foil.

Low-Calorie Yogurt Cheesecake

■

While not calorie-free, this is a low-fat, dieter's dream. Instead of the usual butter-rich cheeses, this is made with easily-prepared, homemade low-fat yogurt cheese. Note that this is a small cake, prepared in a pie plate.

□ ADVANCE PREPARATION: Make the yogurt cheese a day or two before baking the cake; it takes a minimum of 12 hours for all the liquid to drip out of the yogurt. Once prepared, the cheese can be covered and refrigerated for a day or so before use.

Prepare cake a day in advance, so it has time to chill for 24 hours before serving.

□ SPECIAL EQUIPMENT: one 8-inch pie plate or quiche pan, good-quality triple-thickness cheesecloth cut into two 14-inch squares, cotton string, hanging hook or nail, extra bowl

□ BAKING TIME: 25 minutes at 325°F (165°C), plus 5 minutes after the topping is added

□ QUANTITY: one 8-inch cake (serves 8)

□ PAN PREPARATION: Line pan with crumb crust, step 5 below.

CRUMB CRUST:

1 cup graham cracker or zwieback crumbs (3½ ounces; 100 g)
4 tablespoons margarine (½ stick; 60 g), melted

CAKE AND TOPPING:

*2¼ cups homemade low-fat yogurt
cheese made from 6 cups (48 ounces;
1362 g) low-fat, plain yogurt
(instructions follow)*
Pinch of salt
2 large eggs, lightly beaten
*½ cup (3½ ounces; 100 g) granulated
sugar plus 1 teaspoon*
*2 teaspoons grated lemon zest (1 lemon
yields 2 to 3 teaspoons of zest; use 2
teaspoons here, save 1 for garnish)*
*Juice of 1 lemon (about 3 tablespoons),
strained*
1 teaspoon vanilla extract

GARNISH:

*1 teaspoon grated lemon zest reserved
from filling*

1. A couple of days before making the cake, prepare the yogurt cheese. To do this, cut two 14-inch-square pieces of triple-thickness cheesecloth. In a bowl, stir the 6 cups yogurt together with a pinch of salt. Spoon half of the yogurt onto the center of each double-thick cheesecloth square. Gather up the ends of each square, tie them with string, and make a hanging loop; suspend the bundles from a hook or nail set over a bowl; or hang them from the faucet in the kitchen sink, for at least 12 hours, or overnight, until every drop of water stops dripping out. At this point, the cheese is done. Note: The amount of liquid in yogurt varies among brands. Quantities here are approximate, and your yield may vary slightly. If you have any cheese left over, mix it with herbs and use as a spread on crackers.

2. Position rack in center of oven. Preheat oven to 325°F (165°C).

3. Prepare crumb crust: Combine crumbs and melted margarine and toss well to blend. Add a tiny bit more melted margarine if crumbs will not hold their shape. Press crumbs onto bottom and sides of pie plate. Set aside. In hot weather, refrigerate crumb-lined plate.

4. Prepare cake: By hand or with an electric mixer and paddle attachment if available, beat together eggs, 1½ cups of previously prepared yogurt cheese, ½ cup sugar, grated lemon zest and juice. Avoid whipping air into the batter. When it is smooth and creamy, spoon it into the prepared crust.

5. Bake cake in preheated oven for 25 minutes. While the cake bakes prepare topping by blending remaining ¾ cup previously made yogurt cheese, 1 teaspoon sugar, and 1 teaspoon vanilla. When the cake is baked, remove it from the oven and spread on the topping. Return cake to oven to bake for 5 minutes more. Cool on a wire rack, then refrigerate for 24 hours. Garnish with a sprinkle of grated lemon zest. Serve at room temperature.

Grasshopper Cheesecake

■

This recipe combines the richness of cheesecake with the refreshing and mellow flavors of crème de cacao and crème de menthe. I admit that I long resisted the idea of green cheesecake, and as usual, tried it out first on my family. To my surprise, it was an unqualified success, eliciting the comment: "as refreshing as an afterdinner mint!" If you use green crème de menthe, the cake will have a pale green color. If that idea offends you, substitute white crème de menthe.

Prepare Tangerine Cheesecake (page 195) with these changes: For the crust, spread butter generously on bottom and sides of the pan. Sprinkle the butter with about ¾ cup of finely ground chocolate wafers or ground nuts. Pat excess crumbs onto pan bottom. Chill pan.

In the filling, omit tangerine juice, orange liqueur, orange extract, and tangerine zest. Substitute 3½ tablespoons each of crème de cacao and green or white crème de menthe. Add ½ teaspoon peppermint extract or peppermint oil. Stir into batter ½ cup semisweet chocolate minichips (2¾ oz; 80 g) or grated semisweet chocolate.

Omit sour-cream topping. Bake the cake for a full 50 minutes, then turn off oven heat, open the oven door, and leave cake in the oven to cool for 30 minutes. Remove from oven, top with a cardboard disk, and cool completely. Chill as directed.

Top the cake with a layer of sifted unsweetened cocoa powder. Or, for a smashing dinner party finale, pipe sweetened whipped cream rosettes over the cake top and garnish with Chocolate Curls or Chocolate Leaves.

Sponge & Foam Cakes

ABOUT SPONGE AND FOAM CAKES

■

Sponge cakes are light and airy, leavened primarily with eggs beaten to a foam, hence the generic name, "foam cakes." Cakes in this family include sponge cakes, French sponge cakes (génoises), roulades or jelly rolls, angelfood cakes, chiffon cakes, and tortes *(Torten)*. The dacquoise, or meringue cake, is also a foam-type cake. Sponge cakes are both lighter and drier than butter cakes. Moistened with flavored syrups and filled with buttercreams and/or Bavarian creams, or other variations on pastry creams or whipped cream, they form the foundation for many elaborate European desserts.

Whether using whole eggs, yolks, or only whites, the batter is created by whipping eggs with sugar until light in color (sometimes called "lemon-colored"), thick, and at the ribbon stage, when the mixture will form a flat ribbon falling back upon itself when the beater is lifted. At this stage, a line drawn with your finger through the batter will remain visible for at least a couple of seconds. Whisk-type or whipping beaters are always used for this process. With a KitchenAid mixer on speed 8, this can take 3 full minutes; with other mixers it can take up to 6 or 7 minutes.

The air whipped into the egg-sugar mixture during this process contributes to the rising of the sponge cake. When the cake is placed in the oven to bake, the second essential factor in the rising comes into play. In the heat of the oven, the moisture in the batter becomes steam, which rises and escapes through the foam. The heat also causes the air in these bubbles to expand, contributing to the rise.

Once the egg-sugar mixture reaches the ribboning stage, you can add flavoring and fold in sifted flour, a little at a time. Flour is never added all at once, or it sinks to the bottom of the bowl, requiring undesirable extra folding to mix it in. This breaks down the air in the foam and causes a heavy cake.

Some sponge cake recipes add richness and flavor by including melted butter, which must always be added last, after the flour; others supplement the leavening with baking powder. However, the classic foundation formula for a true sponge cake is 1 (2-ounce) egg to 1 ounce of granulated sugar and 1 ounce of sifted cake flour.

Variations in sponge cakes are nearly endless; you can be creative with flavorings and extracts, grated citrus zest, ground nuts, or cake crumbs. To make a chocolate sponge, one third of the flour can be replaced by unsweetened cocoa powder. The butter can be reduced or halved for a chocolate sponge because cocoa contains up to 22 percent butterfat; baking soda should be added to darken the color of the chocolate and make the cake a little lighter in texture. For a softer, silkier texture, sifted cornstarch can be used along with the flour.

There are four basic techniques for making sponge cake: the warm or "génoise" method, the cold batter method, the separated-egg method, and the hot milk sponge method.

The génoise is a whole egg sponge (see page 211). To make a génoise, it is essential to warm the eggs and sugar together before whipping them into a batter. The heat enables the sugar to dissolve completely, helps the eggs whip to a greater volume more quickly, and softens the lecithin, or fat, in the yolks, aiding stabilization of the foam. This method produces an exceptionally light and fine-grained cake. There are several ways to achieve the required warmth. Many recipes call for whipping the eggs and sugar together over a bowl of hot water. Once warmed, the mixture is removed from the heat source and whipped, by hand or machine, before folding in sifted flour and, last, the melted and clarified butter.

While the génoise is always made with a warm egg-sugar mixture, so-called American sponge cakes often use the cold method. The cold method of mixing sponge cake is the easiest and quickest: the room temperature eggs and sugar are whipped to the ribbon stage, the flavoring is added, the sifted flour folded in, and the melted butter incorporated.

The separated-egg method produces the softest, most pliable sponge cake and should be used when the cake will be rolled over a filling, as for jelly rolls, roulades, or a Bûche de Noël. The yolks are whipped with about 1/3 of the sugar in one bowl, the whites are separately whipped with 2/3 of the sugar. Then some of the whites are folded into the yolks before folding in the sifted flour. Last, the remaining whipped whites are folded in. This technique is used with either the génoise or the American sponge recipes.

A hot liquid sponge may be made with hot milk, hot water, hot coffee, or hot fruit juice. Sometimes it also includes butter, cut up and melted in the hot liquid, which should ideally be between 165°F and 175°F when added to the other ingredients. Extra yolks are often added to the whole eggs in this method to allow greater volume and easier absorption of the milk and butter. The eggs may be added whole, for a slightly firmer textured cake, or separated, producing a lighter result. Batter made by the hot liquid method is quite soft. Handle it gently when pouring it into the prepared pan. Bake the cake as soon as the batter is prepared.

Hints and Tips for Sponge Cakes

A well-prepared sponge cake has an even grain, a light texture, with evenly spaced air holes throughout. When the cake comes out of the oven, it should have risen well and be slightly domed in the center; the top should flatten out as it cools. There are a few basic rules to remember when baking sponge cakes:

• Use a perfectly clean, grease-free bowl and beater when whipping eggs, especially when whipping whites. Fat prevents the creation of a good foam structure.

• Sift flour and baking powder well to aerate them and remove all lumps. Sift your sugar if not perfectly lump-free. When folding in flour, add only a little at a time, and be sure to reach well down to the bottom of the bowl to incorporate the batter evenly, avoiding unmixed particles that might create hard bits in the cake. Do not overmix the batter or you break down the foam and produce a heavy cake. Always grease and flour pans; for sponge rolls, line pans with paper and grease the paper. Handle the batter gently to retain maximum volume. Place cakes in preheated oven as soon as pans are filled.

· To fold one ingredient into another, add a little of the second mixture to the first, use a rubber spatula, and cut down through the center of the mixture, turn the spatula, and draw it up along the side of the bowl. Give the bowl a ¼ turn and repeat, turning over the spatula, cutting down through the center and coming up along the bowl side. Add a little more of the second ingredient and repeat. Never stir, never move the spatula back and forth across the mixture; simply cut down, across, and up to distribute and incorporate ingredients without breaking down any aeration of the foam.

Troubleshooting Sponge Cakes

· If the texture is rubbery and tight, or tough and springy: The batter was underwhipped.

· If the cake is dense or heavy, or actually sinks as it cools: The center has collapsed because it was overwhipped and the cell walls burst when expanding in the heat instead of retaining their structure and their air.

· If there are lumps in the cake: The flour and/or baking powder were not carefully sifted, or the sugar not completely dissolved. Or the folding was not done carefully, and bits of dry ingredients were not completely incorporated into the batter. Be sure to scrape down the sides of the bowl and beaters completely.

Sponge Cakes

Génoise (French Sponge Cake)

•

The génoise is a versatile French butter sponge cake. In addition to having a high proportion of eggs and sugar and relatively little fat, the génoise lacks baking powder; it is leavened entirely by a whole-egg foam that is enhanced by having the eggs and sugar warmed together before being whipped. This technique gives the génoise its name: warm method sponge.

The warmth causes many important reactions: it enables the sugar to dissolve in the eggs, it allows the eggs to whip to their fullest, and it softens the fat in the yolks, making it more elastic and better able to envelop the air cells as they are whipped into the foam. The texture of a génoise is light and delicate, with a fine grain. Because of the close cell structure, the cake can easily be split into thin layers by slicing it horizontally with a serrated knife. It has a tendency to be slightly dry, and is usually brushed with a flavored soaking syrup, which adds moisture and flavor. Génoise layers form a perfect base for rich fillings such as mousse or Bavarian creams. Note the four génoise specialties in Elegant and Special Cakes—plus six more suggestions using the génoise foundation in Génoise and Sponge Cake Variations (page 302).

The génoise originated in Genoa, Italy, as *pasta genovese,* a cake flavored with almonds or rum. Though one of the earliest of the Italian cakes, this is still standard in the Italian pastry repertoire. In the sixteenth century, Catherine de Médicis brought this recipe, along with her pastry chefs, with her as part of her dowry when she married Henry II and moved to

France. French *pâtissiers* quickly adopted it, changing the name to *pâte à génoise,* pastry of Genoa, making it a classic of their own. In Britain, the same recipe is referred to as "gateau," and in Germany, *biscuit. Biscuit de Savoie* is yet another European sponge cake, made without any fat but with more eggs than the génoise.

The classic génoise requires the eggs and sugar to be warmed together before being whipped into a batter. There are several ways to achieve this: The easiest but least precise is to set the whole eggs in their shells in a bowl of warm water for about 10 minutes. Then whip the warm eggs together with the sugar in a warmed bowl. The most professional and most reliable method is to combine the eggs and sugar in a bowl set over hot water (such as a double boiler set at a simmer), add a thermometer, and stir the mixture until it reaches 110° to 120°F, when it will feel very warm to the touch and will look like a deep yellow liquid because most of the sugar will be dissolved. At this point the warm egg-sugar syrup is removed from the heat and whipped by hand or electric mixer until cooled, tripled in volume, light in color, and very thick. The batter at this stage will form a flat ribbon falling back on itself when the beater is lifted.

At this point, you gradually sift on and fold in the flour. The melted butter is incorporated with a small amount of the batter, then folded into the remaining batter. This technique blends the butter smoothly and prevents it from causing the batter to decrease in volume as it tends to do when added by itself. Immediately fill the prepared pans and put them into the preheated oven; the foam is delicate and will begin to deflate if not baked at once.

Remember that the tricks of a successful génoise are to prewarm the sugar-eggs, to use a light touch when folding in the carefully sifted dry ingredients, and to bake cakes immediately.

The génoise can be baked in many types of pans: springform, round, or rectangular layers. If you need several layers for your cake, it is best to bake 1 génoise recipe in a 2- or 3-inch deep pan, then slice it into thin layers with a serrated knife (technique on page 424). However, many bakers are uneasy slicing 3 thin layers from 1 cake; if this seems difficult to you, simply bake ⅓ of the batter in one pan and ⅔ in another pan; slice the thicker cake into halves and you will have 3 layers with only one cut. Génoise can also be baked in muffin pans for cupcakes or in a jelly-roll pan to make a sheet cake for Petits Fours (see Index). The sheet génoise can also be cut into sections for stacked cakes such as 7- or 8-Layer Cake. See Génoise Sheet Cakes, following the master recipe.

□ ADVANCE PREPARATION: The génoise can be made in advance, wrapped airtight, and stored at room temperature for several days, for a week if wrapped and refrigerated, and for up to a month if wrapped in heavy-duty foil and frozen. Do not split the génoise into layers until shortly before filling.

□ SPECIAL EQUIPMENT: two 8- or 9-inch round layer pans, 1½ or 2 inches deep, or 1 jelly-roll pan, 10½ × 15 inches, baking parchment or wax paper and scissors, large metal or other heatproof bowl for electric mixer, bottom half of double boiler (or substitute a pan with water in it), candy thermometer or instant-read spot thermometer, optional, three-tiered or box sifter, wax paper, rubber spatula, small saucepan for melting butter, 1½-quart bowl

□ BAKING TIME: 20 to 27 minutes at 375°F (190°C), depending upon thickness of batter in pan.

□ QUANTITY: 6-egg génoise makes 8 cups batter; two 8- or 9-inch round cakes. Each cake can be split into halves or thirds (see page 424 for slicing technique). Halve the recipe (3 eggs; 4 cups batter) to make a single cake, which can be split into 2 or 3 layers.

□ PAN PREPARATION: Spread bottom and sides of pans with solid shortening. Line bottoms of pans with baking parchment or wax paper cut to fit, then grease paper. Dust pans with flour; tap out excess flour.

1½ cups sifted cake flour (5¼ ounces;
  150 g), plus 1 tablespoon
Pinch of salt
6 tablespoons unsalted butter (3 ounces;
  85 g), cut up
6 large eggs
1 cup granulated sugar (7 ounces;
  200 g)
1 teaspoon vanilla extract

SOAKING SYRUP (OPTIONAL):

Basic Soaking Syrup (page 420), with flavoring of your choice

FILLING AND ICING:

Any Mousse, Bavarian Cream, Flavored Whipped Cream, or Buttercream (see Index)

1. Position rack in center of oven. Preheat oven to 375°F (190°C). Prepare pans as described. Sift flour and salt onto a piece of wax paper. Set the sifter on another piece of wax paper on a plate. Pick up the paper containing the flour mixture and gently pour it into the sifter. Just let it sit there waiting to be sifted when needed. Put the plate holding the sifter near the mixer.

Melt the butter in a small saucepan; when melted, skim off and discard any white foamy residue that rises to the surface. Set butter—and a small bowl—aside.

2. Combine eggs and sugar in the large heatproof bowl of an electric mixer. Set this over the bottom of a double boiler containing water that is hot to the touch, about 125°F. If water is too hot, it will cook the eggs rather than warm them. Stir the egg-sugar mixture constantly with a large whisk until it feels very warm to your finger, 110° to 120°F. It will no longer be grainy because the sugar will be dissolved. At once remove the bowl from the heat and attach it to the electric mixer. Whip the egg-sugar syrup on medium-high speed for 3 or 4 full minutes, or until it triples in volume, is very thick and light-colored, and forms a flat ribbon falling back on itself when the beater is lifted. Add the vanilla or any other flavoring and whip for 2 or 3 seconds to blend. Remove bowl from the mixer.

3. Hold the sifter over the batter bowl and sift a few tablespoons of the flour mixture onto the yolk foam. Gently fold it in with a rubber spatula or flat whisk. Repeat about 5 or 6 times to use up flour, always sifting on a little flour and folding it in lightly before adding more.

4. Put about 1½ cups of the batter into the small bowl and fold the melted butter into it. Finally, fold this butter mixture into the entire bowl of batter. Do this lightly without overworking the batter.

5. Divide the batter between the prepared pans. Bake in the center of the preheated oven for 22 to 27 minutes (depending upon the depth of the batter in the pan and the pan size), or until the cake top is golden, springs back when lightly touched, and a cake tester inserted in the center comes out clean. The cake sides will begin to pull away from the pan. Caution: Don't open the oven door wide during the first 15 minutes or the temperature change may cause the cake to fall.

Use the tip of a knife to loosen the cake sides from the pans, then top each cake with a buttered wire rack and invert. Lift off each pan, leaving the cakes on the wire rack to cool. When cold, wrap cakes airtight in plastic bags to prevent drying. Split the cakes into horizontal layers using a serrated knife (see page 424).

6. To assemble the cake, follow specific recipe instructions. The basic method is to set the split layers out flat, cut sides up, and brush on soaking syrup. Spread layers with filling, stack, then frost sides and top. If using a Bavarian cream or mousse or a mixture that must be frozen, assemble the layers and filling in a springform pan; refrigerate or freeze until filling is set, then remove pan sides. Frost top and sides if you wish.

· *Variations:* ·

NUT GÉNOISE:

Prepare basic Génoise, but add ½ cup toasted and finely ground almonds, pecans, or hazelnuts, folded in just after the flour. For an almond génoise, add ½ teaspoon almond extract along with the vanilla.

CHOCOLATE GÉNOISE:

Prepare basic Génoise, but substitute ⅓ cup sifted unsweetened cocoa, preferably Dutch-process, for ⅓ cup of the flour. Add ¼ teaspoon baking soda. Sift cocoa and baking soda together with flour and salt.

LEMON OR ORANGE GÉNOISE:

Prepare basic Génoise, but add 1 teaspoon lemon or orange extract and the grated zest of 1 whole lemon or orange. Combine this flavoring with the melted butter when it is added to the batter.

GÉNOISE SHEET CAKES:

When the basic 6-egg génoise is baked in a jelly-roll pan 10 × 15 inches, it makes one layer a generous ½ inch thick. This cake can be cut into bite-size pieces and sandwiched with buttercream or preserves to make Petits Fours, or sliced crosswise or lengthwise to make narrow layers that are sandwiched with filling (see Seven- or Eight- Layer Chocolate Cake, page 311).

□ BAKING NOTES FOR GÉNOISE SHEET CAKE: When a génoise is baked in a jelly-roll pan, the procedure is the same as for a jelly roll (see Index). Prepare the baking pan with a wax paper or baking parchment lining, then butter and flour the paper.

Bake the génoise at 375°F (190°C) for about 12 minutes, or just until a cake tester comes out clean and the top feels springy; don't overbake or the cake will dry out.

Sift confectioners' sugar over the top of the cake, top with a clean tea towel, then a wire rack or cookie sheet. Invert. Lift off the pan and peel off the paper. With a serrated knife, trim off a scant ⅛ inch all around, removing the crisp edges. If making a roulade, roll the warm cake up in a sugared tea towel. For a flat sheet cake, divide the cake into sections as directed in the recipe. See notes below for a guide.

☐ HANDY MEASURING GUIDE FOR GÉNOISE SHEET CAKES: When a génoise 10 × 15 inches is trimmed ⅛ inch all around, the cake measures 9¾ × 14¾ inches. This can be cut as follows:

3-LAYER CAKE (TO SERVE 14):

Cut the trimmed cake lengthwise into 3 equal strips each 3¼ × 14¾ inches. Fill and stack as directed in the recipe.

4-LAYER CAKE (TO SERVE 8):

Cut the trimmed cake crosswise into 4 equal strips each 9¾ by a generous 3⅝ inches. Fill and stack as directed in the recipe.

7- OR 8-LAYER CAKE (TO SERVE 8):

Cut cake as for 4-layer cake, then use a serrated knife to split each cake strip into halves, making 8 thin layers. Stack 7 or 8 layers to make the cake.

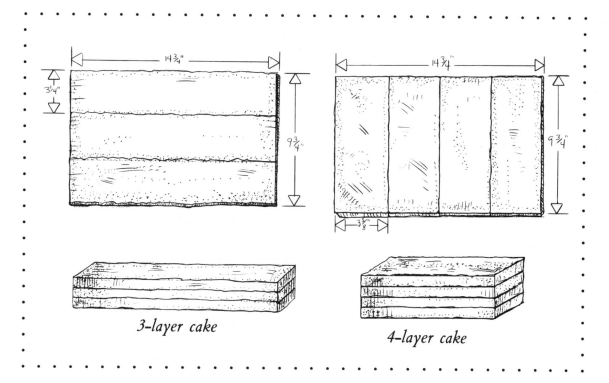

3-layer cake

4-layer cake

American Sponge Cake

The so-called American Sponge Cake includes baking powder, added to the egg foam to aid the leavening. The grain of this cake is open and somewhat coarse when compared with the classic French génoise sponge cake, which is leavened exclusively by whipped egg foam.

To make this cake, follow the recipe for Lemon or Orange Jelly Roll (page 225). Bake the cake in an ungreased 9-inch angel-cake tube pan at 350°F (175°C) for 45 to 50 minutes, or until a cake tester inserted in the center comes out clean.

As soon as the cake is done, invert the tube pan onto its feet, or hang it upside down over the neck of a bottle or funnel (see page 70) for several hours, or overnight, until completely cold.

To remove the cake from the pan, slide the blade of a long thin knife between the cake and the pan sides to loosen the crumbs. Repeat around the sides of the center tube. Top the cake with a plate, then invert and lift off the pan. If your pan has a removable bottom, remove the sides first, then slide the knife between the pan bottom and the cake to release it. Leave the cake upside down on the plate or invert it so it is right side up, whichever looks better. Ice the cake if you wish with any type of Boiled or 7-Minute Icing or Icing Glaze (see Index) or sift on a little confectioners' sugar. Cut the cake with a serrated knife.

Sunshine Cake

This is a classic yellow sponge cake, light in texture, moderately sweet, and wonderful when served with Warm Berry Sauce, fresh fruit, or ice cream.

□ ADVANCE PREPARATION: The cake can be prepared in advance, wrapped airtight, and frozen. However, in my experience freezing dries out the texture; I prefer to wrap the cake airtight and store it at room temperature for a day or two if it is to be made in advance.

□ SPECIAL EQUIPMENT: one 10-inch angel-cake tube pan with feet, or regular tube pan and large funnel or tall bottle from which to suspend inverted tube pan while cooling (see page 70); 3-quart mixing bowl for electric mixer (enough to hold 11 to 12 cups) for whipping egg whites, extra mixing bowl; wax paper or baking parchment, sifter, rubber spatula or flat whisk, long thin-bladed knife, serrated knife, serving plate

□ BAKING TIME: 50 to 55 minutes at 325°F (165°C)

□ QUANTITY: 9½ to 10 cups batter, one tube cake, 10 × 2¾ inches (serves 10 to 12)

□ PAN PREPARATION: Line bottom of pan with wax paper or baking parchment cut to fit. Do not grease pan.

1 cup sifted cake flour (3½ ounces; 100 g)
¼ teaspoon salt
10 large egg whites (about 1½ cups), at room temperature

1 teaspoon cream of tartar
1½ cups sifted confectioners' sugar
  (5¼ ounces; 150 g)
8 large egg yolks
1 teaspoon lemon extract
1 teaspoon orange extract
Grated zest of 1 orange or 1 lemon

S A U C E :

Warm Berry Sauce (page 418), optional

1. Read About Sponge and Foam Cakes. Position rack in center of oven. Preheat oven to 325°F (165°C). Prepare pan as described.

2. Sift together flour and salt onto wax paper and set them aside.

3. In largest bowl (3-quart size) of an electric mixer, whip egg whites with cream of tartar until foamy. Gradually add ½ cup sifted confectioners' sugar and whip until nearly stiff but not dry. Remove bowl from electric mixer and scrape beaters into the bowl. Without washing the beaters, return them to the mixer.

4. In another mixing bowl, stir together the egg yolks, lemon and orange extracts, 1 cup sifted confectioners' sugar, and the grated zest. Using the electric mixer and the same beaters, beat the yolk mixture to blend on very low speed. Increase speed and beat for about 4 full minutes (on KitchenAid at speed #10) or longer on smaller mixers, until yolk batter is thick and foamy and forms a flat ribbon falling back on itself when the beater is lifted.

5. With a rubber spatula, fold the whipped whites over onto themselves once or twice. Fold about 2 cups of whipped whites into the yolk batter with the rubber spatula or a flat whisk. Then alternately fold in remaining whites and the flour, sifting a little of the flour on top of a scoop of whites with each addition.

6. Turn the batter into the prepared pan and bake in the center of the preheated oven for 50 to 55 minutes, or until the top is golden and a cake tester inserted in the center comes out clean. Do not overbake, or the cake will dry out.

7. As soon as the cake is done, invert it onto the feet of its pan, or hang it upside down over the neck of a bottle or funnel; allow it to hang upside down for several hours, or overnight, until completely cold.

To remove the cake from the pan, slide the blade of a long thin knife between the cake and the pan sides to loosen the crumbs. Repeat around the center tube. Top the cake with a plate, then invert and lift off the pan. If your pan has a removable bottom, remove the sides first, then slide the knife between the pan bottom and the cake to release it. Peel off the paper. Leave the cake upside down or, if the bottom appears slightly concave from hanging upside down, invert the cake again, so it is right side up on the plate. To serve, cut the cake with a serrated knife. Top slices with Warm Berry Sauce.

Chocolate Sponge Cake

∎

This is a classic chocolate sponge cake with a light and tender texture and a delicate crumb. It is based on the génoise, or French sponge method, leavened entirely by egg foam, but in this case the eggs are separated. Part of the sugar is whipped into the yolks and part into the whites, following the recipe for Chocolate Sponge Roll.

Follow the recipe for Chocolate Sponge Roll (Bûche de Noël, page 229), but bake the cake in a 9-inch (6½-cup capacity) tube pan. Grease the pan and line bottom with a ring of greased wax paper or parchment; dust with cocoa. Or make a layer cake by baking it in two 8-inch round layer pans, 1½ inches deep, greased, with pan bottoms lined with greased and cocoa-dusted wax paper or baking parchment.

Bake at 350°F (175°C), 25 minutes for 9-inch tube pan and 17 minutes for 8-inch layers, or until a cake tester comes out clean and the cake begins to pull away from the pan sides. Cool cake in its pan(s) for about 5 minutes, then invert onto a wire rack, remove pan, and peel off paper. Cool completely. Note: It is not necessary to hang this sponge cake upside down to cool if baked in a layer or tube pan. Note that the layers may be split with a serrated knife if you wish (see page 424) to make a 4-layer cake.

Ice the cake with Boiled Icing or Seven-Minute Icing or coffee-flavored whipped cream (see Index for recipes). Or, for a gala, fill the 4 layers with Vicky Zeff's Deluxe White Chocolate Mousse Filling, orange-fla-vored, to create my all-time favorite Orange-Chocolate Dream Cake (page 305).

Passover Sponge Cake

∎

This recipe was a specialty of my paternal grandmother, Rebecca Gold. It is a light lemon-orange sponge made with potato flour and matzoh meal rather than wheat flour.

☐ ADVANCE PREPARATION: The cake can be baked in advance and frozen.

☐ SPECIAL EQUIPMENT: one 9-inch angel-cake tube pan with feet, or regular tube pan and large bottle or funnel from which to suspend the inverted tube pan while cooling (see page 70), 1 small and 2 large mixing bowls, sifter, grater, juicer, wax paper or baking parchment, scissors, serving plate

☐ BAKING TIME: 50 to 60 minutes at 350°F (175°C)

☐ QUANTITY: one 9-inch tube cake (serves 8 to 10)

☐ PAN PREPARATION: Do not grease pan.

Grated zest of 1 orange
¼ cup freshly squeezed orange juice
Grated zest of 1 lemon
2 tablespoons lemon juice
5 large eggs, separated
1 cup granulated sugar, sifted (7
 ounces; 200 g)

*¾ cup matzoh meal, sifted (3¼
  ounces; 90 g)*
*½ cup potato flour, sifted (3 ounces;
  85 g)*
½ teaspoon salt
*½ cup light vegetable oil, such as corn
  or safflower oil*

1. Read About Sponge and Foam Cakes. Position rack in center of oven. Preheat oven to 350°F (175°C).

Combine grated zest and juice of orange and lemon in one bowl. Add egg yolks. Whisk well to combine ingredients. Set bowl aside.

2. In the large bowl of an electric mixer, whip the egg whites until fluffy. Gradually add ½ cup granulated sugar, whipping the whites until stiff but not dry. Set whites aside.

2. In a small bowl, combine matzoh meal and potato flour, and set them aside.

In a large mixing bowl, combine remaining ½ cup of sugar and the salt. Stir to blend, then make a hole in the middle of these dry ingredients and pour in the yolk-juice mixture. Add the oil. Whisk well to blend.

3. Whisk about 1 cup of whipped whites into the yolk mixture to lighten it. Then, little by little, fold the yolk mixture into the whites. Finally, fold the matzoh meal–flour mixture into the whipped batter in ¼-cup increments. Use a light touch to maintain batter volume.

4. Turn batter into ungreased tube pan. Bake in the preheated oven for 50 to 60 minutes, or until a cake tester inserted in the center comes out clean.

As soon as the cake is done, invert it onto the feet of its pan or hang it upside down over a tall bottle or funnel. Leave the cake in this position for several hours or overnight, until completely cold.

5. To remove the cake from its pan, slide a knife blade between the cake sides and the pan. Then top the cake with a plate, invert, and tap the pan bottom. Lift off pan. If pan sticks, again work the knife blade between cake and pan to loosen crumbs. The colder the cake, the more easily it will come out of the pan.

Serve the cake plain, or sift on a light coating of confectioners' sugar.

─────────────────────────────
. . . .

Mocha Wheatless Sponge Cake

▪

This light and flavorful sponge cake is made with potato starch (also called potato flour) and is suitable for Passover or wheatless diets. Rice flour may be substituted. Note that both potato and rice flours have a different texture from wheat flour, so the cake will be very slightly different from an ordinary sponge cake.

Note: Both potato flour and rice flour are available in some supermarkets and many specialty, health-food, or gourmet food shops.

□ ADVANCE PREPARATION: The cake can be made in advance and frozen. However, in my experience, freezing dries out the texture; I prefer to wrap the cake airtight and store it at room temperature for a day or two if it is to be made in advance. In fact, with potato flour, the texture improves after 24 hours at room temperature.

□ SPECIAL EQUIPMENT: one 10-inch angel-cake tube pan with feet, or regular tube pan and large funnel or tall bottle from which to suspend the inverted tube pan while cooling (see page 70), wax paper or baking parchment, sifter, rubber spatula or flat whisk, long thin-bladed knife, serrated knife, serving plate

□ BAKING TIME: 60 to 65 minutes at 350°F (175°C)

□ QUANTITY: 9 cups batter, one tube cake 10 × 4 inches (serves 12 to 14)

□ PAN PREPARATION: Line bottom of tube pan with wax paper or baking parchment cut to fit. Do not grease pan.

1 cup sifted potato starch (6 ounces; 170 g) or rice flour
2 tablespoons sifted unsweetened cocoa, preferably Dutch-process
8 large eggs, separated, at room temperature
½ teaspoon cream of tartar
Pinch of salt
1½ cups sifted superfine or granulated sugar (10½ ounces; 300 grams)
1 teaspoon vanilla extract
4 tablespoons strong regular or espresso coffee, made from 1½ teaspoons instant coffee dissolved in 4 tablespoons boiling water
½ teaspoon ground cinnamon
1½ ounces grated semisweet chocolate (45 grams)

TOPPING:

3 or 4 tablespoons sifted unsweetened cocoa

1. Read About Sponge and Foam Cakes. Position rack in center of oven. Preheat oven to 350°F (175°C). Prepare pan as described.

2. On wax paper, sift together potato starch and cocoa and set them aside.

3. In the large bowl of an electric mixer, combine egg whites with cream of tartar and salt. Whip egg whites until foamy, then gradually add ½ cup of the sugar and whip until stiff but not dry. Scrape beaters into bowl, but do not wash beaters. Remove bowl of whites from mixer and set it aside. Return unwashed beaters to electric mixer.

4. In another large bowl, beat the yolks with the electric mixer on high speed for 2 minutes, until yolks are thick and light in color.

Gradually beat in remaining 1 cup sugar, the vanilla, and coffee. Stop the mixer and scrape down the sides of the bowl and the beaters. Then beat on medium-high speed for 2 full minutes.

5. With the mixer on lowest speed, or stirring by hand, gradually add half of the potato starch-cocoa mixture to the yolk batter. Fold in the cinnamon.

6. Fold the whipped whites over on themselves once or twice to amalgamate them, then fold about one third of the whites into the yolk batter. Alternately fold in remaining whites with remaining potato starch-cocoa mixture. Finally, fold in the grated chocolate.

7. Turn batter into the prepared pan and bake in the center of the preheated oven for 60 to 65 minutes, or until the top is springy to the touch and a cake tester inserted in the center comes out clean. Do not overbake or the cake will dry out.

8. As soon as the cake is done, invert it onto the feet of its pan, or hang it upside down over the neck of a bottle or funnel; allow it to hang upside down for several hours, or overnight, until completely cold. To remove the cake from the pan, slide the blade of a long thin knife between the cake and pan sides to loosen the crumbs. Repeat around the center tube. Top the cake with a plate, invert, and lift off the pan. If the pan has a removable bottom, remove the sides first, then slide the knife between the pan bottom and the cake to release it. Peel off the paper. Leave the cake upside down if the top looks good, or invert it once again, so the cake is right side up on the plate. Sift on a few tablespoons of unsweetened cocca for a topping. To serve, cut the cake with a serrated knife.

Jelly Rolls

(Roulades)

ABOUT JELLY ROLLS AND ROULADES

•

The jelly roll, or French *roulade*, is simply a thin sponge cake baked in a broad flat pan and rolled around a filling. Typically, fillings include jelly or preserves, custard, or mousse. When the jelly roll is filled with a buttercream and coated with chocolate icing, it is used for the Bûche de Noël (page 229), or chocolate log cake. It can also be cut into thin spiraled slices to line a mold filled with Bavarian cream, making a Charlotte Royale (see page 336).

The texture of the rolled sponge cake is all-important: it should be light and fine-grained, but it should also be elastic and flexible enough to roll without cracking. There are several techniques for making rolled sponge cakes. The basic génoise, or French sponge

cake, is made with warmed whole eggs whipped to a high foam before the dry ingredients are gently folded in. A variation on this is the Classic Jelly Roll (following recipe), in which the eggs are separated. Part of the sugar is whipped with the yolks and part with the whites, and the flour is folded in last. Separating the eggs helps to make the sponge elastic and particularly well suited to being rolled. The so-called American sponge cake method uses separated eggs but also adds baking powder to supplement the leavening power of the whipped eggs. In my opinion, this method produces a coarser, heavier sponge than the classic recipe; it is my second choice. Angel-Food Cake (page 235) may also be baked in a jelly-roll pan and rolled over filling. The texture of the angel-food cake is light and flexible enough to produce a fine roll.

A jelly roll is always sliced with a serrated knife, using a sawing motion to prevent compressing the roll and squeezing out the filling.

Classic Jelly Roll

∎

This classic French roulade, or jelly roll, is made with a génoise sponge cake. The recipe is my own variation on basic techniques I learned from master Pastry Chef Albert Kumin, director of the Country Epicures' International Pastry Arts Center in Bedford Hills, New York.

Like the regular génoise, this cake is leavened only by whipped egg foam, but in this recipe the eggs are separated. Separating the eggs results in an elastic, flexible cake that rolls easily without cracking. Some cornstarch is added to cut the gluten in the wheat flour and make the texture more tender. Compared to the Lemon Jelly Roll (see page 225), this has a much finer crumb, a closer grain, and a more delicate texture. Use this for an all-purpose jelly roll; flavor it with vanilla, or use lemon or orange if you prefer. To make a Chocolate Sponge Roll, see page 227.

☐ ADVANCE PREPARATION: The cake can be baked in advance, rolled up in a cloth, and left to cool for several hours or overnight. The filled jelly roll can be wrapped airtight and will stay fresh for a couple of days if refrigerated. It can be frozen, but loses its freshness in about a week. Do not freeze if filled with custard or curd fillings, which tend to soften on freezing and make the cake soggy.

☐ SPECIAL EQUIPMENT: one jelly-roll pan 15 × 10 inches, 1 inch deep; wax paper or baking parchment, 2 cups, medium-size mixing bowl, sifter, extra bowl and beater for whipping egg whites, rubber spatula; linen or cotton tea towel somewhat larger than 15 × 10 inches, serrated knife.

☐ BAKING TIME: 11 to 13 minutes at 350°F (175°C)

☐ QUANTITY: 4 cups batter, one 10-inch roll (12 to 14 servings about ¾ inch thick)

☐ PAN PREPARATION: Spread butter or margarine on bottom and sides of jelly-roll pan. Line the pan with wax paper or baking parchment, then butter the paper and dust it evenly with flour; tap out excess flour.

4 large eggs, at room temperature, separated
10 tablespoons granulated sugar (4¼ ounces; 120 g)
½ cup sifted cake flour (1¾ ounces; 50 g)
¼ cup sifted cornstarch (1⅛ ounces; 30 g)
Pinch of salt
¾ teaspoon vanilla extract, or orange or lemon extract (or 1 tablespoon lemon juice) plus grated zest of 1 lemon or orange

UNMOLDING CAKE:

¼ cup confectioners' sugar, sifted

FILLING:

1 cup fruit preserves such as apricot or raspberry, or 3 cups fresh berries mashed and cooked with sugar until thick as jam, or 1 cup (½ recipe) Lemon Curd (page 380). Any mousse or Bavarian Cream can also be used as filling.

ICING:

*¼ cup confectioners' sugar, or Lemon
or Orange Icing Glaze (page 407)*

1. Prepare pan as described. Position rack in lower third of oven. Preheat oven to 350°F (175°C).

2. The sugar is divided in this recipe; I find it avoids confusion to label each sugar container as follows:

Measure 4 tablespoons sugar and put it in 1 cup. Write the number "4" on a piece of paper and set it in the cup. Place remaining 6 tablespoons of sugar in a second cup and identify them with paper marked "6." Sift together the flour and cornstarch into a medium-size bowl.

3. Put the egg yolks in a large mixing bowl and the whites in a medium-size mixing bowl.

Add the salt to the egg whites. With the electric mixer, whip the whites until they are frothy, then gradually add the 6 tablespoons sugar. Whip until the whites are stiff but not dry. They should be glossy and smooth and you should be able to invert the bowl without having the mass of whites move or slide.

Remove bowl from the mixer; scrape the beaters into the bowl. Without washing the beaters, return them to the mixer. Set the whipped whites aside.

4. With the mixer, now whip the yolks with the 4 tablespoons sugar until thick and light-colored. Stop the machine and scrape down the bowl and beaters twice. Add the vanilla extract or other flavoring and/or grated zest. Whip until the yolks form a flat ribbon falling back upon itself when the beater is lifted. This takes about 3 minutes with the KitchenAid mixer on speed #8; with

other mixers it can take 6 or 7 minutes. Set this bowl aside.

5. Fold about one third of the whites into the yolks. Then sprinkle about 3 tablespoons of the flour-cornstarch blend onto the yolk batter and fold it in gently. Continue to fold in the flour-cornstarch in small additions, folding with a light touch to maintain volume. When you near the end of the flour mixture, alternate it with some of the whipped egg whites. Finally, fold in remaining whipped whites. The batter should be light, airy, and smooth.

6. Turn the batter into the prepared pan, smoothing the top and spreading it to the edges with a rubber spatula. Place cake in the preheated oven to bake for 11 to 13 minutes, or until the top is golden and feels springy to the touch and the edges begin to draw away from the sides of the pan. Do not overbake the sponge or it will dry out too much.

7. While the cake bakes, spread the tea towel on a flat surface and sift on ¼ cup confectioners' sugar in a rectangle 15 × 10 inches.

As soon as the cake is baked, invert the pan over the sugared area of the towel. Lift off the pan and peel off the paper. With a serrated knife, slice off a scant ⅛-inch strip of crisp edging around the cake so it will roll more easily (diagram a).

Fold one short end of the towel over a short end of the cake, then roll them together (diagram b). Set the roll seam side down on a wire rack to cool.

8. When the cake is cold, unroll it, spread it with the preserves or other filling (diagram c), and reroll, using the short end of the towel to lift and push the cake as it rolls up (diagram d). Set the cake seam side down and sift con-

fectioners' sugar over the top. Or spread it with Icing Glaze. Cut the cake with a serrated knife (diagram e). If filled with Lemon Curd or other custard, or whipped cream, store the cake in the refrigerator; bring it to room temperature before serving.

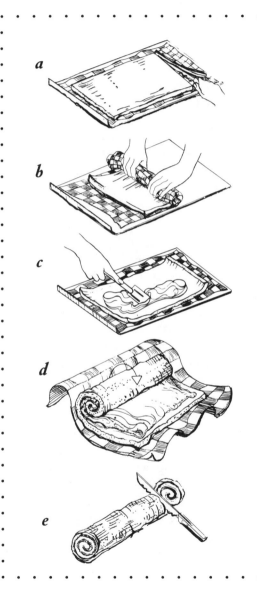

Lemon Jelly Roll

■

This sponge cake is prepared by the so-called American sponge method, that is, with baking powder added to the batter for leavening. The grain of this cake is open and somewhat coarse. When rolled, it may tend to crack a bit because the texture is not as flexible as that of the Classic Jelly Roll leavened entirely by the foam of whipped separated eggs. To make an Orange Jelly Roll, see the variation following the basic recipe.

☐ ADVANCE PREPARATION: The jelly roll can be baked, rolled in a cloth, refrigerated overnight, and filled on the day it is to be served. Or the cake can be filled, then wrapped airtight and refrigerated or, depending on the filling, stored at room temperature for a day or two. If the cake is filled with preserves or jelly, it can be wrapped airtight and frozen; however, custard and curd fillings tend to soften in the freezer and make the cake soggy.

☐ SPECIAL EQUIPMENT: one jelly-roll pan, 15 × 10 inches, 1 inch deep; wax paper or baking parchment; medium-size mixing bowl, extra bowl and beater for whipping egg whites, small saucepan, rubber spatula; linen or cotton tea towel somewhat larger than 15 × 10 inches, sifter, grater, serrated knife

☐ BAKING TIME: 13 to 15 minutes at 350°F (175°C)

☐ QUANTITY: 5 cups batter, one 10-inch roll (serves 8 to 10 generous slices 1 inch thick, or 12 to 14 slices about ¾ inch thick)

□ PAN PREPARATION: Spread butter or margarine on bottom and sides of jelly-roll pan. Line pan with wax paper or baking parchment, then butter the paper and dust it evenly with flour; tap out excess flour.

1½ cups sifted cake flour (5¼ ounces; 150 g)
1½ teaspoons baking powder
¼ teaspoon salt
3 large eggs, separated, at room temperature
1¼ cups granulated sugar (8¾ ounces; 250 g)
Grated zest of 1 lemon
¼ cup freshly squeezed orange juice
¼ cup freshly squeezed lemon juice

UNMOLDING CAKE:

¼ cup confectioners' sugar

FILLING:

1 cup fruit preserves such as apricot or raspberry, or 1 cup (½ recipe) Lemon Curd (page 380)

ICING:

¼ cup confectioners' sugar, or Lemon Icing Glaze (page 407)

1. Prepare pan as described. Position rack in lower third of oven. Preheat oven to 350°F (175°C).
2. Sift together flour, baking powder, and salt onto a piece of wax paper. Set aside.
3. Put egg yolks in the large bowl of an electric mixer. Beat until thick and lemon-colored, then gradually add 1 cup of the sugar while beating on medium speed. Stop the machine and scrape down the bowl and beaters once or twice. Beat until the mixture is thick. It will not form a ribbon.

4. Combine the grated lemon zest and both juices in a small pan. Set over high heat and bring to a boil.

Beat the yolk mixture with the electric mixer on low while pouring in the hot juice. Keep whipping as the liquid is added or the yolks will poach. Gradually increase mixer speed to medium (KitchenAid speed #5) and beat for a generous 30 seconds, until the sugar dissolves and the yolk-sugar mixture cools, thickens, and begins to increase in volume. Scrape down the inside of bowl and the beaters. Turn off the mixer.

5. In another bowl with clean beaters, whip the egg whites on medium-low speed until they look frothy. Then gradually add remaining ¼ cup of sugar, beating the whites at medium-high speed until stiff but not dry.

Use the rubber spatula to fold half of the whites into the yolk batter. Then sprinkle a little of the flour mixture onto the yolk batter and fold it in gently. Continue to fold in the flour in 6 or 7 additions, folding with a light touch to maintain volume. When you near the end of the flour, alternate it with some of the whipped egg whites. Finally, fold in remaining whipped whites. The batter should be light and airy and smooth.

6. Turn the batter into the prepared pan, smoothing the top and spreading it to the edges with a rubber spatula. Place it in the preheated oven to bake for 15 minutes, or until a cake tester comes out clean, the top of the cake feels springy to the touch, and the edges begin to look golden in color and draw away from the sides of the pan.

7. While the cake bakes, set a tea towel out on the counter, smooth it flat, and sift on ¼ cup confectioners' sugar in a rectangle 15 × 10 inches.

As soon as the cake is baked, invert the pan over the sugared area of the towel. Lift off the pan and peel off the paper. With a serrated knife, slice off a ⅛-inch-thick strip around all the edges, removing the cake's crisp border so that it will roll more easily (see Classic Jelly Roll diagrams).

Fold one short end of the towel over a short end of the cake, then roll them together. Set the roll seam side down on a wire rack to cool.

8. When the cake is cold, unroll it, spread it with preserves or Lemon Curd, and reroll without the cloth. Sift confectioners' sugar over the top, or spread with Icing Glaze before serving. Cut with a serrated knife. If filled with Lemon Curd, store the cake in the refrigerator, but serve it at room temperature.

·*Variation:*·

ORANGE JELLY ROLL:

Prepare Lemon Jelly Roll, but substitute orange zest and orange juice for the lemon. Orange marmalade may be used as a filling, or the Lemon Curd may be made with oranges.

Chocolate Sponge Roll or Bûche de Noël

■

This cake is a delight to make. It is easy to prepare, but more important, the results are reliable and delicious. The flavor is intensely chocolate without being sweet, the texture is light and tender, with a delicate crumb, and it rolls beautifully without cracking. The recipe is one I developed following the principles used in the Classic Jelly Roll (see Index). The génoise, or French sponge cake, is the basis for the formula, but the eggs are separated. Part of the sugar is whipped into the yolks and part into the whites. The cake is unmolded onto unsweetened cocoa, which leaves an attractive, finished coating on the filled and rolled cake. It eliminates the need for icing, though you may add any type you wish. This cake may be used for a Bûche de Noël (following), or it may be filled with 1½ cups of whipped cream or any mousse or Bavarian cream (see Index). To bake it as a layer or tube cake, see Chocolate Sponge Cake (page 218).

☐ ADVANCE PREPARATION: The cake can be baked ahead, rolled up in a cloth, and left to cool for several hours or overnight. It can be wrapped airtight and will stay fresh for a couple of days if refrigerated, or longer if frozen. However, it tends to dry out when frozen more than 1 week. Do not freeze if filled with custard.

☐ SPECIAL EQUIPMENT: one jelly-roll pan 15 × 10 inches, 1 inch deep; wax paper or baking parchment, medium-size bowl, sifter, extra bowl and beaters for whipping egg whites, rubber spatula; linen or cotton tea towel somewhat larger than 15 × 10 inches, serrated knife

□ BAKING TIME: 15 minutes at 350°F (175°C)

□ QUANTITY: 4 cups batter, one 10-inch roll (serves 10) This recipe also makes one 9-inch (6½-cup capacity) tube cake or two 8-inch layers

□ PAN PREPARATION: Spread butter or margarine on bottom and sides of jelly-roll pan. Line the pan with wax paper or baking parchment, then butter the paper and dust it evenly with unsweetened cocoa or flour; tap out excess.

4 large eggs, separated, at room
temperature
5 tablespoons sifted cake flour (1 ounce;
30 g)
2 tablespoons sifted cornstarch
⅓ cup sifted unsweetened cocoa,
preferably Dutch-process (¾ ounce;
20 g)
⅛ teaspoon ground cinnamon
¼ teaspoon salt
½ teaspoon baking powder
¼ teaspoon baking soda
¾ cup granulated sugar (5¼ ounces;
150 g)
1 teaspoon vanilla extract

UNMOLDING CAKE:

⅓ cup sifted unsweetened cocoa

FILLING:

¾ cup chilled heavy cream
2 tablespoons sifted superfine sugar

½ teaspoon vanilla extract, or 2
tablespoons dark rum or orange or
hazelnut-flavored liqueur
Or use Viennese Custard Buttercream
(page 377)

1. Prepare pan as described. Position rack in center of oven. Preheat oven to 350°F (175°C).

2. Sift together in a bowl the flour, cornstarch, cocoa, cinnamon, salt, baking powder, and baking soda. Set bowl aside.

3. Put egg whites in the large bowl of an electric mixer and yolks in a medium bowl. Put ½ cup of the sugar in one measure and ¼ cup in another. Set the cups near the electric mixer. The ½ cup of sugar will be whipped into the whites, the ¼ cup of sugar into the yolks. Feel the whites with your finger; they should be comfortably warm, not cold to the touch. Whip the whites on medium speed until frothy, then add about 2 tablespoons of the ½ cup of sugar. Whip for about 10 seconds, then gradually add the rest of ½ cup sugar while increasing the speed of the machine to medium-high. Whip the whites until they are stiff but not dry. They should be glossy and smooth and you should be able to invert the bowl without having the mass of whites move or slide. Scrape the beaters into the bowl. Set the whites aside. Without washing the beaters, return them to the mixer.

4. Using the same beaters and a clean medium-size electric mixer bowl, whip the yolks with the vanilla until pale in color. Add the ¼ cup sugar. Whip the yolk mixture until thick and pale in color. Stop the machine and scrape down the bowl and beaters twice. Continue whipping until the yolks form a flat ribbon falling back upon itself when the

beater is lifted. This takes about 3 minutes with the KitchenAid mixer on speed #8; with other mixers it can take 6 or 7 minutes. Remove bowl from mixer stand and scrape beaters into bowl.

5. By hand with a rubber spatula, fold about one third of the whites into the yolks. Then sprinkle about ¼ cup of the flour-cocoa mixture onto the yolk batter and fold it in gently. Continue to fold in the flour-cocoa mixture in 4 or 5 small additions, adding a small amount of whites occasionally. Fold with a light touch to maintain volume. When you near the end of the flour-cocoa mixture, alternate it with some more of the whipped whites. Finally, fold in remaining whipped whites. The batter should be light and airy and smooth. It should have a fairly even color, but don't worry if there are a few faint streaks of white.

6. Turn the batter into the prepared pan, smoothing the top and spreading it to the edges with a rubber spatula. Place the cake in the preheated oven to bake for 15 minutes, or until the top feels lightly springy to the touch, the sides of the cake begin to shrink away from the pan, and a cake tester inserted in the center comes out dry. Do not overbake the sponge or it will dry out too much.

7. While the cake bakes, set a tea towel on the counter, smooth it flat, and sift on ⅓ cup unsweetened cocoa powder in a rectangle 15 × 10 inches. Note: After use, you can shake this towel outside, then wash with cold water; the dry cocoa will not stain the towel.

As soon as the cake is baked, invert the pan over the cocoa on the towel. Lift off the pan and peel off the paper. With a serrated knife, slice off a scant ⅛-inch strip around the edges of the cake to remove the crisp border so the cake will roll more easily (see Classic Jelly Roll diagrams, page 225).

Fold one short end of the towel over a short end of the cake, then roll them together. Set the roll seam side down on a wire rack to cool.

8. Prepare the filling just before spreading it on the cold cake. To make the whipped cream filling, whip the cream in a chilled bowl with chilled beaters until soft peaks form. Add the sugar and vanilla or other flavoring; use a hand whisk to blend and whip for a few seconds longer. The cream should hold its shape but not be overstiff.

8. When the cake is cold, unroll it, spread it with the filling, and reroll. Set it seam side down, and sift a little confectioners' sugar or unsweetened cocoa on top. I prefer this simple topping for the cake, and like to serve it with a dollop of whipped cream on the side, or a spoonful of vanilla yogurt or vanilla ice cream. However, if you prefer, you can frost the cake with any type of icing (see Index) or whipped cream. Store the cake in the refrigerator and bring it to room temperature before serving. Cut the cake with a serrated knife. For the Bûche de Noël, see the variation following.

· *Variation:* ·

BÛCHE DE NOËL:

In France, this Yule Log Cake is a traditional part of the Christmas celebration. It is a realistic-looking log made of chocolate sponge cake filled with Hazelnut-Chocolate Buttercream or any other flavor of buttercream or mousse you prefer. The icing is Chocolate or Creamy Mocha Buttercream covered with slivers of rough chocolate bark, garnished with meringue mushrooms and green marzipan leaves. The bark, mushrooms, and marzipan can be made ahead, but the Yule Log is best made and served fresh. In a pinch you can fill and frost (but not decorate) the log, wrap it in foil, and freeze it for up to 2 weeks.

CAKE:

Prepare the Chocolate Sponge Roll, roll it in a cocoa-covered tea towel, and set it aside to cool.

FILLING:

Hazelnut-Chocolate Buttercream (page 393)

ICING:

Creamy Mocha Buttercream (page 390)

GARNISHES:

Chocolate Bark (page 452)
3 ounces semisweet or bittersweet chocolate
Meringue Mushrooms (page 459)
Marzipan Leaves and Berries (page 446)

□ ASSEMBLY PROCEDURE: When you are ready to assemble the Bûche de Noël, unroll the cake carefully, leaving it flat on the towel. Be sure your filling is at room temperature, well beaten and creamy. Spread the filling to within ¼ inch of the cake's edges. Reserve a generous ¾ to 1 cup for frosting the outside of log.

Lift one end of the towel to help start the cake rolling over onto the filling. Remove the towel and set the cake, seam side down, on a cake board or rectangular platter. Cover the cake sides, but not the ends, with the icing. To emphasize the bark texture, draw the tines of a fork through the icing to make ridges (diagram a).

Prepare the chocolate bark. Press the chocolate slivers onto the frosted log cake.

Arrange 8 or 9 meringue mushrooms in groups of 2 or 3 along the log. Here and there, position sprays of green marzipan holly leaves around a trio of small red marzipan berries (diagram b).

To serve, slice the cake with a serrated knife.

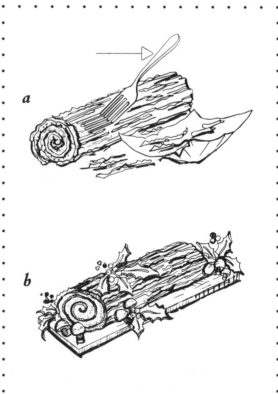

a

b

Angel-Cake Jelly Roll

■

Instead of making a jelly roll with a sponge cake, you can also use angel-food cake. The following recipe is simply half of the Classic White Angel Cake (page 235), with a few modifications in procedure as noted.

☐ ADVANCE PREPARATION: The cake can be baked in advance, wrapped in a sugared tea towel, and allowed to sit for several hours before filling. For best texture, fill the roll shortly before serving; if covered and re-frigerated for more than a couple of hours, the roll may become soggy.

☐ SPECIAL EQUIPMENT: one jelly-roll pan 15 × 10 inches, 1 inch deep; wax paper or baking parchment, triple sifter, rubber spatula or flat whisk; linen or cotton tea towel somewhat larger than 15 × 10 inches, strainer or sifter, serrated knife

☐ BAKING TIME: 25 minutes at 325°F (165°C)

☐ QUANTITY: 4 cups batter, one 10-inch roll (12 to 14 servings about ¾ inch thick)

☐ PAN PREPARATION: Line the pan with wax paper or baking parchment. Do not grease pan.

CAKE:

Prepare half the Classic White Angel Cake recipe (page 235), using a total of ½ cup plus 2 tablespoons superfine sugar and 5 large egg whites. Also you will need ⅓ cup confectioners' sugar to sift over the tea towel before turning out the cake.

FILLING:

1 cup fruit preserves or jam or 2 cups of whipped cream of any flavor or plain sweet-ened whipped cream with sliced fresh ber-ries, or peaches, or other fruit, or Boiled or Seven-Minute Icing or half the recipe (1 cup) for Lemon Curd or any Mousse or Ba-varian Cream (see Index for recipes).

1. Follow the procedure for the Classic White Angel Cake except, in step 2, sift the flour with ¼ cup confectioners sugar and ¼ teaspoon salt and set it aside. In step 3, sift ¼ cup plus 2 tablespoons superfine sugar and set it aside to add to the whipped egg whites.

2. Spread the batter onto the prepared pan, smoothing it out into an even layer without pressing or deflating the whites. Bake the cake for 25 to 30 minutes, until the top looks light beige in color and feels lightly springy to the touch, and a cake tester inserted in the center comes out clean.

3. While the cake bakes, spread a tea towel flat on the table and sift on about ⅓ cup confectioners' sugar in a rectangle 15 × 10 inches. As soon as the cake is baked, slide a knife blade between the cake and the pan sides to loosen the crumbs, then invert the pan over the sugared area of the towel. Lift off the pan and peel off the paper. With a serrated knife, using a sawing motion, slice off a scant ⅛-inch strip around the edges of the cake, removing the crisp border so that the cake will

roll more easily (See Classic Jelly Roll diagrams, page 225).

4. Fold one short end of the towel over a short end of the cake, then roll them together. Set the roll seam side down on a wire rack to cool.

5. When the cake is cold, unroll it, spread it with the desired filling, and reroll. Set it seam side down on a plate, ice if desired, and cut the cake with a serrated knife, using a sawing motion. Refrigerate leftover cake if filled with cream or custard; bring to room temperature before serving.

·*Variation:*·

ZABAGLIONE ANGEL ROULADE:

Prepare Angel-Cake Jelly Roll, substituting 1 tablespoon rum or Marsala wine for the almond extract. Fill the roll with about 1½ cups Zabaglione Cake Filling (page 378). Refrigerate leftovers. Bring the filled cake to room temperature before serving. Just before serving, sift a little confectioners' sugar over the top.

Angel-Food Cakes

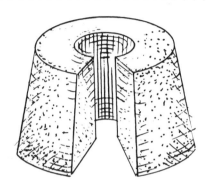

ABOUT ANGEL-FOOD CAKES

■

Angel-food cake was created in the nineteenth century, when baking ovens with reliable heat controls became available. Its origin is disputed, but food historians often attribute the invention to thrifty bakers in the Pennsylvania Dutch community, who, it is said, developed the recipe to use up leftover egg whites.

This delightfully light, fluffy, high-rise cake is basically a sponge cake without egg yolks or fat. Angel-food cake owes its success to a couple of basic tricks and an understanding of the ingredients from which it is made. Angel cake is made with a large quantity of egg whites, which are whipped into a foam; this foam, and the steam that arises when it is heated, provide 100 percent of the cake's leavening. The development and handling of this foam is critical. First, you should understand how to handle egg whites. Review About Meringue (pages 244–248) and About Sponge and Foam Cakes (page 208). Separate the eggs when they come from the refrigerator, then let the whites sit awhile, or, to speed their warming, set them in a bowl inside another bowl of warm water; stir the whites until they are comfortably warm to the touch. Frozen egg whites may be used for angel cakes; they should simply be thawed and brought to room temperature. In case you have forgotten how many whites you have frozen, note that

1 large egg white = 2 generous tablespoons = 1/8 cup; 4 large whites = 1/2 cup; 8 large whites = 1 cup; 10 to 12 whites = 1 1/2 cups

The unused egg yolks may be frozen (see page 31). Whip the whites in an absolutely clean bowl, without any trace of fat or yolk, and use the biggest balloon whisk or electric beater you have. Begin whipping the whites slowly at first to develop many small air cells. Increase speed gradually, as the foam builds. As soon as the whites appear frothy, add a little cream of tartar, an acid that helps to stabilize the meringue, and a little sugar—for sweetening and stability of foam. Part of the total sugar is added in small increments as the whites are whipped, and the rest is sifted with the flour and salt and folded into the whites at the very end. The first trick is to beat the whites to the correct point, because if they are overbeaten, the air cells will enlarge too much and actually collapse when the air in them expands during baking. This can cause the cake to sink, and is the most common cause for angel cake failure. The whites should be beaten until *just before* they are "stiff." When you stop the machine and lift the beater, the whites should hold their shape but the very tip should fall over gently. The whites should be glossy and smooth, and you should be able to invert the bowl without having the mass of whites move or slide. At this stage the whites are not likely to be overbeaten, and there is still a little room for them to expand in the heat of the oven. Also, folding in the dry ingredients works the whites slightly and if beaten "stiff," they risk being overwhipped after folding is accomplished. Note: If your whites are overbeaten and look clumpy instead of perfectly smooth, you can save them by adding some unbeaten whites; read How to Save Overbeaten Whites (page 248).

After the whites reach the correct stage, add the vanilla or other extract and hand-whisk the batter only once or twice, just to combine ingredients.

Now you are ready for the dry ingredients. I prefer to use cake flour in angel-food cakes,

as it contains less gluten and produces a more tender product than all-purpose flour. Be sure to sift the flour well, then resift it with the sugar. Some recipes call for sifting again as the flour is added to the whites; do this if you wish, to ensure lightness.

The type of sugar used can vary; the main point is to have all the sugar dissolved in the batter. Because of the large quantity of sugar, this is best achieved by using either all superfine sugar, or part superfine sugar, added early in the mixing, and part confectioners' sugar, folded in at the end, after the whites are whipped. Granulated sugar may also be used, but be sure it is completely dissolved in the whipped whites: pinch a little of the whites between your fingers; if sugar granules can still be felt, whip longer.

Using a flat whisk or rubber spatula, fold the dry ingredients into the whipped whites with a very light touch to maintain the volume. Review Folding (page 65). Never stir the batter, or the fragile air cells will deflate. It is much better to leave a few traces of flour visible in the whites than to overwork the mixture. Professional chefs often prefer to do the folding with the flat of the bare hand, to control the technique perfectly. If you are adding ground nuts or grated chocolate, fold them in at the very last minute.

The batter is gently scooped into the *ungreased* pan with a rubber spatula. The traditional angel-food pan is a tube, and is used because the central column exposes more batter to the heat and dries out the cake well. However, be aware that many different pans may successfully be used: a regular layer or springform pan, a jelly-roll pan, a loaf pan, or cupcake pan lined with fluted paper liners.

Hints and Tips for Angel-Food Cakes

• There are four important tricks involved in the baking procedure. First, do *not* grease the cake pan; the rising batter must cling to the pan sides and hold itself up instead of sliding down on a slippery, greased surface.

• Second, put the cake in the preheated oven as soon as all the batter is in the pan; do not let the cake stand around or the air cells will begin to deflate, and you need them to make the cake rise.

• Third, bake the cake at the correct heat. Egg whites are protein, and overheating them makes them toughen and tend to shrink. I find that 325°F is the ideal baking temperature. For testing the doneness of an angel-food cake, it is handy to use a thin bamboo cocktail skewer, which is longer than a toothpick or metal cake tester and easier to have at hand than a clean broomstraw.

• Fourth, as soon as the cake is baked, turn the pan upside down and stand it on its feet or hang it upside down over the neck of a bottle or a tall funnel. Or balance the edges of the pan on inverted mugs or cups. The point is to have the cake hang inverted until it is completely cold.

• To cut angel cake, use a serrated knife with a sawing motion or a pronged angel-food cake cutter; this looks like a row of thin nails attached to a bar. Or pull the cake apart with 2 opposing forks. Do not try to cut with a regular knife, pushing down through the cake, or it will compress and flatten.

Troubleshooting Angel-Food Cakes

• Texture of cake very shiny when cut: Egg whites were overwhipped.

• After removing cake from the oven, the cake sinks, collapses, looks concave on top: Egg whites were overwhipped.

• After removing cake from the oven, the cake appears well below the rim of the pan and the center of the cake is peaked like a mountain: Egg whites were underwhipped, creating too little volume.

• Cake is flat and texture is dense: The cake was not inverted to hang unobstructed as it cooled; gravity pulled the delicate structure back onto itself as it cooled while upright in the pan.

- -

Classic White Angel Cake

▪

This is the traditional food of the angels—heavenly, tender, not overly sweet, a perfect light dessert. The basic batter can be combined with ground nuts, or coconut, or a variety of other flavorings to create the variations that follow this recipe. To decorate the cake, you can frost it with swirls of Seven-Minute Icing or simply dust it with confectioners' sugar and serve it with fresh berries and Zabaglione Sauce or Lemon Curd (see Index). Or this recipe can be used as a foundation for a host of gala cakes: bake it in a jelly-roll pan and roll it up with Zabaglione Filling for a great roulade. Or bake it in the tube pan, then hollow out the cake center, fill it with ice cream or mousse, and freeze it for a festive Ice Cream Cake. You can also use this recipe to make cupcakes.

Note: The egg whites for this cake can be whipped in a copper bowl with a large whisk, in a mixing bowl with a hand-held electric beater, or in a bowl with an egg beater. The type of sugar used can vary; the main point is to have all the sugar dissolved in the batter. This is best done either with all superfine sugar or with part superfine sugar and part confectioners' sugar, as in the recipe.

□ ADVANCE PREPARATION: Angel cake can be made in advance and wrapped airtight to keep fresh at room temperature for several days. It can also be wrapped airtight and frozen, though its flavor and texture may deteriorate after a few weeks. Be sure to protect the angel cake in the freezer by placing it in a box; the cake does not freeze solidly and risks being squashed by a heavier object. Defrost the cake and bring it to room temperature before frosting.

□ SPECIAL EQUIPMENT: one 10-inch tube pan; triple sifter, wax paper, rubber spatula or flat whisk, tall bottle or funnel large enough that the tube pan can be hung upside down around its neck while the cake cools; serving plate, serrated knife or pronged angel-food cake cutter

□ BAKING TIME: 45 to 50 minutes at 325°F (165°C)

□ QUANTITY: 8 cups batter, tube cake 10 × 4 inches (serves 10 to 12)

□ PAN PREPARATION: None. Do not grease pan.

1 cup sifted cake flour (3½ ounces; 100 g)
½ cup sifted confectioners' sugar (1¾ ounces; 50 g)

¾ cup superfine sugar (5¼ ounces; 150 g); or substitute a total of 1¼ cups all superfine sugar (8¾ ounces; 250 g)
½ teaspoon salt
1½ cups egg whites (10 to 12 large egg whites), at room temperature
1 teaspoon cream of tartar
1 teaspoon vanilla extract
¾ teaspoon almond extract (optional)

ICING:

A light sifting of confectioners' sugar or any Boiled Icing or Seven-Minute Icing (see Index)

1. Position rack in center of oven. Preheat oven to 325°F (165°C). Read About Angel-Food Cakes.

2. Sift the flour through a triple sifter onto a piece of wax paper. Then resift this flour with ½ cup sifted confectioners' sugar and ½ teaspoon salt. Set this blend of dry ingredients aside.

3. Sift the ¾ cup superfine sugar onto another piece of paper, then pour it into a cup and set it near the electric mixer where you will be beating the egg whites.

4. Test the temperature of the egg whites; they should be comfortable to the touch, not cold. Warm them gently by stirring over a pan of hot water if necessary. Whip the whites on low speed until slightly frothy. Add the cream of tartar and whip the whites for a few seconds, then add 2 tablespoons of the ¾ cup superfine sugar and whip for about 10 seconds longer. Add the remaining superfine sugar gradually, whipping the whites until they are *almost* stiff, but not dry. The whites should be glossy and smooth, and you should be able to invert the bowl without having the mass of whites move or slide.

5. Sprinkle on the vanilla and almond extracts and whisk the whites by hand once or twice, quickly, just to blend in the flavoring.

6. Remove the bowl of whites from the mixer. By hand, using a rubber spatula or flat whisk, fold in the flour-sugar-salt mixture, 3 tablespoons at a time. When adding flour, sprinkle it lightly over the whites or sift it on. Fold with a very light touch, cutting through the center of the whites, down to the bottom of the bowl, and bringing the spatula or whisk up again toward you while giving the bowl a quarter turn. Repeat until all dry ingredients are added and just barely incorporated. Do not stir the batter.

7. Turn the batter gently into the baking pan and smooth the top very lightly with the rubber spatula. Cut through the batter once just to be sure there are no large air pockets.

Set the pan in the center of the preheated oven and bake the cake for 45 minutes, or until it is well risen and golden brown on top, and a cake tester inserted in the center comes out clean.

8. As soon as the cake is done, invert it onto the feet of its pan or hang it upside down over the neck of a bottle or funnel; allow it to hang upside down for several hours, or overnight, until completely cold (see page 70).

To remove the cake from the pan, slide the blade of a long thin knife between the cake and the pan sides to loosen the crumbs. Repeat around the center tube.

Top the cake with a plate, then invert and lift off the pan. If your pan has a removable bottom, you may remove the sides first, then slide the knife between the pan bottom and the cake to release it. Leave the cake upside down, or top it with a plate and invert, leaving it right side up. Ice the cake as you wish; to serve, cut with a serrated knife or pronged angel-food cake cutter.

·*Variations:*·

COCONUT ANGEL CAKE:

Prepare Classic White Angel Cake, being sure to use the almond extract along with the vanilla.

Toss ⅓ cup shredded coconut with the flour-sugar-salt mixture and fold it into the whipped whites at the end of the recipe. Frost the cake with Coconut Seven-Minute Icing (page 399). For a stronger coconut flavor, if you wish, you can also add ¾ teaspoon of coconut extract.

ALMOND ANGEL CAKE:

Prepare Classic White Angel Cake, but use 1 teaspoon of almond extract along with the vanilla. In addition, add 1 tablespoon hazelnut or Amaretto liqueur along with the extracts, and ground nuts prepared as follows:

Prepare ¾ cup finely ground almonds, preferably grated with a hand-held drum-type rotary nut mill (see page 43). If using a food processor, add 2 tablespoons of the premeasured sugar to the work bowl before grinding the almonds. Note: Hazelnuts may be substituted, but not walnuts, which contain too much oil. Combine the ground nuts with ⅓ cup of the flour-sugar-salt blend from step 2. Fold the nut-flour blend into the batter at the very end, using a light touch to maintain volume.

ORANGE ANGEL CAKE:

Prepare Classic White Angel Cake, but substitute 1 teaspoon of orange extract for the almond extract. Add the grated zest of 2 oranges, tossing it with a couple of tablespoons of the flour-sugar-salt mixture so it is not too wet and clumped together, before folding it into the batter at the very end. Frost the cake with Orange Icing Glaze (page 407), or orange-flavored Boiled Icing (page 401).

Double Chocolate Angel Cake

∎

This variation on the classic angel-food cake is made with cocoa as well as grated chocolate folded in at the very end to produce flecks of chocolate throughout the baked cake. You will observe that this recipe uses the same number of egg whites as the Classic White Angel Cake, yet is baked in a smaller pan. This is because the cocoa powder contains butterfat, which weighs down the whipped egg whites somewhat, giving slightly less volume to the cake.

☐ ADVANCE PREPARATION: The cake can be made in advance and wrapped airtight to keep fresh at room temperature for several days. It can also be wrapped airtight and frozen, though its flavor and texture may deteriorate and toughen after a few weeks.

☐ SPECIAL EQUIPMENT: one 9-inch angel-cake tube pan with "feet," or regular tube pan and large funnel or tall bottle from which to suspend inverted tube pan while cooling; triple sifter, strainer or sieve, wax paper, rubber spatula or flat whisk; long thin-bladed knife, serrated knife or pronged angel-food cake cutter, serving plate

☐ BAKING TIME: 55 to 60 minutes at 325°F (165°C)

☐ QUANTITY: 8 cups batter, one 9-inch cake (serves 8 to 10)

☐ PAN PREPARATION: None. Do not grease the pan.

3/4 cup sifted cake flour (2 1/2 ounces; 70 g)
1 1/4 cups sifted superfine or granulated sugar (8 3/4 ounces; 250 g)
1/4 cup sifted unsweetened cocoa powder, preferably Dutch-process (3/4 ounce; 20 g)
1/2 teaspoon ground cinnamon
1 1/2 cups egg whites (10 to 12 large egg whites), at room temperature
1 teaspoon cream of tartar
Pinch of salt
1 teaspoon vanilla extract
1 1/2 ounces grated semisweet chocolate (45 g)

ICING:

2 tablespoons sifted unsweetened cocoa powder or confectioners' sugar, or Boiled Icing (page 401)

1. Position rack in center of oven. Preheat oven to 325°F (165°C). Read About Angel-Food Cakes.

2. Sift the flour through a triple sifter onto a piece of wax paper. Then resift this flour with ½ cup of the presifted sugar, the presifted cocoa, and the cinnamon. Set this blend of dry ingredients aside.

3. Pour remaining ¾ cup sugar through the triple sifter or strainer, then pour it into a cup and set it near the electric mixer where you will be beating the egg whites.

4. Test the temperature of the egg whites; they should be comfortable to the touch, not cold. Warm them over a pan of hot water if necessary. Whip the whites on low speed until slightly frothy. Add the cream of tartar and the salt and whip the whites on medium speed for about 20 seconds. Add 2 tablespoons of the reserved ¾ cup sugar and whip for about 10 seconds longer, then add 2 more tablespoons of sugar. Increase mixing speed to medium-high, then gradually add remaining sugar, a little at a time, while whipping the whites until they are *almost* stiff but not dry. Remove the bowl from the mixer.

5. Sprinkle on the vanilla extract and gently hand-whisk the whites once or twice, just to blend in the flavoring.

6. Fold the flour-sugar-cocoa blend, 3 tablespoons at a time, into the whites using a flat whisk or rubber spatula. When adding this mixture, sprinkle it lightly over the whites or sift it on. Fold with a very light touch, cutting through the center of the whites, down to the bottom of the bowl, and bringing the spatula or whisk up again toward you while giving the bowl a quarter turn. Repeat until all dry ingredients are added and just barely incorporated. Now fold in the grated chocolate, incorporating it with as few folding strokes as possible.

7. Turn the batter gently into the baking pan and smooth the top very lightly with the rubber spatula. Set the pan in the lower third of the preheated oven and bake the cake for 55 to 60 minutes, or until it is well risen and lightly springy to the touch. A cake tester inserted in the cake center should come out clean. Do not overbake, or the cake will dry out.

8. As soon as the cake is done, invert it onto the bottle or funnel and allow it to hang upside down for several hours, or overnight, until completely cold.

To remove the cake from the pan, slide the blade of a long thin knife between the cake and the pan sides and around the center tube to loosen the crumbs. Top the cake with a plate, then invert and lift off the pan. If your pan has a removable bottom, you may remove the sides first, then slide the knife between the pan bottom and the cake to release it. Leave the cake upside down, or top it with a plate and invert, leaving it right side up. Frost the cake as you wish, and serve it by cutting with a serrated knife or angel-food cake cutter or pulling the cake apart with 2 opposing forks.

Chiffon Cakes

Basic Chiffon Cake

•

The chiffon cake is unique in cake history because its birth date is recorded. Food historians credit Californian Henry Baker with inventing the chiffon cake in 1927. He later sold the formula to General Mills, which promoted the cake as well as the vegetable oil that was its "mystery ingredient." As a result of the promotion, cakes baked with oil became very popular in the 40s. They are having a renaissance today because we are so conscious of our cholesterol intake and vegetable oil, of course, contains none.

The chiffon cake has a marvelously light texture, and is big, tall, and only slightly richer than an angel-food cake, in whose pan it is baked. For ease in serving, cut chiffon cake with a serrated knife.

The basic recipe that follows contains whole eggs and makes a plain vanilla cake; to transform this into a completely cholesterol-free cake, omit the yolks and add more whites (see variation, Egg-White Chiffon, following). Follow the other easy variations to make Orange-Lemon Chiffon, Chocolate Chiffon, Mocha Chiffon, and Hazelnut Chiffon.

Note: The chiffon cake, like the angel-food cake, may be hollowed out and filled with Bavarian cream or ice cream (see Index). Frost with an Icing Glaze (see Index) or buttercream, or merely sift on some confectioners' sugar.

□ ADVANCE PREPARATION: The cake can be baked in advance, wrapped airtight, and frozen.

☐ SPECIAL EQUIPMENT: one angel-food tube pan, 10 × 4 inches, preferably with a removable bottom and "feet" on the edge; if there are no feet on the pan, set out a wine bottle or tall funnel from which to hang the cake after baking; an extra large bowl, wax paper or baking parchment, scissors

☐ BAKING TIME: 65 to 70 minutes at 325°F (165°C)

☐ QUANTITY: 9 cups batter; one cake, 10 × 4 inches (serves 14 to 16)

☐ PAN PREPARATION: Cut a paper or parchment liner to fit the bottom of the baking pan. Do not grease the pan.

6 large eggs separated, at room temperature
½ teaspoon cream of tartar
1½ cups granulated sugar (10½ ounces; 300 g)
2½ cups sifted cake flour (8¾ ounces; 250 g)
3 teaspoons baking powder
½ teaspoon salt
¾ cup water
½ cup light vegetable oil, such as corn or safflower oil
2 teaspoons vanilla extract

ICING:

Any Seven-Minute Icing or Boiled Icing (see Index) or Lemon or Orange Icing Glaze (page 407); or top with a light sifting of confectioners' sugar

1. Prepare pan as described. Position rack in center of oven. Preheat oven to 325°F (165°C). Read About Sponge and Foam Cakes.

2. In a large bowl, use the electric mixer to whip the egg whites with the cream of tartar until fluffy. Little by little, add ⅔ cup of the sugar, beating until the whites are very satiny and form nearly stiff peaks. Remove bowl from the mixer. Scrape the beaters into the bowl. Without washing the beaters, return them to the mixer. Set whites aside.

3. In another mixing bowl, sift together flour, remaining granulated sugar, the baking powder, and salt. Scoop a well in the center of this flour mixture. In this well add the 6 egg yolks, the water, oil, and vanilla. With a whisk or wooden spoon, or the electric mixer on medium-low speed, beat the ingredients together until well blended and smooth.

4. In 6 or 7 additions, fold the yolk batter into the whipped whites, working gently so the volume will not be lost. Pour the batter into the ungreased lined pan and bake in the preheated oven for about 65 minutes, or until the top is well-risen and richly golden in color. A cake tester should come out clean.

5. As soon as cake is baked, invert it onto the feet of its pan or hang it upside down over a bottle neck or a funnel; allow it to hang upside down for several hours, or overnight, until completely cold.

To remove the cake from the pan, set the pan upright and slide a long thin knife blade between the cake and pan sides to loosen the crumbs. Repeat around the center tube. Top the cake with a plate, and invert. If the pan has a removable bottom, press on it gently. Lift off the pan. Slide the knife between the pan bottom and the cake to release it. Peel off the paper. Turn cake right side up. Frost as desired. To serve, slice with a serrated knife.

ORANGE-LEMON CHIFFON CAKE:

Prepare Basic Chiffon Cake, but replace the water with orange juice, or use half orange juice and half freshly squeezed lemon juice. Add grated zest of 1 orange and 1 lemon along with 1 teaspoon of vanilla extract. Replace the second teaspoon of vanilla with 1 teaspoon of orange or lemon extract. Frost the cake with Orange or Lemon Icing Glaze (page 407) or Orange Seven-Minute Icing (page 399).

CHOCOLATE CHIFFON CAKE:

Prepare Basic Chiffon Cake, but use only 1¾ cups sifted cake flour (6 ounces; 170 g). Add to dry ingredients ½ cup sifted unsweetened cocoa, preferably Dutch-process (1⅓ ounces; 40 g) and ¼ teaspoon ground cinnamon.

MOCHA CHIFFON CAKE:

Prepare Chocolate Chiffon Cake and add to dry ingredients along with the cocoa and cinnamon 2 tablespoons instant coffee powder.

HAZELNUT CHIFFON CAKE:

Prepare Basic Chiffon Cake or Chocolate Chiffon Cake. After adding the whipped whites, fold in very lightly 1 cup finely chopped toasted hazelnuts (4 ounces; 110 g).

EGG-WHITE CHIFFON CAKE:

Prepare Basic Chiffon Cake, but omit egg yolks. Whip stiff 8 or 9 egg whites (1 cup). This recipe contains no cholesterol.

Cholesterol-Free Lemon Chiffon Cake

■

Completely cholesterol-free, this light, lemony chiffon cake is slightly smaller than the Basic Chiffon Cake and the pan preparation and cooling procedures are different. The result, however, is an excellent light cake made with egg whites. Its refreshingly tart flavor and sponge texture are complemented by a simple Lemon Icing Glaze. As an alternative serve an uniced slice with a Warm Berry Sauce (page 418), or with lemon sorbet and fresh strawberries.

☐ ADVANCE PREPARATION: Cake can be prepared ahead and frozen.

☐ SPECIAL EQUIPMENT: one 9-inch (6½-cup capacity) tube pan, extra mixing bowl, grater

☐ BAKING TIME: 35 to 40 minutes at 350°F (175°C). Note: This cake does not have to hang upside down for several hours while cooling.

☐ QUANTITY: 4 cups batter, one 9-inch tube cake (serves 8 to 10)

☐ PAN PREPARATION: Spread solid shortening on bottom and sides of pan; dust pan with flour; tap out excess flour. (This cake does not have to be baked in an ungreased pan.)

5 large egg whites, at room
    temperature
2 tablespoons sifted confectioners' sugar
1½ cups sifted cake flour (5¼ ounces;
    150 g)
1 cup granulated sugar (7 ounces;
    200 g)
2 teaspoons baking powder
¼ teaspoon salt
½ cup light vegetable oil, corn or
    safflower, for example
Grated zest of 2 lemons
½ cup freshly squeezed lemon juice

ICING:

Lemon Icing Glaze (page 407) or Orange Wine Icing (page 398)

1. Prepare pan as described. Position rack in center of oven. Preheat oven to 350°F (175°C). Read About Sponge and Foam Cakes (page 208).

2. In a large bowl, use an electric mixer to whip the egg whites with 2 tablespoons confectioners' sugar until stiff but not dry. Remove bowl from electric mixer; scrape beaters into bowl. Set whites aside. Without washing the beaters, return them to the mixer.

3. In another large bowl, sift together the flour, granulated sugar, baking powder, and salt. Scoop out a well in the center of the flour and add the oil, lemon zest, and juice. With a whisk or the mixer on medium-low speed, beat until well blended and smooth.

In several additions, fold the batter into the whites, working gently so the volume will not be lost.

4. Pour batter into the prepared pan and bake in the preheated oven for about 35 minutes, or until the top of the cake is golden brown and feels lightly springy to the touch. A cake tester should come out clean. Cool the cake right side up in its pan for 5 minutes, then invert onto a wire rack and lift off the pan. Leave the cake upside down on the rack to cool completely. Ice if desired.

Meringue Cakes

& Dacquoise

ABOUT MERINGUE

Meringue is created by whipping egg whites with sugar to create a foamy structure. It has innumerable uses, all of which take advantage of its uniquely light and airy quality. Meringue is used as leavening in certain cake batters, or to lighten a soufflé, mousse, Bavarian cream, or cake filling. It may be combined with softened butter to create silken buttercream icing or it may be piped from a pastry bag or spread with a spoon into many different shapes and sizes to use as cake layers. When these layers are baked until crisp in a slow oven, they can be filled and frosted with buttercream or flavored whipped cream to form meringue cakes. Meringues can also be formed into cup shapes to hold creams or ice cream and fruit. When baked in a pie plate, meringue forms a crisp shell that when filled with custard or whipped cream is known as Angel Pie. Meringue can also become a dessert in itself—*Île Flottante* (floating Island) or *Oeufs à la Neige* (Eggs in the Snow)—or a dramatic topping for tarts, pies, and cakes (Zuppa Inglese and Baked Alaska).

Meringue may be flavored with any type of extract or citrus zest. When grated or ground nuts are added to a meringue that is shaped into layers for use in a cake or torte, it is called a Dacquoise, or *japonais* or *broyage,* from the French word *broyer* meaning to grind and referring to the nuts.

The amount of sugar combined with the egg whites determines both the final use of the meringue and the method by which it is made.

The classic meringue proportions are 1 ounce of whites (the white of 1 large egg) to 2 ounces of sugar (4 tablespoons or 57 grams).

Soft meringues with a small amount of sugar, about 2 tablespoons per egg white, are easily whipped at room temperature (Cold Method) with a wire whisk in a bowl, preferably copper, or in an electric mixer with whisk beaters. A low-sugar meringue will remain soft inside even if baked or broiled for a short time in the oven, as is the topping for a Baked Alaska.

Sometimes the whites and sugar are whisked together over, but not touching, hot water (Warm or Swiss Meringue Method) until the mixture reaches 120°F and the sugar is dissolved. Then the meringue is whipped until stiff. This method guarantees that no undissolved sugar will bead or weep from the baked product; it makes a very stable meringue. A meringue made by either method may be added to cake or torte batters to provide leavening, or may be folded into mousses or Bavarian creams.

When a larger proportion of sugar is added (3 or 4 tablespoons of sugar per egg white), the resulting meringue may be hard or soft, depending upon how it is baked and whether it is combined with softer ingredients, as when folded into a batter. For the highest sugar-ratio meringue (typically 4 or more tablespoons sugar per white), the sugar can be cooked in water to a syrup (Italian Meringue) before being added to the whipped whites. Since Italian meringues have more sugar than any other type, they are firmer, and make a stable meringue that will not break down or bead when baked. Italian meringue may be combined with softened butter to make a luxuriously satin-textured buttercream, or it can be folded into fillings, toppings, or mousse. It can also be baked slowly at low temperature to make crisp cake layers.

Meringue Basics

Before making meringues, review about Eggs (page 30). Be sure your egg whites are from pure, fresh eggs, with unbroken shells. Bacteria causing a common food poisoning, salmonellosis, can be present in unsanitary egg whites and cannot be destroyed by either the quick cooking given meringue toppings or the low temperature baking used for meringue cakes. For this reason, be sure to refrigerate leftover meringue-topped cakes and cakes that contain whipped egg whites in uncooked fillings or frostings.

There are several important basics to remember when working with meringue: Select a cool, dry day if possible, since humidity may soften meringue. Keep all utensils scrupulously clean; a speck of fat (such as from a broken yolk) in the egg whites prevents them from beating to full volume because the fat becomes suspended in the natural moisture of the whites; it softens the protein, and thus weighs them down. Beware of plastic bowls, which are hard to get grease-free. Similarly, wet mixing bowls or beaters or aluminum bowls may prevent whites from foaming properly.

To separate eggs, see page 31.

Eggs separate most easily when cold, but whites beat to fullest volume when at room temperature (70°F). For this reason, separate eggs as soon as they come from the refrigerator, then let them sit awhile; or set the bowl of egg whites inside another bowl of warm water and stir the whites until they warm up. Frozen egg whites may be used for meringues, but the whites should be defrosted at room temperature. If you are in a hurry, set the container of frozen whites in a bowl of warm, not hot, water to thaw.

What Makes a Meringue?

Egg whites foam because of the peculiar properties of their albumen proteins. Albumen itself is thick and viscous, made up of large molecules that tend to cling together. As air is whipped into liquid whites, the resulting foam depends upon the combined activity of several proteins, which actually bond to each other to form a strong network protecting the cells of air and holding their water in place. Ovomucin and globulins increase the viscosity of the albumen, helping it make a fine foam with many cells. Together with conalbumin, these proteins help stabilize the foam at room temperature and prevent it from draining its liquid.

When meringue is exposed to heat in a warm oven, the molecules of air in the foam cells expand as they are warmed, enlarging the cells; these might actually grow so large they could explode if not for the ability of another protein called ovalbumin to coagulate around and strengthen each cell wall. This prevents the collapse of the wall, even when the meringue is baked and the water in it evaporates. Thus, ovalbumin helps liquid whites turn into solid meringue.

Other ingredients are added to egg whites to improve the quality and stability of the meringue. Acidity (usually in the form of a tiny bit of cream of tartar, vinegar, or lemon juice) lowers the Ph of albumen slightly, stabilizes the meringue, and helps it resist overbeating and leaking of liquid. Add acid to the whites just before you begin to beat them. To

this end, you can also wipe your bowl and beater, before adding whites, with a paper towel dampened with white vinegar (be sure to dry them carefully), or whip the whites in a copper bowl. The copper interacts with the albumen on a molecular level to contribute to the volume and stability of the foam.

Salt is also added to whites just before beating. It is included primarily for taste, though some authorities believe it helps strengthen the albumen proteins.

Sugar is added primarily for flavor; if it is added too early in the whipping process, it can severely hinder the development of the uncooked foam. Generally, a small amount of sugar is added after the whites and acid have been whipped to the fluffy or frothy stage, when they just begin to foam a little. After this, a little more sugar can be whipped in gradually as the whites reach the stiff peak stage. However, if a large amount of sugar is to be added, it is best to fold this in at the very end.

Once the meringue is baking, the sugar helps its stability. The sugar molecules bond with the hydrogen in the water molecules, helping to delay the evaporation of water from the cell walls of the foam until the egg white proteins are set and firmed by the heat.

For meringues, you can use either granulated, superfine, or confectioners' sugar. However, it is important that the sugar granules be completely dissolved in the egg white, or when baked the meringue may "weep" as undissolved sugar granules melt and ooze out. To prevent weeping, use superfine sugar, which has tiny crystals that dissolve quickly; you can make your own superfine sugar by grinding granulated sugar in a food processor fitted with the steel blade. Confectioners' sugar has cornstarch added, and in some preparations the cornstarch may actually help stabilize the meringue. Always sift confectioners' or superfine sugar to avoid any possiblilty of lumps. When a large quantity of sugar is added to a meringue, a small amount of granulated or superfine may be added at the frothy stage as it will dissolve. However, the remaining sugar should be superfine or confectioners' sugar (which dissolves instantly), folded in at the end.

To be sure the sugar is completely melted, pinch some of the meringue between your thumb and forefinger. If it feels grainy, the sugar granules are still whole; if smooth, the sugar is dissolved. Old-timers claim weeping is prevented by sifting a little cornstarch into whites beaten with granulated sugar.

Egg Whites

□ HOW TO WHIP EGG WHITES UNTIL STIFF BUT NOT DRY

To hold its shape, meringue must be properly whipped. For the best results with the least effort, use an electric mixer with the largest balloon beater available and a bowl that fits it most closely. The object is to keep the entire mass of whites in constant movement. The length of the beating time will vary, depending upon your method, from 10 to 30 minutes or more. If you have a strong arm, try using a large balloon whisk and a copper bowl. To avoid fatigue, let your arm from the elbow down do most of the work. Hand-beating will usually result in a slightly greater volume of whites. If you prefer to beat with an electric mixer, and I confess that I do, it is best to stop the mechanical whipping before stiff peaks are reached and finish the job with a hand whisk.

In this way, you control the end result perfectly.

Whip the room temperature (70°F) egg whites with a whisk or electric mixer on low speed at first, increasing gradually to medium speed as the foam builds up. Finally, work up to medium-high as the foam begins to stiffen, look glossy, smooth, and completely amalgamated. This point is reached *just before* the foam is whipped to its maximum volume. The recipe will read: "whip whites until stiff but not dry." This means that when the machine is turned off and the meringue-filled beater or whisk is lifted up in the air, the peak or tuft of meringue on the beater tip will stand straight up without drooping. Ideally, you should now be able to turn the bowl of whipped whites *completely upside down,* and the mass in the bowl should not budge. This is the essential test I use in my baking classes. However, my grandmother's favorite test for whipped whites was to set a whole raw egg, in the shell, on top of the whipped whites. If the egg sinks in no more than ¼ inch, the whites are perfectly beaten. If the egg sinks in farther, the whites are too soft and should be beaten a little longer. If it does not sink in at all, the whites are overbeaten.

If the meringue looks dry, or begins to clump, curdle, or lose its perfectly smooth appearance, the whites have become dry and overbeaten, and the air-cell structure has begun to break down. The mass of whites will slide in the bowl as you turn it over because water has been released from the cell structure of the overbeaten foam. A film of liquid will begin to form in the bottom of the bowl. Occasionally, overbeaten whites will also become grainy.

For every 4 overbeaten whites, you can try whipping in about ¾ of 1 egg white; stir unbeaten white in a bowl, then spoon some into the overwhipped whites and beat again, carefully, for 20 to 30 seconds.

□ HANDY EGG WHITE MEASURE-
MENTS
1 large egg white = 2 generous tablespoons = ⅛ cup
4 large egg whites = 8 tablespoons = ½ cup
4 large whites beaten stiff (with sugar as per recipe) = 4 cups meringue = two 8- or 9-inch meringue cake disks plus a few small meringue cookies. Note: 4 large whites whipped to fullest volume will often yield three 8-inch cake disks.
6 large whites beaten stiff (with sugar as per recipe) = three 8- or 9-inch meringue cake disks plus 6 or 7 small meringue cookies

---

All-Purpose Meringue, Cold and Swiss Methods

■

This is a basic recipe for an all-purpose meringue prepared by two methods: the cold method, when all ingredients are whipped at room temperature, and the Swiss method, when the egg whites and sugar are warmed together before being whipped. The Swiss or warm method is somewhat more stable and long-lived because warming dissolves the sugar completely. Either method can be used for topping cakes, for folding into mousse or Bavarian cream, or for Classic French Buttercream (see Index). Note: Meringue may be flavored, though any flavoring should be added after the meringue is whipped so it does not affect the mounting ability of the egg whites. Suggested flavorings include extracts (vanilla, etc.), grated citrus zest, or sifted unsweetened cocoa (3 tablespoons for 4 egg whites).

□ QUANTITY: 3½ to 4 cups

*4 large egg whites, at room
  temperature*
¼ teaspoon cream of tartar
Pinch of salt
*½ cup superfine sugar (3½ ounces;
  100 g)*
1 teaspoon vanilla extract (optional)

COLD METHOD:

1. Read About Meringue. Place the egg whites in the large bowl of an electric mixer. Test the temperature of the egg whites with your finger; if they are ice cold, put them in a bowl set over another bowl of hot water and stir until the whites no longer feel cold to the touch.

2. Add to the whites the cream of tartar and salt. Beat on low to medium speed until the whites are fluffy. Add the sugar, 2 tablespoons at a time, beating after each addition while increasing mixer speed to medium-high. Beat until the whites look glossy and are nearly stiff but not dry. To be sure the sugar is completely dissolved, rub a little meringue between your fingers; you should not be able to feel the grains of sugar. Finally, fold in the vanilla or other flavoring.

SWISS MERINGUE:

In step 1, combine the egg whites with the sugar and set the bowl over a pan of simmering water. Place a mercury candy thermometer in the bowl. Stir the mixture constantly until the sugar dissolves and the syrup reaches 120°F. Remove from heat at once, add cream of tartar and salt, and whip until stiff but not dry. Finally, fold in the vanilla or other flavoring.

Italian Meringue

■

When a high proportion of sugar will be added to whipped egg whites, it is best done with a cooked sugar syrup. This recipe, called Italian Meringue, produces the most stable type of meringue because the whites are actually cooked by the syrup. This meringue will not break down when baked as cake layers (Dacquoise), added to Bavarian cream or mousse, or used as a topping on Baked Alaska. It can also be whipped with softened butter to make a luxurious, light Italian Meringue Buttercream (page 403). As a general rule, the sugar syrup for Italian meringue is cooked to 238°F to make a meringue of average, all-purpose stiffness. If you prefer a very stiff meringue, the temperature can be higher, up to 248°F. With a reduction in the cooking temperature of the syrup, the same recipe is used for old-fashioned Boiled Icing (see Index). Read About Meringue.

☐ SPECIAL EQUIPMENT: 2-quart heavy-bottomed saucepan, mercury candy thermometer, pastry brush; stand-type electric mixer is helpful but not essential; metal pan of ice water large enough to hold sugar syrup pan

☐ QUANTITY: about 3½ cups

⅓ cup water
¾ cup plus 2 tablespoons granulated
  sugar (6¼ ounces; 175 g)
1 tablespoon white corn syrup, or ⅛
  teaspoon cream of tartar
3 large egg whites
2 tablespoons granulated sugar
1 teaspoon vanilla extract (optional)

1. Put the water in a heavy-bottomed 2-quart saucepan, then add ¾ cup plus 2 tablespoons sugar and the corn syrup or cream of tartar. Stir once or twice. Cook over moderate heat until the sugar is dissolved; swirl the pan several times.

Increase heat to medium-high. Wash down the pan sides with a pastry brush dipped into cold water to remove any sugar crystals; repeat several times. Bring the syrup to a boil, and boil *without stirring* for 7 to 8 minutes, or until the thermometer reads 238°F (soft-ball stage). When the thermometer reads about 228°F and you near the end of the syrup-cooking time, begin to whip the egg whites. Note: It is better to let the cooked syrup wait (standing in ice water) while the whites are being whipped than vice versa.

2. Whip the whites in the large bowl of an electric mixer until fluffy. Gradually add the

2 additional tablespoons of sugar, and increase the mixer speed, whipping until the whites are *nearly* stiff but not dry. Do not overwhip. While whipping, keep a sharp eye on the syrup thermometer.

3. As soon as the syrup reaches 238°F. remove pan from the heat and set it in a pan of ice water near the mixer. The ice water stops the syrup from cooking. Check to see that the whites are stiff and satiny and completely amalgamated.

Turn the mixer on medium-low speed. Wipe ice water from the pan bottom. Slowly pour the hot syrup onto the egg whites in a steady stream directed between the bowl and the beater. Continue whipping until all the syrup has been added. Do not scrape the hardened syrup from the bowl.

The whites will increase in volume as the syrup is whipped in; they will become smooth and quite stiff. Add the vanilla if using it. Turn the mixer down to the lowest speed and whip the meringue until cool to the touch. This can take a while; you can speed the cooling by whipping over a pan of ice water. If making Italian Meringue Buttercream (see page 403), the softened butter is whipped in after the meringue is completely cool.

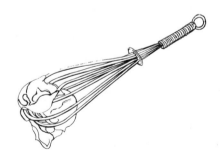

Meringue or Dacquoise Cake Layers

■

This is an all-purpose recipe for meringue cake layers. In the classical French baking repertoire, these crisp-baked disks, or layers, are called *fonds,* or foundations. When ground nuts are folded into the meringue before baking it, the resulting cake is called a Dacquoise. The meringue in the following recipes, with or without nuts, is made by the classic cold method and baked in a slow oven until dried out.

Correctly made meringue layers are light and crisp. They may be filled and frosted with buttercream, Bavarian cream, mousse, flavored whipped cream, or softened ice cream and fresh fruit to make Frozen Meringue Ice Cream Cake, Meringue Cakes, or Dacquoise (see Index for specific recipes).

Note: When meringue layers are filled with whipped cream, they tend to soften on standing. If you want to keep the layers crisp, brush them on both sides with melted chocolate or Apricot Glaze before filling with cream. Read About Meringue.

□ ADVANCE PREPARATION: Meringue cake layers may be made up to a week in advance and stored in an airtight container at room temperature, or they may be frozen. If they soften in humid weather, recrisp them in a 300°F oven for a few minutes, cool them completely, then fill and frost them.

□ SPECIAL EQUIPMENT: 2 or 3 large cookie sheets, large bowl for an electric mixer plus another bowl slightly larger, 8- or 9-inch round template (can be a pot lid or bowl or cake pan), toothpick, pencil, baking parchment (optional); 16-inch-long pastry bag fitted with ½-inch (#6) round tip, sharp paring knife, wire rack, 8- or 9-inch cardboard cake disk, 2-cup measure or large mug (to serve as holder for the pastry bag); wide spatula, rubber spatula, icing spatula

☐ BAKING TIME: 40 to 50 minutes at 300°F (150°C), or until crisp

☐ QUANTITY: Two 8- or 9-inch meringue cake disks about ½ inch thick, plus a few small meringue cookies. Note: If you whip the whites to a great volume, you may occasionally get three 8-inch disks from 4 whites. However, to be sure of making 3 layers, use 6 egg whites; see the variation following.

☐ PAN PREPARATION: Dab a little butter on the pan as an adhesive then add baking parchment cut to fit the pan. Spread softened butter on the baking parchment, then dust it with flour; tap off excess flour. Or generously butter (don't use solid shortening) and flour the baking sheet directly. Use a toothpick or pencil to draw around a template marking two 8- or 9-inch rounds or other shapes on the prepared pans (diagram a, page 252). Set pans aside.

BASIC TWO-LAYER MERINGUE CAKE:

4 large egg whites (½ cup), at room temperature
1¼ cups sifted superfine sugar (8¾ ounces; 250 g)
2 tablespoons sifted cornstarch
¼ teaspoon cream of tartar
Pinch of salt
1 teaspoon vanilla extract

BASIC TWO-LAYER DACQUOISE:

Use above ingredients plus 1 cup (4 ounces; 110 g) toasted and finely ground hazelnuts and almonds, half and half, or all almonds. Do not use walnuts, which contain too much oil. Fold the nuts in at the very end with the sugar and cornstarch.

1. Prepare pans as described. Preheat oven to 300°F (150°C).

Test the temperature of the egg whites with your finger; if they are cold, put them in a bowl set over a larger bowl of hot water and stir until they no longer feel cool to the touch.

2. Put 4 tablespoons of the sugar into a cup and set it aside. Combine remaining sugar with the cornstarch in a sifter and sift them together onto wax paper. If making a Dacquoise, add the ground nuts to this sugar-cornstarch mixture. Set aside.

3. Put the whites in the large bowl of an electric mixer; add the cream of tartar and salt. Beat on low to medium speed until the whites just begin to look fluffy. Gradually add the reserved 4 tablespoons sugar while beating on medium-high speed (KitchenAid #8) until the whites look glossy and are nearly "stiff but not dry." To be sure the sugar is completely dissolved, rub a little meringue between your fingers; you should not be able to feel the grains of sugar.

Sprinkle several tablespoons of the cornstarch-sugar mixture over the whites and fold them in with a flat whisk or rubber spatula; the nuts are included for a Dacquoise. Repeat, lightly folding in the dry ingredients in several additions to maintain volume. Finally, fold in the vanilla and any other flavoring called for in the individual recipe.

4. Prepare the pastry bag by setting it, tip down, in a 4-cup measure. Fold back a 4- or 5-inch cuff, and press in the sides of the bag just above the tip, to plug the opening while the bag is being filled. Spoon in the meringue. Twist the bag closed, and pipe meringue inside the marked shapes on the prepared pans.

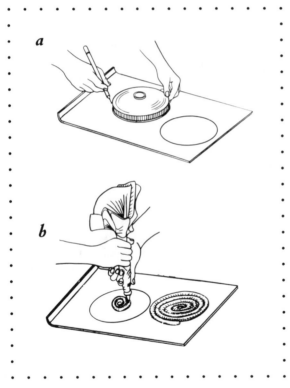

To do this, begin at a point in the center of the marked circle, and gently squeeze out an even column of meringue, holding the bag perpendicular to the pan and slightly above it, so that the meringue falls into place as you guide it in a spiral that completely fills the circle, ending at the drawn ring (diagram b).

Alternatively, you may prefer to begin at the outside of the ring and spiral in toward the center. Or pipe around the outside of the ring, then simply spoon meringue into the center and flatten it very gently with an icing spatula to make a solid disk about ½ inch thick and even on top.

5. Use up any leftover meringue by piping out small cookies or spooning out small nests or cups of meringue.

Bake the meringue in the preheated oven for 40 to 50 minutes, or longer, until the meringue is thoroughly set and a very light beige color. Look in the oven after about 25 minutes; if the meringue is darkening too fast, reduce the heat to 275°F.

Note: If the oven heat is too high, the color of the meringue will darken as the sugar caramelizes; this changes the flavor of the meringue. To achieve a perfectly white meringue, you must bake the layers at 200°F for 90 minutes, or longer, until thoroughly dried out; you can also leave the meringues in the oven, with the heat off, for a couple of hours longer (or overnight) to complete the drying if necessary. Professional bakeries often bake meringue in warming ovens, leaving them for as long as 24 hours.

6. After baking the meringue or Dacquoise cake layers, set the pans on a wire rack for a few minutes. The baked shapes will be slightly pliable while warm. At this stage, use a wide spatula to lift them from the sheet and set them on the wire rack to cool completely. If you have used baking parchment, invert the sheet carefully and peel the paper off the back of the baked shapes.

After cooling the layers on the racks for 15 to 20 minutes, they should be completely crisp; test a small cookie to check texture; it should crack in half. If your shapes are still soft when completely cold, they should be set on baking parchment on a baking sheet and returned to the oven for a little while to dry out further.

7. Once cold and crisp, the layers can be trimmed so that they are all the same size and the complete cake will have a neat appearance. Hold the template against each baked shape and trim the edge with a sharp paring knife; save trimmings to blend with nuts for the final garnish of the frosted cake. Store trimmed meringue or Dacquoise layers in an airtight container with foil or wax paper between the layers, or freeze. Or fill and frost (see the individual meringue or Dacquoise cake recipes).

BASIC THREE-LAYER MERINGUE CAKE MADE WITH 6 WHITES:

Follow the procedure above, but use the following ingredients:

6 large egg whites (¾ cup), at room
temperature
¼ teaspoon cream of tartar
⅛ teaspoon salt
1 cup (7 ounces; 200 g) plus 4
tablespoons sifted superfine sugar
2 tablespoons sifted cornstarch
1 teaspoon vanilla extract

BASIC THREE-LAYER DACQUOISE MADE WITH 6 WHITES:

Use above ingredients and procedure. In step 2, put 6 tablespoons of sugar (instead of 4)

aside in a cup to add to the meringue. Sift remaining sugar with the cornstarch on wax paper. Add 1 cup toasted and ground hazelnuts and/or almonds to the sugar-cornstarch mixture as per the specific recipe. Add ⅛ teaspoon almond extract along with the vanilla.

·*Variation:*·

CHOCOLATE DACQUOISE:

Prepare Basic Three-Layer Dacquoise, but add 2 tablespoons sifted unsweetened cocoa (preferably Dutch-process) to the cornstarch and nut mixture.

Toffee Cream Dacquoise

▪

This cake is too good to be true: 3 crisp meringue-nut layers filled with hazelnut whipped cream and chopped chocolate-coated toffee candy. Frosted with whipped cream and garnished with toasted nuts, it is elegant and rich, but not excessively heavy. It is the perfect choice for a sophisticated birthday party or New Year's Eve celebration, especially when served with Champagne. For Valentine's Day you may wish to make the layers in heart shapes.

This heavenly confection comes to me from my mother, who learned it from her Austrian friend Gusti Wyman. The basic inspiration for the cake, of course, is Viennese, though I have tasted similar confections in Vienna and never found one as good. The secret ingredient, in my estimation, is the quality of the toffee candy; the best results here are achieved with Heath or Skor candy bars, chopped and added to the whipped cream. "Gusti's Meringue Cake," as the original was known, used ½ teaspoon almond extract instead of the nuts in the meringue layers, and omitted the hazelnut liqueur, a variation you may wish to try.

For another variation, substituting raspberries for the toffee, see Raspberry Cream Dacquoise, following the master recipe.

□ ADVANCE PREPARATION: The nuts may be toasted and ground in advance. The meringue layers may be made up to a week in advance and stored in an airtight container, or frozen. In humid weather the meringue layers may soften when stored; if this happens, recrisp them in a 300°F oven for a few minutes, then cool them completely before filling with whipped cream.

The completely filled and frosted cake should be made in the afternoon of the day it is to be served; about 4 hours in advance is fine. This allows the flavors to blend, but the meringue still maintains some crispness. To keep crisp for a longer time, brush melted semisweet chocolate on both sides of each meringue layer.

The completed cake can also be frozen (unwrapped until the cream is set, then wrapped airtight). As the cream never freezes solid, you can serve the cake directly from the freezer, or you can thaw it in the refrigerator for several hours before serving.

□ SPECIAL EQUIPMENT: 2 or 3 flat cookie sheets, 8- or 9-inch round pot or pot lid for a template; 16- to 18-inch-long pastry bag fitted with #6 (½-inch) plain round tip; rubber spatula, sifter, nut chopper or food processor, baking parchment (optional), medium-size bowl; plastic bag and rolling pin (to pound candy), chilled bowl and beater for whipping cream, 8-inch cardboard cake disk covered with foil or flat serving plate. For heart-shaped layers, make an 8-inch cardboard heart-shaped template; cover with foil and use as the supporting cardboard cake disk.

□ BAKING TIME: for meringue layers, 45 minutes at 300°F

□ CHILLING TIME: for filled and frosted cake, 2 to 3 hours minimum, but not longer than 4 hours to keep meringue moderately crisp

□ QUANTITY: one 3-layer, 9-inch cake (serves 10 to 12)

□ PAN PREPARATION: Dab butter on the corners of the cookie sheets, then line the sheets with baking parchment. The paper will cling to the butter. Generously butter the parchment, then dust with flour. Shake the paper over the sink to remove excess flour. Or generously butter (do not use solid shortening or margarine) and flour the cookie sheets directly, tapping out excess flour. Depending upon the size of the cookie sheets, you may fit 2 meringue layers on a sheet. Use the pan or lid as a template. Set it down on the prepared pan and draw around it with a pencil (on parchment) or a toothpick (on a floured pan), leaving a clearly marked circle. Leave a good inch of space, then draw a second circle, if two will fit on one sheet. Draw the third on another sheet. Set aside the prepared and marked pans.

DACQUOISE (MERINGUE-NUT) LAYERS:

1 recipe Basic 3-Layer Dacquoise (page 253), made with 6 egg whites and 1 cup toasted and finely ground hazelnuts or toasted almonds.

FILLING:

1 cup coarsely chopped chocolate-coated toffee candy bars such as Heath or Skor Bars; use best-quality candy (4¾ ounces; 135 g). For 1 cup, use 4 Skor bars (1.4 ounces each) or 4 Heath Bars (1³/₁₆ ounces each)
2 cups chilled heavy cream
5 tablespoons sifted superfine or confectioners' sugar
4 tablespoons hazelnut liqueur, or ¾ teaspoon almond extract
1 teaspoon vanilla extract

GARNISH:

½ cup toasted and ground hazelnuts or toasted sliced almonds (optional)

1. Prepare the meringue layers, bake them, and set them on a wire rack to cool. When cool, use a sharp paring knife to trim the layers to fit the outline of the template. Stack the layers on top of each other (handling them very gently as they are very brittle) to see that they have the same shape and size. Note: Don't panic if a layer cracks; you will put it together with whipped cream and all breaks will be hidden.

2. Break the candy up and place it in a plastic bag. Fasten the top, and use a rolling pin or similar object to pound the candy in the bag until it is coarsely chopped; ⅛- to ¼-inch bits will do fine. Do not make powder.

3. In a chilled bowl with a chilled beater, whip the heavy cream for a few seconds, then begin sprinkling on the sugar as you continue to whip. When the cream is nearly, but not quite, able to form soft peaks, add the liqueur and/or extracts. Continue whipping until almost stiff. Do not overdo it because the folding in of the candy continues to work the cream, and you do not want it to reach the butter stage.

4. Remove about 1¾ cups of the whipped cream to a small bowl and refrigerate it until needed; this will be used to frost the outside of the cake. Fold the chopped toffee into remaining whipped cream to make the cake filling.

5. To assemble the cake, put a dab of whipped cream in the center of a cardboard cake disk or flat plate. If using a plate, protect it from icing with wax paper strips. Set one dacquoise layer on the prepared surface and spread on half of the toffee cream (a generous cup). Cover this with the second dacquoise layer and spread on remaining toffee cream. Top the cream with the third dacquoise layer. Do not press on the top, but check to see that the sides are lined up neatly.

6. Remove the plain whipped cream from the refrigerator, and use it to frost the sides and top of the filled cake.

Finally, if you wish to garnish the cake, pour some toasted and ground or sliced nuts into the palm of your hand and press them very gently onto the lower third of the cake sides, all around (see illustration, page 430).

7. Very carefully, stick 4 or 5 toothpicks into the cake (don't poke hard or you will split the meringue), then top the cake with a sheet of plastic wrap or foil. The picks will keep the wrap away from the cake surface. Refrigerate the cake until ready to serve. Or place it in the freezer until the cream is completely hard. Then remove the plastic wrap and replace it with a layer of heavy duty foil, double-folded to keep out air. Remove the foil as soon as you remove the cake from the freezer, before the cream begins to soften. Defrost the cake in the refrigerator.

Note: In hot weather, always serve this cake directly from the refrigerator, and remember to refrigerate leftovers.

· *Variation:* ·

RASPBERRY CREAM DACQUOISE:

This show-stopping finale for a summer dinner party features raspberries and whipped cream between layers of almond dacquoise. The cake can be frozen well in advance. Because the cream does not freeze hard, it can even be served frozen, though I prefer it freshly assembled and well chilled.

Prepare Toffee Cream Dacquoise, with the following changes:

DACQUOISE:

Make one 3-Layer Dacquoise (page 253) with 6 egg whites and 1 cup ground almonds, and ½ teaspoon almond extract.

FILLING AND ICING:

4 cups fresh raspberries, hulled, quickly rinsed, and drained on paper towels, or 1 box (10 ounces) frozen berries, thawed and drained in a colander
2 cups heavy cream, chilled
3 or 4 tablespoons sifted confectioners' sugar
2 or 3 tablespoons Framboise (raspberry liqueur)

GARNISH:

Fresh raspberries, or candied violets (imported from France and sold in gourmet shops) or Chocolate Curls (page 451) or Chocolate Leaves (page 449); fresh mint leaves in season

1. Prepare the fresh berries, reserving 1 cup fresh whole berries for the garnish and 1 cup for the filling. Mash remaining whole berries with the back of a spoon or in the food processor. Or use drained and thawed frozen berries and omit the berry garnish.

2. Whip the cream to soft peaks, stir in sugar and liqueur to taste, and whip until nearly stiff. Refrigerate 2 cups of this cream for frosting the cake. Stir the crushed raspberries into remaining whipped cream.

3. Assemble the cake as in step 5 above, spreading 1 cup of raspberry cream—dotted with some fresh whole berries if you have them—between the layers. Use 1½ cups of the plain refrigerated whipped cream to frost the outside of the cake. Put remaining whipped cream in a pastry bag fitted with a star tip and pipe shells or rosettes around the

cake top. At this point, the cake can be set unwrapped into the freezer just until the cream is set. Then immediately wrap the cake airtight and return it to the freezer. The berries stay hard once frozen, so I prefer to defrost the cake in the refrigerator for several hours. Just before serving, garnish the cake with fresh berries and mint leaves or candied violets or chocolate curls. Refrigerate leftovers. In hot weather serve the cake directly from the refrigerator.

Chocolate Mousse Dacquoise

·

Toasted almonds and hazelnuts blend with meringue in the 3 crisp layers that form this very special cake. It is filled and frosted with chocolate mousse and garnished with nuts and chocolate curls. If you really want to get fancy, you can cover the entire confection with a solid chocolate skin topped with ruffled chocolate ribbons, making the Chocolate Ruffle Dacquoise, which follows. Note: If you prefer an all-chocolate cake, add cocoa to the dacquoise, making Chocolate Dacquoise layers (page 253).

□ ADVANCE PREPARATION: The nuts may be toasted and ground in advance. The chocolate mousse can be made in advance and chilled for at least 30 minutes to reach spreading consistency. It can also be covered and refrigerated for several hours, or overnight, before being used in the cake. Chocolate curls

can be made a week or so in advance and stored in the refrigerator in an airtight container. The dacquoise cake layers may be made up to a week in advance and kept at room temperature in an airtight container, or frozen. Or you can fill and frost the cake, but omit the chocolate curls, set it in the freezer unwrapped just to set the frosting, then wrap it airtight and freeze. Unwrap while still frozen and thaw in the refrigerator for several hours. Add the chocolate curls shortly before serving. The cake cuts best after 3 or 4 hours in the refrigerator; the layers lose their crispness if left longer. If cake must be assembled more than 3 or 4 hours in advance, keep layers crisp by coating them with melted semisweet chocolate.

□ SPECIAL EQUIPMENT: See recipe for Dacquoise. For the mousse, a double boiler, an electric mixer plus a second bowl and beater for whipping egg whites. For the cake base, it is helpful to have a 9-inch cardboard cake disk. To garnish the cake, a bowl for the chopped nuts and a sifter for the sugar. To cut the cake when serving, use a serrated knife.

□ BAKING TIME: for dacquoise layers, 45 minutes at 300°F (150°C)

□ QUANTITY: one 9-inch 3-layer cake (serves 12)

□ PAN PREPARATION: See recipe for Dacquoise.

DACQUOISE CAKE LAYERS:

1 recipe Three-Layer Dacquoise (page 253) made with 6 egg whites and a half-and-half blend of almonds and hazelnuts.

FILLING AND FROSTING:

1 recipe (6 cups) Chocolate Mousse I (page 375)

GARNISH:

1 cup toasted and ground hazelnuts
* and/or almonds, or toasted sliced*
* almonds*
Chocolate Curls (page 451)
1 tablespoon confectioners' sugar

1. Prepare 3 dacquoise layers. While the layers are baking, prepare the chocolate mousse. Set the mousse in the refrigerator to chill until it reaches spreading consistency.

2. To prepare for assembling the cake, set out a bowl containing toasted sliced or chopped nuts (hazelnuts and/or almonds) to which you should add any crumbs from trimming the baked dacquoise layers. Also set out the previously made chocolate curls.

3. On a 9-inch diameter cake cardboard or a flat plate, put a dab of chocolate mousse, then set down the first dacquoise layer. The dab of mousse keeps this first layer from slipping. Spread about 1¼ cups of mousse on the first layer, top with a second dacquoise round and again add about 1¼ cups of mousse. Top with the last layer. Check the sides of the cake to align the layers neatly.

Frost the sides and top of the cake generously with the chocolate mousse. You will have some mousse left over; this can be sandwiched between the small dacquoise cookies made with the leftover meringue batter, or frozen and served at another time. Or it can be piped through a pastry bag fitted with a star tip, making decorative rosettes around the edge of the cake.

4. To garnish the cake, hold it flat in one hand and with the other gently press the sliced or ground nuts against the lower third of the frosted cake sides (see illustration, page 429). If you plan to freeze the cake, do so at this time (read Advance Preparation).

To complete the cake, cover the top with chocolate curls and sift a fine dusting of confectioners' sugar over them. Refrigerate the cake for 3 or 4 hours for easiest slicing, or until ready to serve. Remember that because the mousse contains uncooked egg whites, leftovers should be refrigerated or frozen.

·*Variation:*·

CHOCOLATE RUFFLE DACQUOISE:

Prepare Chocolate Mousse Dacquoise, but make only half of the Chocolate Mousse I recipe (3 cups) on page 375.

Use about half of the mousse to spread between the cake layers, and the rest to frost the sides and top of the cake with a modest coating. Remember that it will be covered with chocolate. Refrigerate the mousse-covered cake for at least 1 hour while preparing the Plastic Chocolate Coating and Ruffles (page 457). Follow those instructions for covering the cake. Sift on a light dusting of confectioners' sugar just before serving the cake.

Hungarian Coffee Meringue Cake

■

In any French pâtisserie or an Austrian Conditorei, you will find this Gâteau Hongrois Meringué holding court among the most elegant cakes. It is created from 3 meringue layers filled with coffee whipped cream textured with a blend of toasted hazelnuts and almonds. The sides are frosted with coffee cream covered with chopped nuts, and the top is coated with a generous sifting of confectioners' sugar garnished with a few candied coffee beans or whole toasted nuts.

Note: As an alternative, the layers can be filled with Viennese Coffee Custard Pastry Cream (page 378) and frosted with coffee-flavored whipped cream.

□ ADVANCE PREPARATION: The almonds and hazelnuts may be toasted in advance; save a handful of whole nuts for garnishing the cake, then grind the rest. The meringue layers can be made up to a week in advance and stored in an airtight container at room temperature, or frozen. Refrigerate the cake for 3 to 4 hours before serving for ease in slicing. Or freeze the cake, wrapped airtight. Thaw in the refrigerator for several hours before serving. The cake can also be assembled and refrigerated for 24 hours before serving, but the meringue layers will soften.

□ SPECIAL EQUIPMENT: For the Meringue layers, see recipe. For the filling, a nut mill or food processor, a small bowl or cup, and a chilled bowl with a chilled beater; plus a 9-inch cardboard cake disk, icing spatula, sifter, serrated knife.

□ BAKING TIME: for Dacquoise, 40 to 45 minutes at 300°F (150°C)

□ CHILLING TIME: 3 to 4 hours, maximum, in the refrigerator

□ QUANTITY: one 3-layer, 8-inch cake (serves 8 to 10)

□ PAN PREPARATION: See recipe for Meringue Layers.

MERINGUE CAKE LAYERS:

1 recipe Basic Three-Layer Meringue Cake (page 253), made with 6 egg whites

FILLING AND FROSTING:

½ cup whole hazelnuts (2½ ounces; 70 g), toasted and skinned
½ cup whole blanched almonds (2½ ounces; 70 g), toasted
1 tablespoon granulated sugar
1½ cups chilled heavy cream
2 to 3 tablespoons sifted confectioners' sugar
1 teaspoon vanilla extract
1½ teaspoons instant espresso coffee powder dissolved in 1 teaspoon hot water

GARNISH:

⅓ cup confectioners' sugar (1¼ ounces; 35 g)
12 candied coffee beans (optional) or reserved whole toasted nuts

1. Read About Meringue. Toast the nuts (see page 43) and set aside a handful of whole skinned hazelnuts and whole blanched and toasted almonds to garnish the finished cake. Grind the rest of the nuts in a food processor along with 1 tablespoon granulated sugar. Put the nuts in small bowls and set them aside.

2. Prepare three 8-inch meringue layers, bake them, and set them to cool on a wire rack. Use any leftover meringue batter to make smaller shapes or cookies. When the layers are cold and crisp, use a sharp paring knife to trim them to fit the template. Set aside the meringue layer that has the neatest, smoothest top surface to be the top of the cake.

3. With a chilled bowl and chilled beaters, whip the heavy cream until it forms soft peaks. Add 2 to 3 tablespoons sifted confectioners' sugar, the vanilla, and the cooled dissolved coffee mixture. Whip the cream a couple of seconds longer, until stiff peaks form.

4. To assemble the cake, put a dab of whipped cream in the center of the cardboard disk, then set one of the least perfect meringue layers on the disk. The cream keeps the layer from slipping. Now spread about a cup of whipped cream over the meringue layer. Sprinkle on some of the toasted and ground nuts. Top this with the second meringue layer and cover this with 1 cup of whipped cream and some ground nuts. Finally, add the reserved top layer, smoothest and neatest side up. Check the cake sides to be sure they align neatly. Frost the cake sides with remaining 1 cup of coffee-flavored cream.

5. To garnish the cake, hold it flat on the palm of one hand; with your other hand, scoop ground nuts from the bowl and press them very gently against the frosted cake sides, covering them completely. Then set the cake down. Sift a generous ⅛-inch coating of confectioners' sugar over the cake top. Around the edge of the cake set a ring of candied coffee beans or toasted whole skinned hazelnuts and halved, toasted blanched almonds. Refrigerate the cake for 3 to 4 hours for ease in slicing. Note: After refrigerating, you may want to sift on a light touch-up coat of confectioners' sugar if needed. In hot weather, serve the cake directly from the refrigerator and refrigerate or freeze leftovers.

Tortes

ABOUT TORTES

■

Originally, the term *torte,* or *tourte,* referred to breads and sweetened cakes baked in a round form. In the cuisines of Middle and Eastern Europe, particularly in Austria, Hungary, and Germany, tortes, or *Torten,* have developed into a highly specialized art form. They are round cakes, to be sure, but they differ from butter or sponge cakes, for example, because all or part of the flour is replaced by finely ground nuts or other ingredients including poppyseeds, bread, or cake crumbs. Usually lacking chemical leaveners, tortes are lightened by egg foams and whipped egg whites folded into the batter.

Tortes are usually light and spongy, though some can be quite dense, depending upon the ingredients. They should always be somewhat moist rather than dry. Although tortes are flavorful enough to be eaten without icing, or simply dusted with confectioners' sugar, European pastry shops traditionally present them with elaborate ornamentation. Most often, the torte is sliced into 2 or 3 layers and filled with flavored whipped cream or buttercream. The outside of the cake may be coated with a thin skin of marzipan before being frosted with buttercream or glazed with dark glossy chocolate icing. Garnishes range from ground toasted nuts to buttercream rosettes and caramelized sugar cages. Austrian, Hungarian, and German pastry chefs use the torte in the same manner as the French and Italian *pâtissiers* use the génoise or sponge cake—as a base upon which to create artistic culinary fantasies.

Years of restaurant torte-tasting had convinced me that there was an enormous variety of tortes, named for more princes and politicians than one could count. However, closer analysis—a sketch pad and notebook carefully carried on a tasting expedition to Vienna and Munich—revealed that there are really endless variations on a few basic types of tortes.

In the interests of "science," my husband, daughter, and I spent many leisurely October afternoons sampling the legendary tortes of the finest pastry houses, from Vienna's famous Hotel Sacher (see Sachertorte, page 273) to the Sacher's great rival, Demels, Vienna's landmark pastry shop. Demels is an ornate museum of imperial elegance, where for over 200 years the finest cakes and pastries have been baked and served amidst crystal chandeliers, marble floors, muraled walls, and beveled-mirror paneling. Chic blond waitresses in black and white uniforms serve a constant crush of afternoon patrons from marble counters laden with tiered trays of glamorous sweets. Recipes are carefully guarded, and my requests were scornfully denied, but it was worth the considerable price just to taste, to attempt the impossible task of balancing several plates of cake, coffee pots, and cups upon the miniature round marble tabletop while observing the Viennese coffee hour. You have only to see an impeccably soignée matron in black velvet suit and pearls peering intently through her lorgnette at some 100 slices of cake, each wrapped in its own lacy paper, to appreciate the importance of the Selection Process. Cakes are a serious business here.

In Munich, we paid homage to the fabled Kreutzkamm Conditorei. Founded in Dresden in 1825, four generations of the Kreutzkamm family have continually produced exquisite cakes. The *Baumkuchen* or tree cake is one of their most intriguing offerings. This unusual specialty is found in pastry shops throughout the region, but Kreutzkamm's version is reputedly the finest, and we agree. The cake is shaped like a cylinder made from a stack of donuts, with the diameter alternately thick and thin. The cake is sliced crosswise to reveal rings of dough that resemble the growth rings of a real tree. Before modern technology, making the *Baumkuchen* was a slow chore and a fine art. The batter was hand-dripped onto a crank-turned metal arm arranged over hot coals in the fireplace. Today it is rarely made at home; in commercial bakeries, the *Baumkuchen* is baked on a rotating mechanical arm beneath slowly dripping batter. As the heat sets the batter, it forms rings of cake.

In the Palm Court Conditorei behind the Munich's Nymphenburg Palace, we lunched on a nutritious selection of five cakes: blueberry custard cheesecake with a streusel topping; covered apple cake—a heady blend of tart apple slices, raisins and cinnamon enveloped in a sandy-textured crust topped by a lattice of powdered sugar; apple cheesecake —a sugar cookie disk topped by impossibly rich sour-cream cheesecake coated with buttery apple slices and apricot jam; chocolate-cherry torte, about which the less said the better (my notes say "dry, tasteless, boring"), and a divine fresh raspberry torte, in which a biscuit napped with apricot preserves was topped by a syrup-soaked sponge cake followed by a thick layer of whole ruby raspberries embedded in a sweet, clear wine jelly (See Berries in Wine Gâteau in Index).

There are a few points to remember about making tortes. First, be aware that nuts, which are the principle ingredient in many recipes, contain a great deal of oil. This oil is released when the nuts are crushed or improperly ground, and oily nuts clump together; they are not capable of blending properly with whipped egg whites. For light-textured tortes, dry the nuts by toasting them as directed in the recipes. Then grind them with a hand-turned drum-type rotary nut mill (see page 43) to produce a fine, dry, sawdustlike powder. When nuts are ground in the food processor along with a little sugar, they are fairly fine, but never as dry or fine as when ground in a mill; however, the processor is satisfactory for certain recipes, and they are so noted.

It is best to bake tortes in a springform pan with a hinged side and removable bottom. This pan permits minimal handling, and a freshly baked torte is quite fragile. Some cookbooks suggest baking tortes in ungreased pans, but this does not always work, and often the cakes stick. More reliable results are achieved when the pan is paper-lined, greased, and floured.

Many tortes are split into 2 or 3 layers (see page 424) by cutting them horizontally with a serrated knife. If this procedure makes you nervous, you can simply divide the batter among 2 or 3 pans and bake thin layers. If you do this, reduce baking time and watch the cakes carefully.

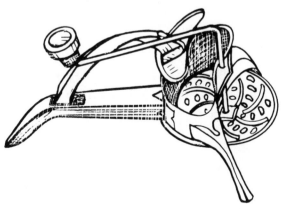

Hazelnut Torte

■

This torte contains a small amount of flour and baking powder, which gives it a slightly drier texture than some of the other tortes in this section. It is particularly well suited to slicing into 3 layers and filling and frosting with flavored whipped cream. Hazelnut Whipped Cream is the traditional choice, but chocolate or coffee cream also blends well with the hazelnut flavor. A touch of cocoa is added to this recipe to enhance the taste without turning it into a chocolate cake. Be sure to toast the nuts to bring out their flavor, and grind them in a rotary-drum-type nut mill so they are dry and powdery.

☐ ADVANCE PREPARATION: The nuts can be toasted and ground in advance. The cake can be baked in advance and frozen. Slice, fill, and frost the cake on the day it is to be served.

☐ SPECIAL EQUIPMENT: jelly-roll pan or roasting pan for toasting nuts, drum-type rotary nut mill; 8½- or 9½-inch springform pan, wax paper or baking parchment, scissors, medium-size bowl, extra mixing bowl and beater for whipping egg whites

☐ BAKING TIME: 25 to 30 minutes at 350°F (175°C)

☐ QUANTITY: 6 cups batter; one 2- or 3-layer 8-inch cake (serves 8 to 10)

☐ PAN PREPARATION: Cut a wax paper or parchment round to fit the baking pan (see page 61). Spread solid shortening on bottom and sides of pan; line pan bottom with the round of wax paper or baking parchment. Grease paper, then dust pan with flour; tap out excess flour.

2 cups hazelnuts that have been
   toasted, and skinned (see page 43)
   and ground to a fine powder in a
   drum-type rotary nut mill (6 ounces;
   160 g)
2/3 cup sifted cake flour (2 1/2 ounces;
   70 g)
1 teaspoon baking powder
1/4 teaspoon salt
1 1/2 tablespoons sifted unsweetened
   cocoa
6 large eggs, separated, at room
   temperature
2/3 cup (4 1/2 ounces; 130 g) plus 2
   tablespoons granulated sugar
2 tablespoons dark rum or hazelnut
   liqueur, optional
1/2 teaspoon ground cinnamon

FILLING AND ICING:

Double recipe (2 cups unwhipped heavy cream) Hazelnut Whipped Cream (page 368)

GARNISH:

1/2 cup toasted and ground hazelnuts, to press onto lower third of frosted cake sides; 8 or 9 whole hazelnuts, to set in a ring around cake top

   Note: For other decorating ideas, see introduction.

1. Prepare pan as described. Position rack in center of oven. Preheat oven to 350°F (175°C) for the cake. Read About Tortes.

After nuts are ground to a fine light powder, put them in a medium-sized bowl and remove any large chunks that fell through the sides of the nut mill. Add the flour, baking powder, salt, and cocoa. Stir lightly to blend; take care not to compact the mixture.

2. In the large bowl of an electric mixer, beat together the egg yolks and sugar until they are thick and light-colored and the mixture forms a flat ribbon falling back on itself when the beater is lifted. This takes 2 or 3 minutes with the KitchenAid mixer on speed #8; with other mixers it can take 6 or 7 minutes. Add the liqueur and cinnamon and beat to blend. Set bowl and beater aside.

3. With a clean bowl and beater, whip the egg whites until stiff but not dry. Stir about 1 cup of whipped whites into the yolk batter to lighten it. Fold in remaining whites in 6 or 7 additions, alternating them with the nut-flour mixture lightly sprinkled on top. Fold with a light touch to maintain batter volume.

4. Turn the batter into the prepared pan and bake in center of preheated oven for about 35 minutes, or until cake is well risen and a cake tester inserted in the center comes out clean.

Cool cake on a wire rack for about 5 minutes. Release the spring and then remove pan sides. Top the cake with another rack or a plate and invert. Lift off the pan bottom; if it sticks, cut around the edge with a knife blade. Peel off the paper. Top the cake with a plate and invert again so it is right side up. Cool completely on a wire rack.

5. On the day the cake will be served, split it into 2 or 3 layers (page 424) with a serrated knife. Set one layer on a cardboard cake disk.

Top with a light sprinkling of hazelnut liqueur if you wish, then add ¾ to 1 cup whipped cream, spread evenly. Top with the middle layer and more cream, then add the cake top, cut side down. Spread cream around the cake sides and top. Lightly press toasted nuts around the lower third of the cake sides and garnish the top with whole nuts set in a ring around the edge. Or fill a pastry bag fitted with a star tip with whipped cream and pipe rosettes around the edge of the cake; top each rosette with a hazelnut. Refrigerate the cake until ready to serve.

Walnut Torte

■

This classic Austrian *Nusstorte* is light, spongy, and moderately moist with a rich nutty flavor achieved by toasting the nuts.

In German and Austrian coffeehouses and pastry shops nut tortes are standard, appearing in myriad guises. Often the nut torte forms the basis for the house specialty. For example, L. Heiner, one of Vienna's exceptional *cafe-conditorei,* serves a delectable *Haustorte* built upon a layer of walnut torte napped by thick apricot preserves; this is topped by chocolate pastry cream blended with whipped cream, alternating with 3 thin layers of dark chocolate sponge. In Munich, the outstanding Kreutzkamm Conditorei features a multilayered *Nuss-Spezial* made of moist, light-textured walnut layers that alternate with a walnut buttercream and a hazelnut buttercream. The torte I sampled was enveloped in a thin skin of marzipan, then topped with an extrasweet coffee glaze dotted with whole hazelnuts. The sides were frosted with mocha buttercream, edged with sliced toasted almonds.

My favorite *Nusstorte* is a specialty of the Cafe Luitpold in Munich. In this house, known for its elegant pastries, an apricot-glazed crisp cookie dough formed the base for 3 light nut layers alternating with almond pastry cream. The top nut layer was spread with vanilla whipped cream and a slice of plain sponge cake. More whipped cream edged with toasted slivered almonds coated the sides, while the top was dusted with confectioners' sugar before being crisscrossed with thin lines of dark chocolate icing studded with candied black cherries. With these inspiring thoughts in mind, try your hand, and be creative in combining imaginative fillings and icings.

Note: For the correct cake texture, the toasted walnuts must be ground in a rotary-type nut mill so they are light, dry, and powdery. Walnuts contain a high proportion of oil; when ground in the food processor, even with granulated sugar, they tend to be too heavy and oily to blend properly with the egg whites in this recipe.

□ ADVANCE PREPARATION: The nuts can be toasted and ground in advance. Cake can be baked ahead and frozen. Slice and fill cake on day of serving, or 1 day ahead. Refrigerate.

□ SPECIAL EQUIPMENT: jelly-roll pan or roasting pan for toasting nuts; drum-type rotary nut mill, medium-size mixing bowl, 9½-

inch springform pan, wax paper or baking parchment, scissors, separate bowl and beater for whipping egg whites, knife with serrated blade

☐ BAKING TIME: 40 to 45 minutes at 350°F (175°C)

☐ QUANTITY: 6 cups batter; one 9-inch 2- or 3-layer cake (serves 8 to 10)

☐ PAN PREPARATION: Cut a wax paper or parchment round to fit baking pan (see page 61). Spread solid shortening on bottom and sides of pan; line bottom of pan with wax paper or baking parchment round. Grease paper, then dust pan with flour or bread crumbs; tap out excess flour or crumbs.

2 cups walnuts that have been toasted (see page 43) and ground in a nut mill to a dry powder (5¼ ounces; 150 g)
⅔ cup untoasted white bread crumbs (1¼ ounces; 35 g)
⅓ cup cornstarch, sifted (1½ ounces; 45 g)
6 large eggs, separated, at room temperature
⅔ cup granulated sugar (4½ ounces; 130 g), sifted
¼ teaspoon salt
Pinch of ground cinnamon
¼ teaspoon almond extract, or ½ teaspoon lemon juice
½ teaspoon vanilla extract

FILLING AND ICING:

Viennese Coffee Custard Buttercream (page 378), or Coffee, Chocolate, or Hazelnut Whipped Cream (pages 368–369); or

½ recipe (3 cups total) Chocolate Mousse Filling (page 375) to fill 3 layers and frost only cake sides. Top cake with Firm Apricot Glaze (page 411) or sifted-on confectioners' sugar.

GARNISH:

½ cup toasted and ground walnuts, or ½ cup halved walnuts to arrange in a ring around the top edge of the cake

1. Prepare pan as described above. Position rack in center of oven. Preheat oven to 350°F (175°C). Read About Tortes.

2. After nuts are ground to a dry, fine, powder, remove any large chunks that may have fallen through the nut mill.

3. In a bowl, combine the ground nuts, bread crumbs, and cornstarch. Set aside.

In the large bowl of an electric mixer, combine egg yolks and all but 3 tablespoons of the sugar. Beat until the mixture is thick and light-colored and forms a flat ribbon falling back upon itself when the beater is lifted. This takes 2 or 3 minutes with a KitchenAid mixer on speed #8; with other mixers it can take 6 or 7 minutes. Add cinnamon and both extracts and beat to blend. Set bowl and beater aside.

4. Using a clean bowl and beater, whip the egg whites until fluffy, add remaining 3 tablespoons sugar and whip until the whites are nearly stiff but not dry.

Stir about 1 cup of the whites into the yolk batter to lighten it. Fold in remaining whites in 4 or 5 additions, alternating with the nut-crumb mixture. Fold with a light touch to maintain volume of batter.

5. Turn batter into the prepared pan and set in the preheated oven to bake for 40 to 45 minutes, or until the cake is well risen, the top feels lightly springy to the touch, and a cake tester inserted in the center comes out clean.

Cool cake in the pan on a wire rack for 15 minutes. Release spring and remove pan sides. Top cake with a rack, invert, and remove pan bottom; if it sticks, use a knife to cut free the edge of the pan. Peel off paper. Top cake with another rack, invert, and cool completely.

Use a serrated knife to cut the cake into 2 or 3 layers (see page 424). Slide a piece of foil or a cardboard disk between the layers to lift them off without breaking them.

Place the bottom layer on a cardboard disk, spread it with about 1 cup filling, top with the middle layer, fill, and add the top layer, cut side down. Spread icing on sides. To garnish, pour some toasted nuts into the palm of your hand and gently press them onto the frosted cake sides. Then frost the top, or leave the top unfrosted and cover it with warm Firm Apricot Glaze.

Almond Torte

∎

This is an old-fashioned, moderately moist, German *Mandeltorte* with a delightfully crunchy nut texture. The almond flavor is heightened by the addition of orange juice and zest. Like most nut tortes, it is excellent served plain, topped only by a sifting of confection-ers' sugar. For a more elegant presentation, it can be sliced into 2 layers and filled and frosted with Light Orange Buttercream, or Orange Whipped Cream, or Viennese Vanilla Custard Buttercream.

Note: The texture of this cake is best if the whole blanched almonds are ground in a nut mill; this produces a fine, dry nut powder that blends well with the batter. However, the nuts, combined with 2 tablespoons sugar, may also be ground in the food processor. If you do this, the nuts will be a little coarser, and you will need to add some cornstarch to the batter to correct the texture of the torte.

☐ ADVANCE PREPARATION: Nuts may be ground in advance. The torte may be baked ahead and frozen. For ease in slicing a single cake into 2 layers, bake the torte a day in advance of slicing. Torte may be wrapped airtight and kept at room temperature for 2 or 3 days. Frosted cake may be prepared a day in advance and kept refrigerated.

☐ SPECIAL EQUIPMENT: wax paper or baking parchment, scissors, drum-type rotary nut mill or food processor; one 9½-inch springform pan or two 9-inch layer pans, clean bowl and beater for whipping egg whites, serrated knife.

☐ BAKING TIME: 50 minutes at 350°F (175°C) for 1 pan; 30 minutes for 2 layers

☐ QUANTITY: 6 cups batter, one 1- or 2-layer 9½-inch cake (serves 8 to 10)

☐ PAN PREPARATION: Cut a wax paper or parchment liner to fit the baking pan (see page 61). Spread bottom and sides of pan with solid shortening. Line pan bottom with wax paper or parchment round. Grease paper. Dust pan with bread crumbs or flour; tap out excess crumbs or flour.

1 cup whole blanched almonds (5 ounces; 140 g)

1 cup granulated sugar, sifted (7 ounces; 200 g)

2 tablespoons cornstarch (optional; see step 2)

½ cup plain dried bread crumbs (2 ounces; 60 g)

6 large eggs, separated, at room temperature

Pinch of salt

Grated zest and juice of 1 orange (about 2 teaspoons grated zest and ⅓ cup juice)

¾ teaspoon ground cinnamon

½ teaspoon almond extract

FILLING AND FROSTING:

Light Orange Buttercream (page 382) or Orange or Almond-flavored Whipped Cream (page 368) or Viennese Custard Buttercream (page 377) flavored with 2 teaspoons grated orange zest or ½ teaspoon almond extract

GARNISH:

½ cup toasted sliced almonds (1¾ ounces; 50 g)

1. Prepare pan(s) as directed. Note that you can either use 1 pan and slice the torte into layers after baking, or divide the batter between two layer pans. Position rack in center of oven. Preheat oven to 350°F (175°C). Read About Tortes.

2. Grind the almonds with a drum-type rotary nut mill (page 43), or combine nuts with 2 tablespoons taken from the measured granulated sugar and grind them in the food processor.

Note that if using the processor, you must add 2 tablespoons cornstarch to the ground nuts to compensate for the fact that they are not as dry when ground this way.

Put nuts in a bowl, add the cornstarch, if necessary, and the bread crumbs. Set aside.

3. In the large bowl of an electric mixer, combine egg yolks and sugar and beat until the mixture is thick and light-colored and forms a flat ribbon falling back upon itself when the beater is lifted. This takes 2 to 3 minutes with a KitchenAid mixer on speed #8, or 6 to 7 minutes with other mixers. Add salt, grated orange zest and juice, the cinnamon, and almond extract. Stir to blend, then whip for 1 full minute.

4. With a clean bowl and beater, whip the egg whites until stiff but not dry. Stir a little of the whipped whites into the yolk batter to lighten it, then fold in remaining whites in 6 or 7 additions.

Finally, sprinkle about ¼ cup of the nut-crumb mixture over the whipped batter. Fold it in. Repeat, adding and folding in the nuts and crumbs, ¼ cup at a time, until all are incorporated. Use a light touch to maintain volume of batter.

5. Turn the batter into the prepared pan(s) and bake in the preheated oven for about 50 minutes for 1 cake, 30 minutes for 2 layers, or until the cake is nicely risen and feels lightly springy to the touch, and a tester inserted in the center comes out clean. Cool the torte in its pan on a wire rack for 15 minutes, then release the spring and remove pan sides, if using a springform pan. Top torte with a plate or another rack, invert, and lift off pan bottom. Peel off paper. Top with another plate and invert. Cool completely.

Once the cake is completely cold (or better yet, the next day), you can slice it into 2 layers with a serrated knife. Set the bottom layer on a cardboard cake disk, add filling, then top with the second layer and frost sides and top. For a garnish, press toasted sliced almonds onto the cake sides.

··

Italian Almond-Chocolate Torte

■

This is my re-creation of *torta di mandorle e cioccolata,* a wonderfully light chocolate-flecked torte I was served last fall in a little trattoria on a side canal in Venice. Perhaps it was the atmosphere—crumbling terracotta and ochre walls, potted red geraniums, and a nearby window of gilded and feathered carnival masks—or the equally colorful display of Venetian pastries presented on a flower-strewn marble tray, but I have been partial to this torte ever since.

Each layer of this cake can be served alone, topped modestly with a light dusting of confectioners' sugar, or the layers can be filled and frosted with sweetened almond or chocolate whipped cream and the cake garnished with chocolate curls or a wreath of chocolate leaves.

□ ADVANCE PREPARATION: The cake may be baked in advance, wrapped airtight, and stored at room temperature for 2 or 3 days. It can also be frozen. Fill and frost with cream at least 3 hours before serving, or the night before; store cake in the refrigerator.

□ SPECIAL EQUIPMENT: two 9-inch cake pans 1½ inches deep, wax paper or baking parchment, box grater, extra bowl and beater for whipping egg whites, food processor or drum-type rotary nut mill, chilled bowl and beater for whipping cream for icing, sifter

□ BAKING TIME: 25 minutes at 350°F (175°C)

□ QUANTITY: 8 cups batter; one 2-layer 9-inch cake (serves 8 to 10)

□ PAN PREPARATION: Cut wax paper or parchment rounds to fit the baking pans. Spread solid shortening on bottom and sides of pans. Line the bottom of each pan with a wax paper or parchment round. Grease paper, dust pans with flour; tap out excess flour.

⅔ *cup blanched, toasted (page 43), and finely ground almonds (see step 1 on next page; 2¾ ounces; 80 g) made from ½ cup whole almonds*
1 *cup granulated sugar (7 ounces; 200 g)*
½ *cup vanilla wafer crumbs (1¾ ounces; 50 g)*
1 *teaspoon baking powder*
¼ *teaspoon salt*
2 *ounces semisweet chocolate, grated (⅔ cup; 60 g)*
1 *ounce unsweetened chocolate, grated (⅓ cup; 30 g)*
6 *large eggs, separated, at room temperature*
¼ *teaspoon almond extract*
Pinch of cream of tartar

WHIPPED CREAM FILLING AND FROSTING:

1½ cups chilled heavy cream
2 tablespoons sifted confectioners' sugar
1 teaspoon vanilla extract (or see Chocolate or Almond Whipped Cream, page 369)

GARNISH (OPTIONAL):

½ cup toasted sliced or ground almonds (1¾ ounces; 50 g)
Chocolate Curls or 8 Chocolate Leaves (page 449)

1. Prepare pans as described. Position rack in center of oven. Preheat oven to 350°F (175°C). Read About Tortes.

Grind the toasted almonds in a drum-type rotary nut mill (page 43) or in the food processor, combined with 2 tablespoons taken from the measured sugar. Nuts should be reduced to a fine, dry powder. Put nuts in a medium-sized bowl.

2. Add to the nuts the vanilla wafer crumbs, baking powder, salt, and all the grated chocolate. Toss the ingredients lightly to blend them together.

3. In the large bowl of the electric mixer, beat the yolks with ¾ cup granulated sugar until the mixture is thick and light-colored and forms a flat ribbon falling back upon itself when the beater is lifted. This takes 2 to 3 minutes with the KitchenAid on speed #8, or 6 to 7 minutes with other mixers. Beat in almond extract.

4. In another mixing bowl with a clean beater, whip egg whites and cream of tartar until fluffy. Gradually add remaining granu-

lated sugar, beating until whites are satiny and stiff but not dry.

Fold the yolk mixture into the whites in 4 or 5 additions. Then sprinkle about ¼ cup of the nut-crumb mixture over the whipped batter and fold it in very gently. Repeat, adding the remaining nut-crumb mixture in 6 or 7 additions, ¼ cup at a time. Fold the dry ingredients in gently to maintain volume.

5. Divide the batter evenly between the prepared pans and bake in the preheated oven for about 25 minutes, or until a cake tester inserted in the center comes out clean. Cool cakes in their pans on a wire rack for about 10 minutes. Top each layer with a rack or plate, lift off pan, and peel off paper. Cool completely.

6. Prepare whipped cream filling, beating cream with sugar and vanilla until soft peaks form. Spread about 1 cup filling between the layers, and spread the rest on the sides and top. Garnish the cake with ground toasted almonds pressed gently onto the cream-covered cake sides, and add chocolate leaves or curls around the top. Refrigerate cake until ready to serve.

Note: Each layer may also be split horizontally in half and filled to make a 4-layer torte.

Passover Nut Torte

■

This easy-to-make torte is suitable for Passover because it is made with matzoh meal rather than cracker or dried bread crumbs, which may, however, be substituted. The recipe was shared with me by Anne Maidman, a family friend and an excellent cook. Note that this is a small, single-layer cake.

☐ ADVANCE PREPARATION: The walnuts can be toasted and ground in advance. The torte can be baked ahead and frozen.

☐ SPECIAL EQUIPMENT: jelly-roll pan or roasting pan for toasting nuts, drum-type rotary nut mill; 2 medium-size bowls, 8- or 9-inch-square baking pan, wax paper or baking parchment, scissors, extra bowl and beater for whipping egg whites

☐ BAKING TIME: 35 to 45 minutes at 350°F (175°C)

☐ QUANTITY: 5 cups batter; one single-layer 8- or 9-inch cake (serves 16)

☐ PAN PREPARATION: Cut a piece of wax paper or parchment to fit baking pan. Spread solid shortening or margarine on bottom and sides of pan. Line pan bottom with wax paper or parchment piece. Grease paper, then dust pan with matzoh meal. Tap out excess meal.

¾ cup walnuts that have been toasted (see page 43) then ground in drum-type rotary nut mill (2 ounces; 60 g)

¾ cup matzoh meal, sifted (3¼ ounces; 90 g)

4 large eggs, separated, at room temperature
½ teaspoon salt
½ cup granulated sugar (3½ ounces; 100 g)
¼ cup honey
¼ cup orange juice, preferably freshly squeezed
¼ teaspoon ground cinnamon

TOPPING:

1 tablespoon confectioners' sugar

1. Prepare pan as described. Position rack in center of oven. Preheat oven to 350°F (175°C).

After grinding nuts to a fine, dry powder, place them in a bowl and add the matzoh meal. Set aside.

2. Place egg whites in the large bowl of an electric mixer and add the salt. Whip whites until fluffy, then gradually add 2 tablespoons of the sugar while whipping until whites are stiff but not dry (see page 247). Scrape excess whites off beaters and return unwashed beaters to mixer.

3. Using the same beater but a clean bowl, beat the yolks, then add all remaining granulated sugar and beat until the mixture is thick, light-colored, and forms a ribbon falling back on itself when the beater is lifted. Add honey, orange juice, and cinnamon. Beat to blend.

4. Stir about 1 cup of whipped whites into the yolk batter to lighten it. Fold in remaining whipped whites in 6 or 7 additions, alternating with the nut-matzoh meal mixture lightly sprinkled on top.

5. Turn the batter into the prepared pan and bake in the preheated oven for 25 to 30 minutes, or until a cake tester inserted in the center

comes out clean. Cool cake in its pan on a wire rack for about 10 minutes. Insert a knife blade between cake and pan sides to loosen crumbs. Top cake with a rack or plate and invert. Lift off pan and peel off paper. Top with another rack and invert. Cool completely on a wire rack.

Sift 1 tablespoon confectioners' sugar over the cake top and cut cake into 2-inch squares to serve.

Poppyseed Torte

•

This classic *Mohntorte* is one of my favorites. Made with ground poppyseeds, it is easy to prepare and stays moist and fresh for at least a week, even without icing or refrigeration.

The recipe is reminiscent of one I tasted in Munich's famous Kreutzkamm Conditorei, a national institution well worth a detour when you are in Munich. My notes from one delicious visit indicate that my eighth! selection was the *Mohntorte,* and it was the favorite of the day. Moist in texture, it was studded with golden raisins and finely chopped citron, topped with a thin skin of marzipan, and glazed with bittersweet chocolate crosshatched with mocha icing.

Mohntorte is excellent unadorned, with only a light dusting of confectioners' sugar on top. If you prefer an icing, choose Cream-Cheese Icing, or let Kreutzkamm be your guide, and go for the Marzipan and Chocolate Glaze (see Index).

☐ ADVANCE PREPARATION. Poppyseeds can be ground in advance, or purchased already ground from a specialty store (see Suppliers, in Index). The cake may be baked in advance and frozen. Well wrapped or in a cake box, it will stay fresh at room temperature for at least a week.

☐ SPECIAL EQUIPMENT: 8½-inch springform or plain round cake pan, wax paper or baking parchment, scissors, blender or electric herb mincer to grind poppyseeds

☐ BAKING TIME: 45 to 50 minutes at 300°F (150°C)

☐ QUANTITY: 3 cups batter; one single-layer 8-inch cake (serves 8)

☐ PAN PREPARATION: Cut a wax paper or parchment round to fit the baking pan. Spread bottom and sides of pan with solid shortening. Line bottom of pan with the wax paper or parchment round. Grease paper, then dust pan with flour; tap out excess flour.

1 cup whole poppyseeds (5 ounces; 140 g, see step 1)

5 tablespoons unsalted butter (2½ ounces; 75 grams), at room temperature

¾ cup granulated sugar, (5¼ ounces; 150 g)

4 large eggs, separated

2 tablespoons golden raisins, coarsely chopped, and/or 2 tablespoons candied citron, chopped (optional)

2 teaspoons grated lemon zest

ICING:

2 tablespoons confectioners' sugar, to sift over cake top, or Cream-Cheese Icing (page 393)

1. Prepare pan as described. Position rack in center of oven. Preheat oven to 300°F (150°C). Read About Tortes.

To grind poppyseeds, put them in an herb mincer (see page 43) until finely ground, or grind ½ cup at a time in a regular blender on high speed for 1 full minute. Stir down the seeds in the blender once or twice. Grind them until no whole seeds remain. Set ground seeds aside.

2. If it is available, attach the flat paddle to the mixer instead of the whip-type beater.

In the large bowl of the electric mixer, cream the butter until soft, then beat in the sugar. Beat until well blended. Add egg yolks, one at a time, beating after each addition. With mixer on low speed, blend in the poppyseeds, raisins, and lemon zest.

3. With a clean bowl and regular whipping beater, whip the egg whites until stiff but not dry. Stir about ½ cup whites into the poppyseed batter to lighten it. In 4 or 5 additions, gently fold remaining whites into the batter.

4. Turn the batter into the prepared pan and lightly smooth the top. Bake the torte in the preheated oven for 45 to 50 minutes, or until a cake tester inserted in the center comes out clean. Cool in its pan on a wire rack for 10 minutes. If using a springform pan, unfasten spring and remove sides. Top torte with a rack or plate, invert, and remove pan. If bottom sticks, cut around the edge with the tip of a knife to loosen cake. Remove pan bottom and

peel off paper. Top torte with another plate or rack and invert. The torte should be right side up; cool it completely on a wire rack. Sift on confectioners' sugar or ice with Cream-Cheese Icing.

Note: If you wish, you can also split the torte into 2 layers with a serrated knife (see page 424), and spread apricot jam between the layers.

Sachertorte

■

The world-famous Sachertorte is much more than a chocolate cake. It is an element of cultural history, a social and political institution, a fascinating story. In fact, it is probably more interesting to read about than to eat. Even the Viennese admit that their intensely chocolaty torte is also slightly dense, just a little dry, and definitely enhanced by a generous dollop of *Schlagobers,* or whipped cream.

The story begins in 1832, when Prince von Metternich, Austria's leading statesman, ordered his pastry chef to prepare a special dessert for a gala dinner. As the chief pastry chef was ill, the task fell to his sixteen-year-old apprentice, Franz Sacher. And the rest, as they say, is culinary history. Chocolate tortes were known before this time, but Sacher produced his own variation, and gave it his own name. It became an instant success, much in demand.

Sacher baked it for the great of his time, while guarding the recipe like a state secret. Finally, he left service, opened his own delicatessen in Vienna, and continued to bake the Sachertorte for his clientele.

Eduard Sacher, Franz's middle son, followed in his father's business. He married a woman named Anna, later a central figure in the story, and in 1876 they opened the Hotel Sacher. Anna became an important socialite and hostess, building the Sacher into a focal point and gathering place for visiting European nobility, aristocrats, and royalty of the Austro-Hungarian Empire. Artists as well as kings enjoyed the splendors of the Sacher, not the least of which was the Sachertorte. Many clients begged the cigar-smoking, elegantly dressed Anna for the recipe, and she often complied. It has been suggested that perhaps she secretly left out an ingredient as a way of safeguarding the cake. Whether or not this is true, many establishments claim to serve Frau Anna Sacher's original recipe. However, no two Sachertortes are the same, and all chefs add their own touches to improve the formula.

The Hotel Sacher flourished for forty years before World War I ended the monarchy and its way of life. The Hotel then went into severe decline, and Anna died in 1930. During this period of economic distress, Anna's son, Eduard, raised cash by selling the Sachertorte recipe to Demel's, Vienna's most celebrated pastry shop. Demel's then claimed it had the original recipe and the only right to call it so. During the next twenty years the Hotel Sacher fell into disrepair, while the torte lived on at Demel's.

In 1951 the Hotel Sacher was rebuilt and refurbished, and the Sachertorte reappeared on the menu. The success of both began to grow once again. In the 1960s, the torte's popularity precipitated what has been called Vienna's Seven Years' War, between the Hotel Sacher and Demel's. Each claimed the right to make and sell "the original Sachertorte." It took a decision from the highest court in Austria to decide in favor of the Sacher, which today is legally permitted to put a round chocolate label marked "original Sacher Torte" on each cake. Light in texture, neither dry nor moist, with a moderately intense chocolate flavor, the torte made at the Sacher is sliced into 2 layers, filled and coated generously with tart apricot jam, and iced with chocolate fudge glaze. Each serving is accompanied by a generous cascade of unsweetened *Schlagobers*. At Demel's, you will be asked whether you wish to have *Schlagobers* alongside your Sachertorte—a fine distinction, but in this city of serious tortes, these things matter. Demel's 2-layer, apricot-jam-glazed and chocolate-iced cake is slightly drier than that of the Sacher, with a medium-strong chocolate flavor; each slice is topped with a chocolate triangle marked "Eduard Sacher Torte."

My own adventure with Sachertorte began last year when, in preparation for a torte-eating visit to Vienna, I tried to arrange in advance a visit to the pastry kitchen of the Hotel Sacher. In spite of making many contacts both here and in Vienna, however, I received no reply at all from the hotel. Even without a kitchen visit, I intended to dine at the Sacher. One bright October afternoon I found myself in the dining room admiring claret-red walls, gold and crystal chandeliers, and overflowing bouquets of voluptuous pink roses while my husband and I waited for our lunch: a Sacher house specialty of boiled beef and applesauce-horseradish sauce. On a whim, I excused myself after ordering and walked into the main parlor outside the dining room. By chance, the manager was there. I explained that, as a food writer and cookbook author, I would be interested in visiting the pastry kitchen. "Impossible," he exclaimed. "We never allow it. One can only make such arrangements months in advance. What a pity. For example," he continued, "I have a request on my desk concerning an American writer named Susan Purdy. I am hoping to hear from her if she ever comes to Vienna." And the rest, as they say . . .

Camera and notebook in hand, I returned at seven the next morning to meet head pastry chef Friedrich Pflieger and his starched-white, chocolate-smudged crew already hard at work on the day's production of *Sachertorten*. It was an impressive operation, as the previously baked, sliced, and glazed cakes were brought out on enormous trays and set in rows before the master. A blond, teen-aged boy hauled over a tub of warm chocolate glaze. With an icing spatula and a few deft strokes, the chef added the finishing touch: he poured chocolate on the cake, smoothed it across, let it drip down the sides, then evened the sides in a quick swipe. Not one excess motion. Without taking his eyes off his production line, the chef explained that for one day's average production of *Sachertorten* alone, the pastry kitchen used some 200 kilograms of bitter chocolate, 3,000 eggs, and 75 kilograms of butter. Daily production varies with the season, from 300 *Sachertorten* (in four sizes plus miniatures), to 2,000 at Christmas. The cake is sold in the

restaurant, of course, but also in the coffee shop and in the special store, where the cakes are mail-ordered around the world. Over 150 cakes a day are mailed in their neat wooden boxes, and at Christmas, the figure soars to between 800 and 1,000 per day. At Demel's, which does a rival business in mail-order *Sachertorten,* the figures are nearly the same. Not bad coverage for the clever invention of a sixteen-year-old boy.

☐ ADVANCE PREPARATION: The cake may be baked in advance, cooled completely, and wrapped airtight. Store it at room temperature for a day or two, or freeze. Thaw completely before slicing into 2 layers, glazing, and icing. Or, if you prefer, the cake may be cut into layers, glazed, and iced with chocolate glaze before wrapping airtight and freezing. For best results, thaw in the wrapping in the refrigerator overnight. Serve at room temperature.

☐ SPECIAL EQUIPMENT: one 8½-inch springform pan or round 8- or 9-inch pan 2 inches deep; double boiler, wax paper or baking parchment, scissors, knife with serrated blade, small saucepan and pastry brush for glaze, paper cone or plastic baggy (optional)

☐ BAKING TIME: 40 minutes at 350°F (175°C)

☐ QUANTITY: 4 cups batter, one 2-layer 8- or 9-inch cake (serves 10 to 12)

☐ PAN PREPARATION: Cut a wax paper or baking parchment round to fit the baking pan (see page 61). Spread solid shortening on bottom and sides of pan, place paper round in pan, spread shortening on paper. Dust inside of pan with flour; tap out excess flour.

3 ounces semisweet chocolate (85 g)

3 ounces unsweetened chocolate (85 g)

¾ cup unsalted butter (6 ounces, 170 g), at room temperature, cut up

¾ cup (2⅔ ounces; 75 g) plus 2 tablespoons sifted confectioners' sugar

6 large eggs, separated, plus 1 extra egg white

¼ teaspoon salt

¾ cup sifted all-purpose flour (3¼ ounces; 90 g)

¼ cup blanched almonds that have been ground to a fine powder in a drum-type nut mill (1 ounce; 30 g)

GLAZE:

1½ cups Apricot Glaze (page 411), warmed before spreading

ICING:

Chocolate Water Glaze (page 410) or Fabulous Chocolate Glaze (page 409). Also, 1 ounce semisweet chocolate, for writing the word "Sacher" on cake top

GARNISH:

1½ cups heavy cream whipped with 2 or 3 tablespoons confectioners' sugar, to serve alongside cake

1. Prepare pan as described. Position rack in center of oven. Preheat oven to 350°F (175°C). Read About Tortes.

Melt chocolate in top pan of a double boiler set over, not in, simmering water. Stir to melt chocolate completely, remove from heat, and set aside to cool until comfortable to the touch.

2. In the large bowl of an electric mixer fitted with a paddle if possible, beat the butter until soft, then add half of the sugar and cream together until well blended and smooth. Add the egg yolks, one at a time, beating well after each addition. With the mixer on low speed, beat in the melted and cooled chocolate. Scrape down inside of bowl and beaters. Beat on medium-high speed for about 30 seconds.

3. In a clean bowl with a whisk beater, combine egg whites and salt. Beat until fluffy. Gradually add remaining sugar and beat until the whites are nearly stiff but not dry.

4. Whisk about 1 cup of the egg whites into the chocolate batter to lighten it. In 1-cup additions, fold about one third of the whites into the chocolate. Fold in about half of the flour, a few tablespoons at a time. Fold in a little more of the whites, then remaining flour and the almonds, a little at a time, and finally remaining whites. The batter will be fairly stiff.

5. Gently spoon batter into the prepared pan. Place pan in center of preheated oven and bake for about 40 minutes, or until a cake tester inserted in the center comes out clean and the cake just starts to pull away from the pan sides.

Set the cake on a wire rack and allow to cool in its pan for about 5 minutes. Top cake with a wire rack, invert, lift off pan and peel off paper. Cool cake completely on wire rack.

At this point, the cake can be wrapped airtight and refrigerated or frozen.

6. On the morning of the day it is to be

served, or one day in advance, slice the cake into 2 layers with a serrated knife (see page 424). Slide a cardboard disk or piece of wax paper between the layers and lift off the one on top. Set it aside.

7. Prepare the apricot glaze. While the glaze warms, set the bottom layer of the cake, cut side up, on a cardboard disk or a piece of foil. Set the cake on a wire rack set over a jelly-roll pan or piece of foil to catch the excess glaze.

When the glaze is warm, spread it over the cake. Place the second layer, cut side down, over the glaze. Pour warm glaze over the cake top. With an icing spatula or knife, spread glaze over cake top and down the sides. Smooth around the sides, letting excess drip down onto the rack. Leave the cake until the glaze sets and feels tacky. Refrigerate to speed this process if you are in a hurry.

8. Prepare the icing while the glaze sets. When ready to ice the cake, be sure the icing glaze is thin enough to pour. Pour icing glaze over cake top and spread it in a fairly thin layer, without going deep enough to pick up apricot glaze, working it down onto the cake sides. Finally, go around the sides, making a smooth surface. Wait until the glaze sets, about 30 minutes (or refrigerate to speed setting), then, if you wish, apply a second coat of icing glaze, for a perfectly smooth finish. Note: Fingerprints will show on chocolate icing glaze, so lift the cake from underneath with a broad spatula.

9. In restaurants, Sachertorte has the word "Sacher" written in script across the top. To do this, prepare a small paper cone (see page 432) or a small plastic baggy. Melt about 1 ounce semisweet chocolate, pour some into the cone or baggy, cut a tiny hole in the tip, and test the flow on the counter. You should have a thin, neatly flowing line. Hold the cone above the cake and write the word "Sacher" with a flourish.

Mocha Torte

∎

Textured with ground almonds and flavored with a harmonious blend of coffee and chocolate, these 3 moist layers are filled with a satiny Mocha Ganache, then frosted with a high-gloss chocolate glaze. For a dazzling dinner party presentation, press toasted almond slices around the cake sides and garnish the top with a ring of alternating dark and white chocolate leaves.

□ ADVANCE PREPARATION: Cake layers may be made ahead and frozen. Or layers can be filled (but not frosted) with ganache, wrapped airtight, and frozen. Defrost filled cake before adding outside glaze. Almonds can be toasted and refrigerated in advance. Chocolate leaves can be made in advance and refrigerated or frozen for a week or two.

□ SPECIAL EQUIPMENT: Wax paper or baking parchment, scissors, three 9-inch round pans, 1½ inches deep, food processor or drum-type rotary nut mill, small bowl; 2 medium-size bowls, 2 large mixing bowls, double boiler, wooden spoon, extra bowl and beater for whipping egg whites, pastry brush. For ganache: hand held electric mixer and large bowl of ice water mixed with ice cubes

□ BAKING TIME: 25 minutes at 350°F (175°C)

□ QUANTITY: 6 cups batter; one 3-layer 9-inch cake (serves 10 to 12)

□ PAN PREPARATION: Cut 3 wax paper or parchment rounds to fit the baking pans. Spread solid shortening on bottom and sides of pans, fit paper liners in each pan, then grease papers. Dust pans with unsweetened cocoa or flour; tap out excess.

12 ounces whole blanched almonds (340 g)
8 large eggs, at room temperature
8 ounces best-quality bittersweet chocolate, Tobler or Poulain Bittersweet Chocolate for Cooks, for example (230 g)
⅔ cup unsalted butter (10⅔ tablespoons; 170 g), at room temperature, cut into small pieces
⅔ cup granulated sugar (4½ ounces; 130 g)
4 tablespoons unsifted all-purpose flour
2 teaspoons instant espresso powder dissolved in 2 teaspoons boiling water
½ teaspoon ground nutmeg
3 tablespoons coffee liqueur (such as Kahlúa)

CAKE MOISTENING LIQUID:

3 tablespoons coffee liqueur

FILLING:

Ganache Chocolate Filling, mocha flavored (page 407)

ICING:

Fabulous Chocolate Glaze (page 409) or Chocolate Water Glaze (page 410)

GARNISH:

1 cup sliced almonds, toasted (3½ ounces, 100 g)
Chocolate and White Chocolate Leaves (page 449)

1. Prepare pans as described. Position racks in center and lower third of oven. Preheat oven to 350°F (175°C). Read About Tortes.

2. Grind almonds in rotary-type nut mill (page 43) or combine almonds and sugar and pulse them together in a food processor until nuts are finely ground. Set nuts and sugar aside.

Separate eggs, putting yolks in a small bowl and whites in the large bowl of an electric mixer.

3. In the top pan of a double boiler set over, not in, hot water, warm chocolate until nearly all melted. Remove pan from heat and stir to complete melting. Stir butter pieces into the warm chocolate, stirring continually until butter is melted.

4. When melted butter-chocolate mixture is smooth, turn it into a large mixing bowl. Immediately stir in the almonds and sugar, the flour, dissolved coffee, egg yolks, nutmeg, and coffee liqueur. Blend very well, beating vigorously with a wooden spoon.

5. In the large bowl of the electric mixer, beat the egg whites until nearly stiff but not dry. Stir about 1 cup of the whipped whites into the chocolate batter to lighten it, then,

½ cup at a time, fold remaining whites into the chocolate batter.

6. Divide the batter evenly among the prepared pans and set them in the oven in a staggered pattern, two on one shelf, one on the other shelf, with space between them for the heat to circulate well. Bake layers for about 25 minutes, or until lightly springy to the touch and a cake tester inserted in the center comes out clean. Cool the layers in their pans for 10 minutes. One at a time, top each one with another rack, or a plate, and invert. Lift off the pan, and peel off the paper. Leave layers upside down on a rack. While still warm, brush 1 tablespoon of coffee liqueur over each layer. While the layers cool completely, prepare mocha-flavored Ganache Chocolate Filling. Whip ganache to spreading consistency.

7. To assemble the torte, set one layer, liqueur-soaked side up, on a cardboard disk or a plate protected by wax paper strips (see page 425).

Spread on a coating of ganache filling about ⅛ inch thick, then top with a second torte layer, liqueur-soaked side up. Add more filling, then top with the third layer, liqueur-soaked side down. Press on the top cake layer gently to compress cake slightly. At this point, before adding the icing, the cake can be wrapped airtight and frozen. Or complete by spreading warm Fabulous Mocha Glaze or Chocolate Water Glaze over the top and sides. Allow a first thin layer of glaze to set for about 30 minutes, then pour on another coat to make the top perfectly smooth. If the glaze has cooled too much to spread easily between coats, set it over warm water to soften before pouring on the second coat. Work the glaze as little as possible for the glossiest finish.

8. Before the glaze sets hard, pick up the torte in one hand, balancing it on your palm, and with the other hand, press toasted sliced almonds all around the bottom edge of the sides (see page 430 for illustration). Note: Beware of fingerprints on the hard glossy glaze. If you wish, alternate dark and white chocolate leaves in a ring around the top of the cake. You can "glue" the leaves in place with dabs of melted chocolate if the glaze has already hardened. Or instead, add a chocolate rose (page 455) to the center of the cake, surrounded by 3 chocolate leaves.

Dobostorte

∎

One of the most glamorous stars of the pastry chef's repertoire, the Dobostorte is a tall stack of thin sponge-cake layers filled with a silken chocolate buttercream and topped with a crisp caramel glaze. But it is much more than just an elegant dessert. The popularity of this torte has come to symbolize the glamour of the nineteenth-century Austro-Hungarian Empire.

The Dobostorte was created in 1887 by József C. Dobos, the chef/owner of Budapest's famed Dobos Pâtisserie. The torte became an overnight success in Hungary, bringing praise and orders from celebrities and royalty as far away as Vienna. The fame of the Dobostorte continued to grow throughout the years, and today it is an international culinary classic. According to George Lang, in his book

The Cuisine of Hungary (Atheneum, 1971), the torte brought such renown to its creator that in 1962, on the seventy-fifth anniversary of its creation, the Hungarian Chefs' and Pastry Chefs' Association placed a wreath on Dobos's grave, held a banquet in his honor, and paraded a six-foot-diameter Dobostorte through the streets of Budapest.

The preparation of the Dobostorte is fairly elaborate but not difficult. The work can easily be spread out over several days. In fact, the torte can be completely made several days in advance of serving, so it is a perfect choice for a gala event. Plan your time wisely. The procedure calls for baking the cake layers first, then making the buttercream, then assembling the cake. Finally, the caramelized sugar glaze is added to the top layer.

□ ADVANCE PREPARATION: Cake layers can be baked, stacked with wax paper between them, wrapped airtight, and frozen for a week or two. Buttercream may be stored, covered, in the refrigerator for several days. The cake can also be filled and the sides frosted a day or two in advance; cover the cake with an inverted bowl or foil and refrigerate. Glaze the top layer on the day the cake will be served.

□ SPECIAL EQUIPMENT: three 8-inch round cake pans or 2 cookie sheets, metal spatula with 6-inch-long blade, knife with long thin blade or broad pancake turner; pastry brush, medium-size heavy-bottomed saucepan, wax paper or plastic wrap, foil, 8-inch cardboard cake disk (optional); kitchen shears or scissors, spoon, toothpicks; apple or potato or piece of styrofoam or clay as a support to hold caramelized nuts; rubber gloves or padded mitt for protection when working with caramel glaze

□ BAKING TIME: 8 to 9 minutes at 350°F (175°C) for each layer

□ QUANTITY: one 6- to 8-layer cake (serves 12)

□ PAN PREPARATION: Turn cake pans upside down. The bottom of each pan now facing up, will be the baking surface. Spread solid shortening over the pan surface, then dust it evenly with flour; tap off excess flour. Or grease and flour cookie sheets, then draw with a toothpick around an 8-inch pot lid, marking several 8-inch disks on the prepared sheets. Note that after each cake layer is baked, the pan must be cooled, wiped clean, and greased and floured once again before baking the next layer.

6 eggs, separated, at room temperature
Pinch of salt
Pinch of cream of tartar
½ cup plus 5 tablespoons granulated sugar (5⅝ ounces; 160 g)
1 teaspoon vanilla extract
1 cup sifted all-purpose flour (4¼ ounces; 120 g)

FILLING AND FROSTING FOR CAKE SIDES:

Double recipe Deluxe French Chocolate Buttercream (page 391)
½ cup Amaretto liqueur or other liqueur with coffee, orange, or raspberry flavor
⅔ cup raspberry or apricot preserves (optional)
½ cup toasted and finely chopped hazelnuts or almonds (1⅓ ounces; 40 g)

1 cup granulated sugar (7 ounces; 200 g)
½ cup water
¼ teaspoon cream of tartar
Butter or vegetable oil, to coat knife

GARNISH (OPTIONAL):

12 whole hazelnuts, skinned (see page 43) and coated with the Caramelized Sugar Glaze

1. Prepare pans as described. Position racks to divide oven in thirds. Preheat oven to 350°F (175°C).

2. In the large bowl of an electric mixer, whip the egg whites with a pinch of salt until fluffy. Add cream of tartar and 2 tablespoons sugar and continue beating until soft peaks form. Add 3 more tablespoons sugar and beat until whites are satiny and stiff but not dry. Clean off beater and set whipped whites aside. Return unwashed beater to mixer.

3. Using a clean bowl, beat egg yolks until light in color, then add ½ cup sugar and beat until the mixture is thick and light and forms a flat ribbon falling back upon itself when the beater is lifted. This takes 2 to 3 minutes with the KitchenAid on speed #8; other mixers take 6 to 7 minutes. Add vanilla and beat to blend.

4. Fold about half of the whites into the yolk mixture. Then sprinkle on about one quarter of the flour and fold it in. Continue alternately folding in flour and whites until all are added. Use a light touch to maintain volume.

5. Scoop up ½ cup plus 1 tablespoon of the batter and turn it onto a prepared cake pan or inside a drawn disk on a cookie sheet. Use a spatula to spread the batter into an even ⅛-inch layer reaching neatly to the edges of the 8-inch circle.

Set the pan in the preheated oven. Stagger 3 pans in a triangular pattern, or if your oven is smaller, bake 2 round layers on each shelf leaving space for the heat to circulate. Rotate pans if necessary, because often they bake more quickly in the rear of the oven. Bake the layers for 8 or 9 minutes. Remove from the oven as soon as they look lightly golden, with a slightly darker edging. Watch the cake, not the clock!

Cool for about 1 minute, then loosen each cake layer from its pan with a long, thin knife blade or a broad pancake turner. Invert the layers onto a wire rack and leave them to cool completely. Cool the pans, then wipe them clean and grease and flour again before baking more layers.

Repeat, using all the batter to make as many layers as you can. The number will vary from 6 to 8, depending upon the thickness of each layer.

6. Set aside the very smoothest layer; this will be coated with caramel glaze and used for the cake top. After all layers are cold, stack them between sheets of wax paper or foil, placing the reserved best layer on top of the pile. Or, wrap the layers in a heavy-duty plastic bag or more foil, and refrigerate for a day or two, or freeze. Unwrap the package and bring the layers to room temperature before frosting with buttercream.

7. Prepare 4 cups (double recipe) of Deluxe French Chocolate Buttercream and chill if necessary. If previously made and refrigerated, bring it to room temperature, then correct the consistency by beating it in the electric mixer.

If you wish, beat in a couple of tablespoons of the same liqueur that you will brush over each cake layer.

8. To assemble the torte, set nearby the ½ cup liqueur, a pastry brush, and a broad icing spatula. Place a dab of buttercream on the center of a cardboard cake disk to hold the cake in position. Or set the cake on a flat plate protected by strips of wax paper (see page 425).

Brush the top of the first layer lightly with a pastry brush dipped into the liqueur. Don't saturate the cake, simply sprinkle or brush on a little moist flavoring. Spread the layer evenly with a generous ¼ cup buttercream. Repeat, adding layers and coating them with liqueur and buttercream. Note: For added flavor, you could also spread the bottom surface of each layer with warm raspberry or apricot preserves before setting it on top of the buttercream.

Arrange layers in a neat stack, and top the last layer with buttercream. Do not add the reserved, best-looking, cake layer. Hold it aside.

To decorate the cake sides, coat them with an even layer of remaining buttercream. Pour some toasted, chopped nuts onto the palm of your hand and gently press them into the frosted sides of the cake. Cover the sides completely. At this point, the cake can be covered and refrigerated for a day or two.

9. To glaze the cake top, set the reserved, best-looking cake layer, smoothest side up, on a wire rack set over foil, or directly on a piece of foil; do not use plastic wrap, the hot glaze will melt it. Nearby, set out a long-bladed sharp knife and some butter or vegetable oil to coat the knife.

Follow the directions to make Caramelized Sugar Glaze.

10. Pour some glaze over the cake layer and spread it evenly with the buttered or oiled knife blade. Use plenty of glaze so that it reaches comfortably to the edges of the cake.

Wait one or two seconds until the glaze just begins to lose its liquidity, then immediately draw the buttered knife blade through it, dividing the disk into 12 even wedges. Cut right through the cake, making separate pieces. To do this, first divide the disk into quarters, then divide each quarter into thirds. Note: Be sure to clean and butter the knife again between cuts if necessary, in order to make neat lines.

After a minute or two, the glaze will be completely hardened. Use kitchen scissors to cut away glaze drips around the edge of the glazed layer if necessary.

11. Optional Garnish: Prepare caramel glaze as in step 9, and follow instructions on page 462 to glaze 12 whole hazelnuts. Stand the glazed nuts in an apple or potato until the glaze is set hard (diagram a).

a

While the glaze in the pot is still soft (return it to heat and stir for a few minutes if hardened), use a drop or two to "glue" 1 glazed nut, flat side down, on the wide end of each wedge of the caramel-glazed layer (diagram b).

12. Set the glazed wedges on top of the cake. The wedges may be placed flat, or angled slightly by pressing one edge into the buttercream topping to give a more decorative effect (diagram c). If the wedges are placed flat on the cake, use your finger to press a little of the chocolate buttercream from the sides up around the edge of the glazed wedges so they appear joined to the rest of the torte. To serve, cut between the glazed wedges.

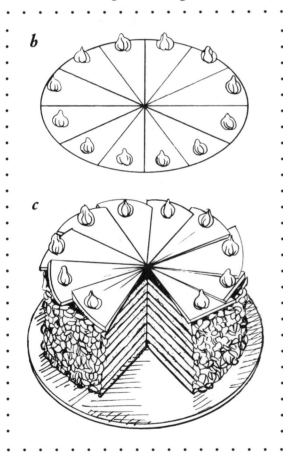

Carrot Torte

Grated carrots are responsible for the richness, moisture, and honeylike flavor of this classic Austrian *Karottentorte*. Because this is not a sweet cake, it is much appreciated by those who shun sugary desserts. Be forewarned, however, this is much lighter and has a less intense flavor than American carrot cake. You can serve *Karottentorte* topped with a light dusting of confectioners' sugar, or dress it up with Cream-Cheese Icing, topped by a molded marzipan carrot (page 446), the way it is presented in Viennese pastry shops.

☐ ADVANCE PREPARATION: Toast the walnuts in advance, as they take about 20 minutes. The cake may be baked ahead and frozen. Wrapped airtight, it will remain fresh at room temperature for several days.

☐ SPECIAL EQUIPMENT: drum-type rotary nut grinder or food processor, 2 medium-size bowls, extra bowl and beater for whipping egg whites, 8½-inch springform pan, wax paper or baking parchment, scissors

☐ BAKING TIME: 90 minutes at 300°F (150°C)

☐ QUANTITY: about 3 cups batter, one single-layer 8-inch cake (serves 6 to 8)

☐ PAN PREPARATION: Cut a wax paper or parchment round to fit baking pan. Spread solid shortening on bottom and sides of pan. Line pan bottom with paper or parchment round. Grease paper. Dust pan evenly with flour; tap out excess flour.

1½ cups shelled walnuts (5 ounces; 140 g)

¼ cup sifted cornstarch (scant 1 ounce; 30 g)

10 tablespoons granulated sugar (4¼ ounces; 125 g)

4 large eggs, separated, at room temperature

⅛ teaspoon salt

2 medium-size carrots, peeled and finely grated to yield 1½ cups packed (7¾ ounces; 220 g)

1 teaspoon vanilla extract

Pinch of ground cinnamon

ICING:

Confectioners' sugar sifted on or Cream Cheese Icing (page 392)

1. Prepare pan as described. Position rack in center of oven. Preheat oven to 325°F (165°C). Read About Tortes (pages 261–263).

Spread walnuts in a roasting pan and toast at 325°F for 15 to 20 minutes, stirring them occasionally. Cool the nuts slightly, then grate them in a drum-type rotary nut mill (page 43) or the food processor. If using the processor, grind nuts along with about 3 tablespoons of the measured sugar. Nuts should be dry and powdery, not oily and clumped. Blend cornstarch into nuts and set mixture aside. Lower oven heat setting to 300°F (150°C).

2. In the electric mixer, whip the egg whites and salt until fluffy. Gradually add half of the sugar, whipping until the whites are stiff but not dry. Scrape whites off the beaters into the bowl, then return beaters, unwashed, to the mixer. Set bowl of egg whites aside.

3. In another bowl, beat egg yolks with remaining sugar until the mixture is very light and fluffy. Beat in the grated carrots, vanilla, and cinnamon.

4. Fold egg whites into the carrot batter in several additions. Lightly fold the nut-cornstarch mixture into the whipped batter in several additions. Use a light touch to maintain volume.

5. Turn batter into the prepared pan, and bake in the preheated oven for about 90 minutes, or until a cake tester inserted in the center comes out clean and sides of cake begin to pull away from the pan. Cool cake on the wire rack for 5 minutes, then remove sides of pan. Top cake with a plate or rack and invert. Remove pan bottom. Top cake with another plate, and invert again, leaving cake right side up to cool completely. Cake will settle and become more dense as it cools. It will be easier to cut the next day, when the texture has become firm. Before serving, sift on confectioners' sugar, or split into 2 layers with a serrated knife (see page 424) and fill and frost with Cream-Cheese Icing.

Elegant & Special Cakes

I have selected this group of cakes because each is special in some way. Many, such as the Hazelnut Marquise, are show-stoppers, others are unusual because of their ingredients (Tiramisú) or presentation (Berries in Wine Gâteau). Any one of them will lend a festive note to an important occasion.

There are many other recipes in the book that would fit this definition. A case in point is the dazzling Chocolate Ruffle Cake, located with the Meringue and Dacquoise Cakes. Others are to be found among the Layer, Sponge, or Fruitcakes, the Charlottes, Tortes, and Cheesecakes. Consult the Index for more "elegant and special" ideas.

Before selecting a cake from this section, read the recipe all the way through; some of the cakes are quick and easy, others complex and time-consuming.

Hazelnut White-Chocolate Marquise

∎

At a Washington, D.C., convention of the International Association of Cooking Professionals, I had the pleasure of attending a master class in baking led by White House pastry chef Roland Mesnier. He presented an elaborate pistachio and white chocolate marquise frozen in a metal ring. With great élan and charm, he dazzled the audience by unmolding the cake with the aid of a flaming propane torch before garnishing it dramatically with a cocoa stencil, fresh berries, and chocolate cutouts.

Inspired by Mesnier, I have adapted and simplified the original notion, omitted the pyrotechnics, and designed a sublime layering of sponge cake and hazelnut-scented white chocolate mousse ribboned with cocoa and nuts. Note that the cake should be prepared well in advance and frozen—the perfect solution for a gala party dessert.

☐ ADVANCE PREPARATION: The génoise sponge cake can be baked and frozen in advance. The assembled cake, before garnishing, can be frozen for up to a week in advance. Remove the cake from the freezer, 3 or 4 hours before serving, unmold, garnish, and refrigerate for at least 3 hours to soften before serving. Do not serve the cake frozen.

□ SPECIAL EQUIPMENT: one 9- or 9½-inch springform pan, aluminum foil, scissors, masking tape, food processor or blender; instant-read spot thermometer, paring knife, plastic wrap or baking parchment, double boiler, paper doily to use as stencil, sifter

□ BAKING TIME: Génoise, 22 to 25 minutes at 375°F (190°C)

□ FREEZING TIME FOR MARQUISE: 5 hours minimum, to set filling

□ THAWING TIME BEFORE SERVING: 3 or 4 hours in refrigerator; let cake stand at room temperature for about 20 minutes before serving.

□ QUANTITY: one 9-inch cake (serves 12)

□ PAN PREPARATION: Make a foil collar to raise the pan height by cutting a strip of aluminum foil, heavy-duty if possible, about 34 × 8 inches. Fold the strip in half lengthwise. Spread softened butter on one side of the foil strip. Generously spread softened unsalted butter on bottom and sides of springform pan. Securely fasten the spring around the pan sides. Wrap the foil collar, butter side inward, around the top edge of the pan so 1½ inches of the collar stick up above the rim of the pan. Fasten the foil collar with masking tape.

CAKE:

½ recipe (3 eggs) Génoise sponge cake (page 211), baked in a 9½-inch springform pan and split into 2 layers or baked in two 9-inch round layer pans

NUT LAYERS:

12 ounces hazelnuts (about 3 cups; 340 g); blanched toasted almonds may be substituted
10 tablespoons granulated sugar (4½ ounces; 130 g)
3 ounces hazelnut liqueur
3 tablespoons unsalted butter, softened

HAZELNUT WHITE-CHOCOLATE MOUSSE (MAKES 6 CUPS):

13 ounces white chocolate, chopped (370 g)
1 cup (2 sticks; 230 g) plus 2 tablespoons unsalted butter, at room temperature
1½ cups (5¼ ounces; 150 g) plus 3 tablespoons sifted confectioners' sugar
8 large eggs, separated, at room temperature
2½ ounces hazelnut liqueur
2 tablespoons sifted unsweetened cocoa
2 tablespoons granulated sugar

CAKE SOAKING LIQUID:

4 tablespoons hazelnut liqueur

GARNISH:

1 cup hazelnuts (4 ounces; 110 g) plus 1 cup reserved nut crumbs from filling

TOPPING:

Unsweetened cocoa

1. Prepare the génoise. If you have made 1 thick layer, split it with a serrated knife. If you have made 2 layers, use the serrated knife to slice the browned "sugar bloom" off the top of each layer, so there is a cut surface that can absorb liqueur.

2. Prepare the nuts: Toast and skin the hazelnuts (see page 43) including those for the garnish, about 4 cups total. In the food processor, chop all the nuts medium-fine; do not overprocess. Remove from the workbowl 1 cup of these nuts and reserve them in a small bowl for garnishing the finished cake.

To nuts remaining in the processor workbowl, add the 10 tablespoons granulated sugar, 3 ounces hazelnut liqueur, and butter and pulse 4 or 5 seconds just to make coarse crumbs; you will have about 3 cups. Remove 1 cup of these flavored nut crumbs and mix them with the nuts for the cake garnish; the remaining flavored nut crumbs are for the cake filling. Set them aside.

3. Set the chopped white chocolate to melt in the top pan of a double boiler placed over, but not touching, hot water. Stir the chocolate from time to time as it melts. Note: The chocolate must not be hotter than 115°F or it will become grainy; it is best to keep it between 100°F and 110°F. Use a spot thermometer to keep track of the melting chocolate. Stir it smooth once it is partially melted, then remove pan from the heat and set it aside. Stir from time to time to keep the chocolate smooth and to cool the mixture.

4. Prepare the mousse: In an electric mixer, cream together the butter and confectioners' sugar. When smooth, add the egg yolks, one at a time, beating after each addition. Beat until light and fluffy, stopping the mixer to scrape down the bowl and beaters several times. With the mixer on lowest speed, gradually beat in the 2½ ounces of liqueur. The batter may look curdled at first; whip on high for several minutes until light, fluffy, and very smooth.

5. Stir the white chocolate again and check the consistency and temperature. Touch it with your finger or use the spot thermometer. It should be smooth, creamy, and at room temperature. If it feels stiff, stir it over warm water for a few seconds. Check the consistency and temperature of the yolk-butter mixture—it should match that of the white chocolate. If one mixture is hotter than the other, they will not blend properly. Fold all the creamy white chocolate into the yolk-butter mixture. The mixture should be light and smooth.

6. In a large clean bowl with clean beaters, whip the egg whites until fluffy, then add the 2 tablespoons granulated sugar and whip until *nearly* stiff but not dry. Don't overbeat. Fold the whites into the mousse.

7. Remove 2 cups of the white chocolate mousse to a separate bowl; sift on and gently whisk in the cocoa. Set this bowl aside.

8. To assemble the cake, place one layer of the génoise, cut side up, in the bottom of the prepared springform pan. Brush on 2 tablespoons of hazelnut liqueur.

Spread 1½ cups of the white chocolate mousse in the pan covering the cake.

Sprinkle on 1 cup of flavored nut crumbs and pat them gently into a flat layer.

Add the cocoa mousse, and top it with another 1 cup of flavored nut crumbs patted gently into a flat layer.

Spread 1½ cups white chocolate mousse

over the nuts and top it with the second génoise layer, cut side up.

Brush 2 tablespoons of hazelnut liqueur on the cake, then spread on remaining white chocolate mousse. The marquise will be about 1 inch above the pan rim at this point, supported by the foil collar.

Lightly cover the pan with plastic wrap, but do not bend the foil collar. Place the cake in the freezer overnight; if freezing it for a longer time, add an airtight foil wrap to protect the cake once it has been frozen solid.

9. About 3 hours before serving, remove cake from the freezer and unwrap it. Soak a Turkish towel in boiling water, wring it out, and wrap it around the cake sides for just a few seconds. Remove the towel and loosen the spring; remove the pan sides. Leave the cake on the pan bottom. If the section that was supported by the collar is slightly wider than the cake sides, smooth it even with the rest, using a knife warmed under hot tap water. Also smooth the cake top flat with a warm knife.

10. In a small bowl, toss together the mixture of flavored nut crumbs and chopped nuts reserved in step 2. To garnish the cake, put some nuts in the palm of your hand and press them onto the cake sides (page 430). Then set a paper doily on top of the cake and sift on a little unsweetened cocoa. Carefully lift the doily straight up and off, leaving a neat lacy design (see page 435). Refrigerate the cake until ready to serve. Store leftovers in the refrigerator or freezer.

Black Forest Cherry Cake

∎

This luscious 4-layer extravagaza is the classic Viennese *Schwarzwalderkirschtorte*. Kirsch, the cherry brandy used, comes from the Black Forest, hence the name in the title, although the cake was actually invented in Vienna. While it looks dramatic, the cake is easy to assemble: the Chocolate Buttermilk Cake is split into 4 layers, brushed with kirsch soaking syrup, and filled with whipped cream and kirsch-soaked tart cherries. It is iced with more whipped cream and garnished with chocolate shavings and curls, whipped cream rosettes, and maraschino cherries. This is a dazzling party cake that really tastes as good as it looks!

Note: You will see that the liqueur in the recipe can be adjusted to your taste or omitted altogether. Bear in mind that the kirsch flavor should be subtle, not overwhelming.

☐ ADVANCE PREPARATION: The Chocolate Buttermilk Cake can be made well in advance, wrapped airtight, and frozen. Thaw and split into 4 layers before assembling the cake. The cherries should be soaked in the kirsch for at least 2 hours before using them in the cake; this can be done the night before. The assembled and iced cake can be held in the refrigerator for several hours before serving; refrigerate leftovers.

☐ SPECIAL EQUIPMENT: serrated knife, aluminum foil or wax paper, large flat serving dish, icing spatula; 2 medium-size bowls, strainer, pastry brush, 9-inch cardboard cake disk covered with aluminum foil, large chilled bowl and beater for whipping cream; 16-inch pastry bag fitted with #6 star tip for decorating cake, vegetable peeler for making chocolate garnish

☐ PAN PREPARATION AND BAKING TIME: See Chocolate Buttermilk Cake.

☐ QUANTITY: one 4-layer 9-inch cake (serves 10 to 12)

CAKE:

1 recipe Chocolate Buttermilk Cake (page 94), baked into two 9-inch round layers

CAKE SYRUP:

1 cup liquid reserved from canned tart cherries
2 tablespoons kirsch, or to taste
2 tablespoons granulated sugar

CHERRY FILLING:

Two 16-ounce cans tart red cherries (not Bing), drained, with 1 cup of the liquid and 4 cups of cherries reserved
¼ cup kirsch

WHIPPED CREAM FILLING AND ICING:

3 cups heavy cream, chilled
4 tablespoons granulated or superfine sugar
3 tablespoons kirsch, or to taste

GARNISHES:

Chocolate Curls (page 451) made with an 8-ounce bar of dark chocolate (226.8 g) such as Hershey's Special Dark, or other fine-quality semisweet or bittersweet chocolate
12 maraschino cherries, well drained, with stems if possible

1. At least 2 hours before beginning to assemble this cake, drain the canned cherries, reserving 1 cup of their liquid for the cake soaking syrup. Put 4 cups of drained cherries into a bowl with ¼ cup of kirsch. Stir occasionally. This can be done the night before making the cake.

2. Prepare the chocolate cake. When layers are cold, use a serrated knife to split them horizontally (see page 424), making 4 layers. On pieces of foil or wax paper, set out the layers, cut sides up.

Set out another piece of foil or wax paper. On this, make the chocolate curls. Note that the chocolate must be at room temperature to peel. If too cold, set it in the oven (pilot light is sufficient) for a few minutes. As you hold the chocolate bar in your hand, body heat warms it. Peel the bar on one side for a little while, then turn the bar and peel on the warmer, underneath side. Reserve the best, biggest curls for the cake top; use the broken shards to press onto the cake sides. Set the chocolate curls aside.

3. Prepare the cake soaking syrup by combining in a bowl the reserved 1 cup of cherry liquid plus 2 tablespoons kirsch and 2 tablespoons sugar. Stir to blend. Brush or sprinkle 3 or 4 tablespoons of the syrup over the cut side of each cake layer. Discard any leftover syrup; do not oversoak the layers or they will become too moist to handle.

4. In a large chilled bowl with chilled beaters, whip the cream with the 4 tablespoons sugar and 3 tablespoons kirsch until stiff peaks form. You will have about 6 cups of whipped cream.

5. Place 1 cake layer, syrup side up, on the cake platter; use a cardboard cake disk beneath the first layer if you wish. Cut strips of wax paper and arrange them beneath the edges of the first layer to protect the platter from icing (see page 425). Spread about 1 cup of whipped cream on the layer, then sprinkle on 1⅓ cups kirsch-soaked cherries. Top this with a second cake layer, syrup side up, another 1 cup of whipped cream and 1⅓ cups cherries. Repeat with the third layer, and position the fourth layer, syrup side down, so the cake top is smooth.

6. Reserve 1 generous cup of whipped cream for garnishing, then frost the cake sides and top, using about 1⅓ cups of cream for the sides and ⅔ cup on top.

Use the palm of your hand to press about two thirds of the reserved chocolate curls gently onto the cake sides.

Put remaining whipped cream into a pastry bag and pipe 12 rosettes around the top edge of the iced cake. Top each rosette with 1 well-drained maraschino cherry, stem up, and pile remaining chocolate curls in the middle of the cake top. Remove wax paper strips protecting the plate.

Refrigerate the cake until 20 minutes before serving time; in hot weather, serve directly from the refrigerator.

Savarin

■

The Savarin is a light, spongy yeast cake baked in a ring mold and soaked with orange and kirsch or rum syrup. A specialty of the French baking repertoire, the savarin uses the same batter and syrup as the individually formed Babas au Rhum. For the background and history of the recipe, see page 357.

Traditionally, the savarin is topped with apricot glaze and decorated with glacéed fruits and sliced almonds. The center may be filled with sweetened, kirsch-flavored whipped cream, pastry cream or custard, or fresh fruits or berries.

☐ ADVANCE PREPARATION: This batter must rise twice, for a total of nearly 2¾ hours, and the baked cake must be soaked in syrup for at least half an hour, so plan your time accordingly. Note: Quick-rising yeast may be used to cut rising time; follow the directions on the yeast package. The baked and cooled cake, without any syrup, may be wrapped airtight and refrigerated for a couple of days, or frozen for about 2 weeks; the syrup, without liquor, may be made in advance and refrigerated in a covered jar.

If made in advance, the cake must be warmed through before being soaked with warm syrup. Once baked and syrup-soaked, the cake keeps very well and may be prepared a day or two before serving.

☐ SPECIAL EQUIPMENT: 2 large and 1 small mixing bowls, 2 saucepans, wooden spoon, grater, wax paper, plastic wrap; 9-inch

(6½-cup) ring mold or 5-cup savarin mold or 1½ quart soufflé dish or casserole, or six 3-inch individual savarin ring molds; soup spoon or bulb baster, pastry brush (optional), toothpick or skewer, large flat dish or pan at least 9 inches in diameter with sides at least 1 inch high

☐ RISING TIME: with regular yeast, about 2¾ hours

☐ BAKING TIME: about 30 minutes at 375°F for large ring mold, 10 to 15 minutes for individual savarin molds

☐ SYRUP SOAKING TIME: minimum 30 minutes

☐ QUANTITY: 1 ring cake (serves 6), or 6 individual ring cakes

☐ PAN PREPARATION: Spread margarine or butter on bottom and sides of the ring mold.

DOUGH:

See Babas au Rhum recipe (page 357)

SYRUP:

See Babas au Rhum recipe, but substitute ½ cup kirsch for the rum if you wish. If you prefer not to use liqueur, substitute 1 teaspoon vanilla, orange, lemon, or rum extract

GLAZE:

1½ cups Apricot Glaze (page 411), warmed just before spreading on savarin

GARNISH:

Glacéed red cherries, angelica (optional), sliced or halved blanched almonds

FILLING:

1½ cups heavy cream, whipped and flavored with 2 tablespoons confectioners' sugar and 2 or 3 tablespoons rum or kirsch; or 1 recipe (2⅓ cups) Crème Pâtissière (page 370), made in advance and refrigerated

OPTIONAL:

2 or 3 cups fresh berries or sliced peaches sprinkled with sugar and kirsch, or macerated in excess savarin soaking syrup

1. Follow steps 1 through 4 of the Babas au Rhum recipe to prepare the batter and let it rise the first time. Grease the mold as directed. In step 5, preheat the oven to 375°F (190°C). Stir down the dough. Note: The following directions will be for a single large ring mold. If using individual molds, follow the same procedure, but decrease the baking time accordingly.

2. Scoop spoonfuls of the dough into the bottom of the prepared pan(s); the large ring mold will be about ¼ to ⅓ filled, the individual ring molds about half filled. Cover the pan(s) with a piece of greased wax paper and place them in a warm draft-free location until the batter has risen almost to the top of the mold(s). This can take from 60 to 90 minutes.

Watch the dough, not the clock. The rising time will depend upon air temperature.

3. Preheat oven to 375°F (190°C). When the dough has risen, place the savarin in the center of the preheated oven. The large ring mold needs to bake for about 30 minutes, the individual ring molds for 10 to 15 minutes. When done, the cake top should be a rich golden brown and a cake tester inserted in the center should come out clean. Note: If the cake top browns too much or too quickly, cover it with a piece of aluminum foil.

6. While the cake bakes, combine all syrup ingredients except the liqueur or extract and simmer them in a saucepan over medium heat for about 10 minutes. Set a strainer over a bowl in the sink. Drain the syrup through the strainer, pressing the fruit slices with the back of a spoon. Discard contents of strainer.

Note: Syrup may be made in advance up to this point and refrigerated in a covered jar until ready to add to the cake.

7. When baked, let the Savarin cool in its pan for about 5 minutes. Prick the top of the cake all over with a toothpick or skewer. Cover the cake with a wire rack or platter, invert, and lift off the mold.

Note: The cake can be baked ahead to this point, cooled completely, wrapped airtight, and refrigerated for a day or two or frozen for a couple of weeks. If made in advance, the frozen or cold cake should be thawed and warmed before soaking with syrup. Set the cold cake in a preheated 300°F oven for about 10 minutes, until warmed through.

At this point, warm the syrup as well; cake and syrup must both be warm for the syrup to penetrate properly. Once the syrup is warm, stir in the kirsch, rum, or extract.

8. As soon as the cake is removed from its mold, still warm, it can be soaked with syrup. To do this, place the cake on a dish or pan with an edge at least 1 inch deep. Spoon the warm syrup over the cake, using a spoon or a bulb baster. Scoop up the excess and baste again every few minutes over a period of at least 30 minutes. Be sure the cake is well saturated; it should hold almost all the syrup like a swollen sponge.

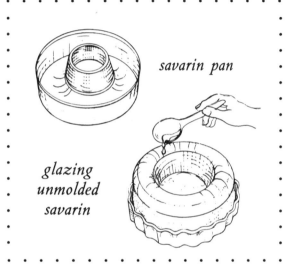

savarin pan

glazing
unmolded
savarin

Cover the cake with plastic wrap and refrigerate, or leave at room temperature until a couple of hours before serving. Sprinkle a few teaspoons of kirsch or rum over the top of the cake if you wish.

8. To glaze the cake:
Note: If you want the cake to stand at room temperature more than an hour before serving, boil the apricot glaze to 228°F (thread stage) before using it. In this way, it will be firm enough to jell and hold. Otherwise, simply boil the glaze until thickened slightly.

Prepare the apricot glaze and brush or spoon it over the cake top and sides. Cut the glacéed cherries into halves and press them into the glaze on the cake, making flower petals; or use the cherries for the centers and almond slices for the petals. Make green stems or leaves from green cherries or green glacéed pineapple or angelica. Brush a second coating of glaze over the design if you wish, for a more finished look.

Serve the decorated savarin as is, or just before serving fill its center with sweetened whipped cream or pastry cream, or fresh berries or sliced fruit tossed with granulated sugar and a little liqueur.

Lime Mousse Cake

▪

Lime Mousse Cake is refreshingly tart and can be made in advance and frozen. The perfect summer dessert, it is simply a lime mousse layered with liqueur-soaked génoise sponge cake. To vary the flavor, substitute other citrus fruits: tangerine or lemon, for example.

□ ADVANCE PREPARATION: The génoise can be made well in advance and frozen. Split the cake shortly before filling it. The assembled cake can be prepared a day in advance and refrigerated, or frozen for up to a week. It must, in any case, be refrigerated for a minimum of 4 hours before serving to set the filling.

□ SPECIAL EQUIPMENT: one 8-inch springform pan, 8-inch cardboard cake disk covered with foil, bowl and beater for whipping egg whites, serrated knife, double boiler, rubber scraper, large mixing bowl containing ice water, whisk, extra bowl and beater for whipping cream

□ CHILLING TIME: minimum 4 hours, to set filling

□ QUANTITY: one 3-layer 8-inch cake (serves 8)

□ PAN PREPARATION: Place foil-covered disk in pan bottom and spread a dab of butter in the center of the disk to hold the cake in place.

CAKE:

½ recipe (3 eggs) Lemon Génoise (page 214), baked in an 8-inch round pan. Cover the cake with foil until ready to split and fill.

CAKE SOAKING SYRUP:

6 tablespoons Grand-Marnier-flavored Cake Soaking Syrup (page 420) or dark rum

LIME MOUSSE CAKE FILLING (6 CUPS):

Zest and juice of 4 limes (about 8 teaspoons zest and ½ cup juice)
1 envelope unflavored gelatin (¼ ounce; 7 g)
¼ cup cold water
3 large eggs, separated, at room temperature
1 cup superfine sugar (7 ounces; 200 g)
2 teaspoons cold water
1 teaspoon cornstarch

3 tablespoons orange-flavored liqueur
(optional)
Pinch of salt
2 tablespoons sifted confectioners' sugar
½ cup chilled heavy cream

GARNISH:

*1 teaspoon grated lime zest, reserved
from filling*

1. Slice the cooled cake horizontally into 2 layers using a serrated knife (see page 424). With cut sides up, brush about 3 tablespoons cake syrup onto each layer. Set one layer, cut side up, into the prepared pan, pressing it gently onto the butter in the center of the cake disk. This holds the cake in place.

2. Set aside 1 teaspoon grated zest for garnishing the finished cake. Put the rest in a small bowl and add the lime juice.

In the top pan of a double boiler, sprinkle the gelatin over the cold water, stir, and set aside to soften for 3 or 4 minutes. Then set the pan directly over low heat and stir constantly until the gelatin dissolves. Remove pan from heat and set aside.

3. Put the 3 egg yolks into the medium-size bowl of an electric mixer and add the superfine sugar and 2 teaspoons cold water. Beat with the electric mixer for about 2 minutes, or until the mixture is thick and pale ivory-colored, and forms a flat ribbon falling back upon itself when the beater is lifted.

4. Check the gelatin; it should still be liquid. If slightly thickened from standing, stir it over low heat for a second to liquefy. Dissolve the cornstarch in the lime zest and juice, then pour the mixture into the melted gelatin. Whisk well. Place the gelatin pan over the bottom half of the double boiler set on the counter, not the stove. Whisk in the whipped egg-sugar mixture. Set the double boiler over medium heat and whisk constantly for about 12 minutes, or until the mixture thickens enough to coat a spoon. Stir in the liqueur, if using it, and cook for about 1 minute longer. Remove pan from the heat. If the mixture is not in a metal bowl or pan, transfer it to one now, to avoid the thermal shock of ice water.

5. To chill the mixture quickly, set the bowl into a larger bowl filled with ice cubes and water, plus 2 tablespoons salt to make it colder. Whisk for 12 to 15 minutes, until the mousse thickens, will mound on a spoon, and looks like soft pudding. When the mousse is nearly thickened, remove it from the ice-water bath while you prepare the egg whites and cream. Do not let the mousse set hard.

Whip the egg whites with a pinch of salt until fluffy, add 1 tablespoon confectioners' sugar, and whip until nearly stiff but not dry.

With a chilled bowl and chilled beater, whip the cream with remaining 1 tablespoon confectioners' sugar until medium stiff. Set meringue and cream aside and return to the mousse. When it has the correct consistency (if it jells too much, stir it over a pan of hot water until soft), fold in the whipped cream, then the meringue. Spoon about half of the mousse on top of the cake layer in the pan. Set remaining cake layer on the mousse, then top with remaining mousse. Smooth the top gently, and sprinkle on the reserved grated lime zest. Cover the pan with plastic wrap and foil, then refrigerate for 4 hours, or freeze.

To unmold the cake, wrap a hot damp towel around the pan sides for a few seconds, then unfasten the spring and remove the pan sides.

Berries in Wine Gâteau

•

I like to call this Berries Under Glass, because the stunning Austrian torte is topped with jewel-red berries set in a clear wine gelatin. I first tasted this *Johannisbeeren torten* in the Cafe Luitpold in Munich, and found variations throughout Bavaria. Use any seasonal berry, from small red currants to rasperries; they sit atop the sponge cake and sparkle in their bed of wine gelatin.

Note: While the recipe calls for a crisp cookie base beneath the sponge cake, this may be omitted if you prefer, or you can use 2 sponge layers. The cookie is favored primarily for its contrasting texture.

☐ ADVANCE PREPARATION: The cookie base can be made ahead and frozen. The sponge génoise can also be baked in advance and frozen. The assembled cake should be refrigerated for a minimum of 3 hours to set the gelatin topping.

☐ SPECIAL EQUIPMENT: one 8½-inch round cake pan plus one 8½-inch springform pan (8-inch size also fine); food processor or large bowl and 2 knives, large bowl of ice water, tea towel

☐ BAKING TIME: cookie base, about 17 minutes at 375°F (190°C); génoise, about 25 minutes at 375°F (190°C)

☐ CHILLING TIME: for assembled cake, minimum 3 hours

☐ QUANTITY: one 8½-inch cake (serves 8)

☐ PAN PREPARATION: Butter bottom of springform pan before baking cookie base. For Génoise, see recipe.

COOKIE BASE:

1 recipe Cookie Base for Cake, Pâte Sablée (page 447)

CAKE:

½ recipe (3 eggs) vanilla-flavored Génoise (page 211), baked in an 8½-inch layer cake

FILLING AND GLAZE:

⅔ cup apricot preserves

BERRIES:

1 pint fresh berries: red currants, rasperries, or strawberries halved or quartered

WINE GELATIN TOPPING:

4½ teaspoons unflavored gelatin
5 tablespoons cold water
½ cup boiling water
3¼ cups slightly sweet non-sparkling white wine such as Moselle, Sauternes, or a California equivalent. Note: If using a sparkling wine, stir well to remove bubbles before adding in recipe.

GARNISH (OPTIONAL):

½ cup apricot preserves, strained
⅔ cup toasted sliced almonds (2 ounces; 60 g)

1. Prepare the Cookie Base for Cake. Roll out and bake the pastry in the bottom of a buttered 8½-inch springform pan at 375°F (190°C) for 17 to 20 minutes, or until golden. Let it cool completely on a wire rack. Remove pan sides but leave the cookie in the bottom of the pan; it will form the base upon which the cake will be "constructed."

Also prepare the génoise, baking it in the 8½-inch cake pan. When baked, allow the cake to cool in the pan for 10 minutes, then remove from the pan and cool it completely on a wire rack.

2. Place the apricot preserves in a small saucepan and warm until it will spread easily. Also prepare the berries: Pick over, hull if necessary, rinse, and dry gently on paper towels.

3. To assemble the cake, spread about ⅓ cup apricot preserves on the cookie base in the springform pan. Cover this with the génoise layer.

Strain remaining ⅓ cup warm apricot preserves and discard the solids. Spread the strained preserves over the top of the génoise layer, making sure to reach the edges all around. This glaze will help prevent the gelatin topping from soaking into the cake.

4. Arrange the berries in the glaze on top of the cake. Refrigerate the cake in its pan while you prepare the gelatin topping.

5. Sprinkle the gelatin over the cold water in a small bowl. Let it stand for about 3 minutes to soften, then add the boiling water and stir until the gelatin is completely dissolved. Add the wine and stir. Set the gelatin bowl into a bowl of ice water and stir on and off for about 15 minutes, until the gelatin thickens and begins to mound on the spoon like a soft pudding; do not let it set hard. At once remove the cake from the refrigerator and spoon the gelatin over the berries on top. Re-

turn the cake to the refrigerator and leave for a minimum of 3 hours to set the topping.

6. To unmold the cake, dampen a tea towel with very hot water, wring it out, and wrap the towel around the pan for a few seconds. Then slowly open the spring on the pan side; the gelatin will pull away from the pan. If the gelatin sticks, run a thin-bladed knife between the cake and the pan sides to loosen. Remove pan sides. Leave cake on pan bottom to serve.

If you want to garnish the sides of the cake, warm remaining apricot preserves and brush it onto the cake sides. Press on toasted almond slices. In hot weather, refrigerate cake until serving.

Cassis Gâteau

■

French pâtissier Robert Dause is an artist as well as a craftsman. His elegant Pâtisserie-Confiserie-Salon de Thé (pastry, candy, teashop) in the Loire Valley village of Azay-le-Rideau is filled with beautiful and delectable specialties that are "handmade" upstairs in the narrow fourteenth-century building where, he assured us, Joan of Arc once lived. She really missed out on the treats, but visitors to the town's two-star château around the corner pay homage to Dause and his cakes. One of his prettiest specialties is the Cassis Gâteau, a rich cassis (black-currant) mousse layered with cassis-flavored sponge cake and topped with a mirrorlike cassis glaze. This heavenly cake is easy on the hostess because it can be made completely in advance.

Note: Cassis (black currant) purée is available canned in many imported food shops; with good success you can substitute fresh or frozen blackberries. Cassis liqueur (Double Crème de Cassis) is available in any liquor shop.

☐ ADVANCE PREPARATION: The génoise cake can be made in advance and frozen. The filled cake must be refrigerated for a minimum of 3 hours to set the filling and topping.

☐ SPECIAL EQUIPMENT: 9-inch round layer pan, 9-inch springform pan, 9-inch cardboard cake disk covered with foil, plastic wrap, aluminum foil, chilled bowl and beater for whipping cream, serrated knife, rubber spatula, large bowl of ice water, tea towel, grater, wax paper, lemon squeezer. For topping: 3 layers of cheesecloth set in a bowl

☐ BAKING TIME: Génoise, about 25 minutes at 375°F (190°C)

☐ CHILLING TIME: minimum 3 hours for filled cake, then 1 hour to set topping

☐ QUANTITY: One 9-inch cake (serves 8)

☐ PAN PREPARATION: Set foil-covered cardboard disk in bottom of the springform pan and put a tiny dab of soft butter in the center of the disk to hold the cake in place.

CAKE:

½ recipe (3 eggs) vanilla-flavored Génoise (page 211) baked in a 9 × 1½-inch round pan.

CASSIS CAKE SOAKING SYRUP:

¼ cup Double Crème de Cassis liqueur

¼ cup Basic Cake Soaking Syrup (page 420)

CASSIS MOUSSE FILLING:
(3 CUPS)

1⅓ cups canned cassis (black currant) purée or canned seedless blackberry purée or 3½ to 4 cups fresh black currants or fresh or frozen blackberries (20 ounces; 560 g). Note: quantity of fresh berries depends upon their size and juiciness
¼ cup cold water
1½ envelopes (3 teaspoons) unflavored gelatin
½ cup boiling water, plain or flavored by pouring over strained berry seeds and pulp (see step 2)
1½ tablespoons freshly squeezed lemon juice
⅛ to ¼ cup granulated sugar, or to taste, depending upon sweetness of berry purée
Pinch of salt
3 tablespoons Double Crème de Cassis liqueur
¾ cup chilled heavy cream

TOPPING:

⅓ cup reserved berry purée from step 2
1 tablespoon granulated sugar
1 teaspoon lemon juice
½ teaspoon unflavored gelatin
1 tablespoon cold water
2 tablespoons boiling water
3 tablespoons Double Crème de Cassis liqueur

1. Prepare the cake, bake it in a 9-inch layer pan, and when it is cold, split it into 2 layers (see page 424). Cover the layers with foil or plastic wrap to prevent drying until ready to use.

In a small bowl, mix together the liqueur and syrup to make Cassis Cake Soaking Syrup. Set the cake layers cut side up and brush each one with 4 tablespoons of syrup. Cover the cake with plastic wrap and set it aside.

2. Prepare the Cassis Mousse Filling: If using canned berry purée, set aside 1 cup for the mousse, and reserve ⅓ cup for the topping. If using fresh berries (washed, drained, and patted dry) or defrosted frozen berries, put them through a food mill to make 1⅓ cups of seedless purée. Do not discard the seeds and pulp that remain in the food mill; reserve them for flavoring the gelatin liquid that follows.

Measure the cold water into a 1½ quart saucepan and sprinkle on the gelatin. Let it sit for 3 or 4 minutes to soften.

Stir in ½ cup boiling water or, if you have prepared your own berry purée, pour the water over the reserved seeds and pulp left in the food mill. Use this flavored water to add to the gelatin mixture. In either case stir the boiling water into the mixture until the gelatin is completely dissolved.

Stir in the lemon juice, sugar, salt, and 1 cup of the berry purée. Taste and add more sugar if necessary. Set the pan over low heat and stir well until the sugar is dissolved; do not boil. If the mixture is not in a metal bowl or pan, transfer it to one now to avoid the thermal shock of ice water.

3. Add 3 tablespoons of cassis liqueur to the fruit mixture. Set the bowl over ice water and stir or whisk on and off for 12 to 15 minutes, or until the mixture feels thick, mounds on the spoon, and has about the consistency of soft pudding. Remove the bowl from the ice water. Do not allow the mixture to jell hard.

The ice water speeds this process, but if you are not in a hurry, you can simply refrigerate the mixture for about 45 minutes, stirring it now and then, until it begins to thicken. Note: If the mousse sets too hard, you can soften it by setting it over hot water and stirring for a few seconds, just to warm it up and relax the gelatin.

4. With a chilled bowl and beater, whip the cream until soft peaks form. Fold the whipped cream into the cooled and thickened berry mixture.

Set 1 cake layer, syrup side up, on the foil disk in the springform pan. Spoon 2 cups of mousse over this layer. Top with the second cake layer, then add remaining mousse, smoothing the top evenly. Cover the pan with plastic wrap and refrigerate the cake for at least 3 hours, to set the filling.

4. Prepare the topping: Put the remaining fruit purée (there should be about ⅓ cup) and 1 tablespoon sugar in a small saucepan and stir over low heat until the sugar dissolves and the purée is soft. Pour the mixture into a bowl lined with 3 layers of cheesecloth and strain, squeezing the cheesecloth to remove all liquid. Discard any solids. Stir in 1 teaspoon lemon juice. Add water if needed to make ¾ cup of mixture.

In a small saucepan, sprinkle ½ teaspoon of gelatin over 1 tablespoon of cold water and set it aside for 3 or 4 minutes. Pour 2 tablespoons boiling water over gelatin and stir. Put the pan on low heat and stir until the gelatin is completely dissolved.

Add the melted gelatin to the fruit mixture, then stir in 3 tablespoons cassis liqueur. Pour this over the cassis mousse on top of the cake and return the cake to the refrigerator for about 1 hour, to set the topping.

5. When ready to serve the cake, dampen a towel with hot water, wring it out well, and wrap it around the outside of the pan for a few seconds. Unspring the pan sides and remove. Lift the cake from the pan bottom or, if not using the cardboard cake disk, leave the cake on the pan bottom. Refrigerate leftover cake.

··

Chestnut Mousse Cake

■

Rum-laced chestnut mousse is studded with chopped candied chestnuts to make the filling for this sublime 3-layer cake. Ice the cake with Chocolate Water Glaze, or garnish the uniced top with whole candied chestnuts, and spread whipped cream and chocolate shavings on the sides.

☐ ADVANCE PREPARATION: The cake must be refrigerated for a minimum of 3 hours for the filling to set before it can be iced and decorated. It is best to prepare this cake one day in advance.

☐ SPECIAL EQUIPMENT: one 8-inch springform pan, pastry brush, icing spatula, 7- or 8-inch cardboard cake disk covered with foil (optional); paring knife, plastic wrap, 2 small bowls, strainer or sieve, 2-quart saucepan, whisk, wooden spoon, large mixing bowl, pastry brush; chilled bowl and beater for whipping cream, plastic wrap

☐ BAKING TIME FOR GÉNOISE: 20 to 25 minutes at 375°F (190°C)

☐ CHILLING TIME FOR ASSEMBLED CAKE: minimum of 3 hours, or overnight, for filling to set

☐ QUANTITY: one 8-inch 3-layer cake (serves 10 to 12)

CAKE:

½ recipe (3 eggs) vanilla Génoise (page 211), baked in an 8-inch pan

CHESTNUTS:

One 10- or 12-ounce jar of candied chestnuts in syrup, drained, with syrup reserved. Set aside several whole chestnuts for garnishing the cake, and coarsely chop the rest.

RUM-CHESTNUT MOUSSE FILLING (5 CUPS):

1 can (15½ ounces) unsweetened chestnut purée
2 cups milk
½ cup (3½ ounces; 100 g) plus 2 tablespoons granulated sugar
2 envelopes unflavored gelatin (each ¼ ounce; 7 g)
1 teaspoon vanilla extract
6 large egg yolks
4 tablespoons dark rum
¾ cup heavy cream, chilled

RUM-CHESTNUT CAKE
SOAKING SYRUP:

7 tablespoons of syrup reserved from candied chestnuts, if there is enough, or make up the difference with 1 more tablespoon of rum or use Cake Soaking Syrup (page 420) plus 2 tablespoons dark rum and 1 teaspoon vanilla extract. Total: about 9 tablespoons syrup, blended in a bowl

ICING (OPTIONAL):

Chocolate Water Glaze (page 410)
½ cup heavy cream, whipped, flavored with 1 tablespoon granulated sugar and 1 tablespoon dark rum

GARNISH:

Chocolate Curls (page 451), or toasted almond slices
Reserved whole candied chestnuts

1. Prepare the génoise and bake in the 8-inch pan. When cold, split it into 3 layers with a serrated knife (see page 424). Wrap the layers in foil or plastic wrap until ready to assemble the cake.

Prepare the chestnuts, reserving the liquid for the syrup and chopping those chestnuts not reserved for garnishing the finished cake. Prepare the Rum-Chestnut Soaking Syrup.

2. Prepare the Rum-Chestnut Mousse Filling: In a 2-quart saucepan, mash the chestnut purée with a fork. Add the milk and sugar and whisk until fairly smooth. Sprinkle on the gelatin right out of the package, then set the pan over medium heat and bring to a boil while stirring continually with a whisk or wooden spoon. Don't worry if there are lumps, the mixture will be strained. When it reaches a boil, remove pan from the heat and stir in the vanilla.

3. In a large mixing bowl, whisk the egg yolks until frothy, then stir in about ½ cup of the hot chestnut mixture while whisking constantly. Transfer the warmed yolks to the hot chestnut mixture in the pan, stirring constantly so the eggs do not poach. Cook, stirring, over medium heat until the mixture thickens slightly. Do not boil. When thick, remove from heat and stir in the rum. Strain through a sieve set over a bowl, then cool in the refrigerator until thickened but not quite jelled. Or, to speed the cooling, stir the mixture over a large pan of ice water.

When the mousse is thick enough to mound on the spoon like a soft pudding, whip the chilled cream to soft peaks. Fold the cream into the cooled and thickened (but not fully jelled) chestnut mixture. At this point it is ready to add to the cake layers.

4. Set a foil-covered cardboard cake disk in the bottom of the springform pan and put a dab of mousse in the center of the disk to hold the cake in place. Put 1 génoise cake layer, cut side up, on the disk. Sprinkle or brush 3 tablespoons of Rum-Chestnut Syrup evenly over the layer. Spread on about one third of the Rum Chestnut Mousse. Sprinkle on half the chopped candied chestnuts, then top with another cake layer. Repeat, adding 3 tablespoons of syrup, one third of the mousse, and remaining chestnuts. Finally, top with the last cake layer, add syrup and remaining mousse, and spread smooth. Top the cake with plastic wrap

and refrigerate for at least 3 hours, or overnight, for the mousse to set.

5. After the mousse is set, remove the cake from the refrigerator, remove the sides of the springform pan, lift the cake on its disk from the bottom of the pan, and set it on the counter. If you don't use the cardboard disk, leave the cake on the pan bottom.

Top the cake with Chocolate Water Glaze. Or simply whip cream with sugar and rum and spread it over the sides of the cake. Garnish the top with several whole candied chestnuts placed in the center and press chocolate curls or toasted almond slices against the sides. Refrigerate the cake in hot weather, but serve it at room temperature.

Génoise and Sponge Cake Variations

■

Endless combinations can be devised by stacking split layers of flavored génoise or sponge cake with mousse, Bavarian cream, buttercream, or flavored whipped cream. Below is a list of suggestions to get you started; for more ideas, look in the Index. Note: If you are intimidated by the thought of dividing one cake layer into thirds, split it into halves instead and divide the filling between 2 layers. Or bake the cake batter in 2 pans, putting ⅓ in one pan and ⅔ in the other; split the thicker cake, thereby gaining 3 layers with only 1 cut.

Chocolate Marquise

■

CAKE:

½ recipe (3 eggs) Chocolate Génoise (page 214), baked in an 8-inch round pan 2 inches deep and split into 3 layers (see page 424)

SOAKING SYRUP:

3 tablespoons chocolate-mint or raspberry liqueur sprinkled on each cake layer. Optional addition: Glaze each cake layer with seedless raspberry jam.

FILLING:

Chocolate Mousse I (page 375). Alternatively, you can fill the cake with Deluxe French Chocolate Buttercream (page 390).

ICING:

Chocolate Ganache Glaze (page 407), or Fabulous Chocolate Glaze (page 409)

GARNISH:

Chocolate Leaves or Curls or a single Chocolate Rose (page 455)

Set a foil-covered 8-inch cardboard cake disk in an 8½-inch springform pan. Put one cake layer—liqueur and jam-glazed side up—on the bottom of the pan. Add ⅓ of the mousse. Top with another prepared cake layer. Repeat. Top with remaining cake layer and spread on remaining mousse. Refrigerate cake for several hours. Unspring pan sides and remove. If you don't use a cardboard disk, leave cake on pan bottom. While cake is cold, spread warm chocolate glaze on top and sides of cake. Refrigerate to set glaze. Add chocolate decorations. Refrigerate cake.

Strawberry Mousse Cake (and Raspberry Variation)

∎

CAKE:

1 recipe (6 eggs) vanilla Génoise (page 211), baked in two 8-inch round pans. Split each layer (see page 424), making 4 layers.

GLAZE:

Strawberry preserves

SOAKING SYRUP:

3 tablespoons kirsch or rum-flavored Cake Soaking Syrup (page 420)

FILLING:

1 recipe Strawberry Mousse (page 337)

ICING:

¾ cup chilled heavy cream, whipped

GARNISH:

Sprig of fresh mint leaves; 1 pint fresh strawberries, rinsed, dried, and hulled; slice half of the berries.

Brush some flavored cake-soaking syrup over each cake layer, then spread each one with strawberry preserves. Set the layers aside; do not stack them.

Set a foil-covered 8-inch cardboard cake disk into an 8½-inch springform pan. Put 1 cake layer, glazed side up, in the pan bottom. Add ¾ cup of the strawberry mousse filling. Repeat three more times, ending with the last of the filling, smoothed flat. Refrigerate for at least 3 hours, to set filling.

Unspring pan sides and remove pan. If you are not using a cardboard cake disk, leave cake on pan bottom. Spread whipped cream on the cake sides and put a small dollop of cream in the center of the top. Set a few whole berries into the cream on top and garnish with the mint sprig. Arrange sliced berries in a border pressed into the whipped cream around the bottom edge of the sides. Serve extra berries alongside cake.

·*Variation:*·

Substitute raspberries for strawberries, use raspberry preserves, and flavor cream with raspberry-flavored liqueur.

Lynn's Devon Lemon Cream Cake

•

This delightfully tart cake is an often requested specialty of Fancy Fare, the North Hatley, Quebec, catering business of my good friend Lynn Pageau.

CAKE:

½ recipe (3 eggs) lemon-flavored Génoise (page 214), baked in an 8-inch round pan and split into 3 layers (see page 424)

FILLING:

1 recipe Lemon Curd (page 380) or Lemon Cake Filling (page 381), less rich than Lemon Curd

ICING:

Lemon-flavored French Buttercream Ménagère (page 393)

GARNISH:

Chopped Candied Lemon Peel (page 448), or grated lemon zest

Set out a foil-covered 8-inch cardboard cake disk and dab a little lemon curd in the center to anchor the cake. Top with 1 cake layer and half of the lemon curd. Cover with a second cake layer and remaining lemon curd. Top with the last cake layer. Frost the cake with Lemon-flavored Buttercream Ménagère, and garnish the top with candied lemon peel or grated lemon zest. Refrigerate, but bring to room temperature to serve.

Grand Marnier Génoise

•

CAKE:

1 full recipe (6 eggs) orange-flavored Génoise (page 214) baked in two 8-inch-square pans. Split each layer horizontally (see page 424) to make four 8-inch-square layers.

SOAKING SYRUP:

Sprinkle the cut side of each cake layer with 3 tablespoons Grand Marnier-flavored Syrup (page 420).

FILLING:

Double recipe (3 cups) Light Orange Buttercream (page 382)

ICING:

Orange Buttercream Ménagère (page 393)

GARNISH:

Grated orange zest or chopped Candied Orange Peel (page 448)

Prepare a foil-covered 8-inch-square cake cardboard. Dab some buttercream or butter in the center of the board to hold the cake in place. Set 1 cake layer, syrup-soaked side up, on the board. Add 1 cup of filling. Repeat twice, layering the flavored cake with the filling and ending with cake. Cover top and sides of cake with icing and add garnish on top. Refrigerate in hot weather.

Gâteau Moka

∎

CAKE:

Chocolate Sponge Cake (page 218), baked in a jelly-roll pan. When cold, trim crisp ⅛-inch edges, then cut the cake lengthwise into 3 strips about 3¼ × 14¾ inches.

SOAKING SYRUP:

Sprinkle about 3 tablespoons coffee-flavored liqueur over each strip of cake.

FILLING:

Viennese Coffee Custard Buttercream (page 378)

ICING:

Mocha Buttercream, any recipe (see Index), or Chocolate Ganache Glaze (page 407)

GARNISH:

Pipe buttercream shell borders on top and bottom edges of cake. Add a row of candied coffee beans or Chocolate Leaves (page 449) down the center of the cake, overlapping the leaves slightly.

Cut a cardboard strip about 3¼ × 14¾ inches and cover it with foil. Dab some butter or buttercream on the board to hold the cake in place. Set 1 cake strip, syrup side up, on the board. Top with half of the filling. Repeat, topping remaining filling with the last cake strip set syrup side down. Refrigerate cake for about 2 hours to allow the filling to become firm. When cake is cold, ice with buttercream or warm ganache glaze. Garnish, then refrigerate cake, but bring to room temperature before serving.

Orange-Chocolate Dream Cake

∎

This is so good I really do dream about it! It is light yet extremely flavorful, rich without being cloying or heavy. A perfect adult birthday cake selection. For a Super-Gala, you could omit the nut garnish and envelop the entire cake in white Chocolate Plastic (page 452) drizzled with melted dark chocolate first to create a striped look topped with a white chocolate ruffle (page 457).

Chocolate Sponge Cake (page 218), baked in two 8-inch round layers. Split each cake horizontally to make 4 layers.

FILLING AND FROSTING:

Fill and frost sides with 1 recipe of Vicky Zeff's Deluxe White Chocolate Mousse (page 373), orange flavored and well chilled. Sift a coating of unsweetened cocoa over the unfrosted top.

GARNISH:

Press toasted sliced almonds onto the cake sides, covering the full width, not just the lower edge. Refrigerate cake until about 25 minutes before serving; in extremely hot weather, serve directly from the refrigerator.

Feather-Topped Truffle Cake

•

This recipe originated as a dark chocolate fudge cake; it was printed years ago in the *New York Times* and was shared with me by my friend Elizabeth MacDonald, a Connecticut artist, potter, and very fine cook. I have added the white chocolate and the topping design and adapted the procedure for the food processor, which makes it one of the quickest recipes in this book. Once all the ingredients are set out and the pan is prepared, it takes 5½ minutes to get the cake into the oven, 7 minutes if you are doing it for the first time. Be sure to read through the whole recipe before starting.

A flourless chocolate cake studded with bits of white chocolate, it is a cross between a satin-smooth creamed fudge and a softly set mousse. Not too sweet, its strong chocolate flavor has overtones of coffee, though other flavors may be substituted. The surprise is in the title: a glamourous feathered pattern is made with melted white chocolate and baked right onto the cake, eliminating the need for any further decoration or icing. Serve it with Champagne Sabayon Sauce (page 379) or unsweetened whipped cream and fresh raspberries.

☐ ADVANCE PREPARATION: The cake must be made at least 1 day in advance. After chilling in the refrigerator, it can be wrapped airtight and frozen. Thaw in the refrigerator for several hours, then bring to room temperature before serving.

☐ SPECIAL EQUIPMENT: paring knife, small double boiler (can be improvised from 2 pans), food processor, 1½-quart saucepan, 2-cup Pyrex measure, small bowl, rubber spatula; 9-inch round cake pan 1½ inches deep with straight sides, wax paper, scissors, paper decorating cone (page 432); Saran or other strong plastic wrap; roasting pan big enough to hold the 9-inch pan in a water bath

☐ BAKING TIME: 35 to 40 minutes at 350°F (175°C)

☐ QUANTITY: one 9-inch cake (serves 10 to 12)

□ PAN PREPARATION: Grease bottom and sides of pan with solid shortening. Line the bottom of the pan with a round of wax paper or baking parchment cut to fit. Lightly grease the wax paper if used but do not grease baking parchment.

4 ounces white chocolate such as Tobler Narcisse, chopped into ¼-inch dice (110 g)
7 ounces best quality semisweet chocolate, chopped (200 g); Nestle's Pure Chocolate Morsels are fine, as is Callebaut Bittersweet and Poulain Semisweet Chocolate for Baking
½ cup water
2 teaspoons instant espresso coffee powder
1 cup granulated sugar (7 ounces; 200 g)
1 cup unsalted butter (2 sticks; 230 g), at room temperature, cut into ½-inch pieces
4 large eggs, lightly mixed in a small bowl

GARNISH FOR CAKE SIDES (OPTIONAL):

⅔ cup toasted sliced almonds (2 ounces; 60 g)

1. Prepare pan as described. Position a rack in lower third of the oven. Preheat oven to 350°F (175°C).

2. Put half of the chopped white chocolate (2 ounces) in a small double boiler set over low heat. Stir on and off until the chocolate is melted and smooth; do not heat above 110°F, or it may get lumpy (see page 47). Test the heat with an instant-read thermometer if you are unsure, but the easiest thing is to remove pan from heat just as soon as the chocolate starts to melt. Stir it until smooth, then set aside. While the first half is melting, sprinkle remaining chopped white chocolate in the bottom of the prepared baking pan. Set this aside.

3. Put the chopped dark chocolate into the workbowl of a food processor fitted with the steel blade. Process for about 60 seconds, until reduced to a fine, even powder. Turn off the machine.

4. In a saucepan, combine the water, coffee powder, and sugar. Stir, then bring to a boil and cook just until the sugar is completely dissolved. At once pour the syrup into a 2-cup Pyrex liquid measuring cup. With the processor machine running, slowly pour the boiling syrup through the feed tube onto the chocolate. Process for about 10 seconds, or until all the chocolate is melted. Scrape down the workbowl and process for another few seconds to be sure the chocolate is all melted and absolutely smooth.

Leave the machine running and add the small pieces of butter, one at a time. Process for about 2 minutes. Scrape down the workbowl and check to see that all the butter is melted into the perfectly smooth batter. Process for 30 seconds more if needed.

With the machine still running, pour the eggs through the feed tube over the chocolate. Process for 2 or 3 seconds, just to blend. If you have not added coffee to the syrup, add another flavoring now and pulse just to blend.

5. Pour the batter over the bits of white chocolate in the prepared pan. Smooth the top as flat as possible.

Check the melted white chocolate; it should be creamy and smooth; if it has begun to thicken, stir it over a pan of hot water for a few seconds. When ready, put it into the paper decorating cone, fold down the top, and follow the Feathered Chocolate Glaze diagrams (see page 441) to create the topping pattern. Briefly, you draw spiral or parallel lines of white chocolate on the cake top, then you pull the blade of a table knife in alternating directions through the lines. Both the spiral and parallel line patterns are quick and easy to do: they take no more than a minute, less time than to describe it.

6. As soon as the pattern is done, place the baking pan inside a roasting pan big enough to hold it with a little room on all sides. Pour hot water into the larger pan until it reaches about ⅓ of the way up the sides of the cake pan. Carefully set the pans in the lower third of the preheated oven. Note: To avoid the danger of splashing water onto the cake while lifting the pan into the oven, I place the pans in the oven before adding the water. Bake the cake for 35 minutes, or until the top feels barely firm and slightly rubbery to the touch; the cake should not stick to your finger. When the pan edge is tapped, the cake center should remain firm, not rippled as if still liquid. Remove pans from the oven, then lift out the cake pan, set it on a wire rack, and cool for 15 minutes. Run a knife blade between the cake sides and the pan.

7. Top the cake with Saran or other strong plastic wrap, cover it with a wire rack, and invert. Lift off the pan and peel off the paper. Top with another sheet of plastic wrap and a second rack and invert once again. Remove the top rack. Carefully peel off the plastic wrap, leaving the feathered pattern facing up.

Note: Be sure to use Saran or other strong plastic wrap for this and not aluminum foil, which sticks to the cake top and mars the surface. Cool the cake completely, then refrigerate for at least 24 hours before serving. Or wrap in plastic wrap and foil, set on a cardboard cake disk, and freeze. If you want to decorate the sides of the cake before serving, press on toasted sliced almonds.

·Other Flavor Variations:·

Omit the coffee and add one of the following: 3 tablespoons any fruit- or nut-flavored liqueur such as hazelnut; Amaretto plus ½ teaspoon almond extract; Grand Marnier or other orange-flavored liqueur plus ½ teaspoon orange extract; Framboise (raspberry liqueur); or Crème de Menthe plus ½ teaspoon peppermint extract.

. . . .

Chocolate Mousse Cake

∎

With a texture somewhere between pudding and cheesecake and an intense chocolate flavor, this cake makes world-class chocoholics swoon. It is one of the cakes I always mention when asked my favorites from this collection. It stands as a monument to good taste without any adornment at all, but if you wish, you can serve it on a platter napped with Crème Anglaise or Champagne Sabayon Sauce. For a party presentation, pipe rosettes of coffee-flavored whipped cream on top of the cake.

Note: I prefer to serve this cake about 1

hour after it is unmolded from its pan, when the inner core is still slightly warm and soft as pudding. The texture of the cake becomes firm as it chills. Though the cake becomes more dense, it is also excellent made a day or two ahead and refrigerated.

☐ ADVANCE PREPARATION: The cake can be made a day or two in advance, covered, and refrigerated. Or cool the cake thoroughly, wrap airtight, and freeze. Defrost in the refrigerator overnight before serving.

☐ SPECIAL EQUIPMENT: 9-inch springform pan, small saucepan, double boiler, chilled bowl and beater for whipping cream, nut chopper or food processor fitted with metal blade

☐ BAKING TIME: 35 minutes at 325°F (165°C)

☐ CHILLING TIME: If not serving cake warm, chill for at least 3 hours.

☐ QUANTITY: one 9-inch cake (serves 12 to 14)

☐ PAN PREPARATION: Generously spread softened butter on bottom and sides of pan.

CRUST:

1 cup pecans or hazelnuts toasted (see page 43) (5 ounces; 140 g)
1 tablespoon granulated sugar
3 tablespoons lightly salted butter, melted

CAKE:

16 ounces best-quality bittersweet or semisweet chocolate, chopped (454 g)
1 cup heavy cream

6 large eggs, at room temperature
1 teaspoon vanilla extract
¼ teaspoon ground cinnamon
⅓ cup sifted all-purpose flour (1½ ounces; 45 g)
¼ cup granulated sugar (1¾ ounces; 50 g)

SAUCE (OPTIONAL):

Crème Anglaise (page 416) or Champagne Sabayon Sauce (page 379)

GARNISH (OPTIONAL):

Candied coffee beans or miniature chocolate chips
½ cup chilled heavy cream, whipped with 1 teaspoon instant coffee powder and 1 tablespoon sugar

1. Prepare pan as directed. Position rack in center of oven. Preheat oven to 325°F (165°C).

Coarsely grind the toasted nuts with the tablespoon of sugar in a food processor or nut chopper; you need about 1¼ cups ground nuts. Combine nuts with melted butter, then press them into an even, fairly thin layer over the pan bottom and 1½ inches up the sides. Set the pan aside. In hot weather, refrigerate the nut-lined pan.

2. In the top pan of a double boiler set over hot, not boiling, water, combine the chopped chocolate with ½ cup of the cream. Stir on and off until chocolate is melted. Remove pan from the heat, stir to blend thoroughly, and set the chocolate cream aside to cool.

3. In the large bowl of an electric mixer, beat the eggs, vanilla, and cinnamon. Add the flour and sugar and beat on high speed until

pale in color and very foamy. The mixture will increase in volume considerably. With a KitchenAid mixer on speed #8, beat for a full 10 minutes; with other mixers it can take 15 to 18 minutes of beating. Don't cheat, the air beaten in now is essential to the texture of the finished cake.

4. In a chilled bowl with chilled beater, whip remaining ½ cup cream until soft peaks form. Set aside.

5. If the top pan of your double boiler is small, transfer the melted chocolate mixture to a large mixing bowl before beginning this step. Stir about 1 cup of the foamy egg batter into the melted chocolate to lighten it, then fold remaining egg batter into the chocolate in 4 additions. Finally, fold in the whipped cream.

6. Turn the batter into the prepared pan, smooth the top, and bake in the preheated oven for 35 minutes, or until the outer third of the top puffs up somewhat; the center will still be soft and flat. Timing is critical here, so watch for the rising of the outer edge and remove the cake when this is clearly visible.

7. Cool the cake on a wire rack for 20 minutes. Remove the sides of the springform pan but leave the cake on the bottom. Either serve the cake in 1 hour, when the center will still be soft (it will not slice neatly), or chill it for 3 to 4 hours to allow the texture to become firm for neat slicing.

8. Once chilled, you can slide the cake from the pan bottom to a flat platter, using a broad spatula. If you wish, decorate the cold cake with piped-on rosettes of coffee-flavored whipped cream garnished with candied coffee beans or miniature chocolate chips. Serve plain or garnished with a sauce or cream (see introduction).

Chocolate Chestnut Fudge Cake

■

This non-cook confection falls somewhere between candy and cake, being a blend of orange-scented bittersweet chocolate and chestnut purée. The recipe was shared with me by a friend when I was an art student in Paris; we used to make it by melting the chocolate on a hotplate and setting the cake out to chill on our "refrigerator"—a broad stone windowsill.

□ ADVANCE PREPARATION: The cake must be made in advance and chilled overnight to set; it can also be frozen.

□ SPECIAL EQUIPMENT: 8-inch cake pan, bowl and wooden spoon, double boiler, grater, potato ricer (optional) or strainer

□ CHILLING TIME: overnight

□ QUANTITY: one 8-inch cake (serves 4 to 6)

□ PAN PREPARATION: Spread softened unsalted butter on bottom and sides of pan.

1 cup plus 2 tablespoons chopped bittersweet or semisweet chocolate (7 ounces; 200 g)
½ cup canned chestnut purée (Crème de Marrons, sold in gourmet shops and many supermarkets; 120 g)
1 cup unsalted butter (2 sticks; 230 g), softened but not melted
2 teaspoons vanilla extract
Pinch of ground nutmeg
3 tablespoons sifted confectioners' sugar

2 tablespoons Grand Marnier or other
orange liqueur
Grated zest of ½ orange

1. Prepare pan as directed. Melt the chopped chocolate in the top pan of a double boiler over hot, not boiling, water.

2. To soften the chestnut purée, press it through a potato ricer or strainer into a mixing bowl. Cream it together with the softened butter until the mixture is smooth. Beat in remaining ingredients, including the melted chocolate. Stir until well blended.

3. Turn the mixture into the prepared pan and refrigerate overnight to set. Cut thin slices and serve directly from the pan, placing the slices on dishes napped with Champagne Sabayon Sauce or garnished with whipped cream and fresh raspberries. If you prefer to unmold the cake, set it on a towel that has been dampened with very hot water. The hot towel should wrap around the pan sides as well. After a few seconds, top the cake pan with a serving plate, invert, and lift off the pan.

Seven- or Eight-Layer Chocolate Cake

■

This recipe is dedicated to my father, Harold Gold, because it was one of his favorite cakes. I remember, as a child, always counting the layers just to check, feeling triumphant when the number varied, as it often did and still does, from the seven we considered traditional to nine or even twelve, depending upon the whim of the chef. Now the choice is yours.

A variation of the multi-layered Dobostorte (page 279), this cake is a composite of several classic recipes: the génoise sponge cake, a deluxe French egg-yolk buttercream, and a dark chocolate glaze. Their general techniques will be outlined below, but for equipment lists and specific instructions, you are referred to each individual recipe.

☐ ADVANCE PREPARATION: The vanilla génoise sponge cake that forms the layers can be made well in advance and frozen. The Deluxe French Chocolate Buttercream can be made several days in advance, brought back to room temperature and whipped before using. The filled and frosted cake can be wrapped in plastic and stored in the refrigerator for several days, or it can be frozen. It is best made a day or two before serving. Bring to room temperature to serve.

☐ EQUIPMENT: For cake, filling and frosting, and glaze, see individual recipes. In addition, you will need plastic wrap, a serrated knife, an icing spatula, and a cardboard cake board 3⅜ × 9¾ inches; you can cut this from the side of a corrugated cardboard box.

Cover the cardboard with foil. You will also need a wire rack set over a tray. If you plan to pipe a decorative buttercream border on the finished cake, prepare a 16- to 18-inch decorating bag with a #6 star tip.

□ QUANTITY: one strip cake, 9¾ × 3⅜ inches (serves 8 to 10)

CAKE:

1 recipe vanilla-flavored Génoise Sponge Cake (page 211) baked as a sheet in a 10- × 15-inch jelly-roll pan (see instructions, page 214). When cold, trim ⅛-inch crisp edges from the sheet cake, then cut it crosswise into 4 equal sections, each about 9¾ × 3⅜ inches. With a serrated knife, halve each section horizontally to make 8 layers, each ¼ inch thick. Stack the layers between sheets of plastic wrap, then wrap the entire stack to keep it fresh until ready to assemble the cake. If you are planning to freeze the cake, do not cut it up until shortly before assembling.

FILLING AND FROSTING:

Double recipe (4 cups) Deluxe French Chocolate Buttercream (page 391)
Chocolate Water Glaze (page 410) or Fabulous Chocolate Glaze (page 409)

GARNISH:

Chopped pistachio nuts or leftover chocolate buttercream piped in a shell border around bottom edge of cake.

1. Prepare the cake as directed in the recipe. Set out the split layers, wrapped, until ready to fill. Be sure the buttercream has been whipped and is at room temperature, smooth and spreadable.

2. Set one ¼-inch-thick strip of cake on the foil-covered board. Top with a fairly thin layer (³⁄₁₆ inch) of chocolate buttercream and cover with another cake strip. Repeat. Remember not to make the filling layers too thick, because there are a lot of them. Continue building up filling and cake layers until the seventh or eighth cake layer (your choice) is set on top, cut side down. Frost the sides, then the top, with the same buttercream, smoothing it as evenly as possible by holding the icing spatula against the cardboard base as a guide while you pull it across the cake sides. Set the cake on a plate in the refrigerator to chill until the buttercream is firm.

3. While the cake chills, prepare the chocolate glaze. Set the chilled cake on a wire rack placed over a tray to catch drips, and pour a generous amount of warm chocolate glaze over it. Tilt the cake to make the glaze flow evenly; help spread the glaze with the icing spatula. Make the top smooth and let glaze drip down the sides. Sprinkle on chopped pistachio nuts if using them. Set the cake aside for at least 30 minutes, until the glaze hardens. In very hot weather, refrigerate to set the glaze. When the glaze is set, you can pipe a buttercream border if you wish. Or press chopped pistachio nuts around the lower edge of the cake (see technique, page 430).

Anna Teresa Callen's Tiramisú

■

Literally meaning "pick me up," *Tiramisú* is an informal Italian peasant dessert. There are endless regional variations, but basically Tiramisú is made with coffee-and-rum-soaked cake or ladyfingers layered with a creamy blend of eggs and mascarpone cheese, topped with chopped semisweet chocolate and cocoa powder.

Tiramisú has recently been "discovered" by Americans because imported mascarpone cheese is now quite widely available. Not long ago, this dessert was little known except to visitors in the Italian countryside, where every family trattoria assembled its favorite ingredients for the dish. Variations include zabaglione or sweetened whipped cream used instead of mascarpone cream, for example, and leftover pound or sponge cake or panettone instead of *savoiardi* (Italian ladyfingers). Marsala, Triple Sec, Sambuca Romana, Strega, and Amaretto vie with rum and coffee liqueur as flavoring agents.

During a recent trip to Italy, our culinary tour was led by the renowned gourmets and Tiramisú aficionados Walter and Molly Bareiss, our gratefully acknowledged guides and hosts in Venice. While we found our favorite Tiramisú at the Trattoria da Romano on the Venetian island of Burano, the Bareiss claim that the finest version is served at the tiny Venetian trattoria, Vini d'Arturo. To their experienced palates, the particular blend of mascarpone, chocolate, and liqueur-soaked cake layered in a deep bowl and served with a spoon by the mama and papa who run this miniature establishment is perfection itself.

This recipe for Tiramisú was shared with me by my friend Anna Teresa Callen, a vivacious and enthusiastic food writer and culinary instructor based in New York. Anna Teresa specializes in the cuisine of her native Italy, including dishes such as this Tiramisú from her family home in the province of Abruzzo.

Note: Imported mascarpone, a soft, mildly tangy double cream cheese, is available in many gourmet and cheese shops. If you cannot find it for this recipe, Anna Teresa recommends substituting a blend of sieved ricotta (6 ounces) and cream cheese (18 ounces). Alternatively, use sweetened whipped cream, alone or blended with Crème Fraîche (page 416), or Zabaglione (page 378).

For the most authentic Tiramisú cake texture, use imported Italian ladyfingers *(savoiardi)* such as Bisconova, found in Italian food shops; these biscuits are crisper than regular American or French ladyfingers and do not get as soggy when soaked with coffee. If substituting sponge cake or soft ladyfingers, sprinkle or brush on the coffee-rum mixture instead of dipping the cake into the liquid.

□ ADVANCE PREPARATION: If using homemade ladyfingers, prepare them well in advance. Assemble the Tiramisú at least 6 hours, preferably 1 day, before serving, for the flavors to blend.

□ SPECIAL EQUIPMENT: 2 bowls, separate bowl and beater for whipping egg whites, soup bowl, serving platter: large oval or rectangular platter with an edge

□ CHILLING TIME: minimum 6 hours, preferably overnight

□ QUANTITY: serves 12

4 large eggs, separated, at room
* temperature*
6 tablespoons granulated sugar
1½ pounds mascarpone cheese (680 g;
* see note above for substitutions)*
4½ ounces coffee-flavored liqueur (Tia
* Maria or Kahlúa, for example), or*
* Amaretto or Sambuca Romana*
¾ to 1 cup strong espresso coffee
1½ ounces dark rum
36 ladyfingers, preferably Italian
* savoiardi*
2 ounces bittersweet chocolate, coarsely
* chopped*
2 tablespoons sifted unsweetened cocoa

1. In the large bowl of an electric mixer, beat the egg yolks until light and lemon-colored. Gradually add 5 tablespoons of the sugar, while continuing to beat.

In a small bowl, stir together the mascarpone and the coffee-flavored liqueur, blending well. Add this mixture to the yolks and sugar, beating to blend.

2. In a clean bowl with a clean beater, whip the egg whites until fluffy, add remaining 1 tablespoon sugar, and whip until stiff but not dry (see page 247). Fold the whites into the yolk-cheese mixture in several additions. Set the bowl aside.

3. Combine the espresso coffee and the rum in a broad soup bowl set near the serving platter. Dip half of the *savoiardi* quickly into the coffee-rum (do not soak them), then arrange them in a single layer on the platter. Spread half of the mascarpone-egg filling over the ladyfingers. Sprinkle on half the chopped chocolate. Cover with another layer of coffee-rum-dipped ladyfingers and top with re-maining mascarpone-egg filling. Garnish the top with sifted-on cocoa topped with remaining chopped chocolate. Cover with plastic wrap and refrigerate for at least 6 hours before serving. Serve with a spoon; tiramisú does not cut into neat slices. Refrigerate leftovers.

Trifle

■

Trifle is an English classic, as popular today as it was in Queen Victoria's time and probably long before. There are as many recipes for trifle as there are chefs serving it, for it is basically a style, or genre, of "sweet," as the English call it, rather than a specific formula. The idea is to line a deep glass bowl with layers of wine-soaked sponge cake or ladyfingers, fruit preserves, sliced fresh fruit or berries, and vanilla pastry cream. Sometimes macaroon crumbs or toasted almonds are included; the top is always lavishly covered with sweetened whipped cream and a sprinkling of toasted almonds or perhaps grated chocolate.

There is plenty of room in this recipe for creative licence: adjust quantities to the size of your guest list; substitute leftover cake or thin-sliced jelly roll; vary the type of wine or use rum, or omit the alcohol and try coffee or fruit purée or fruit juice on the cake; vary the type of jam or fruit preserves; add an additional layer of wine-sprinkled cake in the middle; and select fresh or canned, drained fruit and/or berries in season. You can also prepare individual trifles in goblets or glass bowls.

□ ADVANCE PREPARATION: In order for the flavors to blend and mellow, it is best to prepare the trifle a day, or at least several hours in advance; cover and refrigerate until ready to serve. Note: The Vanilla Pastry Cream must be made in advance and chilled before adding it to the trifle; allow time for this, or prepare Pastry Cream a day in advance.

□ SPECIAL EQUIPMENT: 2-quart glass bowl or soufflé dish; chilled bowl and beater for whipping cream, pastry bag fitted with #6 star tip (optional); frying pan for toasting sliced almonds

□ CHILLING TIME: see Advance Preparation

□ QUANTITY: Serves 4 to 6 (see introduction if you want to enlarge the recipe)

□ BOWL PREPARATION: none

3 ounces ladyfingers, about 12 (page 354), or sponge cake or génoise (page 211), one 9-inch layer split into thirds ¼ inch thick

About ½ cup Marsala, Muscat, or Sauternes wine or cream sherry

¾ cup finest quality jam or preserves (peach, plum, raspberry, or blackberry, for example)

2 cups sliced fresh strawberries or raspberries, picked over, rinsed, dried, and sprinkled with 1 or 2 tablespoons of granulated sugar; or substitute 2 cups sliced and sugared fresh ripe peaches, pears, bananas, pineapple, or other ripe fruit

1 recipe Vanilla Pastry Cream, 2½ cups (page 370), prepared in advance and chilled

¾ cup coarsely crushed crisp macaroons or Amaretti (12 cookies)

¾ cup chilled heavy cream, whipped with 1 tablespoon granulated sugar and ½ teaspoon vanilla extract or 1 tablespoon brandy or wine

2 tablespoons toasted sliced almonds

1. Line a bowl or soufflé dish with the ladyfingers or cake, arranged in a single layer no more than ¼ inch thick. Cut cake pieces to fit side by side, covering the bottom and sides of the bowl. Sprinkle 5 to 8 tablespoons of the wine on the cake.

2. Spread the cake with a coating of jam. Top the jam with about one third of the prepared fruit.

3. Spread on about half of the pastry cream and top this with half of remaining fruit and half of the Amaretti or macaroon crumbs.

4. Add remaining pastry cream.

5. Top pastry cream with remaining fruit and Amaretti crumbs.

6. Spread all the whipped cream on the top, or put the whipped cream in a pastry bag fitted with a star tip and pipe a decorative pattern on top of the trifle. To garnish, sprinkle on the toasted sliced almonds.

7. Cover the trifle and chill for a minimum of 3 hours before serving.

Jo's Blitz Torte

•

Also known as Meringue Cake Torte, or Blintz Kuchen, this delectable cake is a combination of meringue and butter cake layers baked right on top of each other. I have not been able to confirm this, but I suspect the title comes from the fact that, as quick as lightning, *Blitz* in German, or in a wink, *Blinz,* you will have baked 2 cakes at one time. If the technique is a surprise, the result is even more so—a wonderful blend of tender, fine-grained cake and crisp meringue that is then filled with vanilla pastry cream and fresh fruit. This is the perfect summer party cake because the unusual texture showcases the fruit so well. See the several suggestions for different fillings following the master recipe. I have adapted this recipe from one shared with me by my Vermont friend and expert baker Jo Trodgon Sweatt.

☐ ADVANCE PREPARATION: The cake can be prepared a day or so in advance and wrapped airtight. It is better not to freeze it, because the meringue tends to soften. Refrigerate the filled and iced cake; for best texture, assemble it no more than 3 or 4 hours in advance of serving. Make the Vanilla Pastry Cream several hours in advance, or the day before, and chill it before adding it to the cake.

☐ SPECIAL EQUIPMENT: two 8- or 9-inch layer pans 1½ inches deep, small bowl, sifter, rubber spatula, extra bowl and beater for egg whites; for pastry cream, see recipe. In addition, you will need a paring knife, icing spatula, chilled bowl and beater for whipping cream; 8- or 9-inch cardboard cake disk (optional), serving plate

☐ BAKING TIME: 30 to 35 minutes at 350°F (175°C)

☐ QUANTITY: one 2-layer 8- or 9-inch cake

☐ PAN PREPARATION: Spread solid shortening on the bottom and sides of pans, dust them evenly with flour, tap out excess flour.

BUTTER CAKE BATTER:

1 cup sifted cake flour (3½ ounces; 100 g)
1 teaspoon baking powder
⅛ teaspoon salt
½ cup unsalted butter (1 stick; 110 g), cut up, at room temperature
½ cup granulated sugar (3½ ounces; 100 g)
4 large egg yolks, at room temperature
1 teaspoon vanilla extract
⅓ cup milk

MERINGUE CAKE BATTER:

4 large egg whites
¼ teaspoon cream of tartar
1 cup sifted superfine sugar (7 ounces; 200 g)
1 tablespoon granulated sugar blended with 1 teaspoon ground cinnamon
⅓ cup sliced almonds (1 ounce; 30 g) or chopped pecans

FILLING:

½ recipe (1⅓ cups) Vanilla Pastry Cream (page 370), with the following changes: use ¾ cup milk, 3 egg yolks, a scant ½ teaspoon almond extract along with the vanilla, and stir in ¼ cup sour cream at the end. Prepare and chill in advance.

FRUIT:

2 to 3 cups fresh berries, picked over, hulled, rinsed, and dried quickly on paper towels, or peeled sliced ripe peaches or nectarines. Reserve some fresh fruit for garnishing the top of the cake.

TOPPING (OPTIONAL):

1 cup chilled cream, whipped with 2 tablespoons sugar, or 2 or 3 tablespoons confectioners' sugar sifted on the cake

1. Prepare pans as described. Position rack in center of the oven. Preheat oven to 350°F (175°C).

2. Sift together the flour, baking powder, and salt, and set aside. In a large mixing bowl, cream together the butter and ½ cup granulated sugar until completely blended into a smooth, granular paste. One at a time, beat in the egg yolks, then add the vanilla.

With the mixer on lowest speed, alternately add flour mixture and milk, beating after each addition and beginning and ending with flour.

3. Divide the batter evenly between the prepared pans, smoothing the top with a rubber spatula. Set pans aside.

4. In a clean bowl with clean beaters, whip the egg whites and cream of tartar until fluffy. Gradually add 1 cup superfine sugar, whipping until the whites are nearly stiff but not dry (page 247).

5. Divide the meringue evenly between the cake pans, spreading it gently over the butter cake batter. Sprinkle half of the cinnamon sugar over each meringue layer, then top each with half of the sliced almonds.

6. Bake the layers in the preheated oven for 30 to 35 minutes, or until the meringue top is a darkened ivory color and crisp to the touch on top; inside it will still be soft. The cake will begin to shrink from the sides of the pan. Cool the layers in their pans on a wire rack. Run the blade of a knife between the cake and pan sides to loosen, then top each layer with a plate or rack and invert. Lift off the pans.

7. To assemble the cake: On a cardboard cake disk or a plate protected by strips of wax paper (see page 425), place 1 cake layer, meringue side *down*. Spread the buttercake surface with the chilled pastry cream and top it with berries or sliced fruit. Add the second cake layer, meringue side *up*.

8. If you wish, you can top the cake with whipped cream and garnish it with the reserved fruit. Or simply sift on a light dusting of confectioners' sugar and garnish with fruit. Store the cake in the refrigerator.

Baked Alaska

■

For a sensational dinner party finale, create a little drama with this ice-cream cake covered with glazed meringue and set ablaze with burning brandy. You can't beat fire and ice, and your guests will be impressed. For a children's party, forget the brandy, but bring on the cake; kids love this one.

Home bakers used to be intimidated by this "fancy" cake, worrying that the ice cream would melt in the oven during the browning of the meringue. It can in fact happen that the heat of the oven shelf is transferred to the cake pan, warming the ice cream. There is one trick that ensures against this and guarantees success: simply set the hard-frozen cake on a wooden board before putting it into the oven; the wood insulates the frozen cake from the hot shelf.

Baked Alaska can be molded into any shape: rectangle, round, melon (hemisphere), heart, or pyramid, to suggest a few. For easy serving at a party, I like to fashion a long narrow rectangle that can be cut into neat slices.

☐ ADVANCE PREPARATION: This is entirely a do-ahead dessert. The cake can be baked in advance and frozen; the ice cream is store-bought (unless you wish to make it at home, which is far superior). The assembled cake, minus the meringue, may be frozen a week or two in advance. Ideally, right before serving, you should add the meringue, brown it, and present the cake. However, it is often more convenient to add the meringue and

brown it no more than 4 hours in advance, then put the cake in the freezer until ready to serve. The meringue will soften slightly in the freezer and will lose some volume after several hours.

☐ SPECIAL EQUIPMENT: Rectangular cake cardboard cut to fit cake, about 3½ × 15 inches, covered with foil; aluminum foil, icing spatula, loaf pan about 9 × 5 × 3 inches; paring knife, wooden bread board or plank about 4 × 16 inches, covered with 2 layers of heavy-duty foil; 16- to 18-inch pastry bag fitted with #6 star tip, small ladle, matches

☐ FREEZING TIME: 3 hours minimum to freeze ice cream firm before adding meringue and browning in the oven

☐ BROWNING TIME FOR MERINGUE: 2 to 5 minutes at 450°F (230°C), or just until golden

☐ QUANTITY: Serves 12

CAKE:

1 recipe Vanilla or Chocolate Génoise sheet cake (page 211) baked in jelly-roll pan 10 × 15 inches. For sheet cake procedure, see page 214. When cold, slice the cake lengthwise into 3 equal slices. Cover cake with foil until ready to assemble. Note: You can substitute Ladyfingers (page 354) or any layer or pound cake.

FLAVORING SYRUP OR FRUIT GLAZE:

Cake Soaking Syrup (page 420) of any flavor (use just a little, sprinkled on each layer

for flavor), or any flavor of fruit preserves or seedless jam, warmed to spreading consistency and brushed on cake layers

FILLING:

1½ quarts ice cream, any flavor or blend, or pints of several different flavors. Extras: crushed cookies or chopped nuts or chopped chocolate to stir into softened ice cream if desired

MERINGUE:

1 recipe (4 large egg whites) All-Purpose Meringue, prepared by the Swiss Method (warm egg whites and sugar before whipping)

BRANDY BLAZE:

4 empty half-eggshells, reserved from separating eggs,
2 to 3 teaspoons brandy

1. First prepare the cake. Set the 3 cake strips flat on the counter and brush some flavored syrup or warmed fruit preserves over each one.

Place 1 cake strip, syrup side up, on a foil-covered cardboard strip or heatproof platter. Cover the cake strip with a 1-inch-thick layer of slightly softened ice cream. Top it with another layer of cake and another 1-inch-thick layer of ice cream. Cover with the last cake, syrup side down. At once, wrap the entire cake with plastic wrap and foil and put it in the freezer until frozen absolutely hard. This should be done well in advance; the cake must be solidly frozen before adding the meringue.

Note: If you want to add nuts, crushed cookies, etc., to softened ice cream, blend them together in a bowl, then pack them into foil-lined loaf pans and freeze the ice cream solid. Use a hot knife to cut the ice cream into layers and assemble the cake as described.

2. Preheat oven to 450°F (230°C). Prepare the meringue. Spread a generous ¾-inch coating of meringue all over the hard-frozen cake, sealing the meringue right down onto the foil platform. To decorate the meringue, you can swirl the surface with the tines of a fork or, more dramatically, put remaining or extra meringue in a pastry bag and pipe a latticework or striped design over the cake. Or pipe shell borders on the top and bottom edges (see diagram). Place the cake on the foil-covered board and set it in the preheated oven. Bake for 2 to 5 minutes, watching constantly, just until the meringue is golden brown. Remove cake from the oven.

Serve the cake right away or return it to the freezer for several hours. If frozen, allow about 30 minutes at room temperature, depending upon the weather, for the cake to soften slightly before serving.

3. To blaze the brandy: Just before presenting the cake, press the 4 dry half-eggshells into the meringue on the cake top at even intervals. The shells, which serve as hidden brandy cups, may be concealed in the meringue design.

In order to get the brandy to ignite, it must first be warmed. In a small saucepan or metal ladle, warm several teaspoons of brandy over low heat. Pour about ½ teaspoon of warm brandy into each eggshell and touch it with a match. (Note: Don't use too much burning brandy or the shells may ignite.) Bring the cake to the table while the brandy flames. After the flames go out, remove the shells, cut the cake into 1-inch-thick crosswise slices, and serve. Return leftovers to the freezer.

· ·

Ice-Cream Filled Angel Cake

∎

For this quick-and-easy birthday party dessert, the angel-food cake is hollowed out and filled with ice cream. Let the age of the party-goers determine the sophistication of the filling: you can add to the ice cream brandy-soaked raisins, for example, or liqueur, or chopped nuts, candied chestnuts, crushed cookies or candy, or chopped white or dark chocolate. Frost the cake with softened ice cream or flavored whipped cream.

□ ADVANCE PREPARATION: The cake can be baked ahead and frozen, or in a pinch, a store-bought cake can be substituted. The ice cream is store-bought (best quality) or homemade, as you wish. The assembled cake can be frozen up to a week in advance.

□ SPECIAL EQUIPMENT: Long-bladed serrated knife, grapefruit knife, 10-inch cardboard cake disk covered with foil, spoon and mixing bowl in which to soften ice cream, icing spatula, rubber spatula

□ QUANTITY: serves 12 to 14

CAKE:

Store-bought or homemade Angel-food Cake (page 235) baked in a 10-inch tube pan

FILLING:

2 quarts ice cream (different flavors): chocolate and coffee; vanilla and strawberry, etc. Any additional elements (sliced berries, chopped nuts, etc.) to be mixed with the ice cream; ½ cup heavy cream, whipped, can be folded into the ice cream if you wish.

Or use 2 cups heavy cream, whipped and flavored or any mousse or Bavarian Cream or Zabaglione Cake Filling (see Index) instead of the ice cream.

ICING:

Softened ice cream or Flavored Whipped Cream (page 368)

1. To prepare the cake, follow the diagrams that follow. First, use the serrated knife to slice off a 1-inch layer from the top of the cake (diagram a). Set this aside on wax paper. Then carve a trough in remaining cake (diagram b) by making vertical cuts about 1 inch in from the sides, going to within 1 inch of the bottom. Use a grapefruit knife to scoop the cake out from between the 2 vertical cuts. Make this channel neat. Set the cake on the prepared cake disk.

2. Soften the ice cream by beating it in a bowl until it is of spreading consistency. Add flavoring or other additional elements. Or whip the cream and flavor as desired. Spoon the filling into the channel cut in the cake (diagram b). Spread each flavor of ice cream in a separate layer. Smooth the top. Set the top of the cake back in place. Spread icing of your choice all over the cake.

3. Set the unwrapped cake on a tray and place it in the freezer until the icing is firm. Then wrap with plastic wrap and heavy-duty foil and return to the freezer. Remove the cake from the freezer about 30 minutes before serving in wedges (diagram c).

Note: For a birthday cake, you can write a message on the top with tinted whipped cream or buttercream icing.

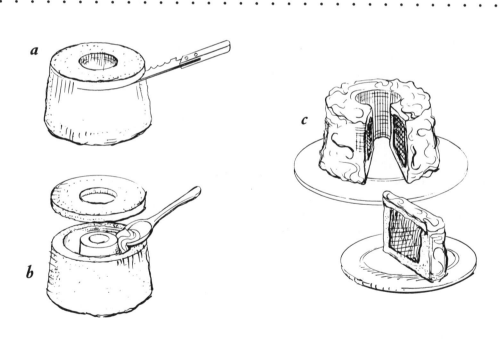

Zuccotto

•

The *zuccotto fiorentino* is a molded dessert whose shape resembles the cupola on the *Duomo,* or cathedral, of Florence. A specialty of this city, the zuccotto filling varies from one chef to the next. Its name derives from its rounded shape: *zuccone* means "gourd," *zucca* refers to a pumpkin-shaped squash, and *zuccotto* means "skullcap."

□ ADVANCE PREPARATION: The pound cake traditionally used as the base can be prepared well ahead and frozen. Slice it just before assembling the cake. The nuts can be toasted and chopped in advance. The vanilla pastry cream should be made in advance and chilled. The assembled *zuccotto* should be refrigerated at least overnight, or up to 2 days before serving. It is not usually frozen, but I have done it without harm for no more than 5 days.

□ SPECIAL EQUIPMENT: 1½-quart hemispherical metal or Pyrex bowl, cheesecloth or plastic wrap, nut chopper or food processor; chilled bowl and beater for whipping cream, 2 mixing bowls, wooden spoon, whisk, knife, rubber spatula, pastry brush

□ CHILLING TIME: minimum overnight, or up to 2 days in advance of serving

□ QUANTITY: Serves 6

CAKE:

1 recipe Best Pound Cake, Praline Variation (page 122)

FLAVORED SYRUP:

3 or 4 tablespoons dark rum
3 tablespoons hazelnut liqueur (optional)
3 tablespoons syrup reserved from candied chestnuts used in filling

FILLING:

About ⅔ cup blanched toasted almonds, coarsely chopped (2½ ounces; 75 g)
About ¾ cup hazelnuts, toasted and skinned (see page 43) and coarsely chopped (3 ounces; 85 g)
4 ounces semisweet chocolate, finely chopped (or use miniature chips; 110 g)
One 10-ounce jar candied chestnuts in syrup, drained, with syrup reserved (see above), chestnuts coarsely chopped
1¾ cups chilled heavy cream
⅔ cup sifted confectioners' sugar (2¼ ounces; 65 g)
2½ tablespoons sifted unsweetened cocoa
½ recipe (1 cup) Vanilla Pastry Cream (page 370), made in advance and chilled
¼ teaspoon almond extract

1. To prepare the mold, line the bowl with several pieces of cheesecloth cut long enough to overlap the edges all around. In a cup, blend the rum, liqueur, and the tablespoons of reserved chestnut syrup.

2. To prepare the cake, cut the loaf into ⅜-inch-thick slices, then halve each slice on

the diagonal, making triangles. Brush a little rum syrup over each slice as you set it into the lined bowl, positioning the triangle points at the center bottom of the bowl and making a star or flower-petal design (said to resemble the divided segments on the rounded top of the cathedral). Line the entire bowl with syrup-brushed triangular slices, cutting small pieces to fit into gaps if needed. Set the bowl aside.

3. In a bowl, combine the nuts, half of the chocolate and all the chestnuts. Set aside.

4. In a chilled bowl with a chilled beater, whip the heavy cream with the sifted confectioners' sugar until soft peaks form. Fold into the cream the nuts, chocolate, and chestnuts. Transfer half of this mixture to another bowl and whisk in the sifted unsweetened cocoa. Set the bowl aside.

5. Whisk the vanilla pastry cream to be sure it is soft, then stir in some of the vanilla whipped cream mixture, whisking it to blend well and lighten the pastry cream. Stir in the almond extract. Finally, fold remaining vanilla whipped cream into the pastry cream, blending the mixture well.

6. To assemble the *zuccotto,* first spoon the chocolate cream mixture into the cake-lined mold. Spread it in an even layer covering all the cake, right out to the edges of the bowl (diagram a).

Into the hollow that is left, pour the vanilla cream mixture, smoothing it flat with a spatula. Cover the top of the cream with slices of cake in any pattern; this will be at the bottom when the cake is unmolded. Fold the cheesecloth flaps onto the cake, then cover the bowl with plastic wrap and foil. Refrigerate overnight, or for up to 2 days.

7. To unmold for serving, remove the wrapping and fold back the cheesecloth flaps. Set a serving plate on the top of the bowl, then invert. Lift off the bowl. Peel off the cheesecloth. Serve the *zuccotto* cut into wedges (diagram b). Store leftovers in the refrigerator. In hot weather, serve it directly from the refrigerator. If you wish, just before serving you can sift a tiny bit of confectioners' sugar over the top of the dome and add a sprig of mint on the top.

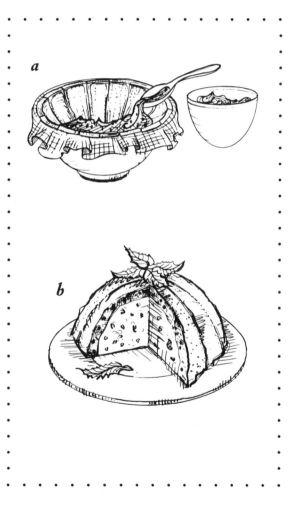

Pumpkin-Pecan Ice-Cream Bombe

∎

This mold of pumpkin pie-flavored ice cream layered with pecan praline crumbs and sponge cake is a showstopper for Thanksgiving or Christmas dinner. The pumpkin pie ice cream is also luscious unadorned, spooned into goblets and accompanied by a crisp pecan cookie or a slice of Carrot Cake (page 103).

☐ A D V A N C E   P R E P A R A T I O N : The génoise sponge cake and the praline powder can be made well in advance and frozen, or the entire bombe can be assembled well in advance and frozen until about 30 minutes before serving time.

☐ S P E C I A L   E Q U I P M E N T : 1½-quart hemispherical bowl (metal or Pyrex is best), plastic wrap, pastry bag fitted with star tip, flat serving plate, foil

☐ Q U A N T I T Y : Serves 8

CAKE:

1 recipe orange-flavored Génoise (page 214), baked in two 8-inch round layers

PECAN TOPPING AND FILLING:

1 recipe Praline Powder (page 444), made with pecans

PUMPKIN PIE ICE CREAM:

1 quart best-quality vanilla ice cream, softened to stirring consistency
1 cup canned unflavored pumpkin (the plain vegetable, not pie filling with cornstarch added)
1 tablespoon granulated sugar
½ teaspoon each of ground cinnamon, nutmeg, and ginger
¼ teaspoon ground cloves
Pinch of salt

ICING:

1 cup heavy cream
2 tablespoons superfine sugar
1 teaspoon vanilla extract, or 2 tablespoons dark rum

GARNISH:

½ cup halved pecans (2 ounces; 60 g)

1. Prepare the génoise, making 2 layers. When cake is cold, slice each layer horizontally into halves (see page 424), making 4 layers each about ½ inch thick. Prepare and set aside the Praline Powder, reserving about ⅓ to ½ cup for topping the completed bombe.

2. In a large mixing bowl, combine the softened ice cream, pumpkin, sugar, and spices. Stir until completely blended; this can be done in an electric mixer on low speed if you wish.

3. Line the round bowl with 1 or 2 large pieces of plastic wrap, allowing the wrap to overhang the bowl edges by about 2 inches. This will facilitate removing the mold.

4. To assemble the mold, cut wedge-shaped sections of the cake and fit them into the bowl with the points in the center of the bottom. Cover the entire bowl surface. Use slivers of cake to fill any gaps if necessary.

Spread a thin layer of softened ice cream mixture over the cake, then sprinkle it liberally with pecan praline powder.

Fill the mold with pumpkin ice cream, top with another layer of praline powder, and cover the top surface with a layer of cake cut to fit the diameter of the bowl. Gently press on the cake to compress the layers.

Pull the overhanging plastic wrap over the top of the cake, then cover with another layer of wrap and a layer of foil. Freeze.

5. Remove cake from the freezer on the morning of the day it will be served. Unwrap the bowl. Top the cake with a plate and invert. Lift off the bowl; peel off the plastic wrap.

6. With a chilled bowl and chilled beater, whip the cream, sugar, and flavoring until nearly stiff. Spread about three quarters of the whipped cream over the surface of the cake. Sprinkle with an even coating of the reserved pecan praline powder. Put remaining cream into a pastry bag fitted with a star tip and pipe a shell border around the base of the mold. Place pecan halves between the shells. Return the bombe to the freezer unwrapped, or lightly wrapped with plastic wrap held away from the cake's surface by a few toothpicks. When the topping is frozen solid, cover it with plastic wrap, then foil. Remove cake from the freezer about 30 minutes before serving; in hot weather serve directly from freezer.

Panforte Di Siena

∎

This nougat candy-cake is a traditional Christmas specialty of Siena, Italy. If it is hard to label, the reason is that there is nothing else quite like the dense fruit- and nut-filled layer scented with honey, spices, and cocoa. The cake is so rich that it is served in very small cubes. In Italy panforte is rarely made at home because it is so widely available in stores, packaged in its characteristic flat, round box wrapped with colorfully printed Florentine paper. If you can't get to Siena for Christmas, try this at home; it is surprisingly easy to make.

☐ ADVANCE PREPARATION: The cake can be made ahead, wrapped airtight, and kept about a month. For longer storage, wrap it well and freeze. Thaw at room temperature before serving.

☐ SPECIAL EQUIPMENT: large saucepan, frying pan, nut chopper or food processor, wax paper, wooden spoon, grater, mixing bowl, baking pan 13½ × 8¾ × 2 inches, sifter, knife, spatula

☐ BAKING TIME: 45 to 50 minutes at 275°F (135°C) plus 5 minutes longer with topping

☐ QUANTITY: 3 pounds (1.3 kg) panforte

☐ PAN PREPARATION: Spread butter on bottom and 1 inch up the sides of pan.

1 cup honey

1 cup granulated sugar (7 ounces; 200 g)

1 cup unsifted all-purpose flour (5 ounces; 140 g)

¼ cup unsweetened cocoa such as Baker's or Droste (¾ ounce; 20 g), unsifted

2 teaspoons ground cinnamon

½ teaspoon ground allspice

¼ teaspoon ground mace

1½ cups toasted (see page 43) and coarsely chopped blanched almonds, (6 ounces; 180 g)

1½ cups unblanched hazelnuts, toasted (see page 43) and chopped coarsely (6 ounces; 180 g)

Grated zest of 1 large orange (2 to 3 tablespoons)

1 pound candied mixed fruits, chopped (454 g)

Confectioners' sugar

1. Prepare pan as described. Position rack in center of oven. Preheat oven to 275°F (135°C).

2. Combine the honey and sugar in a large saucepan and set over medium-low heat. Stir with a wooden spoon for about 10 minutes, or until the sugar melts. Remove pan from heat. Measure the flour, cocoa, cinnamon, allspice, and mace directly into the honey-sugar mixture after it is removed from heat. Immediately stir ingredients together well. Add toasted and chopped nuts, grated orange zest, and chopped candied fruits. Stir hard until mixture is well blended, without any big lumps of fruit.

3. Spoon batter into the buttered pan and spread it evenly. Bake in the preheated oven for 45 to 50 minutes, or until a cake tester inserted in the center comes out clean.

Remove pan from the oven and sift a ⅛-inch-thick layer of confectioners' sugar over the cake top. It should be just thick enough to cover the cake completely. Return pan to the oven and bake for another 5 minutes. Remove from oven and cool on a wire rack.

While the cake is still slightly warm, cut it with a sharp paring knife into ¾-inch squares. To store the cake pieces, wrap them in plastic wrap or foil. When cold, the cake will be quite hard.

Charlottes

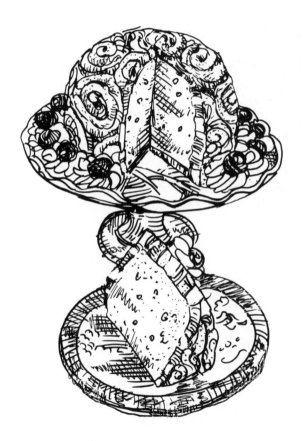

About Charlottes

∎

The charlotte is a molded dessert, assembled in a pan lined with bread, cake, or ladyfingers and filled with fruit, pudding, cream, or a fruit blend.

There are two basic types of charlotte—hot and cold. The oldest type is the fruit charlotte, in which a mold is lined with buttered bread slices and filled with sweetened fruit or fruit purée. This preparation is baked, and served with extra fruit sauce.

The second type of charlotte is unbaked. The simplest form is the peasant charlotte made by layering bread slices dipped into sweetened fruit purée with sliced fruit or berries. However, the most familiar example in the unbaked category is the more elegant Charlotte Russe.

This famous classic was invented in the nineteenth century by the French pastry chef Antonin Carême (see Index). The Charlotte Russe, which Carême also titled *Charlotte à la Parisienne,* is lined with ladyfingers or thin slices of sponge cake and filled with Vanilla Bavarian Cream. Variations on this theme, include Bavarian Cream in many flavors, several of which follow, as well as fillings of mousse, whipped cream, or almond cream and fruit. The charlotte may be prepared a day or two in advance so the Bavarian cream filling has time to set. It is unmolded before serving, and garnished with whipped cream and/or fresh fruit.

When the charlotte is unmolded, its cake casing is completely exposed so it is important to give this casing an attractive appearance. Carême inspired his professional followers to invent elaborate designs cut from the cake

Food historians do not agree about which Charlotte the dish was named for, though they do date its creation in the eighteenth century. According to Jacques Pépin, in La Technique *(Quadrangle, 1976), the fruit charlotte was created to honor Queen Charlotte, wife of England's King George III. However, André Simon, in his* Concise Encyclopaedia of Gastronomy *(1952), claims the dish honors Charlotte Buff, the model for the heroine of Johann Wolfgang von Goethe's popular novel* Die Leiden des Jungen Werthers *(1774).*

pieces lining the mold. For example, he lined the bottom of his *Charlotte à la Parisienne* with dry biscuits cut into diamond shapes to make a double star. Others chefs cut sponge cake into heart shapes, fitting the points together to cover the top of the charlotte, or arranged narrow slices of cake or ladyfingers like the petals of a flower.

The sides of the mold are simply lined with ladyfingers or slices of cake cut to the height of the mold. For a more elaborate presentation, the mold can be lined on the bottom and sides with slices of jam-filled jelly roll. This creates an allover spiral design and is called a *charlotte royale* (page 336). To add flavor, the cake lining the mold may be sprinkled with liqueur or flavored syrup.

Pastry chef Gaston Lenôtre is a master of creative charlottes. One of his pâtisseries in Paris is fortunately just a short distance from the Avenue Foch apartment of Jill and John Guthrie, where my husband and I recently had lunch. Conversation, naturally, turned to cakes, and the fact that the Guthries, having sampled a good number of neighbor Lenôtre's confections, favored above all his *Charlotte Cécile,* our dessert on that sunny fall afternoon. The Cécile is indeed an inspiration: a ring of ladyfingers and a disk of syrup-soaked génoise filled with layers of the richest vanilla Bavarian cream and chocolate mousse. This fantasy is topped with a mountain of chocolate shavings sprinkled with powdered sugar and served with a silken vanilla custard sauce passed in a pitcher.

The cold charlotte is a perfect choice for entertaining, not only because it can be made in advance, but also because you can create any imaginative filling you wish, making the cake as rich as Lenôtre's (see Index for Bavarian cream and mousse recipes) or as light and sugar-free as your conscience dictates. Use any filling set with gelatin and blended with fresh fruit; line the mold with light but flavorful sponge cake or ladyfingers.

The charlotte mold can be the classic French type made of tinned steel in a slightly tapered cylindrical form, or you can use any straight-sided or flared mold of porcelain, Pyrex, metal, or plastic.

. . . .

Chocolate Mint Charlotte

▪

The Chocolate Bavarian Cream filling this charlotte is scented with mint, which cuts its richness. The mold is traditionally lined with ladyfingers, but any thin-sliced sponge or pound cake may be substituted. For an all-chocolate effect, use thin-sliced chocolate sponge cake (page 218). Garnish the top of the charlotte with a sifting of unsweetened cocoa and serve it cold from the refrigerator, adding a dollop of mint-scented whipped cream and a sprig of mint leaves. If you are in a decadent mood, replace the whipped cream with Crème Anglaise or French Sabayon Sauce.

□ ADVANCE PREPARATION: The ladyfingers can be made in advance and frozen, or store-bought ladyfingers may be used, although their taste and texture are not as good as homemade. The assembled charlotte can be made a day in advance of serving; it needs to be chilled for at least 4 hours for the filling to set. The charlotte may also be made in advance, wrapped airtight and frozen; defrost overnight in the refrigerator before serving.

☐ SPECIAL EQUIPMENT: 1½-quart cylindrical French charlotte mold or straight-sided soufflé mold or similar container; 2 small saucepans, scissors, double boiler, strainer or sieve set over a 1-quart bowl, small saucepan, whisk, rubber spatula, chilled bowl and beater for whipping cream, plastic wrap, flat serving plate, sifter

☐ CHILLING TIME: 4 hours

☐ QUANTITY: 8 to 10 servings

☐ MOLD PREPARATION: Cut a round of wax paper to fit the bottom of the mold (see page 61). Spread a thin film of light vegetable oil inside the entire mold, then line the bottom with the paper. Do not oil the paper.

CAKE:

About 24 single homemade ladyfingers, each about 3½ inches long and 1½ inches wide, or 36 single store-bought ladyfingers (1½ packages, each 3 ounces)

CHOCOLATE-MINT BAVARIAN CREAM FILLING (MAKES 3½ CUPS):

6 ounces semisweet chocolate, chopped (180 g)
1 vanilla bean, or 1 teaspoon vanilla extract
2 cups milk
2 teaspoons unflavored gelatin
¼ cup cold water

5 large egg yolks
4 tablespoons granulated sugar
2 tablespoons Crème de Menthe
¼ teaspoon peppermint extract or peppermint oil
½ cup chilled heavy cream

GARNISH:

2 tablespoons unsweetened cocoa powder
½ cup heavy cream, chilled, whipped with 2 tablespoons sifted confectioners' sugar and 2 or 3 drops of peppermint extract, or substitute Crème Anglaise (page 416) or French Sabayon Sauce (page 379)
Fresh mint leaves (optional)

1. To line the mold, cut the ladyfingers into wedges so that when fitted together they make a circle that fits inside the bottom of the paper-lined mold (diagram a). Place the ladyfingers in the mold, rounded side down, so they look attractive when unmolded. Note: If you are making homemade ladyfingers, shape the batter into a disk to fit the diameter of the mold bottom, and use this in place of the petal-shaped wedges.

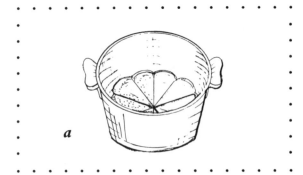

a

Line the mold sides by standing the lady-fingers up on end, side by side, as close as possible to one another. Cut tapers in the ladyfingers if necessary, so they fit the mold. Position these ladyfingers rounded sides out (diagram b). Cut off any ends that protrude beyond the mold top. Reserve scraps to cover top of filled mold.

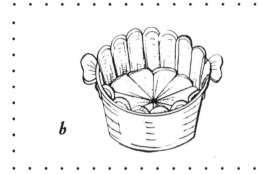

b

2. To make the filling, melt the chopped chocolate in the top pan of a double boiler set over hot, not boiling, water.

While the chocolate melts, prepare a custard sauce: Add the vanilla bean to the milk in a saucepan. If you do not have a vanilla bean, add extract to the finished custard. Heat the milk just until scalding, when small bubbles appear around the sides of the pan; do not boil. Remove the vanilla bean. Set milk aside.

3. Sprinkle the gelatin over the cold water in a small saucepan and set it aside for a few minutes to soften. Then stir over low heat until the gelatin is completely dissolved; do not boil. Set gelatin aside.

4. In a mixing bowl, whisk together the egg yolks and granulated sugar until thick and light. Whisk about half of the hot milk into the yolks, beating constantly so the yolks do not poach, then pour the warmed yolks back into the rest of the hot milk, whisking hard. Heat the milk-yolk mixture over low heat, whisking or stirring constantly with a wooden spoon until the custard thickens enough to coat the back of the spoon. It will not be a very thick custard, but you should be able to draw your finger through the coated spoon and leave a mark that does not close up. Do not boil the custard or it will curdle. Check the gelatin; if it is thickened, stir over low heat until liquefied. Strain the hot custard into a bowl and stir in the dissolved gelatin. Add vanilla extract if using it.

5. Little by little, whisk the melted chocolate into the warm custard, blending completely. Set the chocolate custard aside to cool for a few minutes, then stir in the Crème de Menthe and peppermint extract.

At this point, you can refrigerate the custard for about 1 hour, stirring every few minutes, to chill until it just *begins* to feel thick, mound on the spoon, and look like a soft pudding. To speed this process, you can set the bowl of chocolate custard in a larger bowl containing ice water and stir the custard on and off for about 25 minutes, or just as long as it takes to thicken to the soft pudding stage. If by accident the custard sets too hard, stir it over a pan of hot water just until softened and smooth.

6. Use a chilled bowl and beater to whip the ½ cup heavy cream until soft peaks form. Fold the whipped cream into the chocolate custard. Pour the custard into the lined mold. Top the filling with ladyfingers, and cover the mold with plastic wrap. Refrigerate for at least 4 hours before serving.

7. To unmold the charlotte, remove it from the refrigerator, unwrap it, and top it with a flat serving plate. Invert the mold onto the

c

plate, giving a sharp jerk as you lift the mold straight up; the charlotte will unmold easily onto the plate (diagram c). Peel off the paper if it comes off on top of the charlotte. Sift a very light coating of unsweetened cocoa on top. Whip remaining cream, add the sugar and peppermint extract, and serve in a bowl alongside the charlotte. The whipped cream can also be piped through a pastry bag fitted with a star tube, making shells around the base of the mold. Alternatively, serve the charlotte with Crème Anglaise or French Sabayon Sauce. Garnish it, if you wish, with fresh mint leaves.

Red and White Charlotte

■

I created this recipe for a Valentine's Day party, and I am especially pleased with the result: it is elegant, tastes heavenly, and makes an attractive presentation. The ladyfinger-lined mold encases a rich white chocolate mousse layered with fresh raspberries. Slices of the red and white striped charlotte are served with a tart raspberry sauce.

Note: The recipe calls for a total of 8 cups raspberries (2 quarts), of which 2 cups are for an optional garnish. If you use frozen whole berries you will need only 6 cups because you omit the garnish. Strawberries or other berries (preferably fresh) may be substituted. Vanilla Bavarian Cream (page 335) may be substituted as a filling.

□ ADVANCE PREPARATION: The ladyfingers can be made in advance and frozen, or store-bought ladyfingers may be used, although their taste and texture are not as good as homemade. The assembled charlotte can be made a day in advance of serving; it must be chilled for at least 4 hours for the mousse to set before serving.

□ SPECIAL EQUIPMENT: 2-quart cylindrical French charlotte mold or straight-sided soufflé mold or similar container; double boiler, chopping board and knife, small saucepan, instant read-out spot thermometer (optional); sifter or sieve, medium-size bowl set over a saucepan of warm water, whisk, rubber spatula, food processor or blender, wooden spoon, bowl and beater for whipping egg whites, chilled bowl and beater for whipping cream, medium-size saucepan; plastic wrap, flat serving plate, serving container for sauce

□ CHILLING TIME: 4 hours for filling to set

□ QUANTITY: serves 8 to 10

□ PAN PREPARATION: Cut a round of wax paper to fit the bottom of the mold (see page 61). Spread a thin film of light vegetable oil inside the entire mold, then line the bottom with the paper. Do not oil the paper.

CAKE:

About 24 single homemade ladyfingers (page 354), 3½ inches long and 1½ inches wide, or 36 single store-bought ladyfingers (1½ packages, each 3 ounces)

WHITE CHOCOLATE MOUSSE FILLING (MAKES ABOUT 5 CUPS):

2 cups fresh raspberries, or one 12-ounce package of individually quick-frozen whole berries (These are not packed in juice in a box, but sold frozen in a plastic bag. When frozen, you should be able to feel the separate berries.)
8 ounces white chocolate, chopped (225 grams)
3 teaspoons unflavored gelatin
¼ cup cold water
2 tablespoons heavy cream
4 large eggs, separated, at room temperature
Pinch of salt
¼ cup raspberry liqueur (Framboise)
½ cup heavy cream, chilled

FRESH RASPBERRY COULIS (FRESH RASPBERRY SAUCE):

4 cups fresh raspberries, or thawed frozen berries, drained
⅓ cup sugar, or to taste
¼ cup raspberry liqueur (Framboise), or to taste

GARNISH:

2 cups fresh raspberries, rinsed, stemmed, drained (optional). If using frozen berries, omit the garnish.
Confectioners' sugar

1. Prepare the mold as described. To line the mold, use a thin round of cake or cut ladyfingers into wedges to make a circle fitting the bottom of the paper-lined mold (diagram a, page 330). To line the mold sides, stand the remaining cake slices or ladyfingers on end, side by side, around the mold (diagram b, page 331).

2. To make the filling, first prepare the raspberries. Rinse, stem, and thoroughly drain fresh berries, or thaw and drain frozen berries. Set them aside on paper towels.

3. Chop the white chocolate, and place it in the top pan of a double boiler set over, but not touching, hot water. Stir the chocolate from time to time as it melts. The chocolate must not become hotter than 115°F or it will become grainy; it is best to keep the temperature between 100°F and 110°F. Use a spot thermometer for instant read-out, to keep track as the chocolate starts to melt. As soon as all the chocolate is melted, remove pan from the heat and set it aside. Stir from time to time to keep it smooth.

4. While the chocolate is melting, sprinkle the gelatin over the cold water in a small saucepan. Let it sit for 3 or 4 minutes, until the gelatin swells and softens. Add the 2 tablespoons heavy cream, set the pan over moderate heat, and stir constantly until the gelatin dissolves completely; do not let it boil. Remove from the heat and set aside to cool slightly.

5. Set the bowl containing the egg yolks in another bowl or pan containing water that is hot to the touch, about 120°F. Whisk the yolks with a pinch of salt until they are thick and light-colored; they should be warm to the touch, about 100°F. Be careful not to use boiling water or overheat the yolks, or they will poach. The object here is only to warm the yolks so they will be at the same temperature as the melted chocolate when the two are blended together. When warm, remove the yolks from the water bath, and whisk them very hard for about 1 minute.

6. By this time, the chocolate will have been completely melted, stirred, and set aside to cool slightly. Now stir the melted chocolate again, be sure there are no lumps, and test its temperature. It should be about 100°F on the thermometer, or warm but not hot to the touch, about the same temperature as the whipped yolks.

Whisk the melted white chocolate into the yolks, whisking hard to blend them well. The blend should be smooth and creamy.

7. Whisk in the ¼ cup raspberry liqueur and the melted and cooled gelatin-cream. Whisk the mixture hard. It should be completely smooth.

8. Refrigerate the white chocolate mixture for 15 or 20 minutes, stirring from time to time, until it just *begins* to feel thick, mound on the spoon, and look like soft pudding. Do not allow it to jell completely. If it does set too hard, stir it over a pan of hot water until soft and smooth.

After the white chocolate mixture has begun to chill and thicken, whip the egg whites until stiff but not dry. In a chilled bowl with a chilled beater, whip the ½ cup of cream until soft peaks form.

9. When the white chocolate mixture is ready, fold in the whipped egg whites in several additions, then fold in the whipped cream.

10. To assemble the charlotte: Set out the lined mold, the prepared raspberries, and the white chocolate mixture. Spoon a generous cup of the white chocolate mixture into the lined mold. Smooth it, then add about 1 cup of raspberries. Top this with half of remaining white chocolate mixture, smooth it, and add another layer of raspberries. Finally, add remaining white chocolate.

Top the filling with a layer of cake scraps or ladyfingers. Cover the mold with a piece of plastic wrap and press down gently to compress the layers slightly. Refrigerate the charlotte for a minimum of 4 hours.

11. While the charlotte is chilling, prepare the sauce. In a medium-size saucepan, combine 4 cups fresh or thawed raspberries with sugar to taste and mash the berries slightly with the back of a wooden spoon or a potato masher. Cover the pan, set it over moderate heat, and bring the berries to a boil. Reduce heat, simmer for 3 or 4 minutes, then remove pan from the heat. Taste the berries and add more sugar if needed. If the berries are still whole, purée them in a blender or food processor. Strain the purée if you want to remove the seeds. Stir in the liqueur and chill the sauce until ready to serve the charlotte.

12. To unmold the charlotte, remove it from the refrigerator, unwrap it, and top it with a flat serving plate. Invert the mold onto the plate, giving a sharp jerk as you lift the mold straight up; the charlotte will unmold easily onto the plate. Peel off the paper if it comes off on the top of the charlotte. Sift a very light dusting of confectioners' sugar over the top of the charlotte just before serving.

Garnish the base of the charlotte with fresh raspberries.

To serve the charlotte, nap each individual plate with a couple of tablespoons of raspberry sauce, then carefully set a slice of the charlotte in the center of the sauce. Pass any extra sauce and fresh berries separately.

· *Variation* ·

CHARLOTTE RUSSE

Prepare charlotte above using ladyfingers or sliced chocolate sponge roll (page 227) to line the mold, and fill with Vanilla Bavarian Cream (below) Serve with Fresh Raspberry Sauce.

....

Vanilla Bavarian Cream

∎

This classic Vanilla Bavarian Cream may be served as a dessert by itself or used as a filling to make a molded Charlotte Russe, lined with ladyfingers or sliced chocolate sponge roll.

□ ADVANCE PREPARATION: The Bavarian Cream can be made a day in advance.

□ SPECIAL EQUIPMENT: 1½-quart cylindrical French charlotte mold or straight-sided mold of similar size; 3-quart heavy-bottomed saucepan, wire whisk, large bowl of ice cubes and cold water, double boiler, sieve set over 1½-quart bowl, small saucepan; rubber spatula, chilled bowl and beater for whipping cream, plastic wrap; flat serving plate, sifter

□ CHILLING TIME: 3 hours minimum for filling to set

□ QUANTITY: About 4 cups, 8 to 10 servings; enough to fill a 1½-quart cake-lined charlotte mold.

3 teaspoons unflavored gelatin
¼ cup cold water
2 cups milk
1 vanilla bean, slit lengthwise, or 1½ teaspoons vanilla extract
6 large egg yolks
⅔ cup granulated sugar (4½ ounces; 130 g)
1 teaspoon cornstarch
1 cup chilled heavy cream, whipped

1. Sprinkle the gelatin over the cold water in a small saucepan. Set it aside for 3 to 4 minutes to soften, then stir it constantly over low heat until the gelatin is completely dissolved. Set it aside.

2. Combine the milk and the vanilla bean, if using it, in the 3-quart saucepan and heat until scalding, when little bubbles appear at the edges of the milk. Do not boil. Remove pan from the heat and let stand for 5 minutes for the bean flavor to infuse the milk. Remove the bean. If not using the bean, add the vanilla extract to the finished custard in step 5.

While the milk is heating, combine the egg yolks and ⅔ cup sugar in a large bowl and beat with an electric mixer until the mixture is light and thick and forms a flat ribbon falling back on itself when the beater is lifted. Whip in the cornstarch. Remove bowl from the mixer stand if using one.

3. Pour about 1 cup of the scalded milk into the yolk foam while hand-whisking it vigorously. Return all the warm egg-yolk mixture to the milk in the saucepan and whisk constantly over moderate heat for 7 to 8 minutes,

or until the custard is thick enough to coat a spoon generously. Strain the custard into a bowl. Check the gelatin; if it has begun to thicken, stir it over low heat for a few seconds to be sure it is liquefied and smooth. Stir it into the strained custard and add vanilla extract if using it.

Refrigerate the custard, stirring occasionally, until it begins to thicken, about 30 minutes. Or speed the process by setting the custard pan (metal, not glass) into a large bowl of ice water and stirring on and off for 13 to 14 minutes, or until the custard begins to thicken, mound on the spoon, and resemble a soft pudding. Remove pan from the ice water. Don't let the custard set hard. If this happens by accident, stir it over a pan of hot water for a few seconds until softened and smooth. With a chilled bowl and beater, whip the heavy cream until soft peaks form. Fold the whipped cream into the custard.

4. Pour the cream mixture into the mold. Cover with plastic wrap, and refrigerate for at least 3 hours, or overnight.

....

Strawberry Charlotte Royale

■

While the classic charlotte is lined with ladyfingers or cake, its fancy cousin the royale is lined with jelly-roll slices. The spirals create a decorative pattern in the unmolded dessert. The amount of work needed to make the jelly roll is minimal (it can be done ahead and frozen) and the result is well worth it. In a pinch, however, a store-bought jelly roll can be used, though the flavor and texture will never come close to homemade.

The Charlotte Royale can be filled with any molded filling, but it is particularly good made with a fruit mousse. Be aware that the jelly or preserves in the cake roll should complement the flavor and color of the filling. In summer, make the mousse with whatever berries you have on hand—strawberries, raspberries, blackberries, or blueberries, to name a few. Or you can substitute a purée of any other fruit—passion fruit, mango, cherries, tangerine, kiwi, or cranberries and oranges; see the variations that follow this recipe.

Serve the Strawberry Charlotte Royale garnished with fresh berries or fruit slices and sweetened whipped cream topped with sprigs of mint.

You can also make a Chocolate Royale using slices of Chocolate Jelly Roll filled with any type of preserves, Chocolate Ganache (see Index), or Vanilla Buttercream. Fill the Chocolate Royale with Chocolate Mousse or White Chocolate Mousse (see Index), and serve it with Crème Anglaise as a sauce.

☐ ADVANCE PREPARATION: The jelly roll can be prepared a day or two in advance, wrapped airtight, and refrigerated. Or it can be frozen for up to a week. Thaw it overnight in the refrigerator and slice just before using it.

The assembled charlotte can be made a day in advance of serving; it must be refrigerated for at least 3 hours for the filling to set.

☐ SPECIAL EQUIPMENT: For making the jelly roll, see the recipe. For the charlotte: 1½-quart round-bottomed bowl or hemisphere-shaped mixing bowl, preferably of metal or Pyrex. For the filling: 1½- to 2-quart saucepan, strainer, large mixing bowl filled with ice cubes and cold water; wooden spoon, chilled bowl and beater for whipping cream, rubber spatula, plastic wrap, flat serving plate

□ CHILLING TIME: minimum 3 hours

□ QUANTITY: 10 to 12 slices

□ PAN PREPARATION: Cut a large sheet of plastic wrap and line the mold, pressing the plastic to the mold sides and allowing several inches of plastic to drape over the outer edge all around the mold.

CAKE:

1 Classic Jelly Roll (page 223), spread with preserves that complement the type of fruit in the charlotte filling: strawberry jam for strawberries, orange marmalade for tangerine filling, etc. If you are not sure what type of jam would be best, use all-purpose apricot or currant. For a 1½-quart mold, you will need 16 slices of jelly roll cut approximately ¼ inch thick. A 2-quart mold takes 19 slices. You will have some jelly roll left over if your slices are kept thin.

STRAWBERRY MOUSSE FILLING (3 CUPS):

3 teaspoons unflavored gelatin
¼ cup cold water or fruit juice
½ cup boiling water or fruit juice reserved from straining frozen fruit
1½ tablespoons freshly squeezed lemon juice
2 to 4 tablespoons granulated sugar, or

to taste, depending upon sweetness of fruit
Pinch of salt
1 cup fresh strawberry purée, sieved; or one 10-ounce package frozen strawberries, thawed, drained, and sieved (use fruit and juice to make 1 cup). Or substitute purée of any other berries or fresh fruit.
3 tablespoons fruit-flavored liqueur. For strawberries or raspberries, use Framboise liqueur or Double Crème de Cassis (black-currant liqueur) or Grand Marnier
¾ cup chilled heavy cream

FRESH STRAWBERRY COULIS (FRESH STRAWBERRY SAUCE):

2 cups fresh strawberries, or 1 pint frozen strawberries, thawed
3 to 4 tablespoons granulated sugar
1 tablespoon freshly squeezed lemon juice
2 tablespoons fruit-flavored liqueur, or to taste (same as in filling)

GARNISH:

½ cup chilled heavy cream
1 tablespoon sifted confectioners' sugar
2 tablespoons fruit-flavored liqueur (same as in filling)
2 cups fresh strawberries, rinsed, stemmed, and drained dry

1. Line the mold as described. The extra flaps of plastic wrap will be used to wrap over the bottom of the filled mold.

Use a serrated knife to slice the jelly roll into ¼-inch-thick slices. Position the first spiral slice in the center of the bottom of the bowl. Around this, place the other slices as close to each other as possible without distorting the round shape. Depending on the slope of the bowl sides, you will probably have about 6 slices around the center. Cut wedges from three of the remaining slices to fill in between the curves of cake and cover the entire inner surface of the bowl. Also use scraps of cake to fill in any large gaps between the slices. Reserve 6 slices for covering the filled mold.

2. To make the mousse, sprinkle the gelatin over the cold water in a 1½-quart saucepan. Let it sit for 3 or 4 minutes to soften, then stir in ½ cup of boiling water and stir until the gelatin is completely dissolved. Stir in the lemon juice, 2 tablespoons sugar, the salt, and berry purée. Taste and add more sugar if necessary. Set the pan over low heat and stir well until the sugar is dissolved.

3. Transfer the fruit mixture to a medium-size bowl and stir in the fruit-flavored liqueur. Set the bowl over ice water and stir or whisk on and off for 10 to 15 minutes, until the mixture feels thick, mounds on the spoon, and has about the consistency of soft pudding. Do not allow the mixture to jell hard; as soon as it thickens, remove it from the ice water. The ice speeds this process, but if you are not in a hurry, you can simply leave the mixture in the refrigerator for 45 minutes to 1 hour, stirring it now and then, until it begins to thicken. Note: If the mixture sets too hard, you can soften it by setting it over hot or simmering water and stirring for a few seconds, just to warm it up and relax the gelatin.

4. With a chilled bowl and chilled beater, whip the ¾ cup cream until soft peaks form. Fold the whipped cream into the cooled and thickened berry mixture. Spoon the filling into the lined mold (diagram a) and cover it with more slices of jelly roll. Cover the cake with the ends of the plastic wrap, then cover the entire mold with another piece of plastic wrap and refrigerate it for at least 3 hours, or overnight.

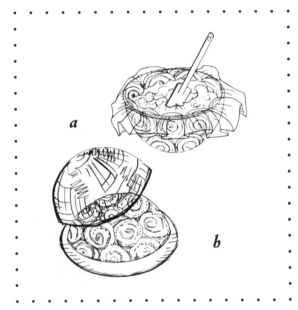

5. To make the sauce, or Fresh Strawberry Coulis, purée the berries in the food processor. Strain out the seeds if desired. Stir in the sugar, lemon juice, and liqueur. Taste and adjust sugar if necessary. Refrigerate until ready to serve.

6. To unmold the charlotte, remove the outer layer of plastic wrap and fold back the flaps of the inner wrapping. Cover the charlotte with a plate and invert. Lift off the mold and peel off the plastic wrap (diagram b). Note: If you wish to get fancy, you can brush

an apricot glaze (page 411) over the top of the unmolded cake, though this is really unnecessary.

For the garnish, whip the ½ cup cream with the confectioners' sugar and the liqueur. Pipe rosettes of cream around the base of the mold and garnish with the fresh berries. Serve the charlotte cut into wedges (diagram c). Pass the fresh berry sauce.

c

For the most elegant presentation, spoon a few tablespoons of berry sauce onto each serving plate, then carefully set down a slice of the charlotte in the center of the sauce. Garnish the slice with several fresh berries and a mint leaf.

·*Variations:*·

Note: Each of the following can be made either as a Royale, lined with sliced jelly roll, or as a plain charlotte, lined with ladyfingers.

FRESH BERRY CHARLOTTE ROYALE:

Prepare Strawberry Charlotte, substituting any other type of berries in season.

PASSION FRUIT OR MANGO CHARLOTTE ROYALE:

Prepare Strawberry Charlotte, substituting 1½ cups thawed frozen passion fruit concentrate for the berry purée in the mousse.

Passion fruit concentrate, frozen or canned, can be obtained at gourmet shops or from some of the sources listed at the end of this book. Fresh mangoes are available in season in supermarkets; be sure the fruit is completely ripe.

TANGERINE CHARLOTTE ROYALE:

Prepare Strawberry Charlotte, substituting 1 can (6 ounces) frozen tangerine juice concentrate mixed with ¾ cup water for the fruit purée in the mousse. Use ⅓ cup sugar, or to taste, and add the grated zest of 2 tangerines or one orange.

CRANBERRY-ORANGE CHARLOTTE ROYALE:

Prepare Strawberry Charlotte, substituting the following cranberry-orange purée for the strawberry purée in the mousse: Rinse and stem 2 cups fresh cranberries. Place them in a saucepan with ½ cup of water, cover, and bring to a boil. Reduce heat and simmer for 3 to 5 minutes, until the berries burst. Put the berries in the blender or a processor fitted with the steel blade and add ⅔ cup sugar. Chop the berries, but do not liquefy them. Add the grated zest of 2 oranges (about 3 tablespoons) plus 2 tablespoons frozen orange-juice concentrate, thawed and undiluted. Blend well. This should give you 1 to 1⅓ cups purée.

Apple Charlotte

■

This is the oldest type of charlotte: an apple compote baked in a mold of buttered bread slices. It resembles a homey apple pie in flavor and looks splendid when unmolded, with crisp golden bread slices arranged in a neat overlapping pattern. It is delicious served at room temperature with Crème Anglaise and Apricot Sauce.

When I first began to make apple charlottes, I experienced several massive failures; I intend to spare you the trouble. I began working with a friend's recipe that required the filling to be "cooked to a thick applesauce." I recalled the apple charlotte served to me by my friend's grandmother, and it was perfectly formed, golden brown, and standing upright as she sliced neat servings. My version collapsed as soon as I lifted the mold, and soft applesauce oozed charmlessly through the splayed bread slices. My second and third attempts were only slight improvements on the first. In another case the sides of the mold held fast but the center caved in. I turned to every cookbook in my considerable collection, and could find no precise description of exactly how thick to cook the fruit to avoid this problem. "Cook until mixture barely falls

from the spoon," "until thick as apple butter," "until a thick, stiff paste," were the most frequent admonishments, with the added warning that the mold would collapse if the fruit were not thick enough. Right. It sure did—time after time, though I increased cooking time and changed techniques. Chef Jacques Pépin's *La Technique* (Quadrangle, New York Times Book Co., 1976) came to my rescue first with the suggestion for cooking the apples in a skillet. The second breakthrough was inspired by *Le Répertoire de La Cuisine,* that indispensable guide to the culinary arts by Louis Saulnier (Barron's Educational Series, 1976), which defined the Charlotte de Pommes as filled with "quarters of apples partly cooked in butter" before baking. This made me think of a compote, rather than an applesauce, and that made all the difference. When apple slices are cooked in butter in a skillet, the large surface exposed to the heat enables them to boil out all their moisture while retaining some of their shape. The end result is a thick, dense compote which has enough body to stand upright in the mold, slice neatly, and have some texture on the tongue, unlike applesauce.

□ ADVANCE PREPARATION: The mold may be lined with buttered bread a little while in advance, but not too long or the bread will become stale; the apple compote may be prepared several hours in advance of assembling the charlotte, though this is not necessary. The charlotte should be cooled for about 60 minutes, minimum, before unmolding, so it sets properly. The sauce and Crème Anglaise may be made on the day they are to be served, or up to 2 days ahead, and refrigerated, covered. Both sauces should be warmed before serving.

□ SPECIAL EQUIPMENT: 2-quart cylindrical French charlotte mold or other straight-sided or flared mold of similar capacity; paring knife, vegetable peeler, cutting board, large mixing bowl, two 10- or 12-inch skillets, wooden spoons, table knife, flat serving plate

□ APPLE COOKING TIME: 30 minutes

□ BAKING TIME: 55 minutes at 400°F (200°C)

□ QUANTITY: serves 8 to 10

□ MOLD PREPARATION: Generously spread a good 2 tablespoons of softened unsalted butter all over the inside of the mold. In very hot weather, store the buttered mold in the refrigerator until ready to add the bread slices. Cut 2 rounds of wax paper to fit the diameter of the top of mold.

BREAD:

One pound loaf of good-quality egg challah or firm white bread, (cut into ¼-inch thick slices about 3½ inches by 2 inches), plus reserved bread scraps

4 to 5 tablespoons unsalted butter, softened but not melted

FILLING:

8 large cooking apples, each about 7 ounces, such as Granny Smith or Greening (about 3½ pounds total), or 10 smaller apples

½ cup dried Zante currants (1¾ ounces; 50 g) or seedless raisins

4 tablespoons freshly squeezed lemon juice

½ cup unsalted butter (1 stick; 110 g) plus 2 tablespoons margarine

½ cup firmly packed dark brown sugar (4½ ounces; 130 g)

Grated zest of 1 lemon

⅓ cup apricot preserves

½ teaspoon ground cinnamon

APRICOT SAUCE:

1 cup Apricot Glaze (page 411), made with 1 cup preserves plus 1 tablespoon granulated sugar and 2 tablespoons apple brandy or rum or orange-flavored liqueur

CUSTARD SAUCE:

1 recipe (2 cups) Crème Anglaise (page 416)

1. Prepare the apple filling first. Peel and core apples and cut into generous ¼-inch-thick slices. Use a ruler to check your measurement; if too thin, they will cook into applesauce, if too thick, they will not soften enough. You will need 10 cups of sliced apples. Put the slices in a large mixing bowl, toss them with the currants, and sprinkle them with the lemon juice to prevent browning before they are cooked.

2. Set 2 skillets on the stove over medium-high heat and melt 4 tablespoons of butter and 1 tablespoon of margarine in each. When melted, add half of the apples slices (5 cups) to each pan. Now you have to pay attention, because you are literally doing two things at once: cooking both pans of apples at the same time. Toss and stir the apples, cooking them uncovered over medium-high heat until they

release their juice and it begins to boil, about 10 minutes.

3. At this point, when the juice is boiling, add 4 tablespoons brown sugar to *each* pan along with half of the grated lemon zest. Stir the mixture in each pan well, to mix the apples with the flavoring.

Keep stirring and tossing the apples. Do not let them scorch or burn on the bottom as the juice begins to evaporate and the mixture starts to dry out.

After 15 to 17 minutes, the apple mixture should hold together in a mass when the skillet is lifted and shaken. At this point most of the liquid is gone, the apple slices are still individually recognizable, and they are fork-tender (diagram a). You should not have apple purée or applesauce. Continue to stir-shake to prevent sticking for a total cooking time of 30 minutes.

4. The apple mixture should now be reduced by half, to a total of 5 cups. Measure the mixture to check. Then combine all the apple mixture in one skillet and set the other skillet aside; it is no longer needed.

Set the skillet containing the apple mixture on the stove. Stir in the apricot preserves and the cinnamon. Simmer the mixture, stirring, for 5 minutes over low heat. It should be thick and not at all liquid, though you should still see individual slices of apple, rather than a purée. Take the pan off the heat, and cool the apples while you line the mold.

5. Preheat oven to 400°F (200°C). Position the rack in the center of the oven. To line the buttered 2-quart mold with bread, cut 8 round-ended wedges each 3 inches long and 2½ inches wide to fit together into a solid petal-shaped disk lining the bottom of the 6-inch diameter charlotte mold.

To line the mold sides, you will need about 13 slices of crustless bread, each 3½ inches by 2 inches. To simplify this, cut the crusts from 6 or 7 slices of 4-inch-square bread, then cut each slice into halves. Spread softened butter on one side of each slice. Arrange the slices standing on their short ends, buttered sides out, overlapping them around the sides of the mold (diagram b). If the slices are too tall, the ends can be trimmed after the mold is filled. Save bread scraps to cover top of the mold.

6. Fill the mold with the apple mixture, mounding it in the center and pressing on it with the back of a spoon to compact it. Spread

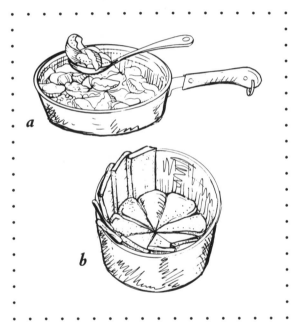

butter on one wax-paper round and set it buttered side down on top of the apples. With the tip of a paring knife, cut off the tips of any bread slices that extend more than ¼ inch above the top of the apple filling.

Set the mold in the preheated oven and

bake for 35 minutes. While the mold is baking, prepare the apricot sauce and the crème anglaise. After 35 minutes, remove mold from the oven, peel off the wax paper round, and again press down the filling with the back of a spoon to compact it. Cover the apple filling with scraps of buttered bread, placed buttered side up. Spread butter on remaining wax paper round and place it, butter down, on the bread. Return mold to the preheated oven to bake for 20 minutes longer. When done, the bread should look golden brown.

7. Remove charlotte from the oven, remove wax paper, and allow the charlotte to cool on a heatproof surface for about 1 hour. When cool, run a knife around the inside of the mold to loosen the bread from the sides. Top the mold with a flat plate, invert, and slowly lift up the mold. If the sides begin to buckle as the mold is lifted, the filling is still too hot; allow it to cool longer. Then lift off the mold completely (diagram c).

Spread warm apricot sauce over the top of the charlotte before serving, and pass the crème anglaise on the side.

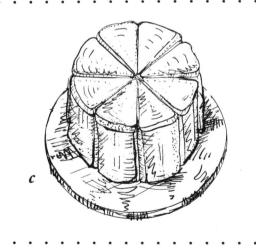

Apricot Charlotte

■

This charlotte is filled with a tart apricot mousse layered with almond slices and halved apricots. When unmolded, it is garnished with sweetened whipped cream and fresh apricot slices.

☐ ADVANCE PREPARATION: The nuts can be toasted well in advance. The charlotte can be made a day or two before serving and left in its pan, covered, in the refrigerator. Or it can be made, unmolded, wrapped airtight, and frozen. Thaw overnight in the refrigerator and bring to room temperature before serving.

☐ SPECIAL EQUIPMENT: 2-quart cylindrical French charlotte mold 4 inches tall and 7 inches in diameter or straight-sided mold of similar size; 2-quart saucepan with lid, strainer and small bowl, small saucepan, paring knife, large bowl containing ice water, wax paper, scissors

☐ CHILLING TIME: 3 hours minimum for filling to set

☐ QUANTITY: serves 8 to 10

☐ PAN PREPARATION: Cut a round of wax paper to fit the bottom of the mold. Spread a film of light vegetable oil inside the entire mold, then line the bottom with paper. Do not oil the paper.

CAKE:

24 single homemade Ladyfingers (page 354), each about 3½ inches long and 1½ inches wide, or 36 single store-bought ladyfingers (1½ packages, each 3 ounces). Or substitute a nut sponge cake (page 286) or Almond Torte (page 267), cut thin.

APRICOT MOUSSE FILLING (MAKES 5 CUPS):

2 or 3 tablespoons apricot liqueur, or peach or orange-flavored liqueur (optional)
8 ounces dried apricots, about 1⅓ packed cups (227 g)
2 cups water
¼ cup cold water
2¾ teaspoons unflavored gelatin
½ cup orange or apricot juice
¾ cup (5¼ ounces; 150 g) granulated sugar, or more to taste
Pinch of salt
Grated zest of 1 orange
2 or 3 tablespoons apricot, peach, or orange-flavored liqueur (optional)
1½ cups heavy cream, chilled
2 tablespoons vanilla extract
6 tablespoons sliced almonds, toasted (see page 43)

GARNISH:

Confectioners' sugar; used only if lining mold with ladyfingers
Apricot Rose (page 458, optional)
½ cup heavy cream, chilled
1 tablespoon granulated sugar
½ teaspoon vanilla extract
1 or 2 fresh apricots, for slices; or canned and drained apricot halves or mandarin orange sections
Apricot Glaze (page 411; use only if lining mold with cake, not ladyfingers)

1. Prepare the mold as described. To line the mold, use a thin round of cake or cut ladyfingers into wedges to make a circle fitting the bottom of the paper-lined mold (diagram a, page 330). To line the mold sides, stand the remaining cake slices or ladyfingers on end, side by side around the mold (diagram b, page 331). Sprinkle apricot or peach liqueur on cake slices in mold.

Note: If soft cake slices tend to fall down from the sides, dab some softened unsalted butter on the mold, then reposition the cake.

2. To make the filling, place the apricots in a 2-quart saucepan, add 2 cups water, and cover. Set over high heat and bring to a boil. Reduce heat and simmer the apricots for 20 minutes. Drain the apricots through a sieve set in a bowl. Reserve the liquid. Also reserve in a small bowl about 20 of the stewed apricot halves to use when layering the charlotte. Put remaining apricots in the food processor fitted with the steel blade, or in a food mill, and purée the fruit. You should have about 1 generous cup of purée. Set this aside.

3. Pour ¼ cup cold water into a medium-size saucepan, then sprinkle on the gelatin. Let it sit for about 3 minutes to soften, then add ½ cup orange or apricot juice, set over low heat, and stir constantly until the gelatin is dissolved. Stir in ¾ cup granulated sugar, a pinch of salt, and the grated orange zest. Continue stirring until all the sugar is dissolved. Remove pan from the heat.

Whisk in the reserved apricot purée and 2 tablespoons apricot or other flavor liqueur if using it. Taste, and add more sugar if needed; the flavor should be quite intense at this point because it will be mellowed later by the addition of whipped cream.

4. Transfer the apricot mixture to a larger bowl and set it into another, still larger bowl of ice water. Stir the apricot mixture until it chills and just begins to thicken. It should mound slightly on a spoon like a soft pudding. Remove it from the ice water; do not let it set hard. If by accident it should set too hard, stir it over a pan of hot water until softened and smooth.

5. With a chilled bowl and chilled beaters, whip 1½ cups heavy cream with 2 tablespoons sugar and 1 teaspoon vanilla until soft peaks form. Fold the whipped cream into the apricot mixture.

6. To assemble the charlotte, set out the lined mold, remaining cake, the toasted almonds, and the apricot mousse.

Spread about 1½ cups of apricot mousse in the lined mold. Smooth it evenly and top with about 2 tablespoons of toasted almond slices. Cover this with a layer of well-drained stewed apricot halves reserved in step 2.

Top the apricots with a layer of ladyfingers or thin-sliced cake, cut into wedges to fit the round shape.

Repeat, adding 1½ cups apricot mousse topped by 2 tablespoons toasted almond slices, more apricot halves, and ladyfingers or cake. Top this with 1½ cups apricot mousse, remaining almonds, and the final layer of ladyfingers or cake, cut to fit the mold. If any ladyfingers or cake slices extend above the top of the mold, cut them off. Press down gently to compress the layers.

7. Cover the top of the mold with plastic wrap and refrigerate for at least 3 hours, or overnight, to set the mousse.

8. To unmold the charlotte, unwrap it and run a thin-bladed knife between the ladyfingers or cake and the pan sides. Cover the top of the mold with a flat plate and, holding both the mold and the plate, invert. Give one sharp downward shake, then lift off the mold. Garnish as follows:

With a lining of ladyfingers, sift a tiny bit of confectioners' sugar over the top, and set an apricot rose in the center. Whip the ½ cup heavy cream with the sugar and vanilla and pipe it through a decorating tube fitted with a star tip, making rosettes around the base of the charlotte. Between the rosettes, you can arrange fresh or canned and drained apricot slices or mandarin orange segments.

With a lining of cake, prepare Apricot Glaze. No more than 2 hours before serving, spread the warm glaze on the top of the unmolded charlotte, letting it drip down the sides. Finish as above, piping rosettes of whipped cream around the base and adding the fruit and the apricot rose if you wish.

Individual Portion Cakes

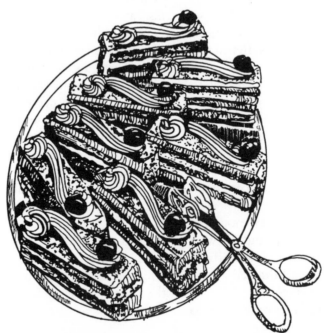

Cupcakes

Like poundcakes, which originally contained 1 pound of each ingredient, cupcakes are so-called because all ingredients were originally measured out by the cup. In fact, the 1896 first edition of Fannie Merritt Farmer's *Boston Cooking-School Cook Book* has a recipe for "Cup Cake" that calls for 1 cup butter, 2 cups sugar, 3 cups flour, and 4 eggs—a variation on the classic 1-2-3-4 Cake recipe (see Index). When the cake was baked in small individual tins, it was also referred to as cupcake, but this nomenclature is a later development. The original name derived from the recipe quantities, not the baking pans.

GENERAL INSTRUCTIONS

Equipment

Cupcakes are baked in muffin pans. Select pans made of the heaviest gauge metal for consistently good results. As a general rule, the pans are prepared for baking by spreading them with solid shortening or spraying them with a nonstick coating; they may also be lined with paper or foil baking cups. The liners guarantee that the cakes will not stick to the pans, thus aiding serving and cleanup, but they also hold moisture in the cupcakes, allowing them to stay fresh longer.

Recipes to use for Cupcakes

Any recipe for layer, butter, pound, or angel cake makes fine cupcakes. Many coffee cakes can also be baked in cupcake pans, as can fruitcakes, nut cakes, and tea cakes. When baking Christmas fruitcakes as individual cupcakes, take care to reduce the baking time or the cupcakes will dry out too much. See Index for recipes. Note: If you are not using paper cupcake liners, prepare the muffin cups in the manner suggested for cake pan preparation— i.e., grease, or grease and flour. There is one notable exception: angel-food cake, which is baked in an ungreased pan. To make angel-food cupcakes, you must grease and flour the muffin pan if not using the paper liner; otherwise, the cupcake will stick. Angel-food cupcakes do not need to be inverted until cold as do large angel cakes.

To Adapt Cake Recipes to Cupcakes

As a basic rule of thumb, remember that a 2-layer 8-inch butter cake yields 3 to 4 cups of batter. A 2¾-inch diameter cupcake contains about ¼ cup batter; therefore, 3 cups batter makes 12 cupcakes and 4 cups batter makes 16 cupcakes. The yield will be slightly greater for smaller cupcake tins. To gauge the yield, note that many of the layer-cake recipes in this book indicate the number of cups of batter made in the notes on quantity.

Baking Procedure

Fill the prepared pans about ⅔ full with batter. To keep the heat in the pan evenly distributed and to avoid burning the surface of the pan, fill any unused cups about half full of water before baking. Oven temperatures for cupcakes follow the temperatures given in the recipes for the cakes; however, reduce the baking times. As a general rule, when the oven is 350°F (175°C) to 375°F (190°C) the cupcakes are baked for about 20 minutes. The timing will vary depending upon the type of batter and size of the cups, so watch closely and test for doneness by looking for a nice rise, a golden color, and a cake tester that comes out clean when poked in the center of a cupcake.

Freezing Cupcakes

Cupcakes may be wrapped airtight and frozen; this is an excellent way to have on hand individual portions of cake for picnics, children's parties, or packaged lunches.

To Ice Cupcakes

Any type of icing may be used. An easy way to ice cupcakes with Boiled or Seven-Minute Icing is simply to hold the cupcake by the bottom and dip it into the soft icing; lift the cup up, invert and twist, making a swirled peak (diagram a).

DECORATIVE CUPCAKE IDEAS

■

Surprise Cupcakes

Tuck a small "surprise" of raisins, nuts, chopped apricots, dates, chocolate, or jam on top of half of the cupcake batter before adding remaining batter and baking it. You will discover the hidden surprise when you bite into the cupcake.

Children's Decorative Cupcakes

For children's school parties, it is fun to make faces or write names on the cupcakes (diagram b). An inverted ice-cream cone makes a clown hat; use the sugar cone, which is narrower than the cake-type cone. Hair can be fashioned of tinted coconut (see Index). Draw features with colored icing pressed from a decorating tube or use melted chocolate in a paper decorating cone (page 432). Alternatively, use raisins or candy to make the features. Make big eyes with wafer candies for the base and cinnamon hots or other small round candies

b

"glued" on top with frosting. Make whiskers and moustaches with shoestring licorice. The project will be most successful and most appreciated if your children help with the decorating.

Flat-bottomed cake-type ice-cream cones can be used as baking containers for cupcake batter. Children love these cupcake-cones. To make them, fill the cones ⅔ full with batter, about 2 generous tablespoons. Place the filled cones on a flat baking sheet and bake for about 25 minutes, or until a cake tester inserted in the center of the cupcake comes out clean. Eat the cake and its container (diagram c).

To make individual birthday cakes, serve each child a decorated cupcake with a birthday candle in the top.

c

Petits Fours

*P*etits fours take their name from *four,* the French word for oven. As these little cakes were originally baked after the main cakes were done but while the oven was still hot, they became known as *petits fours.* They are fancy little finger cakes that go perfectly with chilled Champagne and garden parties. As an art form, the *petit four* is unique, for it must be lovely to look at, appealingly decorated, very tasty, and very delicate.

Many cakes can be used to make *petits fours.* Some bakers favor the firm grain of pound cake, but I find that the best all-purpose recipe is the Génoise, or French Sponge Cake. Chocolate Petits Fours can be made with the Chocolate Sponge Cake (page 218). There are endless possibilities for variation in the flavoring and decorating of *petits fours;* see the index for specific recipes. Following you will find a few suggestions to get you started.

The cake is traditionally baked in a sheet or jelly-roll pan, cut into strips, sliced into 2 or 3 layers, and filled with fruit preserves or buttercream. Then it is cut into shapes: fingers, squares, diamonds, or rounds, for example. If you are working in advance and using preserves as the filling, it is a good idea to arrange the filled layers on a tray and weight them with another tray or cookie sheet topped by a few heavy cans; after being "pressed" for several hours, the layers are well bonded to the filling and do not separate later. This is especially important for 3- or 4-layer *petits fours.* At this stage, bakers sometimes brush warm fruit preserves over the top of the filled layers and cover them with a coating of rolled marzipan (see Index), to give an absolutely smooth surface for the fondant to cling to.

The filled *petits fours* may either be fondant-glazed directly, or first frosted with buttercream icing. Remember to chill frosted or jam-glazed *petits fours* before pouring on the warm fondant.

Fondant is used for several reasons: it seals the cake's surface and keeps it moist and fresh, and it has a beautiful high gloss finish. The best type of fondant to use is Classic Poured Fondant (page 412); this type lasts longest and has a gloss that does not break down. Quick Mock Fondant (page 414) can also be used, though it is slightly less glossy and less durable. For directions on covering *petits fours* with fondant, see the fondant recipe. Very pale colors are traditionally used to tint fondant for these small cakes, and garnishes are best kept simple.

crescents, diamonds, circles (diagram a). Keep the cake covered with plastic wrap so it does not dry out while waiting to be glazed.

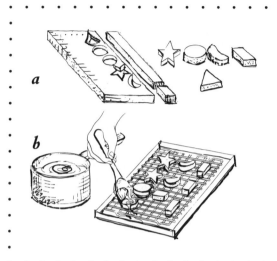

Basic Petits Fours Recipe

■

CAKE:

Génoise Sponge Cake (page 211), baked in a jelly-roll pan. This cake will be about ½ inch thick. You can simply cut it into halves, spread half with warm preserves, and top it with the rest of the cake. Or you can cut the entire sheet into thirds and use a serrated knife to slice each third horizontally into halves, making 6 layers each about ¼ inch thick; fill and stack two, three, or four of these thin layers.

Finally, slice the filled layers into 1½-inch squares or 1- × 3-inch fingers, or use canapé cutters to cut a variety of bite-size shapes:

FILLING:

Any type of fruit preserves, warmed to spreading consistency, or any buttercream icing. Keep in mind that the filling and icing fondant flavors should be compatible, and the fondant color should relate to the taste (yellow for lemon, etc.). Rolled marzipan may also be used as a filling in combination with preserves.

GLAZE:

Classic Poured Fondant (page 412) is the first choice; Quick Mock Fondant (page 414) is also good, though less showy and somewhat less long-lived. Set the chilled *petits fours* on a rack over a tray and spoon on the fondant. Let the fondant dry (diagram b).

Note: Sometimes the fondant does not quite cover the bottom edges of the *petit four;* in this case, let the fondant glaze harden completely, then hold the *petit four* by the top edge and dip the bottom into melted semisweet chocolate. Stand the *petit four* upside down on parchment until the chocolate is hard.

GARNISHES:

See Cake Decorating (page 435) for ideas. However, *petit four* designs should be kept small, in scale with the *petit four* itself. Use chopped nuts (pistachios are traditional) or individual slices of toasted almonds, or model tiny rose buds and leaves from tinted Marzi-

pan (page 446). Form small meringue hearts or finely traced birds by "drawing" with meringue squeezed from a paper decorating cone onto parchment paper; once air-dried, or gently baked in the oven, the meringue shapes are stiff and can be lifted from the paper and set on the cakes. Or draw swirled lines of slightly darker-colored fondant with a paper decorating cone (page 432). For a touch of color, use 1 silver dragee or candied violet, a bit of angelica or candied orange peel, or a dot of melted chocolate. Make Chocolate Lace designs by drawing lacy patterns with melted chocolate squeezed from a paper cone onto parchment paper (see below); when the chocolate sets, it will be stiff enough to lift and set atop a *petit four.*

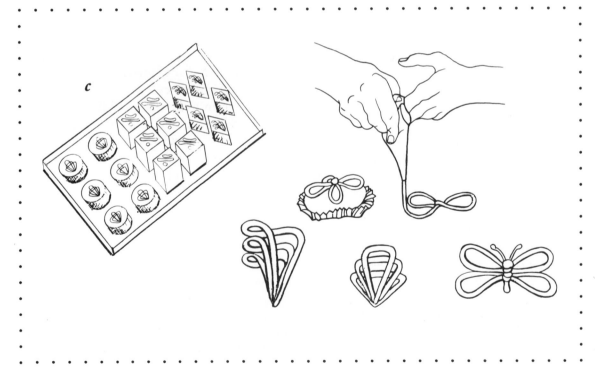

Fluted paper cups for *petits fours* are sold in gourmet and specialty shops. When presenting *petits fours* for a party, set each one in its own paper cup, or arrange a group on a doily.

·Petit Four Suggestions (see Index for specific recipes):·

CHOCOLATE (MASTER TECHNIQUE):

Prepare Vanilla-flavored Génoise or Chocolate Sponge cake baked in a jelly-roll pan. Cut the cake lengthwise into thirds, then use a serrated knife to split each third horizontally, making 6 layers, each ¼ inch thick. Fill and stack groups of 3 or 4 layers, using any chocolate buttercream recipe. Or fill with apricot or raspberry preserves, warmed to spreading consistency. Cut the filled cakes into individual *petit four* shapes. Frost each *petit four* all over with any chocolate buttercream.

To garnish, roll each *petit four* in chocolate shavings (crushed Chocolate Curls, see Index) or chocolate "shots" or "jimmies." Or chill the *petits fours* until the buttercream is hard, then coat them with chocolate fondant and garnish them with 1 small chocolate leaf or designs drawn with vanilla royal icing piped from a paper cone.

CHOCOLATE BOXES:

Prepare Chocolate Petits Fours, Master Technique, but garnish with 4 cutout squares of Plastic Chocolate pressed onto the frosted sides to form a box. Pipe a buttercream or sweetened whipped cream rosette on the top and garnish with a single miniature semisweet chocolate bit or 1 segment of mandarin orange, well dried and brushed with Apricot Glaze.

MOCHA PETITS FOURS:

Prepare Chocolate Petits Fours, Master Technique, but fill with any Mocha Buttercream. Cut individual *petit four* shapes. Frost each *petit four* with Mocha Buttercream and garnish with a candied coffee bean. Or chill the buttercream-frosted *petits fours,* then coat them with coffee-flavored Fondant garnished with crisscrossed lines drawn with melted dark chocolate piped from a paper cone.

CHESTNUT PETITS FOURS:

Prepare Vanilla-flavored Génoise baked in a jelly-roll pan, and cut the cake as for Chocolate Petits Fours, Master Technique. Brush each cake layer with Chestnut-Rum Cake Soaking Syrup (page 420). Fill with Chestnut Buttercream, stacking the cake in groups of 3 layers each. Cut individual *petit four* shapes. Frost each *petit four* with Chestnut Buttercream. Chill, then top with Fabulous Chocolate Glaze or Chocolate Water Glaze. Garnish with a small marzipan flower and leaf or a zigzag of lines drawn with rum-flavored Royal Icing piped from a paper cone.

LEMON PETITS FOURS:

Prepare Lemon-flavored Génoise baked in a jelly-roll pan and cut as for Chocolate Petits Fours, Master Technique. Brush each cake layer with Triple Sec or orange-flavored Cake Soaking Syrup and fill with Lemon Curd. Cut individual *petit four* shapes. Frost with Lemon Buttercream Ménagère (page 393). Chill, then glaze with pale yellow Fondant. Garnish with a chip of candied lemon peel or a swirl of dark yellow fondant accented with 1 silver dragee.

ORANGE PETITS FOURS:

Prepare Orange-flavored Génoise baked in a jelly-roll pan and cut as for Chocolate Petits Fours, Master Technique. Brush each cake layer with Orange Cake Soaking Syrup (page 420), and fill with any Orange Buttercream or Orange-Chocolate Buttercream. Cut shapes and frost with Orange Buttercream. Chill, then glaze with pale orange Fondant and garnish with candied orange peel or grated orange zest. If using orange-chocolate filling, top with a piece of Chocolate Lace (page 352).

ZABAGLIONE PETITS FOURS:

Prepare Vanilla-flavored Génoise baked in a jelly-roll pan and cut as for Chocolate Petits Fours, Master Technique. Brush each cake layer with Marsala wine or dark rum and fill with Zabaglione Cake Filling. Chill to set filling, then coat with rum-flavored vanilla Fondant and top with a candied violet.

Ladyfingers

■

Ladyfingers are delicate finger-shaped sponge biscuits. When properly made they have a light eggy flavor, a slightly soft interior with a tender, spongy crumb, and a crisp outside crust that results from a dusting of sugar just before they are baked. Homemade ladyfingers bear little resemblance to the soft, cottony product sold in the supermarket under the same name. They are easy to prepare once you know the tricks, and there are a few; when you have mastered the art, you will find it a breeze to whip them up to line a charlotte mold or Baked Alaska, or just to serve plain alongside fresh berries and cream.

In the French pastry repertoire, ladyfingers fall into the family of *petits gâteaux secs* (little dry cakes, literally); they are known as *biscuits à la cuiller*, or "spoon cookies," because until the beginning of the nineteenth century when the pastry bag was invented, they were formed by dropping the batter from a spoon.

The basic technique for this classic recipe is the same as that used for making sponge cakes. Egg yolks and sugar are ribboned together with flavoring, while the egg whites are stiffly beaten in a separate bowl. Finally, some of the whites are folded into the yolks, then remaining whites are alternately folded in along with the sifted flour. This last step is the critical stage, folding must be gentle and light to maintain full volume, and you must stop while there are still powdery streaks of flour visible. If you fold until flour is completely blended in, the batter will be overworked and will deflate when the fingers are shaped. The ladyfingers then spread and flatten in the oven.

□ ADVANCE PREPARATION: Ladyfingers can be baked ahead, wrapped airtight, and kept at room temperature for a week, or they can be frozen.

□ SPECIAL EQUIPMENT: 2 or 3 flat cookie sheets, 16- to 18-inch-long pastry tube fitted with ½-inch, #6 plain tip, regular-size strainer or sieve and small (2½- or 3-inch diameter) strainer; separate bowl and beater for whipping egg whites, rubber spatula, 4-cup Pyrex liquid measuring cup or jar of similar size

□ BAKING TIME: about 15 minutes at 300°F (150°C)

□ QUANTITY: 24 to 30 ladyfingers, 1½ × 4 inches; enough to line a 2-quart French charlotte mold, or any mold of equivalent size.

Double the recipe to line the top and bottom of the mold with disks made of ladyfinger batter, and also to line sides with regular ladyfingers.

□ PAN PREPARATION: Spread pans with butter, not solid shortening, then dust with flour; tap out excess flour. Alternatively, you can dab a little butter in the corners of the pans, then line them with baking parchment. Spread butter on the parchment, then dust with flour; tap out excess. The butter "glues" the paper onto the sheets.

⅔ cup sifted cake flour (2½ ounces; 70 g)
3 large eggs, separated, at room temperature
½ cup (3½ ounces; 100 g) plus 1 tablespoon sifted superfine sugar
1 teaspoon vanilla extract
Pinch of salt
Confectioners' sugar

1. Prepare pans as described. Put together the pastry tube and tip and set it nearby. Position racks so the oven is divided into thirds. Preheat oven to 300°F (150°C).

2. Sift the flour, then return it to the sifter and gently set it down in a small bowl. Set this aside until needed. The flour will later be sifted directly onto the batter.

3. In the large bowl of an electric mixer, beat the egg yolks with ½ cup of the superfine sugar and the vanilla until the mixture is thick and light-colored, and forms a flat ribbon falling back upon itself when the beater is lifted. This takes 2 to 3 minutes in the KitchenAid mixer on speed #8, or 6 to 7 minutes with other mixers. Once or twice, stop the machine and scrape down the beater and the inside of the bowl.

4. With a clean bowl and beater, whip the egg whites with a pinch of salt until foamy. Add remaining 1 tablespoon superfine sugar and whip until the whites are nearly stiff but not dry. It is important to catch this stage; the whites should look shiny, and you should be able to invert the bowl without causing the mass of whipped whites to slide.

5. Using a rubber spatula, scoop about one quarter of the whites into the yolk mixture and fold them lightly together. Streaks of the whites should remain visible.

Sift about one quarter of the flour over the whipped batter, fold the mixture once or twice, then add another quarter of the whites and fold gently. Repeat, alternately sifting on the flour, adding some of the whites, and folding them very lightly into the batter. Use all remaining flour and whipped whites.

To fold correctly (see page 65), use one hand to move the rubber spatula in a gentle motion, cutting down through the center of the batter, then up and over the top; with the other hand, give the bowl one quarter turn. Repeat. Leave some powdery flour streaks showing. Do not blend thoroughly. Do not mix or stir.

6. Set out a 4-cup measure or jar as a holder for the pastry bag while you fill it. Fold down a generous 4- or 5-inch cuff, then press the side of the narrow end of the bag into the base of the metal tip (diagram a) so the batter does not run out when the bag is filled.

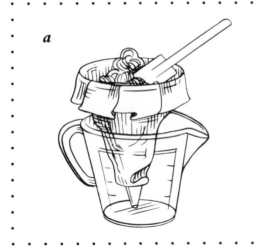

a

Add about one third of the batter. Lift up the bag cuff, twist it closed just above the batter, and pipe out neat single-line fingers about 3 to 3½ inches long and 1 inch apart on the prepared sheets. The batter should not spread and flatten, but rather should stay in place and remain slightly rounded after piping. If it flattens and runs, you have over-folded and deflated the whites; you can still

bake the fingers but their shape will be flatter and wider than otherwise.

7. Put a couple of tablespoons of confectioners' sugar into the smallest sifter and sift an even dusting of sugar over the top of each ladyfinger on the cookie sheet (diagram b).

Then hold the cookie sheet on a slant, or invert it over the sink, and give it a tap to shake off excess sugar. The batter will not run if it has the correct consistency.

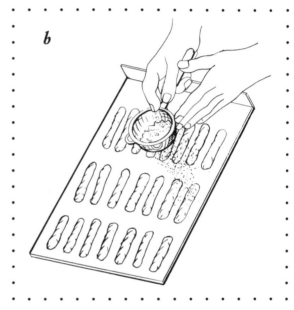

b

8. Set the ladyfingers in the preheated oven and bake for about 15 minutes, or until they are a pale golden color around the edges; the tops will have a slightly crackled appearance, dotted with some of the sugar. Let the ladyfingers cool for 2 or 3 minutes, not longer or they start to stick, then lift them with a spatula and cool them on a wire rack. If baking them on parchment, you can cool the ladyfingers on the sheets, then peel off the parchment backing.

Babas Au Rhum

•

These individual cakes, or *babas,* are made from a light, spongy yeast dough soaked with orange-rum syrup. Babas are decorative, individual-portion desserts, glazed with apricot preserves and garnished with candied fruits or topped with fresh berries and rum-flavored whipped cream.

☐ ADVANCE PREPARATION: This batter must rise twice, for a total of about 2¾ hours, and the baked cakes must be soaked in syrup for at least half an hour, so plan your time accordingly. Note: Quick-rising yeast may be used to save time; follow directions for procedure on the yeast package.

The baked and cooled babas may be wrapped airtight and refrigerated for a week, or frozen. To thaw and warm them, place the frozen babas on a baking sheet in a preheated 300°F oven for about 5 minutes; they should be warm through before soaking them with warm syrup.

Once the cakes are soaked in syrup they keep well in the refrigerator and may be prepared a day before serving.

☐ SPECIAL EQUIPMENT: 2 large and 1 small mixing bowls, 2 saucepans, wooden spoon, paddle or dough hook for electric

It is a curious footnote to culinary history that this French specialty was probably invented by the Polish King Stanislas Leszczynski (Stanislas I). Whether this was a true invention, or simply a rum-soaked variation on a traditional Polish kugelhopf, no one disputes the fact that King Stanislas named the cakes after Ali Baba, a character in his favorite book, The Thousand and One Nights. *In 1736, Stanislas abdicated the Polish throne and settled in France, at Lunéville. During this period, it is believed that a pastry cook named Sthorer discovered the raisin-studded, rum-soaked baba, found it worthy, and introduced it in his Parisian pastry shop. In the early nineteenth century, a raisinless, ring-shaped variation was created by another Parisian chef named Julien, who flavored his soaking syrup with kirsch and named his version of the cake after the brilliant historian of good food and good living, Jean-Anthelme Brillat-Savarin. Today, it is known to us as a Savarin (see Index). This is one more proof that, as Julia Child says, most recipes are "research and development" rather than original creations.*

mixer (optional), grater, wax paper, baba molds about 2 inches in diameter and 2 inches deep, or popover or muffin tins 2 or 3 inches in diameter; large flat plate or pan with at least a 1-inch-deep edge, strainer, plastic wrap, soup spoon or bulb baster, pastry brush (optional), paring knife, toothpick or skewer

☐ RISING TIME: about 2¾ hours

☐ BAKING TIME: 10 to 15 minutes at 400°F (205°C)

☐ SYRUP SOAKING TIME: minimum 30 minutes

☐ QUANTITY: 9 babas, 3 inches in diameter, or 20 babas, 2 inches in diameter

☐ PAN PREPARATION: Spread margarine or butter in the molds.

DOUGH:

¼ cup warm water (105° to 110°F)
¼ cup granulated sugar (1¾ ounces; 50 g)
1 envelope active dry yeast (¼ ounce; 7 g)
¼ cup milk
4 tablespoons unsalted butter or margarine (½ stick; 60 g), cut up
1 whole large egg plus 2 large yolks
1 whole orange, zest grated and orange reserved for syrup
⅛ teaspoon salt
1¾ cups sifted all-purpose flour (7½ ounces; 110 g)

SYRUP (3¼ CUPS):

1½ cups water
1½ cups granulated sugar (10½ ounces; 300 g)

2 thick slices of lemon
Reserved orange, cut crosswise into three ¼-inch-thick slices, pits removed
1 cinnamon stick, 2 or 3 inches long
3 or 4 whole cloves
½ cup dark rum

GLAZE:

1 cup Apricot Glaze (page 411)
⅛ cup dark rum

GARNISHES (OPTIONAL):

Almond slices, julienne orange zest, glacéed cherries, fresh berries, sweetened rum-flavored whipped cream

1. Measure the warm water into a small bowl. Add 1 teaspoon of the sugar and sprinkle on the package of yeast. Stir the mixture and set it aside for about 5 minutes, until it becomes bubbly.

2. Scald the milk in a saucepan set over moderate heat. Remove pan from heat, add butter, and stir until the butter melts. Set aside to cool.

3. In the large bowl of an electric mixer, beat the whole egg plus extra yolks for about 1 minute, until light in color. Gradually add remaining sugar and beat well for about 30 seconds. Stir in the cooled milk mixture, then the grated orange zest and salt. Beat again. Test the temperature of the batter; it should be lukewarm, not hot. Add the yeast mixture and beat just to mix. With the mixer on lowest speed, gradually add the flour. Scrape down inside of bowl and the beaters.

If your mixer has a dough hook or flat paddle, attach one of these. Beat the batter slowly for 4 to 5 minutes longer; this is really a kneading process. With the KitchenAid mixer, use speed #2 for 5 minutes.

Instead of using the mixer, you can slap the dough mass back and forth inside the bowl until it begins to hold its shape and become less sticky; add a tiny bit more flour if needed; work the dough on a very lightly floured countertop until you can pick it up in one mass and twist and stretch it about 12 inches without its falling apart. This takes 6 or 7 minutes by hand. Remember that the dough should always stay soft and spongy, never firm as a bread dough.

4. Grease a large clean bowl with a little butter or margarine. Scrape all the dough from the mixer into the bowl, cover with a buttered piece of wax paper, and place in a warm, draft-free location (the oven with heat off and a pan of hot water set on the oven floor, for example) until batter has doubled in bulk, about 1½ hours. Watch the dough, not the clock; the rising time depends on the temperature surrounding the dough.

5. While the batter is rising, prepare the pans as described and set them aside. When the dough has risen, remove it from the oven if that was its rising location. Position the rack in the center of the oven. Preheat oven to 400°F (205°C).

Stir down the dough to remove excess gas bubbles (it will be too sticky to punch down as you would a bread dough).

6. Spoon the batter into the greased molds, filling them about ⅔ full. Cover them with a sheet of buttered wax paper and set the tray(s) in a warm, draft-free location (not the hot oven) until the batter rises almost to the rim of the cups. This can take an hour or longer. Add a few spoons of water to any empty muffin cups so the heat will be even and the tray will not burn. Set the babas to bake in the center of the preheated oven for 10 to 15 minutes, or until they are golden on top and a cake tester inserted in the center of a cake comes out clean. While the babas bake, prepare the syrup.

7. Combine all syrup ingredients except the rum and simmer in a saucepan over moderate heat for about 10 minutes. Set a strainer over a bowl in the sink. Drain the syrup through the strainer, pressing the fruit slices with the back of a spoon. Discard the solids left in the strainer.

Note: The syrup may be prepared ahead up to this point and refrigerated in a covered jar for a few days.

When ready to use the syrup, warm it well, then stir in the rum.

8. When baked, cool the babas in their pans for about 5 minutes. Use the tip of a knife or a fork to pry them gently out of their molds.

Prick the top of each baba with a toothpick or skewer. Then set them upside down in a shallow flat dish or pan with an edge at least 1 inch deep. The bottoms of the babas are more porous than the tops, and will more easily absorb the syrup. For this to work properly, the babas should still be warm (not hot) from the oven, and the syrup should be warm as well. If the babas are cold, or were frozen, warm them through completely in a preheated 300°F oven for about 5 minutes before soaking with syrup. Spoon the warm syrup over the warm babas, or baste them with a bulb baster. Repeat on and off for about 30 minutes, until the cakes are well soaked.

The babas should absorb nearly all the

syrup, like a swollen sponge, but they should hold their shape.

Cover the soaked babas with plastic wrap, and leave at room temperature or refrigerated until an hour or two before serving. Drain the babas on a rack.

9. Glaze and garnish babas: Sprinkle each one with a few drops of dark rum, then brush the top of each baba with apricot glaze, warmed in a saucepan to spreading consistency.

If you wish, garnish the top with an almond slice, a curl of orange zest, or half a glacéed cherry. Serve on a plate, or in a fluted paper cup set on a plate. If you wish, pass excess syrup in a pitcher.

As a variation, you can macerate several cups of fresh berries in rum or the baba syrup, then serve them alongside the babas, garnished with a little sweetened rum-flavored whipped cream.

Old-Fashioned Country Shortcake

∎

Shortcake is an all-American classic with many regional variations. New Englanders, myself included, favor unsweetened baking powder biscuits, while Southerners prefer sweet biscuits made with heavy cream. A plain eggy spongecake is sometimes served as the base, as is angel-food cake, Scotch shortbread, or even a flaky piecrust. But in my opinion, anything other than a rough, lumpy biscuit is

an imposter, a City Shortcake, rather than the Real Thing, which has just the right texture to absorb the tart berry juices and balance the rich taste of the sweetened whipped cream.

Note: This recipe is for old-fashioned unsweetened baking powder biscuits; add sugar if you wish. You may bake the cake in 2 thin layers, in which case each layer will have a rather crisp top, or in 1 medium-thick layer, in which case you will split the baked cake, resulting in 2 softer, more porous surfaces upon which to pile the berries and cream. Or you may make 12 individual biscuits, which are split before being filled with berries and cream.

☐ ADVANCE PREPARATION: The shortcake can be baked in advance; wrapped airtight, and frozen. Or it can be made a day in advance, wrapped airtight, and stored at room temperature. To avoid soggy cake, do not assemble until just before serving.

☐ SPECIAL EQUIPMENT: sifter, 8-inch round cake pan 2 inches deep or two 8-inch pans 1½ inches deep, or a cookie sheet (for individual biscuits); chilled bowl and whisk or beaters for whipping cream, bowl for berries

☐ BAKING TIME: 12 to 15 minutes at 450°F (232°C)

☐ QUANTITY: one 2-layer 8-inch cake (serves 8), or 12 individual biscuits

☐ PAN PREPARATION: Spread baking pan(s) with solid shortening or butter.

CAKE:

2 cups sifted all-purpose flour (8½ ounces; 240 g)
1 tablespoon baking powder

¾ teaspoon salt
2 tablespoons granulated sugar
  (optional)
¼ cup unsalted butter (½ stick; 60 g),
  at room temperature, cut up
¾ cup milk or heavy cream

FRUIT:

1 quart fresh ripe strawberries,
  washed, gently patted dry or drained
  on paper towels, and hulled (or
  substitute any other type of berries)
½ to ¾ cup granulated sugar (3½
  ounces; 100 g), or to taste

TOPPING:

Butter, optional
1 cup heavy cream, chilled
2 tablespoons sifted confectioners' sugar
1 teaspoon vanilla extract

1. Prepare pan as directed. Position rack in center of oven and preheat oven to 450°F (232°C).

2. Sift flour, baking powder, salt (and sugar if using it) into a large mixing bowl. Cut in the butter until the mixture resembles coarse meal. Lightly stir in the milk or cream until dough is just blended and clumps together.

3. To make individual shortcakes, drop 10 to 12 three-inch rounds of batter from a spoon onto the greased cookie sheet.

If you are making 2 cake layers, divide the dough equally between 2 prepared cake pans. Smooth the top more or less flat with the back of the spoon. Or spoon all the dough into a slightly deeper cake pan to make a single cake that will be split horizontally after baking.

4. Bake the cake(s) in the center of the preheated oven for 12 to 15 minutes, or until golden brown; the thicker cake may take a minute or two longer, and is done when a cake tester inserted in the center comes out clean. Cool the pan on a wire rack for a minute or two, then remove the cake(s) and cool on a rack. If splitting the single biscuit cake layer, wait until it is cold, then use a serrated knife to slice it horizontally with a sawing motion. If making individual biscuits, "saw" them into halves while still warm and spread them with butter if you wish.

5. To make the filling, select about 12 perfect whole berries and set them aside. Slice remaining berries and stir them together in a bowl with ½ to ¾ cup sugar. Set the bowl aside.

6. Assemble the shortcakes shortly before serving time to prevent the biscuits from becoming soggy. Gather all the ingredients. Then, in a chilled bowl with chilled beater, whip the cream with the confectioners' sugar and vanilla until soft peaks form.

To assemble the individual shortcakes, set 1 biscuit half, cut side up, on a plate, top with some whipped cream and sliced berries, then add the second half, cut side down. Top with more whipped cream and garnish with a few choice whole berries.

To assemble a single large cake, place 1 shortcake or 1 layer, cut side up, on a serving plate. Top it with about half of the whipped cream and half of the sugared, sliced berries. Cover with the second shortcake or layer, cut side down, and top with remaining sliced berries. Spoon on remaining cream and garnish with the reserved whole berries.

Charley's Lemon Squares

■

Susan "Charley" Kanas and I have been friends for thirty years and I still cannot believe my good fortune. To share her friendship and also her recipe for Lemon Squares is almost too much to ask. An artist living in Paris, Charley bakes these delicacies for us whenever we visit, which is never often enough. Having the recipe helps.

Tart lemon custard covers a marzipan-coated shortbread to make a perfect blend of crisp and creamy, sweet and sour.

☐ ADVANCE PREPARATION: The squares can be baked in advance and stored in a covered container.

☐ SPECIAL EQUIPMENT: 8-inch-square baking pan 2 inches deep; grater, lemon squeezer, sifter, rolling pin

☐ BAKING TIME: 20 minutes at 350°F (175°C) for cake layer alone, then 25 minutes longer with topping added

☐ QUANTITY: 16 squares

☐ PAN PREPARATION: None; do not grease the pan.

1 cup sifted all-purpose flour (4¼ ounces; 120 g)
½ cup unsalted butter (1 stick; 110 g), softened but not melted
6 tablespoons sifted confectioners' sugar
½ teaspoon salt
3½ ounces marzipan, store-bought or homemade (page 446)
2 large eggs
1 cup granulated sugar (7 ounces; 200 g)
½ teaspoon baking powder
Freshly squeezed juice of ½ large lemon (2 tablespoons)
Grated zest of ½ lemon

GARNISH:

1 tablespoon confectioners' sugar

1. Position rack in lower third of oven. Preheat oven to 350°F (175°C).

2. In a mixing bowl with a wooden spoon, or in an electric mixer, cream together the flour, butter, 4 tablespoons of the sifted confectioners' sugar, and ¼ teaspoon salt. Press this mixture into an even layer in the bottom of the ungreased baking pan. Place it in the preheated oven and bake for 20 minutes.

3. While the cake bakes, roll out the marzipan in remaining 2 tablespoons of confectioners' sugar to form an 8-inch square. As soon as the cake comes from the oven, place the marzipan on top of the baked dough and set the cake aside on a wire rack.

4. In a mixing bowl, combine all remaining ingredients except the grated lemon zest and the garnish sugar, and beat them together with the electric mixer until pale in color and very foamy (a full 3 minutes with the KitchenAid mixer on speed #5, or 4 minutes with smaller mixers). Pour the lemon foam over the marzipan in the pan and sprinkle on the grated lemon zest. Return pan to the oven and bake for 25 minutes longer, or until no imprint of your finger remains in the center of the cake when touched. Cool the pan on a wire rack. When cold, sprinkle on 1 tablespoon confectioners' sugar. Cut into 2-inch squares and serve directly from the pan.

Gâteau Romanoff

•

Strawberries Romanoff is one of the simplest and most elegant of preparations—sliced strawberries and softened vanilla ice cream blended with kirsch-scented whipped cream. Serve this over a slice of angel-food cake for a summer evening dessert to remember. If you cut the cake slices ahead of time, you can whip up the "Romanoff" at the last moment and serve a very large crowd with little trouble. For a variation, try Strawberries à la Ritz (Romanoff with fresh whole raspberries added).

CAKE:

Angel-Food Cake (page 235)

TOPPING:

Strawberries Romanoff (page 420) or Strawberries à la Ritz (page 420)

Vassar Devil

•

This devilish confection occupies a singular place in the memory of my days as a Vassar student. Late night hours spent lingering over term papers, and another helping of cake. Including the recipe in a book helps mitigate my guilt and proves at last that the cake, as well as the education, was for a purpose.

A thick slab of Devil's Food Cake covered with a scoop of vanilla ice cream, warm fudge sauce, and whipped marshmallow topping, this dessert is still the specialty of the Vassar College Alumnae House Restaurant and Pub. No one at the "Pub" knows where it came from or how long it has been on the menu, but countless generations of satisfied alumnae can vouch for its pedigree.

CAKE:

Devil's Food Cake (page 97), cut into 3-inch squares

ICE CREAM:

Best-quality vanilla ice cream

CHOCOLATE SAUCE:

Rich Chocolate Sauce (page 419)

MARSHMALLOW TOPPING:

Store-bought whipped marshmallow topping, warmed slightly to pouring consistency

Cut squares of cake, top each with a scoop of ice cream, and pour on very warm Rich Chocolate Sauce and whipped marshmallow topping.

·*Variation:*·

VASSAR ANGEL:

Another "Pub" specialty, the Vassar Angel is just as wicked as its counterpart and runs it a very close second in popularity. To make it, prepare as above, but replace the chocolate cake with a wedge of vanilla Angel-Food Cake (page 235).

Madeleines

•

Just as literary gourmets associate madeleines with Marcel Proust, who found their taste so evocative of his youth, travelers to France know that these buttery, shell-shaped tea cakes are the hallmarks of the towns of Commercy, in Lorraine, and of Illiers-Combray, where Proust lived.

□ ADVANCE PREPARATION: Madeleines may be made and frozen, or stored at room temperature for a few days if wrapped air-tight; however, they are never as good as when freshly baked.

□ SPECIAL EQUIPMENT: madeleine mold. With shells of any size. Our tray has shells about 2¾ × 1¾ inches.

□ BAKING TIME: 8 to 10 minutes at 450°F (230°C)

□ QUANTITY: 3 cups batter, about 2½ dozen madeleines 2¾ × 1¾ inches; yield depends upon shell size

□ PAN PREPARATION: Spread shell-shaped depressions with solid shortening or soft butter, then dust evenly with flour; tap out excess flour. Note that the pan should be greased and floured again before baking every batch.

2 large eggs (warmed by setting whole in a bowl of warm water for 10 minutes)
⅔ cup granulated sugar (4½ ounces; 130 g)
1 teaspoon vanilla extract, or grated zest of 1 orange or 1 lemon, or 1 teaspoon orange-flower water, or 1 tablespoon rum
1 cup sifted cake flour (3½ ounces; 100 g)
¾ cup unsalted butter (1½ sticks; 170 g), melted and cooled

1. Prepare pan as described. Position rack in center of oven. Preheat oven to 450°F (230°C).

2. Warm the mixing bowl by rinsing it with hot water. Dry the bowl well. Add the warmed eggs, sugar, and flavoring of your choice. Beat on high speed for 3 or 4 minutes, or until the batter is thick and light-colored, and forms a flat ribbon falling back on itself when the beater is lifted.

3. Resift about half the flour directly onto the egg batter. Fold it in very lightly in 8 to 10 strokes. Repeat, sifting on and folding in remaining flour.

Finally, dribble on the butter and gently fold it in. Do not overwork the batter or it will lose volume and lightness.

4. Spoon the batter into the prepared shell molds, filling each about ¾ full. Bake in the preheated oven for 8 to 10 minutes, or until madeleines are golden brown and slightly domed on top. They will feel slightly springy to the touch. Remove madeleines from the pan and cool them on a wire rack. When the pan cools enough to touch comfortably, re-grease and flour the shell molds. Bake remaining batter in batches until it is all used.

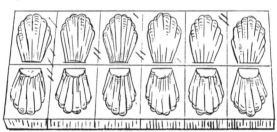

Fillings, Frostings, Icings & Glazes, Sauces & Syrups

Fillings

ABOUT WHIPPING CREAM

■

There is a wide variety of creams on the market, each with specific characteristics that must be understood by the baker. Read about Cream, page 29.

"Heavy" or "Heavy Whipping" cream is what you want to use, as both have the essential 36 to 40 percent butterfat content, whether stated on the carton or not. A well-prepared whipped cream should be smooth, light, and able to hold its shape; it should not be lumpy, yellowish, or buttery, all indications of overbeating and separation of cream into butter and water. If the whipped cream is too soft, it was not whipped enough, or was too fresh, too warm, or too low in butterfat.

Sweeteners for Whipped Cream
Superfine, granulated, or sifted confectioners' sugar can be used in whipped cream, but should be added after the cream is partially whipped. If added too early, the sugar can impede whipping. Confectioners' sugar contains about 3 percent cornstarch, which acts as a mild stabilizer; use this sugar if you will hold the cream before serving it. Honey can be substituted for sugar in whipped cream if the honey is liquefied and strained. Stir the honey gently into the cream after it is whipped stiff.

How to Whip Cream
To whip cream properly, be sure the cream, bowl, and beater are chilled. In hot weather, whip the cream over a pan of ice water.

To whip cream by hand, use a large balloon whisk or rotary beater, and a large bowl, preferably metal, which holds the cold once chilled. You can do the job more quickly and easily with an electric mixer, its largest balloon beater and its metal bowl well chilled. Put the bowl and beaters in the freezer for a few minutes to accomplish the task quickly.

The colder the cream and utensils, the firmer the butterfat in the cream and the thicker and stiffer the whipped results. As cream is whipped, it passes through several stages.

Stages of Whipped Cream

CHANTILLY CREAM:

This is when soft peaks appear, before the cream is really firm. Chantilly cream is best for adding to mousses and Bavarian creams or Strawberries Romanoff. This is also the point at which flavoring and/or sugar should be added to cream that will be whipped more.

CREAM BEATEN STIFF:

The best idea is to hand-whisk your cream from the Chantilly stage to stiff, even if you started the job with an electric mixer. By hand, you can prevent overbeating by controlling and observing the exact moment when the cream stiffens.

At the stiff stage, swirl lines from the beaters are clearly visible in the cream; they do not melt away. Firm peaks hold on the beater. Be careful about this stage; it occurs quickly; the time differs, depending on what type of mixer or hand utensil you use, and the beating should be halted at once. If you beat too long, you will have butter. To rescue slightly over-whipped cream, gently whisk in 2 tablespoons cold milk or unwhipped cream; it sometimes works.

How to Hold Cream Whipped in Advance

You don't want to leave the dinner table hastily and rush into the kitchen to whip the cream at the last minute, and it is not really necessary to do so. To hold regular (unstabilized, see below) whipped cream, be sure to add confectioners' sugar so as to benefit from the stabilizing power of its cornstarch content. To hold this cream for several hours, put it into a cheesecloth-lined strainer set in a bowl and refrigerate. Straining will eliminate any liquid that drains out.

To Stabilize Whipped Cream

Professional bakers add gelatin or cornstarch to their whipped cream to guarantee that it will remain stiff for approximately 24 hours. This stabilized cream can also be guaranteed to hold shape when piped through a pastry bag in fancy shapes.

GELATIN STABILIZER:

For every 1 cup of chilled heavy cream to be whipped, dissolve 1 teaspoon unflavored gelatin in 2 teaspoons cold water. Heat the gelatin until melted, then cool it but keep it liquid. Whip the cream until soft peaks form (Chantilly stage), then slowly add the gelatin while hand-whisking until stiff.

CORNSTARCH STABILIZER:

For every 1 cup of chilled heavy cream to be whipped, add 2 tablespoons confectioners' sugar and 1 teaspoon cornstarch. Combine the sugar and cornstarch in a small saucepan and gradually stir in 1/4 cup of heavy cream. Bring it to a boil, stirring constantly, and simmer for a few seconds until thickened. Remove from the heat and cool to room temperature. Whip remaining cream until it begins to thicken, just when the beater marks begin to show. Hand-whisk in the thickened cream mixture and whisk until stiff peaks form. (Cornstarch method derived from the article "Sugar in Baking and Cooking" by Rose Levy Beranbaum in the *Research Report of the International Association of Cooking Professionals,* Vol. 1, No. 2, Oct. 1985). In this method, the cornstarch present in confectioners' sugar, plus a little extra, is enhanced as a stabilizer because it is cooked.

Handy Measurement Notes for Whipping Cream

· Cream approximately doubles in volume when it is whipped; 1 cup chilled heavy cream = 2 cups whipped.

· To frost the top of an 8- or 9-inch cake you will need 1 cup whipped cream; to fill between 2 layers this size, you will need 1 cup whipped cream; to frost the sides of a 2-layer 8- or 9-inch cake, you will need about 1 cup whipped cream. Therefore, you will need a total of 3 cups whipped cream to fill and frost a 2-layer cake.

· To fill and frost a 3-layer cake you will need 4 cups whipped cream.

· For every 1 cup cream to be whipped, allow 2 tablespoons sifted confectioners' sugar and 2 tablespoons flavoring liqueur, or to taste.

Flavored Whipped Cream Filling and Topping for Cakes

∎

Unless otherwise noted in the recipes below, whip the chilled cream just to Chantilly stage, or soft peaks, add the flavoring extract or liqueur and sugar, then whip or hand-whisk to stiff peaks. Chill, or use the cream immediately.

□ QUANTITY: All variations make 3 cups whipped cream, to fill and frost a 2-layer 8- or 9-inch cake; use 2 cups chilled heavy cream to make 4 cups, whipped, for a 3-layer cake.

"DIET" CREAM:

To lower the butterfat content of the cream, use half whipped cream and half stiffly beaten egg whites, folded in.

RUM CREAM:

1½ cups chilled heavy cream
3 tablespoons rum, or 1 teaspoon rum extract, or to taste
3 to 4 tablespoons sifted confectioners' sugar

AMARETTO OR ALMOND CREAM:

1½ cups chilled heavy cream
3 tablespoons Amaretto liqueur plus ½ teaspoon almond extract
3 to 4 tablespoons sifted confectioners' sugar

CASSIS CREAM:

1½ cups chilled heavy cream
4 tablespoons Double Crème de Cassis liquer (black-currant flavor, tints cream pink)
3 tablespoons sifted confectioners' sugar

HAZELNUT (FILBERT) CREAM:

1½ cups chilled heavy cream
3 tablespoons hazelnut liqueur
3 tablespoons sifted confectioners' sugar, or to taste

¾ cup toasted (see page 43) and
  ground hazelnuts (3 ounces;
  90 g)

Note: Fold all nuts into stiff whipped cream, or use only ⅓ in the cream and reserve remaining nuts to garnish the frosted cake. Hazelnut Praline Powder (see Index) can be substituted for the toasted and ground nuts; if using praline, omit sugar.

MINT CREAM:

1½ cups chilled heavy cream
3 tablespoons white Crème de Menthe
  liqueur (green type will tint cream
  green) plus scant ½ teaspoon
  peppermint extract
4 to 5 tablespoons sifted confectioners'
  sugar, or to taste

ORANGE CREAM:

1½ cups chilled heavy cream
Grated zest of 1 orange
3 tablespoons orange-flavored liqueur
  (Curaçao, Grand Marnier, etc.)
Generous ½ teaspoon orange extract
3 tablespoons sifted confectioners' sugar

APRICOT CREAM:

1½ cups chilled heavy cream
3 tablespoons apricot liqueur, or to
  taste
4 tablespoons sifted confectioners' sugar

PEACH CREAM:

1½ cups chilled heavy cream
3 tablespoons peach liqueur, or to taste
½ teaspoon orange extract
3 or 4 tablespoons sifted confectioners'
  sugar

GINGER CREAM:

1½ cups chilled heavy cream
3 tablespoons confectioners' sugar sifted
  together with generous ½ teaspoon
  ground ginger
1 to 2 tablespoons crystallized ginger,
  minced fine, or to taste

Note: Whip the cream to soft peaks, add the sifted ginger and sugar. Whip stiff, then fold in the minced crystallized ginger.

COFFEE CREAM:

4 teaspoons instant espresso coffee
  powder dissolved in 1½ cups chilled
  heavy cream
4 to 5 tablespoons sifted confectioners'
  sugar, or to taste

COCOA CREAM:

1½ cups chilled heavy cream
4 tablespoons confectioners' sugar sifted
  with 1½ tablespoons unsweetened
  cocoa and a pinch of ground
  cinnamon

CHOCOLATE CREAM (CALLED IN AUSTRIA "PARISCREME"):

1½ cups chilled heavy cream
4 ounces bittersweet chocolate, chopped
  fine

Note: Put cream in a saucepan and bring just to a boil. Remove from the heat and stir in the chopped chocolate; be sure it is completely dissolved. Chill until very cold, then whip. Sifted confectioners' sugar may be added to taste if you wish.

MOCHA CREAM:

Prepare Cocoa or Chocolate Cream (preceding recipes), but add 2 teaspoons instant coffee powder dissolved in the chilled cream before whipping.

ORANGE-CHOCOLATE CREAM:

Prepare Cocoa or Chocolate Cream. Add 3 tablespoons orange-flavored liqueur and grated zest of 1 orange. If desired, add ½ teaspoon orange extract to enhance orange flavor.

PRALINE CREAM:

1½ cups chilled heavy cream
½ to ¾ cup Praline Powder (page 444)
½ teaspoon almond extract (optional), if needed to enhance the flavor

Note: Whip cream, then fold in powder and extract.

BUTTERSCOTCH CREAM:

1½ cups chilled heavy cream
1 cup firmly packed dark brown sugar (9 ounces; 255 g)
1 teaspoon vanilla extract

Note: Combine all ingredients in a bowl. Stir well to soften and partially dissolve the sugar. Whip stiff.

MAPLE CREAM:

1½ cups chilled heavy cream
½ cup pure maple syrup

Note: Whip the cream to soft peaks. Fold in the syrup. Hand-whisk to stiff peaks.

Vanilla Pastry Cream (Crème Pâtissière)

∎

Vanilla Pastry Cream is a classic thickened custard used as a filling in cakes and pastries. You can vary the quantity of eggs from the traditional 6 yolks to 2 cups of milk to 4 yolks (my preference) or just use 2 whole eggs; remember, the more yolks, the richer the sauce.

By changing the flavoring, you can create endless variations on this recipe; see 12 suggestions following the master recipe. For a lighter, fluffier texture, you can also fold in some whipped cream or meringue.

☐ ADVANCE PREPARATION: Pastry cream can be made ahead and refrigerated, covered, for a week.

☐ SPECIAL EQUIPMENT: 2½-quart heavy-bottomed nonreactive pan, whisk, sieve, mixing bowl, plastic wrap

☐ QUANTITY: about 2⅓ cups

⅔ cup granulated sugar (4½ ounces; 130 g)
2 tablespoons cornstarch
2 tablespoons all-purpose flour
Scant pinch of salt
4 large egg yolks, or 2 to 3 yolks, or 2 whole eggs
2 cups milk
1 vanilla bean, slit lengthwise, or 2 teaspoons vanilla extract
2 tablespoons unsalted butter

1. On a piece of plastic wrap, combine the sugar, cornstarch, flour, and salt. In a saucepan,

combine and whisk together the egg yolks and milk, or whole eggs if using them. Gather the corners of the plastic wrap and pick up the starch mixture; pour it on top of the eggs and milk and whisk well to be sure all the cornstarch and flour are dissolved. Add the vanilla bean (if using vanilla extract, add it at the end of the recipe).

2. Set the pan over moderate heat and cook the custard for about 12 minutes, until thickened and brought to a boil. To do this, stir on and off for the first 5 minutes, then stir constantly for about 7 minutes longer, until the cream really thickens and reaches a boil, when you will see fat heavy bubbles work their way to the surface and burst between stirs. Occasionally, use a whisk instead of a spoon, to break up any lumps. Boil for 1 full minute while stirring constantly, covering the entire bottom of the pan with the spoon. Remove pan from the heat. The cream is cooked when smooth and thick enough to leave a clearly defined line when you draw your finger through the cream coating the back of the spoon.

3. Remove the vanilla bean, rinse it, and set it aside to reuse. If you have not used the bean, stir in the vanilla extract at this point. Add the butter and whisk until melted and blended in. Pour the cream through a sieve into a bowl. Stir in additional flavoring if using it. To prevent a skin from forming on top of the cream, press a piece of platic wrap into the surface or dab the cream with butter or sift on a light coating of confectioners' sugar. Cool. Cover and refrigerate.

· *Variations:* ·

LIQUEUR-FLAVORED PASTRY CREAM:

Prepare Vanilla Pastry Cream. Add 2 tablespoons dark rum, kirsch, or other liqueur of your choice, stirred into the cream along with the vanilla extract.

PRALINE PASTRY CREAM:

Prepare Vanilla Pastry Cream. Fold into the finished, warm cream ½ cup Praline Powder (page 444).

HAZELNUT PASTRY CREAM:

Prepare Vanilla Pastry Cream. Fold into the finished, warm cream ½ cup Praline Powder (page 444) made with hazelnuts. Add 1 or 2 tablespoons hazelnut liqueur.

ALMOND PASTRY CREAM:

Prepare Vanilla Pastry Cream. Fold into the finished, warm cream ½ cup Praline Powder (page 444) made with almonds. Add 1 teaspoon almond extract. Or, instead of praline powder, you can use ½ cup ground blanched almonds to make this into Frangipane Cream.

ORANGE PASTRY CREAM:

Prepare Vanilla Pastry Cream. Add 1 tablespoon grated orange zest to the milk-yolk mixture before cooking. Stir 2 or 3 tablespoons orange-flavored liqueur into the finished, warm cream. Do not strain the cream or the orange zest will be lost.

COFFEE PASTRY CREAM:

Prepare Vanilla Pastry Cream but dissolve 1½ tablespoons powdered instant coffee into the milk before whisking it into the egg yolks.

CHOCOLATE PASTRY CREAM:

Prepare Vanilla Pastry Cream. Melt 3 or 4 ounces finest-quality semisweet or bittersweet chocolate in the top pan of a double boiler, then stir it into the finished, warm cream. The amount of chocolate used depends on the intensity of flavor desired; I prefer the maximum.

MOCHA PASTRY CREAM:

Prepare Vanilla Pastry Cream. Melt 3 ounces semisweet chocolate in the top pan of a double boiler. In a small bowl, dissolve 4 teaspoons powdered instant coffee in 1 tablespoon hot water. Stir into this 1 cup of the finished, warm cream. Add to the entire cream mixture and whisk in the melted chocolate.

BUTTERSCOTCH PASTRY CREAM:

Prepare Vanilla Pastry Cream. Substitute ½ cup dark brown sugar for all the granulated sugar.

PASTRY CREAM SAINT-HONORÉ:

Saint-Honoré is the patron saint of bakers. Prepare Vanilla Pastry Cream. Make a meringue by whipping 2 large egg whites with a pinch of salt and 3 tablespoons sifted confec-tioners' sugar (see About Meringue, page 244). When whipped until stiff but not dry, fold the whites into the hot pastry cream. The heat of the cream must poach the whites to create the correct consistency. Chill.

DIPLOMAT CREAM:

Prepare Vanilla Pastry Cream; chill. Stir or whisk the cool pastry cream until soft and smooth. Whip ½ cup chilled heavy cream to soft peak stage with 2 tablespoons confectioners' sugar and ½ teaspoon vanilla extract. Fold whipped cream into chilled pastry cream. Use immediately.

INSTANT PASTRY CREAM:

For desperate moments when time is precious, prepare 1 small package "instant-type" French vanilla pudding using 1 cup milk. Whip ½ cup heavy cream to soft peaks and fold it into the pudding along with 1 teaspoon vanilla and/or almond extract. Or, for an even better (though packaged) flavor, use "cooked-style" pudding prepared as directed on the box. Fold in the whipped cream and extract.

Vicky Zeff's White Chocolate Mousse

∎

This luxurious mousse is a specialty of our good friend Vicky Zeff, the talented young woman in charge of the kitchen at Long Pond Inn in Mahopac, New York. Vicky's impressive credentials include working at Régines in Paris and at Michel Guérard's restaurant in Eugénie-les-Bains.

Vicky likes to use this recipe as a filling for wedding cakes. On less formal occasions she serves the mousse in stemmed goblets topped by raspberry or coffee liqueur or garnished with fresh berries. The tartness of the fruit provides a counterpoint to the intense sweetness of the white chocolate; for the same reason, she often adds to the mousse a strong flavoring agent such as orange liqueur and grated orange zest. I have also successfully added (separately) praline powder and grated bittersweet chocolate. I like to use the mousse for filling and frosting the Chocolate Sponge Roll (page 227), served garnished with fresh raspberries or sliced ripe peaches. Note that the mousse freezes well, either before or after being spread on a cake.

□ ADVANCE PREPARATION: The mousse should be made several hours in advance or the day before it is needed so it can chill and thicken to spreading consistency. It can be kept covered in the refrigerator for up to 1 week, or frozen. When frozen, it does not harden completely, so it may be served directly from the freezer.

□ SPECIAL EQUIPMENT: Double boiler, instant-read spot thermometer, rubber spatula, chilled bowl and beater for whipping cream, hand-held electric mixer (optional), or whisk

□ QUANTITY: about 2¾ cups; about 8 individual servings if used alone as a mousse dessert, or enough to fill and frost one Chocolate Sponge Roll

4 tablespoons unsalted butter (2 ounces; 60 g), softened but not melted
1 cup heavy cream, chilled
6 ounces white chocolate (170 g), chopped fine
4 large egg yolks

FLAVORING (OPTIONAL):

Orange: 3 or 4 tablespoons orange liqueur (Grand Marnier or Cointreau, for example) plus grated zest of ½ large orange, about 1½ teaspoons. For even stronger flavor, add more liqueur or ½ teaspoon orange extract (my preference).
Praline: ½ teaspoon almond extract, or to taste, plus 3 or 4 tablespoons Praline Powder (page 444) folded in at the end of the recipe
Black and White: 3 to 4 tablespoons grated bittersweet chocolate, folded in at the end of the recipe

1. In a bowl, beat the butter with a wooden spoon or electric mixer, until creamy; at this stage it will incorporate well with the chocolate. Set the butter aside; do not refrigerate.

In a chilled bowl and with a chilled beater,

whip the cream until soft peaks form (Chantilly stage). Fold in any flavoring liquid or extract or grated zest. Refrigerate cream until needed.

2. Place the chopped white chocolate in the top pan of a double boiler set over, but not touching, hot water. Stir the chocolate as it melts. Use a spot thermometer if possible to check that the temperature stays between 100°F and 110°F; it will feel warm, not hot, to your fingertip. If the chocolate heats above 115°F it risks clumping and becoming grainy. If you suspect it is too hot, set the white chocolate pan in another pan of cold water and stir. When the white chocolate is partially melted, remove pan from the heat and stir until completely melted, perfectly smooth and creamy. Note: If your white chocolate should overheat and stiffen, you can smooth it out by whisking in warmed heavy cream, a few drops at a time.

3. With a hand-held electric beater or whisk, beat the yolks, one at a time, into the melted chocolate. Don't panic when the chocolate stiffens after adding the first yolk; this is normal. The mixture smooths out as more yolks and the butter are added. Beat in the softened butter, 1 teaspoon at a time.

After the mixture is completely smooth and at room temperature, not hotter, check the whipped cream. If it has softened on standing, whisk it briskly until it returns to the soft peak stage. Then whisk about ½ cup of this cream into the chocolate to lighten it. Finally, fold in the rest of the whipped cream as well as any flavoring such as grated chocolate or praline powder, if using it. Cover and refrigerate the mousse until it reaches spreading consistency, 3 or 4 hours. Note that this mousse stays somewhat soft even when thoroughly chilled; it may also be frozen. In hot weather, serve it directly from the refrigerator or freezer.

· ·

Chocolate Mousse

∎

Here are 2 types of chocolate mousse. Each can be served alone as a dessert or can be used to fill or frost cakes. They are quite different. The first is intensely chocolate, made with whipped egg whites but without whipped cream. It is best used for coating a layer cake, where a richer blend may be overwhelming. The second, Chocolate Mousse II, is the same as the first preparation but with the addition of whipped cream; it is much richer and creamier. Use it for fillings or for a molded charlotte.

Remember that chocolate mousse contains uncooked egg whites and should be refrigerated.

☐ ADVANCE PREPARATION: Chocolate mousse can be made in advance and chilled. When prepared for a cake filling it may first need to be refrigerated to thicken to spreading consistency.

☐ QUANTITY: 6 cups, to fill and frost a 2- or 3-layer 8- or 9-inch cake or dacquoise (meringue-nut layer cake); there will be some mousse left over for piping decorations on the cake or to be frozen for a dessert. As a mousse served alone for dessert, the recipe serves 8 to 10.

Note: Halve the recipe (3 cups total) to fill a 3-layer cake and frost the sides but not the top. Coat the top with Apricot Glaze (page 411) or Chocolate Glaze (page 409) or sifted confectioners' sugar.

CHOCOLATE MOUSSE I:

12 ounces semisweet or bittersweet chocolate (340 grams)
1 teaspoon instant espresso coffee powder, dissolved in 2 teaspoons hot water
¾ cup unsalted butter (1½ sticks; 170 g), at room temperature, cut up
5 large egg yolks (Note: if halving the recipe, use 3 yolks)
8 large egg whites
3½ tablespoons sifted superfine sugar

FLAVORING (OPTIONAL):

2 tablespoons dark rum, brandy, or hazelnut or Amaretto liqueur

1. Melt the chocolate in the top pan of a double boiler set over, not in, hot water. Stir in the coffee and the butter and beat until completely melted and smooth. Remove from heat and cool until comfortable to touch. When cool, add the yolks, one at a time, beating after each addition.

2. In the large bowl of an electric mixer, beat the whites until fluffy, add the sugar gradually, and beat until stiff but not dry. Test the temperature of the chocolate. It should be at body temperature (neither hot nor cold) or it will not blend properly with the egg whites; fold the chocolate into the whites in 4 or 5 additions. Note: If the chocolate is too warm,

set it in the refrigerator for a minute or two; if too cold, stir it over a bowl of warm water for a few minutes. The mousse should have an even color, with no streaks of egg white visible. Refrigerate for about 25 minutes to bring it to spreading consistency before filling and frosting a cake.

Note: The mousse will become dry on the surface after an hour or so; if used to frost a cake, press nuts or other garnishes such as chocolate curls into the mousse as soon as the cake is frosted, while the surface is still soft.

·*Variation:*·

CHOCOLATE MOUSSE II:

Prepare Chocolate Mousse I. Whip 1 cup heavy cream with 2 tablespoons confectioners' sugar until soft peaks form. Fold the whipped cream into the mousse right after folding in the egg whites.

Note: The addition of this cream will increase the quantity to 8 cups. If you need less, use only half of the cream (½ cup) or use only 4 egg whites, beaten stiff, plus 1 cup cream. Excess chocolate mousse may be frozen in a covered container.

To fill a 2-quart charlotte mold with this mousse, you need only half of the recipe for Chocolate Mousse I plus ½ cup heavy cream whipped. Quantity: 4 cups mousse.

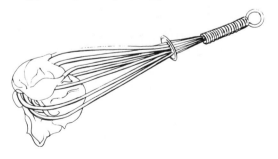

Eggless Custard Buttercream

∎

If you want the satiny texture of a custard buttercream without the richness or fat of egg yolks, make this cornstarch-thickened custard icing. Be sure to boil the cornstarch-milk mixture to eliminate the taste of uncooked starch.

☐ ADVANCE PREPARATION: The buttercream can be prepared up to a week in advance and refrigerated, or it can be frozen. Bring to room temperature and whip before spreading on a cake.

☐ SPECIAL EQUIPMENT: medium-size mixing bowl, cup, 2-quart saucepan, large bowl of ice water

☐ QUANTITY: 3 cups, to fill and frost an 8-inch 2- or 3-layer cake.

1 cup plus 2 tablespoons unsalted
butter (2¼ sticks; 260 g), softened
but not melted
4 tablespoons cornstarch
1¼ cups milk
⅔ cup granulated sugar (4½ ounces;
130 g)

FLAVORING:

2 teaspoons vanilla extract or 1 tablespoon
instant coffee powder dissolved in the milk;
or 3 or 4 ounces semisweet chocolate, melted
and cooled

1. In a bowl, beat the butter with a wooden spoon until soft and smooth; at this stage it will be easily incorporated into the custard.

2. In a small bowl, dissolve the cornstarch in ¼ cup of the measured milk. Combine remaining milk with the sugar (and coffee if using it) in a 2-quart saucepan set over moderate heat. Bring the mixture to the boiling point, stirring on and off to dissolve all the sugar.

3. Stir the cornstarch mixture to be sure it has not settled. Whisk some of the hot milk into the cornstarch mixture to warm it, then pour the cornstarch mixture into the saucepan and whisk the ingredients over moderate heat for about 4 minutes while it comes to a full boil. Boil, stirring, for 30 full seconds. The custard should be thick and smooth like a pudding. Remove pan from the heat and whisk hard until custard is smooth and glossy. Add the vanilla extract, or melted and cooled chocolate if using it.

4. Transfer custard to a clean metal bowl and stir it over ice water for a couple of minutes, until completely cool to the touch throughout. If too warm, it will melt the butter. With an electric mixer, beat the custard for a few seconds. With the mixer running, beat in the smooth butter, 1 tablespoon at a time, beating on high speed after each addition. After all the butter is incorporated, whip the mixture on high speed for a full 30 seconds. Use the buttercream at once or cover and refrigerate.

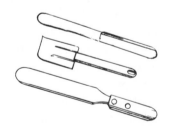

Viennese Custard Buttercream

•

Butter is beaten into vanilla custard to make this rich and creamy blend used for filling and icing classic Viennese tortes and layer cakes. For Chocolate and Coffee Custard Buttercreams, see the variations following the master recipe.

□ ADVANCE PREPARATION: The buttercream can be made up to a week in advance and stored, covered, in the refrigerator. Bring it to room temperature and whip to soften before using.

□ QUANTITY: 2½ cups, to fill and frost an 8- or 9-inch 2-layer cake

1 cup unsalted butter (2 sticks; 230 g),
*   softened but not melted*
1½ vanilla beans, slit lengthwise, or
*   1½ teaspoons vanilla extract*
1 cup milk
3 large egg yolks
½ cup granulated sugar (3½ ounces;
*   100 g)*
1 tablespoon cornstarch

1. Beat the butter with a wooden spoon until soft and creamy, so it will be easily incorporated into the custard. Set the butter aside; do not chill it.

2. In a 2-quart saucepan, combine the vanilla beans and ¾ cup of the milk and set over moderate heat. Scald the milk until small bubbles appear around the edges. Remove the milk from the heat and set it aside for the vanilla beans to infuse for about 5 minutes,

then remove the beans. Or add vanilla extract at the end of the recipe.

While the milk heats, whisk together in a medium-size bowl remaining ¼ cup milk, the egg yolks, sugar, and cornstarch.

3. Whisk the hot milk into the yolk mixture, then return the yolk-milk mixture to the saucepan and whisk it constantly over moderate heat until it just reaches the boiling point; this will take about 7 minutes. Don't stop whisking or the custard will cook on the bottom. When done, it will be as thick as a pudding and generously coat the whisk.

At once, remove pan from the heat and whisk the custard hard until it looks smooth, satiny, and not at all separated. If you have not used vanilla beans, whisk in vanilla extract now. Chill the custard in the refrigerator, or speed the process by stirring it over a pan of ice water until it is completely cool to the touch throughout. If too warm, it will melt the butter.

4. With an electric mixer, beat the custard for a few seconds; leave the mixer running and begin to add the softened butter, 1 tablespoon at a time. Beat on high speed after each addition, then go back to medium-high speed and add more butter. Scrape down the sides of the bowl and the beaters several times during this process. When the butter is added slowly enough and beaten sufficiently, you will have a perfect emulsion, like a mayonnaise, and it will not separate. If, however, separation starts, just beat on high speed with a little more softened butter until smoothed out. After incorporating all the butter, whip the buttercream on high speed for 1 full minute. Use immediately or store in a covered container in the refrigerator.

·Variations:·

CHOCOLATE CUSTARD BUTTERCREAM:

Prepare Vanilla Custard Buttercream, but add 2 or 3 ounces of melted and cooled semisweet chocolate to the cooled custard *before* adding the butter.

COFFEE CUSTARD BUTTERCREAM (2½ CUPS):

Follow the basic procedure for vanilla Viennese Custard Buttercream using these ingredients:

1 cup unsalted butter (2 sticks; 230 g), softened but not melted
⅓ cup granulated sugar (2¼ ounces; 65 g)
2 tablespoons cornstarch
Pinch of salt
2 tablespoons instant coffee powder or 1 tablespoon instant espresso coffee powder
¾ cup warm water
3 large egg yolks

1. Beat the butter until creamy. Put the sugar, cornstarch, and salt in a heavy 2-quart saucepan. In a small bowl, dissolve coffee powder in the warm water, then whisk in the yolks. Whisk the coffee-yolk mixture into the dry ingredients in the pot. Set over heat and whisk constantly while bringing just to the boiling point, when the custard will be as thick as a pudding.

2. Remove custard from the heat, whisk hard, then stir it over a pan of ice water until completely cool to the touch. With an electric mixer, beat the custard, then beat in the soft butter, 1 tablespoon at a time. Scrape down bowl and beaters. Beat the finished mixture on high speed for 1 full minute. Buttercream should be perfectly smooth.

Zabaglione Sauce and Zabaglione Cake Filling

■

Zabaglione *(Zabaione)* is an easily prepared wine custard made by whipping egg yolks, sugar, and Marsala or other wine in a double boiler. Traditionally served in wine goblets as a dessert in itself, zabaglione can also be served with sliced ripe peaches or berries and a piece of sponge or chiffon cake. When a little gelatin is added to the recipe, it will hold its shape when used as a cake or jelly-roll filling (see variation following).

Zabaglione may be served warm as soon as it is made, or it can be chilled and served cold, or even frozen. Note that chilling, or adding gelatin, reduces the volume, and the recipe should be doubled for the cold method. For a fluffier consistency, the chilled sauce can also be folded into whipped heavy cream. In my opinion, any way you eat zabaglione is heavenly, though I prefer it the way I tasted it the first time: very warm over fully ripe sliced peaches, served under a grape arbor in the garden of a sunny Roman trattoria.

Zabaglione was invented by the Italians, who taught it to the French. In France they call it *sabayon,* and replace the Marsala with dry white wine or Champagne to make Champagne Sabayon Sauce. Germans and Austrians make a similar sauce, called *Weinschaum* or *Weinschaumsaucen* (hot wine sauce).

☐ QUANTITY: warm, about 2 cups; four ½-cup servings as a dessert, 6 servings as a sauce over sliced cake. Cold, about 1½ cups, 3 servings

4 large egg yolks
4 tablespoons granulated sugar
8 tablespoons Marsala wine

Note: The classic zabaglione is made with the ratio of 1 egg yolk to 1 tablespoon sugar and ½ a large eggshell of Marsala or other wine.

TRADITIONAL WARM METHOD
(MAKES ABOUT 2 CUPS):

Off the heat, in the top pan of a double boiler, stir together the egg yolks and sugar. Then set the pan over, not touching, gently boiling water. Whisk constantly, gradually adding the wine. Whisk until the mixture foams, doubles in volume, and thickens, 4 to 5 minutes. During the later stage of whisking, lower the heat so the water just simmers. The sauce is done when it generously coats a spoon and falls from it in thick, heavy drops. "Cook until the spoon cries only one tear," explained Italian cooking authority Giuliano Bugialli at a master class I recently attended. Serve the sauce immediately, while still warm.

COLD METHOD
(MAKES ABOUT 1½ CUPS:

Double the recipe for more than 3 servings, as chilling reduces the volume.

The advantage of this method is that the zabaglione can be made up to 6 or 8 hours in advance. Prepare a large bowl of ice cubes and cold water; set it aside. Proceed as for warm method, whisking the yolk-sugar-wine mixture in the top pan of a double boiler for 4 to 5 minutes, until increased in volume and thick enough to coat a spoon generously. At once, remove the top pan of the double boiler from the heat and set it into the pan of ice water. Whisk the zabaglione over ice water until the sauce is completely cold. At this stage, you can fold in whipped cream or other flavoring if you wish. Pour the cold zabaglione into a bowl or serving goblets and refrigerate until needed. Or cover with plastic wrap and freeze. Serve cold or frozen (the texture never completely solidifies even when frozen).

·*Variations:*·

Add to the basic recipe:
• 1 cup whipped heavy cream, folded into cold zabaglione
• 1 teaspoon vanilla extract, stirred in after cooking is complete
• Southern Italian Style: Replace the Marsala with dry white wine and add the grated zest of 1 orange or tangerine.
• French Sabayon Sauce: replace Marsala with dry Champagne (Champagne Sabayon Sauce) or use a dry white wine or cream sherry; or flavor a white wine zabaglione with Grand Marnier or other liqueur.

• Fold a drained purée of fresh strawberries or raspberries and 1 cup whipped cream into the finished and cooled sauce just before serving.

• Creole Style: Prepare cold method zabaglione with dry white wine and 2 teaspoons grated orange zest. Into the finished sauce fold 1 cup whipped heavy cream and 1½ teaspoons instant coffee powder dissolved in 3 tablespoons dark rum. Top with a little grated bittersweet chocolate.

Zabaglione Cake Filling

■

This filling is made by adding a little gelatin and whipped cream to the basic Zabaglione Sauce. Prepare the filled cake in advance and refrigerate it about three hours for the filling to set; be sure to bring it to room temperature before serving. It is soft and delectable, yet holds its shape when sliced.

□ QUANTITY: 2 cups, to fill a 3-layer 8- or 9-inch cake: 1½ cups will generously fill 1 jelly roll.

1. Prepare Zabaglione Sauce, cold method, with 4 egg yolks. Add 1½ teaspoons unflavored gelatin plus ½ cup chilled heavy cream, whipped, following this procedure:

First set out a large bowl containing ice cubes and cold water. In a small saucepan, sprinkle 1½ teaspoons gelatin over ¼ cup of cold water. Let this sit for about 3 minutes to soften the gelatin, then stir the mixture over low heat until the gelatin is dissolved completely. Do not boil. Remove pan from the heat and set it aside.

2. Follow the basic procedure to whisk yolks, sugar, and Marsala in the top pan of a double boiler until increased in volume and thick enough to coat a spoon generously and fall from it in a thick, heavy ribbon. At this stage, whisk in the dissolved gelatin.

3. Remove the top pan from the lower and set it into the ice water. Whisk the custard in the ice-water bath on and off for about 10 minutes, until custard is cold and beginning to thicken. When ready, it will mound on the spoon like a soft creamy pudding; it will hold its shape softly on the spoon and be neither runny nor hard and rubbery. Note: If the custard sets too hard and jells, just put the bowl over a pan of hot water and whisk for a few seconds until the custard softens and smooths out. Then proceed.

4. While the custard is chilling, whip the cream. As soon as the custard is at the pudding stage, fold in the whipped cream. Spread the custard on a jelly roll or between cake layers. Refrigerate the cake until about 30 minutes before serving; serve at room temperature.

Lemon Curd

■

Traditionally rich, this version of lemon curd is made with 5 egg yolks, and it is worth every one of them. The result is absolutely smooth and deliciously tart—perfect for filling a sponge cake or angel-food roll. It is equally good as filling for a vanilla or citrus-flavored layer cake, and is an old-fashioned favorite for filling a wedding cake, though the quantity must be increased for a multilayered cake. Note: Most classic versions of Lemon Curd are thickened exclusively with the egg yolks in the recipe; however, for cake filling, I find the addition of cornstarch gives a better texture.

☐ QUANTITY: scant 2 cups, enough to fill two jelly rolls. Will also fill a 3-layer 8- or 9-inch cake.

½ cup unsalted butter (1 stick;
  110 g), cut up
1 cup granulated sugar
Grated zest of 2 lemons, about 5
  teaspoons
⅓ cup freshly squeezed lemon juice
1 whole large egg plus 5 egg yolks
1 tablespoon cornstarch, dissolved in 2
  tablespoons cold water

1. Place the butter in the top pan of a double boiler set over simmering water. When the butter has melted, stir in the sugar, lemon zest, and juice. Whisk on and off until the sugar is melted, about 5 minutes.

2. Combine the whole egg and egg yolks in a small bowl and whisk them together until well blended. Whisk in the cornstarch and water mixture.

Pour about one quarter of the hot lemon mixture into the yolks while whisking hard, so the yolks become warm but do not poach. Pour the warmed yolks into the rest of the hot lemon mixture in the top pan of the double boiler, again whisking the mixture hard to avoid poaching the eggs.

3. Cook the custard over simmering water, whisking continually, for a good 5 minutes, until it is thick enough to coat the back of a spoon generously. A line drawn down the back of the spoon with your finger should not close up readily. Remove pan from the heat, pour the lemon curd into a clean bowl, and top it with a piece of plastic wrap to prevent formation of a skin. If you have time, set it aside until cool, then refrigerate. It will thicken more as it cools.

To speed the cooling, you can set a metal pan of the double boiler right into a large bowl of ice and cold water and stir the lemon curd until it is cool. Then you can refrigerate it until thick enough to spread; do not put it on a cake until completely cold.

Lemon Cake Filling

■

This old New England recipe for a tart cornstarch custard is used for filling jelly rolls or layer cakes. It is extremely flavorful, but contains much less fat than the Lemon Curd (preceding recipe), a consideration for cholesterol watchers. See the variation for Orange Cake Filling, following.

☐ ADVANCE PREPARATION: The filling may be made a day or two in advance and stored, covered, in the refrigerator.

☐ SPECIAL EQUIPMENT: 2-quart saucepan, grater, rubber spatula, 1½-quart bowl, plastic wrap

☐ QUANTITY: 2 cups to fill 2 jelly rolls or to fill one 3-layer 8-inch or 9-inch cake

*¾ cup granulated sugar (5¼ ounces;
    150 g)*
3 tablespoons cornstarch
2 teaspoons all-purpose flour
Pinch of salt
1¼ cups water
2 large egg yolks
*Grated zest of 1 lemon, about 2
    teaspoons*
¼ cup freshly squeezed lemon juice
*1 tablespoon unsalted butter or
    margarine, cut up*

1. In a 2-quart saucepan off the heat, combine the sugar, cornstarch, flour, and salt. Slowly stir in the water, blending with a spoon or whisk until no lumps remain. Set the pan over high heat and stir constantly until the mixture comes to a full rolling boil. Boil for 1 full minute while stirring constantly. The mixture should be very thick and smooth.

2. In a 1½-quart bowl, whisk the egg yolks with the lemon zest and juice, then whisk vigorously while adding about half of the hot thickened cornstarch mixture. Return the warmed yolk mixture to remaining hot mixture in the pan and whisk over low heat for 3 minutes.

3. Remove pan from the heat, add the butter, and stir until it is melted. Cool the custard, top with plastic wrap to prevent a skin from forming, and refrigerate until needed. The custard thickens more as it cools.

·Variation:·

ORANGE CAKE FILLING (MAKES 2 CUPS):

Follow the procedure for lemon filling, but use the following ingredients:

*½ cup plus 2 tablespoons granulated
    sugar (4¼ ounces; 120 g)*
3 tablespoons cornstarch
2 teaspoons all-purpose flour
Pinch of salt
1½ cups orange juice
2 large egg yolks
Grated zest of 1 orange
*1 tablespoon unsalted butter or
    margarine, cut up*

Combine the sugar, cornstarch, flour, and salt in a pan. Slowly stir in 1¼ cups of the orange juice, stirring until no lumps remain. Use a whisk if necessary. Bring the mixture to a full boil, stirring constantly. Boil for 1 full minute. In a small bowl, whisk the egg yolks with remaining ¼ cup orange juice and the orange zest. Whisk in half of the hot mixture, pour the warmed yolk mixture into the pan, and stir over low heat for 3 minutes. Stir in butter. Cool.

Light Orange Buttercream Filling

■

In this buttercream recipe, some of the classic butter and egg yolks are replaced with a cornstarch-thickened sauce, thus reducing the fat content. I like to use this as a cake filling, but it can also be used to frost cakes. To change the flavor of the recipe, replace the orange juice with milk so the custard is neutral in taste before adding your own flavoring.

□ SPECIAL EQUIPMENT: double boiler, grater, large bowl of ice water, heatproof bowl or top pan of double boiler, rubber spatula

□ QUANTITY: 1½ cups; double this recipe to fill and frost a 2-layer 8-inch cake.

1 tablespoon cornstarch
½ cup orange juice
1 tablespoon lemon juice
Grated zest of 1 orange
1 large egg yolk
½ cup unsalted butter (1 stick; 110 g), softened
1½ cups sifted confectioners' sugar (5¼ ounces; 150 g), plus ½ cup more if needed

1. Off the heat, in the top pan of a double boiler, whisk the cornstarch into ¼ cup of the orange juice, stirring until the cornstarch is dissolved. Add remaining orange juice, the lemon juice, grated orange zest, and egg yolk and whisk well. Set the pan over gently boiling water and whisk constantly for about 4 minutes, or until the mixture becomes a thick, creamy custard.

2. Remove pan from the heat and set it into a bowl of ice water. Continue to whisk until the custard is cool to the touch. Beware, for if too warm, it will melt the butter when it is added. Remove bowl from the ice water bath.

3. Using an electric mixer or a wooden spoon, beat the butter until very soft and creamy. Then gradually add 1 cup of the sifted confectioners' sugar, beating until smooth. You may want to cover the mixer with a tea towel while the sugar is beaten in to prevent flying powder. With the mixer on low speed, gradually beat the cooled custard, a little at a time, into the butter-sugar blend. Beat well after each addition. Beat in the final ½ cup of sugar and beat on high speed until smooth. If the mixture starts to curdle, whisk it over a pan of warm water until smooth, or add another ½ cup sugar and beat on high speed. Chill the buttercream if too soft to spread.

....

Lane Cake Filling

■

Laden with chopped nuts and fruit, this bourbon-scented custard is used to fill the Alabama specialty known as Lane Cake (page 84).

□ QUANTITY: 2 generous cups, to fill one 3-layer 8- or 9-inch cake

8 large egg yolks
1 cup sugar (7 ounces; 100 g)
⅓ cup lightly salted butter or margarine (5⅓ tablespoons; 80 g)
½ cup chopped maraschino cherries, or 3 tablespoons apricot preserves
1 cup pecans, finely chopped (4 ounces; 110 g)
¼ cup dried pitted dates, chopped (1¾ ounces; 50 g)
½ cup seedless raisins (preferably half golden, half black), finely chopped (2½ ounces; 70 g)
½ cup sweetened shredded coconut (1½ ounces; 45 g)
3 tablespoons bourbon whiskey
Grated zest of 1 orange
¼ teaspoon ground nutmeg

1. In the top pan of a double boiler over moderate heat combine the egg yolks, sugar, and butter. Whisk constantly while cooking for about 20 minutes, or until all the sugar is dissolved and the custard thickens enough to coat a spoon.

2. Remove pan from the heat and stir in all remaining ingredients. Cool completely. When cold, divide the filling into halves and spread between the layers of the 3-layer Lane Cake. Frost the cake with Boiled Icing (see page 400). Note: This filling can be made a day ahead and refrigerated. Bring to room temperature and stir until smooth enough to spread.

Toppings

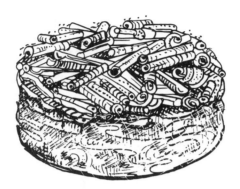

Toasted Coconut Topping

∎

Use this to garnish the top and/or sides of a "tropical" cake.

☐ QUANTITY: 1 cup, to top one 8- or 9-inch cake or one 8 × 12 sheet cake

1 cup sweetened shredded or flaked coconut, or grated fresh coconut

Spread coconut on a sheet of foil with the edges turned up and bake in a preheated 375°F (190°C) oven for 6 to 8 minutes, tossing the coconut occasionally to color it evenly until golden brown. Cool and add to cake as a garnish.

Streusel Nut Topping

∎

Use this crunchy nut-crumb topping on fruit crisps, coffee cakes, or fruit-nut cakes; it adds texture and is not as sweet as regular icing.

☐ ADVANCE PREPARATION: Streusel topping can be made ahead and frozen or stored in a covered jar in the refrigerator for several days before using. Leftover streusel can be frozen.

☐ QUANTITY: about 2½ cups. Use 1½ cups to top a 9-inch cake, 1¾ cups to top a cake 11¾ × 7½ inches, the full recipe (2½ cups) to top a cake 13 × 9 inches, and 1½ times the recipe (3¾ cups) to top a cake 15 × 10½ inches.

⅔ cup firmly packed light or dark brown sugar (4½ ounces; 130 g)
7 tablespoons butter or margarine (100 g), at room temperature, cut up
½ cup plus 2 tablespoons all-purpose flour (3½ ounces; 100 g)
1 cup finely chopped walnuts (4 ounces; 110 g), or use pecans or almonds
½ teaspoon each of ground cinnamon and nutmeg

Combine all ingredients in a mixing bowl. Crumble and pinch them together with your fingertips, making pea-size crumbs. Spread the mixture evenly over the cake before baking as directed in recipe. Note: If the butter or margarine is too warm, the mixture will cling together and refuse to crumble; chill if necessary.

Meringue Crumb Topping

■

Crumbs of crisp flavorful meringue make a delicious topping when sprinkled over a cake frosted with whipped cream, buttercream, or mousse. The scraps may be left over from trimming meringue or dacquoise cake layers into neat rounds, or you can make the meringue specifically for decorative purposes, following the recipe for cake disks or plain meringue (page 250). Use a decorating bag fitted with a ¼-inch plain tip to pipe the meringue into long ropes or fingers. Flavor the meringue after it is whipped with some unsweetened cocoa powder (3 tablespoons for 4 egg whites) to make chocolate meringue topping. Once the meringue ropes or fingers are baked crisp, break or cut them into short lengths and press them gently onto a frosted cake.

One of the most glamorous examples of a cake decorated with meringue topping is found in the Paris pastry shops of Gaston Lenôtre. Lenôtre, on the rue d'Auteuil, was the scene of one glorious day's orgy where, though I was firmly asked not to photograph the cakes, I made elaborate notes and sketches. My slightly sticky records recall "Concorde," constructed from 3 crisp chocolate meringue layers filled and frosted with chocolate mousse. The outside of the cake is entirely covered with short logs of chocolate meringue with a little confectioners' sugar sifted over the top. Instead of topping the cake with Lenôtre's signature chocolate seal, you might gild the lily and add a Chocolate Leaf or Rose (see Index).

Frostings, Icings & Glazes

All-Purpose Frosting

·

This quick-and-easy recipe is a so-called American-style frosting; it is less rich than a buttercream.

☐ QUANTITY: about 2½ cups, to fill and frost an 8- or 9-inch 2-layer cake

4 tablespoons unsalted butter or
margarine or solid white vegetable
shortening
Pinch of salt
1 teaspoon pure flavoring extract
(vanilla, almond, lemon, or orange)
4 to 4½ cups sifted confectioners' sugar
(16 ounces; 454 g)
5 tablespoons milk, or as needed

In an electric mixer, cream the butter or margarine until soft. Beat in the salt and flavoring extract. With the mixer on lowest speed, gradually beat in the sugar and milk. Scrape down the sides of the bowl and the beater. Beat on high speed until creamy. Add more milk if needed to reach spreading consistency. This can be made in advance and stored, covered, in the refrigerator for up to 1 week. Bring to room temperature and whip smooth before using.

Royal Icing

·

This icing becomes very hard when air-dried. Use it for trimming and decorations. To avoid a crust forming on the icing while it is being used, cover the bowl with a damp towel or plastic wrap; store pastry tube filled with leftover royal icing in a plastic bag.

☐ QUANTITY: 2 cups, enough to make decorations for one 8- or 9-inch 2- or 3-layer cake

2 large egg whites
⅛ teaspoon cream of tartar
Pinch of salt
3½ cups sifted confectioners' sugar
   (12¼ ounces; 350 g), or as needed
2 tablespoons lemon juice, or as needed

Combine the egg whites, cream of tartar, and salt in a mixing bowl and beat just to blend. With the mixer on lowest speed, add the sugar, ½ cup at a time, beating smooth after each addition. Add just enough lemon juice to bring the icing to spreading consistency. Scrape down the bowl and beaters. Beat on high speed until well blended. Sift in more sugar if the icing is too thin, add juice if too stiff.

Confectioners' Frosting

■

This creamy icing is the one to use for forming roses and leaves for wedding cakes because the solid shortening gives it body and holds up, especially in warm weather. You can also use this for frosting any type of cake, but it will be less rich and flavorful than a classic buttercream. For flavoring ideas, see Basic Quick Buttercream on the following page.

☐ QUANTITY: about 3 cups, to fill and frost an 8- or 9-inch 2-layer cake

½ cup unsalted butter or margarine (1
   stick; 110 g), at room temperature
½ cup solid white vegetable shortening
   (3 ounces; 85 g)

1 teaspoon pure flavoring extract
   (vanilla, almond, lemon, or orange)
4½ cups sifted confectioners' sugar (16
   ounces; 454 g), or as needed
2 tablespoons milk, or as needed

In an electric mixer, cream the butter and shortening until smooth and well blended. Add the flavoring extract. With the mixer on lowest speed, gradually beat in the sugar. Scrape down the sides of the bowl and the beater. Add the milk and beat on high speed until frosting is light and fluffy. Add 1 or 2 tablespoons more milk if too dry. Cover the icing with plastic wrap or a damp cloth to prevent drying until ready to use. Store it in a covered container in the refrigerator for up to 2 weeks. Whip before using.

·Variation:·

CHOCOLATE
CONFECTIONERS' FROSTING:

Prepare the basic recipe, but beat into the finished icing

4 ounces unsweetened chocolate, melted,
   plus 2 tablespoons milk.

Basic Quick Buttercream

■

This all-purpose buttercream is less rich than the classic French buttercream and contains a larger proportion of confectioners' sugar. Note the ten flavor variations following the basic recipe.

□ QUANTITY: about 2½ cups, to fill and frost an 8- or 9-inch 2-layer cake

½ cup unsalted butter (1 stick; 110 g),
*   softened but not melted*
1 large egg yolk (optional)
Pinch of salt
1 teaspoon vanilla extract
4 to 4½ cups sifted confectioners' sugar
*   (16 ounces; 454 g)*
5 or 6 tablespoons heavy cream or
*   milk, or as needed*

In an electric mixer or food processor, cream the butter until soft, then beat in the egg yolk if using it, the salt, and the vanilla. With the mixer on low speed or pulsing the processor, add about ¼ cup of the sugar. Beat smooth. Alternately add cream and remaining sugar, blending smooth between additions. Scrape down sides of bowl. Add more cream if too stiff. Chill the icing to harden if too soft.

·Variations:·

LEMON:

Omit the vanilla; use 1 teaspoon grated lemon zest plus 1 or 2 tablespoons fresh lemon juice as part of the liquid.

ORANGE:

Omit the vanilla; use grated zest of ½ orange and substitute orange juice for the cream.

PINEAPPLE:

Omit the vanilla; add 1 teaspoon lemon juice and ⅔ cup drained crushed pineapple. Add more sugar if needed.

SOUR CREAM:

Substitute sour cream for the heavy cream. Especially good when used with chocolate flavoring.

ALMOND:

Omit the vanilla; use ¾ teaspoon almond extract, or to taste.

ALMOND-PRALINE:

Add to finished almond buttercream ½ cup Almond Praline Powder (page 444).

MAPLE-PRALINE:

Add 1 teaspoon maple extract along with the vanilla and stir into the finished buttercream ½ cup Praline Powder made with walnuts (page 444).

CHOCOLATE:

After adding the first ¼ cup of sugar to the mixture, beat in 4 to 6 ounces melted and cooled semisweet chocolate; use only as much cream as necessary to reach spreading consistency.

Increase the vanilla to 2 teaspoons; before adding, dissolve in the vanilla 2 teaspoons instant coffee powder.

CREAMY MOCHA:

Contains no egg yolks. Try this for frosting the Bûche de Noël (page 229).
Follow the basic procedure but use the following ingredients:

¾ cup unsalted butter (1½ sticks; 170 g), at room temperature
2 ounces semisweet plus 1 ounce unsweetened chocolate (85 g), melted in a double boiler
1½ teaspoons instant coffee powder dissolved in 2 teaspoons vanilla extract
Pinch of salt
3 cups sifted confectioners' sugar (10½ ounces; 300 g)
3 to 6 tablespoons heavy cream, as needed

. . . .

Classic French Egg-Yolk Buttercream

∎

Also called Mousseline Buttercream, this is the best there is—rich, silky, and well worth the extra trouble of cooking a sugar syrup to whip into the yolks before adding the butter. For a lighter version, you can add some meringue—see Classic French Buttercream with Meringue, following the master recipe. Other variations include Deluxe French Chocolate Buttercream (used to fill and frost Dobostorte, see Index), Coffee, Orange, Lemon or Lime, and Orange-Chocolate Buttercream.

This is a good icing choice for a Wedding Cake (page 109); you will need 4 times the basic recipe to coat a 3-tier cake.

☐ ADVANCE PREPARATION: This buttercream can be made up to 2 weeks in advance and refrigerated; it can be frozen for up to 2 months. Bring it to room temperature and whip to soften it before using.

☐ SPECIAL EQUIPMENT: double boiler, 2-quart heavy-bottomed saucepan, wooden spoon, candy thermometer, electric mixer

☐ QUANTITY: 2 cups, to frost top and sides of an 8- or 9-inch 2 layer cake
Note: To double this recipe, use 1 cup granulated sugar (200 g) and 1½ cups butter (3 sticks; 340 g); other ingredients double evenly.

1 cup unsalted butter (2 sticks; 230 g), softened but not melted, cut up
½ cup plus 1 tablespoon granulated sugar (rounded 3½ ounces; 100 g)
⅛ teaspoon cream of tartar
¼ cup water
4 large egg yolks

FLAVORING (OPTIONAL):

2 teaspoons vanilla extract or 2 tablespoons liqueur (fruit or nut flavor) or rum or brandy. Other variations follow recipe.

1. In a mixing bowl, use a wooden spoon to work the butter until softened and creamy; at this stage it will properly blend into the buttercream. Set butter aside.

2. In a saucepan, combine the sugar, cream of tartar, and water. Stir a few times, then cook over moderate-high heat until the sugar is dissolved and the syrup looks clear. Raise the heat and begin to cook down the syrup. Several times during this period, wash down the pan sides with a pastry brush dipped into cold water to remove any sugar crystals. Bring the syrup to a gentle boil, and boil *without stirring* for 6 or 7 minutes, or until the candy thermometer reads 238°F.

3. While the sugar boils, put the egg yolks in a heatproof bowl and beat with an electric mixer for several minutes until pale in color and foamy. They should form a flat ribbon falling back on itself when the beater is lifted.

As soon as the syrup reaches the proper temperature, turn the electric mixer to medium-low speed and pour the hot syrup into the yolks in a slow steady stream directed just between the bowl and the beater; if you pour on top of the beater, threads of the sugar syrup will harden too quickly. Do not scrape out the syrup bowl, use only the syrup that pours easily; the rest will be hardened. Beat the mixture until the bowl feels cool to the touch, for 8 to 10 minutes; time depends upon weather as well as bowl temperature. To speed the cooling, you can set the bowl into a pan of ice water and use a hand beater. The buttercream will thicken as it is whipped and cooled.

4. Stick your finger into the buttercream; it should feel cool to the touch; if too hot, it will melt the butter.

With the mixer still running, add the butter, 2 teaspoons at a time. If the bowl temperature is correct, the icing should form a smooth mayonnaiselike emulsion. Continue to add butter slowly, beating well after each addition. Then beat for a full 3 minutes longer, or until the mixture is smooth and fluffy. Note: If making this buttercream in advance to be stored, put it in a covered container unflavored and refrigerate. It is best to add the flavoring just before use.

5. When ready to use the buttercream, whip it until smooth, then beat in the flavoring liqueur, or see the suggestions following. If necessary, chill the buttercream to spreading consistancy. Note: If the buttercream has been refrigerated or frozen, bring it to room temperature and whip before spreading. It may tend to curdle if whipped while too cold; to remedy this, whip it over a pan of very warm water, but do not let the buttercream melt. Or beat in 4 to 8 tablespoons of softened unsalted butter.

· *Variations:* ·

DELUXE FRENCH CHOCOLATE BUTTERCREAM:

Melt 4 ounces semisweet chocolate in the top pan of a double boiler. Let cool and stir into 1 recipe of finished Classic Buttercream.
Note: To fill and frost the Dobostorte (page 279), double the recipe, making 4 cups icing; see the Quantity note on the previous page about doubling ingredients.

COFFEE EGG-YOLK BUTTERCREAM:

Prepare Classic recipe. For flavoring use 2 tablespoons coffee liqueur plus 2 teaspoons instant espresso powder dissolved in 2 teaspoons hot water.

ORANGE, LEMON, OR LIME EGG-YOLK BUTTERCREAM:

Prepare Classic recipe. For flavoring use 2 tablespoons orange liqueur plus the grated zest of 1 orange or 2 lemons or 2 limes and ¾ teaspoon orange or lemon extract.

ORANGE-CHOCOLATE EGG-YOLK BUTTERCREAM:

Prepare Deluxe French Chocolate Buttercream and add 2 tablespoons Grand Marnier and the grated zest of 1 orange.

CLASSIC FRENCH BUTTERCREAM WITH MERINGUE:

Prepare ½ recipe All-Purpose Cold Method or Swiss Method Meringue (page 248), using 2 egg whites plus 4 tablespoons sugar. Prepare Classic Buttercream recipe or any variation. After beating in the butter and flavoring, fold in the meringue. This lightens the buttercream and also makes it spread farther. The 2-egg meringue will add 1½ cups volume to the basic buttercream recipe.

French Buttercream Ménagère (Homestyle Buttercream)

■

Because this recipe contains only 2 egg yolks, it is less rich than Classic French Buttercream. It is really a compromise between the classic recipe and Quick Buttercream (see Index), which is made entirely without egg yolks but with a great deal more sugar.

You can adapt this recipe to any flavor; note lemon, orange, chestnut, chocolate velvet, hazelnut-chocolate variations following the basic recipe. Note that the buttercream hardens as it is chilled; in very hot weather, refrigerate cakes iced with this buttercream.

☐ QUANTITY: about 2 cups, to frost top and sides of 8- or 9-inch 2 layer cake

1 cup unsalted butter (1 stick; 110 g),
*   softened but not melted*
2 large egg yolks
Pinch of salt
1 teaspoon vanilla extract
1½ to 2 cups sifted confectioners' sugar
*   (about 7 ounces; 200 g), as needed*

With an electric mixer, cream the butter until smooth, then add the egg yolks, one at a time, beating after each addition. Add the salt and vanilla and a little of the sugar and beat smooth, then gradually beat in additional sugar until the buttercream reaches spreading consistency. If it starts to look curdled, add a little more sugar and beat on high speed. Chill to stiffen if too soft to spread.

LEMON BUTTERCREAM MÉNAGÈRE:

Prepare basic recipe, but add the grated zest and strained juice of 1 lemon. You will need about 2 cups sugar; use a few tablespoons more sugar to smooth out the buttercream if it begins to curdle.

ORANGE BUTTERCREAM MÉNAGÈRE:

Prepare basic recipe, but add the grated zest of ½ an orange, ½ teaspoon orange extract, and about 3 tablespoons orange juice or orange-flavored liqueur, or as needed. You will need about 2 cups sugar; use a few tablespoons more sugar to smooth out the buttercream if necessary.

CHESTNUT BUTTERCREAM MÉNAGÈRE:

Prepare basic recipe, but flavor with ⅔ cup chestnut purée, 1 more teaspoon vanilla extract, and 3 tablespoons dark rum or brandy. Use 2 cups sugar, or as needed to reach desired consistency.

CHOCOLATE VELVET BUTTERCREAM:

Chop 4 ounces semisweet chocolate (115 g) plus 2 ounces unsweetened chocolate (55 g) and melt them together in the top pan of a double boiler. Remove chocolate from the heat and set it aside to cool to room temperature, not more than 70°F. Prepare basic recipe; beat in the cooled melted chocolate before adding the egg yolks. Use about 1½ cups sugar. This makes about 2⅔ cups.

HAZELNUT-CHOCOLATE BUTTERCREAM:

To the Chocolate Velvet Buttercream above, add ½ cup finely chopped toasted hazelnuts and 2 to 4 tablespoons (to taste) of hazelnut liqueur.

Cream-Cheese Icing

■

This is the traditional icing for Carrot Cake (page 103). It is quick and easy to make, and the slight tang of the cream cheese cuts the sweetness of the sugar, making it an excellent, not-too-sweet topping for many cakes: chocolate, spice, or nut, for example. Prepared in the food processor, Cream-Cheese Icing can be ready in about 1½ minutes. See variations for Orange and Chocolate Cream-Cheese Icing following the basic recipe.

☐ QUANTITY: 2½ cups; enough for an 8- or 9-inch 2 layer cake, or a 9-inch tube cake, or a 9 × 13-inch sheet cake

8 ounces cream cheese (227 g), at room temperature
8 tablespoons lightly salted butter, at room temperature
1½ teaspoons vanilla extract
4 cups sifted confectioners' sugar (14 ounces; 400 g)

In the workbowl of a food processor fitted with the metal blade, or with an electric mixer or wooden spoon, blend the cream cheese and butter together until very smooth and creamy. Beat in the vanilla. Gradually add the sifted sugar, beating until smooth. The longer you beat, the softer the frosting will become. When soft enough to be spread, frost the cake. Refrigerate in hot weather.

· Variations: ·

ORANGE CREAM-CHEESE FROSTING:

Prepare Cream-Cheese Frosting, but add 1 or 2 tablespoons frozen concentrated orange juice and the grated zest of 1 orange.

CHOCOLATE CREAM-CHEESE FROSTING:

Prepare Cream-Cheese Frosting but add 3 to 4 tablespoons sifted unsweetened cocoa, to taste. If the frosting is too stiff, thin it with a few drops of cream or milk.

Quick Coconut Icing

Cream cheese cuts the sweetness of this coconut icing, and using the food processor makes it quick work.

☐ QUANTITY: 2 cups, to frost top and sides of an 8-inch 2-layer cake or the top of one 8 × 12-inch sheet cake

8 ounces cream cheese (227 g)
3/4 teaspoon coconut extract
6 tablespoons heavy cream
5 tablespoons canned sweetened coconut cream, such as Coco Lopez
2 1/2 to 3 cups sifted confectioners' sugar (8 3/4 ounces; 250 g), or as needed

GARNISH:

1 cup sweetened shredded coconut, to sprinkle on the frosted cake

In a bowl, or in the workbowl of the food processor fitted with the metal blade, combine the cream cheese, coconut extract, heavy cream and coconut cream. Slowly add the sifted sugar, blending until smooth. Add more sugar if the icing is too soft. Spread icing on cake, then sprinkle with coconut.

Sour-Cream Nut Icing

•

This Kentucky recipe is the traditional filling and frosting for Gold Layer Cake (page 81). Note that the icing takes about 1 hour to cook, with attention on and off, so plan your time accordingly. The result is a rich, thick, tangy caramel icing unlike any other, and worth the time involved.

☐ SPECIAL EQUIPMENT: double boiler

☐ PREPARATION TIME: 70 minutes

☐ QUANTITY: 3 cups icing, to fill and frost a 2-layer 8-inch cake

8 large egg yolks
1½ cups sour cream
1½ cups firmly packed dark brown sugar (13½ ounces; 385 g)
2 teaspoons vanilla extract
1½ cups finely chopped walnuts or pecans (6 ounces; 170 g)

1. In the top pan of a double boiler, whisk together the egg yolks and sour cream. Crumble and whisk in the brown sugar. Set top pan over the bottom pan containing some hot water. Bring this water to a boil, then reduce heat and simmer for about 1 hour and 10 minutes. During the first 30 minutes, whisk the icing mixture every 5 minutes or so to keep it from sticking. After that, whisk on and off to keep the mixture smooth as it begins to thicken. When done, it will be thick like sour cream and reach a temperature of 170°F.

2. When thick, stir in the vanilla and nuts. Let the mixture stand off the heat until cool and comfortable to touch. As it cools, it will thicken enough to spread.

Peanut Butter Icing

•

If you like peanut butter, you will love its flavor blended with honey and butter in this creamy icing. Note that the recipe is small and can easily be doubled.

☐ QUANTITY: 1⅓ cups, to cover a sheet cake 8 × 12 inches. Halve the recipe to frost the top of an 8- or 9-inch-square cake; double the recipe to fill and frost a 2-layer 8-inch cake.

4 tablespoons lightly salted butter (½ stick; 60 g), at room temperature
½ cup honey
1 cup peanut butter, smooth or chunky

In a medium-size bowl combine all ingredients and beat by hand or with an electric mixer until creamy and smooth. Spread on cooled cake.

To broil this icing, set the frosted cake about 2½ inches below the heat source of a preheated broiler for a minute or two, watching constantly lest it burn. The icing should look golden brown and bubbly when done.

Penuche Icing

•

Like a buttery caramel fudge, this icing is wonderful on spice or nut cakes. The process resembles that for making fudge and requires serious stirring to get the correct texture, but the result is worth it.

□ QUANTITY: 3 generous cups, to fill and frost a 2- or 3-layer 8- or 9-inch cake

2 cups firmly packed dark brown sugar (18 ounces; 510 g)
1½ cups granulated sugar (10½ ounces; 300 g)
¼ teaspoon salt
¾ cup milk
6 tablespoons lightly salted butter (85 g), cut up
2 tablespoons light corn syrup
2 teaspoons vanilla extract

1. Combine all ingredients except the vanilla in a 2-quart heavy-bottomed saucepan. Stir to blend, then set over moderate-high heat and bring slowly to a boil. This takes about 8 minutes. Cover the pan for 3 minutes at the beginning to allow condensation to melt down any sugar crystals that may form on the pan. Do not stir. Boil the syrup without stirring for 1 full minute.

2. Remove pan from the heat and set it in a large pan of ice water. Stir the penuche now and then for about 10 minutes, until icing is lukewarm to the touch. Stir in the vanilla.

3. At this point beat the penuche like fudge. Use a wooden spoon and hand-beat for 10 to 15 minutes, until it reaches spreading consistency. Spread icing on the cake. The icing will air-dry and lose its stickiness in about 30 minutes, but the inside will remain like fudge.

Brown-Sugar Caramel Icing

•

Like Penuche, this icing has a fudgelike consistency and a strong caramel flavor, but is easier to make. Use it for caramel cake or white, yellow, or nut layer cake. For a spice cake, use the variation for Sugar'n Spice Icing.

□ QUANTITY: 1½ cups icing, to ice the top of a sheet cake 8 × 12 inches or the top and sides of a 2-layer 8-inch cake; double the recipe to both fill and frost a layer cake

1 cup firmly packed dark brown sugar (9 ounces; 255 g)
6 tablespoons milk or heavy cream
5 tablespoons lightly salted butter (75 g)
2 cups sifted confectioners' sugar (7 ounces; 200 g)

In a 2-quart saucepan, combine the sugar, milk, and butter. Bring to a boil over moderate heat, stirring constantly. Boil for 2 full minutes, stirring. Remove from heat and cool until comfortable to touch. Stir in the sifted sugar and beat well until the icing reaches spreading consistency.

Variation:

SUGAR 'N' SPICE ICING:

Prepare Brown-Sugar Caramel Icing, but substitute light brown sugar. After stirring in confectioners' sugar, add ¾ teaspoon vanilla extract, ¾ teaspoon lemon juice, 1 generous teaspoon ground cinnamon, and ½ teaspoon each of ground ginger, nutmeg, and allspice. If doubling the recipe, do not double the spices; prepare as listed here, then adjust quantities to taste.

Broiled Caramel-Nut Icing

■

This is one of the few icings you can successfully put on a warm-from-the-oven cake. It is good on oatmeal, spice, white, or yellow cakes.

□ QUANTITY: 1 generous cup, to top an 8- or 9-inch square cake. Double the recipe for a larger sheet or a layer cake.

4 tablespoons unsalted butter (60 g), melted
½ cup firmly packed dark brown sugar (4½ ounces; 130 g)
¼ cup light cream or milk
½ teaspoon vanilla extract
⅛ teaspoon each of ground cinnamon and nutmeg
⅛ teaspoon salt
1 cup finely chopped pecans (4 ounces; 110 g), or chopped walnuts, and/or shredded sweetened coconut

Combine all ingredients and beat them thoroughly in a bowl. Spread the icing over the warm or cold cake and put it 4 to 5 inches beneath the heat source of a preheated broiler. Broil for about 3 minutes, or just until the icing is light brown and bubbly; watch carefully lest it burn. Remove cake from the broiler and cool the icing completely before serving the cake.

Mocha Frosting

■

□ QUANTITY: 3 cups, to fill and frost the top and sides of a 2 layer 8- or 9-inch cake. Double recipe to fill and frost a 2- or 3-layer cake generously, or to frost a 4-layer cake. For Mocha Fudge Cake (see Index), use sweetened whipped cream for the filling; frost with this recipe, mixed until soft enough to spread without pressing on the cake so the whipped cream is not forced out.

½ cup unsalted butter (1 stick; 110 g), at room temperature
6 cups sifted confectioners' sugar (21 ounces; 600 g)
⅓ cup sifted unsweetened cocoa (¾ ounce; 20 g)
7 tablespoons strong coffee, or 1 tablespoon instant espresso powder dissolved in 7 tablespoons boiling water
2 teaspoons vanilla extract

In the large bowl of an electric mixer, beat the butter until very soft and creamy. With the mixer on very low speed, beat in about 2 cups of the sugar. Stop the mixer and scrape down bowl and beaters. Add remaining sugar and the cocoa alternately with the coffee, beating until very smooth and creamy. Beat in the vanilla. Note: For an even richer icing, use ¾ cup butter.

In the large bowl of an electric mixer, cream the butter until soft and smooth. Add 1 cup of the sugar and the orange juice and beat until creamy. Don't worry if mixture looks curdled. Little by little, add remaining sugar, beating slowly. Beat in the lemon juice, orange extract, and grated zest. Add the sherry and beat until smooth. Add more sherry if needed; or add some sugar if the icing is too thin—it should be slightly thinner than a regular buttercream when spread on the cake.

Orange Wine Icing

∎

Dry sherry cuts the sweetness of this icing and gives it a refreshing and sophisticated flavor. For a nonalcoholic icing you can substitute orange juice or cream. To make Orange Madeira Icing, use Madeira wine instead of sherry.

□ QUANTITY: 1½ cups icing, to frost two 8- or 9-inch layers or one 9-inch (6 cups) tube cake. Double the recipe to fill and frost 2 or 3 layers or a large sheet cake.

5 tablespoons unsalted butter (70 g)
3 cups sifted confectioners' sugar (10½ ounces; 300 g)
3 tablespoons freshly squeezed orange juice
1 teaspoon freshly squeezed lemon juice
½ teaspoon orange extract
1 generous teaspoon grated orange zest
2 tablespoons dry sherry or orange liqueur or Madeira wine

Seven-Minute Icing

∎

Seven-Minute Icing is really a quick and easy version of Boiled Icing (page 400), and the results are similar: a white satin meringue with a texture somewhere between whipped cream and melted marshmallows. Seafoam Icing, Maple, Coconut, Orange, Lemon, and Peppermint Seven-Minute Icing are variations that follow the master recipe. Note that Seven-Minute Icing can be used for Lord or Lady Baltimore Cake instead of the classic Boiled Icing.

□ QUANTITY: 3 cups, to fill and frost a 2-layer 8- or 9-inch cake

2 large egg whites
1½ cups granulated sugar (10½ ounces; 300 g)
5 tablespoons cold water
2 teaspoons light corn syrup
¼ teaspoon cream of tartar
1 teaspoon vanilla extract

1. Combine all ingredients except the vanilla in the top pan of a double boiler set over boiling water. Immediately begin beating with a whisk or hand-held electric mixer. If using the mixer, start at medium-low speed for 4 minutes, then increase to high for the final 3 minutes. With a whisk it can take up to 13 or 14 minutes. Whip until the icing is a satiny foam that holds very soft peaks and mounds on the beater.

2. Remove pan from the heat, stir in the vanilla, then beat hard for 1 full minute longer, or until the icing is a little thicker. Spread on the cake at once. After it air-dries, the outer surface will lose its stickiness but the inside will remain soft. Don't ice cakes with this more than 6 hours in advance, because the icing tends to become granular after long standing.

· Variations: ·

SEAFOAM ICING:

This has a caramel flavor and makes 4 cups. Prepare Seven-Minute Icing, but replace the granulated sugar with 1½ cups firmly packed dark brown sugar (13½ ounces; 385 g). If you wish, add ½ teaspoon almond extract along with the vanilla.

MAPLE SEVEN-MINUTE ICING:

Prepare Seven-Minute Icing, but replace the sugar with ¾ cup pure maple syrup. This whips to stiff peaks in about 6 minutes. Note: Don't freeze a cake covered with this icing; when it thaws, the icing breaks down and gets runny.

COCONUT SEVEN-MINUTE ICING:

Prepare Seven-Minute Icing, but add ½ teaspoon coconut extract and stir in ½ cup sweetened shredded coconut. Spread more coconut on the frosted cake.

ORANGE SEVEN-MINUTE ICING:

Prepare Seven-Minute Icing, but substitute ½ teaspoon orange extract for the vanilla and add 2 teaspoons grated orange zest.

LEMON SEVEN-MINUTE ICING:

Prepare Seven-Minute Icing, but use only 3 tablespoons water plus 2 tablespoons lemon juice in the pan at the start. Add to the finished icing 1 teaspoon grated lemon zest.

PEPPERMINT SEVEN-MINUTE ICING:

Prepare Seven-Minute Icing, but add ½ teaspoon oil of peppermint or peppermint extract and 4 tablespoons finely crushed peppermint candy. If you must, tint this icing a very light pink or green with a drop of vegetable food coloring.

Boiled Icing

•

Shiny, sticky, and luxurious, the peaks of the marshmallowlike boiled icing remind me of childhood birthday cakes. Also known as Divinity or White Mountain Icing, this is in fact a classic Italian Meringue with a slight adjustment in the cooking temperature of the syrup that is poured over the whipped egg whites. Endless variations are possible; recipes follow for Rocky Mountain, Beige Mountain, Lane Cake Icing, Lord and Lady Baltimore, Lemon, Orange, Cocoa, and Coconut.

☐ SPECIAL EQUIPMENT: 2-quart heavy-bottomed saucepan, mercury candy thermometer, pastry brush, electric mixer, metal pan of ice water for cooling sugar syrup (optional)

☐ QUANTITY: about 3½ cups, to fill and frost an 8- or 9-inch 2 layer cake

¾ cup plus 2 tablespoons granulated
*   sugar (6¼ ounces; 175 g)*
⅓ cup water
1 tablespoon white corn syrup, or ⅛
*   teaspoon cream of tartar*
3 large egg whites
2 tablespoons granulated sugar
1 teaspoon vanilla extract (optional)

Follow the procedure for making Italian Meringue. To summarize, combine sugar, water, and corn syrup in a saucepan; heat to dissolve the sugar, then bring to a boil. Boil without stirring (wash down pan sides with a pastry brush dipped into water to remove sugar crys-

tals) until the recommended temperature is reached (see below). When almost at the end of the boiling time, begin to whip the egg whites. Whip until fluffy, add 2 tablespoons sugar, and whip until stiff but not dry.

Note carefully: For Boiled Icing, boil syrup for about 7 minutes, until the candy thermometer reads 230°F. Lift the pan from the heat (the syrup continues to cook from internal heat) and watch thermometer until it reaches 235°F, *not* 238°F as required for Italian Meringue. At 235°F the syrup will make a thin thread when dropped from the side of a metal spoon. At this point, not a higher temperature, pour the syrup slowly over the whipped whites with the electric mixer running on medium speed. Continue to whip for 3 to 4 minutes longer to thicken and cool the icing. Whip in the vanilla or other flavoring.

When the icing is cool, stiff, and very glossy, apply it to the cake. Use an icing spatula or the back of a spoon to create characteristic swirls. As the icing cools, the outer surface dries and loses its stickiness, but the inside it will remain creamy.

·Variations:·

ROCKY MOUNTAIN ICING:

Use this to fill a 1-2-3-4 Cake (page 76), turning it into Rocky Mountain Cake. Prepare Boiled Icing, adding the vanilla. Reserve 1 cup of the icing and set it aside. Into the rest stir 1 cup sweetened flaked coconut, ½ cup chopped seedless raisins, ½ cup currants, 1 cup chopped blanched almonds, and ¼ teaspoon almond extract. Use the fruited icing to fill the 3 layers of the cake. Spread the reserved plain icing on the cake top (do not ice the sides at all) and sprinkle with ½ cup flaked coconut.

BEIGE MOUNTAIN ICING:

Prepare Boiled Icing, but substitute 1½ cups firmly packed brown sugar for the granulated sugar.

LANE CAKE ICING AND LADY BALTIMORE ICING:

Both are the same as regular Boiled Icing, made with vanilla extract.

LORD BALTIMORE ICING:

Prepare Boiled Icing, adding the vanilla. Reserve a scant 2 cups of icing. Fold into remaining icing 2 teaspoons lemon juice, ½ teaspoon orange extract, ½ cup crushed crisp macaroon cookies (not powdered), ¼ cup toasted sliced almonds, ¼ cup chopped toasted pecans, and 12 glacéed red cherries, chopped. Use the fruited icing to fill the 3 layers of the cake. Spread the reserved plain icing on the top and sides. If you don't have quite enough icing for a generous side coat, spread it thinner around the lower edges and press on toasted sliced almonds.

LEMON BOILED ICING:

Prepare Boiled Icing, but substitute 1 tablespoon lemon juice for the vanilla extract and add ½ teaspoon grated lemon zest.

ORANGE BOILED ICING:

Prepare Boiled Icing, but substitute 1 tablespoon frozen orange-juice concentrate, thawed but not diluted, for the vanilla extract. Add 2 teaspoons grated orange zest.

COCOA BOILED ICING:

Prepare Boiled Icing, but sift 4 tablespoons unsweetened cocoa into 1 cup of the finished and cooled icing. Stir this into the entire batch and whip to blend.

COCONUT BOILED ICING:

Prepare Boiled Icing, but add 1 teaspoon coconut extract. You can stir into the icing 1 cup sweetened flaked coconut if you wish, or (as I prefer) sprinkle the flaked coconut on top of the icing after it is spread on the cake, working quickly before the surface dries.

Swiss Meringue Buttercream

■

This light, fluffy icing is buttery and not too sweet. It has a luscious satin texture and white color, and is perfect for summer wedding cakes that must be on display in warm weather. The technique is quick and easy: a Swiss Meringue (page 249) is made by warming egg whites with sugar, whipping them to stiff peaks, then beating in softened sweet butter. The result is similar to Italian Meringue Buttercream (following recipe), but the method is quicker.

☐ ADVANCE PREPARATION: The texture and spreading quality of this buttercream are best when it is freshly made. However, it may be refrigerated a week in advance or frozen for up to 1 month. Bring to room temperature and whip before using.

□ SPECIAL EQUIPMENT: large metal bowl for electric mixer, pan containing hot water upon which the metal bowl can sit, wooden spoon, separate bowl and beater for softening butter, mercury candy thermometer or spot instant-read thermometer

□ QUANTITY: about 3 cups, to fill and frost an 8- or 9-inch 2 layer cake

4 large egg whites (½ cup)
¾ cup granulated sugar (5¼ ounces; 150 g)
1¼ cups unsalted butter (2½ sticks; 285 g), softened but not melted
¼ teaspoon cream of tartar
Pinch of salt

FLAVORING:

1 teaspoon vanilla (or other flavor) extract; or 1 tablespoon grated orange or lemon zest plus 1 teaspoon orange or lemon extract; or
4 squares semisweet chocolate, melted and cooled, then whipped into 1 cup of the finished buttercream before being blended into the whole mixture

1. Combine the egg whites and sugar in the large metal bowl of an electric mixer and set it over a pan of simmering water on the stove. Put the candy thermometer in the bowl. Stir the whites and sugar frequently as they warm to 120°F and the sugar dissolves. As the temperature rises, stir more often.

While the sugar syrup is warming, cream the butter by hand or with an electric mixer, beating until butter is soft and smooth. At this stage it will incorporate easily with the butter-

cream. Set the butter aside; do not chill it.

2. As soon as the egg-white and sugar syrup has reached the correct temperature, add the cream of tartar and salt and whip with the electric mixer until stiff but not dry. The whites will be very shiny. With the mixer on medium speed, continue whipping until the whites are cool to the touch throughout; this can take about 10 minutes. Touch the bowl as well as the whites to check the temperature; if too warm, the whites will melt the butter.

3. When egg whites are cool to the touch, continue to whip them while adding the softened butter, 1 small spoonful at a time. Whip after each addition. The buttercream will start to deflate when the first few spoons of butter go in, but by the end it will look thicker and fluffier. When the butter is all in, add the flavoring of your choice and whip for a few seconds to blend. Use at once or refrigerate in a covered container for later use.

Note: For a 3-tiered wedding cake you will need at least 8 to 9 cups of icing. For best results, I prefer to make 1 double recipe and 1 single recipe. Do not triple the recipe unless you have professional equipment, very large and heavy-duty.

For a wedding cake that must stand outside in extremely hot weather, you could replace up to half of the butter with solid white vegetable shortening; it will hold up better. You may want to increase the flavoring to compensate for loss of the butter flavor; taste and adjust as needed.

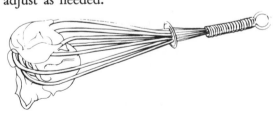

Italian Meringue Buttercream

■

This elegant, light-textured buttercream is not too sweet, holds up well in hot weather, and will take any type of flavoring. To make it, a cooked sugar syrup is whipped into beaten egg whites, then softened butter is added. The technique is more exacting than that used for the Swiss Meringue Buttercream (preceding recipe), which it resembles, but it is not difficult. Because the sugar syrup is cooked, this is even more stable and long-lived than the Swiss buttercream and is an excellent choice for a summer wedding cake; in extreme heat, it is a better choice than Swiss buttercream. For a richer version, you can add some Vanilla Pastry Cream, to make Deluxe Meringue Buttercream, following the master recipe.

□ ADVANCE PREPARATION: This buttercream spreads most perfectly and the texture is lightest when it is freshly made; however, it can be made in advance and stored covered in the refrigerator for up to 1 week, or it can be frozen for up to 1 month. Bring buttercream to room temperature and whip it smooth before using. Note: For a 3-tiered wedding cake you need about 2½ times this recipe. For best results, make single-recipe batches as needed unless you have professional equipment, very large and heavy-duty, to take the volume of doubling the recipe. Use freshly made buttercream if possible, then chill or freeze the frosted wedding cake layers.

□ SPECIAL EQUIPMENT: 2-quart heavy-bottomed saucepan, mercury candy thermometer, pastry brush, mixing bowl and wooden spoon, stand-type electric mixer (helpful but not essential), metal pan of ice water to hold sugar syrup pan

□ QUANTITY: about 3½ cups, to fill and frost an 8- or 9-inch 2-layer cake

1⅓ cups unsalted butter (2 sticks plus 5⅓ tablespoons; 310 g), softened but not melted
1 recipe Italian Meringue (page 249) as follows:
⅓ cup water
¾ cup plus 2 tablespoons granulated sugar (6¼ ounces; 175 g)
1 tablespoon white corn syrup, or ⅛ teaspoon cream of tartar
3 large egg whites
2 tablespoons granulated sugar

FLAVORING (SELECT ONE):

1 teaspoon vanilla or other extract;
Grated citrus zest and/or juice;
1 tablespoon instant espresso coffee powder dissolved in 1 tablespoon coffee liqueur or hot water;
3 or 4 ounces melted bittersweet chocolate;
4 ounces melted and cooled white chocolate, preferably Tobler Narcisse;
3 tablespoons rum or brandy or liqueur (fruit or nut flavor);
¼ to ⅓ cup Praline Paste (page 444), amount to taste, softened with a little cream

1. In a bowl, with a hand-held beater or wooden spoon, work the butter until softened and creamy; at this stage it will properly blend

into the meringue. Set the butter aside; do not chill.

2. Read the recipe for Italian Meringue. Briefly, combine in a saucepan and bring to a boil the water, ¾ cup plus 2 tablespoons sugar, and corn syrup or cream of tartar. Set the candy thermometer in the pan. Several times during the cooking, wash down the pan sides with a pastry brush dipped into cold water to remove any sugar crystals. Allow the syrup to boil *without stirring* for about 8 minutes, or until the thermometer reads 238°F (soft-ball stage). Near the end of the sugar-cooking time (at about 228°F), begin to whip the egg whites. When fluffy add 2 tablespoons granulated sugar to the whites and whip until *nearly* stiff but not dry. Do not overwhip. Keep a sharp eye on the syrup thermometer.

3. As soon as the syrup reaches 238°F, no higher, remove it from the heat and set it near the mixer in a pan of ice water to stop the cooking. Check the egg whites; they should be satiny and stiff but dry. With the mixer running on medium-low speed, slowly pour the hot syrup over the beaten whites in a thin, steady stream. Continue whipping after all the syrup is in. The whites will increase in volume and be satin-smooth and quite stiff. Keep the mixer on medium-low speed and whip the meringue for 10 to 15 minutes, or until thoroughly cool to the touch throughout. Feel the bowl as well as the meringue. To speed this process, you can also use a hand-held mixer and whip the meringue over a pan of ice water.

4. As soon as you are sure that the meringue is cool enough not to melt the butter, you can begin to add it. Although the butter was beaten earlier, give it a few turns now just to be sure it is soft.

With the mixer on medium speed, add the soft butter, 1 tablespoon at a time, to the meringue. Beat after each addition as if making a mayonnaise. If meringue starts to curdle, increase mixer speed to high and blend, then lower speed and continue adding butter. When completely smooth, stir in the flavoring of your choice, a few drops at a time. Use the buttercream immediately if possible, or store in a covered container in the refrigerator or freezer. If chilled, bring it to room temperature and whip before spreading it on a cake.

·*Variation:*·

DELUXE MERINGUE BUTTERCREAM:

This is regular Italian Meringue Buttercream enriched with Vanilla Pastry Cream. This icing can be frozen for several months without changing texture. Bring it to room temperature and whip before spreading on a cake.

Prepare ½ recipe Vanilla Pastry Cream (page 370). Set the cream aside to cool. Start preparations for the Italian Meringue Buttercream. In step 1, beat 1 cup of the cooled vanilla pastry cream into the softened butter. Set this aside. Continue making the syrup and beating it into the whipped egg whites. In step 3, beat the enriched butter into the Italian Meringue. Add flavoring (see master recipe for suggestions). Praline is a classic flavoring choice with this recipe.

Tangerine Glaze for Cheesecake

∎

This tangy glaze garnished with tangerine segments is the perfect topping for Tangerine Cheesecake, but it also adds a flourish to plain cheesecake or sponge cake. For variations, substitute regular, blood, or mandarin oranges, and orange juice.

☐ QUANTITY: about 1⅛ cups, to top one 9- or 10-inch cake

½ cup granulated sugar (3½ ounces; 100 g)
2 tablespoons cornstarch dissolved in ⅓ cup cold water
⅔ cup fresh or frozen tangerine juice
1 or 2 drops each of red and yellow vegetable food coloring (optional)
3 tangerines, peeled, pitted, divided into segments with membranes removed

1. In a saucepan combine the sugar, dissolved cornstarch mixture, and juice. Stir smooth and bring to a boil while stirring constantly. Boil for 1 full minute. If you wish, stir in just enough food coloring for an orange tone. Taste and adjust for sweetness if necessary. Cool the sauce.

2. When the cheesecake is completely cold, stir the glaze to be sure it is at spreading consistency, then spread a generous ½ cup on the cheesecake. Drop peeled tangerine segments or other sliced fruit into remaining glaze and stir gently just to coat. With tongs, lift the fruit to the top of the cake and arrange in a decorative pattern. Pour remaining glaze over the cake top. It takes about 1 hour in the refrigerator for the glaze to set.

Strawberry Glaze

∎

This fruit-filled glaze is perfect on vanilla or citrus-flavored cheesecakes, but it also makes a fine topping for plain sponge cakes. Use any type of fresh berries in season, or substitute frozen berries.

☐ QUANTITY: 1½ cups, to top one 9- or 10-inch cake

1 quart ripe strawberries (20 ounces; 560 g), or other berries, washed and hulled
½ cup granulated sugar (3½ ounces; 100 g), or to taste, depending on sweetness of berries
1½ tablespoons cornstarch dissolved in ¼ cup cold water
2 teaspoons lemon juice
1 tablespoon butter

1. Pick over the berries; crush enough of the least perfect looking ones to make 1 cup pulp. Place the pulp in a 1½-quart saucepan along with the sugar and dissolved cornstarch mixture. Stir well and bring the mixture to a boil over moderate heat. Stir constantly while boiling for 1½ to 2 minutes, until the glaze

is thickened and clear. Remove pan from the heat and add the lemon juice and butter, stirring until the butter melts. Cool the glaze to room temperature.

2. When the cheesecake is completely cold, arrange reserved whole berries on top, then spoon on about ⅔ cup of the glaze. Chill the cake; it will take about 1 hour in the refrigerator for the glaze to set. Pass any remaining glaze, to serve as a sauce, in a small bowl at the table.

ABOUT ICING GLAZE

∎

Icing glazes blend confectioners' sugar and flavoring liquids plus, occasionally, melted butter and cream. Glazes are meant to flow smoothly and drip, they are not thick enough to spread with a knife. Because glazes are made with confectioners' sugar, which contains cornstarch and has a raw taste when uncooked, be sure to use sufficient flavoring.

Icing glazes are used when a rich, thick frosting is undesirable, for example, on certain chiffon, spice, fruit, or nut cakes. Often the glaze is used on a ring-shaped cake, where it covers the top and drips down the sides. On holiday cake rings and loaves, glazes can be decoratively studded with candied fruits and nuts.

Vary the amount of liquid in the recipe to control the fluidity of the glaze, making it softer if you wish it to drip down the cake sides, or stiffer if you prefer a thicker, less transparent look. Vary the flavor of the glaze to match that of your cake; use maple or cinnamon for a spice cake, lemon or orange

for a fruit or nut cake, and vanilla if you are not sure which way to go.

Since the glaze is thin, it will not conceal uneven blemishes in the cake's surface. To remedy this, you can sprinkle the glaze, before it hardens on the surface, with finely chopped nuts, toasted coconut, finely crumbled praline powder (page 444) nutmeg, cinnamon, or a little grated lemon or orange zest. Be sure to select a garnish that goes with the icing. Or you can apply 2 coats of glaze. To do this, spread one thin coat to seal the crumbs on the cake's surface, then add a second coat that flows easily and drips down the cake sides; even with 2 coats, the total glaze should be quite thin.

Basic Icing Glaze

∎

☐ QUANTITY: about ½ cup glaze, enough to top one 8- or 9-inch square or tube cake or a sheet cake 8 × 12 inches. Double the recipe to top a sheet 9 × 13 inches or a tube cake 10 × 4 inches.

*1⅓ cups sifted confectioners' sugar
    (4¾ ounces; 135 g)*
*1 to 2 tablespoons cream, or more as
    needed to thin the glaze*
1 tablespoon unsalted butter, melted

FLAVORING:

*½ teaspoon lemon or orange extract; or
    1 teaspoon vanilla extract; or 3 or 4
    drops of maple extract (as it is*

stronger); or 1 tablespoon very strong coffee; or 1 to 2 tablespoons bourbon or fruit or nut liqueur used in place of the cream

Combine all ingredients in a small bowl, beat well, and check flavor and consistency. Add more cream to thin, more sifted sugar to thicken the glaze. It should drip from a spatula in a sheet when at the correct consistency.

Orange Icing Glaze

▪

☐ QUANTITY: 1 scant cup, to top an 8- or 9-inch tube cake. Double the recipe for a 10-inch tube cake.

*1½ cups sifted confectioners' sugar
   (5¼ ounces; 150 g)
1 teaspoon grated orange zest
3 tablespoons orange juice
2 teaspoons freshly squeezed lemon
   juice
1 tablespoon unsalted butter, melted*

Combine all ingredients and blend until smooth. Adjust for consistency and flavor.

·Variation:·

LEMON ICING GLAZE

Prepare Orange Icing Glaze but substitute grated lemon zest and use all lemon juice. Another possibility, which is a little less sharp, is to use the lemon zest but keep the blend of orange and lemon juice.

Ganache: Icing Glaze or Chocolate Filling

▪

A blend of melted chocolate, heavy cream, and flavoring, ganache is a versatile mixture. Its flavor is intensely chocolate, less sweet than a buttercream, and its texture is silky smooth. When warm, ganache flows like cream and can be poured over cake as an icing glaze; it will set with a dark color and high gloss but remain like fudge under the surface. At room temperature, it can be whipped until fluffy and light-colored (ganache soufflé), then spread as a filling and icing on cakes. It can also be piped through a pastry bag to make decorations.

Note: Two methods for preparation are given here—the conventional method in which the chocolate is melted in the double boiler with the cream, and the quicker food-processor method in which the hot cream is poured through the feed tube onto the machine-ground chocolate.

The ganache can be prepared ahead and refrigerated, covered, until needed. Bring to room temperature, or warm in a double boiler, before applying as a glaze; whip before using as a filling.

☐ SPECIAL EQUIPMENT [depends upon method used and whether the ganache is used as a glaze or a whipped filling]: double boiler, hand-held electric mixer or food processor, saucepan, large bowl containing ice and ice water

☐ QUANTITY: about 2⅓ cups before whipping. As a glaze, makes enough for two 9-inch 2-layer cakes. When whipped, makes enough to fill three 9-inch layers or to fill and frost a 2-layer 8-inch cake. Make half of the recipe if using ganache only to fill between 2 layers.

8 ounces best-quality semisweet or bittersweet chocolate, such as Lindt Excellence or Tobler Tradition, chopped fine (or use some milk chocolate if you want a sweeter ganache)

1 cup heavy cream

2 or 3 tablespoons liqueur (coffee, fruit, or nut flavor, or rum or brandy), or 1 teaspoon vanilla or other extract Note: For Mocha Ganache, use 2 teaspoons instant coffee powder dissolved in 1 tablespoon hot water or 3 tablespoons coffee liqueur; for Raspberry Ganache, use 3 tablespoons Chambord liqueur.

1½ tablespoons white corn syrup (optional), used only in ganache icing glaze, to ensure smoothness

□ CONVENTIONAL METHOD (ABOUT 2⅓ CUPS): Combine the chocolate and cream in top pan of double boiler set over, not in, hot water. Heat until the chocolate melts. Remove from heat and stir to blend well. Stir in the liqueur and corn syrup if using it.

To use the ganache as a dark chocolate glaze, let it cool until just barely lukewarm, then pour generously over a cake set on a rack over a tray. Tilt the cake to help the glaze flow. Note: For the smoothest finish, first give the cake an undercoating of Apricot Glaze (see page 411) or buttercream. Chill the coated cake before pouring on the glaze.

To use the ganache as a spreadable filling or icing, set the bowl of melted chocolate in a larger bowl of ice water. Note: If the bowl is tippy, set it on a ring made from a draped tea towel. With a hand-held mixer, beat the chocolate mixture for about 5 minutes, or until ganache is cool, lighter in color, nearly double in volume, and has become thick and creamy. At this stage, it should be of spreading consistency. If necessary, adjust the consistency by adding more cream to soften it, or chilling to harden.

When you first apply whipped ganache, you will see lots of air bubbles. As you work the ganache with the icing spatula as it is applied, the texture smooths out perfectly and the bubbles disappear.

□ FOOD PROCESSOR METHOD (ABOUT 2 CUPS): Break the chocolate into chunks, put it in a processor fitted with the metal blade, and process to a fine powder. Place the cream in a pan over moderate heat and bring just to the boiling point. Do *not* boil. With the machine running, pour the hot cream slowly through the feed tube onto the chocolate. Blend until completely smooth. Twice, stop machine and stir down the sides. Add liqueur or other flavoring and corn syrup if using it. Pulse to blend.

To use this as a glaze, pour the warm, fluid ganache on the cake, spreading gently with a spatula as needed. To use as an icing and/or filling, cool without stirring (for darker color), or stir it over ice water until cool (for a lighter tone), then whip to spreading consistency. Note: For a more intense chocolate flavor, you can increase the quantity of chocolate to 12 ounces, but leave the other ingredients unchanged.

FRANNI'S GANACHE GLAZE (1 CUP):

This recipe comes from Franni's Café-Pâtisserie in Montreal and is used atop their Mosaic Cheesecake (page 192). It is a wonderful all-purpose glaze for any type of cake.

6 ounces semisweet or bittersweet chocolate (170 g), broken up, or 1 cup chocolate morsels
¼ cup unsalted butter (½ stick; 57 g)
½ cup heavy cream
½ teaspoon vanilla extract
½ teaspoon rum or brandy
2 tablespoons sifted confectioners' sugar

Use the Food Processor Method: grind the chocolate into powder in the processor, scald the butter and cream in a saucepan, then pour the hot mixture over the chocolate with the machine running. Scrape down the bowl, add flavorings and sugar, and process until smooth. Spread over cake while still warm. Note: Half of this recipe (½ cup) is sufficient to cover one 9½-inch cheesecake.

Fabulous Chocolate Glaze

∎

This superb and foolproof chocolate glaze sets with a firm surface and high gloss, though inside it retains the texture of a creamy fudge. It gives cakes and tortes a professional bakery look and taste. Be sure to use the finest chocolate you can find, for the glaze takes its flavor from the chocolate, even if liqueurs or extracts are added. Note that this is not a sweet glaze; it will be exactly as sweet as the chocolate you use, as no sugar is added.

The chocolate glaze is applied to the cake when warm, and flows on, spreading easily. After about 30 minutes, it sets. Use it for Sachertorte (page 273) or any other fine chocolate or nut cake or torte. To achieve a perfectly smooth surface on the cake, apply 1 thin coat of glaze, let it harden for 30 minutes, then apply a second coat.

Note: Fingerprints will mark the glaze, so be careful. Lift the finished cake from underneath, using a broad spatula or cake cardboard.

□ QUANTITY: 1½ cups glaze, enough to coat a 2- or 3-layer 9-inch cake

½ cup plus 1 tablespoon unsalted butter (4½ ounces; 130 g), at room temperature, cut up
9 ounces best-quality semisweet or bittersweet chocolate, such as Lindt or Tobler, cut into small pieces
1½ tablespoons corn syrup

FLAVORING:

Mocha: 1 teaspoon instant espresso coffee powder dissolved in 1 tablespoon boiling water
Orange: 2 tablespoons Cointreau or other orange liqueur plus 1 teaspoon orange extract
Hazelnut: 2 or 3 tablespoons hazelnut liqueur
Brandy: 2 or 3 tablespoons any brandy
Nonalcoholic flavoring: 1½ teaspoons any pure extract such as vanilla, almond, or orange

1. Combine the butter, chocolate, and corn syrup in the top pan of a double boiler set over, not in, hot water. When melted remove from heat and stir until very smooth and glossy. Stir in the flavoring.

2. Place the cake on a wire rack over a tray. While the glaze is warm, pour 1 thin layer, about ½ cup for an 8-inch cake, on top of the cake and allow it to flow. With an icing spatula, spread the glaze evenly so it drips down onto the sides. Spread more glaze around the sides. Set the cake aside for about 30 minutes, until the glaze no longer feels tacky to the touch (test a side, not the top, or the fingerprint will show). In hot weather, refrigerate to set.

While the first coat hardens, press a piece of plastic wrap or wax paper directly onto the top of remaining glaze to prevent it from forming a skin. If this glaze has cooled and stiffened at all during the wait, set it back over hot water for a few minutes and stir until warm and smooth. Then pour a second coat of glaze over the cake. Use the spatula with a *very* light touch to smooth the warm glaze across the top. Allow the glaze to set for at least 30 minutes without touching it. It will harden and become very glossy.

Chocolate Water Glaze

∎

This is my adaptation of a glaze developed by Albert Kumin of Country Epicure's International Pastry Arts Center in Bedford Hills, New York. Kumin devised this glaze when pastry chef at the Four Seasons Restaurant in New York City, and he has continued to favor it because the water, which replaces the traditional cream, gives a better gloss and holds up longer. The flavor is equally good. The recipe is easy to follow if you whisk in enough water at one time to prevent the chocolate from seizing. This glaze sets with a fine gloss and retains a fudgelike consistency underneath. It can be frozen.

□ QUANTITY: about 1½ cups, more than enough to glaze one 9-inch 2- or 3-layer cake

12 ounces best-quality semisweet or bittersweet chocolate
6 tablespoons very hot water

1. Melt the chocolate in the top pan of a double boiler set over hot, not boiling, water. Stir until smooth. Whisk the hot water into the chocolate all at once (*not* slowly or the chocolate may seize) until the chocolate is satiny smooth. It will have the consistency of softly whipped cream. If you wish the glaze more liquid, whisk in 1 or more tablespoons hot water.

2. Set the cake on a rack over a tray and pour a generous amount of glaze in the center. Tilt the cake to help the glaze flow; spread it with an icing spatula. Set aside, or refrigerate in hot weather, to set the glaze. The gloss disappears when refrigerated, but returns at room temperature. Beware of fingerprints on the glaze; they show.

Cocoa Icing Glaze

■

□ QUANTITY: 1⅓ cups, to glaze the top and sides of an 8- or 9-inch 2-layer cake or torte

½ cup sifted unsweetened cocoa, preferably Dutch-process (1⅓ ounces; 38 g)
½ cup granulated sugar (3½ ounces; 100 g)
½ cup heavy cream
¼ cup unsalted butter (½ stick; 60 g), cut up

Combine all the ingredients in the top pan of a double boiler set over hot, not boiling, water and stir until the mixture is shiny and smooth, about 5 minutes. Remove pan from the heat and set it aside to cool for about 5 minutes. Pour the glaze over the top of the cake, and use an icing spatula to spread it evenly over the top and around the cake sides. Refrigerate the cake to harden the glaze.

Apricot Glaze

■

This is an all-purpose glaze used to undercoat cakes before icing, or to top fruitcakes and savarins.

□ QUANTITY: 1 cup, to coat a 2-layer 8- or 9-inch cake

1 cup apricot preserves, best quality

Stir preserves over medium heat in a small saucepan until melted. Stir and cook about 2 minutes longer, bringing preserves to a boil. Cook until thick enough to coat a spoon. Strain preserves through a sieve. Cool slightly and use pastry brush to coat the cake with lukewarm glaze as directed in recipe. Chill cake to set the glaze.

Firm Apricot Glaze

■

This recipe is preferred when a glazed cake top must be held several hours before serving. The addition of gelatin keeps the glaze from melting.

□ QUANTITY: ½ cup to top an 8- or 9-inch cake

½ cup apricot preserves, best quality
1½ teaspoons unflavored gelatin
2 tablespoons kirsch, or other fruit-flavored liqueur or fruit juice

Stir preserves over medium heat in a small saucepan until melted. Strain preserves through sieve. Remove solids, then return strained preserves to saucepan. Add gelatin and liqueur. Stir over medium heat until gelatin completely dissolves. Bring to boil for barely 30 seconds, then cool slightly. Apply lukewarm glaze to cake. Chill cake to set glaze.

Classic Poured Fondant

∎

Fondant is a satin-smooth sugar icing poured while warm over cakes or petits fours. In addition to its glossy sheen, fondant has the virtue of sealing moisture in a cake and guarding its freshness. It is, however, extremely sweet and should be used as a very thin coating layer.

The classic fondant recipe combines water, sugar, and corn syrup (which helps prevent crystallization of the sugar) or cream of tartar or lemon juice. The fondant is boiled to the soft-ball stage, then poured onto a slab and worked or kneaded with a dough scraper until it becomes opaque in color and takes on a satiny gloss. At this stage, the fondant is scooped into a jar and "ripened" for at least 12 hours; then it is ready to use. It can be stored in the refrigerator for up to a year.

It sounds a formidable task, and many cookbooks recommend purchasing prepared fondant from bakers' supply houses, but actually fondant-making is not difficult at all. Simply follow the instructions carefully, and select a dry day.

To use the fondant for an icing, the basic preparation must be melted in a double boiler and thinned to pouring consistency with a little warm Stock Syrup (see Index). Flavoring and coloring are added at this time. Specific instructions follow.

☐ QUANTITY: about 1 pound, 1½ cups

☐ SPECIAL EQUIPMENT: mercury candy thermometer, 2-quart heavy-bottomed, non-reactive saucepan or copper sugar pot, pastry brush set in a glass of cold water, Pyrex measure of ice water and teaspoon (for testing soft-ball stage); dough scraper or putty knife (reserved for cooking) or pancake turner; jelly-roll pan (preferable because the edges contain the poured syrup, the metal keeps the fondant warm a little longer than marble to facilitate kneading, and the tray can be lifted to a comfortable angle) or a marble slab (traditionally used because it stays cold and cools the fondant quickly)

1 cup water
2¼ cups granulated sugar (1 pound; 454 g)
2 tablespoons light corn syrup, or ¼ teaspoon cream of tartar

1. Combine the water, sugar, and corn syrup or cream of tartar in a saucepan. Swirl the pot to moisten the sugar, then set it over moderate-low heat for about 5 minutes, stirring occasionally, until the sugar is dissolved.

Rinse the jelly-roll pan with cold water (do not dry) and set it nearby. Or simply ready the clean marble slab. Set out the dough scraper or other spatula.

2. Raise the heat to medium-high and place the candy thermometer in the pot, resting the tip in the syrup. Boil the syrup without stirring at all for 12 to 13 minutes, or until it reaches the soft-ball stage, 235°F. During this boiling, every few minutes dip the pastry brush into cold water and wash down the inside of the pan to prevent sugar crystals from forming. As the syrup approaches the correct temperature, test it by dropping some syrup into ice water; it should form a soft ball between your fingers. Do *not* overcook the syrup; if boiled to too high a temperature, it will not form fondant properly.

3. As soon as the correct temperature is reached, immediately pour the hot syrup onto the dampened pan or the slab. Let the syrup sit for a few minutes until cool enough to touch comfortably, 110°F. Test the temperature, if you wish, with a spot instant thermometer; don't try to knead the fondant while it is too hot.

4. To work, or knead, the fondant, use the dough scraper or other spatula to lift the edge of the mass, turn it over, and spread or smear it across itself. Repeat, working the fondant for 7 to 10 minutes, depending on its temperature, so that it traps air, turns white, and cools. After a while the fondant will feel too stiff to work any longer. If this happens too quickly, simply cover it with an overturned bowl for a few minutes; the bowl will contain the heat, and the moisture will soften the fondant. Continue kneading. You can also knead the fondant for 3 or 4 minutes with your hands, turning it over and pushing it down. Note: If the syrup will not knead to a stiff mass, it was not boiled to a high enough temperature. Add a little water, return the syrup to the pot, and reboil.

5. Once the fondant is satiny, with a high gloss and opaque white color, it can be stored. If it will be used the next day, scrape it up and put it into a small nonferrous saucepan or bowl. Top with a damp cloth, then with foil, and refrigerate overnight, or for up to 24 hours before using. For longer storage, scrape the fondant into a wide-mouthed jar, cover with a lid, and refrigerate for up to a year.

Flavoring and coloring are added to the fondant just before using it.

TO USE FONDANT:

First, you will see that the fondant is extremely hard. Before it can be used, set the bowl or jar of fondant in a pot of warm water; take care that thermal shock does not crack the glass jar. Allow the fondant to warm enough for you to scoop out the desired amount.

As a rule of thumb, 1 cup of fondant will coat an 8- or 9-inch cake or an equivalent surface of *petits fours*. Always use more than you actually need; you must pour on a very generous amount for the correct flow and coverage.

Scoop the amount of fondant to be used into a small saucepan, set this into a larger pan containing some hot water, and place over low heat. Heat the fondant to no more than 95°F. In another pan, heat a little Stock Syrup (page 422). Stir the fondant as it melts, add a little warmed stock syrup to thin it to the correct pouring consistency, and stir in a small amount of flavoring (go slowly, flavoring to taste) and coloring (use the tiniest drop of vegetable food coloring for a very pale tint, never a bold hue).

For flavoring you can use rum, brandy, liqueur; vanilla, almond or other flavor extract; coffee; lemon, lime, or orange juice or extract; peppermint extract or oil; grated orange or lemon zest; or chocolate (melt 1 ounce unsweetened chocolate and stir it into 1 cup of slowly melting fondant).

CAKE PREPARATION FOR FONDANT:

Before using fondant, it is best to coat your cake or *petits fours* with a smooth skin of buttercream or fruit preserve glaze (see Index) to give the fondant a smooth surface. After frosting or glazing the cake(s), chill them in the refrigerator or freezer until very cold before pouring on the hot fondant. The cold surface prevents the warmth of the fondant from melting the underglaze of buttercream or preserves. The cold also helps the fondant to set up quickly.

POURING ON
THE FONDANT:

Set the chilled cake(s) on a wire rack set over a jelly-roll pan or other flat pan with an edge. When the fondant is thin enough to flow easily, stir it well to smooth it and remove any skin that may have formed on top. Do *not* whip air in while stirring.

Pour a generous amount of fondant over the center of the cake, allowing it to flow. It may help to tip the rack so the fondant can run over the surface more easily. Use an icing spatula to touch up any bare spots, but beware, for pressure with the spatula can cause the underglaze to spot through. Avoid pouring on more fondant because it sets so fast you will have too thick a coating. Try to let the fondant flow itself, dripping down the edges of the cake. If necessary, you can spread some fondant on the sides after the top coat is set. See illustrations for Petits Fours, page 351.

To coat *petits fours,* either pour on the fondant or hold the bottom of each piece of neatly preglazed firm-textured cake and dip it top first into the fondant. Or hold the pieces with a fork while dipping. Set *petits fours* bottom up on a rack to drip-dry. When the fondant has set hard, you can conceal the finger-holding bare spots by dipping the bottom

edges in melted chocolate or more fondant. It looks very pretty if the second half is dipped in a darker shade of the first fondant color.

Note: If you want the edges of a large cake completely coated instead of glazed with drips from the top, the easiest thing to do is spread a buttercream around the sides after the top has been coated with fondant and set firm.

TO DECORATE FONDANT:

Decorate the fondant surface after it has hardened. An easy and elegant trim is simply to put some fondant of the same or a slightly darker color into a paper cone (page 432) and draw a flower or geometric design on the cake or *petit four.* Top the design with a single silver dragee or candied violet. For other ideas, see Petits Fours (page 350).

Quick Mock Fondant

■

This is an easy recipe for mock poured fondant. It makes a fine satin-finish glaze that gives the effect of the classic fondant, but it lacks the high gloss and texture of the real thing. Nevertheless, it can be used on cakes, tortes, or *petits fours* for a smooth fancy coating.

Note: Because fondant is poured on, it is a fairly thin glaze that takes the shape of the surface below. To be sure this surface will be smooth, it is best to coat the cake with buttercream or Apricot Glaze (page 411) before adding the fondant. Chill the cake to harden the glaze so it will not be melted by the warm fondant.

☐ ADVANCE PREPARATION: Mock Fondant can be made in advance and refrigerated in a covered jar for several weeks. Rewarm to about 95°F before using. Refrigerate leftovers for later use.

☐ SPECIAL EQUIPMENT: 1½-quart heavy-bottomed saucepan, sifter, instant-spot thermometer (optional but handy), wooden spoon, wire rack, cookie sheet, icing spatula, rubber spatula, pan of ice water

☐ QUANTITY: 1⅓ cups, enough to glaze the top and sides of a 2- or 3-layer 8- or 9-inch cake or one 10-inch single layer cake or an equivalent area of petits fours. This recipe can successfully be doubled or tripled.

5 tablespoons water
1 tablespoon light corn syrup
3½ cups sifted confectioners' sugar
  (12¼ ounces; 350 g)

FLAVORING:

½ teaspoon flavoring extract (orange, almond, vanilla, etc.); or 2 tablespoons fresh lemon juice; 1 teaspoon instant coffee powder dissolved in 1 teaspoon hot water; 2 tablespoons any liqueur or brandy or rum. For chocolate flavor and color, melt 1½

ounces semisweet chocolate and stir into fondant. For chocolate flavor but white color, use 2 tablespoons white Crème de Cacao. For green color and mint flavor, use green Crème de Menthe.

COLORING:

Fondant icing should be pale in color. Use tiny drops of vegetable food coloring or beet juice (pink), concentrated undiluted frozen orange juice (orange or yellow), or coffee (beige).

1. Combine the water, corn syrup, and sugar in a saucepan and stir until blended. Set over low heat and stir until completely smooth and warm to the touch (92° to 95°F on the spot thermometer). Be careful not to let the fondant heat above 100°F. Stir in the flavoring and coloring if using either. Set the fondant pan into a pan of ice water to stop the cooking. Wipe the pan bottom before pouring the fondant to prevent drips.

2. Set the chilled cake on a wire rack set over a cookie sheet to catch drips. Pour a generous quantity of warm fondant over the top of the cake. Tilt the rack to help the fondant spread. Spread icing around the sides and touch up bare spots with a spatula. Air-dry to set the fondant. Do not rework the fondant or you will lose the shine and smooth coating. Scrape up and save leftovers.

Note: In hot humid weather, this fondant tends to soften after a day at room temperature; do not ice cakes too far in advance.

Sauces & Syrups

Crème Fraîche

■

While there is no exact American duplicate of the classic French *crème fraîche,* the following recipe will give you a satisfying approximation. Serve *crème fraîche* over fresh sliced fruit or warm fruit cobbler, or alongside a slice of rich dark chocolate cake.

☐ QUANTITY: about 1 cup

1 cup heavy cream
½ cup sour cream (4 ounces; 110 g)

In a mixing bowl, whisk the creams together. Cover with plastic wrap, and let sit at room temperature for about 8 hours, until thickened. Line a strainer with a double thickness of paper towels or a coffee filter and set it over a bowl. Turn the cream into the lined strainer and let it drain overnight, or up to 24 hours,

in the refrigerator, covered with plastic wrap. Discard the thin liquid and store the thicker cream left in the strainer in a covered glass jar in the refrigerator; it will keep for about a week.

Vanilla Custard Sauce (Crème Anglaise)

■

A rich custard sauce primarily thickened with egg yolks, this is pure heaven served with Chocolate Mousse Cake, Chocolate Truffle Cake, or any fruit Charlotte (see Index for recipes).

The addition of a little cornstarch in this recipe is insurance for smooth thickening; however, do not expect this to be as thick as a pastry cream or pudding. It is a soft sauce.

□ ADVANCE PREPARATION: The sauce may be made early in the day, or up to 2 days ahead, and stored, covered, in the refrigerator. To serve warm, reheat it in a double boiler, stirring over warm, not hot, water.

□ SPECIAL EQUIPMENT: 2-quart heavy-bottomed, nonreactive saucepan, whisk or electric mixer, 2 bowls, wooden spoon, double boiler, strainer, mercury candy thermometer (optional)

□ QUANTITY: 2 cups

1 vanilla bean, or 2 teaspoons vanilla
  extract
1¾ cups milk
4 large egg yolks
1½ teaspoons cornstarch
4 tablespoons granulated sugar

ADDITIONAL FLAVORING
(OPTIONAL):

1 tablespoon orange-flavored liqueur or dark rum

1. If using a vanilla bean, slit it lengthwise, place it in a saucepan with the milk, and bring slowly to a boil. During this time, beat together in a bowl the egg yolks, cornstarch, and sugar until the mixture is thick, light-colored, and forms a flat ribbon falling back on itself when the beater is lifted.

2. When the milk just boils, remove it from the heat. Pour about half of the hot milk onto the yolk mixture in a slow stream while whisking constantly. Then pour the warm yolk mixture into the saucepan with remaining milk. To be safe, you can now set the pan in the bottom of a double boiler. Or set di-

rectly on low heat and watch it very closely. Stir the sauce constantly with a wooden spoon until thick enough to leave a clearly defined line when you draw your finger through the cream on the back of the spoon (170°F).

3. Remove custard from the heat and strain it into a bowl. Do not overcook, or it will tend to curdle, though the cornstarch helps prevent this. At this point, stir in the vanilla extract and any other flavoring if using it. Cool the sauce completely, then cover and chill.

Hard Sauce

■

This is the brandy sauce traditionally served with Old English Plum Pudding (page 134). The sauce is also good on spice cake and fruit cake, and can be thinned with a little warm cream to make a softer topping or icing.

□ QUANTITY: about 2 cups

1 cup unsalted butter (2 sticks; 230 g),
  at room temperature
4½ cups sifted confectioners' sugar (1
  pound; 454 g)
¼ cup brandy, or as needed

With an electric mixer or in a food processor fitted with the metal blade, beat the butter until soft. Add the sifted sugar, beating very slowly until combined. Add the brandy, beating smooth. Add more brandy or some cream to bring the sauce to the correct consistency;

it should be thick but creamy. It will stiffen if stored in the refrigerator, and should be brought to room temperature for serving.

Warm Berry Sauce

•

This quick and easy-to-make sauce is delightful served warm over slices of sponge cake for a family dinner or an elegant Sunday brunch. I also like it on vanilla ice cream and waffles. Use fresh or frozen raspberries, blueberries, strawberries, or whatever is in season.

☐ QUANTITY: 3 cups

2 cups fresh berries, rinsed, hulled, and sliced, or an equivalent amount of frozen berries
⅓ to ½ cup granulated sugar (amount depends upon type and sweetness of fruit; 2¼ to 3½ ounces; 65 to 100 g)
1½ to 2 tablespoons freshly squeezed lemon juice, to taste
Grated zest of ½ lemon, about 1½ teaspoons
½ cup water
1 teaspoon cornstarch dissolved in 2 tablespoons cold water

Combine all ingredients in a saucepan set over moderate heat. Stir gently and bring to a gentle boil. Stir until the sauce is clear and thickened. Remove from the heat. Reheat sauce just before serving.

Hot Lemon Sauce

•

This old-fashioned New England specialty is served warm over gingerbread fresh from the oven. The sauce can be made in advance and refrigerated, but it should be warmed before serving.

☐ QUANTITY: about 1⅓ cups

1 cup granulated sugar (7 ounces; 200 g)
½ cup lightly salted butter (1 stick; 110 g)
¼ cup water
1 egg, lightly beaten
1 teaspoon grated lemon zest
3 tablespoons freshly squeezed lemon juice

Whisk together all ingredients in a 1½-quart heavy-bottomed saucepan set over moderate heat. Bring to a boil, whisking constantly. Boil for 1 full minute. Remove from heat. Serve warm.

Butterscotch Sauce

■

A rich buttery sauce with a thick, creamy consistency. Serve this warm over unfrosted vanilla, spice, or sponge cake and/or ice cream.

□ QUANTITY: 1 cup

¼ cup unsalted butter (½ stick; 60 g)
½ cup firmly packed light brown sugar (3½ ounces; 100 g)
½ cup heavy cream
Pinch of salt
1 teaspoon vanilla extract

Melt the butter in a medium-size, heavy-bottomed saucepan. Add the sugar, cream, and salt and stir until well blended. Bring to a very gentle boil and cook for about 5 minutes, stirring occasionally. Remove from the heat and stir in the vanilla. Serve warm or cold; the sauce thickens as it cools. Store refrigerated in a covered jar.

Rich Chocolate Sauce

■

This is the ultimate sauce to top cake and ice cream. For the most intense chocolate flavor, use 4 ounces semisweet and 4 ounces unsweetened or bittersweet chocolate; if you prefer a sweeter mixture, use all semisweet. This sauce is quite thick.

□ ADVANCE PREPARATION: Can be made up to a week ahead and stored in a covered jar in the refrigerator. Warm over low heat before serving.

□ SPECIAL EQUIPMENT: double boiler, whisk, rubber spatula

□ QUANTITY: about 1¼ cups

8 ounces semisweet chocolate, or substitute 4 ounces bittersweet or unsweetened chocolate for half the semisweet
½ cup heavy cream

FLAVORING (OPTIONAL):

1 teaspoon vanilla extract; pinch of ground cinnamon; 1 or 2 tablespoons rum, or orange, raspberry, or almond-flavored liqueur, or to taste

Melt the chocolate in the top pan of a double boiler set over simmering water. Remove pan from the heat just before all the chocolate is melted. Whisk or stir until completely smooth, then add half of the cream all at once and whisk it into the chocolate until smooth. Add remaining cream and whisk until the mixture is smooth, glossy, and thick. Whisk in the flavoring liquid. Serve warm. Thin with more cream if desired. Note: You can also make this in the food processor by chopping the chocolate, then processing it until powdered. Heat the cream to the boiling point and slowly pour it through the feed tube onto the chocolate with the motor running. Process until completely smooth and melted. Add flavoring and pulse.

Strawberries Romanoff

■

This gorgeous concoction is heavenly by itself, served in goblets, and even better over a slice of angel-food or sponge cake. To make a variation on this theme called Strawberries à la Ritz, purée a pint of strawberries and a pint of raspberries and fold them into the sweetened cream and ice-cream mixture.

☐ QUANTITY: 6 to 8 servings

☐ SPECIAL EQUIPMENT: 2 bowls, wooden spoon, chilled bowl and chilled beater for whipping cream

1 quart ripe strawberries, picked over, hulled, rinsed, and dried; reserve a few whole berries for garnish
¼ cup granulated sugar (1¾ ounces; 50 g)
1 pint vanilla ice cream
1 cup chilled heavy cream
½ teaspoon vanilla extract
¼ cup Cointreau or Curaçao or kirsch

Place the berries in a bowl, slicing about 7 or 8 into quarters. Sprinkle with the sugar and toss to coat the berries. Refrigerate for a couple of hours. Shortly before serving, remove the ice cream from the freezer and soften to stirring consistency. Whip the heavy cream with the vanilla until nearly stiff. Fold the whipped cream into the softened ice cream, then fold in the liqueur and the sugared berries. Top with the whole reserved berries. Serve immediately, alone or over cake.

Cake Soaking Syrup

■

This flavored syrup is brushed or sprinkled on split layers of génoise or sponge cake to add flavor and moisture before filling. Beware of adding too much alcohol to the syrup, it may overpower the flavor of your cake.

Add the syrup to the cake layers in an allover pattern, taking care to reach the outer edges as well as the center. Do not saturate the cake or it will fall apart when the layer is lifted.

As a general guide, use:

2⅓ to 3 tablespoons flavored syrup brushed on each ¼-inch-thick sponge cake layer;

3 to 4 tablespoons flavored syrup brushed on each ½-inch-thick layer; for a moist ½-inch layer you can use up to ⅓ cup of syrup.

☐ QUANTITY: 1½ cups, enough for two or three 8-inch cakes

1 cup granulated sugar (7 ounces; 200 g)
1 cup water

FLAVORING:

3 tablespoons fruit- or nut-flavored liqueur or rum or brandy; or 1 teaspoon extract (vanilla, maple, rum, etc.); or 3 or 4 tablespoons strained fruit purée

Combine the sugar and water in a heavy-bottomed saucepan; boil, stirring, to dissolve all the sugar. Remove pan from the heat, cool, and store the syrup. Add flavoring just before filling a cake. The syrup can be refrigerated in a covered jar for about 6 weeks.

·*Variations:*·

ORANGE OR GRAND MARNIER SYRUP:

3 tablespoons Grand Marnier or other orange liqueur

ALMOND SYRUP:

1 teaspoon vanilla extract, 2 tablespoons Amaretto liqueur, ¼ teaspoon almond extract

RUM SYRUP:

3 tablespoons dark rum plus 1½ teaspoons vanilla extract

COFFEE SYRUP:

2 teaspoons instant coffee powder dissolved in 1 tablespoon hot water

Note: Warmed pure maple syrup, unadulterated, or the syrup from poached fruit or fruit packed in cans, may also be used as soaking syrup; taste first and adjust the flavor if necessary.

Stock Syrup

∎

This classic syrup formula is used to thin fondant icing or chocolate glaze. With the addition of a flavoring extract or liqueur it can also be brushed over sponge cake in the same way you use Cake Soaking Syrup (preceding recipe).

□ QUANTITY: about 2¼ cups, enough to thin several batches of fondant or to spread on the layers of two 2-layer 8- or 9-inch cakes

1¼ cups water
2¼ cups granulated sugar

Combine the water and sugar in a 2-quart heavy-bottomed saucepan. Stir to moisten the sugar. Bring to a boil over moderate-high heat; swirl the pan gently to be sure all sugar is dissolved. Remove pan from the heat and cool the syrup. Store the syrup in a covered jar in the refrigerator for several months, or flavor and use it right away. Note: Remove and flavor only the amount of syrup needed at one time.

Decorating
Cakes

To Prepare Cakes for Filling and Decorating

■

Before baked cake layers can be filled or frosted, they are prepared by one of the following methods:

1. Often a sponge cake, génoise, or torte will be cut horizontally into thin layers before filling. To do this, first set the cake on a cardboard disk, a turntable or lazy Susan, or a piece of foil. Place one hand flat on the cake top and with the other, hold a serrated knife blade against the side of the cake. Turn the cake away from the blade as you make a gentle sawing motion, cutting a shallow groove into the cake all the way around the edge (diagram a). This marks the layer. Then go around again, sawing deeper, but not quite through; finally, cut clean through. Slide a cardboard cake disk, a sheet of foil, or an edgeless cookie sheet between the layers for support and lift off the top layer. Never lift the layer without supporting it, or it may crack.

Another method for splitting a sponge cake is to cut a groove in the cake with a serrated knife as described, then wrap a length of strong button thread or dental floss around the groove. Cross the thread ends, and keep pulling with even pressure until you sever the layer. (diagram b). Support and remove the layer as described.

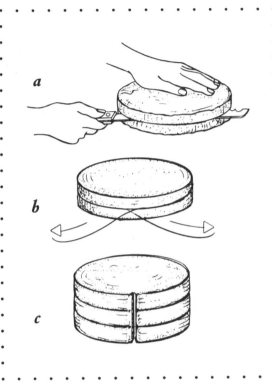

a

b

c

When cutting layers, you may wish to make a very shallow vertical groove in the side of the cake before you begin the layers. This notch will be a guide when reassembling the cake, so the layers line up properly (diagram c).

2. If the baked shape is to be altered, it should be cut now. (Review Shaped Cakes, page 441.) Cut a pattern or template out of paper, set it on the cake, and mark around the edge with a toothpick or a knife tip. Remove

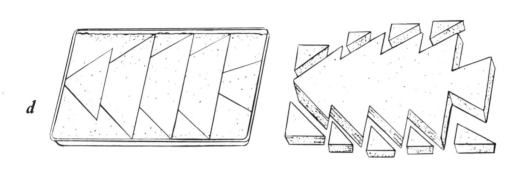

d

the template and cut around the marked line with a serrated knife (diagram d). For intricate shapes, a grapefruit knife can be helpful. For pound cake or butter cake, a paring knife works more easily than a serrated blade. (Note: Freeze cake scraps for snacks or crumbs or shortcake.)

3. If the top of any layer of the cake is domed, level it off with a long-bladed serrated knife, so your filled cake will be flat when the layers are stacked (diagram e). This is essential when making a wedding cake, which must be perfectly flat, but may be overlooked in a casual cake.

4. When ready to frost the cake, brush all the surface crumbs off the sides and top with your hand or a pastry brush.

5. Put a dab of jam or icing in the center of a cake cardboard or flat plate or turntable. This icing is just to hold the cake in place.

6. To protect the serving plate while icing the cake, cut 4 or more narrow strips of wax paper or parchment and set them around the bottom of the cake, sliding them slightly underneath. This paper covers the plate edges,

and will be pulled out once the decorations are complete (diagram f).

7. Apply flavored syrup or filling between the layers and assemble them.

8. If a smooth icing surface is important, paint on a layer of warm Apricot Glaze (page

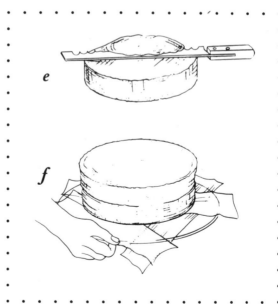

e

f

411). Use a jam that complements the flavor of your cake and its icing.

First set your cake on its cardboard on a wire rack set over a jelly-roll pan (to catch drips). Use an icing spatula to spread the glaze over the top first, then down and around the sides. Remember that a glaze is not an icing and should not be as thick. Glazes are meant to be thin, unless used in a heavy coat for a cake topping. Some glazes, particularly chocolate glazes, are poured onto the cake, then spread across the top and around the sides with an icing spatula (diagram g). If necessary, scrape up the dripped glaze, warm it if thickened, and reapply it to the cake.

The round is picked up on a piece of wax paper, foil, or a rolling pin (like lifting up a piecrust) and draped over the cake. Then with dry hands (coated with a little confectioners' sugar if needed) you gently mold the coating to the cake, firming and smoothing it over the top first, then down the edge, over the sides, and around the bottom (diagram h). With a sharp paring knife, trim the bottom edge; some bakers turn the cake upside down and fold the excess onto the bottom. Or, for a total seal for a fruitcake, you can even put a disk of marzipan on the bottom of the cake. In Britain, Christmas fruitcakes are so sealed before being decorated with royal icing.

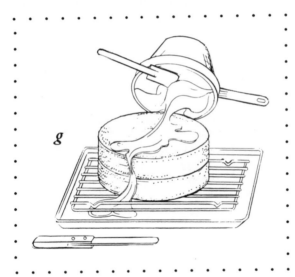

ABOUT CAKE FROSTING
AND DECORATIONS

9. Sometimes a glazed undercoat is topped by another layer—rolled fondant or marzipan—to protect the cake and hold in moisture as well as to provide an absolutely silken surface for decorating. The marzipan or fondant (see Index) is rolled into a round between 1/8 and 1/16 inch thick and as big as the diameter of your cake plus twice the height of a side.

This is a subject for a book in itself. However, the fact is that with a few tools and some basic techniques, one can easily achieve very elegant results in cake decorating. Less is more; cakes actually look more appetizing and appealing when their decorations are understated rather than overdone. This chapter will present the paper decorating cone as well as the basic

QUANTITY CHART FOR FILLING AND FROSTING CAKES

■

CAKE SHAPE AND SIZE:	CUPS OF ICING NEEDED
8- or 9-inch round layer, to cover top only, for filling or frosting	½ to 1
10- to 12-inch round layer, top only	1 ⅓
14-inch round layer, top only	1½
2-layer 8- or 9-inch round cake, top and sides plus filling	2½ to 3½
2-layer 8- or 9-inch round cake, top and sides only, no filling	1½ to 2½
2-layer 8- or 9-inch round cake, sides only, no filling, no icing on top	1 to 1½
3-layer 8- or 9-inch round cake, top and sides plus filling	4
8-inch square cake, top only	¾ to 1
8- × 2-inch cake, top and sides	1½ to 1¾
8- × 12-inch sheet cake, or 9 × 13-inch sheet cake, top only	1½ to 2
10½- × 15½-inch sheet cake, top only	2
9- × 5 × 3-inch loaf, top only	½ to ¾
9- × 5 × 3-inch loaf, top and sides	1½
9- to 9½- × 3¾-inch tube, top and sides	2½ to 3
10- × 4-inch tube, top and sides	3 to 4
2- to 3-inch diameter cupcake	2 tablespoons
12 cupcakes	1 to 1½ cups
To glaze one 9-inch round cake	1 cup glaze
To cover with meringue the top and sides of one 8- or 9-inch cake	3½ to 4 cups meringue made with 4 egg whites
To fill 1 10-inch jell roll (made from 15- × 10-inch sheet cake).	1 to 1½ (up to 2 cups for whipped cream)

decorating bag, a few standard tips, and some elementary all-purpose borders and designs. For additional ideas for quick and effective decorations see the Index for Cake Decorating Ideas.

Quantity Chart for Filling and Frosting Cakes

The amount needed for each cake will vary with the type of icing, the thickness it is spread, and the quantity used between the layers, if any. You may prefer to fill the cake with preserves, fruit slices and whipped cream, or another type of icing. Changing the filling adds variety to the cake and also allows more icing for decorating the outside. In the table on page 427, the icing quantities are given only as a general guide. Fluffy or boiled icing requires about ⅓ more than a buttercream. Icing glaze is applied when soft and runny and will be much thinner than an icing that is spread on the cake. Specific icing yields are given with each recipe. If you are planning to decorate the cake after frosting it, make at least ½ recipe more icing.

Icing for Decorations

The consistency of the icing is very important: use a fairly soft icing to spread all over the cake. Use a medium-stiff icing to pipe borders that must hold their shape. Use a fairly soft icing for writing that must flow evenly yet hold its shape without drooping. Use a stiff icing containing a high ratio of solid white shortening to make flowers with three-dimensional petals. To select the correct icing, see the recipe suggested along with the cake, or check the Index.

Coloring Decorative Icing

U.S. Certified food colors are those that meet FDA purity guidelines and are considered edible. Approved colors will be labeled FD & C (Food, Drug, and Cosmetic Act). In the small amounts that these colors are added to cake icing, they are probably perfectly safe to use and ingest. However, the safety of some of the approved colors has been questioned, and many home cooks prefer to avoid them altogether. If you want a substitute, look for natural substances with coloring properties: undiluted frozen orange-juice concentrate or egg yolks will tint icing a yellow color, as will saffron and turmeric (though the latter leaves a curry flavor). Beet juice, cranberry juice, and many types of strained berry preserves produce shades of pink and rose; coffee tints icing beige, and chocolate can be blended in varying amounts for a wide range of beige-to-brown tones. You should be aware of the properties of the coloring used: liquid vegetable food colors are water-based and may adversely effect certain icings. For example, they may not blend well with some types of buttercream, and if added to melted white chocolate, they may cause it to seize and harden into an unusable mass. It is usually preferable to use professional bakers' paste or powder colors, which are available in many gourmet and cookware shops, department stores, and baking and candy supply houses (see Index for Suppliers).

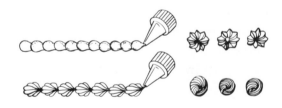

How to Frost a Cake

First prepare the cake for icing following the guidelines on page 424; to do this, use a serrated knife to level the layers. Brush off the crumbs. Split the cake into thinner layers if you wish, making a vertical notch to help realign the layers later.

Set out a cardboard cake disk cut to fit the layers. Dab a little icing on the disk to anchor the cake in place. Set the first layer on the disk. (diagram a). Add filling on top of this layer, then add the next layer. Repeat, adding and filling all layers. Check to see that the layers are lined up evenly.

If you are concerned that the filling may bleed out and discolor the icing (strawberry preserves and white boiled icing for example), first pipe a ring of icing around the edge of the layer to be filled; then spread the filling inside the ring. This icing ring acts as a dam to prevent the filling from reaching the outside of the cake (diagram b).

If you have a decorating turntable, place the cake on it. You may want to anchor the cake to the turntable with a dab of icing. To prevent crumbs from getting into the icing, brush the cake off. If you wish, you can spread warm apricot jam glaze (page 411) over the cake top and sides to guarantee crumb-free icing. Chill the glazed cake to set the glaze before adding the icing.

Spread a generous amount of icing around the cake sides, then on the top (diagram c). Finally, smooth the sides and top, removing

excess icing. It is better to start with extra icing, building up a good layer, than it is to press against the sides and lift crumbs in an attempt to spread a skimpy amount of icing. If using a turntable, hold your spatula upright against the side of the cake in a fixed position while rotating the turntable away from the blade (diagram d). This smooths the sides. To even the top of a very large cake, you can use a metal ruler wider than the cake's diameter, drawing the ruler across the top in a single motion (e), making a flat surface. This can also be done in several motions with a long spatula. Finally, smooth the top edges by sweeping the spatula from the rim of the cake toward the center. If you have trouble getting the top perfectly smooth, dip the blade of your longest spatula in hot water, shake it off, and draw it across the cake top, smoothing the surface.

How to Decorate Cake Sides with Nuts or Crumbs

Use toasted and ground or chopped nuts, or toasted and sliced almonds, or crushed cake,

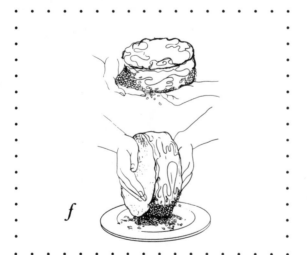

cookie, or meringue crumbs. Put ¾ to 1 cup nuts or crumbs in a bowl (the exact amount depends upon the cake size and the density of nuts you wish on the cake). For ease in applying the nuts, it helps to have the cake fastened with icing to a cardboard cake disk. Pick up the cake with one hand and with the other scoop up some nuts or crumbs into the palm of your hand. Press the nuts or crumbs up against the cake sides with your hand, allowing the excess to fall back into the bowl or onto wax paper (diagram f). You can also achieve this effect by frosting only the cake sides, not the top, then holding the cake by its top and bottom and rolling the frosted sides in nuts or crumbs (see below, left).

PASTRY BAGS AND TIPS

For piping icing, meringue, or whipped cream into decorative patterns on cakes, a decorating tube or pastry bag fitted with a fancy tip is the answer. Pastry bags are the easiest to use because they are flexible, fit into your hand well, and release their contents with slight finger pressure. Metal syringe-type tubes are handy for writing icing messages, called "the sweetest calligraphy of them all" by food writer George Lang. Small paper or parchment cones are easy to make and perfect for piping soft icing or melted chocolate into decorative patterns.

Pastry bags lined with plastic or made of nylon are the best type to use because they are flexible and do not absorb fat. Bags are available in sizes from 7 inches to nearly 24 inches long; select one larger than you think you need. Use the smallest bags for delicate designs, the largest for piping stiff batters or foams. For general all-purpose decorations, I use a 16-inch nylon bag. Wash the bags in hot water and air-dry them after use. The decorating tip can be dropped inside the bag so it sticks out of the hole (diagram a), or you can use a coupler assembly, usually sold with the tips. This is most convenient because the coupler allows you to change tips simply by removing an outer ring (see diagram b). If you drop the tip inside the bag, you must remove the icing to insert another tip into the bag, a rather messy procedure. Alternatively, you can just hold a new tip over the outside of the old one, changing the configuration of the icing design as you continue to squeeze the bag. This usually works, but occasionally icing oozes out between the tips.

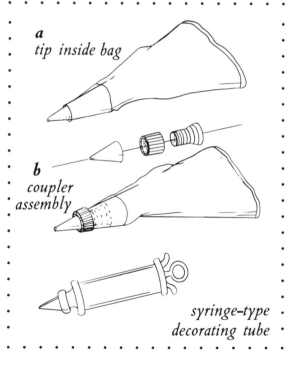

a
tip inside bag

b
coupler assembly

syringe-type decorating tube

How to Fill a Pastry or Decorating Bag

To fill the bag, fold back a 4- or 5-inch cuff. It may help you to stand the bag tip down inside a measuring cup. Use a broad spatula to add icing, filling the bag no more than half full. With your fingers, squeeze the icing down into the tip and twist the bag closed. The icing is forced into the tip; press out a little icing to be sure there is no air trapped in the tip (diagram c).

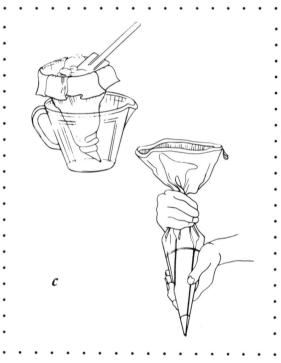

c

How to Use the Bag

To use the bag, hold the twist-closure between the thumb and fingers of one hand; with this gesture you hold the bag closed and apply pressure to squeeze out the icing. The other hand guides the bag (diagram c) and helps support its weight. For most designs, the bag is held at either a 90-degree or 45-degree angle to the cake top.

How to Make Paper Cones

To make a paper cone, cut a wax paper or parchment triangle about 12 by 15 inches. Pull the long side of the paper around its midpoint, making a cone. Hold the cone tight while wrapping the second point around; tuck in all the ends (diagrams a through f). Cut a tiny bit off the cone tip to make a round tip or cut a triangle-shaped hole to make icing leaves or petals. Or, you can simply drop a metal decorating tip into a paper cone (the best way to guarantee an even line). Fill the paper cone, then fold down the top. This cone can be held and used with one hand. After use, the paper cone is discarded, but save the metal tip if using it. Baking parchment triangles 15 × 15 × 21 inches, 100 to a pack, are sold in some gourmet and cookware shops; this is a convenient way to have readily available decorating cones. The paper cones are used almost exclusively by professional chefs for doing fancy work and piping melted chocolate. In an emergency, you can also use a small plastic bag. Fill the bag, twist it closed, and cut a pin-size hole in one corner, or drop in a metal decorating tip.

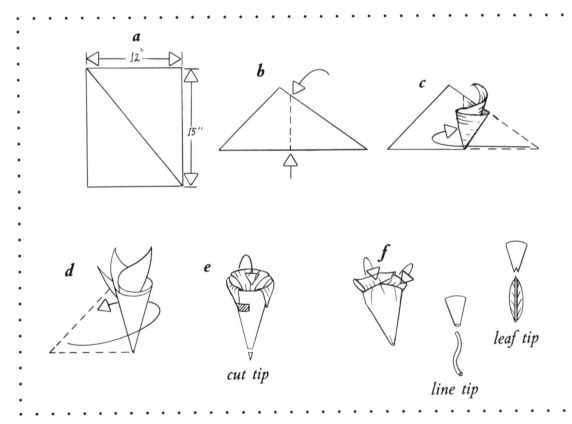

a

b

c

d

e

cut tip

f

line tip

leaf tip

About Decorating Tips

Decorating tips come in hundreds of sizes and shapes. Be sure that the tips you select fit the size of your decorating bag; small tips will fall out of the end of the large bags. For our purposes, we recommend the use of a star tip, preferably #6, ½ inch, for use with the 16-inch pastry bag. You should have an open star and a partially closed star, a plain round tip for writing, a leaf tip, and a rose petal tip for making roses and other flower petals and ribbons. A basket-weave tip is essential for achieving the correct basket texture.

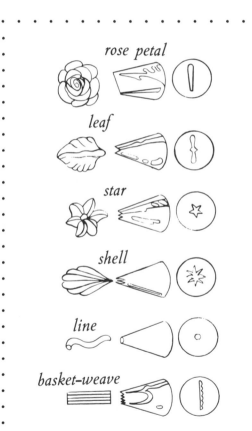

rose petal

leaf

star

shell

line

basket-weave

The most common border designs used in this book are shells and rosettes. To make shells, use the #6, ½-inch, slightly closed star tip, or #18, 22, 25, 26, 27, 28, or 30. Hold the star tip at a 45-degree angle to the cake top. Press out the icing, lift the tip slightly as the shape bulges out, then press down gently onto the cake while releasing pressure and pulling sharply away, forming a tail. To make a shell border, repeat, beginning the next shell on the tail of the last. As you proceed with the border you will feel a rocking motion with your hand. You can also curve the shells to alternate sides, like a series of opposing commas. A single shell with a long tail is called a claw; a series of side-by-side claws makes another decorative border.

To make rosettes, use the slightly closed star tip, #14, 16, 18, 21 or 22, for example, or the #6, ½-inch, star tip. Hold the tip perpendicular to the cake top. Press out icing, then pull up sharply while giving a circular twist to the bag. To make a more twisted rosette, move the bag in a small circle as you press out the icing. To make stars or small flowers use the open star tip #4 and repeat the above motion without the twist at the end. If you make the small stars side by side, you have an attractive border.

The plain round tip, #2, 3, 4, 5, and 7, for example, can be used for writing, dots, beads, strings or ropes, and flower stems or vines. It can also be used for scroll work. Draw a design, or trace one, onto a piece of paper, then top it with baking parchment, which is transparent. "Draw" the icing lines directly over the drawing. If you do this with royal icing or melted chocolate, let the design harden, then peel off the parchment. These delicate shapes (butterflies, flowers, lace) can stand up in the icing on cakes or *petits fours* for fancy decorations.

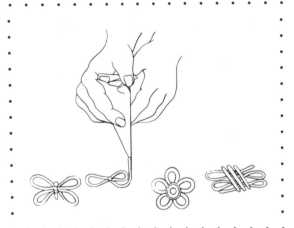

To make a simple basket-weave design, you will need both the plain round tip and the basket-weave tip #47. To make this design, first pipe 2 vertical lines an even distance apart using the round #3 or #4 tip. Second, with the basket-weave tip, pipe 3 horizontal lines crossing the first 2 at the top, middle, and bottom. Now draw one new vertical line in the middle that extends from the top to the bottom of the 3 basket-weave lines. Again using the basket-weave tip, pipe 2 horizontal lines filling in the weave between the original 2 verticals (diagrams a, b, c). Repeat, continuing the pattern and keeping the intervals even.

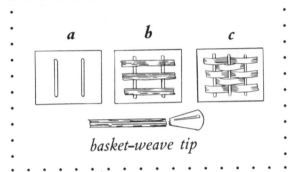

basket-weave tip

Hints for Successful Decorating with Tips

The amount of pressure on the pastry bag, the size of the tip, and the consistency of the icing will determine the amount of icing flowing out. By increasing the pressure and moving the bag slowly, you can increase the size of the line being piped. Practice on wax paper on the table before making designs on the cake. Be sure to sift confectioners' sugar through a fine sieve before making icing that will be piped through a small round tube; the smallest lump in the icing can block the tip. If this happens, use a toothpick poked into the tip to release the blockage. After use, soak decorating tips in hot water until clean; use a toothpick to free icing stuck in small openings.

CAKE DECORATING IDEAS AND TECHNIQUES

•

The following suggestions include a wide variety of cake decorating ideas. Most are quick and easy for a fast effect with minimum skill and effort; some are more complex, but none requires artistic skill or experience. There are many other decorating and garnishing ideas within the recipes throughout this book. Use this section for reference and as a starting place for your own ideas; often just looking at the illustrations will get your creativity going. If inspiration fails you, fall back on a simple border of piped icing shells or rosettes; they always look elegant and give a fine finish to a cake without much extra work. Or, where appropriate, top a simple whipped-cream icing with a border of fresh whole berries garnished with mint leaves. When in doubt, remember: keep the decorations simple. A lot of effort goes into making a cake and its appearance should add to, never detract from, the impression it makes. For other decorating ideas, see Index for Cake Decorations, Chocolate Leaves, Plastic Chocolate, Meringue Mushrooms, Shaped Cakes, and Molded Cakes.

Fresh Flowers

This is the quickest, easiest, and most effective way to decorate a cake. Fresh flowers provide instant decoration. For suggested flowers and ways to add them to cakes and to keep them fresh, see Wedding Cakes (page 107).

Stencil Designs

Paper doilies make excellent stencils for cake tops, and plastic doilies are sold in some cookware shops for this purpose. Stencils make instant decorations on plain or frosted cake tops.

To use, simply set the stencil (doily) flat on the cake top. Sift on confectioners' sugar for a white design or unsweetened cocoa for a dark design on a white cake. Very carefully lift up the stencil, leaving the design below (diagram a, page 436).

Comb Designs

Decorating combs are flat metal triangles with teeth of different sizes on each edge. These are sold in cookware shops; a clean new hair comb or a serrated knife blade makes a fine substitute. To use a comb, first frost the cake with a buttercream or sugar icing. Smooth the surface flat, then put the comb against the surface and draw it across in a wavy pattern. You can hold the comb against the sides and repeat the design, or press sliced toasted nuts onto the cake sides (diagram b, page 436).

Paper Strip Designs

This is a variation on the stencil. Use this technique on an uncoated cake or on a cake topped with any icing, glaze, or even with chocolate curls or shavings. Simply cut 3 or 4 strips of paper longer than the width of the cake. Set the paper strips at evenly spaced intervals across the cake (diagram c, page 436). Sift confectioners' sugar or unsweetened cocoa, depending upon the color desired, over the cake top. Carefully lift off the paper strips, leaving stripes on the cake (diagram d, page 436). A plaid effect is created by repeating the design in the opposite direction.

a *stencil*

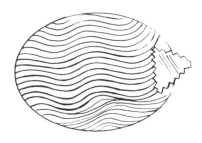

b *decorating comb*

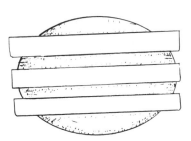

c *paper strips*

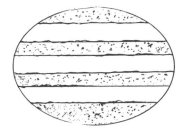

d *paper strips removed*

e *birthday cake*

f *whipped cream lattice*

g *fork drizzle*

h *chocolate-dipped nuts*

Chocolate on Chocolate Designs

Frost the cake with any chocolate icing or glaze (see Index for recipes). Chill the cake to set the icing or glaze. Melt about ⅓ cup semisweet chocolate morsels (60 g) with 1 tablespoon butter in the top pan of a double boiler. Stir the mixture until perfectly smooth. Put the melted chocolate into a paper decorating cone (page 432) with a small round hole in the tip; or use a #2 round metal tip. Pipe the chocolate into the pattern shown: it is simply 2 sets of intersecting straight lines set off to one side of the cake. Write a message in the large open space using the melted chocolate remaining in the cone. If you want to get fancy, put a real rose (or a Chocolate rose, see page 455) at the point where the lines intersect (diagram e). The color contrast on this cake comes from using different shades of chocolate for the icing. Unsweetened or bittersweet chocolate on a milk chocolate glaze (medium-brown) gives good contrast. Use this same design with white chocolate lines on a dark chocolate cake; omit the butter when melting white chocolate.

Whipped Cream Lattice

Flavored Whipped Cream (page 368), including chocolate or coffee whipped cream, can be piped through a pastry bag fitted with a star tip. In addition to the obvious rosettes and border designs, you can pipe overlapping parallel lines to create a lattice pattern (diagram f). Make one row around the edge of the top and another row around the bottom edge as borders. This is particularly attractive on a rectangular cake. If the whipped cream must be held for several hours before serving, use Stabilized Whipped Cream (page 367).

Drizzled Lines

This is a variation on the chocolate decoration above, but much easier. Simply melt the unsweetened chocolate with butter as directed but omit the paper cone. Prepare a previously frosted cake. Dip a fork into the slightly cooled chocolate, then drizzle parallel lines across the cake top in one direction, then in the other, creating a crosshatched pattern. The melted dark chocolate will stand out even on a milk chocolate icing, but can be used on any other icing as well. Instead of dark chocolate, try white chocolate lines drizzled on dark chocolate icing (diagram g).

Chocolate-Dipped Nuts

Melt 1 or 2 ounces of semisweet or bittersweet chocolate in the top pan of a double boiler or in the microwave. Stir smooth. Hold blanched almonds with a pair of tweezers or your fingertips and dip them up to their center in the melted chocolate. Set them on foil and refrigerate to set the chocolate. Arrange the half-dipped nuts in 1 or 2 concentric rings on the cake top (diagram h). As a bonus, these chocolate-dipped nuts can be stored in the refrigerator for a week or two and make good "candies" to pass after dinner.

Chocolate Curls

White or dark chocolate curls are quick and easy to make. Prepare your cake with a buttercream icing. Make the Chocolate Curls (see page 451) and arrange them either in a random jumble covering the top or in neat rows (diagram i, page 438). To highlight dark chocolate curls, you can sift a tiny bit of confectioners' sugar over them. To get fancy, you can cut paper strips (see Paper Strip Designs, above) and sift on stripes of sugar over the curls.

i chocolate curls

j chocolate rose and leaves

k wreath

l ribbon Edging

Chocolate Shavings

Bittersweet or semisweet chocolate can be shaved across a grater, with the shavings falling directly onto a frosted cake. Cover the top completely. Press more shavings onto the cake sides or press on ground nuts.

Caramel-Glazed Nut Borders

Dip any type of nuts (hazelnuts, walnut or pecan halves, blanched almonds) into Caramel Glaze (page 462). When the amber glaze is hard, remove the dipping toothpicks and set the shining nuts in a ring around the edge of the cake top. Select nuts that go with the flavor of the cake.

Caramel Cage

See page 463.

Feathered Chocolate Glaze

See page 439.

Cut-Out Chocolate Shapes

See page 456.

Chocolate Ruffles

See page 457.

Chocolate Roses

See page 455.

Use the dark or white chocolate plastic roses or apricot roses in combination with Chocolate Leaves, (diagram j, above).

Chocolate Leaves or Wreath

See page 449.

Make a border design around a cake top by setting chocolate leaves end to end or overlapping them slightly. You can alternate white and dark chocolate leaves for added drama. To make a wreath cake, cover the top of a tube cake with overlapping rows of chocolate leaves (diagram k). For a Christmas wreath, add a frosting or satin fabric bow.

Ribbon Decoration

For a stunning decoration, simply wrap a wide piece of satin or metallic ribbon around the cake and fasten it with a little frosting "glue." For a "country" look, use gingham or floral ribbon. If the ribbon is too stiff for the frosting to hold it, use a straight pin but be sure to remove it when removing the ribbon before serving (diagram l).

Portrait Cake

This is fun for adults as well as children. If you feel artistic, look at a photograph and try for a likeness; otherwise, make it a caricature, picking up obvious characteristics (red hair, blue eyes, freckles) (diagram m).

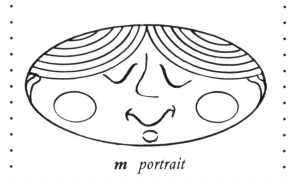

m portrait

Measles or Chicken Pox Cake

This is for children, to brighten an otherwise uncomfortable time. Draw the face and hair with colored buttercream. Apply "measles" all over the face with tiny cinnamon hots or other round red candies. For a "thermometer" in the mouth, use the stem of a candy cane or a striped candy stick (diagram n).

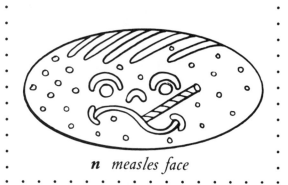

n measles face

Feathered Chocolate Glaze

■

This technique looks so professional that it is intimidating to many inexperienced bakers. Actually, it is one of the easiest and quickest designs to make. It always works, and always gets rave reviews for its elegant appearance. Don't be afraid to try it, just look at the diagrams first; it takes longer to describe than to do it.

The idea is to frost the cake or torte with

any fondant or glaze, then pipe fine lines of a contrasting color icing across the top. Both icings must be soft enough to flow slightly; this does not work well with buttercream. When a knife blade is pulled through the lines in alternating directions, a classic wave pattern is produced. This is the design commonly used on Napoleon pastries and the German chocolate torte called Prinzregententorte.

Note: You can vary the technique by using white lines on a dark cake or dark lines on a light cake.

☐ SPECIAL EQUIPMENT: paper cone (see page 432), wire rack set over jelly-roll pan, icing spatula, thin-bladed knife and damp cloth, small plastic bag

BASE COAT ICING:

Classic or Mock Fondant, any flavor (page 414), or any chocolate glaze such as Ganache Icing Glaze (page 407), Fabulous Chocolate Glaze (page 409), or Chocolate Water Glaze (page 410).

LINE ICING:

Melted white chocolate (page 47); or Basic Icing Glaze, sifted confectioners' sugar and water (page 406) for white lines. For dark lines on a light cake, melt 2 ounces semisweet chocolate with a teaspoon of marga-

rine or solid shortening. Put the line icing into a paper cone with a small round hole in the tip; fold over the cone ends to seal, then set the filled cone in a plastic bag to prevent icing from drying out before use.

CAKE:

Any layer cake or torte. To give the glaze a smooth surface to adhere to, the cake may be previously undercoated with Apricot Glaze (page 411) or any buttercream, and chilled in the refrigerator until the undercoating is set.

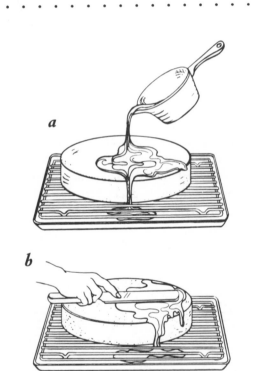

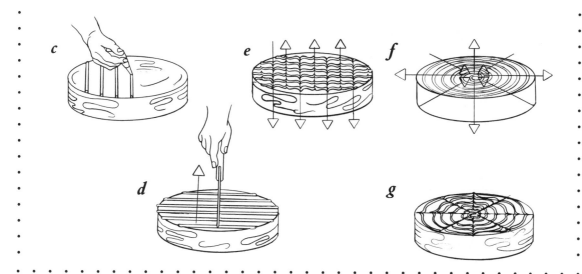

1. Place the prepared cake on a wire rack set over a tray. Warm and stir the base coat glaze until it reaches pouring consistency. Pour a generous amount of glaze onto the center of the cake, then tilt the rack to help the glaze flow evenly (diagram a). Guide the glaze with an icing spatula; it should coat the top and sides evenly but be fairly thin (diagram b). Work quite quickly as the glaze thickens as it cools.

2. While the base coat glaze is still soft on top, squeeze a little line of icing out of the paper cone to test the flow, then draw parallel vertical lines about 1 inch apart across the top of the cake (diagram c). Turn the cake 180 degrees so these lines are now horizontal. Draw a thin knife blade through the lines at 1½-inch intervals (diagram d). Begin in the center of the cake and work toward the edges to keep the spacing even. Now turn the cake entirely around and again draw the knife through the lines, going between your previ-

ous lines (diagram e) and pulling in the opposite direction to make a series of connected brackets. Remember not to cut with the knife, just pull it lightly through the surface. This technique can also be used to make a spiral pattern (diagram f). To do this, first pipe a spiral on the cake top, then draw the knife from the center to the rim at even intervals in alternating directions (diagram g).

SHAPED CAKES

■

For special occasions such as birthdays, anniversaries, and holidays you may wish to make a cake in the shape of a number, letter, train, clown, or other figure. These can be done in a variety of ways with a variety of baking pans, and the subject is material for a book in itself. However, here I want to give just a few ideas and general tips to guide the creative process.

First, select a cake batter with a firm grain; any layer, pound, or butter cake is fine. Avoid cakes containing chunks of nuts or raisins or chocolate bits, which will obstruct neat edges when the cake is cut into shape, or will weaken the structure when the cake is used to form a "built" figure made of several pieces joined together.

Consider the baking pan(s) you will use. Specialty pans formed into fancy shapes are sold in many cookware and gourmet shops as well as in hardware and department stores; always select the heaviest quality pan available. Santa Claus, Christmas Tree, Snoopy, and a host of other shapes are common. The most imaginative and useful to own is the Educated Cake Pan (see Suppliers in Index) made by Burvelle. It is basically a rectangular pan with a variety of modular blocks that can be moved around in endless combinations to create baking areas of the desired shape; the little blocks can also be used to bake cube-shaped cupcakes—a good way to use up extra batter or form modular building blocks for cake constructions.

These pans are not necessary, however. First, in a private home (as opposed to a commercial bakery) specialty cakes are a sometime thing for which you really do not need an expensive piece of equipment; second, with a little ingenuity and imagination, you can usually improvise with your present equipment and come out with equally satisfying results.

Consider the size of the finished cake: the easiest and most common shapes are made from sheet cakes baked in a large rectangular roasting pan approximately 11 or 12 × 17 inches. This rectangular flat shape is excellent

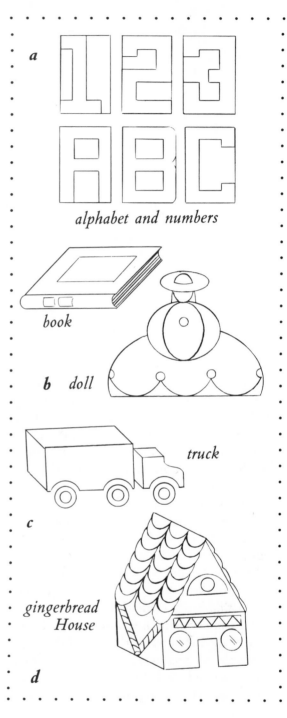

a alphabet and numbers

book

b doll

truck

c

gingerbread House

d

for cutting into all the letters of the alphabet, and all the numbers. The flat rectangle is also used to create an opened or closed book-shaped cake. For these cakes, see diagram a.

To make a hemisphere-shaped skirt for a doll cake, you can bake the cake in a rounded bowl. Cut a hole in the center of the inverted cake and insert a small doll, leaving her torso sticking up. Decorate the skirt with icing, and add a hat of fresh flowers or ribbon and lace. For the dress bodice, use a piece of lace, or icing piped directly onto the doll; an inexpensive plastic doll from the five- and ten-cent store in the best for this purpose (diagram b).

Trucks and trains can be fashioned from cakes baked in loaf pans or 8-inch-square pans. For wheels, use Oreo cookies or other round cookies or candies (diagram c).

A gingerbread house can be made from a solid rectangle of cake as well as from the traditional gingerbread cookie dough. To make a solid gingerbread cake house, use loaf-shaped cakes or 8-inch cake pans as basic building blocks and follow a pattern and decorative ideas from a traditional gingerbread house (diagram d).

As a general guide, it is important to make a sketch of the finished shape before going to the trouble of baking a cake, only to find it is not a practical shape. Avoid thin shapes, which will be fragile; stick to sturdy forms and simple ideas; a bold statement is most effective. Use decorative icing piped through a bag or fresh flowers or candies and cookies for decorative trimmings. If you need more ideas, look at the cake shapes below or see illustrations in children's books. For very elaborate sculptured cakes (a portrait head, a piano), first model the shape from clay to simplify the form and determine the most efficient cake pan to use. Use buttercream icing as glue to fasten all pieces as well as to decorate the finished shape.

Use a serrated knife to cut shapes from cake. Keep the cut edges neat. Brush crumbs from cut surfaces. For small curved cuts, use a serrated grapefruit knife.

Assemble the cake on a sturdy base. Try covering a cookie sheet or flat tray with foil, or use a foil-covered jelly-roll pan. A mirror makes an attractive base; bind the edges, which may be sharp, with masking tape or colored cloth Mystic tape.

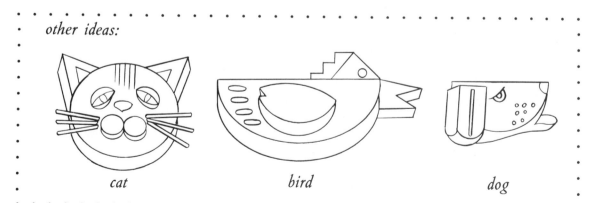

other ideas:

cat   *bird*   *dog*

Special Effects, Flavorings, & Decorative Techniques

Praline Powder and Praline Paste

•

Nut brittle is called praline, *pralin* in French. To make it, sugar is caramelized with toasted almonds and/or hazelnuts, then poured onto a slab and allowed to harden. When this brittle candy is powdered it makes "praline," or praline powder, an extremely flavorful preparation that is added to buttercreams, mousses, Bavarian cream, or whipped cream, or used to decorate cakes or other desserts. Note that the classic proportions for making praline require an equal weight of nuts and sugar. The water in this recipe is added to smooth the melting of the sugar; it quickly evaporates.

To vary the flavor, praline powder can be made with pecans, walnuts, or other nuts, instead of the classic almonds and hazelnuts. Skins may be left on the almonds to add flavor, although they are always removed from the hazelnuts.

Note: Many recipes require the nuts to be toasted before they are added to the syrup at the amber stage; this is fine for hazelnuts, because they have to be toasted anyway to have their skins rubbed off before use. However, with almonds and other nuts, you can save time and achieve the same result simply by putting the untoasted nuts directly into the syrup as soon as the sugar has melted. In this manner, the nuts are cooked along with the sugar syrup, and the flavor of the finished product is excellent.

When praline powder is worked in the food processor for about 6 minutes, it becomes a paste, like a nut butter. This is called Praline Paste, and can also be used to flavor icings or creams.

☐ ADVANCE PREPARATION: Praline powder can be made well in advance and refrigerated in an airtight container for several months or stored at room temperature for about 2 weeks.

☐ SPECIAL EQUIPMENT: 1½-quart heavy-bottomed saucepan, rough-textured towel (for skinning hazelnuts), mercury candy thermometer (nice but not essential), marble slab or jelly-roll pan or cookie sheet lightly coated with flavorless vegetable oil or butter, blender or food processor, airtight storage container, pastry brush

☐ QUANTITY: about 1½ cups

1 cup whole blanched almonds (5 ounces; 140 g); or use half whole hazelnuts, toasted and skinned (directions follow), plus half whole blanched almonds (either toasted in advance or added to the melted sugar syrup)
1 cup granulated sugar (7 ounces; 200 g)
6 tablespoons water

TO TOAST NUTS:

Spread nuts on a roasting pan and put in a preheated 325°F (165°C) oven for 8 to 10 minutes. Toss nuts occasionally, until they are golden and aromatic.

TO REMOVE HAZELNUT SKINS:

Place the hot hazelnuts in a textured towel and rub them well to remove their skins. Set the nuts aside.

1. Combine the sugar and water in the saucepan or a copper sugar pot, and set over moderate heat. Swirl the pan, or stir once or twice, until the sugar is dissolved. Bring to a gently bubbling boil for a full 3 minutes, swirling the pan occasionally and washing down the pan sides with a pastry brush dipped into cold water to dissolve any sugar crystals that may have formed.

2. Add the nuts (if *not* previously toasted); swirl the pan gently to coat nuts with melted sugar syrup, then return the syrup to a boil. Without stirring, cook over medium-high heat for 12 to 15 minutes after reaching the boiling point. Occasionally wash down the pan sides with a brush dipped into cold water.

3. At this point, the syrup should have reached the hard-crack stage (295° to 310°F) and become light amber in color. If using *toasted* nuts, stir them in now. Cook until the syrup just begins to darken slightly, at about 335°F. Then pour out the nuts and syrup onto the oiled pan. Spread the nuts in a single layer with the back of a spoon and set them aside to cool.

4. When the nut brittle is cold, break it up into small pieces. In several batches, process it to fine crumbs or powder in a food processor or blender, or with a mortar and pestle. Note: As the nut brittle cools, it may appear slightly cloudy. Don't worry; this is caused by the oil and moisture content of the nuts, which varies. Store the praline powder in an airtight container.

PRALINE PASTE:

□ QUANTITY: about 1 cup

Prepare Praline Powder. Leave it in the food processor or blender and work it for 6 to 10 minutes longer, until the nut oils are released and the mixture resembles a slightly dry nut butter. Processing time and texture vary with the oil content of the nuts. Store the paste in an airtight container in the refrigerator. Use the paste to flavor cake fillings, creams, and buttercream icing.

Marzipan

■

Marzipan is almond paste combined with egg whites and sugar to make a smooth blend that may be modeled like clay or rolled out into sheets. Bakers' supply houses sell ready-made marzipan, but you can prepare your own quickly and easily using canned or packaged almond paste available in the supermarket.

□ QUANTITY: about 2 cups

1 cup canned pure almond paste
(8 ounces; 220 g)
1 large egg white
2 teaspoons almond extract
2 cups sifted confectioners' sugar
(7 ounces; 200 g)

Note: Instead of the canned almond paste, which is quite stiff, you can substitute a 7-ounce roll of plastic-wrapped Odense (Dan-ish) brand "Pure Almond Paste," which is already soft and needs nothing added to it.

If using the canned almond paste, crumble it into a bowl, add the egg white, extract, and sugar. Mix with a spoon or your sugared hands or the paddle attachment of an electric mixer until the mixture forms a ball. Sift in extra sugar if it needs to be drier. Knead until smooth and satiny.

If using the store-bought soft almond paste, it can be used as is, without adding sugar or egg white. The 7-ounce roll will make one 10-inch disk about 1/16 inch thick. To cover a 2-layer 9-inch cake with this almond paste, you need 1½ rolls, or 10½ ounces.

Whichever you are using, almond paste or marzipan, divide it into the required amounts and roll it out with a sugared rolling pin on a surface also dusted with confectioners' sugar. Or, break off small lumps and mold them into roses (see rose-making directions on page 455), or form fruit shapes.

Marzipan or almond paste may be colored with paste or liquid vegetable food colors. Use

the tiniest amount possible, knead it into a small ball of marzipan dough, and work until the color is even. Add more color if necessary, but remember that pale tints are the most appetizing. Color may also be brushed on molded shapes by using liquid food coloring thinned with water to the desired shade. Stems for fruit can be made with whole cloves or bits of toothpick dipped into green food coloring. Leaves can be cut from paper or modeled from green-tinted marzipan.

After forming marzipan flowers, leaves, fruits, or other designs, let them air-dry for several hours or overnight. Store them in an airtight container at room temperature.

Cookie Base for Cakes

■

Fancy European tortes and gâteaux made of sponge cake with cream filling are frequently built upon a crisp cookie base. This gives the cake a firm foundation as well as a contrast in textures. The cookie base is actually a sweetened piecrust pastry, *pâte sablée,* containing an egg yolk and sugar.

□ ADVANCE PREPARATION: The pastry dough can be made well in advance and frozen.

□ SPECIAL EQUIPMENT: bowl, 2 knives or food processor

□ QUANTITY: enough for a single layer base about ¼ inch thick for an 8- to 9-inch cake

1 cup (5 ounces; 140 g) plus 2 tablespoons unsifted all-purpose flour
½ cup sifted confectioners' sugar (1¾ ounces; 50 g)
¼ teaspoon salt
⅛ teaspoon ground nutmeg
6 tablespoons unsalted butter, cut up
3 tablespoons margarine or solid shortening
1 large egg yolk
2 or 3 tablespoons ice water, as needed

1. Combine the flour, sugar, salt, and nutmeg in a large bowl or in the work bowl of a food processor fitted with a metal blade. Combine the ingredients or pulse the processor to blend. Add the butter and margarine or shortening and use 2 cross-cutting knives or pulse the processor to combine the fat and flour until the mixture resembles dry rice.

2. Add the egg yolk, a tablespoon or two of ice water, and blend, or pulse a couple of times, only until the pastry begins to clump together. Add a tiny bit more water if the dough is too dry. When the dough will cling together when pinched between your fingers, remove it from the bowl and turn it out onto wax paper. Wrap it into a ball and chill for about 30 minutes.

3. Roll out and bake as per directions in the cake recipe.

Candied Citrus Peel

∎

I first attempted making candied citrus peel over 20 years ago, but my efforts were disappointing and varied from thin hard crisps to soft flabby strips. On rare occasions I achieved the ideal crisp-outside chewy-inside texture, but reliable results eluded me. I sought advice from a friend's grandmother, famous for her candied peel, and was advised to blanch the peel 3 times to remove its bitterness, then cook the peel in sugar until I "felt" it was done when I bit into it. Her friends, she said, always asked her to make it for them; they couldn't duplicate her success, even with her recipe. I understood. My first breakthrough came when a chef explained the correct syrup temperature (230°F), which automatically controls the texture. More recently, I learned a simplified blanching technique from the *Chez Panisse Desserts* cookbook by Lindsey Remolif Shere (Random House, 1985), and I gratefully acknowledge adapting her method here.

There are three points to note when preparing citrus peel. First, the thickness of the peel, second, the blanching technique which removes the natural bitterness, and third, the time and temperature for boiling the peel in syrup. Follow the recipe carefully; it works. Note: Before starting, wash whole fruit to remove any possible chemical residue.

☐ ADVANCE PREPARATION: Candied peel will last at least a year if packed in layers of granulated sugar in an airtight container and kept in a cool, dry location or the refrigerator.

☐ SPECIAL EQUIPMENT: paring knife, cutting board, 1½-quart heavy-bottomed, nonreactive saucepan, strainer or colander, mercury candy thermometer or instant spot thermometer, pastry brush and glass of cold water; tongs, soup bowl or pan with sides, wax-paper-covered tray or cookie sheet with sides or wire rack set over wax paper

☐ QUANTITY: about 2 cups

FRUIT:

About 2 cups loosely packed peel cut from 4 oranges or 6 lemons or limes or 2 grapefruits (see step 1)

SYRUP:

1 cup granulated sugar (7 ounces; 200 g)
½ cup water
2 tablespoons light corn syrup, or ¼ teaspoon cream of tartar

COATING:

1 cup granulated sugar (7 ounces; 200 g) plus extra for layering peel if it is to be stored

1. With a sharp paring knife, quarter the oranges or grapefruit, then remove the quarter-segments of peel. With lemons and limes, slice off the peel, cutting right down to the beginning of the fruit. Cut wide strips of peel and leave on the white pith. Ideally, orange peel should be about ⅛ inch thick, though if more it does not matter. Do not cut off the peel with a vegetable peeler; the zest alone is too thin to give the correct texture.

2. Put the peels into a saucepan, cover with cold water, and bring to a boil. Lower the heat and boil gently for 15 minutes. Turn off the heat and let the peel stand in the hot water for 15 minutes. Drain in a colander and rinse with cold water. The peel will be soft. Grapefruit peel is more bitter than the others and is best blanched in 3 changes of cold water, each brought to a boil, then simmered for 10 minutes.

3. With a teaspoon, carefully scrape off and discard the soft white pith inside each segment of peel. It is easily removed. Slice the peel to the desired thickness—¼-inch-thick strips are most common.

4. Combine in the saucepan the sugar, ½ cup water, and corn syrup or cream of tartar. Stir, then bring to a boil, swirling the pan several times to dissolve the sugar. Wash down the pan sides with a pastry brush dipped into cold water. When the syrup boils and looks clear, add the prepared peels. The syrup should cover the peels. Put the candy thermometer into the pan. Boil the peel gently over moderate heat for about 30 minutes, or longer, until the syrup reaches 230°F (thread stage, just before soft-ball stage) and most but not all of the syrup has been absorbed. With a slotted spoon, transfer the peel to a bowl or pan of sugar. Toss the peel in the sugar, then set the pieces on the paper-covered tray or rack to air-dry. After drying for several hours or overnight, the peel should be crisp outside but flexible and chewy inside. If too flabby and soft, it was not cooked long enough at a high enough temperature; if it is crisp enough to crack when bent, it was cooked at too high a temperature. Store the peel in layers of sugar in an airtight container.

5. To use the candied peel as a garnish, it can be diced or left in thin strips. To make a delectable candy even more so, dip all or half the length of each strip into melted semisweet or white chocolate; use this to garnish the tops of cakes. Set candy-dipped strips on wax paper and refrigerate to set the chocolate. Chocolate-covered peel can be made well in advance and stored in a cool place.

Chocolate Leaves

■

Chocolate leaves are made by coating real leaves with melted chocolate. When the chocolate is hard, the real leaf is peeled away, leaving an edible garnish for cakes. Both white and dark chocolate are used for making leaves; the procedure is the same, though solid shortening is not used with the white chocolate. Before starting to make the chocolate leaves, read About Chocolate (page 45), particularly noting How To Melt Dark or White Chocolate (page 47).

☐ ADVANCE PREPARATION: Chocolate leaves can be prepared well in advance and stored in a protective airtight container in the refrigerator for a week or two; leaves can also be frozen for several months.

☐ SPECIAL EQUIPMENT: double boiler, leaves (see Note following), wax paper, tray, pastry brush or small spatula for applying chocolate (though I prefer to use my finger)

☐ QUANTITY: As a rough guideline, 1 ounce of melted chocolate will coat about 6 leaves, depending upon their size; 8 ounces will make roughly 50 leaves. 5 to 6 leaves are enough to top a 9-inch cake, but you should always make extras in case some break. Excess melted chocolate can be poured into a paper muffin cup and chilled, to be stored and reused for another purpose.

☐ A NOTE ABOUT LEAVES:

For the prettiest effect, use gracefully shaped leaves with a waxy surface and a pronounced pattern of veins on one side. Lemon, magnolia, camellia, gardenia, ivy, and rose leaves work well. However, be aware that certain types of leaves can be poisonous! If you are uncertain, check with a nursery or a botanist or the state agricultural extension service. I use lemon or camellia leaves from a local florist, who also supplies them to neighboring restaurants. Be sure to wash and dry the leaves before using them to remove any chemical sprays. If you have a misshapen or extra-large leaf, simply cut it to size with scissors before coating it with chocolate; or cut it to the desired shape; for example, a rounded leaf can be turned into a maple or holly leaf before coating it with chocolate.

8 ounces semisweet chocolate, milk chocolate, or white chocolate (230 g), chopped
2 teaspoons solid white shortening (used only with dark chocolate)

1. Melt the chocolate, and shortening if using it, in the top pan of a double boiler over hot (125°F) water. If using white chocolate, be particularly careful not to let the water get too hot or the white chocolate will become grainy and lumpy; use a spot thermometer to be sure the white chocolate gets no hotter than 115°F;

ideally, keep the temperature between 100° and 110°F and the water beneath it about 125°F. Stir the chocolate to blend it smooth. Set it aside to cool until comfortable to the touch.

2. Set clean, dry leaves, vein-patterned sides up, on a wax-paper-covered tray. (Note: The most pronounced vein pattern is generally on the underside of the leaf.) With a pastry brush, small spatula, or your fingertip, spread a generous ⅛-inch layer of chocolate on the leaves, one at a time (diagram a). Remember that you should be covering the side of the leaf where the vein markings are most visible. Brush the chocolate out to the edges, but not over them. Try to avoid thinning the edges too much. Set the coated leaves, chocolate side up, on a wax-paper-covered tray and place the tray in the refrigerator or freezer for a few minutes, until the chocolate is hard-set.

3. To make curled leaves, allow the chocolate leaves to cool partially, then set them onto the curved surface of a French-bread pan or a

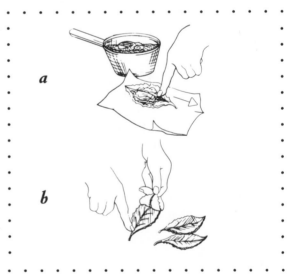

tube-shaped cake pan and chill to set. If curved too soon, the melted chocolate will all run to the middle of the leaf.

4. When the chocolate is completely set, remove the firm leaves from the refrigerator or freezer. Allow the leaves to stand at room temperature for 30 to 60 seconds. Carefully break off any uneven chocolate edges that wrap over onto the front of the real leaves. Then, starting at the stem end, peel the real leaves away from the chocolate (diagram b). Take care to handle the chocolate leaf as little as possible to avoid leaving fingerprints. Set the chocolate leaves back on the tray or in a protective container and refrigerate or freeze them until needed. Reuse the real leaves, coating them with more chocolate as long as they hold their shape, but get fresh ones for each new batch of chocolate leaves.

Note: If this is your first time, it is best to make a few test leaves at the start to determine the quality of the chocolate coating. Chocolate leaves should have a delicate appearance; ease up if you made the chocolate too thick. If, on the other hand, the chocolate shatters when the leaf is peeled away, apply more chocolate the next time and warm the leaf a little longer before peeling it off.

Chocolate Curls

▪

Professional pastry chefs make chocolate curls, or long fat chocolate cigarettes, by spreading a coating of melted chocolate over a marble slab. When the chocolate (usually a coating chocolate) is nearly set, they draw a wide-bladed sharp knife across the surface, causing a thin sheet of chocolate to roll up on itself in a long curl. It takes practice, but this is the classic technique.

Curls can be made with either white or dark chocolate; white curls are dramatic on a dark chocolate icing and dark chocolate curls can be highlighted with a faint sifting of confectioners' sugar.

An easy method to produce small but acceptable chocolate curls is to draw a swivel-type vegetable peeler across the surface of a thick candy bar or piece of block chocolate. Be sure you work over a sheet of wax paper and lift the completed curls with toothpicks poked into their sides. The trick is to have the chocolate at the correct temperature. If it is too cold and hard, the curls will crumble or shave; if too soft, they will collapse. The easiest thing to do is set the chocolate in a barely heated oven for 10 to 15 minutes. Some ovens are warmed sufficiently by their pilot lights. In warm weather, use the sun. Often just the heat of your hand holding the chocolate will warm it; work on one side of the chocolate bar, then turn it around so the warmer side (previously resting on the palm of your hand) is facing up. If the chocolate feels too soft, chill it slightly; experiment until it works. Chocolate curls can be stored in a protective airtight box in the refrigerator or freezer.

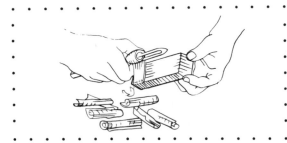

Grated Chocolate

■

To grate or shave chocolate for a decorative topping or to press onto iced cake sides, simply take a piece of block chocolate, a chocolate bar, or a 1-ounce square of chocolate and pass it across the medium-size holes of a box grater. This can be done over a piece of wax paper or directly over the cake top. Unused grated chocolate can be stored in the refrigerator or freezer in an airtight container; it requires no thawing before use.

Chocolate Bark

■

Melt chocolate in the top pan of a double boiler. Spread it in a ⅛-inch-thick layer on wax paper or foil. Set the paper on a tray and refrigerate it for about 5 minutes, until choco-

late is hard. Remove the paper from the refrigerator. Hold the paper in your hands and bang it back and forth, splintering the chocolate into long slivers. Press the slivers onto the surface of a frosted cake to create a barklike effect. This is most commonly used for the Bûche de Noël or Yule Log Cake (page 229).

Plastic Chocolate Ribbons and Roses

■

For years I avoided making this marvelous material for 2 reasons: first, I feared it was too complex and second, most recipes called for ingredients I don't have around on a regular basis: gum tragacanth and cocoa butter. Recently, a friend in Canada taught me the following simple formula, and now nothing can stop me. Try it, if you like shaping things with your hands; it couldn't be easier or more fun. Note: Ribbons and roses can also be made with Marzipan (page 446).

When melted white or dark chocolate is blended with light corn syrup it becomes a very pliable substance perfect for shaping into cake decorations. This so-called plastic chocolate is more flexible than plain chocolate, though that is fine for making chocolate leaves or curls. Plastic chocolate is best for modeling into lifelike roses, rolling flat into ribbons, or cutting out with cookie or canapé cutter shapes for flat or interlocked 3-dimensional shapes.

☐ ADVANCE PREPARATION: Plastic chocolate can be stored refrigerated for up to 12 months.

☐ SPECIAL EQUIPMENT: double boiler, instant-read-out spot thermometer (optional), plastic wrap, rolling pin, dough scraper or spatula, 6-inch icing spatula, hand-cranking pasta machine (optional)

☐ QUANTITY: ¾ to 1 cup plastic chocolate. White chocolate makes 8½ ounces, 245 grams. Dark chocolate makes 9 ounces, 255 grams. One batch makes 5 or 6 roses or a complete "skin" to cover a 9-inch 3-layer cake.

7 ounces semisweet chocolate or white
chocolate (200 grams), chopped fine
¼ cup (2 ounces) light corn syrup
Confectioners' sugar (for white
chocolate), or unsweetened cocoa (for
dark chocolate)
Note: White chocolate can be delicately
tinted with confectioners' paste or
powdered (not liquid) colors.

1. The procedure is the same for dark or white chocolate. Place the chopped chocolate in the top pan of a double boiler set over 125°F water. At this temperature the white chocolate, especially, will remain perfectly creamy and smooth. When melted at too high a temperature, the protein in white chocolate can stiffen and the mixture become lumpy or granular. Stir the chocolate until melted and completely smooth; it should be 100°F to 110°F, not higher.

Remove pan from the heat and use a rubber spatula to scrape the melted chocolate into a clean bowl. Set the chocolate aside for about 5 minutes, until lukewarm.

2. Pour on the corn syrup *all at once* and stir with a wooden spoon for about 10 seconds, until the chocolate thickens and looks dull. It is important not to add the syrup slowly. Note: If you overbeat the white chocolate, the syrup may start to separate out. Ignore it, and carry on.

3. Place the lump of chocolate on a square of plastic wrap, press it into a flattish package, and wrap well. Set the wrapped chocolate in a cool place (on a marble counter or in a cool pantry) for 45 to 60 minutes. This period of chilling and firming is important. In the heat of midsummer, I have had to refrigerate my chocolate to firm it, and this has done it no harm other than to make it more difficult to soften for shaping.

4. After firming, the chocolate must be rolled out and folded several times. Working the chocolate develops its plasticity. If the chocolate is too hard, first bring it to room temperature, or at least to a flexible stage. Working and kneading the chocolate with warm hands may do this, but if it has been refrigerated and is really hard, you can speed the warming—very carefully—by placing the unwrapped chocolate on a piece of paper in the microwave. For white chocolate, use Defrost for 3 to 6 seconds; for semisweet chocolate go to 10 seconds and test for softness. If still hard, try 2 seconds more and retest. When partially soft, knead the chocolate with your hands.

If you are working with both white and dark chocolate on the same day, always work white chocolate first, so the dark does not discolor the white. This is especially important when kneading on the countertop or when rolling the chocolate in a pasta machine.

5. Before rolling out white chocolate, sprinkle some confectioners' sugar on a cool counter and on a rolling pin; for dark chocolate, use unsweetened cocoa. Roll the chocolate into a strip about 4 inches wide and 15 inches long. Fold the strip into thirds like a letter and roll again (diagram a). Repeat 3 or

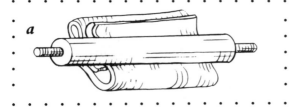

4 more times. This process resembles working with puff pastry, giving the dough 4 turns. After rolling, the chocolate should be smooth, flexible, and easy to handle. Wrap the chocolate in plastic wrap and set it aside until ready to mold. Or refrigerate for later use.

CHOCOLATE RIBBONS:

BY HAND:

Bring the chocolate to flexible consistency. Roll it with the rolling pin to the desired

thickness, usually ¹⁄₁₆ inch, bearing in mind that it should look delicate but still be strong enough to handle. Cut the rolled chocolate ribbon into strips and set them on your cake. You can make a bow (diagram b) or a 2-toned ribbon by combining a wide ribbon of one color with a narrow ribbon of another color set on top of it and rolling them both together (diagram c).

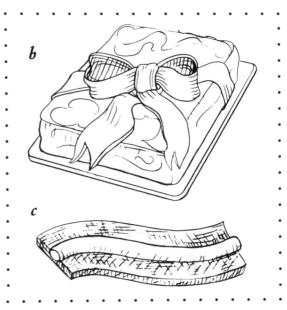

WITH THE PASTA MACHINE:

To make ribbons, break off about one third of the total plastic chocolate and shape it into a flattish rectangle. Dust it lightly with either confectioners' sugar or cocoa (remember to do white chocolate first). Pass the chocolate through the widest setting of the machine, then fold it, reshape it, and pass it through once more. Repeat, but reduce the setting one notch. Repeat until desired thickness is reached. To make striped ribbons, you can add a white strip on top of a chocolate strip or vice versa, and roll them both together; however, in my experience this usually results in wavy or crooked lines.

CHOCOLATE ROSES:

There are two basic ways to fashion chocolate roses: by hand, shaping the petals with an icing spatula, and by rolling the chocolate thin with a rolling pin or pasta machine and then cutting out petals with a knife or scissors. Whichever method you use, the assembly technique is the same. The icing spatula technique is adapted from one I learned from Chef Albert Kumin.

To shape the petals with an icing spatula, form the chocolate into a cylinder roughly 1¼ inches in diameter and set it on the counter. Hold one hand on the roll, and with the other hand, use a small icing spatula to spread or smear some chocolate from the end of the roll onto the counter. Make a rough petal shape about 1½ inches square. Fan out the chocolate until the rounded outer edges are so thin they trail away; the petal will be thicker where it joins the roll (diagram a). Cut the petal loose from the roll (diagram b), then slide the spatula beneath it and scrape it off the counter (diagram c). Repeat, making between 7 and 12 petals for a full-size rose.

To make petals from plastic chocolate that has been rolled out flat, simply cut out 1½-inch squares, then round them into petal forms.

To give dark or white chocolate plastic a sheen, and to remove the cut-edge look, set the petals flat on the counter and lightly polish them by rubbing with the "pinky" side of your fist, moving your hand lightly and rapidly in a circular motion on top of the petal.

To fashion a budlike core for the rose, or to make a bud that stands alone, form a lump of chocolate into a cone about 1½ inches tall and about ¾ inch wide at the base. Be sure the tip is very pointed (diagram d).

To add petals for the bud, place 3 petals against the cone so each petal faces the others and joins them at the sides. The point of the cone barely peeks out from the center. If you look straight down on the bud at this stage, it should look like a 3-bladed propeller (diagram e). Pull each petal around in the same

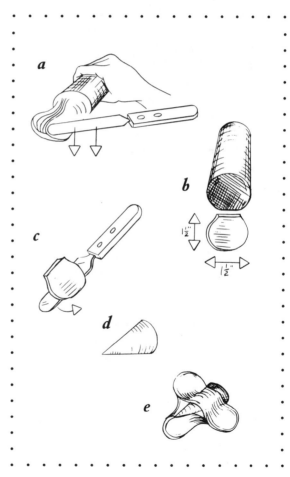

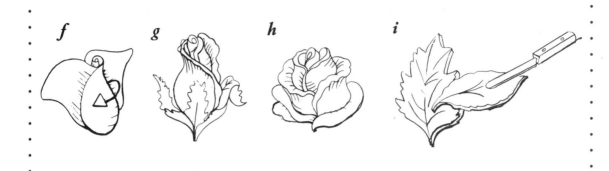

direction, turning the petals slightly downward as they go (arrow, diagram f). Pinch the top edges of each petal, making them thin and delicate. Roll back the edges of each petal for a lifelike appearance. To complete a bud, pinch the cone in at the bottom, rounding the bud form as shown (diagram g). Cut off excess base.

To complete the single bud, you can cut out 3 small narrow leaves, press the back of a knife into the chocolate to make veins, and press the leaves around the base of the bud.

To make a full-size rose, omit the leaves and keep adding petals to the bud. As you add petals, overlap each one about ⅓ before adding the next. After the 3 petals that form the bud, add 4 petals in one round, then 5 in the next round. Pinch the base of each petal to the bottom of the bud to fasten it. When the rose is the correct size, again pinch the base to round it. Cut away excess base, making a flat bottom. With a delicate touch, roll back the top edges of each petal, then open the petals up slightly, giving the rose a lifelike appearance (diagram h). Stand the rose on a dish until the chocolate hardens, then set it on your cake.

The roses can be made weeks in advance and kept at cool room temperature or refrigerated in protective covered plastic boxes.

To make Chocolate Leaves to accompany the buds or full-sized roses, use rolled white or dark plastic chocolate cut to leaf shapes, pressing the back of the knife into the leaf to make veins (diagram i). Or use melted chocolate spread on real leaves (page 449).

Cut-Out Plastic Chocolate Shapes

■

These are the easiest of all the shapes to make. Simply follow the directions for rolling out plastic chocolate. To make decorative shapes, use cookie or canapé cutters, or a paring knife drawn around a homemade cardboard template, cutting or stamping out the pieces. If the shapes are to be set flat on the top or sides of a frosted cake, the chocolate can be about ¹⁄₁₆ inch thick.

To make chocolate sections to go around the sides of a cake, cut rectangles (diagram a) and press them into the buttercream or whipped-cream icing in an overlapping pattern all around.

To make interlocking, free-standing shapes, cut 2 shapes (a tree, for example), then make a slot in the center from the top to the middle of one shape and from the middle to the bottom of the other. Set one shape into the other, crossing them so the shape stands by itself (diagram b).

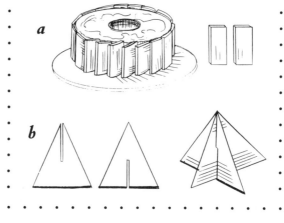

Chocolate Ruffles

■

This oft-copied decoration was perfected in Paris by pâtissier Gaston Lenôtre, whose pastry shops all offer the glamorous Meringue d'Automne. Basically 3 crisp meringue layers filled with a chocolate mousse, the exciting thing about the cake is its icing. The entire cake is cloaked in a skin of leathery chocolate (rather than a glaze or icing), and the top is a mass of stiff chocolate ruffles. A light dusting of confectioners' sugar just before serving adds just the right highlight. The effect is dramatic, to say the least, but it is not at all hard to copy once you know the tricks.

The biggest secret is the use of plastic chocolate (page 452). Professional bakers make the wrapping layer with plain melted couverture chocolate, spread flat, partially stiffened, then picked up and draped around the cake. The chocolate must be at exactly the right temper-

ature, but often becomes brittle, cracking apart. This is definitely not for beginners. However, with plastic chocolate, it is a piece of cake. In fact, 1 recipe (7 ounces chocolate plus 2 ounces corn syrup) makes exactly the amount needed to cover one 9-inch 3-layer round cake.

To do this, sprinkle a little cocoa on the counter and the rolling pin, then roll out the flexible chocolate into a strip 5 × 30 inches. If the counter is well coated, the strip will not stick. Pick up the strip and drape it around the cake, setting the bottom edge of the strip even with the bottom of the cake and draping the excess over onto the cake top. It should reach nearly to the center, but not cover the top completely. The chocolate ruffle will fill in the center. Overlap the ends of the strip, and use your hands to mold the chocolate gently to the cake. Gather and pleat the top so it is fairly flat (diagram a, page 458). To make ruffles for the top, you have two choices. The quickest and easiest is not actually the prettiest, but it may be close enough. For this, you need a second batch of plastic chocolate; roll the

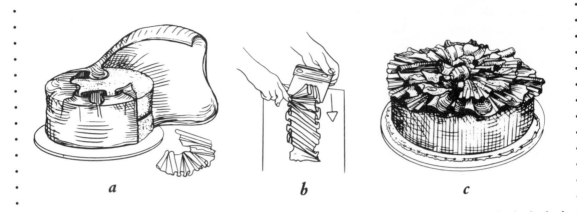

| *a* | *b* | *c* |

chocolate very thin, cut it into strips about 2 inches wide, and gather one long edge, making a ruffle. Set sections of ruffle in concentric circles on the cake top, adding a small curl in the center. Sift a tiny bit of sugar on top.

To make more authentic, lacier ruffles, melt about 8 ounces semisweet chocolate in the top pan of a double boiler. Spread the melted chocolate onto the back of a jelly-roll pan 10 × 15 inches to a thickness of about ⅟₁₆ inch. Set the chocolate aside in a cool room, or refrigerate, just until "leather hard," when an edge can be picked up and bent without cracking; do not chill hard.

With a 3-inch-wide putty knife or dough scraper, make the ruffles by scraping the chocolate toward yourself in strips. The trick to getting it to gather is to hold one finger at the side of the strip as it is formed, causing the chocolate to gather up by your finger and fan out on the other side (diagram b). Set sections of ruffled chocolate around the cake top, making concentric circles and adding a small curl in the center (c). Sift a tiny bit of confectioners' sugar on top.

Apricot Roses

∎

To decorate an apricot-flavored cake, nothing is as elegant as an apricot rose. It is a cinch to make if you cut the petals out of a sheet of pure dried apricot "leather" (also called fruit roll), sold in health-food stores, delicatessens, and supermarkets. If you don't have the fruit roll, you can substitute sheets of rolled dried apricots. Note: Fruit leather and fruit roll are made in many fruit flavors; you can select the color and flavor that best complements your cake (cherry, raspberry, strawberry, orange, etc.) instead of apricot, if you wish. These roses can be prepared up to 2 weeks in advance and refrigerated.

☐ EQUIPMENT: scissors or kitchen shears, wax paper, rolling pin for apricot halves, toothpicks, tray

☐ QUANTITY: One average "fruit leather" roll (the type sold in the health-food store or deli, not the boxed supermarket variety) usually weighs 1 ounce and comes rolled in a 7-inch–diameter disk. It will make 1 rose with 12 petals. The boxed supermarket Fruit Roll-Ups, such as those made by General Mills, weigh ½ ounce each and come in 4½-inch squares. You will need 2 roll-ups to make 1 rose.

If using dried apricot halves, you will need about 15 large moist halves to make 2 roses.

TO MAKE ROSES WITH APRICOT LEATHER:

Cut the fruit leather with its paper backing in place. Peel off the backing before using the cut shapes to form the rose. Shape the roses following the directions and diagrams for plastic chocolate roses on page 455. Briefly, start with the central bud, cutting a rectangle about 3 × 1½ inches, then rolling it up into a cone. Around this add the petals. Cut the petals about 1½ inches square, then round the top edges, shaping the roses as directed. To make the petals adhere, simply press the pieces together; the warmth of your fingers will make them stick. If you have scraps left over, overlap them and pinch them together to make larger pieces for more rose petals. After adding enough petals, pinch the base firmly, then roll back the top edge of each petal with your fingertip to open out the rose and make it look lifelike. Use the scissors to cut away excess base.

TO MAKE ROSES WITH DRIED APRICOT HALVES:

Place several moist apricot halves, sticky side down, on a piece of wax paper. Cover with another paper and roll out apricots until very thin. Repeat, rolling out all the pieces. To see how the rose bud and full rose will look, see the diagrams on page 456.

To form the central bud, roll 1 apricot half, sticky side in, onto itself, forming a tight cone. Press it together to make it firm. To add a petal, press the base of 1 rolled apricot half, sticky side in, onto the central bud. Pinch it at the base to make it stick. Add another petal overlapping half of the first. Add 2 or 3 more petals, depending upon the size of the apricot halves and the desired rose size. If you need to hold the base together, push a toothpick through the bottom of all the petals. With knife or shears, trim off the excess base below the petals, making a flat stand.

To give a lifelike look to the petals, use your fingertip to roll or curl the petal tops outward, opening up the rose.

Set the roses on their flat stands on a plate or tray and refrigerate or freeze (to speed up setting) until firm.

Meringue Mushrooms

■

Meringue mushrooms are traditionally used to garnish the Bûche de Noël or Yule Log Cake (see Index). They also make attractive decorations or dessert treats in their own right. Maida Heatter, the acknowledged master of this confection (as well as many others), tells me the meringues that she keeps in her southern Florida home have lasted for over a year; moreover, she says she has no trouble producing them in a tropical kitchen, though she prefers air conditioning and avoids humid days. These lifelike mushrooms are less temperamental and easier to make than one would think, and the fact that they keep so well means they can be prepared well in advance. I have adapted the following technique, more or less, from *Maida Heatter's Book of Great Desserts,* Alfred A. Knopf, Inc., 1975.

☐ ADVANCE PREPARATION: Meringue mushrooms should be stored at room temperature in a loosely covered container, not airtight. They should remain crisp for months, even up to a year. Do not freeze them.

☐ SPECIAL EQUIPMENT: 16- to 18-inch pastry bag fitted with ½- to ¾-inch round tip, 2 cookie sheets, aluminum foil, small strainer, 4-cup Pyrex measure (as a stand for filling the pastry bag), rubber spatula, flat tray, double boiler, teaspoon, 2 empty egg cartons for supporting cooling mushrooms (if you don't have any empty egg cartons remove the eggs temporarily), paring knife

☐ BAKING TIME: 1 hour at 225°F (107°C)

☐ COOLING TIME IN OVEN WITH HEAT TURNED OFF: 30 to 45 minutes

☐ QUANTITY: about 3 dozen mushrooms; quantity depends upon size

☐ PAN PREPARATION: Cover cookie sheets with foil

MERINGUE:

1 recipe All-Purpose Meringue (page 248), Cold or Swiss Method, made with:
4 large egg whites, pinch of salt, ¼ teaspoon cream of tartar, 1 cup superfine sugar (note increase over
original recipe, which calls for ½ cup sugar) and 1 teaspoon vanilla extract

GARNISH:

2 tablespoons unsweetened cocoa
2 ounces semisweet chocolate

1. Prepare the pans as directed. Set a small strainer in a cup or small bowl and add a couple of tablespoons of cocoa. Do not sift, just leave it until needed. Position the oven shelves to divide the oven in thirds. Preheat oven to 225°F (107°C).

2. Prepare the meringue as directed in the recipe, beating whites, salt, and cream of tartar until fluffy, then gradually whipping in the sugar, 2 tablespoons at a time. After all the sugar has been added, whip the whites for an additional 7 to 8 full minutes, to be sure they are stiff and satiny and contain no grains of undissolved sugar. Pinch the meringue between your fingers; you should not feel any sugar granules. Total beating time from start to finish is between 15 and 18 minutes.

3. Spread a dab of meringue under each corner of the foil on each cookie sheet to hold it in place. To prepare the pastry bag, set it tip down in a 4-cup measure and fold back a 4- or 5-inch cuff (see illustrations, page 431). With a rubber spatula, transfer all or most of the meringue to the pastry bag. Lift up the bag cuff and twist the ends closed.

4. Pipe the mushroom stems first. Hold the bag at right angles to 1 foil-covered cookie sheet. With the tip pointing straight down, squeeze gently on the bag while lifting it slowly up. The idea is to pipe a small stem about 1 to 1½ inches tall, slightly fatter at the

base, sticking straight up off the sheet. Leave about 1 inch of space and repeat. Make many stems in rows. Don't worry if some are irregular or fall over. Sift a little cocoa on the stems, then put them right into the oven, on the top shelf.

To pipe the mushroom caps, hold the pastry bag at right angles to the foil and form even rounds of meringue about 1 to 1½ inches wide and ¾ inch thick. These should vary in size somewhat, just as real mushrooms do (diagram a). Space the caps about ½ inch apart on the sheet. Use your fingertip to smooth any peaks on top of the meringue caps. Sift a little cocoa over the caps, then set them in the oven. Continue making stems and caps to use up remaining meringue. Be sure you have extras, as some always break. Save scraps to garnish cakes.

5. Bake the stems and caps in the preheated oven for about 1 hour. Then turn off the oven heat and prop the door open but leave the meringues in the oven to continue drying out for another 30 to 45 minutes. The meringues are done when they are crisp, dry through, and stiff enough to be lifted off the foil. They become crisp as they cool. Break 1 piece into halves to test it. Bake them longer if needed; they must be hard.

Remove meringues from the oven and carefully peel off the foil. Set the shapes on a clean flat tray, or on more foil.

6. Melt the chocolate in the top pan of a double boiler set over hot, not boiling, water.

7. To assemble the mushrooms, the caps must be prepared. Cradle each cap in the palm of your hand while using the tip of a paring knife to "drill" a hole gently in the flat underside for the stem to fit in. Don't press on the cap.

8. Dip the tip of each stem in melted chocolate, then gently poke the tip into the prepared depression in the underside of the cap (diagram b). Set the mushrooms upside down in an egg carton until the chocolate is hard. Refrigerate the mushrooms to speed the setting if the weather is hot.

9. Store the mushrooms in a loosely covered container at room temperature.

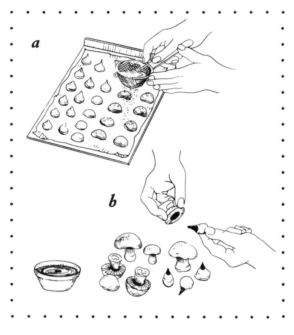

Caramelized Sugar Glaze and Cage

■

When caramelized sugar is cooked to the hard-crack stage, it can be used for many decorative purposes: to coat nuts, small pastries, or an entire cake top (see Dobostorte, page

279). It can also be used to make a caramel cage. One of the most attractive cake presentations I have seen was in a master class taught by Jacques Pépin, when he made a raisin and bourbon chocolate cake coated with sifted confectioners' sugar and topped with a caramel cage. The effect is dazzling and the work is minimal once you get the knack and learn the tricks. Don't be afraid to try it.

I tried for a long time to make make caramel cages in the so-called traditional manner, applying the caramel directly to a greased bowl. I consistently had trouble lifting off the cages, because the temperature was critical: too hot and they would bend, too cold and they would crack. My young daughter watched my efforts one day and asked why I didn't cover the bowl with foil first to make removal easier. Why not indeed. Ever since, my caramel cages work perfectly every time.

□ ADVANCE PREPARATION: Caramelized sugar can be made in advance and stored in a covered wide-mouthed container for months. To use it, rewarm to pouring consistency. Save leftover glaze. In hot weather, a caramel cage should be refrigerated lest heat and humidity cause it to melt. Generally, even in summer, it will last 1 day at room temperature; refrigerated, it will last for several days.

□ SPECIAL EQUIPMENT: 1½-quart heavy-bottomed saucepan, mercury candy thermometer (optional), pastry brush set in a glass of cold water. For glazing nuts: toothpicks, foil, apple or block of clay or styrofoam as a drying stand. For making caramel cage: round-bottomed stainless-steel or Pyrex bowl for a mold. Small molds can be made from Pyrex custard cups or the backs of metal ladels; aluminum foil and protective mitt or rubber gloves, spoon or fork

□ QUANTITY: about 2 cups, enough to glaze 12 nuts plus an 8- or 9-inch cake top, or to make several 7- to 9-inch caramel cages

2 cups granulated sugar (14 ounces; 400 g)
½ cup water
¼ teaspoon cream of tartar dissolved in 1 teaspoon water
For caramel cage: vegetable oil or solid shortening

TO MAKE THE CARAMEL:

Combine the sugar, water, and dissolved cream of tartar in a saucepan and set over moderate heat. Swirl the pan, or stir once or twice, cooking until the sugar is dissolved and the syrup looks clear. Raise the heat and begin to cook down the syrup. Several times during this period, wash down the pan sides with a pastry brush dipped into cold water to remove any sugar crystals from the pan sides. Bring the syrup to a gentle boil and boil *without stirring* for 10 to 14 minutes, or until the syrup is pale yellow in color and the thermometer reads 300°F, the hard-crack stage. At this point a drop of syrup will form a brittle ball when dropped into ice water. If you wish the syrup to have a darker amber color, let it cook to about 340°F. At once remove pan from the heat. At this stage the glaze can be poured on pastries or cakes, or can be used to coat nuts or make caramel cages.

TO MAKE CARAMEL-GLAZED NUTS:

Stick a toothpick in the end of each nut. Set out a piece of foil and on top of it place an apple or block of clay for a holder (diagram a). Grasp the toothpick and dip each nut into the warm caramel, then stand the toothpick up in the apple or other support. Leave until the caramel is hard; in very hot or humid weather, refrigerate to set the glaze. Remove picks and break off any caramel threads before serving.

a

TO MAKE A CARAMEL CAGE:

1. First select a bowl for the cage mold that is slightly smaller in diameter than your cake; or make a very small cage molded over a soup ladle to sit as a centerpiece in the middle of the cake.

2. To prepare the mold, which will be the outside surface of the bowl or ladle, cover it completely with a piece of aluminum foil. Tuck the ends of the foil inside the bowl rim. Smooth the foil absolutely flat onto the mold. Spread oil or solid white shortening over the foil.

3. Prepare the caramel as directed. Allow the caramel to cool just until thick enough to make long threads when dripped from a spoon, about 220° to 225°F.

4. Put a rubber glove or protective mitt on the hand that will be holding the mold (to avoid sugar burns) and lift the greased mold with one hand while the other hand dips a spoon or fork into the caramel and drips long

continuous threads in figure eights from one side of the bowl to the other (diagram b). Overlap the threads to make a strong, evenly spaced skeleton all around. Drip a few extra lines around the bottom edge of the cage to give it extra support. Set the bowl down (dome up) on the table and wait a few minutes for the glaze to set. In hot weather, place the mold on a tray and refrigerate until the caramel is hard. When ready, remove the foil from the bowl, then peel the foil away from the caramel cage. Set the finished cage on top of the iced cake (diagram c). To serve, remove the cage before slicing the cake.

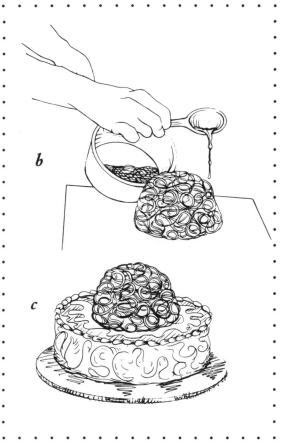

b

c

MOLDED CAKES

■

Two-piece metal cake molds are made in a variety of shapes including lambs, rabbits, footballs, and Santa Clauses. The molds are sold in specialty cookware shops, and their quality varies considerably. To ensure success in turning out a neatly shaped, thoroughly baked cake, it is best to use heavy-gauge metal, preferably 1/16-inch-thick aluminum, cast in 2 pieces. Thinner, less expensive aluminum molds will work, but manufacturer's directions should be carefully followed.

Molds fit together in different ways. One type has 2 solid pieces that clamp together to make a complete form; these have a steam vent hole in one half. Other molds are 2 pieces joined with a clamp that also forms a stand. In this case, the batter is poured into the top of the mold and baked on its stand set on a baking sheet. In both cases, look for halves that fit together neatly.

GENERAL INSTRUCTIONS FOR USING A TWO-PIECE CAKE MOLD:

Molds are sold with manufacturer's directions, and these should be read and followed. However, some general directions apply to the use of all molds:

First select a cake that has a firm grain and rises nicely; most layer cakes or pound cakes work well. The average mold will hold 3 to 4 cups of batter, or a standard-size cake mix (17 or 18 ounces). If your mold holds less batter than you have mixed, use the excess to make cupcakes. Do not add chunks of nuts or raisins to the cake batter as they weaken the cake; save them for decorations.

To prepare the mold, spread the inside of both halves with a generous coating of solid shortening or softened butter. Dust the greased surfaces with flour, then invert the pans and tap out excess flour. Be sure the vent hole is not plugged. Add cake batter to just below the rim, or joint, of the bottom half. Use a wooden spoon to stir gently through the batter to remove any air pockets. Attach the top half of the mold, lock it in place according to accompanying directions, and use strong cotton string or picture wire to tie the halves together. If you have the type of mold with an open top, fasten the halves, set the mold firmly on its stand, open top up, on a baking sheet, and fill 2/3 with batter.

Generally, molded cakes bake at about 375°F for approximately 1 hour. To test the cake for doneness, insert a cake tester or toothpick through the steam hole or open top of the mold into the cake. Set the mold, steam-vent side up, on a wire rack and allow the cake to cool for about 15 minutes.

To unmold the cake, remove the top half and let the cake sit on the rack for another 5 minutes. Then remove the cake from the bottom half of the mold. Let the unmolded cake sit on its side on a wire rack until completely cold before standing it upright. If necessary, cut off any uneven lumps of cake to flatten the standing surface.

After You've Baked

· HOW TO CUT AND SERVE CAKES ·

ifferent types of cakes and icings require different techniques and equipment. If you have gone to all the trouble of making a cake, you will want to present it with a flourish, serving neat slices that show it off to advantage.

☐ LAYER CAKES: For most layer cakes, use a knife with a thin, sharp blade. It is helpful to have a wedge-shaped pie server to support and lift out each cut piece. Round layer cakes are cut like pies, into wedges (diagram a). Make the wedges significantly smaller for very rich or very sweet cakes.

Extra-large layer cakes, 12 or 14 inches in diameter or more, should be cut like wedding cakes. To do this, make a dot in the exact center of the cake. Divide in half the distance from the dot to the outer edge. At this point, hold the knife perpendicular to the top of the cake and cut, with a sawing motion, an inner circle. Cut wedge-shaped sections from the outer ring, then cut the central circle into wedges (b). Alternatively, you can cut the entire cake into quarters (c), then cut each quarter into narrow slices.

☐ SHEET CAKES: Use a thin, sharp knife. Sheet cakes are cut into halves or thirds, then into smaller rectangles or squares or diamonds (d and e). Most sheet cakes are served directly from the pan.

☐ TUBE CAKES: Tube cakes are cut into wedges (f). Cut thinner wedges for extra-rich cakes. Angel-food, sponge, and chiffon cakes are cut with a serrated knife worked with a gentle sawing motion. Or you can use the specially designed multipronged wire "cake breaker." Angel-food cakes can also be broken with a fork, or with 2 forks back-to-back, prying gently in opposite directions.

☐ LOAF CAKES: Use a thin sharp knife or a serrated knife. Cut the loaf into slices, crosswise (g). Vary the thickness of the slices depending upon the richness of the cake.

☐ JELLY ROLLS/ROULADES: Use a thin sharp knife or a serrated knife. Cut crosswise, making pinwheel-shaped slices (h). If the cake

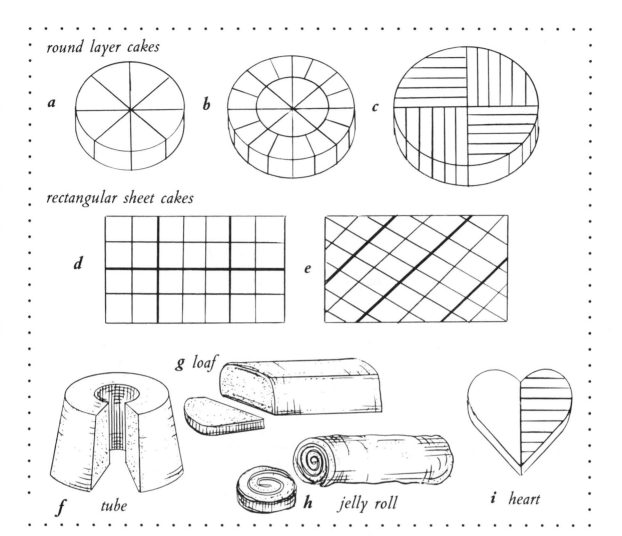

round layer cakes

a **b** **c**

rectangular sheet cakes

d **e**

g *loaf*

f *tube* **h** *jelly roll* **i** *heart*

is a sponge-type with a cream or custard filling, it is usually not practical to make slices thinner than ½ to ¾ inch.

□ HEART-SHAPED CAKES: Cut lengthwise into halves, then cut crosswise slices in to the midline (i).

□ CHEESECAKES: Cut cheesecake into wedges with a sharp thin knife that has been dipped into hot water then wiped off after each cut. Or cut with strong thread (see page 186).

□ SPECIAL ICINGS: If the icing is sticky or fluffy, it will tend to stick to the knife blade. Stand a tall glass of water nearby when cutting the cake, and dip the knife into water between slices. If the blade gets coated, wipe it clean before cutting.

□ WEDDING CAKES: See page 116.

· HOW TO FREEZE & STORE CAKES ·

*T*he freezer is a great convenience in baking. It is essential for stockpiling all types of ingredients, from nuts to flour, but it is even better for storing baked cake layers. Take careful note of the following hints and tips about freezing, however, because some items do well, others do not, and you do not want to put a lot of work into a cake only to have it spoil in the freezer.

Your freezer should maintain a temperature of 0°F. Keep an auxiliary freezer thermometer on a shelf to be safe. The fast freeze shelf may be as low as −10° to −20°F, but the main section should hold constant at 0°F to no more than 5°F.

I can not recommend freezing unbaked cake batters as they tend to shrink and can cause cakes made from them to fall. However, if you must freeze batter, do so for no longer than 6 months.

Most baked cakes can be frozen with success. Cheesecakes are really the best. If they are properly wrapped, you cannot detect the fact that they have been frozen. Cakes with high fat content freeze very well, butter cakes, for example. These will keep frozen for 6 to 12 months if carefully wrapped. Angel cakes and sponges freeze without harm, although I notice a flavor change in sponge cakes after a couple of months and try not to freeze them longer than that. Watch out for spice cakes; after as little as 6 weeks, the spices tend to change their flavors in the freezer. As a general rule, it is best to freeze unfilled, unfrosted cakes; frosted cakes can be frozen, but for no longer than 2 months. After this, flavors and textures may change.

Many fillings deteriorate when frozen, especially those made with eggs. Some types of filled cakes also get soggy when frozen.

Cake icings containing butter and confectioners' sugar freeze well, but those made with brown sugar or egg whites or syrups tend to crystallize when frozen. Boiled icing gets sticky when it thaws.

How to Freeze Cakes

•

To Prepare Cakes for the Freezer

As a general rule, unfrosted cake layers must be completely cooled on a wire rack, then, if you wish, slipped onto a cardboard cake disk. Wrap the layer with plastic wrap or foil, then place it inside a heavy-duty plastic bag; gather the ends of the bag, put it to your mouth and suck out all the air, then wire the bag tightly closed. Some bakers repeat this process, sealing cakes in 2 plastic bags, to ensure no air or moisture gets in to spoil the cake. You may prefer to use freezer paper and heavy-duty foil, folded in double folds to exclude all air, instead of the plastic bags. In either case, the wrap must be airtight.

To freeze decorated cakes, first set them on a cookie sheet or a flat tray, uncovered, in the freezer, if possible, on the fast-freeze shelf. If the icing has a delicate design, arrange a few well-placed toothpicks sticking up around the top so that, after freezing, the wrapper will not touch the icing's surface. Leave the cake until the icing freezes hard, then remove the cake and work quickly to wrap it. Envelop it loosely in plastic wrap, freezer paper, or foil with double folds; then use heavy-duty plastic bags for an airtight outer layer. Finally, to avoid the cake being crushed by a frozen chicken, place it in a cardboard box and label it carefully. I like to freeze wrapped cakes in airtight plastic Tupperware cake containers.

To Thaw Frozen Cakes

Leave your cakes wrapped until they thaw out. When thawing, the moisture will cling to the outside of the wrapping and not to the cake; this moisture could ruin the glaze on a frozen chocolate cake if it thawed unwrapped.

Thawing cakes wrapped, in the refrigerator, is the best method, but takes at least three times longer than thawing at room temperature. Thaw cheesecakes overnight in the refrigerator. Layer cakes with butter icing I leave in their wrappings on the kitchen counter for about 2 hours before serving. Note that 4-layer cakes or loaf fruitcakes will take considerably longer than a 2-layer cake to thaw; plan for it.

Also consider the fact that some cakes are delicious to eat frozen, so if you are faced with a frozen cake and a time crisis, cut thin slices and pretend it is supposed to be served that way. You may discover something wonderful.

Can Cakes Be Refrozen?

Yes. But it is best to cut off the frozen portion you want, then rewrap and quickly return the still-frozen cake to the freezer.

Freezing Do's and Don'ts

· Do not freeze custards or cream fillings unless the recipe so specifies.

· Do not use jelly-based fruit glazes on cakes that are to be frozen.

· Do not freeze cream cheese alone unless mixed into icings or in combination with other ingredients, as for a cheesecake; cream cheese turns grainy when frozen alone.

· Do not freeze sour cream, it separates.

· Do not freeze chocolate in bulk for storage; you can freeze chocolate decorations, leaves, etc., for a short period of time to harden the chocolate. However, when I have a small amount of leftover melted chocolate, I often pour it into a paper muffin cup and freeze it to harden before wrapping it in a plastic bag. I have stored these in the freezer for a few weeks without harm. Read About Chocolate (see Index).

• Do not freeze cakes covered with marzipan or rolled fondant icing; the humidity will cause both of these toppings to loosen and separate from the cake.

• Do not freeze cake decorations made from marzipan; freezing causes marzipan to collect surface moisture.

• Do freeze (provided wrapped airtight):
Bavarian Creams
Mousses
Spices, fresh or dried
Milk and cream
Eggs (see page 31 for instructions)
Butter or margarine
Flour
Sugar, including especially brown sugar, which does not get lumps in the freezer
Nuts, whole or chopped
Crumbs (cookie, cake, cracker, etc.)
Fresh fruit mixtures cooked with sugar, or fresh fruits packed whole with sugar (berries or sliced peaches, etc., for use in cake fillings)
Buttercream flowers, set on foil or wax paper, then loosely wrapped with foil or plastic wrap. Set them on the cake frozen, thaw before serving.

HOW TO STORE CAKES

•

Freshly baked cakes with sugar or butter-based fillings and icings should be stored at room temperature for a couple of days, covered with a cake cover (metal or plastic) or set into a plastic, airtight cake holder with a lid (Tupperware, for example).

Cakes can also be stored on the serving platter topped by a large, inverted bowl. Cakes with boiled or fluffy cooked egg-white icing are best eaten the same day, but can be stored at room temperature under a bowl if a spoon is left under one edge of the bowl to allow a little air circulation.

If the cake contains custards, uncooked eggs, whipped cream, or soft meringue (not a stiff dacquoise), it should be refrigerated. Always store cheesecakes in the refrigerator. To prevent the odors of other foods from penetrating your cakes, loosely wrap the cakes with plastic wrap, tucking the ends of the plastic beneath the cake dish, before putting them into the refrigerator. If you have a fancy or delicate icing atop the cake, put a few well-placed toothpicks in the icing before wrapping; the picks will hold the wrap above the surface of the cake.

Store marzipan decorations at room temperature, wrapped if necessary, so they air-dry and harden; do not refrigerate them or they may become covered with beads of moisture. Do not refrigerate cakes decorated with fondant or marzipan coatings; the humidity from the refrigerator loosens the coating from the cake. Note that cakes are coated with these substances in order to seal out the air and retain freshness, so refrigeration is not needed anyway.

Sliced cakes can be kept fresh by pressing a piece of wax or parchment paper flat against each cut surface.

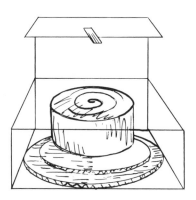

*A*fter a short time working with this book, your cakes will no doubt be in such demand that you will be packing them up to take to parties, catered events, and weddings. It is great to be in demand, but it can be tricky to transport cakes. Read the suggestions below before setting off with your cake.

Before transporting a cake, be sure it is anchored to a cardboard cake disk the same diameter as the cake with a few dabs of icing. Then, put a dab of icing in the center of a cardboard disk 1 or 2 inches larger than the first and anchor the first disk and the cake to it.

Finally, set the double-boarded stationary cake into a cardboard cake box close to the size of the bottom cake disk so it will not slide around too much. The larger disk will prevent the cake itself from sliding into the box sides. Cake boxes are available from bakers' supply houses or from individual bakeries, which often are willing to sell you a dozen or so at little cost. Often this box is of soft or flexible cardboard; if traveling far, or by car or public transportation, it should usually be set into a sturdy cardboard carton for protection.

If transporting your cake in hot weather, be sure it travels in an air-conditioned vehicle. Beware of hot car trunks and buttercream icings. You may want to double-box a cake on a hot day, putting frozen ice packs wrapped in plastic bags between the two boxes, to keep the temperature cold enough. Or line a cardboard box with ½ to 1-inch-thick panels of stiff styrofoam insulation (sold in hardware and building supply stores). For large, or wedding, cakes, cut down one side panel of the cardboard carton so the cake will slide easily in and out; for traveling secure the panel with tape.

When traveling with a decorated cake, be sure to pack a supply of extra icing in a plastic bag. Bring along an icing spatula or small knife (to do patch-up work) and a decorating tube or pastry bag and tips if the cake has fancy work, borders, or flowers, etc.

If you are decorating the cake with fresh flowers (see Index), do not apply the flowers until the cake is assembled at its final destination. Transport the flowers with their stems wrapped in wet paper towels or newspaper, then set into water.

For birthdays and holidays, one is often inspired to send a cake to a child at school or a friend far away. It can be a great idea from start to finish if you excercise some caution and judgment. Avoid cakes that must be refrigerated or have egg or cream fillings that might spoil in transit. Select pound cakes, fruitcakes, or cakes made with fruit (applesauce, date-nut or its variations, Williamsburg Orange Wine, with currants and nuts); many of the cakes in the Coffee Cakes section of this book are good candidates. Writing in royal icing (such as a Happy Birthday greeting) will survive the trip; raised 3-dimensional

flowers and leaves may not; if decorating the cake, be practical, or wrap and send molded marzipan flowers that are fairly substantial and air-dried; pack and seal these alongside the cake, rather than setting them on top, lest they break off.

Wrap the cake as if you were going to freeze it (see Index), with an inner and outer airtight covering to maintain freshness. Select an inner box made of cardboard, plastic, or tin. Surround the cake with cushioning material—bunched sheets of newsprint, unflavored, unsalted popped corn, or styrofoam beads. Or roll up sheets of plastic bubble-wrap (2 layers of plastic with air bubbles sandwiched between them). Finally, suspend this box in a sturdy mailing carton and again pack it with cushioning material so it cannot slide around. Seal as usual and mark the outside of the box "PERISHABLE, HANDLE WITH CARE," or "FRAGILE AND PERISHABLE, HANDLE WITH CARE." If you have questions about mail regulations, or length of time in transit, inquire at your nearest post office or United Parcel Service (UPS) office.

Appendices

· RECIPES FOR SPECIAL NEEDS ·

Note: See index for page numbers; listed in order of appearance in text.

☐ EGG-FREE RECIPES:
Eggless Chocolate Cake
Crazy Mixed-Up Chocolate Cake
Chocolate Pudding Cake
Eggless Custard Buttercream

Toasted Coconut Topping
Streusel Nut Topping
All-Purpose Frosting
Confectioners' Frosting
Creamy Mocha Buttercream
Cream-Cheese Icing
Quick Coconut Icing
Mocha Frosting
Peanut Butter Icing
Penuche Icing
Brown-Sugar Caramel Icing
Broiled Caramel-Nut Icing
Orange Wine Icing
Basic Icing Glaze
Fabulous Chocolate Glaze
Ganache Chocolate Filling or Icing Glaze
Chocolate Water Glaze
Cocoa Icing Glaze
Crème Fraîche
Hard Sauce

Warm Berry Sauce
Butterscotch Sauce
Rich Chocolate Sauce
Strawberries Romanoff
Cake Soaking Syrup
Praline Powder and Paste
Candied Citrus Peel
Plastic Chocolate Ribbons and Roses
Caramelized Sugar

☐ RECIPES MADE WITH ALL EGG YOLKS:
Gold Layer Cake
Lady Baltimore Cake
Vanilla Pastry Cream (Crème Pâtissière)
Vicky Zeff's White Chocolate Mousse
Viennese Custard Buttercream
Zabaglione Sauce and Cake Filling
Lemon Curd
Lemon Cake Filling
Lane Cake Filling
Light Orange Buttercream Filling
Classic French Egg-Yolk Buttercream
French Buttercream Ménagère (Homestyle)
Vanilla Custard Sauce (Crème Anglaise)

☐ RECIPES MADE WITH ALL EGG WHITES:
Lord Baltimore Cake

Lane Cake (made without filling)
Fresh Coconut Cake
Angel-Cake Jelly Roll
Angel-Food Cake
Egg-White Chiffon Cake
Swiss and Italian Meringue Cakes
Seven-Minute Icing
Boiled Icing
Swiss and Italian Meringue Buttercream

□ CHOLESTEROL-FREE RECIPES
(NO YOLKS OR BUTTER):
Chocolate Pudding Cake
Passover Sponge Cake
Angel-Cake Jelly Roll
Classic White Angel Cake
Egg-White Chiffon Cake
Cholesterol-Free Lemon Chiffon Cake
Meringue or Dacquoise Cake Layers
Meringue Crumb Topping
Royal Icing
All-Purpose Frosting (made with margarine
and skimmed milk)
Seven-Minute Icing
Boiled Icing
Tangerine Glaze
Chocolate Water Glaze
Fondant
Candied Citrus Peel
Caramelized Sugar

□ CHOLESTEROL-FREE AND
FAT-FREE (NO YOLKS, BUTTER, OIL,
OR SHORTENING):
Same as Cholesterol-Free *except* for:
Egg White Chiffon (contains oil)

□ LOW CALORIE AND LOW FAT
RECIPES:
Low-Calorie Yogurt Cheesecake
"Diet" Whipped Cream

□ WHEAT-FREE CAKE RECIPES:
Mocha Wheatless Sponge Cake
Feather-Topped Truffle Cake
Chocolate Chestnut Fudge Cake

□ SUGARFREE, HONEYFREE CAKES:
Susan Richman's Sugarfree, Honeyfree Orange Cake

□ PASSOVER RECIPES:
Passover Cheesecake
Mocha Wheatless Sponge Cake
Passover Sponge Cake
Passover Nut Torte
Feather-Topped Truffle Cake
Chocolate Chestnut Fudge

□ FASTEST CAKE RECIPES
(QUICK-AS-A-MIX):
Crazy Mixed-Up Chocolate Cake
Lemon-Blueberry Pudding Cake
Chocolate Pudding Cake
Feather-Topped Truffle Cake (omit topping)

□ HOLIDAY GIFT CAKES:
Anna's Swedish Butter Cake
Swedish Sandcake
Marvelous Mud Cake
English Fruitcake
Apricot-Nut Fruitcake
Bourbon-Pecan Cake
Williamsburg Orange Wine Cake
Kugelhopf
Gingerbread
Cranberry Orange Loaf
Cranberry Apricot Loaf
Lemon Tea Cake
Ukranian Poppyseed Loaf
Applesauce Cake
Panforte Di Siena

At altitudes above 3,000 feet, adjustments must be made in your baking techniques because of the decrease in air pressure and the low humidity of the atmosphere.

In general, the higher the altitude, the more adjustments must be made. For this reason, it is always best to use recipes created for your region. If you have moved from New England to the Rockies and suddenly find your most reliable recipes no longer work, do not despair. Consult the Agricultural Extension Service of a nearby university, or your state department of agriculture, or the U. S. Government Printing Office for a booklet on high altitude cooking. Sometimes the home economics department of a local high school can be helpful.

A decrease in atmospheric pressure causes several reactions in baking. For one thing, gases expand more easily, so as a cake bakes it may rise so much that it collapses. For this reason the amount of leavening used in the batter must be reduced. The amount of baking powder or baking soda should be decreased by about one third at 3,500 feet, by one half at 5,000 feet, and by two thirds above 5,000 feet. Note: Some cakes depend on baking soda to neutralize acid in chocolate or buttermilk, as well as to provide leavening power by producing carbon dioxide when reacting with the acids; in these recipes you cannot reduce the baking soda more than ½ teaspoon per 1 cup sour milk or cream. For fruitcakes, some authorities believe all leavening should be omitted at high altitudes.

Because air expands more at high altitudes, you should slightly underbeat your eggs. To help control the whipping volume, beat them cold, when they will be harder to whip than if warm.

Another problem is that as altitude increases both the air pressure and the boiling point of water decrease. At sea level water boils at 212°F; at 3,000 feet above sea level, at 207°F; at 5,000 feet, at 203°F. Because air pressure is less and the boiling point is lower, more water evaporates in the baking process. This causes baked products to dry out. It also leaves a different ratio of ingredients in the cake—less moisture and a higher relative concentration of sugar. Extreme excess of sugar can cause a cake to fall. It also leaves telltale white spots on the surface of the cake. Some authorities recommend a change in the sugar-to-flour ratio in the recipe. For example, using half as much sugar as flour. But this changes with each type of cake, and sponge cakes do not react the same way as butter cakes.

Low humidity is particularly a problem with flour, which may be much drier (contain much less internal moisture) at high eleva-tions. When dry flour is used in baking, more water is required to balance it. Again, recipe proportions must be adjusted, and either less flour or more water added to the batter. Stor-ing flour in moistureproof containers is a help, but it does not entirely solve the problem.

Another side effect of high altitude is that cakes tend to stick more when being removed from their pans. Be sure to grease and flour the pans well, especially if using decorative molds.

As a general rule of thumb to guide you in adapting "sea level recipes," i.e., any recipe not specifically designed for your altitude, you can start by trying to reduce the sugar in your recipe 1 to 3 tablespoons per cup of sugar used; increase the liquid by 1 to 4 tablespoons; reduce the amount of butter in pound or heavy-butter cakes by about 2 tablespoons; reduce each teaspoon of baking powder by up to ¼ teaspoon; and increase the oven temper-ature by 25°F.

· ABOUT CAKE MIXES ·

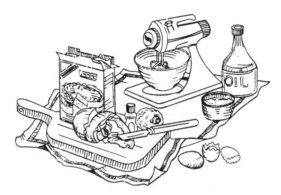

*F*irst let me publicly acknowledge that I have used a cake mix on occasion, though the occasion is rare. While I am not philosophically opposed to mixes, I usually object on flavorful grounds; they taste like chemicals to me. Also, mixes usually have a characteristic texture, more soft and cottony than any homemade cake. There are reasons for these characteristics, all having to do with laboratory technology. For the serious baker, it is worth looking at mixes carefully to study how they contrast and compare with homemade cakes from the point of view of taste, texture, and time.

Anyone who has ever eaten a cake made from a mix has noticed the light, high rise and tender crumb. Why, some ask, can't I get the same texture in a homemade cake? The answer lies in a chemistry lab, but briefly, the fact is that you do not have access to the same ingredients used in commercial mixes. Read About Flour and About Fat (see Index). All

commercial flour is bleached, either by aging or by chemicals. Flour for cake mixes is specifically formulated and generally bleached with chlorine gas, among other agents. This alters the character of the starch, and the fatty substances called lipids, in the gluten; it inhibits the gluten development of the flour, slowing or stopping elasticity. According to Harold J. McGee in *On Food and Cooking; The Science and Lore of the Kitchen* (Charles Scribner's Sons, 1984), chlorine-treated flour can "tolerate more structure-enfeebling ingredients," such as sugar and fat, than can normal flour. Thus more sugar and fat are used, making mixes sweeter and softer than homemade cakes using store-bought flour.

Special emulsifiers are added to the vegetable shortening in cake mixes. High-ratio emulsified shortening contains mono- and diglycerides for greater absorption and retention of moisture and liquid. With the stabilizing influence of these emulsifiers, the air cells in whipped batters remain at optimal size and the cakes rise to great height.

Take a close look at the ingredients label on a cake mix and you will find any number of items you know you don't add at home. For example: propylene glycol mono-esters "for smooth texture," polyglycerol esters "for smooth texture," cellulose gum or xanthan gum "for smooth batter," not to mention artificial coloring and flavoring.

These chemicals have a great deal to do with artificially constructing specific textures and maintaining shelf life. I am more concerned about natural products and my family's health. Think about this the next time you opt to save 20 minutes by preparing a cake mix for your child's birthday party.

DO CAKE MIXES SAVE TIME?

∎

Do cake mixes really save time? Sure, but that depends upon the recipe you compare it to. Many mixes have pound and/or pudding cake variations using extra ingredients, adding to cost, effort, and time expended. Naturally, many fancy homemade cakes are time-consuming, but I have long contended that some homemade cakes are just as quick to prepare as mixes. Recently my baking assistant Barbara Cover and I did some time tests to prove our point.

Working with chocolate cake recipes, we compared a Chocolate Cake and a basic Devil's Food Cake (dump and blend method) with a Devil's Food Cake Mix to which oil, eggs, and water were added.

First we assembled all our ingredients. We mixed the batters with the same stand-type electric mixer. Working with a stop watch, we compared the entire preparation procedure from the greasing of the pans to the measuring, combining, and beating together of the ingredients, right up to the moment when the cakes were set in the oven.

The Devil's Food Cake Mix, which required only that the dry ingredients be beaten with eggs, oil, and water, took 9 minutes total time.

Our scratch chocolate Crazy Mixed-up Chocolate Cake (page 102), which resembles the mix because it uses dry ingredients blended with oil and water, cut the time to 4 minutes, 35 seconds!

With our scratch Devil's Food Cake (page 97), including sifting of the dry ingredients, the preparation time was 28 minutes. When sifting was eliminated, we shaved 2 minutes. Note that this is a butter cake, in which the butter and sugar are ideally creamed together before adding the other ingredients. By skipping the creaming, we shaved off another 2 minutes (24 minutes total).

The bottom line: some scratch recipes are even quicker to make than mixes. Some take slightly longer, but just slightly. Our Lemon-Blueberry Pudding Cake (page 180) takes 8 to 9 minutes. Many conventional recipes can be adapted for use in the food processor (see Index) to cut down further the conventional preparation times.

ADAPTING CAKE MIXES

∎

While I am not an avid supporter of cake mixes, I readily acknowledge their importance as convenience foods in our busy lives. Everyone uses them at some time, so we must be practical and find ways to adapt box recipes to enhance their flavors and textures.

Most mixes offer variations for pound cake, which add additional eggs and sometimes sour cream. Others add instant pudding mix, which contains powdered eggs and milk. These items enhance the richness and moisture of the cake, making the texture a little more dense and homey. Here are some other home-style "additives":

• Alter the cake's flavor by replacing the water with fruit juice.

• Substitute cream sherry or other wine for the water in a pound cake mix; or add 2 or 3 tablespoons of brandy or liqueur to the batter.

NUT CAKE:

To any pound cake, add ¾ cup finely chopped walnuts or pecans or toasted hazelnuts (filberts).

ORANGE CAKE:

Replace the water with orange juice and add the grated zest of 1 orange. Try this with Devil's Food Cake, adding 1 teaspoon orange extract as well for chocolate-orange flavor. Ice with Orange Glaze or Orange-Chocolate Buttercream (page 392).

MOTHER'S ORANGE-LEMON CAKE:

Make yellow cake mix blended with instant lemon pudding mix, ½ cup oil, and 4 large eggs. For liquid, use 1 cup orange juice and the grated zest of 1 lemon or orange. Bake the cake in a tube pan. Two or three minutes after removing the cake from the oven, while it is still hot, pour over it a glaze made with ⅓ cup orange juice stirred into ⅔ cup sugar. Cool the cake in the pan before unmolding. Ice with Orange or Lemon Glaze (page 407).

DOUBLE CHOCOLATE POUND CAKE:

Add to the regular or pound/pudding cake mix 4 ounces grated semisweet chocolate plus 1½ cups semisweet miniature chocolate bits and ¼ teaspoon ground cinnamon.

MAC SQUIRE'S CHOCOLATE RUM CAKE:

Make dark chocolate cake blended with instant dark chocolate pudding mix, 4 large eggs, and ¾ cup oil. For liquid, use ¾ cup dark rum. Bake in a tube pan.

STREUSEL COFFEE CAKE:

Make yellow pound cake mix. In a separate bowl, prepare streusel ingredients from the recipe on page 385. Place half of the batter in a bundt pan, sprinkle on half the streusel, add remaining batter, and top with remaining streusel before baking.

ENGLISH SPICE CAKE:

To a yellow cake mix, add 1 teaspoon ground cinnamon, ½ teaspoon each of ground nutmeg and mace, a pinch of ground ginger, and 2 tablespoons caraway seeds (optional). If you wish, you can replace the water with cider and add ½ cup finely chopped walnuts or currants.

COFFEE-FLAVORED CAKE:

Make any yellow cake mix. Replace the water in the recipe with strong coffee, or add 1 tablespoon instant coffee powder to the dry ingredients. Top the baked cake with a glaze made by stirring 2 tablespoons strong coffee into ⅔ cup sifted confectioners' sugar. For Mocha Cake, try this with a chocolate cake mix.

COCONUT CAKE:

Add to white cake mix 1 teaspoon coconut extract, ⅓ cup canned sweetened coconut cream, and ¾ cup flaked sweetened coconut.

NINA BACON'S SHERRY-POPPYSEED CAKE:

Make a yellow cake mix blended with 1 package instant vanilla pudding. Add ⅓ cup poppyseeds, ½ cup dry sherry, ½ cup oil, 1 cup sour cream, and 4 large eggs. Bake in two 9-inch layers at 350°F (175°C) for 60 minutes. Fill and frost with Cream-Cheese Icing (see page 393), or fill with lingonberry jam and sift confectioners' sugar over the top. Note: This recipe was shared with Nina by the chef at the Fire and Ice Restaurant in Middlebury, Vermont.

NANCY LIEBERMAN'S HOT BUTTERED-RUM PECAN CAKE:

Make a yellow cake mix blended with 1 package instant vanilla pudding. Add ½ cup white rum, ½ cup water, ½ cup vegetable oil, and 4 large eggs. Make a soaking syrup by bringing to a boil in a saucepan 1 cup firmly packed light brown sugar, ½ teaspoon ground nutmeg, ½ cup butter, and ¼ cup water. Remove from heat and stir in ¼ cup rum. Spread butter on bottom and sides of a 10-inch bundt pan; dust with flour, tap out excess flour. Chop 1 cup of pecans and sprinkle half on the bottom of the prepared pan. Turn the batter into the pan and top with remaining chopped nuts. Bake at 325°F (165°C) for 60 minutes. Pour warm soaking syrup over the cake as soon as it comes from the oven. Cool the cake in its pan before unmolding.

· SUPPLIERS OF SPECIAL ·
INGREDIENTS & EQUIPMENT

Bridge Kitchenware Corp.
214 East 52nd Street
New York, N.Y. 10022
212-688-4220
(baking pans and miscellaneous cooking equipment and utensils)

Educated Cake Pan
Burvelle Enterprises
7010 Cherrytree Avenue
Citrus Heights, California 95621
916-969-2253
(special modular pan for shaped cakes)

International Pastry Arts Center
525 Executive Blvd
Elmsford, New York 10523
914-347-3737
(chocolate, chocolate molds)

Kraft-Rosenblum (Flying Foods)
2101-91st Street
North Bergen, New Jersey 07047
201-854-1100
(unusual fruits and ingredients, especially mango, cassis, and passion fruit concentrate and purée)

Maid of Scandinavia
3244 Raleigh Avenue
Minneapolis, Minnesota 55416
612-927-7996
(baking supplies, utensils, chocolate)

Paprikas Weiss Importer
1546 Second Avenue
New York, N.Y. 10028
212-288-6117
(imported spices, flavorings, poppyseeds, Middle European foods, baking utensils, chocolate)

Williams-Sonoma Mail Order Dept.
P.O. Box 7456
San Francisco, California 94120-7456
415-421-4555 (Customer Service)
(baking equipment, miscellaneous utensils, chocolate)

Wilton Enterprises, Inc.
Caller Service 1604
2240 West 75th Street
Woodridge, Illinois 60517
312-963-7100
(cake decorating supplies)

· INDEX ·

483

INDEX

494

INDEX